football fans guide

Janet Williams

Victoria Bennett James Hilton

With additional research by Chris Worrall, Adam Bonner, Eddie Allcorn, Tim Capp and Mark Johnson

CollinsWillow

An Imprint of HarperCollins*Publishers*

Arena magazine listed JANET WILLIAMS as one of the twenty most powerful people in football... along with Stan Collymore's mum and West Ham's mascot 'Herbie the Hammer'. She has the ability, said the magazine, to make or break the football fan's day out! After all, she's had enough bad days herself during three decades as a supporter of a lower division team. With 14 years as a journalist and researcher, and a degree in geography – not to mention an uncanny homing instinct for pizza restaurants – Janet claims to be ideally qualified to write a fan's guidebook.

VICTORIA BENNETT is a one-time average left-back who does not respond well to being called 'Blondie' or asked 'what shape is a football?' She's a long-suffering fan of a notoriously unsuccessful 'sleeping giant' club, with a palate for real ale and meat-and-potato pies. She spends the rest of her time uncovering the history of sports writing for her PhD, freelance writing and dreaming of playing for her team.

JAMES HILTON feels he has been destined for life as a football researcher since, at his first league football match many moons ago, he missed the winning goal whilst queuing for a burger. Having since developed a passion for writing, and a degree in communications, James thinks his early promise as a football food researcher has been fulfilled by working on this book!

First published in 1995

Second edition 1996

Third edition published in 1998
by CollinsWillow
an imprint of HarperCollins*Publishers*
London

1 3 5 7 9 8 6 4 2

A CIP catalogue record for this book is available from the British Library

ISBN 0 00 218855 4

Designed by Design in Print Limited

Cartoons by Tony Eagle, Cris Glascow, Phil Maynard and Pete McKee

Maps and ground plans by Mark Pringle

Printed in Great Britain by Caledonian International Book Manufacturing Ltd, Glasgow

The Publishers and Authors have done their best to ensure the accuracy of all the information contained herein; they cannot accept responsibility for any loss, injury or inconvenience sustained by any reader as a result of information or advice contained in this guide. Suggestions for improving this guide are welcome from all football fans. Please write to: The Editor, CollinsWillow, HarperCollins*Publishers*, 77-85 Fulham Palace Road, London W6 8JB.

Contents

Introduction

After a gap of two years, the *Football Fans Guide* is back! Not only has it been totally updated, to include all the new grounds, but it also has a whole new set of cartoons, new art design and two new authors, Victoria Bennett and James Hilton. But our aim remains the same: to produce the best, most accurate, comprehensive, readable and humorous football guidebook on the market.

Ask yourself if the following scenario sounds familiar. You take half a day off work. As you set off north (or south) at 3.30 pm, it starts to sleet. There are traffic jams on the M1/M6/M5 or M40 (or indeed all four). By the time you race through the turnstiles, your team is already 0-1 down, and it goes downhill from there. Your feet slowly freeze to the floor. You arrive back home at 1.30 am and bid your friends farewell with: 'Great, I had a wonderful time', and mean it. If this rings true, then this book is for you.

We've changed the format slightly for this new edition of the 'FFG'. We've dropped the programme review and the description of the club shop, and introduced website addresses, more train information and details of local Saturday sports papers and radio phone-ins. In the past, few away fans have called in to these local phone-ins ... now's your chance!

THE RESEARCH

We've always believed that the only way to compile a football guidebook is to visit all 92 Premiership and league grounds ourselves, to speak with the locals, gather the compliments and complaints of the visitors, consult with the club and, perhaps most importantly of all, speak with each club's police liaison officer. The locals know the best cafés and restaurants, the niftiest short cuts and the best places to park. Visiting fans know which pubs make them welcome and which ones don't. Most clubs are happy to provide basic information on pricing, facilities for the disabled and plans for ground relocations and improvements. Some agreed to meet the authors and even gave guided tours. Only two (Newcastle United and Blackburn Rovers) declined to give any information at all.

Safety has always been of paramount importance to the *Football Fans Guide,* which is why in all cases we consult with the local police. They know where the nutters hang out on matchdays. They know the best and the worst pubs, and the ones visiting supporters should avoid at all costs! Sometimes they suggest specific road routes for away fans, which on paper can look a very long way round. There's usually a reason for this: for example, the police are often concerned about visiting fans, with away colours on show in the car, getting caught in stationary traffic exactly where home supporters pour out of pubs on the way to the ground.

Once each club's entry was written up, we sent copies to the club representative, the police and the home supporters. Most were kind enough to read it through and send it back to us. Their suggestions and corrections were then incorporated into the text.

The 'FFG' is compiled by the three authors, with the help of many other wonderful people. Some simply take the time to tell us what they think of their cups of coffee as we go round asking opinions at half-time. Others have gone where the authors feared to tread (the gents' or the ladies' loos, depending on the gender of the researcher!). A number of people responded to our advert in *FourFourTwo* magazine and began filling in our 'Travelling Fan's Forms'. These are basic questionnaires asking about ground facilities (the food, the loos, the view etc), and for any tips on parking, pubs and the like. Supporters filled them in on their travels, giving us a wonderful picture of life throughout the divisions. Doncaster fans wrote in wonder at the quality of the graffiti at Barnet and complained that only home fans had ketchup at Scunthorpe ('It's an oasis of condiments in there. This away end is a disgrace to the catering services of north Lincolnshire.') A Gillingham fan found some 'unique strains of bacteria living on the walls' of the gents at York. An Everton supporter overheard workmen in the loos at Bolton trying to locate the source of a leak into the refreshment bar below. A Preston supporter wrote in glowing terms about the 'Egon Ronay' food at Northampton Town. The names of those who helped in this way are recorded at the end of the book, but we'd like to single out Eddie Allcorn, Daniel Magill, Mark Cassidy, Dave Kreamer, Steve Exley, Chris Worrall and the wonderful supporters of Doncaster Rovers. Most importantly, all their work means that the 'Food and Drink' and 'Visitors' Toilets' sections are in many cases compiled from several reports and are not just the opinion of one researcher.

THE TEXT

How to get there: Here we'd like to point out that this book is for the independent travelling football fan. It is not intended for use by coaches. Coach parties should contact the local police football liaison officer for directions, meeting points and other vital information.

In all cases, the road directions have been driven in person by one of the authors, and in many cases checked by another. It's actually not that easy to drive along with a map in one hand and a dictaphone in the other! But it does mean we can note exact distances, signposts and landmarks. And yes, this has meant more wear-and-tear on the authors' cars. No major accidents to report this time round, despite a joint mileage of about 50,000 miles. We've driven at night, in fog, in snow, in blinding sunshine and through blinding migraines. We've been cut up on motorways; had people signal right on roundabouts only to turn left at the last minute; taken two-and-a-half hours to drive five miles on the M6; we've had a strange rubber bouncy-thing on the M25 smash a front indicator light ... all the normal experiences of travelling fans in other words! And then Janet drives into the car park railings at Tescos!!

Last Midweek Trains: A number of supporters suggested that the *Football Fans Guide* should give more detailed rail information especially for those trying to get home after a midweek game. The idea seemed simple. In practice, it wasn't. Yes, the telephone rail enquiry line gives out train information, but gives different train times to different callers! And of course, we can't give train times to every town in Britain. Hence the information under 'Last Midweek Trains' can only be an indication as to whether it's possible to get home after a night match. Fans will still have to double-check on (0345) 484 950. More information, including cut-price ticket deals, can be obtained on the following numbers: Virgin (0345) 222 333; Connex (0870) 603 0405; Great Western (0345) 000 125; Great North-Eastern (0345) 225 225: Midland Mainline (0345) 125 678: Anglia (01603) 764 776; Thameslink (0345) 300 700; Great Eastern (to East Anglia) doesn't have a booking line. The London Underground information line is (0171) 222 1234.

Cost: Wherever possible, admission prices are given for season 1998/99. A few clubs had not finalised prices by the time this book went to print. In these cases prices are given for season 1997/98.

Visitors' Toilets: Forget the FA Cup, the UEFA Cup, the Cup Winners' Cup. All league clubs have, in season 97/98, been vying for the FFG's most-coveted MATITLA ('Most Awful Toilet in the League Award'). The outright winner was: Darlington. And was the club overawed by this? Were they grateful? No, all they did was to announce that they're about to be demolished! Runners-up for this prestigious award were: Hull, Wigan, Blackpool, York, Mansfield, Plymouth, Southampton and Aston Villa. Other special category winners were: Female MATITLA – Swansea; Funniest Graffiti – Barnet; Best for Wildlife – Cambridge; Deepest Puddle – Chelsea; Weirdest feature – Portsmouth for the traffic cone and Brentford for the pie tins. The best football toilets were: Premier League – Arsenal and Manchester United; First Division – Port Vale, QPR, Wolves, WBA and Crewe; Second Division – Bristol City and Wycombe; Third Division – Scarborough.

Food and Drink: The authors of the *Football Fans Guide* and all the football fans who help in its production, have been sampling football food since season 1994/95. So don't believe other publications claiming to be the first to carry out such a survey! We have also always given the date, or dates, on which we visited each ground. This shows that we always attend a full league or cup match, not pre-season friendlies. Our survey is, of course, only valid for that one day. The following week new caterers may take over, or a new line introduced. We found a marked improvement overall between season 95/96 and 97/98. Next season the food could be even better, or a lot worse!

Overall, our top five clubs for football food are (in alphabetical order): Cambridge, Crewe, Leicester, Liverpool and Northampton. 'Highly recommended' awards went to: Orient, Rochdale, Rotherham, Plymouth and Preston.

A number of clubs had excellent pies and/or pasties. After hours of debate we chose our top ten as: Crewe, Mansfield, Millwall, Notts County, Rochdale, Rotherham, Preston, Plymouth, Sheffield Wednesday and Wolves.

The best tea was at: Colchester, Darlington, Leyton Orient, Luton, Macclesfield, Mansfield, Oldham, Plymouth, Preston and QPR. However, even though Halifax Town wasn't in the league during our research, it still won the 'BAFTA' (Best Away Football Tea Award), with Macclesfield and Plymouth a very close second.

The worst tea was at: Bolton, Bristol City, Chester, Gillingham, Grimsby, Ipswich, Lincoln, Millwall, Newcastle and Wycombe.

Overall, our choices for the 'YUK-OH' Award for worst football food were: Arsenal, Bristol City, Burnley, Leeds and Wigan (with Coventry a close runner-up).

Special awards 'for making a bit of an effort' go to: Bolton for the Hollands pies and peas on a plate with a fork; Macclesfield for the chip butties and pizza; Stockport for the jacket potatoes; Swindon for the free biscuits; Walsall for the excellent Balti pies; Watford for the baguettes; and York for the pies, peas and chips.

Pub Guide: This is where we come to the classic author opt-out. The authors cannot guarantee the safety of any supporter inside or outside any of the pubs listed, or anywhere else for that matter.

What we have done is taken every possible care to find safe, well-run pubs which accept visiting supporters. We consulted the local police, spoke to the home supporters, and checked with every landlord or landlady to ensure they were happy to be listed. Only when the fans, the police and the pubs themselves agreed, did we put the pub in the book. However, pubs change hands and change their policies. So, wherever possible, we have included the pub phone numbers, allowing fans to check in advance that visiting football supporters are still welcome. NB The London Police declined to advise the authors on the pubs listed in the London Guide.

Some of the pubs do occasionally close on matchdays. This will often be on police advice, or the landlord may choose to close for derby matches. Please be understanding.

Moreover, each pub agreed to be listed in the entry for one club (except for those listed under the 'London Guide'). In other words, a pub which welcomes fans in

Rochdale, for example, may not welcome supporters passing through Rochdale to other games. Please do not assume that because a pub is listed it automatically welcomes fans from every sundry club playing in the area.

Some excellent, football friendly pubs declined to be listed in the book. Obviously this was disappointing, but we could not ignore their wishes. Hence if your own favourite pub isn't included, the chances are the landlord didn't want it to be. So, yes, we do know about that fantastic football pub in Wolverhampton ... the landlord's said 'no' three years running! However, it's also possible of course that we simply didn't know of the pub's existence. Therefore we'd love further recommendations, from supporters, landlords or breweries.

Most importantly, coach parties should note that it is illegal to have alcohol on board, or for any passengers to be drunk. This applies to coaches, trains and to any vehicle adapted to carry more than eight passengers, and in fact carrying at least two passengers. So that does indeed mean minibus passengers, too. The pubs listed in the book have agreed only to accept the independent travelling football fan – not coachloads of them. Coach parties should always notify the local police football liaison office in advance, and follow police instructions.

Safety Factor: Incidents such as the trouble in Rome or Marseilles, or in the car park at Barnsley in 1998, attract huge media attention. Yet overall, trouble at football matches is rare, and the ordinary supporter intent on simply enjoying the match is most unlikely to encounter any problems. Most football-related violence appears to be arranged in advance, by mobile phone, between the rival hooligans. Still, there are a few clubs where supporters should take extra care, and these are highlighted in the text. It is patently obvious, however, that the authors of this guidebook cannot possibly predict or prevent trouble at football matches, which can flare up at any time and occasionally in the most unlikely places. To be as safe as possible, therefore, don't wear colours outside football grounds, and certainly not in town centres or pubs.

Unofficial Websites: The authors have done their best to track down all the websites for each club. In many cases we were unable to list them all because of lack of space. And of course we may have missed some, while others will already have changed their addresses or closed down. The *Football Fans Guide* is hoping to set up its own website soon, with comprehensive listings to other club sites, as well as updated travel information. We have not listed all the Nationwide, Carlingnet, Teamtalk, or 'Shaggy's Guide' pages, mainly because they are readily accessible.

London/Nottingham Road Guides: As in these cities there's more than one club, and the inherent duplication of road directions, we have provided general road guides, to be used in conjunction with specific directions under each relevant club entry.

REFERENCES

The *Football Fans Guide* was compiled mainly through primary research ... in other words, we drove the road directions, checked out the pubs, went to matches and spoke to supporters. However, we have used one excellent book to double-check some of our facts and figures: *The Football Grounds of Britain* (CollinsWillow), by Simon Inglis. It's the definitive book on the history and architecture of football grounds, and a brilliant piece of work. Buy a copy now!

THE IMPORTANT LEGAL BIT

The *Football Fans Guide* must be one of the most plagiarized books in Britain. Large chunks of it, usually the road directions, regularly appear in matchday programmes, fanzines, websites, newspapers, and local and national magazines. We need to make it clear that the entire book is copyright. The unauthorised reproduction of any part of the text, the maps or the cartoons is illegal and will result in prosecution. Researching the *Football Fans Guide* is expensive: we have to buy match tickets, programmes, fanzines, food and drink; pay for petrol, hospitality (ie. drinks to fanzine editors and the like), and sometimes for overnight accommodation. We rely completely on the sale of the book to recoup these expenses. If you copy the book you are in effect stealing from the authors.

KEY TO ABBREVIATIONS

Text Directions

LHS Left-hand side
RHS Right-hand side
s/p Signposted
n/s No signpost
(*) Denotes where to pick up road route when coming from an alternative direction. In other words, if coming in 'From West', follow the route described until the text says 'then as From South(*)'. At this point look for the (*) sign in the directions From South, and continue from this point. From here, both routes From South and From West are running along the same roads.

Ground Plans

Dark shading refers to home supporters' stands/terraces, light shading to stands/terraces for visiting supporters.

Maps

Roads with dark shading refer to major routes, while those in light shading refer to all other minor roads. All maps are drawn in North-South orientation, with varying scales. New for this edition are pub locations denoted by circled numbers.

Underground station
Parking
Overland station
Pub location

London Guide

This London Guide provides general information, useful to supporters travelling to any London club. For example, we have not been able to list any pubs at Chelsea, so visiting fans have to look further afield ... there are some suggestions here. We're assuming many fans will travel by London Underground, so we've concentrated our pub searches around tube stations. The London Guide also has some general road directions, which link with routes outlined under particular clubs. For example, supporters living in South London can drive one of the routes below to Putney Bridge, and pick up directions from there to Stamford Bridge under the entry for Chelsea FC. Hammersmith Bridge is expected to reopen in April 1999.

TO BLACKWALL TUNNEL FROM THE NORTH

Exit M25 at junction 27 and follow signs to 'London (NE), M11' onto the M11 southbound. After 7.1 miles, where the road divides, bear left (s/p A12 London E., The City) onto the North Circular Road. After 4.8 miles, the North Circular ends in a roundabout. Here, turn right (3rd exit, s/p The City A13) onto the A13. Follow signs to 'The City, Blackwall Tunnel' for 4.1 miles, where the Blackwall Tunnel is signposted left. See entries for Charlton FC and Millwall FC from here.

TO NORTH CIRCULAR ROAD

a) From M1: For North Circular Road westbound (Brentford, Fulham, Chelsea, QPR, Kew Bridge): Continue on M1 to end of motorway. At roundabout, turn right (s/p A406 North Circular Road West, Heathrow), under railway bridge. Straight on at next roundabout onto the North Circular Road. For North Circular Road eastbound (Tottenham, West Ham, Leyton Orient, Blackwall Tunnel): Exit M1 at junction 2 (s/p North Circ. Road East A406, The City A1) onto the A1 Great North Road. Follow signs for The City A1 for 1.7 miles to junction, and turn left onto the North Circular Road.

b) From A1(M): Exit M25 at junction 23 (s/p A1(M), Hatfield, A1081 Barnet, A1 London NW). At motorway roundabout (South Mimms) take 2nd exit (s/p London A1) onto the A1. Straight over 1st roundabout (Stirling Corner) after 2.7 miles, and left at the next (Apex Corner, s/p Central London A1 (A41)) after 1.5 miles. Follow signs to 'Central London A1, A41' for 1.7 miles, over Mill Hill roundabout to Fiveways Junction. Here, follow signs for 'West End A41, North Circular Road' under flyover onto the A41. Exit A41 after 1.9 miles (s/p North Circular Road, The West A4, M4). The roundabout is the junction with the North Circular Road. Turn left for Arsenal, Tottenham, West Ham, Blackwall Tunnel. Turn right for Brentford, Fulham, Chelsea, QPR and Kew Bridge.

TO PUTNEY BRIDGE FROM THE SOUTH

From M25, onto the A3: Continue on A3, following signs to Central London for 15.6 miles, and exit at Tibbets Corner (s/p Westminster, West End, Putney A219). At roundabout turn left (1st exit, s/p West End A304, Westminster A3212, Putney, Fulham) onto the A219. After 1.0 miles, at junction with the South Circular Road (A205), go straight on (s/p West End A304, Westminster A23) into Putney High Street. Putney Bridge is 0.4 miles straight ahead.

TO KEW BRIDGE FROM THE SOUTH

Exit M25 at junction 12 (s/p M3 Basingstoke, Southampton, Sunbury), and keep right where the road divides (s/p London SW, Sunbury M3) onto the M3. Go straight on for 11 miles, following signs to Central London A316 to fifth roundabout. Here, take 1st exit (s/p Kew Bridge A205, The West A4). After 1.4 miles past Kew Green with its pubs and restaurants, and after another 0.3 miles over Kew Bridge. Turn left at junction to Brentford FC, right to the Chiswick Roundabout. At the Chiswick Roundabout follow signs to Central London A4 onto the A4 and pick up routes to Fulham FC and Chelsea FC.

TO HAMMERSMITH ROUNDABOUT FROM THE SOUTH

Exit M25 at junction 12 (s/p M3 Basingstoke, Southampton, Sunbury), and keep right where the road divides (s/p London SW, Sunbury M3) onto the M3. From here, follow signs to 'London A316' for about fourteen miles, onto the dinky flyover over the Hogarth Roundabout. Where road divides after 0.3 miles go straight on (s/p Central London, Hammersmith A4), joining the A4. At the Hammersmith Flyover junction after 0.8 miles, keep in left-hand lane and exit the A4 (s/p Hammersmith (A306, A315, A219)). Follow signs to Oxford (A40) for 0.3 miles to T-junction in front of Hays Accountancy Personnel. This is the Hammersmith Roundabout.

LONDON RAIL GUIDE

These are the last midweek trains from London: in other words, these are the trains to catch after an evening game. Obviously, it's not possible to reach some destinations:

To Derby and Sheffield, from St Pancras, 22.00; to Leicester, from St Pancras 23.20; to Nottingham, from St Pancras, 22.00, 23.20; to Liverpool, from Euston 21.05; to Manchester, from Euston, 22.05; to Birmingham, from Euston, 22.45 and 23.45; to Preston, from Euston, 20.35; to Leeds, from Kings Cross, 21.30 and 23.10; to York, from Kings Cross, 22.00; to Southampton, from Waterloo, 22.55, 23.55; to Portsmouth Harbour, from Waterloo, 22.20; to Swansea, from Paddington, 22.00; to Plymouth, from Paddington, 20.35. Please double-check on (0345) 484 950.

LONDON PUB AND FOOD GUIDE

One of the best-known football friendly pubs is at Liverpool Street Station:

The Hamilton Hall (Upper Level, Bishopsgate Entrance) (0171) 247 3579

Weatherspoons (with guests). Huge pub in what used to be the ballroom of the Great Eastern Hotel ... there are cherubs on the ceiling! Bar meals served all day. No under-18s admitted. Open: all day.

In the station itself is a McDonalds, a Burger King and 'Le Croissant'. Outside on Bishopsgate is a KFC and three sandwich shops, some of which open on Saturdays.

ON THE CIRCLE AND DISTRICT LINES

Near VICTORIA, try:

The King's Arms 77 Buckingham Palace Road (0171) 834 7324

Scottish and Newcastle (plus guests). A wonderful 'traditional English pub' with an excellent menu (eg fish and chips £4.95, avocado bake £7.25) served in the restaurant upstairs. Families welcome in restaurant. Open: all day.

The Stage Door 3 Allington Street (0171) 834 7055)

Scottish and Newcastle. A 'traditional drinkers' pub', all dark wood and barrels, serving a full menu (sandwiches, fish and chips, pies) all day. TV. Open: all day.

Just outside Victoria Station, on Victoria Street, is an American Steak House, an 'ASK Pizza', a Pizza Express and a Bella Pasta. Just round the corner, on Buckingham Palace Road, is a Balti House and two theme-cafés, the 'Internet Café', and the 'Space Café'.

SLOANE SQUARE is a good station for supporters heading to Chelsea. Head straight out of the station towards Peter Jones into King's Road. It's a 20-30 minute walk along King's Road, and then right along Edith Grove or Gunter Grove, to Stamford Bridge, passing a huge array of eateries and fashionable shops en route.

SOUTH KENSINGTON is a very 'French' area: Bute Street in particular has some very quaint coffee shops and brasseries. Just outside the station is a great little Italian restaurant called 'Diva', but it doesn't always open on Saturdays. There's also a 'Seasons Traditional Fish and Chip' restaurant on Thurloe Street, two café/brasseries on Exhibition Road, and a KFC, a 'Bosphorous' kebab shop and a 'Bella Pasta' on Old Brompton Road. A good pub almost opposite the station is:

The Norfolk Tavern (part of the Moat House Hotel) at 2/10 Harrington Road (0171) 344 9988

Bass (with Brakspear Ales). A bright, friendly bar, all white wood, and a big-screen TV. Meals such as pizza, pasta, combo dishes, served 12-9. Families welcome. Open: all day.

GLOUCESTER ROAD is much more American/touristy, and is great for a pre-match meal. Right outside the station are: Pizza Piazza, KFC, Haagen Dazs, Burger King, All Bar One, Dino's Restaurant, the Texas Lone Star, and 'Seasons Traditional Fish and Chips' restaurant.

EARLS COURT is, of course, very Australian, and is excellent for food and drink. On Earls Court Road are: a Bakers Oven, an Angus Steak House, a McDonalds, a Pizza Hut and a Hippo's Pizza. On Hogarth Road are Thai, Chinese and Tandoori restaurants, a chique sandwich bar called 'Get Stuffed' and the classy 'Little French Restaurant', where main courses cost about £7. The two pubs to try are:

The King's Head 17 Hogarth Place (0171) 244 5931

Bass. A top-class smart traditional pub, serving bar meals 12-3, 4-7. TV. Open: all day.

The Prince of Teck 161 Earls Court Road

Independent (with Youngs plus guests). The landlord calls it an 'Australian dirty pub', by which he means (we think) that it's a lot of fun! Anyhow, it has boomerangs on the walls and a stuffed kangaroo on the counter. Bar meals 12-3, 6-9, families welcome upstairs. TV. Open: all day.

Right opposite GUNNERSBURY station is **The World Famous John Bull** at 590 Chiswick High Road (see under Brentford entry). This pub is tremendously football-friendly - many fans have such a good time they prefer to stay in the pub and miss the game!

HIGH STREET KENSINGTON is a major shopping centre, with a scattering of eateries including a McDonalds, a Pizza Hut, an Angus Steak House and a Pizza Inn.

ON THE JUBILEE LINE

BAKER STREET is a popular meeting place. Try:

The Globe 43-47 Marylebone Road (0171) 935 6368

Scottish and Newcastle. Well-known ultra-football-friendly pub, one of the best in London. On most days it serves classic traditional fish and chips (in newspaper wrapper!), though when it's really busy (eg Wembley days) it can only serve sandwiches and the like. Big-screen TV, patio. Families welcome to 7 pm. Open: all day.

The Allsop Arms 137-143 Gloucester Place (0171) 723 5864

Scottish and Newcastle (and guests). A wonderful homely traditional pub, and a great place for pies! It serves 'Traditional Great British Pies' for £4.75, as well as other main meals, unless it gets very busy. Big-screen TV and darts. Families welcome to 9 pm. Open: all day.

The Volunteer 245 Baker Street (by the Sherlock Holmes Museum) (0171) 486 4091

Bass. A classic city pub serving 'something a little different' for food ... like 'Cajun chicken and pepper on toast', 12-7 (again only sandwiches when it's very busy). Big-screen TV. Families welcome to 9 pm. Open: all day.

Baker Street is excellent too for food. Right outside the station are: a Pizza Express, Pizza Hut, Jenny's Restaurant, McDonalds, Garfunkels, Deep Pan Pizza, various cafés and a Brasserie.

Arsenal

Highbury

Address: Arsenal Stadium, Avenell Road, Highbury, London N5 1BU
Telephone: Club (0171) 704 4000
Recorded Information (0171) 704 4242
Box Office (0171) 704 4040
Arsenal ClubCall (0891) 202 020
ClubCall/Ticket Information (0891) 202 021
Gunners Shop (0171) 704 4120
Arsenal World of Sport (0171) 272 1000

A visiting American asked us where he should go for a 'real British soccer match experience.' A number of sarcastic remarks sprang to mind of course, but the most sensible suggestion was Arsenal. It's simply that Highbury on a matchday retains a real atmosphere of yesteryear. The streets, shut to traffic, are full of souvenir stands and burger bars, programme sellers and mounted police. And the sections of the ground visible from the streets add to the overall picture: even the old wooden noticeboards are adorned with the Arsenal crest and two small football designs. Highbury is deep within London commuting territory. From this, the good news is that public transport is excellent. The bad news is that parking on all the roads near, and not so near, the ground is for residents only. For those looking for sustenance, however, there are pubs, cafés and restaurants to suit all tastes within easy walking distance.

HOW TO GET THERE

As parking near Highbury is extremely difficult, it's a very good idea to travel to the ground by public transport. Otherwise leave at least an hour for the stretch between the M25 and the ground:

BY CAR: From North (M1): Exit M1 at junction 2 (s/p North Circ. Road East A406, The City A1). Follow signs for 'The City A1' for 1.7 miles to junction with North Circular Road. Turn left onto North Circular and move immediately into right-hand lanes for the A1 (s/p City A1), which branches off to the right. At junction/lights after 1.9 miles head towards the Esso petrol station, and get in left-hand lanes following signs for 'London A1' into Archway Road. Straight on for 1.5 miles, under high bridge and past 'Welcome to Islington' sign, to Archway Corner (the almost-rectangular roundabout sign). Here, take 2nd exit (s/p City A1, then Nags Head, Highbury Corner), remaining on A1. Straight on for 1.6 miles to traffic lights (landmarks to look out for just before this junction are the University of North London, Ladbrokes, Sunrise Foodshop and the Eastern Health and Beauty Centre). Here turn left (no signpost) into Drayton Park. Straight over mini-roundabout, and ground is on RHS after 0.4 miles.

From East: Exit M25 at junction 25 (s/p A10 Enfield, Hertford). At roundabout follow

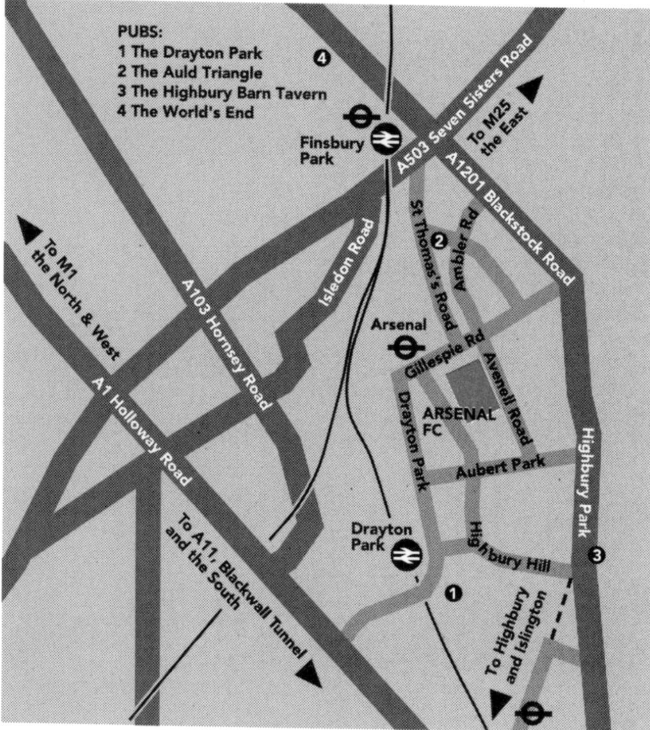

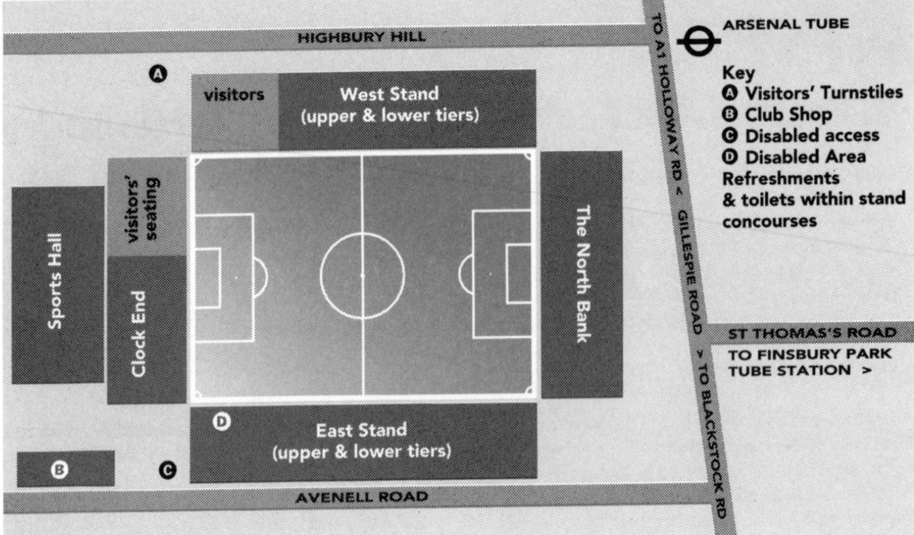

signs to 'A10 Central London, Enfield' onto the A10. Follow Central London signs for 5.0 miles to the Great Cambridge Junction. Here go straight on (s/p Central London A10). After 0.9 miles the road divides: turn right (s/p West End A40, Wood Green, Hornsey) onto The Roundway. After 0.5 miles, turn right at lights (s/p West End A400) and then immediately left (s/p West End, Hornsey, Manor House) into Westbury Avenue. At crossroads/lights after 0.6 miles, by Burger King and Turnpike Lane tube station, turn left into Green Lanes. After 1.5 miles turn right at lights by Manor House tube station (s/p West End A503, Finsbury Park, Holloway) into Seven Sisters Road. After 0.5 miles turn left (s/p Arsenal, Crouch End) just past the KFC and the Happening Beigel Bakery into Blackstock Road. To ground, turn right after 0.4 miles into Gillespie Road.

From South (Blackwall Tunnel) (For directions to tunnel see London Road Guide): Out of tunnel, go straight on (s/p Stratford, Dalston A102) remaining on the A102. Exit A102 after 1.2 miles (s/p A11 City) and turn left at roundabout onto Bow Road. After 0.9 miles, just past Mile End tube, turn right (s/p Hackney A1205) onto the A1205 Grove Road. Straight on for 1.1 miles, over one roundabout, to second roundabout by Huttons. Here, turn left into Victoria Park Road. At T-junction after 0.5 miles, opposite Elbe Footwear, turn right onto Mare Street. After 0.8 miles, just after the Hackney Empire and the KFC Express, turn left at lights (s/p Clapton, Dalston) into Graham Road. Go straight on for 1.6 miles to Highbury Corner roundabout. Follow signs to 'The North, Nags Head' onto the A1 Holloway Road. Turn right after 0.5 miles at lights by Cooperative Funeral Service into Drayton Park.

PUBLIC TRANSPORT: The best policy by far is to travel to Highbury by public transport: Here are a few suggestions:

a) Park at Cockfosters or Oakwood tube stations, and take the Piccadilly Line to Arsenal. Exit M25 at junction 24 (s/p Potters Bar A111), and head south on the A111 (s/p Cockfosters). Cockfosters station is on the LHS after about 2.5 miles, just after the Jet station. The car park costs £1.70 per day Monday-Saturday, free Sundays/Bank Holidays. To get to Oakwood, continue past Cockfosters station for 0.4 miles to the next roundabout, and turn left (s/p Enfield A110) into Bramley Road. Oakwood is on the RHS after another 0.6 miles. There's street parking before and after the station.

b) Take the overland railway routes. Drayton Park, Finsbury Park and Highbury and Islington stations are on the Great Northern Line which runs from central London (either Moorgate or Kings Cross) to various points north, including New Barnet, Potters Bar, Hatfield, Welwyn Garden City, Hertford North, Stevenage, Cambridge, Peterborough and Kings Lynn.

FROM RAILWAY/UNDERGROUND STATIONS:

a) Arsenal (Underground: Piccadilly Line, Zone 2): The station is right by the ground.

b) Drayton Park (Great Northern Line): 5-10 minute walk. Turn left out of station into Drayton Park. This road becomes Gillespie Road at Arsenal tube station. The away turnstiles are on the road opposite the tube station, Highbury Hill.

c) Highbury and Islington (North London Link Line/Great Northern Line. Underground: Victoria Line, Zone 2): On exiting station, bear left to main road. Cross road towards the Barclays Bank, and go straight on into

Highbury Place. Keep straight on, with the park on the LHS. Where road ends, cross Highbury Crescent, and go straight on along pathway. At clock tower turn left into Highbury Hill. This long road leads to the away turnstiles.
d) Finsbury Park (Great Northern Line. Underground: Victoria Line, Zone 2): About 0.5 miles. There are three exits from the station. The best idea is to follow signs to 'Station Place', which is by the Arsenal World of Sport shop. Turn right out of the station, along by the shop, and cross the main Seven Sisters Road into St. Thomas's Road. Where road divides, bear right, keeping on St. Thomas's Road to the ground.
Last Midweek Trains: Good services on all lines. From Finsbury Park, for example, there are trains to Moorgate at 22.06 and 22.20; to Kings Cross at 22.02, 22.08 and 22.17; and to Stevenage via Welwyn Garden City at 21.41, 22.11 and 22.41. Please double-check on (0345) 484 950. For midweek trains from the main London stations, see London Guide at front of book.
BY BUS: Nos. 4, 19 and 236 run along Highbury Grove to Blackstock Road, from where it's a 5-10 minute walk to the away turnstiles.

PARKING

By far the best advice anyone can give about parking at Highbury is: DON'T. Near the ground, there's a strict residents-only parking policy, and supporters' cars will be towed away. That said, those who arrive early enough can find spaces in Drayton Park or the roads south of the ground between Highbury Park/Highbury Grove and Green Lanes, where there are fewer restrictions.

THE GROUND

Highbury ... excellent ground, great team, good facilities, loads of character. There's just one problem: it's not big enough. Both the fans and the club eye the likes of Old Trafford and worry about being left behind. The club wants to raise the ground capacity from 38,500 to about 50,000, preferably by developing the present site. However, local opposition is fierce, the East Stand is a listed building, and the West and North Stands back onto houses in Highbury Hill and Gillespie Road. The obvious alternative is for Arsenal to relocate. The club famously announced, in January 1998, that it was considering moving to Wembley. It subsequently backed down, but other sites, including one at King's Cross, remain a possibility.

For season 98/99 at least, Arsenal will continue to play at Highbury. While the East and West Stands were built in the 1930s, both the North Stand and the Clock End have been redeveloped within the last five years at a cost of more than £25 million. Facilities in the North Stand in particular are excellent, with plush padded seats, loads of legroom, spacious concourses and kiosks serving smoked salmon beigels. Facilities are not quite as palatial for visiting fans in the Clock End. Expect more

'Won't be long ref! Just watching the first half highlights.'

standard football food, and the view from the back is obstructed by thick pillars. Supporters always stand up when the ball heads into the far corner, then stand up again to watch the action replays on the huge video screens!
Total Capacity: 38,500. For away fans: approximately 3,000. Turnstiles 69-76.
Cost (98/99): Adults £16. No concessions for visiting supporters.
Disabled Facilities: Space for 10 disabled fans and ten helpers in the South-West corner. *Disabled Toilet:* Nearby. *Cost:* Free for disabled and helper. *Booking:* Essential, two months in advance. *Parking:* Those with orange disabled badges can park in Elwood Street, on a first-come, first-served basis. Places start filling up by 1 pm. *For the Blind:* There are 66 seats for the blind/partially-sighted in the North-West corner.
Programme: £2.
Visitors' Toilets: *Male:* To go off at a tangent, as this book is apt to do, the loos at Arsenal brought back memories of a scene in the film 'The Last Emperor', where the emperor, now imprisoned, is told by his fellow inmates to pee against the side of the bucket, as otherwise the noise wakes them all up! It's the same at Highbury – fans said the curious plastic-type urinals were, well, 'loud'. Fans also noted the 'watery' floor, but were mightily impressed that there was a man diligently mopping it all up. *Female:* Still the tops! Immaculate as ever, clean, with nicely scented soap.
Food and Drink: The slow service didn't put supporters into a very good mood: 'Twenty minutes I

waited for this burger (£2.50),' said one 'and it's burnt! The chips are soggy too!' Nearly all fans thought the chips were overpriced: '£1.10 for 75 mm of chip,' said one disgruntled fan (14.10.97, 26.10.97).

PUB GUIDE

The Drayton Park (1) 66 Drayton Park (0171) 359 3915
Scottish and Newcastle/Courage/Watneys. Attractive Victorian-style pub, extremely welcoming and football-friendly. TV. Open: all day.

The Auld Triangle (2) (formerly the Plimsoll Arms) 52 St Thomas's Road (0171) 354 2869
Free House/Courage. Forget the old Plimsoll Arms ... the Auld Triangle has been done-up in traditional style, with wood everywhere! It's very football-friendly, says the landlady, with a great matchday atmosphere. Bar snacks served 12-3. Big-screen TV. Families welcome. Open: all day.

The following pubs are all within two to three minutes walk of Highbury and Islington station. The station is on a major roundabout, Highbury Corner. The 'The Famous Cock Tavern' is next to the station. The 'Hen and Chickens' is visible from the station entrance, with the 'Alwyne Castle' further down the same road. For the 'Tut 'N Shive', turn right out of the station and follow the roundabout sign to 'The City A1' into Upper Street.

The Famous Cock Tavern 259 Upper Street (0171) 226 4627
Ambitious Pub Group. Large characterful pub, mightily popular on matchdays. Full meals and snacks served weekends 12-6 weekdays, 11-3, 5-8. TV. Families welcome. Open: all day.

The Tut 'N Shive 235 Upper Street (0171) 359 7719
Whitbread (with Flowers and Trophy). Cosy one roomed pub with wooden floors and panels. Big screen TV. Open: all day.

The Hen and Chickens 109 St Paul's Road (0171) 704 7620
Bass (with London Pride, Caffreys). Bright traditional one-roomed pub with a theatre upstairs. Bar snacks served all day. 2 TVs. Open: all day from 12.

The Alwyne Castle 83 St Paul's Road (0171) 288 9861
Bass (with Caffreys). Large well-decorated pub, serving bar snacks 12-3. Big-screen TV, patio. Families welcome. Open: all day.

The Highbury Barn Tavern (3) 26 Highbury Park (0171) 226 2383
Greenalls (with Directors, Flowers, Tetleys). Large, traditional pub in an 18th century building, which certainly knows the way to a football fan's heart ... i.e. big-screen TV, table football, pool, darts and a full ('Brew 'n Chew') menu served all day. Families welcome. Open: all day.

The World's End (4) 21-23 Stroud Green Road (0171) 281 8679
Free House (real ales). Large attractive bright pub with wooden floors and a big-screen TV. Highly recommended! The landlord describes it as 'very vibey' but all ages welcome. Open: 11-midnight.

FOOD GUIDE

Near the ground, there's the 'Golden Fish Bar' (hamburger and chips for £1.20) on the corner of Gillespie Road and Avenell Road, and the small 'Arsenal Cafe'. In addition, numerous mobile burger vans emerge on matchdays. Nearby Blackstock Road and Highbury Park offer a huge range of outlets, mostly offering all-day breakfasts and the like. Of these, locals recommend the 'Arsenal Fish Bar' on the corner of Blackstock Road and Riversdale Road. Further up the Blackstock Road are the more upmarket 'Bodari Indian Restaurant' and the Italian 'San Daniele Del Friuli'.

Fans arriving at Highbury and Islington tube station have a good, though slightly more limited, choice. Head towards the 'Hen and Chickens' pub, into St Paul's Road. Almost opposite the pub is the upmarket 'Gill Wing Café', with breakfast at £3.95 and meals from £5.95. Further along the road are a burger/kebab bar, a pizza restaurant and another cheerful café.

LOCAL MEDIA

Local Radio: Capital Gold 1548 AM; GLR 94.9 FM; XFM 104.9.
Radio Phone-ins: Capital Gold, Saturdays 2-6.30, midweek 7-10 (or 7-8 if no match). Call (0845) 35 60 7080.
Saturday Sports Paper: None.

MISCELLANEOUS

Safety Factor: Very few problems here.
Rivals: The rivalry with Tottenham dates back to 1913 when Arsenal moved to North London. Manchester United is disliked 'because they keep winning!'
Fanzines: 'Highbury High', PO Box 16198, London, N1 9WF; 'One-Nil Down, Two-One Up', PO Box 10794, London, N10 2DW; 'The Gooner', BCM Box 7499, London, WC1N 3XX.
Best Unofficial Websites:
Arseweb:
http://www.netlink.co.uk/users/arseweb/index/html
Arsenet: http://www.isfa.com
James Killeen's Pages:
http://www.iol.ie/~killeen/arse/htm
Chris Parry's Pages: http://www.interstate.co.uk/arsenal/
Internet Soccer Fans Info:
http://www.isfa.com/ira/arsenal/
Steve Gleiber's Pages:
http://www.users.fl.net.au/~steve/index.htm
Tourist Information: Islington (0171) 278 8787.

Aston Villa

Villa Park

Address: Villa Park, Trinity Road, Birmingham, B6 6HE
Telephone: Club (0121) 327 2299
Ticket Office (0121) 327 5353
Shop (0121) 327 2800
ClubCall (0891) 121 148
Ticket Information Line (0891) 121 848
Official Website: http://www.astonvilla-fc.co.uk/

Villa Park is a whopping great Premiership ground, with one of the tallest stands in the world, less than half a mile from two major motorways, the M6 and the A38(M). Yet so many fans complain about getting lost and missing the start of the game! And why? Because of the maze of terraced streets to the south and east of the ground, the pre-match traffic gridlock and the difficulty of finding a safe parking place. The key is to allow plenty of time to park up in one of the many official and semi-official car parks and to walk to the ground. Or take the train, as the station's two minutes from the away turnstiles. Unusually for the Premiership, there's a pub close to the ground welcoming away supporters, and some decent chippies just down the road.

HOW TO GET THERE

BY CAR: The routes below take supporters either to the ground, or to a good area for car parking. The car parks, most of which are at local schools, are all marked on the map.

From North-East (M1-M42-M6): Exit M1 at junction 23A (s/p A42 (M42), The South West, Tamworth, Birmingham) onto the M42. Exit M42 after 29.7 miles at junction 8 (s/p Birmingham Central, E, N and W, M6) onto the M6 northbound. Exit M6 after 5.0 miles at junction 6 (s/p A38(M), Birmingham (Cen), A38 Birmingham NE)(*)and then follow signs to 'A38, Birmingham (NE), Lichfield' to the Salford Circus

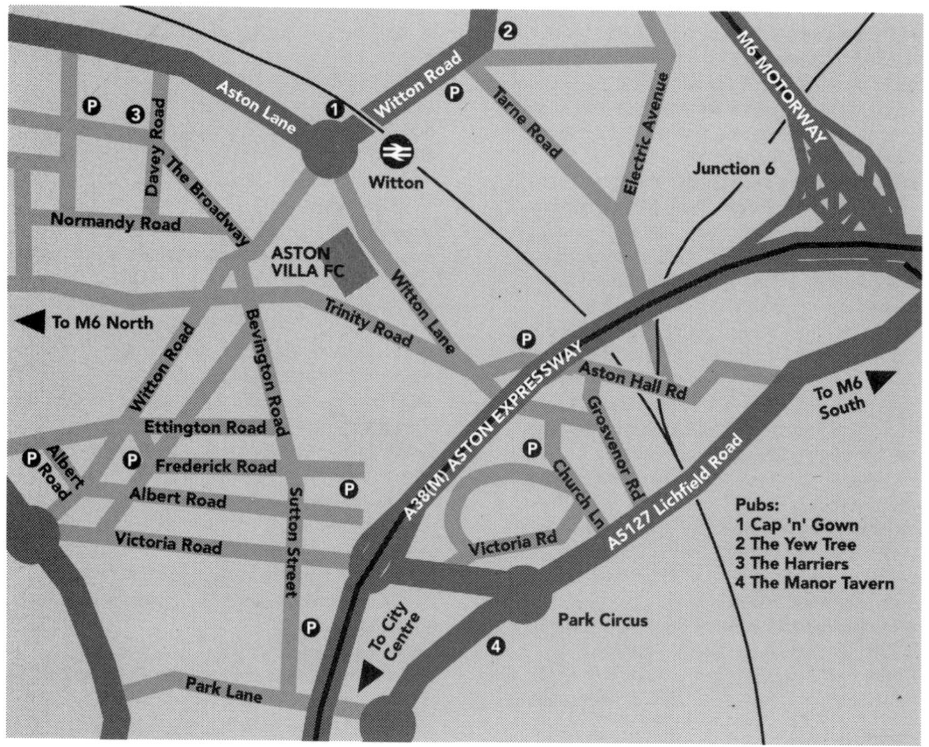

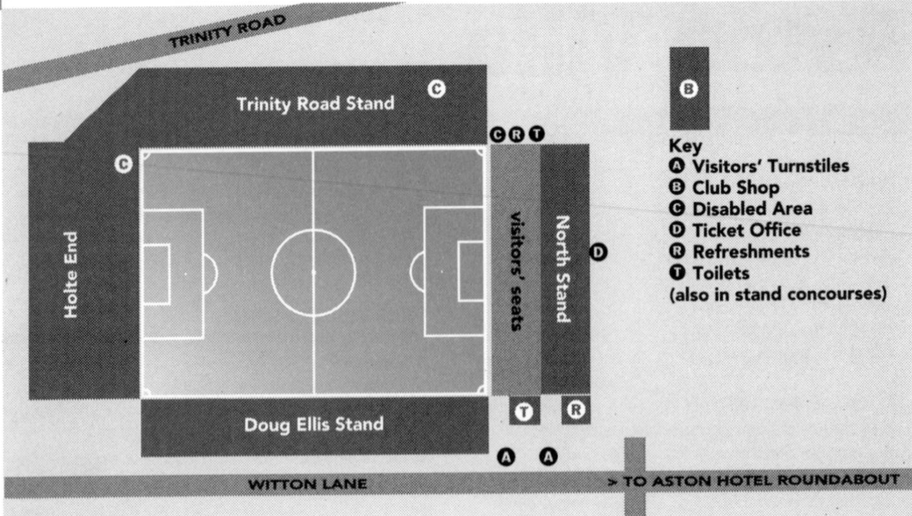

roundabout. Here turn right (s/p City Centre A5127) onto Lichfield Road. After 0.2 miles, where road divides, by the 'Reservoir' pub, keep in the right-hand lanes, and then filter right in front of the 'King Edward VII' pub (s/p Witton, Aston Villa, Junction 6 Industrial Park) onto Aston Hall Road. After 0.4 miles, by 'Priory Castor' turn left (no signpost) under railway bridge, towards the Vauxhall garage (remaining on Aston Hall Road). The Aston Villa Leisure Centre car park is almost immediately on the RHS. To get to the ground, continue along Aston Hall Road, and turn right into Witton Lane.

From South (M1 or M42-M6): Exit M6 at junction 6 (s/p A38(M), Birmingham (Cen), A38 Birmingham NE). Then as From North-East(*).

From North-West (M6): Exit M6 at junction 7 (s/p A34, B'ham (N), Walsall). At roundabout/junction follow signs to Birmingham A34 onto the A34 dual carriageway. Keep on the A34 for 2.8 miles, passing the 'Tennis Court' pub on the LHS, to where the road divides. Here, keep right, following 'City Centre A34' signs over the flyover and through an underpass. Immediately after the underpass move into left-hand lanes and turn left at lights (s/p Aston, Lozells, Handsworth) in front of the Saddam Hussein Mosque into Trinity Road. For the parking at the Sacred Heart RC Primary School, take 1st left turn into Earlsbury Gardens, or take street parking in this area. To ground, continue on Trinity Road, crossing Witton Road after 0.6 miles, and ground is straight ahead.

From South West (M5): At end of M5, where road divides, keep left (s/p London M1 and M40, Birmingham N and E) onto the M6 eastbound. Exit M6 at junction 7 or 6, picking up road directions as above.

FROM RAILWAY STATION (Witton): Two minute walk to ground. *By foot:* Down pathway to main road and turn left, passing the 'Cap 'N' Gown' to roundabout. Turn left to away turnstiles.

Last Midweek Trains: Trains run from Witton to Birmingham New Street at 22.03 and 22.41. Trains from New Street run to: London at 21.55, 22.50 and 23.09; to Manchester/Leeds at 22.01 and 23.30; to Derby and Sheffield at 22.25; and to Bristol at 22.27 and 23.00. Please double-check on (0345) 484 950.

BY BUS: The no. 7 runs from Birmingham city centre, the no. 11 takes the 'Outer Circle' route, and the no. 440 runs from Perry Barr to Bearwood and Handsworth.

PARKING

Street parking round Villa Park is generally not safe and, as in other large cities, youngsters offer to 'look after' the car for a fee up to £4. There are a large number of official and semi-official car parks (see map). The two main car parks are at the Aston Villa Leisure Centre on Aston Hall Road, and the Brookvale Road Car park, at the junction with Tame Road (1,000 spaces, £4). Space is also available at the following schools: Aston Tower on Upper Sutton Street; Mansfield Green on Albert Road, near junction with Mansfield Road; the King Edward Grammar School and the Prince Albert school, both on Albert Road; the Broadway School on The Broadway, near 'The Harriers'; the Manor Park Primary on Church Lane; and the Sacred Heart R.C. Primary on Earlsbury Gardens.

THE GROUND

A home supporter once described Villa Park as 'a good ground, but not a great one.' The problem is that each

stand has been developed independently, and together they don't quite gel. The spectacular Holte End, which holds 13,600 supporters, is the largest end-stand in Europe ... fans in the south corner have a fine view of the pitch, Trinity Road and Aston Park beyond! The Doug Ellis and North Stands are both two-tier cantilever constructions, large, smart but nothing out-of-the-ordinary. The Trinity Road Stand, now over 70 years old, retains the most character, with its slender pillars and ornate balcony painted in claret, blue and white. Keen to further increase the ground capacity, the club has been looking at ways to enlarge the Trinity Road Stand. The latest plans envisage removing the roof and the decorative gables, and building out over Trinity Road. The plan has, however, already run into local opposition. Away fans are housed in the bottom tier of the North Stand. There are no pillars, but fans often stand up if play heads to the far touchlines.

Total Capacity: 39,339. For away fans: 3,086.

Cost (98/99): Adults £17, no concessions for away fans.

Disabled Facilities: Space for visiting disabled supporters is limited, but the club hopes to gain extra spaces at the back of the North Stand Lower. Please contact Kim Graham in the ticket office for more information. *Disabled Toilet:* Nearby. *Cost:* Free for disabled, £17 for helper. *Booking:* Essential. *Parking:* By request, subject to availability. Please call Anne-Marie on (0121) 327 5399. *For the Blind:* 12 seats with commentary on headphones, in the Trinity Road Stand Lower. No charge for blind supporter, £17 for helper.

Programme: £2.

Visitors' Toilets: *Male:* There are loos at both sides of the away end, but most fans head for the ones at the far side, by the Trinity Road Stand, which are a lot less smelly. *Female:* Our embarrassed male researcher finally found a female willing to go and check out the loos, only for her to come charging out again after ten seconds convinced it was a wind-up. She'd just seen one of the biggest spiders this side of the Atlantic.

Food and Drink: Not bad at all: the pies and pasties (£1.50) were hot – some almost too hot – with plenty of filling. The hot dogs and burgers (£2) were also good, but came with undercooked onions whether fans wanted them or not (13.8.97).

PUB GUIDE

The Cap 'n' Gown (1) 458 Witton Road (0121) 344 4514
Carlsberg/Tetley (with Ansells Mild). A large friendly pub, due for renovation in the summer of 1998, welcoming both home and away supporters. Baguettes. TV. Families welcome. Disabled facilities. Open: all day.

The Yew Tree (2) Brookvale Road (0121) 356 1751
Courage (with Theakstons). Traditional pub, popular with both sets of supporters. Meals served to 1.30, and there's a snack-bar in the car park on matchdays. TV, patio. Children welcome to 9 pm. Open: all day.

The Harriers (3) The Broadway (0121) 356 5119
Allied Domecq/Ansells. Cheerful, modern-style pub, welcoming home and away fans. Big-screen TV, pool table. Open: 12-3, 5-11; from 5.30 for midweek games.

The Tennis Court Walsall Road (A34), Perry Barr (on route in from M6 junction 7) (0121) 311 2971
Bass. This is an ideal sports-friendly pub, with several large rooms, two big-screen TVs, table football, pool, darts and a beer garden. 'Sizzler' meals served 12-2 and midweek also 5-7. Disabled facilities. Open: all day.

The Manor Tavern (4) Portland Street (0121) 326 8780
Ansells (with Tetleys Smooth Flow). A friendly, old-fashioned pub with lounge, public bar and pool room. Opens from 10.30 for breakfast (£2.50) and serves bar snacks all day. TV. Open: Saturdays from 10.30, otherwise from 11.

FOOD GUIDE

On Witton Road, almost opposite the 'Cap 'n' Gown', is a row of shops including the recommended 'Silver Sands' Caribbean café/takeaway, and the 'Balti Kitchen'. Just round the corner, in Manor Road by Witton Station, is the 'Villa Fish Bar', which also serves chicken and kebabs. There's a fish-and-chip shop on The Broadway, by 'The Harriers', while home fans recommend the 'Witton Fish Bar and Kebab House' on the junction of Witton Road and Bevington Road.

LOCAL MEDIA

Local Radio: BBC Radio WM 95.6 FM; Capital Gold 1152 AM.

Radio phone-ins: Radio WM, Friday evenings 7-9, until 6 pm on Saturdays and to 10 pm after midweek games, call (0121) 432 2000; Capital Gold 1152 AM, Fridays 6-7.30 pm, Sat 5-7 pm, call (0121) 359 5599.

Saturday Sports Paper: The 'Sports Argus' pink.

MISCELLANEOUS

Safety Factor: The major problem here is car crime.

Rivals: Historically it's Birmingham City, but the two clubs haven't been in the same division for ages.

Fanzines: 'Heroes and Villains', PO Box 1703, Perry Barr, Birmingham, B42 1UZ; 'Witton Wag', PO Box 26, Wednesbury, West Midlands, WS10 9YT; 'The Holy Trinity', 216 Brandwood Road, Kings Heath, Birmingham, B14 6LD.

Unofficial Websites:
http://freespace.virgin.net/mac.mccolgan/h&v/
http://members.tripod.com/~site_11/villa.html
Villa Web: http://www.gbar.dtu.dk/~C937079/AVFC/
'The Villan': http://www.villan.demon.co.uk/
http://www.geocities.com/Colosseum/Field/6089/

Tourist Information: (0121) 693 6300.

B

Barnet

Underhill Stadium

Address: Underhill Stadium, Westcombe Drive, Barnet, Hertfordshire EN5 2BE
Telephone: Club (0181) 441 6932
ClubCall (0891) 121 544

Barnet is a prosperous little town, just south of the M25, in the middle of the Green Belt. No London gridlocks here! For the football fan, everything's within walking distance. The ground itself is in a residential area, so parking's not a problem, and the nearest pub, just two minutes walk away, is very football-friendly. And just round the corner is one of the best fish-and-chip shops for miles. Those with a little more time to spare can amble up Barnet Hill to the High Street, which has many pubs, a beigel café and an excellent traditional fish and chip restaurant.

HOW TO GET THERE

BY CAR: From All Main Routes: Exit M25 at junction 23 (s/p A1(M) Hatfield, A1081 Barnet). At roundabout follow signs to 'Barnet A1081' onto the A1081 St Albans Road. At lights/T-junction after 2.4 miles, by KallKwik, bear right (n/s) into Barnet High Street. At lights by church and the 'Crown and Anchor', go straight on into Barnet Hill. (*)After 0.6 miles turn right at lights just before the 'Old Red Lion' into Underhill, then first left into Barnet Lane. Ground is on LHS after 0.1 miles.
From North London: Exit A406 North Circular Road onto the A41 northbound (s/p A41 The North A1). At lights after 0.5 miles, by Hendon Central tube station, go straight on (s/p Mill Hill A41, Colindale A5150). From here, follow signs for 'The North A1' for 4.8 miles to

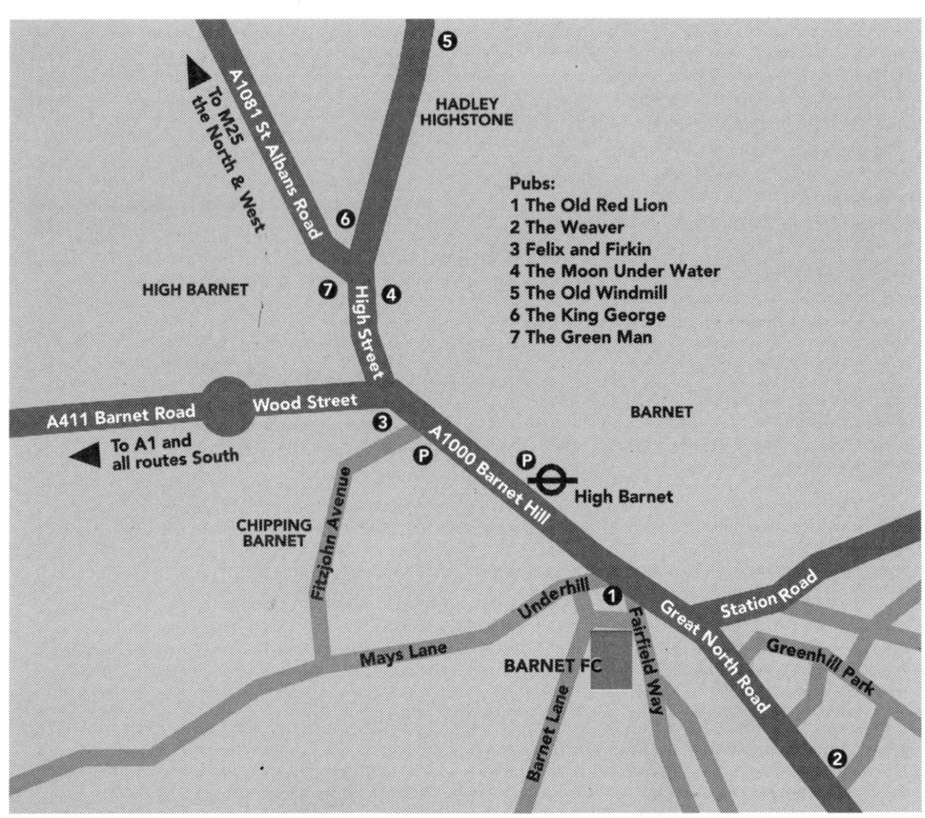

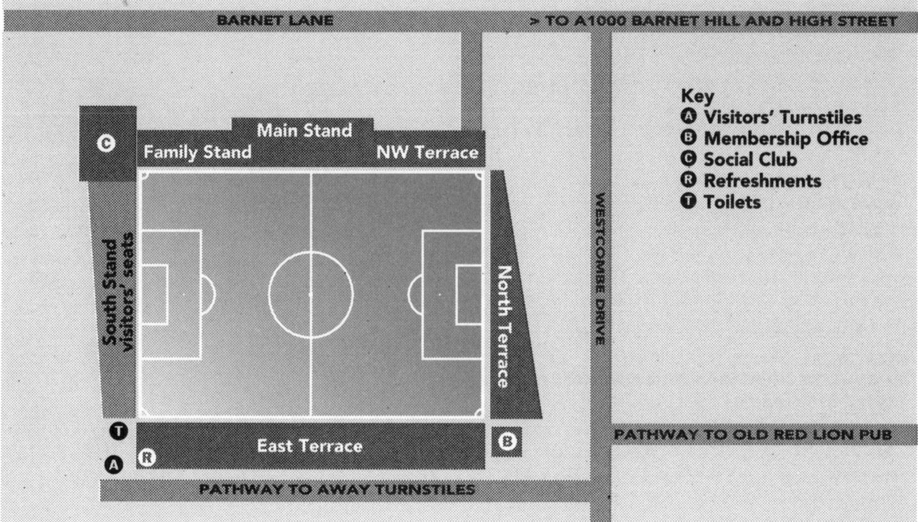

Stirling Corner roundabout (the one with 'Bennigans' on it). Here, turn right (s/p Arkley, Barnet A411) onto the A411. Go straight on at roundabout after 2.5 miles, by the 'Black Horse' pub, remaining on the A411. At junction/lights after 0.3 miles by the church and the 'Bull Theatre', go straight on into Barnet Hill. Then as From All Main Routes(*).

FROM UNDERGROUND STATION (High Barnet, Northern Line, Zone 5). NB It can take an hour from the centre of London to High Barnet on this line: *By foot:* 5-8 minute walk. Head up slip-road to main road (Barnet Hill) and turn left, down the hill. Turn right in front of the 'Old Red Lion'. Walk through pub car park to pathway leading to Westcombe Drive.

FROM RAILWAY STATION (New Barnet, 20 minutes from King's Cross): *By foot:* Up steps from platform, and turn left along footbridge. At station building, turn right towards the bus stops. Follow road round, going straight over mini-roundabout, and turn left along Station Road (the main road). At junction/lights after 0.6 miles turn right (s/p High Barnet) onto the Great North Road. First left into Fairfield Way, first right into Westcombe Drive. *Last Midweek Trains:* From New Barnet, trains back to King's Cross run at 21.47, 22.17, 22.47 and 23.17. For onward connections, see London Guide at front of book. Please double-check on (0345) 484 950.

BY BUS: The following run along Barnet Hill: nos. 34 (to Walthamstow), 84 (to St Albans), 107 (to Edgware), 234 (to Muswell Hill), 263 (to Archway), 307 (to Brimsdown).

PARKING

Street parking is available around the ground, and off the Great North Road (eg Greenhill Park, Richmond Road). Football fans can use the car park at High Barnet tube station (£1.90 all day). The shoppers' car park on Fitzjohn Avenue (£1 for 4 hours, £1.50 for 6 hours) is convenient for those having lunch along the High Street ... the turning is off Barnet Hill, by the 'Felix and Firkin' and the big red lion sign. Fans can also park at the 'Felix and Firkin' (£1.50 all day).

THE GROUND

Underhill, said a Barnet fan, 'is neat and intimate, but leaves a lot to be desired ... it's still non-league.' The ground has fallen foul of FA regulations which stipulate that league venues must have a capacity of 6,000, including 2,000 seats. Underhill has neither, and for many months the club has been campaigning to build a £14 million state-of-the-art leisure complex at Copthall Athletics Stadium near junction 2 of the M1. Local residents' associations are strongly opposed, and a public enquiry was called in June 1998. Barnet FC has until the end of season 98/99 to move, or to redevelop Underhill, so its future remains uncertain. For season 98/99 at least, away fans are housed on a bank of uncovered temporary seating behind the goal at what home fans term 'the bottom end.' In other words, the pitch slopes toward the visitors, affording them a good view even of the action at the opposite goalmouth!

Total Capacity: 4,057. For away fans: 787.

Cost (98/99): Adults £10, no concessions for away fans.

Disabled Facilities: Space for about six visiting supporters in front of the Family Stand. *Disabled Toilet:* In the social club. *Cost:* Free for disabled, £10 for helper. *Booking:* About two days in advance. *Parking:* None available. *For the Blind:* No special facilities.

B

Programme: £1.50.

Visitors' Toilets: *Male:* One supporter had sat in a cubicle dripping depression. He'd written on the walls: 'We're so s*** it's unbelievable' and 'Why do we come all this way to watch this cr**?' And under a more upbeat 'CUFC For Ever!' he'd simply added 'Oh God!' *Female:* It's share and share alike here, as there was just one bar of soap between three sinks!

Food and Drink: Tip – buy the burgers (£1.60) before the game, when they're 'nice and hot'. By the end of half-time they were 'cool and tasteless!' Word got round that the pies (£1.30) were excellent – so much so, that even the ball went into the snack bar in the Main Stand! The coffee and tea (both 50p) were good (8.11.97).

PUB GUIDE

The Old Red Lion (1) Great North Road (0181) 449 3735
McMullens. Popular traditional-style pub, the nearest to the ground. Football menu served 11-2.30, 6-11. TV, darts. Doorman on matchdays. Open: all day.

The Weaver (2) 27 Greenhill Parade (0181) 449 9292
Free House (real ales). Characterful pub packed with bric-a-brac. Full meals to 8.30 pm. Families welcome. Open: all day.

The Felix and Firkin (3) 31 High Street (0181) 449 0099
Firkin. Classic Firkin pub serving a full menu all day. Six TVs, big-screen TV, table football, beer garden. Disabled facilities. No entry for under-18s. Open: all day from 12.

The Moon Under Water (4) 148 High Street (0181) 441 9476
Free House/J.D. Weatherspoons. A smart pub, ideal for a pre-match meal. Beer garden, no smoking area. No entry for under-18s. Open: all day.

Also recommended: **The Old Windmill (5),** 12 Hadley Highstone, a well-furnished Patrician Inns pub with real ales and bar lunches; **The King George (6),** 149 High Street, a smart quiet Bass pub; **The Green Man (7),** 143 High Street, a friendly McMullens pub with four pool tables, and serving full meals 12-2, 7-9.30. There's also a cluster of pubs around New Barnet railway station, including the excellent **Railway Tavern** at 3 East Barnet Road.

FOOD GUIDE

The nearest takeaway to Underhill is the highly-recommended 'Fresh Fry Fish and Chips' on the Great North Road near 'The Weaver'. Almost opposite is 'Café Jose', a smart delicatessen with three or four tables and a takeaway service. For a greater choice, head up Barnet Hill. 'The Blue Fin' fish and chip shop serves Peter's Pies (£1.20), while opposite is 'Barnet Kebab', Perfect Pizza and Domino's Pizza. Also nearby are: 'George's Café' and the 'Just Delight Café'; the 'Original Pasta Bar' offering twenty vegetarian dishes from about £8, and the 'Continental Bakery'. Bear right at the church for the smart 'Café Pacino', Pizza Hut, McDonalds and Greggs Bakers. At the end of the street is the recommended 'Whitecaps' fish and chip restaurant.

'I wish he'd do his 60 yard dribbles when we kick DOWN the slope!'

LOCAL MEDIA

Local Radio: BBC Three Counties Radio 103.8 FM, 630 MW; Capital Gold 1548 AM; GLR 94.9 FM.

Radio Phone-ins: Three Counties Radio, Friday nights 6-7, Saturdays 2-2.30, 5-6 pm, call (0645) 455 5555; Capital Gold, Sat 2-6.30, midweek 7-10 (or 7-8 if no match). Call (0845) 35 60 7080.

Saturday Sports Paper: None.

MISCELLANEOUS

Safety Factor: Some trouble in the latter half of the season, but away from the ground on the Great North Road.

Rivals: Enfield (or 'the E-word'), Stevenage, Fulham, Orient, Northampton and Colchester.

Fanzines: 'Two Together', 5 Trellis Drive, Lychpit, Basingstoke RG24 8YU.

Unofficial Websites:
'Two Together': http://www.twotogether.demon.co.uk/
http://members.tripod.com/~BagleyR/index.html
http://members.aol.com/TWebb2581/Barnet.htm

Tourist Information: No local office.

Barnsley

Oakwell

Address: Oakwell Ground, Grove Street, Barnsley, South Yorkshire, S71 1ET
Telephone: Club/Box Office (01226) 211 211
ClubCall (0891) 211 152

Talk about a transformation! Ten years ago, Barnsley was a seriously unfashionable club, playing at a windswept traditional ground with acres of terracing and just 2,000 seats. In 1997/98, the club had Premiership football, a packed 19,000 all-seater stadium, and a reputation as the never-say-die footballing underdog. Despite relegation, the club is now so fashionable that Barnsley car stickers have appeared in the most obscure London sidestreets.
For most visitors, the trip to Oakwell is stress-free. The road route is well-signposted and passes a couple of excellent pubs, the car park's close to the turnstiles, and the town centre's just a short walk away.

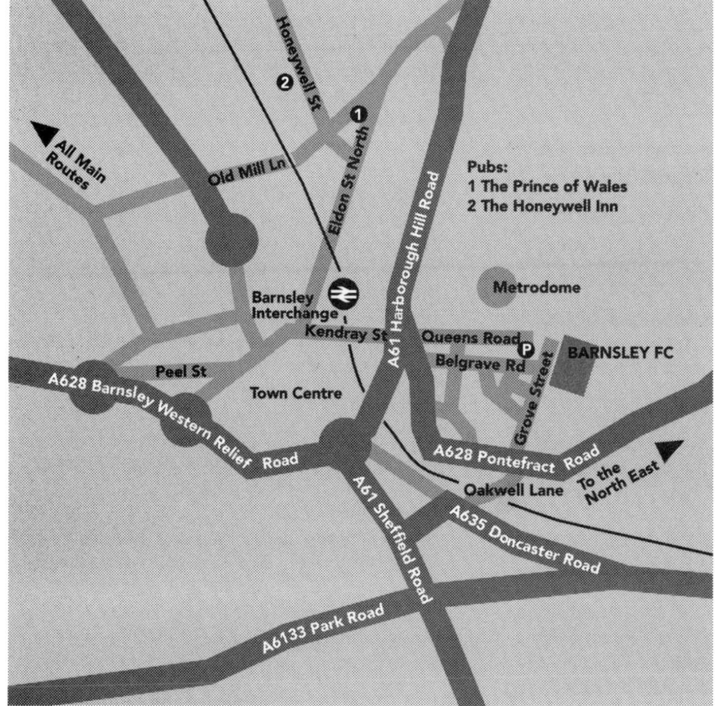

HOW TO GET THERE

BY CAR: The local police are keen to keep football fans away from the congested town centre and advise all to take the following route: Exit M1 at junction 37 (s/p Barnsley, Manchester A628) and at roundabout follow signs to 'Barnsley A628' onto the A628 Dodworth Road. After 0.3 miles turn left (s/p Barnsley FC, Barnsley General Hospital, Huddersfield (A637)) into Pogmoor Road. Past the hospital entrance after 1.1 miles and after a further 0.1 miles turn right at crossroads/lights in front of the Orchard Views Home for the Elderly, into Gawber Road (s/p Barnsley FC, but not very prominently). After 0.3 miles, all traffic turns left by Raley's Solicitors into Victoria Road. At crossroads/lights by Howard and Co. after 0.3 miles, go straight on into Old Mill Lane. Past 'Prince of Wales' pub after 0.3 miles, and get in right-hand lane at major junction/roundabout. Here, follow signs to 'Sheffield A61' (and Football Ground/Metrodome) up into Harborough Hill Road. After 0.3 miles branch left (s/p Metrodome/Football Ground) and then immediately left again (s/p Visitors' Parking) into Queen's Road. The club's official visitors' car park is at top of road on RHS.

FROM RAILWAY STATION (Barnsley Interchange): From Platform 1: leave station without crossing the railway line. Turn right to main road, then left away from the level crossing, past the bingo hall. Cross the slip road and walk under bridge. Cross road and turn left up the slip road. Take 1st right into Queen's Road, towards 'Queen's Road Dental Care'. Road leads to ground. *Last Midweek Trains:* Trains run to Sheffield up to 23.25,

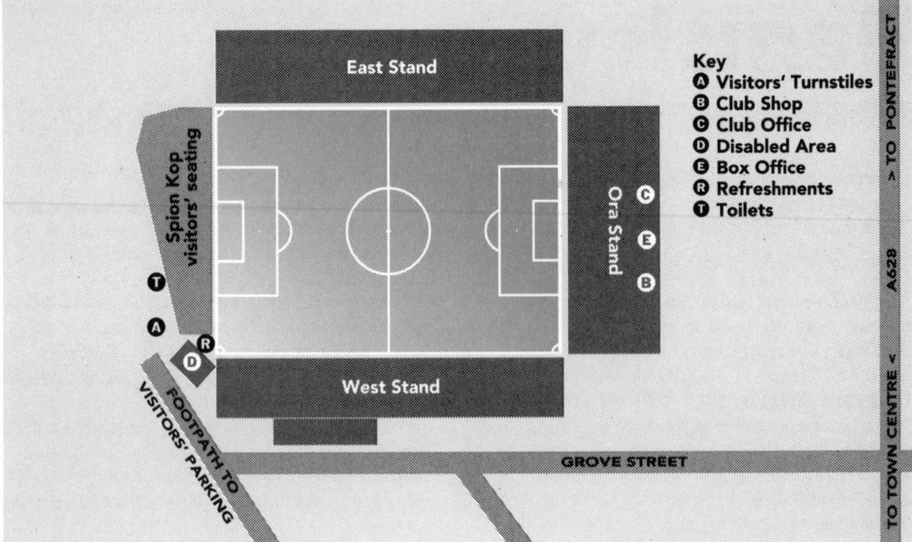

but from there the choice is limited. There are no connecting trains to London after 21.32. Trains do run to Leeds (23.14, not Friday), and to Newcastle, via Doncaster (23.09). Please double-check on (0345) 484 950.

BY BUS: From the town centre bus station, it's quicker to walk. However, if needs be, frequent buses (e.g. nos. 36, 37, 38, 211, 245 and 247) run from Stand D2 or D3 along Pontefract Road.

PARKING

The best option is the official visitors' car park (£2), at the top of Queen's Road. It rarely gets full. There are a number of informal car parks along Pontefract Road, charging about £2, but these can be a good walk from the ground and car crime is not uncommon.

THE GROUND

'It's only half-built,' said one Tykes fan. 'We desperately need a new away end, and part of the main stand is more than ninety years old ... stick it in a museum!' The developed sections of Oakwell – the 7,500-seater East Stand, complete with executive boxes, and the 4,500-seater Ora Stand – are very impressive indeed, and would grace any Premiership venue. The remaining half of the ground remains a bit of a headache. To comply with Taylor Report regulations, the club put seats onto the part-uncovered West Stand paddock and the uncovered Spion Kop, which is allocated to the visiting supporters. This leaves away fans at risk from sunburn and showers, though – as the terracing was reprofiled – the view is surprisingly good. The club has made the rebuilding of the Spion Kop a priority, and has planning permission for a development to mirror the Ora Stand opposite. The work, however, depends on available cash and Barnsley's league status.

In the meantime, the club is building a Football Academy behind the Spion Kop, with several pitches and smart little stands to house up to 2,000 spectators for Barnsley junior games! How times have changed.

Total Capacity: 19,000. For away fans: 2,036, and up to 4,200 for cup ties.

Cost (98/99): Adult £15, concessions (juniors/OAPs) £9, available on a reciprocal basis, i.e., if the away club offers concessions to Barnsley fans.

Disabled Facilities: Excellent! Between 6 and 8 places are available in a special stand, shared with home fans, between the Spion Kop and the West Stand. It's fully enclosed, and therefore warm and protected from the elements, though some fans lament the loss of matchday atmosphere from being behind glass. *Disabled Toilet:* One male, one female nearby. *Cost:* Free for disabled, £10 for helper. *Booking:* Yes, through own club. *Parking:* Spaces available in the car park behind the Ora Stand, on a first-come, first-served basis. If that's full, the visitors' car park is close to the disabled entrance. *For the Blind:* Ten headsets with hospital radio commentary in the disabled stand.

Programme: £1.80.

Visitors' Toilets: *Male:* 'If you fancy sponsoring a queue, that's the one,' said a visiting fan, surveying the line of desperate fans seething its way up the back steps. One despairing Everton supporter couldn't wait, and was summarily thrown out. The facilities, once reached, turned out to be 'decent enough'. *Female:* On first sight it appeared that Barnsley FC had provided separate toilets for fat and thin people! It turned out that one was wheelchair-friendly, though the other door was still frighteningly narrow.

Food and Drink: When asked about his food, one fan launched into a good old rant along the lines of 'they've run out of pasties, sausage rolls, and burgers' ... and then gave his pie seven-out-of-ten. Given the lack of choice, most fans wolfed down the meat-and-potato pies (£1.55), which were hot, spicy and above average (14.3.98).

PUB GUIDE

The following three pubs are all on the main route, detailed above, to Oakwell from the M1:

The Prince of Wales (1) Eldon Street North (01226) 247 609

Wards (with Lambtons Smooth). Popular, traditional pub attracting a good range of supporters, and with a great matchday atmosphere. Bar snacks (such as pie and peas, hot dogs) served 11.30-2.30. Darts, pool, TV, beer garden. Families welcome. Disabled facilities. Open: all day from 11.30. There's a shortcut to the ground from the pub. The landlady points fans in the right direction.

The Honeywell Inn (2) Honeywell Street (01226) 295 013

John Smith. Small traditional friendly local with separate pool room, TV, darts and beer garden. Open: 11.15-4, 7-11; from 5.30 for midweek games.

The Travellers Rest Intake Lane (01226) 281 440

Tom Cobleigh. An unusual Tom Cobleigh pub this one, as it's small and traditional, with TV, pool and darts. Excellent menu served 12-8 pm. Open: all day from 12. How to get there: Turn left just before the 'Tom Treddlehoyle' pub.

FOOD GUIDE

The nearest fish and chip shop to Oakwell is in Langdale Road, but it closes at 2 pm. The best alternative is 'Oakwell Sandwiches', on the corner of Pontefract Road and Grove Street, which offers baps for 90p or £1.30, hot sandwiches, pork pies and sausage rolls.

It's only a short walk from Oakwell to the town centre, but it's a very good idea indeed to cover away colours there, especially after the match. The 'I'm Mustard' coffee lounge on Kendray Street, near the station, has an all-day breakfast for £2.50, and OAP specials. Behind the station, in Midland Street, is the 'Minerva Fish and Chips, Grill and Coffee House', a shopper-style café with a huge menu, and children's meals at £1.75.

The main pedestrianised shopping centre is south of Kendray Street. The covered Alhambra Centre has a coffee shop and houses the second Barnsley FC shop 'Reds in Town'. For McDonalds, go straight on up Kendray Street, turning left at the Barnsley Chronicle into Eldon Street. In Burlington Arcade, off Eldon Street, is a traditional fish and chip restaurant/takeaway called

'Prince's Fish' with cod at £1.55 and pies at £1.05. For Indian food, home fans recommend the 'India Gardens' on Peel Square above the 'Corner Pin', and 'Jalsa' on Pitt Street.

LOCAL MEDIA

Local Radio: BBC Radio Sheffield FM 88.6, 104.1, 94.7; Hallam FM 97.4, 102.9 and 103.4 FM. Barnsley FC has its own matchday radio station, Oakwell 1575 AM.

Radio Phone-ins: BBC Radio Sheffield, 'Praise or Grumble', 5 pm. Call (0114) 268 2222; Hallam FM, Saturdays 5-6, and after midweek games to 10 pm. Call (0114) 285 2050.

Saturday Sports Paper: The excellent 'Green 'Un'.

MISCELLANEOUS

Safety Factor: The more successful the club, the more idiots come out of the woodwork, and there was trouble following the home match against Liverpool in late March 1998. Such confrontations are rare, and more than half of Barnsley's 97/98 home matches passed without a single arrest. And, as Oakwell is now all season-ticket, Barnsley FC has been able to identify trouble-makers and ban them from the ground. Still, as a precaution, the police advise visiting fans to cover colours after the match.

Rivals: In the Premier League, it's Sheffield Wednesday, but home fans say they still get far more worked up over the rivalry with Huddersfield Town.

Fanzines: 'Better Red Than Dead', 15C Courcy Road, Hornsey, London, N8 0QH.

Unofficial Websites:
http://members.aol.com/Jlister/bfc/bfc.htm
Copacabarnsley: http://upload.virgin.net/d.penty/copacabarnsley/Copacabarnsley.htm
Supporters' Site: http://www.barnsley.fc.co.uk/

Tourist Information: (01226) 206 757.

B

Birmingham City

St Andrew's

Address: St Andrews Ground, Birmingham B9 4NH
Telephone: Club (0121) 772 0101
ClubCall (0891) 121 188
Ticket Information (0891) 332 988
Official Website: http://www.bcfc.com/

Stand in the main car park at St Andrew's, and the view over the Birmingham city centre skyline, a mile to the west, is spectacular. The area immediately around the ground has been completely redeveloped under a city regeneration scheme, with urban wasteland transformed into a modern housing estate built around old canals. This hasn't greatly helped football supporters, as the streets are all coned off, and it takes ages to walk from one side of the ground to the other around houses and railway lines. Visiting fans are strongly advised to eat and drink away from the ground, as the choice nearby is severely limited.

HOW TO GET THERE

BY CAR: From North: Exit M6 at junction 6 (Spaghetti Junction, s/p A38 (M) Birmingham E & Cen, A38 Birmingham (NE), Lichfield). Where road divides keep right (s/p Birmingham E & Cen) onto the Aston Expressway. (*)Exit Expressway after 1.1 miles (s/p Convention Centre, Nat. Indoor Arena, Ring Road). At roundabout turn left (s/p Ring Road East, Solihull A41, Coventry A45) onto the Dartmouth Middleway. Go straight over the next three roundabouts and under two railway bridges. At fourth roundabout (Garrison Circus), start thinking about parking – it's left into Garrison Lane, straight on to the Bordesley Circus Roundabout and right into the Great Barr Street industrial estate.

From North-East (M1-M42-M6): Exit M1 at junction 23A (s/p A42 (M42), The South West, Tamworth, Birmingham) onto the M42. Exit M42 after 29.7 miles at junction 8 (s/p Birmingham Central, E, N and W, M6) onto the M6 northbound. Exit M6 after 5.0 miles at junction 6 (s/p A38(M), Birmingham (Cen), A38 Birmingham NE)(*). Where road divides keep right (s/p Birmingham E & Cen) onto the Aston Expressway. Then as From North(*).

From South-East (M40/London): Exit M40 at junction 3A (s/p The North, M1, B'ham East, North and Central) onto the M42 northbound. (*)Exit M42 at junction 4 after 2.6 miles (s/p Henley, Shirley A34) and

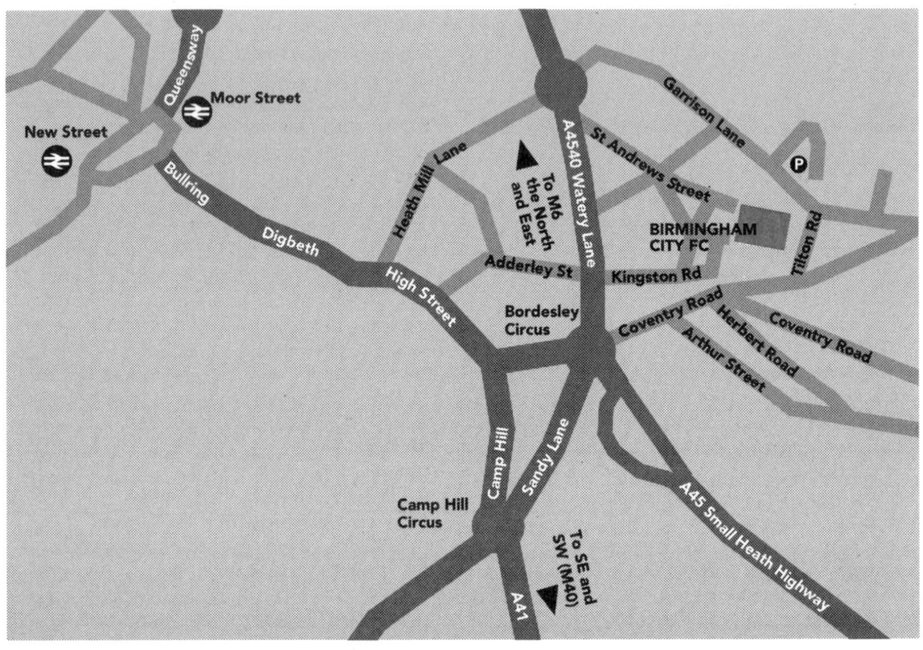

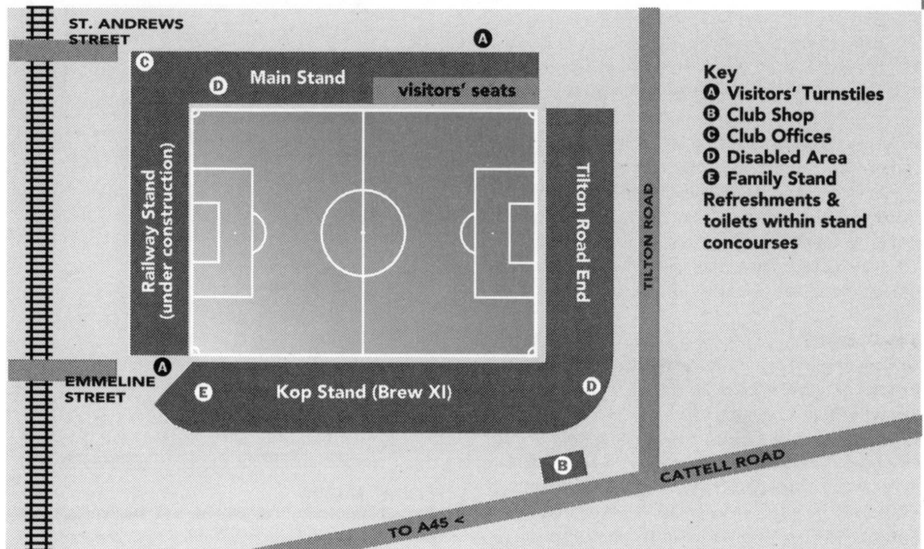

at roundabout turn left (s/p Birmingham, Shirley A34) onto the A34. Continue on the A34 for 7.7 miles, over four roundabouts and through the suburb of Sparkbrook (where the road becomes the A41) to the Camp Hill Circus roundabout. Here, take 3rd exit (s/p Ring Road and North, M6, Coventry A45) onto the A4540 Sandy Lane. At roundabout after 0.3 miles, go straight on (s/p Small Heath, Bordesley Green) to ground, or look for parking.

From South-West (M5-M42): At junction 3A follow signs for 'The North, B'ham East, North and Central' onto the M42 northbound. Then as From South-East(*).

FROM RAILWAY STATION (Birmingham New Street): *By taxi:* £3-£3.50. *By bus:* Nos. 15, 15a and 17 run along Coventry Road. *By foot:* Bear left out of the station, past the taxi ranks, and take the steps down into the Bull Ring underpass. To get out to Digbeth is not easy ... head through St Martin's Subway and carry straight on into Bell Street Subway. At the end of the passage turn left, in front of the Bull Ring Shopping Centre Entrance (s/p Moor Street Station, Bull Ring Market). Head straight toward the market and back into underpass opposite (s/p Moor Street Station). Turn right at crossroads, past Janson Hong Kong Supermarket and bear right, out of underpass towards the NCP car park into Digbeth (the main road). After 0.7 miles, where the road divides, bear left (s/p Coventry, Small Heath), under railway bridge to Bordesley Circus roundabout. The ground is visible from here.

Last Midweek Trains: Trains run to London at 21.55, 22.50 and 23.09; to Manchester/Leeds at 22.01 and 23.30; to Derby and Sheffield at 22.25; to Nottingham at 22.25; and to Bristol at 22.27 and 23.00. Please double-check on (0345) 484 950.

BY BUS: In addition to those listed above, nos. 96 and 97 run from Carrs Lane (just behind the High Street by Marks and Spencer) to Garrison Lane. After the game, it's usually as quick to walk.

PARKING

There's a small car park at the ground (£3) though it may not be open during the redevelopment work. The Century car park off Garrison Lane also charges £3. Otherwise it's street parking, but as there is some car crime, keep valuables out of sight. The roads immediately around the ground are coned off on matchdays, so fans have to look further afield:

a) Early birds can park on St Andrews Street behind the BP garage.

b) From Bordesley Circus roundabout, follow signs to 'Ring Road North and M6' into Watery Lane, and take first left turn into Adderley Street. This is an industrial area, with plenty of unrestricted parking. Don't block entrances as the factories remain open evenings and Saturdays.

c) From Bordesley Circus roundabout, follow signs to 'Small Heath, Bordesley Green, Birmingham City FC', towards the 'Watering Hole', into Coventry Road. The sidestreets here, such as Herbert Road, offer good parking.

THE GROUND

Until the summer of 1998, one half of St Andrew's was in the Premier League and the other in Division Two. The linked Kop and Tilton Road stands opened in 1994, winning awards for design and for supporters' facilities.

The other two sides, the Main Stand and the Railway End, were both well over thirty years old, with facilities to match! However, work is now underway to replace the Railway End with a two-tier, 8,000-seater stand to bring the overall ground capacity to around 30,000. The building work, which is costing £4.1 million, should be complete by February 1999. In the meantime, away fans are being moved from the Railway End to the Main Stand paddock. In theory it's covered, but in practice the rain blows right in to the back row, so bring waterproofs. When the Railway Stand is complete, the club plans to allocate the top tier to families, and the bottom tier to the visiting support.

Total Capacity: 21,000, rising to 30,200 when the redevelopment is complete. For away fans (Main Stand Paddock K) 1,000-4,000.

Cost (98/99): 'A' category match: Adults £15, 'B' category: £13.50. No concessions for away fans.

Disabled Facilities: Six spaces for visiting supporters in Paddock F of the Main Stand. *Disabled Toilet:* Nearby. *Cost:* £5 for disabled, £7 for helper. *Parking:* None available. *Booking:* Essential, call extension 247 at the club. *For the Blind:* Headphones available, please book.

Programme: £1.70.

Visitors' Toilets: *Male:* Home fans in the Main Stand in season 97/98 reported that the loos there are dark and dingy. Their advice? 'Bring a torch.' *Female:* Someone's been wielding a paintbrush, but one supporter said the loos still 'looked and smelled like an old shed.'

Food and Drink: (Main Stand): Forest fans recommended the steak-and-kidney pies (£1.50) ... 'nice thick gravy and a good amount of filling.' The meat-and-potato version needed lots of sauce to spice it up, but the burgers (£2) were 'much better than expected'. Most fans thought the coke (£1.10) was expensive, while the tea (60p), the powdered milk variety, was drinkable after a good stir (21.3.98, 5.5.98).

PUB GUIDE

For safety reasons, the police advise visiting fans to drink away from St Andrew's, perhaps using one of the pubs listed under other clubs in the Birmingham area. Those driving in along the A34 or the A45 pass a number of family-style pubs en route.

FOOD GUIDE

Around the ground the choice is very limited. Home fans recommend 'Fat Terry's' hot dog stand near Kingston Road, and the chip shops along Digbeth. Those driving in on the A34 pass a McDonalds, a Burger King and several American-style family diners. There's another Burger King at New Street Station and the city centre's just round the corner ... come out of the station and bear left at the main roundabout. Take first left, by Ladbrokes, into the High Street.

BIRMINGHAM CITY F.C.
KEEP RIGHT ON TO THE
END OF THE ROAD .....
eagle

LOCAL MEDIA

Local Radio: BBC Radio WM 95.6 FM; Capital Gold 1152 AM; BRMB 96.4 FM.

Radio Phone-ins: Radio WM, Friday evenings 7-9, until 6 pm on Saturdays and to 10 pm after midweek games, call (0121) 432 2000; Capital Gold, Fridays 6-7.30 pm, Saturdays 5-7 pm, call (0121) 359 5599.

Saturday Sports Paper: The 'Sports Argus' pink.

MISCELLANEOUS

Many clubs have gypsy curses, and Birmingham City is no exception. The club's stadium tour guide says that, many years ago, a gypsy horse, employed to roll the pitch, keeled over and died. It was buried in the goalmouth at the Tilton Road End ... hence the strange bump that's still there today! In a desperate attempt to lift the curse, one former manager is rumoured to have relieved himself on all the four corners of the pitch!

Safety Factor: Birmingham does have a small active hooligan element, which appears at high-profile matches. One area for potential trouble is where both home and away fans head out of the ground behind the Kop Stand.

Rivals: The favourite Blues ditty is 'Sh** on the Villa'. But after Villa player Savo Milosevic demonstrated his dislike of his own fans, the song quickly became 'Spit on the Villa'. Wolves and West Brom are nicknamed 'the Yam Yams' because of the Black Country accent.

Fanzines: 'Wake Up Blue', 137 Custard Factory, Gibb Street, Digbeth, Birmingham, B9 4AA; 'The Zulu', PO Box 5454, Redditch, B98 8QN; Blues News, PO Box 4093, Birmingham B16 9LF

Unofficial Websites:
http://welcome.to/planetblues
http://sotv.demon.co.uk/

Tourist Information: (0121) 693 6300.

Blackburn Rovers

Ewood Park

Address: Ewood Park, Blackburn, Lancashire BB2 4JF
Telephone: Club (01254) 698 888
Ticket Sales (0321) 101 010
Ticket Information (0891) 121 014
ClubCall (0891) 121 179
Official Website: http://www.rovers.co.uk

Blackburn has, since the club's rise to the very top, become one of the most eagerly anticipated trips for many Premiership supporters. It's a compact and friendly northern town, now easier to reach by road via the new M65, and well-served by rail. There are a number of football-mad pubs near the ground, as well as some good eateries just across the road from the 'Jack Walker Stand'. In particular, check out the European football memorabilia in the 'Fox and Hounds', personally collected by the landlord!

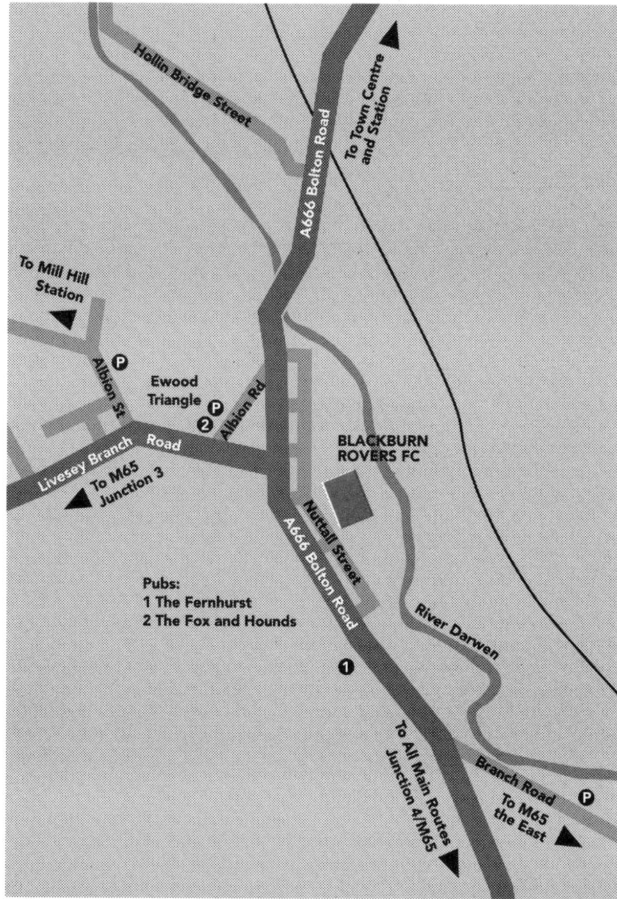

HOW TO GET THERE

All roads to Ewood Park lead to what for simplicity we've dubbed the 'Ewood Triangle'. It's basically a large roundabout, with the 'Shamus O'Donnells' pub on one corner, and McDonalds to one side.

BY CAR: From All Main Routes: Exit M6 at J29 (s/p M65 Burnley, Blackburn, Preston Sth), and at motorway roundabout take 3rd exit (s/p M65 Burnley, Blackburn) onto the M65. Exit M65 at junction 4 (s/p Ewood Park), and follow signs to 'Blackburn A666' onto the A666 Bolton Road. (*)Follow this road for about a mile, passing 'The Fernhurst' pub on the LHS. The ground is down the sidestreets on the RHS.

From South and North, via pubs and takeaways on the Livesey Branch Road: Exit M6 at J29 (s/p M65 Burnley, Blackburn, Preston Sth), and at motorway roundabout take 3rd exit (s/p M65 Burnley, Blackburn) onto the M65. Exit M65 at junction 3 (s/p A674 Blackburn W). Take first exit at roundabout (s/p Blackburn A674) onto the A674. (*)After 0.7 miles, turn right at T-junction/lights. After 0.8 miles turn right at mini-roundabout by the 'Fieldens Arms' (s/p Darwen A6062) into Livesey Branch Road. Follow this road for 2.5 miles, passing 'The Brown Cow' and 'The White Bull' pubs to the 'Ewood Triangle'. Go round the one-way system, following signs to Bolton, onto the A666 Bolton Road. Ground is down sidestreets on the LHS.

From East (M61): Exit M61 at junction 8 onto the A674. Follow signs to 'Blackburn A674' through

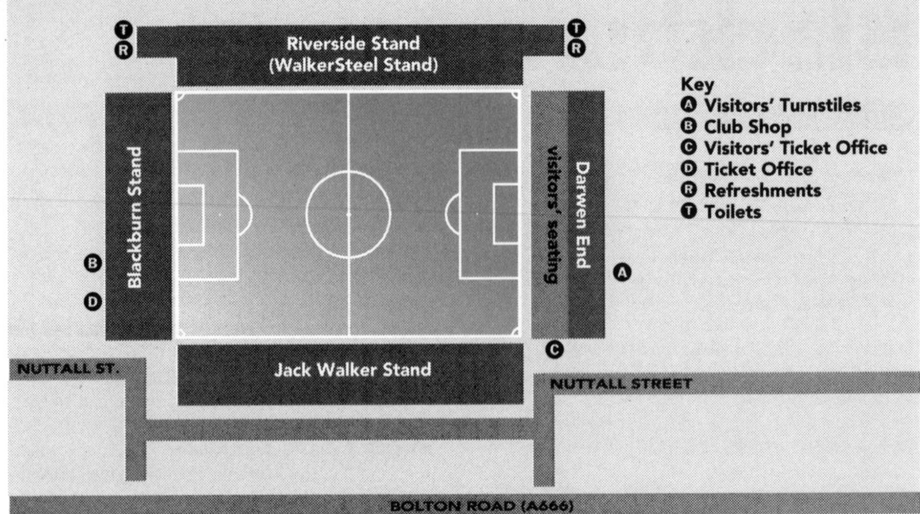

open countryside to roundabout by the Houghton Arms. Here, go straight on (s/p Blackburn A674) onto the A674. Then as From South and North(M6-M65)(*).

From Bolton (A666): Continue on A666 through town of Darwen, passing the 'Golden Cup' pub on LHS. Pass under M65 motorway, then as From East (M65).

FROM RAILWAY STATION (Blackburn): 1.6 miles. *By taxi:* £2.20-£2.50. *By bus:* The bus station is right outside the railway station, and plenty of buses travel down Bolton Road on their way to Darwen. The best bets are: From Stand M – Nos. 2, 3, 4, 5, 346 and 603; From Stand N – Nos. 19, 20, 21, W1, X25 and X26; and From Stand O – Nos. 223, 67, 30, 237, 535 and 823. *By foot:* Turn left out of the station, and left again down Bridge Street. The road bends round to the right to a T-junction. Here, turn left. Cross the road, go under bridge and take right fork (s/p Bolton A666). Walk for 1.0 miles to the 'Ewood Triangle' – turn left for 'The Fernhurst' and the ground, right for the 'Fox and Hounds' and McDonalds.

Last Midweek Trains: There are trains to Manchester at 22.02 and 23.13, as well as to Blackpool North at 23.35, Preston at 23.33 and Burnley at 23.11. It's not possible to reach London after an evening game. Please double-check on (0345) 484 950.

FROM RAILWAY STATION (Mill Hill): This station, about 0.5 miles from Ewood Park, is one stop from Blackburn Station on the local Preston line. *By foot:* Turn left out of station onto New Chapel Street. Walk a couple of hundred yards, past a row of shops, then turn left into New Wellington Street. This bends right into Moorgate Street. At the end of the street turn left onto Livesey Branch Road, and the 'Ewood Triangle' is a five minute walk ahead.

BY BUS: See above.

PARKING

Street parking is very limited. However, there are a number of options:

a) 'The Fernhurst' pub has a matchday car park for around 60-70 cars (£3).

b) The 'Youth Aid' car park (£3) off Albion Road (one side of the Ewood Triangle).

c) Albion Mill car park on Albion Street (£2), see map.

d) Industrial estate car parks on Branch Road charge between £1.50 and £2.

THE GROUND

Blackburn fans have seen more changes in the last ten years than most supporters experience in a lifetime! Multi-millionaire Jack Walker has fulfilled every supporter's dream, taking his favourite club from the lower reaches of the old Second Division to the very top. He's sunk a fortune into Ewood Park, financing the construction of the Darwen End and the Blackburn and Jack Walker Stands, to bring the capacity to over 31,000. And there are moves afoot to turn the only remaining 'original' part of the ground, the Riverside (WalkerSteel) Stand, into a 15,000-seater development, complete with exhibition hall and hotel. Away fans are housed in the lower tier of the Darwen End, although they were moved to the upper tier, on an experimental basis, towards the end of the 97/98 season. The facilities are excellent.

Total Capacity: 31,367. For away fans: 5,000.

Cost (98/99): Darwen End, Upper and Lower Tiers:

Adults Category A match £22, Category B match £18. Concessions (OAPs, under 15s) £10.
Disabled Facilities: Space for 20 visiting supporters at pitch level in front of the Darwen End. *Disabled Toilets:* Between the stands. *Cost:* £18 or £20 for disabled, free for helper. *Booking:* 24 hours in advance – call Colin Barcley on (01254) 263 794. *Parking:* Limited availability, please book through Mr Barcley. *For the Blind:* Radio headsets available with commentary from Radio Rovers, allowing fans to sit where they wish. Please book through John Aitken on (01254) 725 573.
Programme: £1.70.
Visitors' Toilets: The facilities are excellent. *Male:* So this is how the other half lives! Music while you pee! *Female:* 'Much better than at Barnsley, not as good as Bolton' was the assessment of one well-travelled Wimbledon fan.
Food and Drink: The burger (£2.10) was tasty but rather cold, while the hot dogs (£2) were 'nice, tasty, but a bit dry'. Take a spoon for the meat-and-potato pies (£1.50), described as 'hot, tasty and messy.' The coffee (80p) was good, but the tea (65p) had one fan rushing back to the beer counter for a pint! (8.11.97, 25.4.98)

PUB GUIDE

McEwans lager (£2/pint) and Matthew Brown bitter (£1.90/pint) are served in the concourse in the Darwen End. However, there are four friendly pubs to try (though note that some may become 'home only' on big matchdays). Near the ground are:
The Fernhurst (1) 466 Bolton Road (01254) 581 827
Thwaites. Huge, popular pub with a large matchday car park (£3), from where a trailer serves burgers, hot dogs etc. Children welcome in TV room. Pool table, darts. Disabled facilities. Open: Saturday matchdays 12-3.30, Monday-Friday all day from 12.
Fox and Hounds (2) Albion Road (on the Ewood Triangle) (01254) 671 497
Thwaites. Small football-crazy pub, with loads of memorabilia from Rovers' recent forays into Europe. Separate pool room. Sandwiches. Two TVs. Families welcome. Open: all day from 11.30.

In addition, there are two small friendly pubs on Livesey Branch Road, a ten-minute walk from Ewood and handy for those walking from Mill Hill station: **The Brown Cow** is a traditional Whitbread pub with pool table and darts; **The White Bull** is a Thwaites pub with pool table and TV. Both come highly recommended.

Those approaching Blackburn on the A666 from Bolton pass **The Britannia** on Bolton Road, a small friendly Thwaites pub with pool and darts rooms.

FOOD GUIDE

Fans don't have to wander far: opposite the ground on Bolton Road are three outlets. A kiosk sells good value pies for 70p-80p, although unsurprisingly the 'Shearer Pie', as sampled a couple of years ago, is no longer available! The 'Mother Riley' café does traditional sit-down meals such as roast beef and Yorkshire pud for £2.99, while a nearby chippy has fish and chips for £2.10, and pies for 70p-80p. There's a McDonalds on the Ewood Triangle: it has a 'Walk Through' instead of a 'Drive Through' service. Weird!

LOCAL MEDIA

Local Radio: BBC Radio Lancashire; Red Rose Gold 999 AM; matchday broadcasting on Radio Rovers 1404 AM.
Radio Phone-Ins: BBC Radio Lancashire, Saturdays 6-7 pm, call (01254) 583 583; Radio Rovers also has a post-match phone-in.
Saturday Sports Paper: None.

MISCELLANEOUS

Safety Factor: No problems.
Rivals: The rivalry with near-neighbours Burnley continues, despite the gulf between the two teams. Some of the newer Blackburn fans perhaps dislike Manchester United a touch more, while new in at no. 3 comes Newcastle United ... maybe a connection here with some chap called Shearer?!
Fanzines: 'Loadsamoney', 44 Tiverton Drive, Blackburn, BB2 4NR; '4000 Holes', PO Box 609, Ribchester, Preston, PR3 3YT.
Unofficial Websites:
Supporters' Site: http://www.brfc-supporters.org.uk/
http://www.pnolan.demon.co.uk/brfc/index.htm
http://www.blackburn.demon.co.uk/brfc/html
Tourist Information: (01254) 53277.

Blackpool

Bloomfield Road

Address: Bloomfield Road, Blackpool, FY1 6JJ
Telephone: General Enquiries/Shop
(01253) 405 331
Ticketline (01253) 404 331
ClubCall (0891) 121 648
Official Website:
http://www.cyberscape.net/users/bfc/

In many smaller towns, the biggest landmark is often the football ground itself, especially if it's still got traditional floodlights. Not in Blackpool! Bloomfield Road is dwarfed by two major constructions: Blackpool Tower of course and the 'Pepsi Max Big One' rollercoaster. A glimpse of either sends many footie fans' brains into a spin, as this is the top choice for a raucous weekend away. The ground itself is a five minute walk from the sea front, with huge, cheap car parks right next door. Blackpool is also served by two railway stations, both within walking distance of Bloomfield Road, and there's a choice of about 200 fish-and-chip shops!

HOW TO GET THERE

BY CAR: From all directions: Exit M6 at junction 32 (s/p M55 Blackpool, Fleetwood, Preston North) onto the M55. Go straight on for 13.1 miles, picking up the signs for Main Parking Areas. At the first roundabout (with the strange sculpture) go straight on (s/p Blackpool Main Car and Coach Parks) into Yeadon Way. At roundabout after 1.9 miles go straight on (s/p All Other Parking Areas). From here follow signs to the Lonsdale Parking - this leads to the large parking areas on Seaside Way next to the ground.

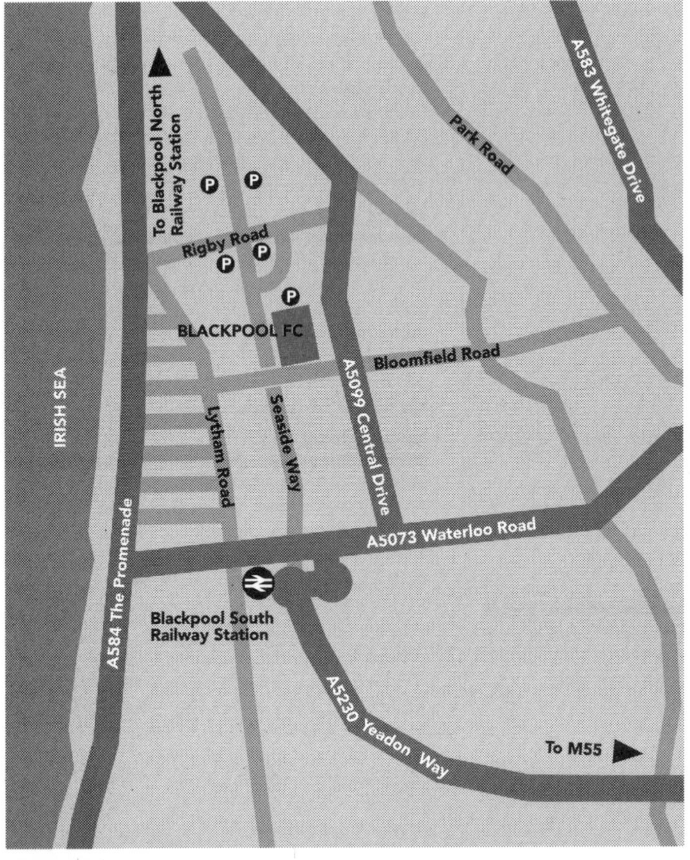

FROM RAILWAY STATIONS:
Trains run from Preston to either Blackpool North or Blackpool South.
(a) Blackpool North: 1.5 miles. *By taxi:* £3 plus 20p per passenger. *By bus:* See below. *By foot:* Head across forecourt and through underpass. Turn left up steps to main road (Talbot Road) and turn right to seafront. At seafront turn left along the Promenade. After 1.3 miles, bear left at lights into Lytham Road (s/p Car Park, South Station, Airport). After 0.3 miles turn left by the Scotch Café into Bloomfield Road. Remember too that Blackpool's famous trams run along the seafront.
(b) Blackpool South: *By taxi:*

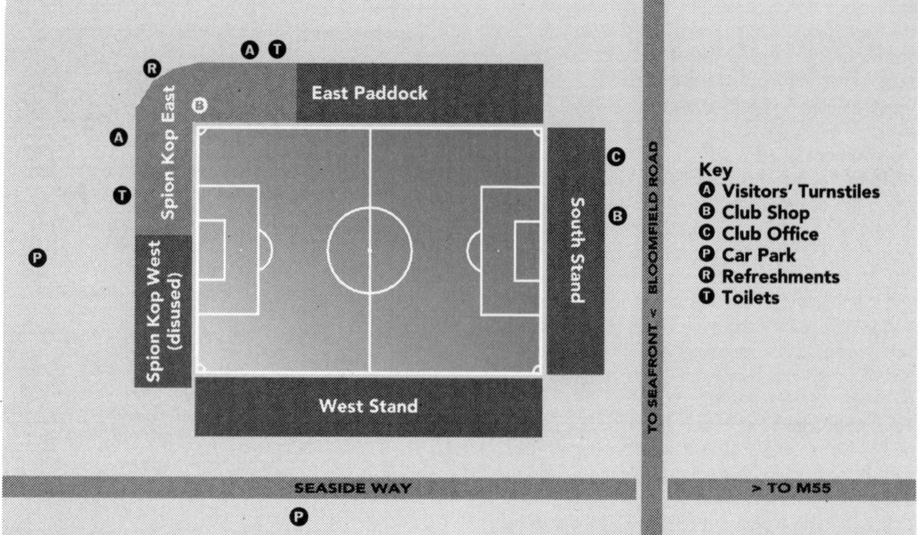

£1.80 plus 20p per passenger. *By bus:* See below. *By foot:* Up to main road and turn left. At first lights turn right (s/p Football Ground) by William Hills into Lytham Road. After 0.3 miles turn right by Scotch Café into Bloomfield Road.

Last Midweek Trains: Blackpool North has the better service, with trains at 21.55 and 23.08 to Manchester Piccadilly. The 21.55 train arrives in time for connections to Leeds and Sheffield. There are no connecting trains to London. Please double-check on (0345) 484 950.

BY BUS: Fans arriving via Blackpool North railway station are well set, as the bus station is in Talbot Road, next to the station. The most frequent services are nos. 22 and 22A, which stop at the junction of Bloomfield Road and Central Drive. Bus nos. 11, 11A, 12 and 12A run along Lytham Road. All the services run in the evenings, apart from the 12A. Those arriving at Blackpool South railway station can catch the nos. 11, 11A, 12 and 12A along Lytham Road.

PARKING

The main car parks are on either side of Seaside Way. The charge in winter (ie when the resort is out of season) is 70p for 15 hours – obviously this will be higher and parking will be more difficult in the peak holiday season. The car parks nearest the ground are Lonsdale, Rigby Road, Bloomfield 3 and Bloomfield 4. These are now covered by CCTV.

THE GROUND

Blackpool fans have eyed with some concern the new grounds and stands opening at other north-west clubs such as Preston, Burnley, Bolton, Tranmere and even Rochdale. One depressed supporter pointed out that when Wigan moves to a new stadium, Bloomfield Road will become 'the worst ground in the region, if not the country'! A little harsh, perhaps, but the grand old terraces of Bloomfield Road have most definitely seen better days.

Blackpool FC is acutely aware of the problems, and is keen to build a new ground at Whyndyke Farm, at the end of the M55. The plan is for the football stadium, which would initially have about 28,000 seats and a retractable roof, to be just one part of an extensive leisure complex, hosting shows, conferences, exhibitions and other sporting events. These commercial activities would in theory generate income 365 days a year, helping to take Blackpool FC up through the divisions. However, the financial situation is complex: the club has been the subject of a takeover bid, and no starting date for the work has yet been set. 'Still', said one Blackpool supporter, 'Let's hope the pie eventually falls out of the sky!'

Back at good old Bloomfield Road, away fans are still housed in one corner of the ground on either the uncovered Spion Kop East or the covered East Paddock North, or both. The view from the Spion Kop East is generally better, but the wind off the Irish Sea can be more than bracing!

Total Capacity: 11,295. For away fans: 2,532. Turnstiles 9 and 10. Visiting supporters with children are, for some matches, welcome in the Family Area. Contact the away club in advance for details.

Cost (98/99): Terrace: Adult £10, concessions (OAPs/Juniors) £7.

Disabled Facilities: Space for 12 supporters and

helpers by the players' tunnel and at the north end of the West Stand. *Disabled Toilet:* In supporters' bar. *Cost:* Free for disabled, £10 for helper. *Booking:* Only for all-ticket games. *Parking:* Not available. *For the Blind:* Headphones with match commentary available, please book.

Programme: £1.70.

Visitors' Toilets: *Male:* 'A dark and dingy wall, and a smelly wall at that', wrote one visitor. The sink appeared to have been made out of an old drinking fountain! Apart from a recent lick of paint, there's probably been little improvement since Blackpool were in Division One and the players were wearing baggy shorts! *Female:* A York fan complained about the 'dodgy lock, dodgy toilet seat ... in fact dodgy everything!' Most fans, male and female, struggled to think of any worse toilet facilities they'd seen anywhere on their travels.

Food and Drink: Two choices here. The burger van next to the turnstiles sold a very tasty hot dog (£1.60) and lukewarm cheeseburgers (£1.70). The tea (60p) and coffee (60p) were most welcome on a cold day. Coke and Sprite in bottles (95p) were a good idea, but the staff had to keep the bottle top for 'safety reasons', leaving fans with half a litre of liquid to drink all at once or to leave on the terrace to get kicked over! A kiosk by the terrace sold meat-and-potato, steak-and-kidney and cheese-and-onion pies (all £1). One fan devoured one of each and declared the steak-and-kidney the winner (22.11.97, 20.12.97).

PUB GUIDE

With more than 2,500 licensed premises in Blackpool, no-one is likely to leave town thirsty. Unfortunately, because fans of many clubs converge on Blackpool for the weekend, plus other parties for stag-nights and the like, the police prefer guidebooks like this not to name any specific establishments. In general, home fans drink inland, while away fans head for the promenade. Those who like 'Fun Pubs' will have a grand time. Connoisseurs of good beer, however, tend to steer clear of the lot and stay in Preston! NB The police warn that any drunk fans trying to enter Bloomfield Road will be arrested. They also carry out random stop checks on coaches, and any operators found in breach of the alcohol regulations will be reported to the Traffic Commissioner.

FOOD GUIDE

Where do we start?! The choice is endless. Near the ground, head for Lytham Road, which runs parallel to Seaside Way. 'The Frying Squad', an eat-in or takeaway chippy, offers fish-and-chips for £2.15. The 'Cosy Caff' does roast dinners (pork, beef, lamb or chicken) for £3.50, but not much in the way of vegetarian food. The 'Lytham House Kitchen' is a typical Chinese takeaway with a large selection, most dishes costing £3.70.

Further afield, try the myriad of takeaways and

Due to a slight mix-up in the planning applications...

restaurants along the seafront, including Harry Ramsdens by the North Pier. To get to the seafront, cross Lytham Road and go down any of the streets opposite. Turn right for the Tower and Golden Mile, left for the Pleasure Beach.

LOCAL MEDIA

Local Radio: BBC Radio Lancashire 103.9 FM; Red Rose Radio 999 AM; The Wave 96.5 FM.

Radio Phone-ins: BBC Radio Lancashire, Saturdays 6-7 pm, call (01254) 583 583.

Saturday Sports Paper: None.

MISCELLANEOUS

Safety Factor: As mentioned above, Blackpool can be a magnet for fans of many clubs on any one weekend, so care should be taken around the town. The area around Bloomfield Road is well policed, and problems at the ground itself are rare.

Rivals: 'Nobb End' and 'The Clampets'. That's Preston and Burnley to you and me!

Fanzines: 'Another View From The Tower', PO Box 106, Sale, Cheshire M33 7AA; 'Do I Like Tangerine', 89 South Park, Lytham, Lancs, FY8 4QU.

Unofficial Websites:
'BASIL': http://www.blackpool.co.uk/basil/
http://www.geocities.com/Colosseum/Stadium/2169/
'It's not Orange': http://www.blackpool.net/bfc/

Tourist Information: (01253) 621 623 or (01253) 403 223.

Bolton Wanderers

The Reebok Stadium

Address: Reebok Stadium, Burnden Way, Lostock, Bolton BL6 6JW
Telephone:
Club (01204) 673 673
Ticket Enquiries/Credit Card Booking (01204) 673 601/2/3
ClubCall (0891) 121 164
Official Website: http://www.boltonwfc.co.uk/

Without a doubt, the design of the Reebok Stadium is the most innovative and spectacular of all new British football grounds. With its maze of white roof supports, curved stands, towers and inward-leaning floodlights, it's visible from miles around, and cars on the nearby M61 slow down in admiration. The ground's about five miles from Bolton town centre, in the commuting suburb of Horwich. And it's exchanged the terraced houses and excellent pie shops of the old Burnden Park for a huge retail and leisure park, where most restaurants and bars are highly suspicious of football fans. A warmer welcome can be found, however, a little further afield. Parking is easy though expensive, but rail links are poor.

HOW TO GET THERE

BY CAR: From South (M6-M60-M61): Exit M6 at junction 21A (s/p Manchester, Bolton, Leeds, M62) onto the M62. Exit M62 after 9.2 miles at junction 12 (s/p Leeds M60 (M62), Bolton, Preston M61), onto the M60 northbound. Exit M60 after 2.5 miles (s/p Bolton, Preston M61) onto the M6 (*). At junction 2 after 1.0 miles, bear left where road divides (s/p M61 Preston) remaining on the M61. Exit M61 after 7.5 miles, at junction 6 (s/p Chorley, Horwich A6027). At roundabout turn right onto Burnden Way.
From East (M62 from Leeds): As it passes north of Manchester, the M62 becomes the M60. Exit M60 at junction 15 (s/p M61, Bolton, Preston) onto the M61. Then as From South(*).
From North: Exit M61 at junction 6 (s/p Horwich, Bolton North A6027), and at roundabout turn left into Burnden Way.
FROM RAILWAY STATIONS: There are plans for a new rail link to the ground, but until then the nearest station is the suburban stop at Lostock, served by infrequent trains from Bolton. There are no taxis. *By foot:* Turn left out of car park up to main road, and then left and right down Regent Road. At T-junction after 0.7 miles, by Holly Vale, turn left. At roundabout after 0.9 miles turn left and ground is ahead.

The nearest mainline stations to the Reebok are Bolton and Wigan. From Bolton (5 miles): *By taxi:* About £8. *By bus:* The no. 539 runs directly to the ground at 8 and 38 minutes past the hour. Special buses are laid on if a large number of away supporters are expected. From Wigan: *By taxi:* £7-£8.
Last Midweek Trains: The last train from Lostock to Bolton is at 23.59, and from Bolton to Manchester up to midnight. The last train from Wigan to Manchester is at 23.08. Trains from Manchester run to York and Newcastle at 21.50, to York at 22.47, and to Nottingham and Derby at 22.28. It's not possible to get to London after a midweek game. Please double-check on (0345) 484 950.

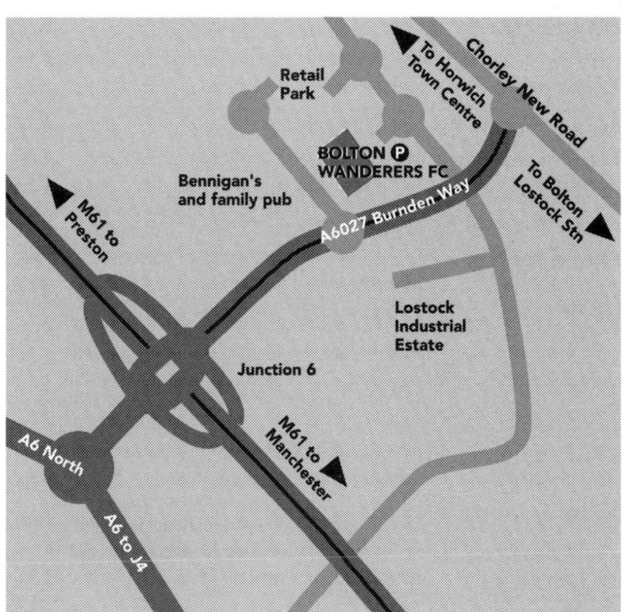

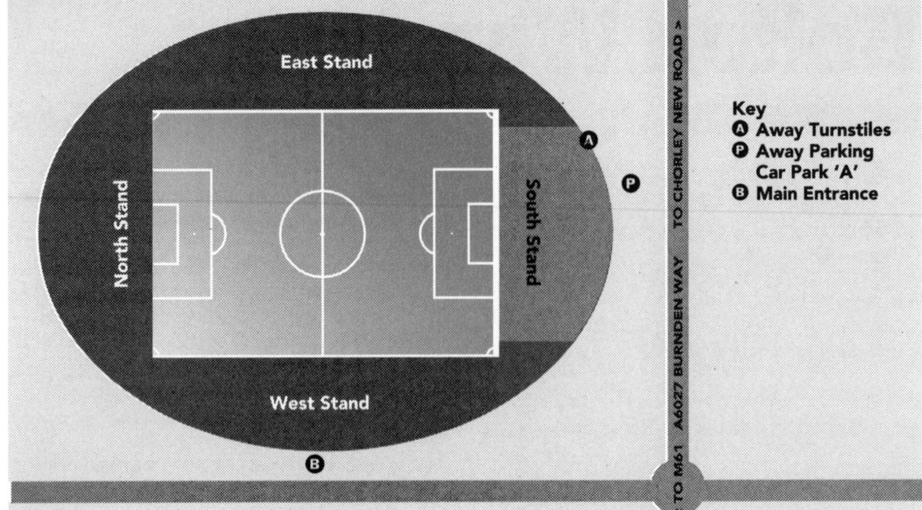

BY BUS: See above. The club runs special buses from Bolton town centre and outlying areas to the Reebok, costing £1 return. Ask the club for further details.

PARKING

For an easy, but expensive life, follow the signs to the away parking at the stadium (£5). Expect to wait at least half an hour to get out again, as the police hold cars back to give the away coaches a clear run down Burnden Way. The coaches exit from the opposite side of the car park, and once they're gone, cars can take the same route (watch out for this as it's a nippy way of jumping the queue!) There's parking at a college on Victoria Road, off the Chorley New Road. Some fans park on the opposite side of the M61, or on the Lostock Industrial Estate on Lostock Lane. A lot of the off-street parking on this estate, however, is already allocated to home fans.

THE GROUND

When Bolton Wanderers FC first mooted the possibility of moving from the historic but outdated Burnden Park, there was uproar. Supporters, understandably attached to their 100-year-old stomping ground, threatened to boycott any new stadium and tear up their season tickets. The club launched a PR campaign, pointing out the impossibility of redeveloping Burnden Park. But it was the club's season in the Premier League 1995/1996 which did the trick, as Bolton fans visited other top-class grounds and compared them unfavourably with their own.

And once the £30 million Reebok stadium opened, there was no looking back. One fan wrote: 'Burnden Park had open terracing, restricted viewing and primaeval loos. The Reebok Stadium doesn't.' Although the inside of the Reebok is a bit of a disappointment compared with the futuristic design of the outside, the facilities are very good indeed. It complies with, or exceeds, all FIFA recommendations, and fans enjoy the best legroom in the league! Visiting fans are allocated part of, or all of, the South Stand behind the goal. The top-floor refreshment area has a view out over the motorway and beyond, and sells a decent pie too. The only possible compaint would be that, with a large away crowd, everywhere was crowded.

Total Capacity: 25,000. For away fans: Up to 5,000.
Cost (98/99): Upper Tier: Adult £17, OAPs £11, juniors £9. Lower Tier: Adult £14, OAPs £11, juniors £9.
Disabled Facilities: Ample space for all either at ground level or in a special enclosure in the NE corner. Entrance on the west side of the ground, by the ticket office. *Disabled Toilet:* In all stands. *Cost:* Free for disabled, matchday price for helper. *Booking:* Essential. *Parking:* Available. *For the Blind:* Loop system available.
Programme: £2.
Visitors' Toilets: *Male:* It was simply one almighty scrum, and fans were mightily unimpressed. An Everton fan, at the Reebok for the first-ever Premier game, discovered a teething problem. Inside the male loos were two stewards, with ladders, discussing whether the leak in the snack bar was coming from the toilets. He decided against having a half-time drink! *Female:* Now everyone will have missed a goal or two through having to nip out during the match. At Bolton, at least one knows who's scored thanks to the matchday radio commentary piped into the loo block!! Overall, no complaints.

Food and Drink: The highlight, unusually, was the cheese-and-onion pie (£1.50). One supporter said: 'Holland's cheese pies – you can't beat 'em wherever you go in the world.' Generally fans liked all the pies, and were impressed with the choice of steak-and-kidney, meat-and-potato and chicken-and-mushroom, all of which contained good chunks of meat. For an extra 30p, the pie came complete with mushy peas, on a plate with a fork. Classy, eh? The tea (80p) however, was gritty and tasted of disinfectant, but the Kenco coffee (90p) was good. But most fans stuck with the excellent beer (John Smiths) and the drinkable lager (McEwans) (1.9.97, 18.4.98).

PUB/FOOD GUIDE

The nearest traditional food outlet to the Reebok is 'Settles' corner shop, at the top of Burnden Way, which sells home-made pies at 60p, pasties at 50p and bacon-and-egg in a barmcake for £1.17. On the retail park west of the ground is a 'Bennigan's American Tavern' and a family pub, neither of which run a bar on matchdays. Football colours are not allowed on anyone over 12-years-old. Their car park charges £10, but in return supporters receive a £10 voucher to spend on meals, which isn't a bad deal considering it's £5 for the normal matchday car park. To the east of the ground is a Pizza Hut, a McDonalds, a KFC, and – in an arcade – 'Old Orleans', 'Mamma Amalfi' and a 'Seattle Coffee Co.'. The Asda has a café. There's a cinema too if any of the family prefer a film to the football!

The pubs near the Reebok are home-only, and the ones further away are not keen on attracting large numbers of visiting supporters. However, there are a number of country-style, family-friendly pubs along the A6 which runs parallel to the M61. To reach the A6, exit the A61 at junction 4 (s/p Atherton, Leigh). At motorway roundabout turn left (s/p Walkden A6). At next roundabout turn right onto the A6. Keep going straight on, and eventually the road comes out almost opposite the Reebok at junction 6. 'Quincey's' American diner, on the A6 near junction 6, comes highly recommended for families. It has a huge menu, including grills, salads, Tex Mex and pasta, and an outdoor children's play area. Parties of ten or more need to book on (01942) 812 468.

LOCAL MEDIA

Local Radio: BBC Radio Lancashire 95.5 FM, 103.9 FM and 104.5 FM; GMR 95.1 FM; Piccadilly Radio 1152 AM.
Radio Phone-ins: BBC Radio Lancashire, Saturdays 6-7 pm, call (01254) 583 583; GMR, Saturdays 1-3 and 5-7, and after midweek games. Call (0161) 228 2255; Piccadilly Radio, Saturdays 5-6, call (0161) 288 1152.
Saturday Sports Paper: The 'Manchester Pink'.

MISCELLANEOUS

Safety Factor: The police say the stadium has been well-designed, and there's been little trouble.
Rivals: 'Any different rivals?' we asked innocently. 'Oh no,' said our Bolton fan. 'Just Manchester United.' However, he did mention in passing a First Division rivalry with Wolves.
Fanzines: 'White Love', PO Box 150, Bolton, BL2 1GY; 'Tripe 'N' Trotters', Bolton Enterprise Centre, Washington Street, Bolton, Lancs BL3 5EY.
Unofficial Websites: 'London Whites': http://www.hankins.demon.co.uk/bwscl/globetrotters/html
'Gareth Langmead':
http://www.landmead.u-net.com/
'Druid's Den':
http://www.freeway.co.uk/druid/index.html
'Wanderers Web':
http://www.geocities.com/Colosseum/Bleachers/3034/
'Tripe 'N' Trotters:
http://members.xoom.com/tripentrotters/
Tourist Information: (01204) 364 333.

Bournemouth

Dean Court

Address: Dean Court Ground, Bournemouth BH7 7AP
Telephone: Club/Ticket Office (01202) 395 381 ClubCall (0891) 121 163
Official Website: http://www.afcb.co.uk/

On 21 January 1997, with the club on the brink of bankruptcy, about 500 Bournemouth fans travelled to Bristol City to watch what they believed would be their team's last match. A few days later, supporters organised a meeting. So big was the response that a larger venue had to be booked to seat 2,000, and loudspeakers set up for the 2,000 outside! The evening raised £35,000 to keep the club afloat while a supporters' consortium negotiated a successful takeover. AFC Bournemouth is now a 'Community Club' and a friendly one at that. Bournemouth's survival was excellent news for visiting supporters, who never like to miss a trip to the seaside, even if the beach is a ten minute drive away! Dean Court is in King's Park in the upmarket suburb of Boscombe. Parking is easy, and there are welcoming pubs within walking distance.

HOW TO GET THERE

BY CAR: From North and East (M3/M27): Exit M3 at s/p 'So'ton Docks, Bournemouth, M27 West'. Follow signs for 'M27 West' onto the M27 (which becomes the A31). After 20.6 miles, exit A31 (s/p Bournemouth A338, Christchurch B3073). At the (Ashley Heath) roundabout, turn left (s/p Bournemouth A338, Christchurch B3073) onto the A338. (*)After 7.7 miles, exit A338 (s/p Boscombe A3049, and then King's Park, Littledown). At roundabout turn left into Littledown Avenue, then first right into Thistlebarrow Road.
From West A31 (from roundabout junction with A347): At roundabout turn left (s/p Ringwood A31), remaining on the A31. Go straight on, following signs for Ringwood, over three roundabouts for 2.8 miles, then exit A31 (s/p Bournemouth A338, Bearwood B3081). At (Ashley Heath) roundabout turn right (s/p Bournemouth A338, Christchurch B3073) onto the A338. Then as from North and East(*).
Tip: If you get lost, try to pick up signs to Boscombe, as Boscombe town centre is close to King's Park and Dean Court.

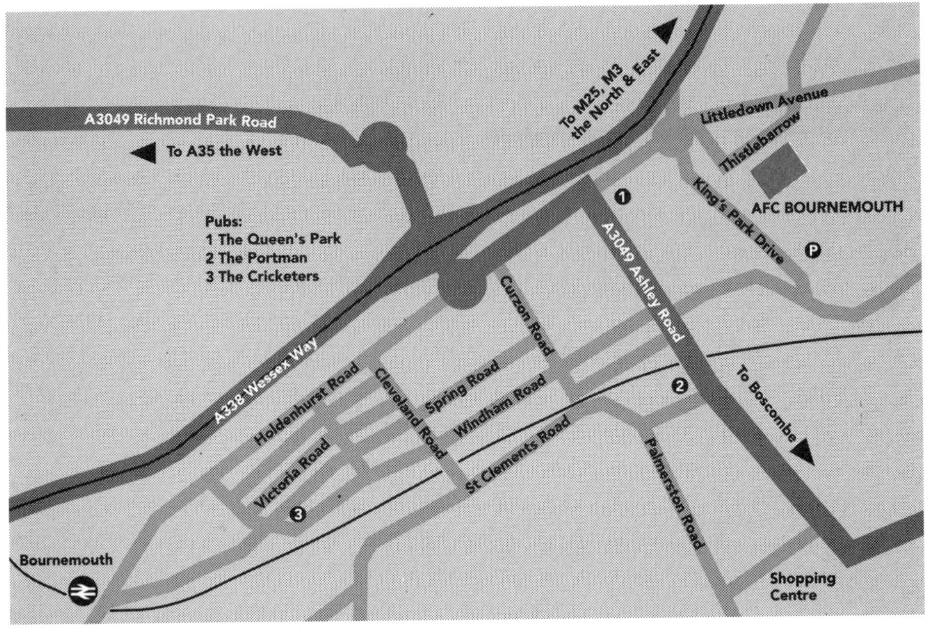

FROM RAILWAY STATION (Bournemouth Central): About 1.5 miles. *By taxi:* £3.60-£3.80. *By bus:* The bus stop is on the main road outside the station, by the Texaco garage. Only the yellow corporation buses go to Dean Court. Take nos. 68, 33 or 25, which go to the 'Queen's Park' pub. *By foot:* Turn left out of station and left again along Holdenhurst Road. At roundabout by Halfords take 2nd exit, remaining on Holdenhurst Road. Go straight on for about a mile, over one roundabout and through the traffic lights by the 'Queen's Park' pub. Go straight on at roundabout into Littledown Avenue, and first right into Thistlebarrow Road.

Pokesdown, a local station, is about 15 minutes' walk from Dean Court, though not all trains stop here. *By foot:* Turn left out of station, and first left down Clarence Park Road. At end of road, turn left along pathway between railings, passing cemetery on LHS. At end of the path, the ground is straight ahead across the park.

Last Midweek Trains: Trains run frequently to Southampton Central (21.05, 21.55, 22.02 and 23.02). There's a train to Waterloo at 22.02, arriving 00.55. For onward connections, see London Guide at front of the book. Please double-check on (0345) 484 950.

BY BUS: Nos. 25, 34, 35 and 68 run from the square in the town centre to the ground. The no. 35 runs from Boscombe.

PARKING

Finding a parking space is easy, as the club and the council have huge car parks at the ground, but take a copy of 'War and Peace' for the wait to get out again. Some cars are stuck for up to an hour. The club car park costs £1 while the council car park charges 60p for four hours. The council car park clears first, but the police direct traffic south towards Boscombe so fans have to work their way back to the A338. One alternative is to park near 'The Portman' pub and walk across the park, or try the sidestreets off Holdenhurst Road.

THE GROUND

Major plans for the redevelopment of Dean Court were put on hold following the club's brush with bankruptcy in 1997. However, the new board splashed out on paint to smarten up the South Stand, and blocks of the Main Stand were renamed after former players (e.g. the MacDougall Stand, the Redknapp Stand and the Newsham Centre Stand). Apart from that, the ground is exactly as it ever was. As one supporter mused: 'It's a bit crumbly, but it's home'. The board says that once the club's financial future is secure, it will consider the redevelopment of Dean Court – planning permission has already been granted to turn it into a 12,000 all-seater stadium – or a move to a new site. Visiting supporters are allocated seats in Block A of the renamed 'Norris Stand', and the uncovered Brighton Beach End terrace. The terrace is shallow and although the fences have gone, the posts that held it up remain.

Total Capacity: 10,770. For away fans: Standing 2,620, turnstiles 21-25. Seating: 160, turnstile 25.

Cost (98/99): Terrace: Category 'A' match, adults £9.50, concessions £5, category 'B' match £8.50/£5. Seating: £15, £12.50, £11.50.

Disabled Facilities: Space for about six visiting fans in a covered enclosure in front of the South Stand. *Disabled Toilet:* Nearby. *Cost:* Free for disabled and helper. *Booking:* Essential. *Parking:* Orange badge holders can park at the ground. *For the Blind:* Two rows

....AND IT'S
SUPER BOURNEMOUTH,
SUPER BOURNEMOUTH F.C.
FRIZZELL
eagle

at the top of E Block in the Main Stand, but no commentary available. The club plans improvements.
Programme: £1.60.
Visitors' Toilets: *Male:* 'Large and grotty, but not disgraceful ... just old and neglected, like the rest of this place,' said a visiting fan. *Female:* York fans decided the tide must be in, as the facilities were flooded, as well as being cold and smelly. Of the three loos, only one was working, and the seats were hanging off.
Food and Drink: Gills fans said the catering was the worst they'd come across all season: the bovril (80p) was revolting, the hot chocolate tepid and the cheeseburgers cold and soggy. However, it was a noon Boxing Day kick-off and they did lose 0-4. In April, a Wycombe fan said his 'Fleur de Lys' pasty (£1.30) had 'superb pastry' and 'a good filling', whilst York fans said the tea (80p) was lovely (26.12.97, 4.4.98).

PUB GUIDE

Visiting supporters are welcome in the Supporters' Social Club (entry £1), but need to book 48 hours in advance. The club is a Free House, with two pool tables, snooker and TV. Open: 11-2.45, 4.45-11; from 6 pm midweek.
Queens Park (1) 482 Holdenhurst Road (01202) 397 499
Whitbread (with Boddingtons and guests). Large football-friendly pub with a great matchday atmosphere. Sandwiches and bar snacks, including toasties at £1.95 and 'big breakfasts' at £3.25. TV. Open: all day.
The Portman (2) 97 Ashley Road, Boscombe (01202) 393 499
Eldridge Pope (Thomas Hardy Country Bitter and guest beer). Large pub with comfortable lounge bar as well as two pool tables, big-screen TV and darts. Open: Friday-Sunday all day; from 5.30 for midweek games.
The White Horse 947 Christchurch Road, Pokesdown (near local station) (01202) 425 268
Eldridge Pope. Traditional drinkers' pub with comfortable lounge bar and separate public bar. Bar snacks served all day. Two pool tables, TV, darts. Open: 11-3, 5-11.
The Cricketers (3) 41 Windham Road (01202) 551 589
Ushers of Trowbridge. Large 'community' pub with real open fires and loads of cricket paraphernalia. Food served 12-2. Large-screen TV, darts. Open: all day.

FOOD GUIDE

For the best choice, head across the park to Boscombe, where there's a shopping precinct with a Burger King, McDonalds and the highly recommended 'Bosphorous' kebab shop. Nearer the ground, try the café in the cricket pavilion, which serves good value snacks. Holdenhurst Road, which runs between the ground and Bournemouth station, has many outlets. And there's a group of takeaways on Christchurch Road, including a fish-and-chip shop, pizza, and 'Dixie's Chicken', which home fans say is 'the best'.

LOCAL MEDIA

Local Radio: BBC Radio Solent, 96.1 FM; Classic Gold 828 AM; Capital Gold 1557 AM.
Radio Phone-ins: Radio Solent, Saturdays pre-match 1.10-2.30, call (01703) 631 316; Capital Gold, Saturdays 2-6.30, midweek 7-10 (7-8 if no match). Call (0845) 35 60 70 80.
Saturday Sports Paper: The Southampton-based 'Sports Echo' produces a Bournemouth edition of the Saturday 'Pink', but it doesn't arrive until 7.30 pm. Fans can buy the Southampton edition earlier at the Roundhams services on the M27.

MISCELLANEOUS

AFC Bournemouth took 34,000 fans for the trip to Wembley in the Auto Windscreens Cup Final in 1997/98. A sign on the door of the Dean Court social club reads: 'Supporting Boscombe is not just for Wembley, it's for life.'
Safety Factor: No problems, a very friendly club.
Rivals: Any West Country teams, particularly those in Bristol, plus south coast rivals Brighton ('the seaweeds'). But Bournemouth fans have mixed feelings towards traditional adversaries Southampton after the club played a fund-raising match for free.
Fanzines: 'Community Service', 60 Colomb Street, Greenwich, London, SE10 9HA.
Unofficial Websites: http://www.homeusers.prestel.co.uk/rose220/afcb1.htm
http://www.xs4all.nl/~basstits/b_index.htm
http://www.maths.soton.ac.uk/rpb/AFCB.html
Tourist Information: (01202) 451 700.

Bradford City

Valley Parade

Address: Valley Parade, Bradford, West Yorkshire BD8 7DY
Telephone: Club (01274) 773 355
Ticket Office (01274) 770 022
Club Shop (01274) 770 012
Bantams Leisure (01274) 770 012
ClubCall (0891) 888 640

Anyone visiting Bradford expecting Satanic mills and clanking looms will be sorely disappointed. But those who look forward to the best Chicken Vindaloo this side of Delhi certainly won't be! Bradford remains THE place for curry, but the town is perhaps equally well-known for its starring role in the controversial TV series 'Band of Gold' and for its amazing 'Museum of Photography, Film and TV', which gives visitors the chance to write and read the news (... 'and the latest from Wembley, Barnet have won the Cup for the third year running ...'). Valley Parade is difficult to find by road, as it's to the north of Bradford, away from the main motorways. Parking's not easy either, but there are good football-friendly pubs within easy walking distance.

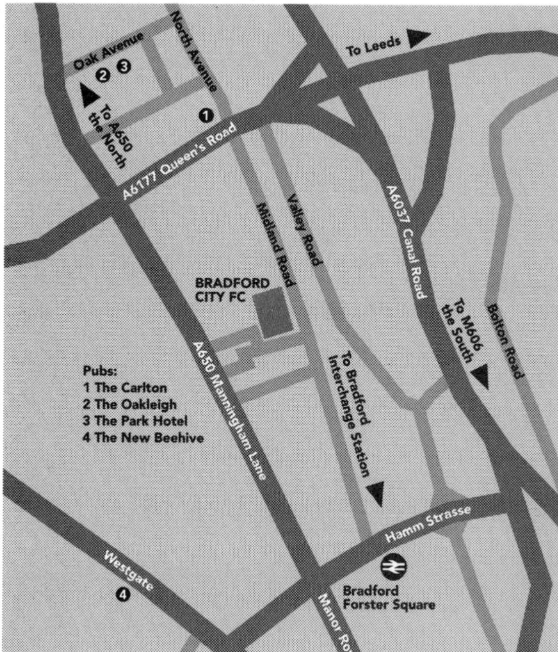

HOW TO GET THERE

BY CAR: From South (M606): Continue to the end of the M606. At roundabout turn right (5th exit, s/p Valley Parade, Ring Road A6177, Keighley) onto Rooley Lane. Straight on at roundabout after 0.7 miles (s/p Ring Road A6177, Keighley A650), and left at the next after 0.4 miles (s/p City Centre, Keighley A650) into Wakefield Road. Straight on at next two roundabouts, following signs to 'City Centre A650'. Move into outside lane, following the signs to 'Keighley, Skipton A650' through several sets of lights onto the A650 dual carriageway, Shipley Airedale Road. Go straight on for 1.8 miles, and then turn left (s/p Valley Parade, just after Food Giant and by The Car Pavilion) into Station Road. Left again into Queen's Road, and left after 0.1 miles (s/p Valley Parade) into Midland Road.

From North (via A650): Past the 'Bankfield Hotel' on LHS, into Saltaire. At roundabout take 4th exit (s/p Bradford A650) onto Bradford Road, passing a KFC on RHS. Straight on for 2.5 miles, passing the 'Cartwright Hotel' on LHS to crossroads/lights. Turn left (s/p Ring Road A6177, Leeds A647) into Queen's Road. After 0.2 miles turn right (s/p Valley Parade) into Midland Road.

From Leeds (from Leeds Old Road, B6381): Pass 'White Bear' pub on LHS, then turn right at crossroads/lights (s/p Ring Road A6177, Harrogate A658) onto the A6177 Killinghall Road. Turn left after 1.1 miles (no signpost – it's the turning just before the 'Save' petrol station on RHS) into Northcote Road. At junction after 0.8 miles, follow signs to 'Ring Road A6177', passing the 'The Bolton' pub on RHS. Straight on at next junction (s/p Ring Road A6177, Keighley A650), and then turn left (s/p Valley Parade) into Midland Road.

FROM RAILWAY STATIONS:

a) Bradford Interchange: About 1.3 miles. *By taxi:* About £2.50. *By bus:* The bus station is part of the interchange, so catch any of the buses listed below. *By foot:* Straight out of main entrance and down steps into Bridge Street. Straight on at crossroads, over Hall Ings, and turn right at next crossroads into Market Street. At end of road turn left by Barclays Bank up Cheapside, which becomes Manor Row.

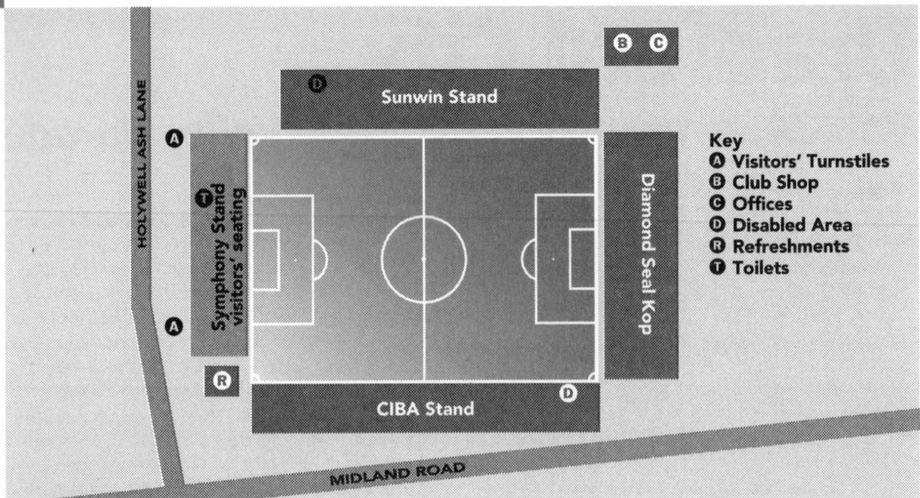

(*)Pass Bradford Forster Square station on RHS. At top of hill, cross dual carriageway at pedestrian lights and turn right down dual carriageway (Hamm Strasse) following signs to Keighley, Wakefield A650. Take next left (s/p City Centre North) into Midland Road.
b) Bradford Forster Square: About 0.7 miles. *By foot:* Head diagonally across the car park and up cobbled slope to main road. Turn sharp right into Manor Row. Then as from Bradford Interchange(*).
Last Midweek Trains: There are no trains to London after a midweek game. From Bradford Interchange, the 21.55 goes to Manchester Victoria, and the 22.04 to Sheffield via Leeds. From Forster Square the 22.10 goes to Newcastle via Leeds. Please double check on (0345) 484 950.
BY BUS: Numerous buses to Valley Parade leave from Stand B12 in the Interchange, such as the 622-626, 648-656, 658-671, 677-680, 755, 811 and the 812.

PARKING

Horrendous, as many of the roads around the ground are now residents' parking. About 200 spaces are available along Midland Road, with cars parking across the pavement on one side of the road, and nose-to-tail along the other. The club recommends the Manningham Middle School car park on Manningham Lane, next to the 'Belle Vue' pub.

THE GROUND

So it happened at last: the dinky little Midland Road Stand – one of the shallowest in the League – has gone, replaced with the single-tier 5,000-seater 'CIBA' Stand! And now, with the 1999 deadline drawing near, the Diamond Seal Kop, one of the largest remaining football terraces in the country, is expected to be the next to go. The home fans protest that the Football Licensing Authority itself has declared the terrace to be safe. But the law hath spoketh, and the club says it must be demolished at the end of season 1999/2000.

Away fans are allocated the smart two-tier Symphony Stand, built in 1991. If a small away contingent is expected the lower tier is closed. This is no great loss as the back is open, allowing in rain, snow and icy winds. The facilities are good, but four slender posts block the view from some seats, and fans towards the back need necks like ET to see the near touchline.

Groundaholics might like to know that the Midland Road Stand was dismantled and taken over to Barrow FC. However, it's still in its packaging, as Barrow still hasn't got planning permission to rebuild it.
Total Capacity: 18,018. For away fans: Seating 1,840 (Symphony Stand) and, if required, 1,800 in the CIBA Stand.
Cost (98/99): Seating: Adult £13, concessions (OAPs, juniors, students) £8.
Disabled Facilities: Space for 49 disabled supporters in the CIBA Stand and Sunwin Stand. Entry through gates by Turnstiles 1-2. *Disabled Toilet:* Nearby. *Cost:* Joint ticket for disabled and helper costs £13. *Booking:* Essential. *Parking:* Available, by the Diamond Seal Kop on Midland Road. *For the Blind:* Headphones and commentary in the CIBA and Sunwin Stands.
Programme: £1.80.
Visitors' Toilets: *Male:* These toilets are surely the narrowest in the league, leaving little space for those trying to get in and out. Only nimble feet kept fans out of the line of fire! *Female:* Hooligan proof ... as indicated by the steel doors, breeze blocks and trough sink. There was no soap, no hot water and no hand-dryers, but the facilities were very clean.

Bradford – probably the best curries in the world.

Food and Drink: 'Very Hot Pies' read the warning notice. And they were. One Birmingham fan confirmed that the energy radiating from his steak and kidney pie (£1.40) could probably heat the Bradford conurbation for several weeks, but added that it was tasty too. The chicken-and-mushroom variety was also very good (14.3.98).

PUB GUIDE

The Carlton Hotel (1) Queen's Road (opposite junction with Midland Road) (01274) 542 874
Tetleys. Popular hotel with separate pool room, serving snacks from 12-2.30. TV. Families welcome. Disabled facilities. Open: all day.

The Oakleigh (2) 4 Oak Avenue (01274) 544 307
Free House/Mansfield (with guest beers). Large friendly open-plan bar with beer garden. Pool, TV. Disabled facilities. Open: all day from 12. Next door, **The Park Hotel (3)** is under the same management, and tends to be quieter. It has pool tables and a large beer garden. Accommodation is available at reduced rates for people who mention the *Football Fans Guide.*

The Spotted House 22a Keighley Road (01274) 721 784
Bass. Excellent pub with a good matchday atmosphere and lots of pinball machines, jukeboxes and the like. Pool table, TV. Families welcome. Open: all day.

The New Beehive (4) 171 Westgate (01274) 721 784
Free House (with four permanent and four guest beers). An Edwardian gas-lit tavern, with six small rooms, each with its own character. Bar snacks served 12-2.30, pool, skittle alley, TV, beer garden, children's room. Open: all day. Accommodation available.

The Bolton 1025 Bolton Road (en route in From Leeds) (01274) 559 021
Bass (with Caffreys). The landlady describes the pub as a 'good friendly local'. Bar snacks. TV. Open: all day.

FOOD GUIDE

Surprisingly, for one of the food capitals of the world, the choice round Valley Parade is limited to two takeaways on Manningham Lane. The nearest decent curry house is the 'Westgate Tandoori' on St Thomas Road, but it doesn't open until 7 pm. The chef at the 'Nawaab' on Manor Row (near Forster Square station) recently came runner-up in an international competition. It's popular so please book on (01274) 720 371 (unfortunately not open Saturday lunchtimes). The greatest concentration of restaurants is on the other side of town, near Bradford University. The 'Shah Jehan' at 30 Little Horton Lane (open 12-2, 5-midnight) has won the 'best Bradford curry' award two years running: book on (01274) 390 777. The award-winning 'Mumtaz Paan House' on Great Horton Road also takes bookings on (01274) 571 861. It opens all day from 11 am. Two other old favourites come highly recommended: 'The Sabraaj' at 3 Morley Street (01274) 724 316 and 'The Kashmir' 27 Morley Street (01274) 726 513.

LOCAL MEDIA

Radio: Bradford City has its own station, Bantams 1566 AM; BBC Radio Leeds 92.4 FM.
Radio Phone-ins: Bantams, Saturdays 5.15-6 pm, call (01274) 771 677; BBC Radio Leeds, Saturdays 5-6 pm, call (0113) 244 3222.
Saturday Sports Paper: The Saturday 'pink'.

MISCELLANEOUS

In the old days, pre-match and half-time entertainment at Valley Parade meant standing and watching the rain pouring off the stand roof. No more! The new-style razzmatazz includes an 'American-style announcer' and the Bantam Belles cheerleaders, whose routines threaten to delay the kick-off as they never finish in time. The BCFC mascots are another source of amusement. The rooster 'Billy Banter' has been compared to 'the constipated penguin from Wallace and Gromit', while the 'City Gent' is so well-rounded, one wag suggested he held the answer to the eternal question 'who ate all the pies?'
Safety Factor: No trouble in 1997/98 season, but it's not a great idea to wear colours in the town centre.
Rivals: Huddersfield Town, Leeds United and Burnley.
Fanzines: The excellent 'City Gent', PO Box 56, Bradford BD13 4YU.
Unofficial Websites:
'City Gent': http://www.legend.co.uk/citygent/
'News Pages': http://web.ukonline.co.uk/n.ackroyd/
Tourist Information: (01274) 753 678.

B

Brentford

Griffin Park

Address: Griffin Park, Braemar Road, Brentford, Middlesex, TW8 0NT
Telephone: Club (0181) 847 2511
Clubcall (0891) 121 108

Here's an enjoyable challenge for the football fan: to down a pint (or two) at the four pubs which mark the corners of Griffin Park. The drinking isn't really the challenge ... the difficult part is negotiating the west London traffic and finding a parking place, while still leaving time for the pub tour! Griffin Park is one of those grounds pointed out as 'what-IS-that-ground-over-there' by thousands of motorists passing by on the nearby elevated section of the M4. So, for the footie fan, it's easy enough to find. It's surrounded by suburban terracing – pleasant, hanging-basket territory, this – but still, the choice of food near the ground is severely limited.

HOW TO GET THERE

BY CAR: From All Routes Outside M25: Exit M25 at junction 15 (s/p M4, Heathrow Terminals 1,2 & 3, London (W)) onto the M4 eastbound. After 8.3 miles exit M4 at junction 2 (s/p A4, N and S Circular A406 (A205), Chiswick A315), onto slip road down onto the A4, which runs underneath, and parallel to, the M4. At Chiswick Roundabout after 0.7 miles, there's a choice of directions:

a) To the main parking area: go right round the roundabout and head back up the A4 (s/p The West, Heathrow A4, M4). Keep in the two right-hand lanes (s/p Staines, Hounslow A4) and go straight on for 1.5 miles, to junction/lights. Here, turn left (s/p Brentford A3002) into Boston Manor Road. Somerset Road, which leads to one of the best parking areas, is on the RHS after 1.0 miles.

b) To the ground: take 4th exit (s/p S. Circular A205, A316, M3 Richmond) onto Chiswick High Road/Kew Bridge Road. (*)Straight on for 0.3 miles to junction/lights (Kew Bridge Junction). Here, keep in lane for the A315 and go straight on (s/p Hounslow, Brentford A315), towards 'The Plough'. At lights after 0.5 miles turn right (by McDonalds) into Ealing Road, which runs past Griffin Park.

From South London (for directions to Kew Bridge see the London Guide): Over Kew Bridge to the Kew Bridge Junction. Here turn left (s/p Hounslow, Brentford A315) into Kew Bridge Road. At lights after 0.5 miles turn right (by McDonalds) into Ealing Road.

FROM RAILWAY STATIONS:

a) Brentford: South West trains run from Waterloo and Vauxhall to Weybridge via Brentford. *By foot:* Head up to the main road and turn left. Take first main left turn into Windmill Road, and first right (s/p Methodist Church)

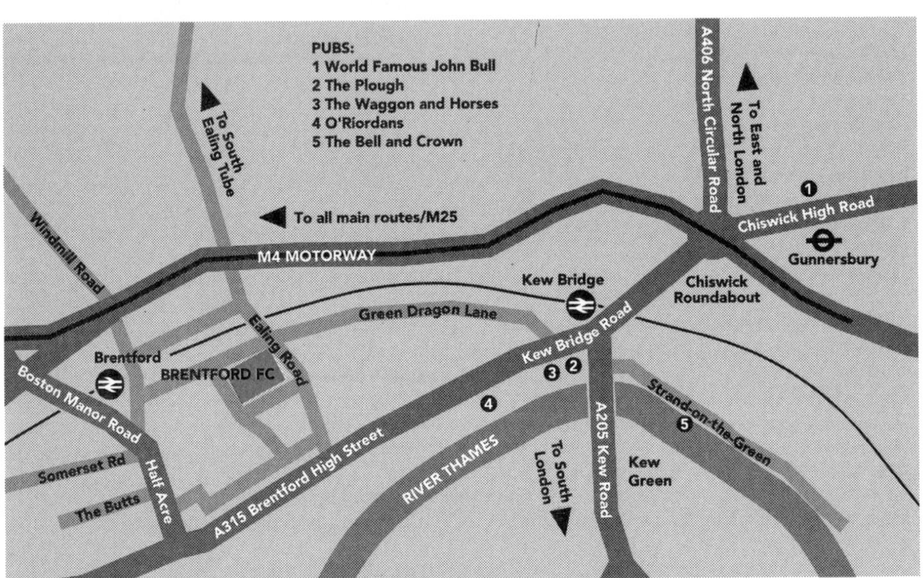

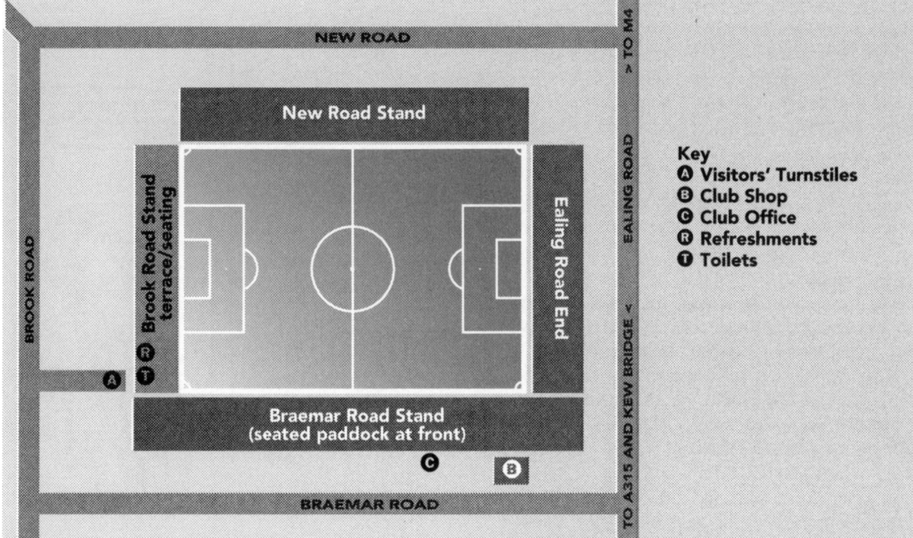

into Clifden Road. After 0.2 miles turn right into Brook Road and away turnstiles are on the LHS.

b) Kew Bridge: This station is on the same line as Brentford station, but is closer to 'The Plough', 'The Waggon and Horses', and the Strand-on-the-Green. It's 0.4 miles to the ground: take steps up from platforms to main exit and turn right. Keep going for 0.3 miles, then turn right by McDonalds into Ealing Road.

Last Midweek Trains:

a) From Brentford. To central London 21.41 and 22.11; to Weybridge 22.15 and 23.15.

b) From Kew. To London Waterloo 21.43 and 22.13; to Weybridge 22.13 and 23.13.

FROM UNDERGROUND STATION: Gunnersbury (District Line, Zone 3): 1.3 miles to ground. *By foot:* Exit station into Chiswick High Road and turn left. After 0.3 miles, at Chiswick Roundabout, take 2nd exit (s/p S. Circular A205) into Chiswick High Road, which becomes Kew Bridge Road. Then as by car From All Routes (*).

BY BUS: The E8 is a frequent service from Hanwell along Boston Manor Road, while the E2 runs from West Ealing along Windmill Road. The no. 65 runs from south of the river, over Kew Bridge. Nos. 237, 267 and H29 run along Kew Bridge Road. The main night bus is the N97, Brentford High Street to central London.

PARKING

It's street parking only, and woe betide the latecomer. One of the best places to try is Somerset Road and the Butts Estate (see map).

THE GROUND

All talk of Brentford FC moving from Griffin Park to a new stadium (location unspecified) has died away, and the club has been busy upgrading the existing facilities. In the summer of 1996, 4,000 seats were added to the New Road terrace, and 1,000 extra seats to the Braemer Road paddock. This left the open Ealing Road End as the only terracing for home fans, though the more vociferous have set up shop in the New Road Stand, to be nearer, one presumes, to the visitors.

Away fans, in the two-tier Brook Road Stand, were unaffected by the changes and still have a choice of covered terrace or top-tier seating. Two fans sneezing on the terrace sound like the Roker Roar, and envious home supporters are keen to swop ends to take advantage of the excellent acoustics. They wouldn't be so keen on the view, which is generally poor. As one visiting Gills fans wrote: 'A top tip is to push the kids out of the way and stand right at the front!'

Total Capacity: 12,763. For away fans: Seating 636, standing 1,627. Turnstiles in Brook Road.

Cost (97/98): Seating: Adult £14, juniors and OAPs £11. Terrace: Adult £9, concessions £6.

Disabled Facilities: Space for 18 in Block E of the Braemar Road Stand. *Disabled Toilet:* by St John's Ambulance Station. *Cost:* Free for disabled and helper. *Booking:* Essential. *Parking:* None available. *For the Blind:* Room for 14 in the Braemar Road Paddock.

Programme: £1.50.

Visitors' Toilets: *Male:* Here's one for the Guinness Book of Records: Griffin Park's attempt to break the world record for the number of people crammed into a public toilet!! *Female:* No smell, thankfully, and an interesting lighting arrangement ... are those really silver pie cases surrounding the light-bulbs?

Food and Drink: The burgers (£2) were a good size, came with freshly fried onions, and smelled great, but were disappointing. After a deal of chomping, most fans blamed the stale-tasting bread. The pies (£1) were tepid-to-cold, so go for the good-sized hot-dogs (£2) and sausage rolls (£1) which Preston fans thought were good value (2.9.97, 18.10.97, 21.10.97, 14.2.98).

PUB GUIDE

By an arrangement made in heaven, Griffin Park has a pub on each corner: 'Excellent, every one of them', said a tipsy Preston fan. Gillingham supporters recommended **The Griffin,** while the **New Inn** is particularly welcoming. Slightly further afield, try:

The World Famous John Bull (1) 590 Chiswick High Road (0181) 994 0062

Scottish and Newcastle. Large, unbelievably football-friendly pub where fans are sorely tempted to stay and miss the match altogether. Bar meals served all day. Table football, darts, pool, TV. Open: all day.

The Plough (2) 24 Kew Bridge Road (by Kew Bridge) (0181) 560 5621

Scottish and Newcastle. Large traditional sports-friendly pub with big-screen TV and excellent food. Full menu served until 6 pm (9 pm midweek). Bar snacks available all day. Pool table, patio. Open: all day.

The Waggon and Horses (3) 26 Kew Bridge Road (0181) 560 3590

Fullers. Right next door to 'The Plough' and just as welcoming. Full menu served 12-4. Pool table, TV, darts, beer garden. Open: all day.

O'Riordans (4) 3 Brentford High Street (0181) 560 5543

Free House. Highly recommended Irish pub with real atmosphere. Bar food 12-2. Families welcome. TV.

FOR FAMILIES:

Two pubs to try: **The Bell and Crown (5)** 11-13 Thomas Road, Strand-on-the-Green, is a lovely traditional pub right on the river, serving excellent food all day; **The Royal Harvester** on Boston Manor Road, Hanwell is a huge friendly Harvester/Bass pub. Please book on: (0181) 567 3711. Open: all day.

How to get there, from Chiswick Roundabout: Exit roundabout at s/p The West, Heathrow A4, M4. Keep straight on for 1.5 miles, following signs to Staines, to crossroads. Here, turn right (s/p Hanwell A3002) into Boston Manor Road. Pub is on the RHS after 0.9 miles.

FOOD GUIDE

Near the ground the choice is between the 'Oriental' takeaway opposite 'The Griffin' and the 'Albany Fish Bar' on Albany Road. Also on Albany Road is the 'Brentford

Kebab House', which does puddings such as trifle and cheesecake! There's a McDonalds on the corner of Ealing Road and Brentford High Street. Just a short drive away, on the other side of Kew Bridge, is a classy area of pubs and restaurants around Kew Green. They include a Pizza-Pasta and the excellent 'Franco Al-Bocconvino' restaurant (corner Gloucester Road).

LOCAL MEDIA

Local Radio: Capital Gold 1548 AM; GLR 94.9 FM.

Radio Phone-ins: Capital Gold, Saturdays 5-6.30 pm; midweek every night 7-8 or after live match commentary. Call (0845) 35 60 70 80.

Saturday Sports Paper: None.

MISCELLANEOUS

Brentford fans avoided the nightmare that is Wembley Park station by travelling to their 96/97 play-off final by barge along the Grand Union Canal, livening up a sleepy west London Sunday morning with fog horns and booming renditions of 'We're the famous Brentford FC and we're going to Wembley'. The return trip was a little quieter: they lost.

Safety Factor: Bring your granny.

Rivals: Traditional rivals Fulham are regarded with green-eyed envy.

Fanzines: 'Beesotted', 19a Stanley Road, Teddington, Middlesex, TW11 8TP; 'Thorne in the Side', 25 Shaftesbury Crescent, Laleham, Middlesex, TW18 1QL.

Unofficial Websites:

http://village.vossnet.co.uk/b/beesfan

http://freespace.virgin.net/h.hobbs

Tourist Information: (0181) 940 9126.

Brighton & Hove Albion

Withdean Stadium

Registered Office: 118 Queen's Road, Brighton BN1 3XG
Telephone: Club (01273) 778 855
ClubCall (0891) 800 609
Club Shop (01273) 776 969
Official Website: http://www.seagulls.co.uk/

NB Brighton & Hove Albion plan to play their home games at Gillingham's Priestfield Stadium until October 1998, and then at Withdean Stadium in Brighton. If in doubt, check the matchday venue with the club.

After a truly dismal year in exile in Gillingham and months of negotiations with the local council, Brighton & Hove Albion are at last returning to Brighton. Their new ground is at Withdean, an upmarket residential area, nearly three miles north of the town centre. Many local residents are bitterly opposed to the football club landing on their doorstep, and to allay their fears the club has signed a number of stringent planning restrictions. The result is that football fans MUST NOT park anywhere near the stadium. The club has set aside two areas for free park-and-ride schemes (see road directions below). Alternatively travel by train to nearby Preston Park. Those prepared to walk the odd half mile or so will find friendly pubs, but takeaways are few and far between.

HOW TO GET THERE

BY CAR: These are directions to the park-and-ride schemes, at Mill Road and Mithras House.
From North (A23): Approaching the junction with the A27, keep in the right-hand lanes (s/p Brighton A23) to roundabout (by the Q8 service station). Here turn right (s/p Mill Road) into Mill Road, from where buses take supporters to Withdean Stadium. Alternatively, it is walkable, about a mile mostly downhill, assuming supporters will be allowed to cut through to the south, along the path by the windmill. The path comes out opposite Mill Rise ... head down the hill towards the row of shops (which has a newsagents and an Indian takeaway, open from 5 pm). Keep on the main road, which becomes Dene Vale, to T-junction by the 'Eldred News'. Here turn right along Eldred Avenue to ground.
From West (A27): Exit A27 at signpost 'Brighton A23'. At first roundabout turn right (s/p Brighton A23) over the A27, and go straight on at the second roundabout. At next roundabout (by the Q8 service station) go straight on (s/p Mill Road) into the Mill Road, from where buses take supporters to Withdean Stadium.
From East (A27): a) To the Mithras House park-and-ride: Exit A27 at signpost 'Brighton A27, A270' and follow 'Brighton A270' signs onto the A270 Lewes Road. Mithras House is well signposted, on the left after 1.9 miles. b) To the Mill Road park-and-ride: Exit A27 at signpost 'Brighton, London, Gatwick A23'. At roundabout after 0.2 miles turn left (s/p Brighton, London, Gatwick). At next roundabout (by the Q8 service station) go straight on (s/p Mill Road) into Mill Road, from where buses take supporters to Withdean Stadium.

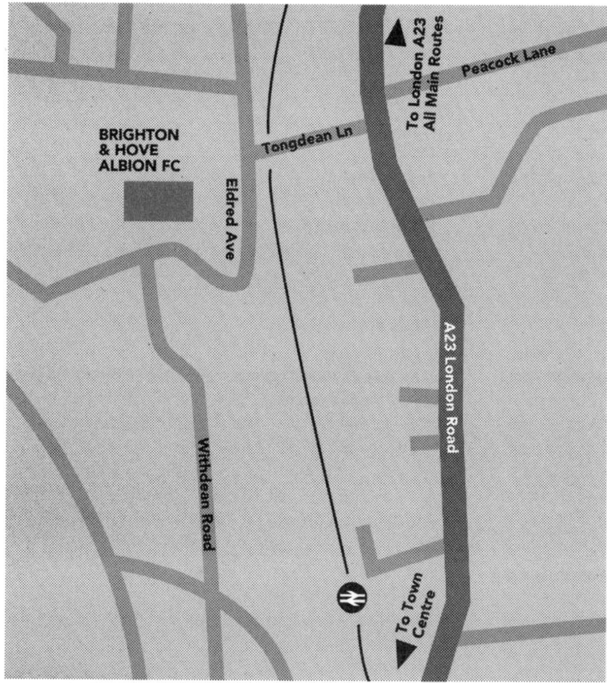

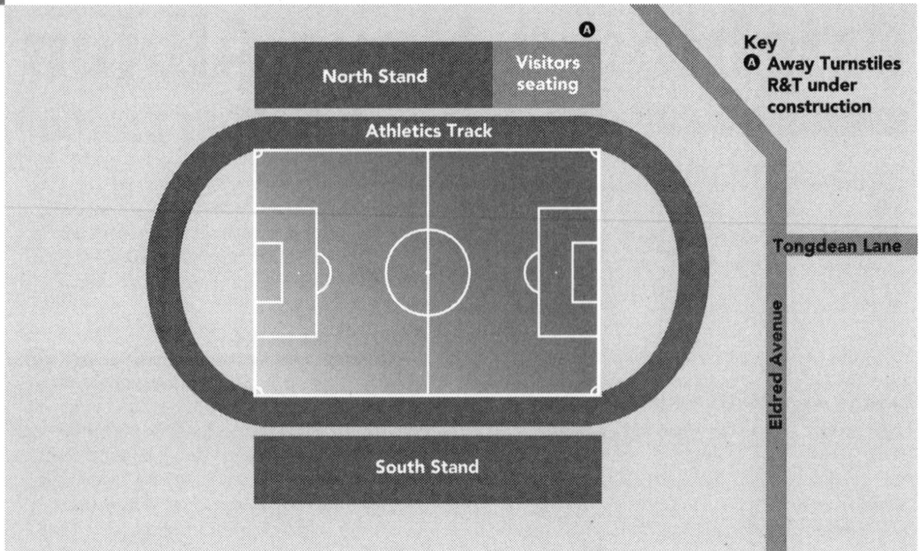

FROM RAILWAY STATION (Preston Park, with Connex and Thameslink trains): 0.7 miles. *By foot:* Come down steps from platform into underpass, and head towards the main exit (ie not the one with the steps to a pathway). Head straight down the road ahead (Clermont Road) and at T-junction after 0.15 miles, by Bernadette's R.C. School, turn left into London Road (A23). Turn left after 0.45 miles (s/p Withdean Sports Complex) into Tongdean Lane, under narrow railway bridge. Turn right, and first left to away turnstiles.
Last Midweek Trains: Trains from Preston Park to London Bridge leave at 21.43 and 22.43; to London Victoria at 22.03 and 23.05; to Portsmouth Harbour, via Haywards Heath, at 21.43. Please double-check on (0345) 484 950.
BY BUS: Special park-and-ride buses run from Mill Road and from Mithras House (see road directions above).

PARKING

As mentioned at length above, football fans must use one of the two designated park-and-ride schemes, Mill Road or Mithras House, so allow lots of extra time. Mill Road will become one-way only, westbound. The only alternative is to park a long way east or south of the ground.

THE GROUND

Withdean is principally an athletics stadium, with a football pitch laid out inside the eight-lane running track. The south side is bordered by woodland, and the north by a large family pub and indoor tennis courts. The club plans to build a large bank of uncovered seating to the south, and a small covered stand to the north, part of which will be allocated to visiting supporters. It does not have permission to build stands or terracing behind the goals, so with capacity limited, every match will be all-ticket. New refreshment kiosks and toilet blocks are under construction, as well as new turnstiles. Away fans are likely to enter the stadium from the north, alongside the pub. Brighton & Hove Albion have permission to play at Withdean for three years while the search continues for a site for a new stadium.
Total Capacity: 6,000. For away fans: 250.
Cost (98/99): TBC, but concessions will be available.
Disabled Facilities: Space at pitch level on both sides of the ground. Parking also available. Please book through Brighton & Hove Albion. *For the Blind:* No special facilities.
Programme: £1.70.

PUB GUIDE

The Preston Brewery Tap 197 Preston Road (on the A23 about 0.6 miles south of the ground, by the Shell petrol station) (01273) 508 700
Courage (with Marstons Pedigree, Ruddles, John Smiths Smooth). Smart traditional pub in a Victorian building, and very sports-friendly too. Excellent menu served 12-2, 7-9 (unless it's too busy). Darts, TV, beer garden. Families welcome. Open: all day.
By the Mithras House park-and-ride:
The Royal Hussar 5 Pelham Terrace (A270 Lewes Road) (01273) 603 901

Corporate Catering (with Courage Best, John Smiths Smooth). Large traditional locals pub with public bar with pool table, and quieter lounge bar. Bar snacks (burgers, baguettes, all-day breakfast etc) served 12-7. Darts, TV. Families welcome in beer garden. Live music Saturday evenings. Open: all day.

FOR FAMILIES:

The Black Lion Hotel London Road, Patcham (the A23 north of the ground) (01273) 552 886 Bass/Harvester. Wonderfully friendly pub/restaurant in an imposing detached building, on the A27 but in Old Patcham village. Bar with big-screen TV and bar billiards, plus snacks (sandwiches £2.50, burgers £4.65) served 12-10. Restaurant, open from 12-11, has a huge menu, including pasta, salads, steaks, fish and vegetarian dishes, costing £6-£9. Children's menu from £1.45. Booking advisable. Large beer garden, bouncy castle in the warmer months.

The Preston Park Hotel London Road (the A23, opposite Clermont Road). This is a smart hotel bar which serves food from 11-2 and from 6 pm, although snacks are usually available at all times (chef willing!) The menu, at £6.95, includes Thai Green Chicken Curry, salad bowls and burgers and wedges.

FOOD GUIDE

For those using the Mill Road park-and-ride, the only choice is the 'Q8' garage on the main roundabout, which has sandwiches and provides hot water for Pot Noodles and the like. The nearest chippy to the ground is the 'Happy Inn' on Eldred Avenue (open from 5 pm). Just off the A27, the Old London Road near the 'Black Lion Hotel' has the fantastic 'Village Bakery' (open 8.30-4) with a huge range of pies and pasties (eg curry, steak-and-kidney, broccoli and cheese) all for 75p or less. Also on Old London Road are a Tandoori restaurant and the family 'Coach House Tea Rooms'. At the junction of Ladies Mile Road and Mackie Avenue, there's a fish and chip shop open lunchtimes and evenings (burgers £1.15, home baked pies £1.40); a Tandoori (open from 5.30 pm) and a bookies. By the Mithras House car park are two Indian takeaways, a café and the 'Ocean' fish and chip shop.

LOCAL MEDIA

Local Radio: South Coast Radio 1323 and 945 AM; Surf 107.2 FM; Capital Gold 1323 and 945 AM, with local sports coverage; BBC Southern Counties Radio 95.3 FM.

Radio Phone-ins: Possibly on Capital Gold, listen out for details.

Saturday Sports Paper: The 'Sports Argus'.

MISCELLANEOUS

Safety Factor: Few problems expected.

Rivals: The nearest club to Brighton is Crystal Palace or, as 'Build a Bonfire' calls them, 'Crystal Palarse'. Leyton Orient aren't popular either.

Fanzines: 'Seaside Saga', PO Box 2187, Hove, East Sussex, BN3 4RF; 'Scars and Stripes', 10 Greenland Close, Durrington, Worthing, West Sussex, BN13 2RP; 'Build a Bonfire', 22 Harding Avenue, Eastbourne, East Sussex, BN22 8PH.

Unofficial Websites:
http://homepages.enterprise.net.gjc/

Tourist Information: (01273) 292 599.

B

Bristol City

Ashton Gate

Address: Ashton Gate, Bristol, BS3 2EJ
Telephone: Club/Ticket Office (0117) 963 0630
Ticket Hotline (0117) 966 6666
ClubCall (0891) 121 176
Official Website: http://www.bcfc.co.uk

All those driving to Ashton Gate from the M5 can admire a view over the very best bits of Bristol – viz, the elegant suspension bridge and the imposing terraced houses of the posh suburb of Clifton. Unsurprisingly, the dullest suburbs, the retail parks and industrial estates, surround the football ground. For the footie fan, all is not lost. Just round the corner is a shopping street with loads of places to eat and drink, including an excellent pie shop, while the more adventurous can walk to a newly developed area of Bristol Docks, which has some truly characterful pubs. For everyone, there's just one warning: arrive early to avoid an almighty bun-fight for parking spaces.

HOW TO GET THERE

BY CAR: From East: Exit M4 at junction 19 (s/p Bristol M32) onto the M32. At end of motorway after 4.9 miles turn left (s/p All Other Routes, Broadmead, Temple Meads). Get in right-hand lanes into underpass (s/p Temple Meads, Bristol Airport). After underpass, get in lane for 'Flyover Only'(**) (s/p City Centre, Bedminster, Bristol Airport) and over flyover. At next two roundabouts follow signs to 'Taunton A38, Weston A370' onto Coronation Road, running parallel to the River Avon. After 1.5 miles the road divides. Keep left (s/p Bath A4, Wells A37, Taunton A38) onto A3029 Brunel Way. For the ground, keep in the left-hand lane and come off the road at the next exit (s/p Taunton A38) into Winterstoke Road.
(**)NB: The police warn that the flyover is about to be demolished, to be replaced by a roundabout.

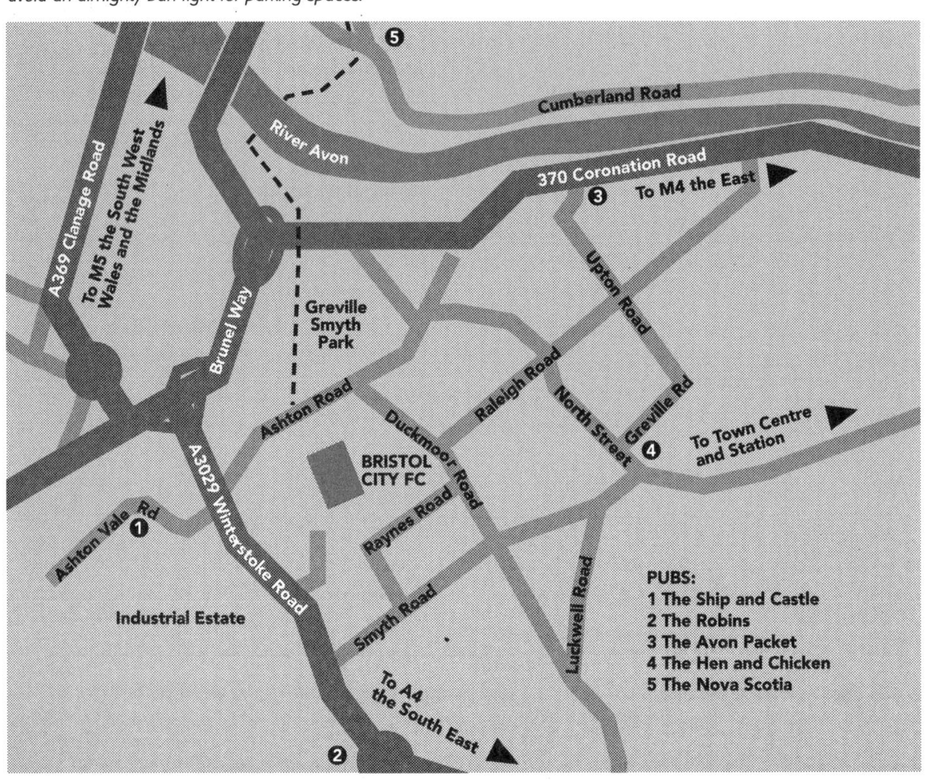

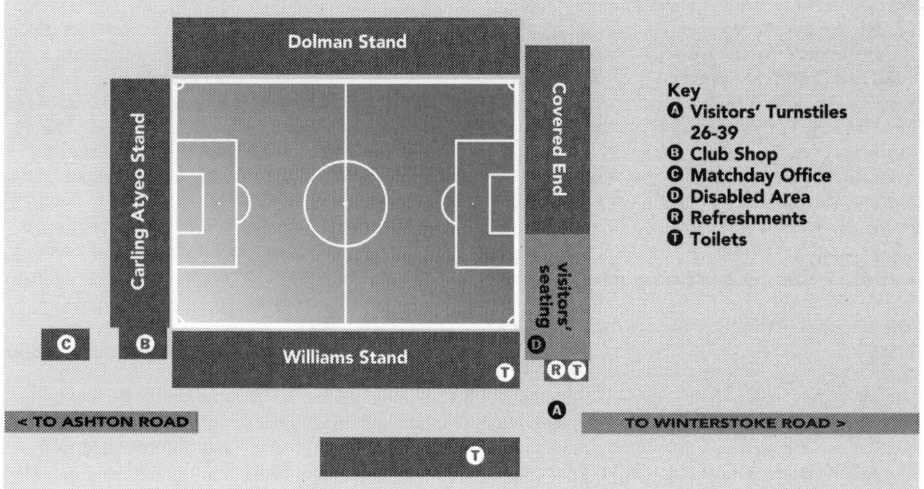

From South-West, Wales and Midlands: Exit M5 at junction 19 (s/p Services, Portishead, Docks A369). At roundabout follow signs to 'Easton-in-Gordano, Clifton' onto the A369. Go straight on, following signs to 'Bristol A369', for 5.0 miles – through Abbots Leigh and Leighwoods – to roundabout. Here, take 2nd exit (s/p Weston A370, Taunton A38), through underpass to a T-junction. Go straight across (s/p Taunton A38, Bath A4), towards the Mercedes Benz garage, into Winterstoke Road.
FROM RAILWAY STATION (Temple Meads): 2.6 miles to ground. *By taxi:* £4.50-£5. *By bus:* The no. 528 runs to the ground.
Last Midweek Trains: Bristol Temple Meads: The last train to London is at 21.25. To Cardiff, trains run at 21.49, 21.59 and 23.04.
BY BUS: In addition to the no. 528 from the station, the nos. 21 and 22 run from Redcliffe Hill/City Centre to Ashton Gate.

PARKING

Parking in season 98/99 is likely to be very difficult, because of new restrictions and Bristol City's promotion. A couple of areas to try are the industrial estate on Winterstoke Road (see map), and along Ashton Drive, by 'The Robins' pub. Another idea, especially for those coming in from the M5, is to park to the north of Brunel Way, in the 'Ashton Court Estate'.

Another good idea is to park in Hotwells, where there are the excellent pubs detailed below. Hotwells is signposted off the A3029 heading north into the city, just after the bridge over the River Avon. The road goes down to the 'Rose of Denmark', where there's a car park. For the other two pubs, continue round the one-way system (s/p Weston, Historic Harbour, and then Avonmouth A4). There is a short cut to the ground from near 'The Nova Scotia': Head along Avon Crescent past the Howard restaurant, to the junction with Cumberland Road. Cross the road and through the little gate, across the railway line and bear right to the river, passing the P&O distribution centre. Turn left over the railway bridge, and immediately up the path on the LHS. The ground is visible from the ridge.

THE GROUND

'From the outside, without traditional floodlights, it does look like a B&Q', commented one City fan. 'But inside it's one of best grounds in the division.' Indeed, both the atmosphere and appearance of Ashton Gate improved with the addition of seating, in 1997, in front of the Dolman Stand which had until then presented a blank wall to the pitch. The smart Atyeo Stand, opened in 1994, is the main home end and houses the 'Cider 'Eds' matchday band, and right noisy it is too. Visitors are allocated sections of the Covered End. It's cavernous with several large pillars, so fans are continually standing up to see near-touchline action. The facilities, however, are good and the roof provides what City fans call an 'annoyingly good atmosphere'.
Total Capacity: 21,300. For away fans (covered seating): Up to 5,000. Turnstiles 26-39.
Cost (98/99): Category 'A', TBA, expected to be: Adults £16; Category 'B': £14/£11/£9. Category 'C': £13/£10/£8.
Disabled Facilities: 20 spaces available for visiting fans. *Disabled Toilet:* Nearby. *Cost:* Free for disabled, full price for helper. *Booking:* Essential. *Parking:* Possible – please call Andrew Thomas at the club. *For the Blind:* Headphones with commentary in the Williams Stand.
Programme: £1.80.
Visitors' Toilets: *Male:* Cor blimey mate and no mistake. Fans thought they'd wandered into the Bristol

Ritz by some secret tunnel. *Female:* 'These are smart', said one surprised Northampton fan on entering what must be some of the best loos on the football circuit.

Food and Drink: You know when you've done lots of washing-up, and all the suds have gone, so you drain away the water to start again? Well, the tea (75p) at Ashton Gate was the colour of that water. And tasted worse! Go for the excellent bovril (75p) instead. Most fans found that the burgers (£1.80), without any onions or sauces, were bland (28.1.98).

PUB GUIDE

NEAR THE GROUND:

The Ship and Castle (1) Ashton Vale Road (0117) 902 0059

Courage (and guest ale). Small traditional local, described by one stalwart as 'a real nice friendly pub'. Sandwiches. Darts, pool, TV, beer garden, skittle alley. Families welcome. Open: all day.

The Robins (2) Winterstoke Road (0117) 953 3138

Courage. Large modern-style pub close to the away turnstiles. It usually welcomes all, but occasionally becomes 'home only' for higher profile games. Darts, pool, TV. Families welcome. Open: all day.

WITHIN EASY WALKING DISTANCE:

The Avon Packet (3) Coronation Road, Southville (0117) 987 2431

Courage. Small two-roomed pub in an 18th century building with a bear-pit in the backyard! Sandwiches. Darts, outdoor pool table, TV. Open: all day.

On North Street it's worth checking out the **Hen and Chicken (4),** a huge Mr Qs pub under new management and newly-redecorated.

The following pubs are in Hotwells (see under 'Parking' above), and again are within walking distance.

STAND UP IF YOUR LEGS HAVE CRAMP,
STAND UP IF YOUR LEGS HAVE CRAMP....
OL CITY
GLASCOW

The Nova Scotia (5) Nova Scotia Place, Cumberland Basin is a wonderful traditional Courage pub right on the dockside, with walls covered in maps and prints. It also does excellent bar food; **The Pump House** Merchants Road is a characterful Marstons pub converted from a 19th century pump house, serving a full menu; **The Rose of Denmark** at 6 Dowry Place, Hotwells, is a traditional Ansells pub with, says the landlord, the cheapest food in Hotwells.

FOR FAMILIES:

A Harvester pub called **The Smyth Arms**, in Ashton Lane, by Long Ashton, accepts restaurant bookings from visiting supporters. Please call on (01275) 392 245.

FOOD GUIDE

The section of North Street between the 'Hen and Chicken' pub and Ashton Road is by far the best bet for pre-match food. Home supporters recommend the 'Metro Café' and 'Pacific Fish and Chips'. Nearby is a small outlet called 'Clarks Pies', highly recommended by the hordes of locals buying their lunch there. Nearer the ground are a couple of cafés, one of which, the 'Robins Café', is right on the Ashton Road entrance. In addition, the locals recommend two fish and chip shops: the 'Parkway Chippy', on Ashton Road, between North Street and the ground, and the 'Lucky House', opposite 'The Robins' pub on Ashton Drive. Both do Chinese food too.

LOCAL MEDIA

Local Radio: BBC Radio Bristol, 1548 MW; GWR 96.3 FM.

Radio Phone-ins: BBC Radio Bristol, Friday night 7-8 pm, call (0117) 923 8877.

Saturday Sports Paper: The 'Green 'Un'.

MISCELLANEOUS

Safety Factor: Bristol City does have a hooligan following, but it prefers to seek out and fight the opposition's idiots rather than the average football fan. Obviously derby days can be tense, as Sky viewers witnessed last season when both City and Rovers fans staged pitch invasions. Such problems inside the ground, however, are rare.

Rivals: Bristol Rovers: 'no other team comes close.'

Fanzines: 'One Team in Bristol', PO Box 4-2, Burnham On Sea, Somerset, TA8 2YZ; 'The Cider'Ed', 3 Ravenswood Road, Redland, Bristol, BS6 6BN; 'Come In No. 7 Your Time Is Up', 27 Chichester Way, North Yate, Bristol, BS17 5TA.

Unofficial Websites:

http://www.netcouk.co.uk/~cornolio/city.html

The Gate: http://www.freckleton.demon.co.uk/

http://www.homeusers.prestel.co.uk/oaen

http://www.nott.ac.uk/~pmymjaa/t_darker.htm

Tourist Information: (0117) 926 0767.

Bristol Rovers

The Memorial Ground

Registered Office: The Beeches, Broomhill Road, Brislington, Bristol, BS4 5BF
Stadium: Memorial Ground, Filton Avenue, Horfield, Bristol, BS7 0AQ. Club Shop/Commercial Department: 411-413 Gloucester Road, Horfield, Bristol, BS7 8TS
Telephone: Registered Office (0117) 977 2000
Shop/Commercial Department (0117) 924 7474
Rovers Hotline (0891) 664 422
Supporters Club (0117) 961 1772

In 1998 it finally happened: the last remnants of Eastville Stadium, Bristol Rovers' spiritual home, were demolished. Rovers fans went into mourning, remembering its stonking matchday atmosphere, the flower beds, and the gasworks which gave the club its nickname. The current Rovers team is now well ensconced about a mile to the north-west at the Memorial Ground, a stadium shared with the rugby club. It's in the suburb of Horfield, and yes, that is in Bristol, an important point for Rovers fans with painful memories of their recent ten-year exile in Bath. For visiting fans, life is easy. The Memorial Ground is just a short drive from the M32, the pubs are friendly, and the nearby Gloucester Road is lined with cafes and takeaways. The biggest problem is actually finding the away turnstiles, which are hidden down a sidestreet.

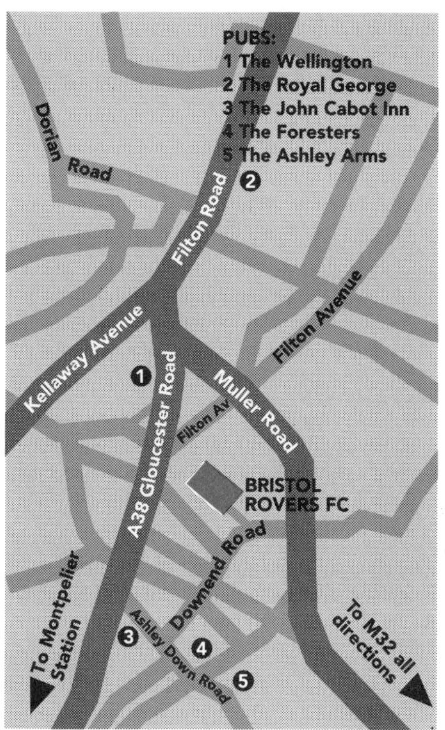

HOW TO GET THERE

BY CAR: From West, East and North: Exit M4 at junction 19 (s/p Bristol M32) onto the M32. After 3.1 miles, exit M32 at junction 2 (s/p B4469 Fishponds, Horfield). At roundabout turn right (3rd exit, s/p A38 Bristol Eastville Stadium, Eastgate Shopping Centre, Horfield and Southmead). Immediately the road divides: branch right (s/p Horfield, Southmead B4469 (A38)) onto Muller Road. Straight on, up the hill, for 1.4 miles to traffic lights. Here, there's a signpost right to Horfield Health Centre and Library. Don't follow it! Instead turn left (no signpost) into Filton Avenue. The ground is on the LHS after 0.1 miles.
From South-East: Exit M5 at junction 16 (s/p Thornbury, Filton A38). At roundabout turn right (s/p Filton A38) onto the A38. Straight on, keeping on the A38 Gloucester Road, for 4.3 miles, passing through Patchway, past Filton Airport, the Royal George and Wellington pubs to traffic lights (just past a small shop called Satellite Warehouse and before Polypipe Timber). Here, turn left (n/s) into Filton Avenue. Ground is on RHS after 0.1 miles.
FROM RAILWAY STATIONS: a) Bristol Temple Meads: About 3.5 miles. *By taxi:* Up to £6. Allow extra time for the matchday traffic congestion. *By bus:* Take the no. 8 or 9 to the Broadmeads Shopping Centre. The buses stop at the back of Debenhams. Cross the road towards the 'Bristol Fashion' pub. Bus nos. 70 and 73 run to Filton Avenue, while the no. 75 runs along Gloucester Road. All services are frequent.
b) Bristol Parkway: About 2 miles. *By taxi:* £5-£6. *By bus:* The no. 73 runs from Parkway to Filton Avenue.
c) Montpelier is a small suburban station about 1.5 miles from the Memorial Ground. Trains to and from Temple Meads run roughly hourly, but no taxis wait outside. *By bus:* Nos. 70, 75 and 77. *By foot:* Turn right out of station along Station Road, passing the Royal Mail on the LHS, to junction by the Cat and Wheel. Turn right into Cheltenham Road, across mini-roundabout and under railway bridge to traffic lights. Bear right, between 'Bottoms Up' and the 'Prince of Wales' into Gloucester

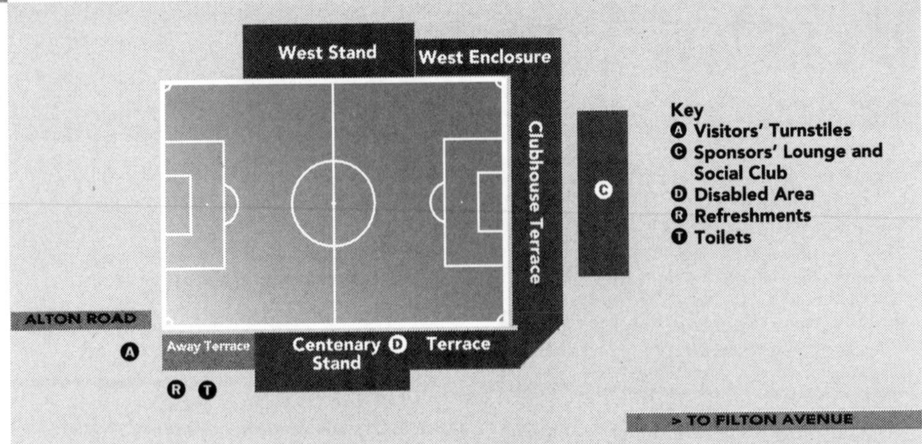

Road. After 1.2 miles turn right by Horfield Methodist Church into Filton Avenue.
Last Midweek Trains: a) Bristol Temple Meads: To London 21.25, to Cardiff 21.49, 21.59 and 23.04.
b) Bristol Parkway: The last train to London is at 22.00. Trains to Cardiff leave at 21.30 and 22.23.
c) Montpelier: Last train to Temple Meads is at 21.46. Please double check on (0345) 484 950.
BY BUS: Nos. 70, 75 and 77 run from the city centre.

PARKING

Remember the adage 'he who hesitates is lost'. The Memorial Ground version is 'he who hesitates loses the parking space and drives around highly irate for hours'. In other words, it's street parking for everyone and there are a lot more fans than streets. For an easy life, park near the junction of Ashley Down Road and Gloucester Road, have a drink at the 'Foresters' and then amble over to the ground.

THE GROUND

Despite a lot of redevelopment work, the Memorial Ground still looks like a rugby stadium, which is, after all, exactly what it is. This is principally because the local council insisted that the West Stand, rebuilt two years ago, must be exactly the same size as the old one, extending just a short distance either side of the centre circle. The stand, which has just 450 seats, looks good, but Anfield it ain't. Apart from the older Centenary Stand, the rest of the ground is covered or uncovered terracing. So of course away supporters need to bring umbrellas, furry mitts or sunglasses, depending on the time of year. The terracing is steep, so the view is generally good (except for one floodlight pylon). Facilities still have a definite temporary feel, but are actually pretty good.
Total Capacity: 9,275. For away fans: 740. Some seating can be made available through prior arrangement with the visiting club. Turnstiles in Alton Road.
Cost (98/99): Adults £10, concessions (OAPs and juniors) £6.
Disabled Facilities: Generally up to five visiting disabled supporters are welcome, though more space can be made available with prior notice. *Disabled Toilet:* One in each area of the ground. *Cost:* Free for disabled, full price for helper. *Booking:* Essential. *Parking:* None available. *For the Blind:* Very limited space, with seating next to the hospital radio commentary.
Programme: £1.70.
Visitors' Toilets: *Male:* The words 'absolutely' and 'spotless' don't usually come up together as a phrase to describe football toilets, but yes, that's what one Gillingham fan wrote after his visit to the Memorial Ground. *Female:* Welcome to the Bristol Rovers obstacle course. First challenge: to enter, and then close, the door in the narrowest cubicles in the football league. Second challenge: to turn the extremely stiff lock. Third challenge – and the most difficult – open that lock again. That said, everything was very clean.
Food and Drink: Most visiting Wycombe fans thought the 'Proper Cornish Pasties' (£1.30) were just that: 'This is the real thing', said one. 'Not the normal rubbish we get'. The vegetarian pasty had to be heated up specially, which took 15 minutes, and was edible enough, which is more than could be said for the cheese-and-onion variety, which a couple of fans chucked after a couple of bites. Eleven-year-old Karen, a foodie in the making if ever we saw one, was unimpressed with the sausage roll (70p): 'Nice sausage, but the crust is very crumbly in a not very nice way', she said (13.9.97, 24.2.98).

PUB GUIDE

The Wellington (1) Gloucester Road (by Horfield Common) (0117) 951 3022
Scottish and Newcastle. Big, detached traditional pub, with a good matchday atmosphere, and usually very busy. Varied menu served all day, plus a post-match BBQ on sunnier afternoons. Darts, TV, beer garden. Families welcome. Open: all day.

The Royal George (2) 2 Filton Road (0117) 951 9335
Scottish and Newcastle. A traditionally football-friendly pub which may shut for a few weeks in autumn 1998 for complete renovation. The landlady, however, says it will remain football friendly. 'Red Hot Value Menu', including 8 oz rump steak and chips for £2.99, served all day. Two pool tables, big-screen TV, darts, beer garden. Open: all day.

The John Cabot Inn (3) 385 Gloucester Road (0117) 924 0480.
Intrepreneur (with Pedigree, Courage Best and occasional guest beer). Smart traditional pub, welcoming 'well behaved fans'. The menu, served 11-2.30, is particularly good, making this an ideal place for a family pre-match meal. Good vegetarian selection. Large family room/lounge, plus separate children's room with TV/video. Disabled facilities. Open: all day.

The Foresters (4) 94 Ashley Down Road (0117) 924 3852
House of Bellingham (with Courage). Traditional, football-friendly locals pub, with a good matchday atmosphere. Bar snacks and sandwiches served all day. Darts, pool, 2 TVs. Children welcome up to 8 pm. Open: all day on football-match days.

Also recommended: **The Ashley Arms (5)** 112 Ashley Down Road, a bright, sports-friendly Bass pub, renowned for its frequent food and beer promotions. Bar meals 12-2. Big screen TV, pool. Open: all day.

FOOD GUIDE

Nearby Gloucester Road provides an excellent food choice. The locals strongly recommend 'The Bristol Fryer' (near the junction with Quarrington Road). A little further down the road is Clancy's Bakers/Coffee Shop which has a tasty all day breakfast for £1.99. This area of Bishopston is paired with a town in Southern India, and the theme is continued in the series of Indian restaurants. Rovers supporters recommend the 'Ghurkhas', close to Clancy's Bakers.

A row of shops in Ashley Down Road has a good Chinese, the recommended 'Fish-and-Chip Bar' and the 'Big Bite' café. The latter offers a full breakfast for £2 and tea for 30p, so is pretty popular!

LOCAL MEDIA

Local Radio: BBC Radio Bristol, 94.9 FM in Bristol, 104.6 FM in Bath, 95.5 'across the west'; GWR 96.3 FM.
Radio Phone-ins: BBC Radio Bristol, Friday night 7-8 pm, call (0117) 923 8877 or (01823) 323 001.
Saturday Sports Paper: The much-recommended 'Green 'Un', published by the *Bristol Evening Post.*

'He heard that a cat was being allowed in to games without paying!'

MISCELLANEOUS

One of the biggest talking points in Bristol sporting circles last season was the disappearance of Arnie, the Memorial Ground's large grey cat. A great rugby fan, he took delight in chasing the ball and stalking the touchline. One day, after one of the team's cat(haha)strophic away drubbings (76-0 or something similar), Arnie vanished. Most feared he'd successfully transferred to a better side, or that both clubs were so poor they weren't feeding him enough. Whatever, a couple of weeks later, Arnie reappeared some three miles down the road, and after suitable negotiation agreed to return home. He's now back to his best egg-chasing ways and the sign remains in the club office: 'Last one to leave, please put the cat out'.

Safety Factor: Trouble inside the ground is rare, and wearing colours is fine. That said, there was fighting in nearby pubs on derby days versus Plymouth and Exeter in season 97/98.

Rivals: Rovers supporters save their venom for one club only – Bristol City.

Fanzines: 'The 2nd of May', 17 Glyn Road, Hackney, London E5 0JB; 'The Black Arab', PO Box 1740, Chipping Sodbury, Bristol, BS37 6BF.

Unofficial Websites: Bristol Rovers Online:
http://www.geocities.com/Colsseum/6542/
http://www.btinternet.com/~uk/BristolRovers/
http://www.coley.u-net.com/rovers/
http://www.btinternet.com/~uk/BRFC/
http://www.geocities.com/Colosseum/Stadium/4720/
Black Arab: http://www.godjira.demon.co.uk/

Tourist Information: (0117) 926 0767.

Burnley

Turf Moor

Address: Turf Moor, Brunshaw Road, Burnley, Lancashire BB10 4BX
Telephone: Club (01282) 700 000
Ticket Office (01282) 700 010
Club Shop (01282) 700 016
ClubCall (0891) 121 153
Official Website: http://www.clarets.co.uk/

Burnley is a small Lancastrian town with a huge passion for football. Even with the club towards the bottom of the Second Division, crowds regularly topped 10,000, which as a percentage of the town's total population is phenomenal. Loyalty is strong, and Manchester United shirts are rare! Burnley is best approached from the south, in bright sunlight after a light fall of snow. Then the moors are stunningly beautiful and the cross-country route from Todmorden well worth the effort. Unfortunately, most football fans see Turf Moor, and Burnley's terraced streets, through torrential rain or sleet! The ground is just east of the town centre, and parking is usually easy. But most visiting fans drink well away from the ground.

HOW TO GET THERE

BY CAR: There are now Football Trust roadsigns, though they are rather small.
From West (M6-M65): Exit M6 junction 29, and follow signs onto the M65 eastbound. Exit M65 after about 18 miles at junction 10 (s/p Burnley, Clitheroe A671). (*)At motorway roundabout, take 5th exit (s/p Burnley A671) and at next roundabout, by the Little Chef, turn left (s/p Burnley Town Centre) onto the Westway. At traffic lights after 0.2 miles branch right (s/p Burnley FC) into Trafalgar Street. At next two roundabouts, follow signs for 'Rochdale A671' onto Centenary Way (dual carriageway). Straight over roundabout after 0.5 miles (s/p Skipton, Keighley M65), and after a further 0.3 miles turn right, by 'The

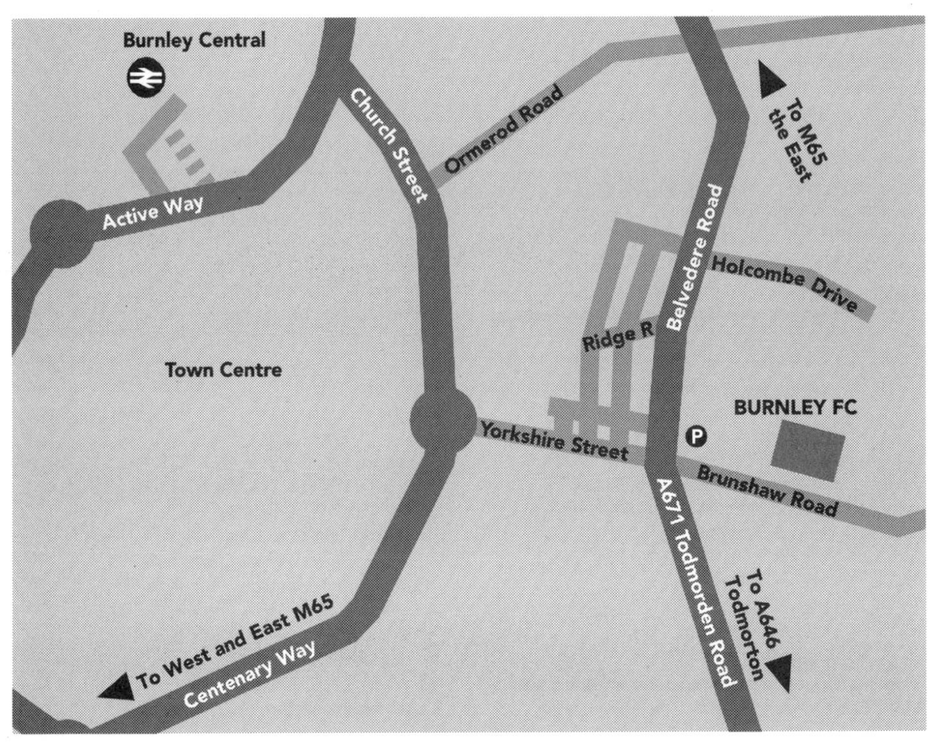

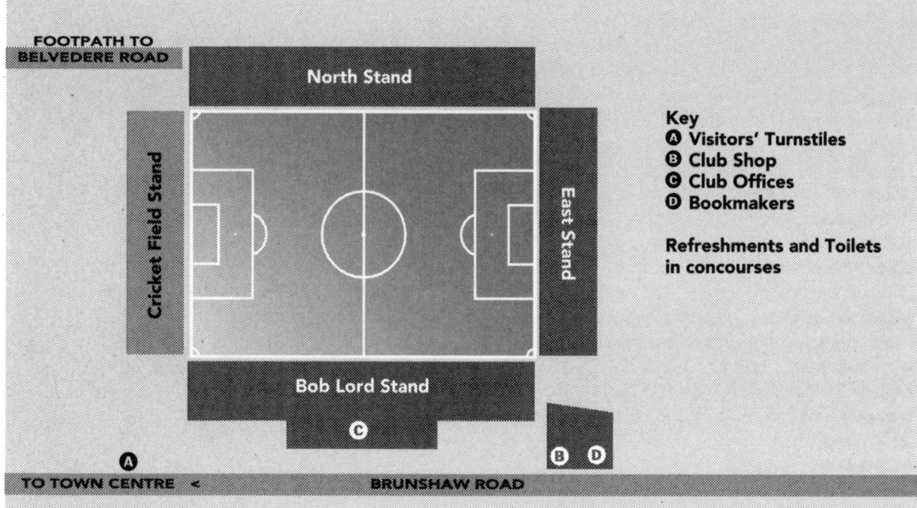

Sparrowhawk Hotel', into Ormerod Road. At crossroads after 0.2 miles, turn right (n/s) into Belvedere Road. Look for parking from here. The ground is on the LHS after 0.4 miles.

From East: Exit M65 at junction 10 (s/p Burnley, Clitheroe A671). Then as From West(*).

From South-East (A646 via Todmorden): Pass through village of Holme Chapel. Just past village, turn right (s/p Worsthorne, Burnley FC) into Red Lees Road. After 2.6 miles, having passed through the suburb of Overtown, turn right (s/p Football Visitors' Car Parking Area) into Ridge Avenue, which becomes Ormerod Road. At crossroads after 0.8 miles turn left into Belvedere Road.

FROM RAILWAY STATION (Burnley Central): About 0.7 miles. Turn right out of station down Railway Street. Turn left, following the Town Centre pedestrian sign, down pathway, through a retail park and down steps to main road. Cross the dual-carriageway (Active Way) at the pedestrian crossing and go straight on into Standish Street. At the end of Standish Street there is a short cut straight ahead into Market Square. Alternatively, to take in more restaurants, bear right, then left under the bridge towards Burger King. Turn left in front of Burger King (s/p Bus Station). Pass Pizza Hut and bakers on RHS, McDonalds on LHS and keep straight on where road bends to the right (ie heading towards Sainsbury's). Cross road towards Sainsbury's and turn right. At roundabout turn left (s/p Halifax A646, Rochdale A671) into Yorkshire Street.

Last Midweek Trains: No trains to London, Sheffield or Leeds after a midweek game. Trains do, however, run to Preston (21.57, 23.06) and to Blackburn and Manchester at 21.57. Please double-check on (0345) 484 950.

FROM RAILWAY STATION (Burnley Manchester Road, on the line from York to Blackpool North): About a mile. Turn right out of station onto Halstead Street to main road. Cross road and turn left. Bear right at the roundabout (s/p Halifax A646, Burnley FC) into Centenary Way. After a few minutes' walk, the ground is visible ahead.

Last Midweek Trains: Last train to York is at 21.51. No trains to Blackpool North after a midweek game.

BY BUS: Nos. 4 and 7 to Worsthorne run every 15 minutes, nos. 589 and 592 to Halifax and Rochdale run every half hour.

PARKING

The cricket club by the ground has a good, safe car park (£2), entrance off Belvedere Road. Otherwise, it's street parking. Away coaches/minibuses are parked at the junction of Belvedere Road and Ormerod Road. There's also street parking on the roads off Belvedere Road. Don't leave valuables or away colours visible in the car.

THE GROUND

Turf Moor's famous terraces, the open Bee Hole and the covered Longside, were demolished in 1996, replaced by the 6,500-seater East Stand, and the two-tier James Hargreaves (North) Stand, with seating for 8,600, 22 executive boxes, and excellent acoustics. Home fans warn those sitting near the front to bring waterproofs, as the rain (the horizontal Lancashire variety) still cascades in! The new stands, built at a cost of £6.5 million, are both Premiership standard, leaving the other two stands, constructed in the 1970s, looking somewhat outdated. That said, the view from the Cricket Field Stand behind the goal, which houses the visiting supporters, is excellent and fans can normally sit where they like. The facilities are just about adequate, though supporters appreciated the little TV set perched on top of the refreshment kiosk, which relayed the match live to those in the queue.

Total Capacity: 22,546. For away fans: Up to 4,100.

Cost (98/99): Adults £12, concessions (juniors/OAPs) £6.

Disabled Facilities: Space for 20 visiting fans in a raised enclosure in the Cricket Field Stand. Entrance in Brunshaw Road. *Disabled Toilet:* Nearby. *Cost:* Free for disabled, £9 for helper. *Booking:* Advisable, through Burnley FC ticket office. *Parking:* Possible to drop off, but please arrive early.

Programme: £1.70.

Visitors' Toilets: *Male:* 'Was there anything unusual about the Burnley loos?' we asked one seasoned traveller. 'Nothing,' he replied. 'Unless you include loos that weren't blocked, were well lit, didn't stink and had working soap dispensers!' *Female:* One fan simply said they were 'damp'!

Food and Drink: The meat-and-potato pie (£1.20) had a rock-hard burnt top, like a slab of concrete, attached to squashy pastry, so as soon as you tried to pick it up, the whole lot ripped apart! This was a dodgy moment, as the unappetising filling was as hot as molten lava. The tea (90p) ran out at 3.50 pm. 'NO TEA?', exclaimed one aghast fan after another. Beer and lager is on sale at £1.80 a pint (16.8.97, 20.9.97, 2.5.98).

PUB GUIDE

There are plenty of good pubs in Burnley, but for safety reasons the police have advised this book against making any specific recommendations. The obvious alternative is to stop en route, eg. via Todmorden on the A646 (directions above).

FOOD GUIDE

Yorkshire Street has the best selection: 'Paradise' has Indian dishes from £3.70, and chicken burger and chips at £1.70; 'Carolina Chicken' is a KFC-style restaurant where chicken burgers and chips are again popular at £1.99; 'Sun Ye' does the usual 'everything with chips' menu, as well as Chinese dishes from £3.80. In the town centre, St James's Street has a Burger King, a McDonalds, a Pizza Hut and a bakers. Gillingham fans recommend the 'El Greco' café by the bus station, which serves huge chunks of pie, peas, chips, gravy and bread and butter for £3.50, as well as milkshakes made with real milk for £1.

'Wake up you dozy old sod!'

LOCAL MEDIA

Local Radio: BBC Radio Lancashire 95.5 FM; Red Rose Radio 999 AM.

Radio Phone-Ins: BBC Radio Lancashire, Saturdays 6-7 pm, call (01254) 583 583.

Saturday Sports Paper: None.

MISCELLANEOUS

Safety Factor: As Burnley fans can be a mite territorial, visiting fans should approach with caution. Colours are not advisable.

Rivals: Blackburn Rovers, of course, even though many of Blackburn's new wave of supporters aren't even aware of the rivalry.

Fanzines: 'The Claret Flag', 9 Romney Avenue, Burnley, BB11 2PG; 'Kicker Conspiracy', 15 Woodlands Close, Bradley Grange, Huddersfield, West Yorks, HD2 1QS; 'Bob Lord's Sausage', 14 Bridge Street, Padiham, Burnley, BB12 8LA.

Unofficial Websites:
'The Claret Flag': http://dspace.dial.pipex.com/ajobes
http://www.zen.co.uk/home/page/trevor.ent/
http://www.theturf.demon.co.uk/burnley.htm
http://www.soft.net.uk/pizzaman/Claretsupdate/
http://www.geocities.com/Colosseum/Track/2593/longside.htm.

Tourist Information: (01282) 455 485.

Bury

Gigg Lane

Address: Gigg Lane, Bury BL9 9HR
Telephone: Office (0161) 764 4881
Clubline (0930) 190 003
Ticket-Line (0930) 190 097
Club Shop (0161) 705 2144

Bury FC hasn't appeared on 'Match of the Day' much in recent years, but it does have a new claim to TV fame: Jimmy McGovern used Gigg Lane to recreate the tragic events of Hillsborough for his TV drama. Bury is, of course, already renowned nationwide for its black puddings and the illustrious Neville family. Dad Neville Neville and mum Jill dedicate their time to Bury FC as Commercial Manager and Secretary ... now if only their sons graced the pitch! There's not much for hungry supporters around the ground except for a few burger vans, but the compact town centre is only about ten minutes' walk away. And there are plenty of football-friendly landlords nearby, on hand with a pint and a 'barmcake'.

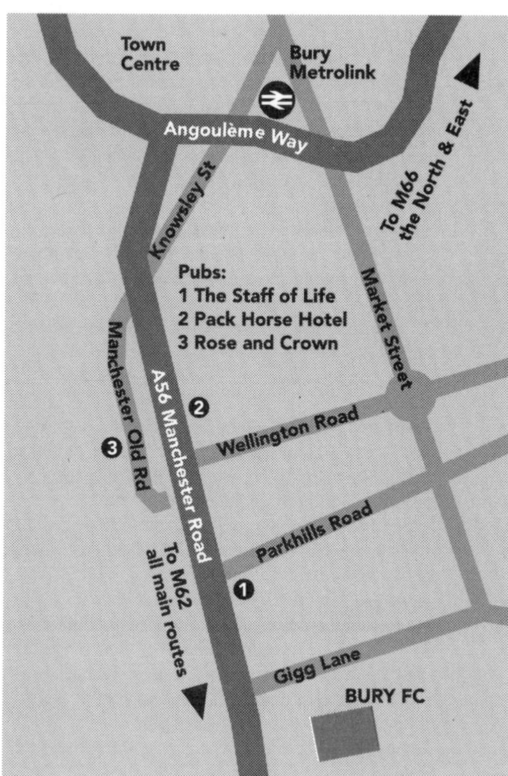

HOW TO GET THERE

BY CAR: All Main Routes: Exit M60 at junction 17 (s/p A56 Whitefield, Salford). At roundabout follow signs to 'Whitfield A56, Radcliffe (A665), Bury A56' onto the A56. After 0.3 miles go straight over double traffic lights passing McDonalds on LHS (s/p Bury A56, Radcliffe A665). At lights after 0.8 miles (just after the 'Bull's Head' pub) bear right (s/p Bury A56). Straight on at lights after 1.0 miles (s/p Town Centre). After 1.0 miles turn right (s/p Football Ground) into Gigg Lane. Ground is on RHS after 0.1 miles.

From North and East (via M66): Exit M66 at junction 2 and follow signs to 'Bury A58, Football Ground' onto the A58 Rochdale Road. After 0.5 miles turn left at traffic lights by the Crown Hotel (s/p Football Ground) onto Heywood Street. After 0.4 miles turn right at second mini-roundabout (s/p Football Ground, Manchester, Salford B6219) into Wellington Road. At next mini-roundabout turn left into Market Street. Straight on over mini-roundabout after 0.1 miles and right at T-junction after 0.2 miles into Gigg Lane.

FROM METROLINK STATION (Bury): 0.7 miles to ground. Trams run from Manchester Victoria and Manchester Piccadilly. *By taxi:* £1.50. *By bus:* Nos. 90, 92, 134, 135 and 137 run every ten minutes down Manchester Road past the end of Gigg Lane. *By foot:* This route takes in a couple of the pubs listed below. Turn left out of station along covered passageway and past various bus-stops. At T-junction with Haymarket Street (by the bingo hall) turn left. Straight over crossroads, down Knowsley Street. This comes out opposite the 'Jolly Waggoners' and a white monument. Here, turn left along the Manchester Road, towards the 'Staff of Life'. Turn left after about 0.5 miles into Gigg Lane. *Last Midweek Trains:* The Metrolink has a frequent service up to 23.02 to both Manchester mainline stations. From Manchester, trains leave to: York and Newcastle at 21.50; to York at 22.47; to Nottingham and Derby at 22.28; to Liverpool at 22.07, 23.12 and 23.15; to Leeds at 22.43, 23.50 and 1.50; to Birmingham at 21.40 (via Manchester airport) and 22.33 (via Crewe). There is no service to London after a midweek game.

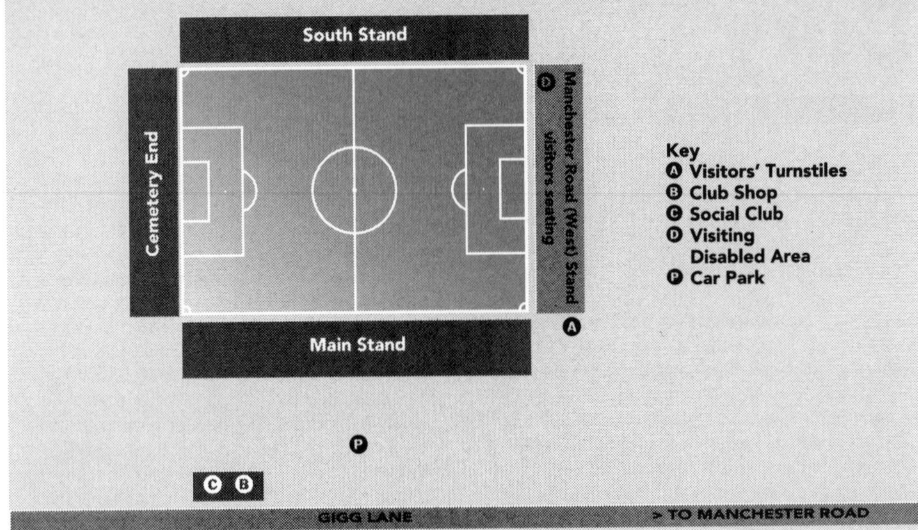

Please double-check on Metrolink (0161) 205 2000, and Rail Enquiries on (0345) 484 950.
BY BUS: As above.

PARKING

Much of Gigg Lane itself is coned off, but the side streets are not, and there's a good deal of space. Holy Cross College on Wellington Road provides matchday parking for £3. The police advise mini-buses to park in the coach-park on Gigg Lane.

THE GROUND

Bury fans have for some years been making the most of their last remaining terrace, at the Cemetery End. After all, it was the only feature of Gigg Lane which might make the supporters of nearby Manchester United remotely jealous ... Bury fans had standing space, Red fans didn't. But work began in the summer of 1998 to convert the Cemetery End into an all-seater stand. Visiting fans are housed in the Manchester Road Stand. It's covered, but four stanchions obstruct the view near the goalmouth. Note when booking tickets in advance, the seating is lettered with A as the back row.
Total Capacity: 11,840. For away fans: Seating 2,676 Manchester Road (West) Stand. Turnstiles 14-19.
Cost (98/99): Adults £14, concessions (juniors/OAPS) £8. The club welcomes away fans into the Family Stand, blocks G, H & J of the Main Stand. A family ticket, which admits one adult and one child, costs £15, extra children £5; two adults and two children costs £28.
Disabled Facilities: Bury FC's disabled supporters have a sponsored mini-bus, only missing away games when the host club has no facilities for them. It comes as no surprise therefore, that facilities at Gigg Lane are very good. For away fans, there's room for 6 wheelchairs and helpers in the Manchester Road Stand. *Disabled Toilet:* In South Stand and Starkies Restaurant. *Cost:* Free for disabled and helper. *Booking:* In advance via the away club ticket office. *Parking:* Available, please book. *For the Blind:* 12 seats in the Main Stand family section have headphones for hospital radio commentary. No entry fee.
Programme: £1.80.
Visitors' Toilets: *Male:* There's a light, a roof and running water, and that's about it folks - obviously the budget for ground improvements didn't stretch to here! *Female:* All-seater stand, same old ancient loos. We're all for preserving footballing traditions, but this is ridiculous! There were frames on the walls, but no mirrors inside, while toilet paper was the only home comfort.
Food and Drink: The pies (£1.55) were warm, the pasty crusty and the filling very grey. That said, fans liked them: 'Slightly spicy and very good,' said one. The pasties (£1.50) also got the thumbs-up, but the tea (70p) and coffee (80p) were, wrote an Ipswich fan: 'Typical football fare. In other words, weak, uninteresting and expensive' (18.1.98, 25.4.98).

PUB GUIDE

Bury Social Club welcomes visiting fans both before and after the match as long as it's not too busy, charging £1 for non-members. There's a bar serving food, a large-screen TV and a separate children's area.
The easiest pubs to find are along the A56 Manchester Road or the roads turning off it:

The Staff of Life (1) 111-113 Manchester Road (0161) 764 6246
Tetleys (with JW Lees bitter). The closest pub to the ground, and most hospitable it is too. Public and lounge bars, and separate pool room. Darts, 2 TVs. Sandwiches and pies if away fans have travelled a long way. Children welcome in the lounge. Open: all day. B&B for £12.50.
The Pack Horse Hotel (2) 201 Manchester Road (0161) 761 5635
Whitbread. A newly-refurbished sports-mad pub with a big-screen TV, pool table, and separate room with darts and pub games. Beer garden. The landlord organises football quizzes and provides huge home-made sandwiches. Families welcome. Open: all day.
Rose and Crown (3) (formerly The Tap and Spile) 36 Manchester Old Road (0161) 764 6461
Free House (with 8 real ales and two own-brand ales). A traditional pub, recently refurbished with dark wooden decor, highly recommended by home supporters. It won a CAMRA award for 'Pub of the Season, Winter 1997/98'. Barmcakes (muffins) on matchdays. Open: Monday-Thursday 12-3, 5-11; Friday/Saturday all day.
The Blue Bell 840 Manchester Road (on the A56, 1.7 miles from M60) (0161) 766 2496
Joseph Holts (Manchester Independent Brewery). Large pub, catering for all tastes with a quiet lounge and a separate room with the jukebox, darts, cards and dominoes. Open: all day from 12.

FOOD GUIDE

The only takeaway within easy striking distance of Gigg Lane is 'Fish and Chips' in Market Street, which also does burgers and sandwiches. The 'Blue Sky Fishbar'/Chinese takeaway on Redvales Road doesn't open until 5 pm.

Otherwise, it's a good idea to stop off at one of the many takeaways along the A56. They include a McDonalds, 'Antonio's' (which has pizzas, kebabs and chicken), the attractive bistro-style 'Peppe's Pizzeria', a 'Prime Pizza', and the 'Tong Feng' Chinese takeaway. Supporters looking for a sit-down meal before an evening game could try the 'EstEstEst' Trattoria (2.2 miles from the M60). It's a large lively modern-style Italian restaurant, where children have fun choosing toppings for their pizzas. Large parties should book on (0161) 766 4869.

It's only a few minutes' walk from Gigg Lane to the town centre. Near the Metrolink is a Pizza Hut, a Burger King and a wonderful traditional fish-and-chip restaurant/takeaway called 'The Cornmarket' on Haymarket Street, which also has a children's menu. Just round the corner in Market Street is the 'Spice Hut' which opens at 5 pm – the 'very hot' vindaloo sounds a challenge (from £2.90). Opposite is the recommended Met Theatre Bar.

LOCAL MEDIA

Local Radio: GMR 95.1 FM.
Radio Phone-ins: GMR, Saturdays 1-3 and 5-7, and after midweek games. Call (0161) 228 2255.
Saturday Sports Paper: *The Manchester Evening News* produced the 'Manchester Pink' which includes coverage of Bury.

MISCELLANEOUS

Bury's long ball techniques, which elevated them into the First Division, are fast becoming folklore. Home fans have dubbed the old 'hoof down the centre' as the 'paradise alley' pass. And supporters joke that new floodlights, erected in 1997, were initially pointing upwards, as this was the best way to keep the ball illuminated!

And for those seeking lesser-known statistics, Bury fans say that their away support, as a percentage of the home support, is the highest in the league.
Safety Factor: No problems except at local derbies.
Rivals: First and foremost Bolton, now nicknamed 'Horwich Wanderers' or 'Horwich Amateurs' at their ground, the 'White Elephant'. Second and third come Rochdale and Preston.
Fanzines: 'Where Were You at the Shay?', 38 Manchester Old Road, Bury BL9 0TR; 'The Hatchet', 101 Brecon Drive, Bury, BL9 9LQ; 'Dead and Bury(ed)', 7 Winchester Close, Brandlesholme, Bury, Lancashire, GL8 1YQ.
Unofficial Websites:
'Unofficial Bury FC':
http://www.buryfc.creations.co.uk/main.htm
'Gordo's Site':
http://freespace.virgin.net/gordon.sorfleet/enter.htm
Tourist Information: (0161) 705 5111.

Cambridge United

The Abbey Stadium

Address: Abbey Stadium, Newmarket Road, Cambridge, CB5 8LN
Telephone: Club/Ticket Office (01223) 566 500
Commercial/Club Shop (01223) 566 503
Abbey Update (0891) 555 885

Remember those scenes from the TV series 'Porterhouse Blue', the pubs on the River Cam, college courtyards, streets filled with students on bicycles? Well, stuff all that because the Abbey Stadium is two miles from the city centre, bordered by a stagnant stream, allotments and the main road to Newmarket. The road is great for those looking for paint, a new vacuum cleaner or a used car, but not so good for football fans after a decent meal and a pint. The best bet is to use the Coldham's Common car park, eat and drink in the nearby Greyhound pub and then hike across the fields – over various piles of horse manure and under the railway line – to the ground.

HOW TO GET THERE

BY CAR: From North (A1): Exit A1 onto A14 (s/p London E, M11, Huntingdon, Cambridge A14). After 17 miles, the road divides – keep in the left-hand lanes (s/p Cambridge A1307, Newmarket, Felixstowe A14). After 0.7 miles the road divides again – keep left (s/p Newmarket, Felixstowe, Harwich A14) remaining on A14 which becomes the Cambridge Northern Bypass. (*)After 4.6 miles exit A14 (s/p Cambridge B1047). At T-junction/lights turn right (s/p Fen Ditton, Cambridge Airport) onto the B1047. At T-junction/lights after 1.4 miles turn right (s/p Cambridge, Hanger 17), and straight over roundabout by Racehorse pub (s/p Ring Road, City Centre) into Newmarket Road. Ground is on LHS after 0.3 miles.

From East: Exit A14 at s/p 'Cambridge A1303, Burwell B1102', and at roundabout turn left (s/p Cambridge A1303, Airport) onto the A1303. Keep straight on, remaining on the A1303 and following Cambridge and City Centre signs, for 2.5 miles to roundabout by Racehorse pub. Here, go straight on (s/p Ring Road, City

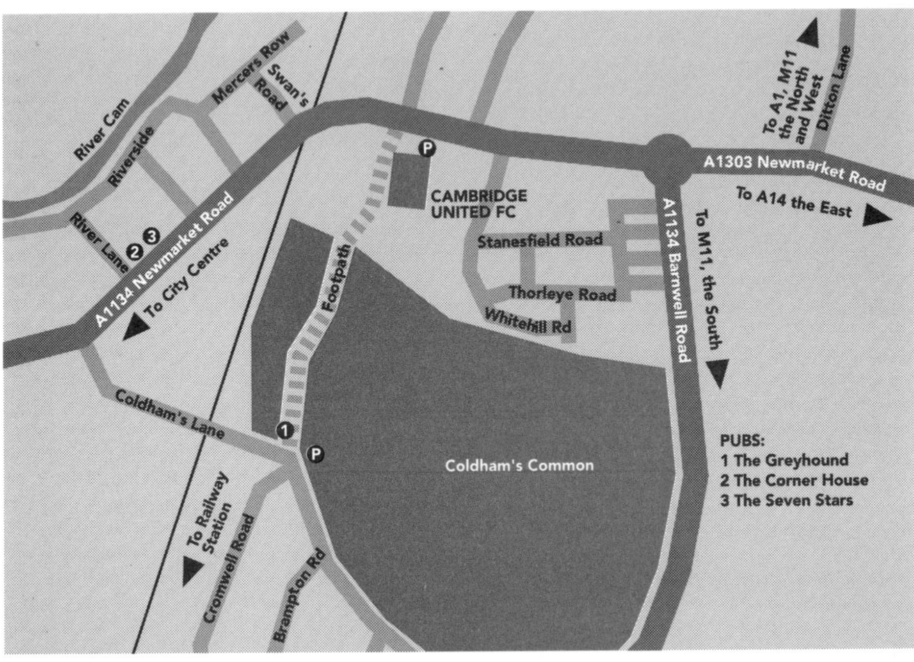

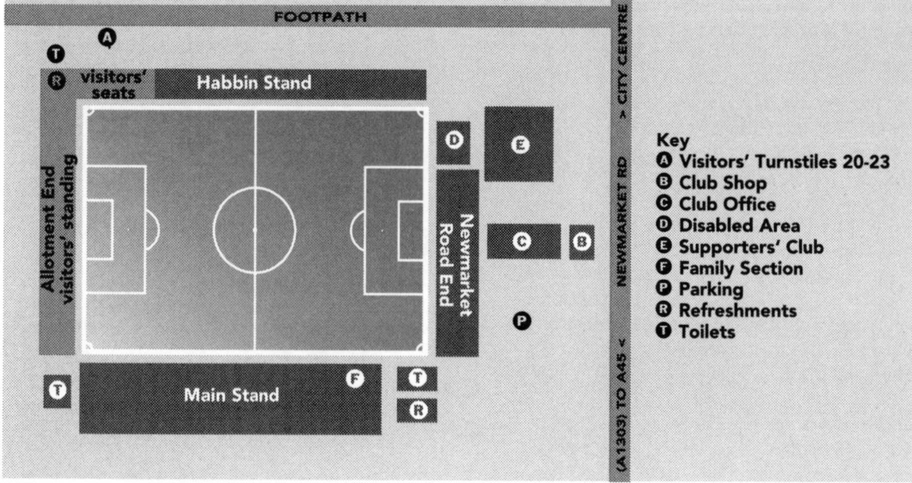

Centre) into Newmarket Road.

From South: Exit M11 at junction 11 (s/p Cambridge South, Harston A10). At roundabout turn right (s/p Cambridge A1309). At traffic lights after 1.5 miles turn right (s/p Ring Road, Cherry Hinton) into Long Road. At crossroads/lights after 1.1 miles go straight on (s/p Ring Road) into Queen Edith's Way. At next roundabout after 0.3 miles turn left (s/p Ring Road) into Mowbray Road. Follow Ring Road signs for 1.6 miles, over three roundabouts, to a fourth roundabout, by Sainsbury's (it's the one where the advance signpost has two red triangles on it). Two choices here: a) For the Coldham's Common parking and the Greyhound pub, turn left (no s/p) into Coldham's Lane – the car park is on the RHS after 0.5 miles. b) For the ground, take 2nd exit (s/p Ring Road) into Barnwell Road. At next roundabout turn left into Newmarket Road.

FROM RAILWAY STATION (Cambridge): About 2 miles. *By taxi:* About £4.50. *By bus:* Until 6 pm, Cambus no. 1 runs every 8 minutes to the Emmanuel Street city centre bus station. After 6 pm the no. 95 runs hourly, at 28 minutes past. Cambus nos. 3 and 3B run from the Emmanuel Street bus station to the ground every 10 minutes until 6 pm. After that, Myall Coaches runs an hourly bus, no. 93, starting at 7.05 pm. *By foot:* Walk up main road opposite station entrance. After 0.1 miles turn right (s/p Youth Hostel) into Tenison Road. At lights after 0.1 miles (cyclists' s/p Romsey, Cherry Hinton) into Devonshire Road. At junction by White Swan pub after 0.4 miles, turn right into Mill Road. Over bridge and take 3rd left into Sedgwick Street. Keep on the left hand pavement and, at roundabout after 0.3 miles, by fancy dress and motorbike shops, bear left into Cromwell Road. This road comes out by Coldham's Common. The floodlights are visible from here.

Last Midweek Trains: Trains leave to London at 23.14, and to Peterborough at 21.54 and 23.14. Please double check on (0345) 484 950.

BY BUS: See above.

PARKING

The site of the demolished Corona Works building on Newmarket Road has been turned into a club car park, available to all (£2.50). For away fans, the best bet is the parking (£1.50) on Coldham's Common (see road directions above). From here, it's a 7-8 minute walk across fields to the away turnstiles, and fans also miss the post-match Newmarket Road traffic jams.

The alternative is street parking. Try the roads on the Mercer's Row Industrial Estate (signposted off the Newmarket Road), or the Whitehill Road area (see map) – the turning is by the Abbey Guest House off the Newmarket Road.

THE GROUND

After ten years of fruitless searching for a site for a new ground, Cambridge United announced, in October 1997, plans to redevelop the Abbey Stadium. It said that the work, which would be carried out in stages, would turn the ground into a 10,000 all-seater stadium, with 'some of the best-appointed facilities in the city'. However, for season 98/99 at least, visiting fans remain on the open Allotment End, where facilities are mediocre. However, some covered terracing and seating is also available and the bacon butties are still excellent!

Total Capacity: 9,617. For away fans: Seating (Habbin Stand) 366. Standing (Allotment End, mainly uncovered) 1,950.

Cost (98/99): Seating or standing: £8, no concessions for away fans.

Disabled Facilities: Limited space in a covered enclosure at pitch level at the Newmarket Road End. *Disabled Toilet:* Nearby, next to the Ground Control Room. *Cost:* Free for disabled, £8 for helper. *Booking:* Essential. *Parking:* Limited spaces available, please book. *For the Blind:* No special facilities.
Visitors' Toilets: *Male:* 'Well, it's covered, I'll give it that' said one fan, adding: 'It's better than Rotherham's anyway – though that isn't hard'. *Female:* Mobile phone call: 'Hello, is that the BBC? Is David Attenborough there? I have something here in the toilets at Cambridge United FC which might be of interest ... What is it? It's a frog of course. Species Ohgawdwotsthatipus'. In fact it was a rather cute frog, and undoubtedly in the coolest place on a hot August afternoon!
Food and Drink: In February 1998, with new caterers installed, supporters were very impressed ... one gave the bacon rolls twelve-out-of-ten, while the Cornish pasty was described as 'really nice'. The cheese pasty and the burgers ('bigger than at other grounds') were also recommended. Indeed, the club is proud that, on very limited resources, its catering won two awards in 97/98. Bibs on, folks!! (16.8.97, 7.2.98).

PUB GUIDE

Away fans are welcome in the Cambridge United Supporters Club, though there is a small entrance charge for non-members.
The Greyhound (1) 93 Coldham's Lane (01223) 247 075
Free House. Friendly pub with everything to suit the football fan. Food served all day. Children welcome up to 7 pm. Pool, darts, big-screen TV. Open: all day.
The Corner House (2) 231 Newmarket Road (01223) 500 257
Greene King. Smart, traditional pub serving bar meals 12-2.30. Pool, darts, TV. Families welcome. Open: Saturdays all day from 11.30; midweek from 5 pm.
The Seven Stars (3) 249 Newmarket Road (01223) 574 150
Greene King. Small traditional pub, serving bar meals. Pool, darts. Families welcome. Open: all day from 12.
In the side-streets between the station and the ground are the following excellent pubs. You'll need a map to find them, however: **The Live and Let Live** at 40 Mawson Road is a characterful Free House in a turn-of-the-century corner house, with gas lighting, wooden floors and paneling. It also has excellent home-made food; **The Salisbury Arms** at 76 Tenison Road is a highly-recommended Charles Wells pub, serving a full menu 12-2, and from 6-8 for evening games.
The Blue Lion is in Fen Ditton, en route in From North:
The Blue Lion 2 Horningsea Road. (01223) 292 113
Greene King. Large, busy roadside pub serving food 12-2.15 and 6.30-9.30 pm. Pool, darts, beer garden. Open: 11.30-2.30, 5-11.

'Remember that irate horse I scared off last season? We won't see him again!'

FOR FAMILIES:
The Green Man in Trumpington High Street (en route From South M11) is a Whitbread/Beefeater restaurant in a 450-year-old building. Open: all day.

FOOD GUIDE

Near the ground, the choice is limited to two fish-and-chip shops: 'Edward Durrant', about 0.4 miles from the Abbey along the Newmarket Road towards town, and 'Beijing', on Barnwell Road, near the roundabout junction with Newmarket Road. For a wider choice, try the revamped Grafton Shopping Centre, about a mile from the ground. To get there, continue along Newmarket Road towards town, over a bridge to large roundabout. Here turn left (s/p Railway Station) and the shopping centre is signposted right.

LOCAL MEDIA

Local Radio: BBC Radio Cambridgeshire 96 FM, 1026 MW; Q103 FM; Chiltern Super Gold 792 AM.
Radio Phone-ins: Radio Cambridgeshire, 5.30-6 pm, call (01223) 252 000.
Saturday Sports Paper: None.

MISCELLANEOUS

Safety Factor: Very few problems here.
Rivals: It'll always and forever be 'Pizzaboring' at 'Cripple Sidings Lane' – so named after the track which runs alongside the London Road ground. Stevenage made few friends (make that no friends whatsoever) in their two FA Cup games against Cambridge in 1997.
Fanzine: 'The Abbey Rabbit', 27 Martin Way, Letchworth, Herts, SG6 4XU.
Unofficial Websites:
http://www.cambridgeunited.com/
Tourist Information: (01223) 463 385.

Cardiff City

Ninian Park

Address: Ninian Park, Sloper Road, Cardiff CF1 8SX
Telephone: Club/Ticket Office (01222) 398 636
Shop (01222) 666 699
Bluebird ClubCall (0891)121 171
Official Website: http://www.styrotech.co.uk/ccafc

Many lower division football fans must have visited Ninian Park over the years and never seen anything of the city of Cardiff. Access to the ground by road is incredibly easy ... turn left off the M4, left again after six miles, and straight into the club car park. And that suits visiting fans down to the ground: they head straight to the stadium and race home again as fast as the car park queues allow. It's a shame, as Cardiff is great for shopping and sightseeing, and is packed with characterful pubs and restaurants. Ninian Park is in the middle of an area once known as Temperance Town, so unsurprisingly the nearest decent pubs and eateries are a good half mile away. Train travellers have a better time of it, as the city centre is just round the corner from the railway station.

HOW TO GET THERE

BY CAR: From all directions: Exit M4 at junction 33 (Cardiff West, Barry, Penarth A4232), and at roundabout follow signs to 'Cardiff West' onto the A4232. Exit A4232 after 6.1 miles (s/p Leckwith Industrial Estate, Athletics Stadium B4267). At roundabout turn left (s/p City Centre B4267) onto the B4267 Leckwith Road. The main car park is on RHS after 0.4 miles.

FROM RAILWAY STATION (Cardiff Central): 1.1 miles. *By taxi:* About 2.50. *By bus:* The bus station is outside the railway station. Nos. L1 and L2 leave from Stand C5 at quarter to and quarter past the hour, to the Athletics Stadium. City Circle Bus no. 1 leaves from Stand E4 at 25-past and 5-to the hour, and runs along Sloper Road. *By foot:* Turn left out of station, down to main road by 'HyperValue', and turn left. Over bridge by Qualitex Printing and through traffic lights. Keep straight on, passing the 'Ocean Palace Chinese Restaurant and Takeaway', 'Plaice Takeaway' and a newsagents after about 0.3 miles. Just after Gulf petrol station after a further 0.8 miles, take left fork where road divides (s/p Penarth B4267, Dinas Powys). At T-junction turn left into Leckwith Road. Under railway bridges, and then left into Sloper Road. Ground is on LHS after 0.1 miles.
Last Midweek Trains: The last train to London leaves at 21.25, and there are no trains to Birmingham or

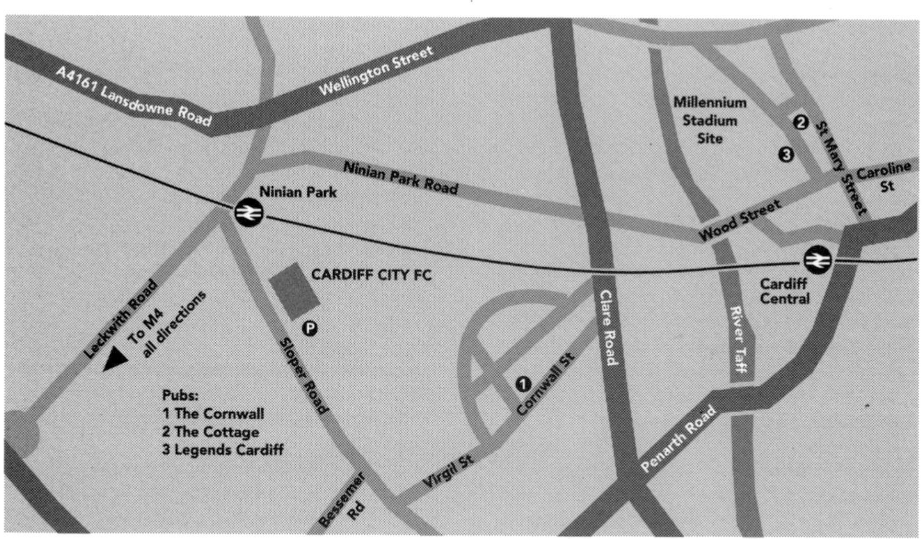

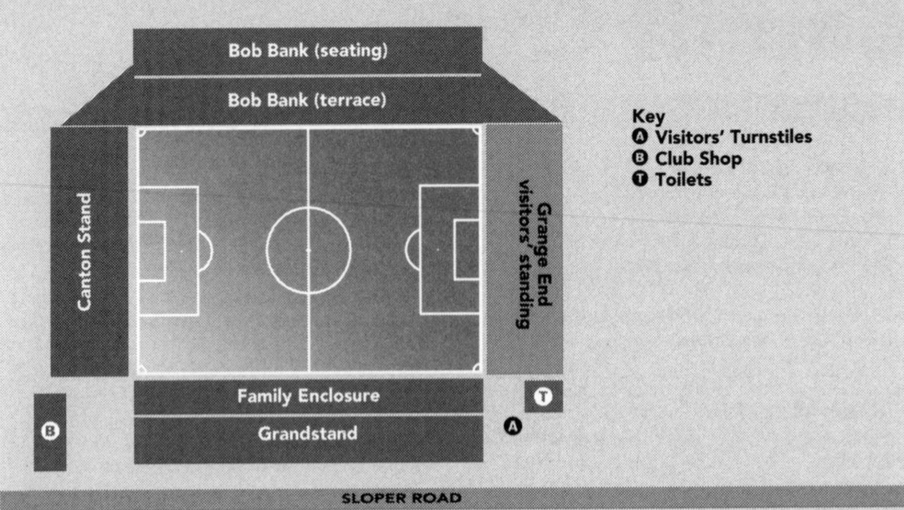

Manchester. Please double-check on (0345) 484 950.
BY BUS: As above.

PARKING

Nearly all visiting fans park in the car park (£1.20) at the Athletics Stadium, opposite Ninian Park. The streets near the ground (e.g. Newton Road) are residents only parking on matchdays. There is street parking in the area round Bessemer Road and along Virgil Street.

THE GROUND

All Cardiff fans agree that something needs to be done about Ninian Park. But what exactly? Some want to demolish it and move to a new site. Others would prefer to spend millions renovating the ground to its former splendour: 'Why move to a B&Q, when we already have a Marks and Spencers?' said one supporter. If the club is to move, it has two main options: to ground-share at the new £120 million, 75,000-seater Millennium Stadium, which is replacing the Arms Park rugby stadium, or to move to a massive leisure complex in the Cardiff Bay development. While the debate continues, and the club looks for new investors, the team continues to play at Ninian Park. It's a grand old stadium, with a huge main stand and open terracing, which has most certainly seen better days and bigger crowds. For season 98/99 away fans are being moved to the open Grange End terrace.
Total Capacity: 14,601. For away fans: 1,800.
Cost (98/99): TBA, but no more than: Adults £8, concessions £4.
Disabled Facilities: Space for up to 16 visiting fans in a disabled section in the family enclosure, shared with the home support. *Disabled Toilet:* At back of family stand. *Cost:* Free for disabled and helper. *Booking:* Advisable. *Parking:* None available. *For the Blind:* No special facilities.
Programme: £1.60.
Visitors' Toilets: *Male:* Fans were fascinated by a cobweb 'you could stand your drink on.' It's not recorded whether anyone actually tried to! The loo roll looked like it had been wet, then dried, several times. Lincoln fans had managed to BURN the words 'Beck Out' into the foam cladding on the pipes! *Female:* Nothing like the Gents at all. A visiting Doncaster fan went as far as to describe them as 'upmarket', very clean, with sink, soap, paper towels and a mirror. No complaints here!
Food and Drink: A problem here with heat, or more to the point, the lack of it! The corn-beef-and-vegetable pasty sounded great but wasn't very warm and didn't taste of much 'which is why I covered it in tomato sauce', said one hungry supporter. The hot dog sausage (£1.50) was hot and tasty but surrounded by bread which felt like it had just come out of the freezer. Similarly, the pies (£1) were extremely spicy but lukewarm. Fans liked the bacon rolls (£1.50), but said they weren't as good as the ones at Cambridge United (14.3.98).

PUB GUIDE

The nearest friendly pub to Ninian Park is:
The Cornwall (1) 92 Cornwall Street (01222) 232 379
Brains (a Cardiff brewery). A super friendly local, welcoming both sets of fans. Hot and cold snacks on demand, though large groups should book in advance.

Darts, bar billiards, TV. Car park, walking distance to ground. Open: all day.
To get there: Continue along Sloper Road, passing Ninian Park on the LHS. After 0.5 miles turn left, just after the Gulf petrol station, into Virgil Street, which becomes Cornwall Street.
In the city centre, St Mary Street, near the railway station, has a series of pubs, cafés and restaurants. Of the pubs, the most football-friendly are:
The Cottage (2) 25 St Mary Street (01222) 230 600
Brains. A long, narrow pub, more than 100 years old, well-renovated and very welcoming. The landlord describes it as 'quiet and traditional', and it's a great place for a pre-match meal. All the food, which includes steak-and-ale pie, liver-and-onions, fish-and-chips, is home-made, served 12-3. Open: all day from 12.
Legends Cardiff (3) (formerly Rosie O'Briens)
96 St Mary Street (01222) 235 066
Allied Domecq. A recently-renovated modern-style pub/bar, with big-screen TV and a good snack menu served 12-2. 'Picasso would be proud of the pictures we have on the walls', says the landlord, who adds that the pub serves the best pint of Stella in town. Families welcome. No colours after 7 pm, when the pub becomes a 'nite-spot'.
To get to St Mary Street: From railway station, walk straight ahead, passing the Burger King on the RHS. At T-junction by 'Clinton Cards' and 'Greggs' bakers, turn right along Wood Street towards Brains Brewery. At T-junction turn left into St Mary Street. From Ninian Park: go back down Sloper Road to the junction with Leckwith Road and turn right. Take first right into Ninian Park Road, and go straight on for about a mile, passing Cardiff Central railway station on the RHS. The road ends in a T-junction – this is St Mary Street. A number of multi-storey car parks are well signposted. Don't wear club colours in the city centre.

FOOD GUIDE

The only outlet near the ground is a corner shop at the junction of Broad Street and Leckwith Road. On Cornwall Street, near 'The Cornwall' pub – about half a mile from the ground – is a fish and chip shop.

For those arriving by car, there's a Burger King at the services on junction 33 of the M4. A retail park called 'Culverhouse Cross', just off the A4232, has a McDonalds. The turning is 3.1 miles from the M4, signposted 'Cardiff (W) A48, Cardiff Airport'.

Train travellers have a greater choice. There's a Burger King just outside the station, and a series of cafés on Wood Street, the main road into the city centre. 'Marlowes' offers triple-decker sandwiches from £2.75, burgers at £3.80 and a choice of main meals. Almost next door is 'Rascals' café/diner, with breakfasts and full meals for £3.50 or less. There's also a Wimpys. For a classic takeaway, home fans recommend Caroline Street, commonly known as 'Chip Shop Street'. To get there, turn right along St Mary Street, and then first left. 'Dorothy's' claims to be 'Caroline Street's longest-established and friendliest fish and chip bar and café', while 'Rosarios Steak House and Restaurant' is the best bet for a sit-down meal. It has all the classics, as well as Greek dishes and a children's menu.

St Mary Street also has a McDonalds, a Fatty Arbuckles American diner, and the rather upmarket 'Louis Restaurant and Coffee Shop'. Near 'Legends Cardiff' is the 'Laurel and Hardy Dining Co', advertising 45 main meals for £2.99, while at the end of the road, towards Cardiff Castle, is a Bella Pasta, a Pizza Hut and a Pizza Express.

LOCAL MEDIA

Local Radio: BBC Radio Wales 882 MW; Red Dragon 103.2, 97.4 FM.
Radio Phone-ins: BBC Radio Wales, Saturdays 6-7, call (01222) 578 928; Red Dragon, Saturdays 5.30-6 pm, call (01222) 231 010.
Saturday Sports Paper: *The Western Mail* produces the 'Sports Echo'.

MISCELLANEOUS

Safety Factor: Cardiff City says it's doing everything possible to eliminate its small hooligan element. All known troublemakers have long since been banned from the ground. Even so, it's an extremely good idea not to wear club colours outside the ground, or to have any showing in cars. This applies to all games, not just high profile or local derby matches.
Rivals: First and foremost, Swansea City. Then there's a 'bit of a rivalry with Wrexham'. And, if they're in the same division, Bristol Rovers, Bristol City, Swindon and Reading. In other words, any club within 50 miles!
Fanzines: 'The Thin Blue Line', PO Box 265, Cardiff CF2 3YH; 'Watch the Bluebirds Fly', 49 Nant-y-Fedw, Ynysboeth, Abercynon, Mid Glamorgan.
Unofficial Websites:
'Cardiff City Online':
http://ds.dial.pipex.com/m4morris/ccafc.htm
'Independent Supporters':
http://www.uwcm.ac.uk/uwcm/mg/bloo/giz.html
Tourist Information: (01222) 227 281.

Carlisle United

Brunton Park

Address: Brunton Park Stadium, Carlisle CA1 1LL
Telephone: Club/Ticket Office (01228) 526 237
Red Fox Clubcall (0891) 230 011
Official Website: http://www.carlisleunited.co.uk/

Here's a horror story: the Cambridge United Supporters' Coach sets out at midday for an evening match at Carlisle. After battling through blizzards and the inevitable jams on the M6 through Birmingham, it arrives at the ground at 9 pm, just in time to see Carlisle's three goals. Yes, the Carlisle trip really is the test of the loyal supporter. The nearest major club to Brunton Park is actually Queen of the South in Dumfries, while the nearest English club is Newcastle, 50 miles to the east. Brunton Park is dead easy to find, and there's a large club car park. Many fans then walk into town either to check out the pubs, or to admire the castle and city walls ... or both!

HOW TO GET THERE

BY CAR: From All Routes (M6): Exit M6 at junction 43 (s/p Carlisle A69), and follow the A69 towards Carlisle. Brunton Park is on the RHS after 1.1 miles.
FROM RAILWAY STATION (Carlisle): About 1 mile. *By taxi:* £1.60. *By bus:* Nos. 70, 74 and 685 all run along Warwick Road. *By foot:* Straight out of the main station entrance, straight over traffic lights, keeping the Citadel and old city wall on LHS, into The Crescent. Follow the road as it curves to the left, and then turn right by Mr Jingles Coffee House onto Warwick Road. From here it's a 15-minute walk to the ground.
Last Midweek Trains: There are no trains south out of Carlisle after an evening game. Please double-check on (0345) 484 950.
BY BUS: See above.

PARKING

Away supporters are strongly encouraged to use the official club car park, which is well signposted off Warwick Road. Visitors are advised against parking in the streets off Warwick Road, where car crime is a problem.

THE GROUND

Carlisle fans headed into season 1998/99 knowing that their team plays at one of the best stadiums in their division... sadly, though, this was because they'd once again been relegated into the basement. Work is in progress to turn Brunton Park into a 28,000-seater stadium. The East Stand, seating 6,000, was built in 1995, and – much to the amusement of visiting fans – appears to have been built fifty seats too long. This is because the club plans eventually to demolish the Waterworks End and move the pitch several yards to the north. The section of the East Stand with a view of the doomed terrace is roped off, with the away fans in the next section, separated from the home support by some black matting. The food and toilet facilities are good.
Total Capacity: 16,300. For away fans: Seating (East Stand) 1,903. An additional 990 spaces are available on the Waterworks End open terrace for large away contingents. Entrance via turnstiles 17-21.
Cost (98/99): Adults £11, concessions £6.
Disabled Facilities: Space for 16 visiting supporters in the East Stand. *Disabled Toilet:* Nearby. *Cost:* Free for disabled and helper. *Booking:* Essential. *Parking:* None available. *For the Blind:* No special facilities.
Programme: £1.50.
Visitors' Toilets: *Male:* Clean, spacious with all the necessities. *Female:* Pretty good, though Gills fans found all the loos blocked. Either all female fans had curries

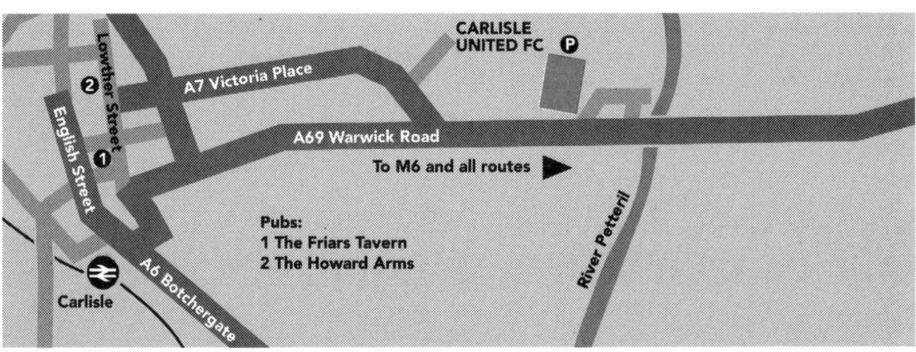

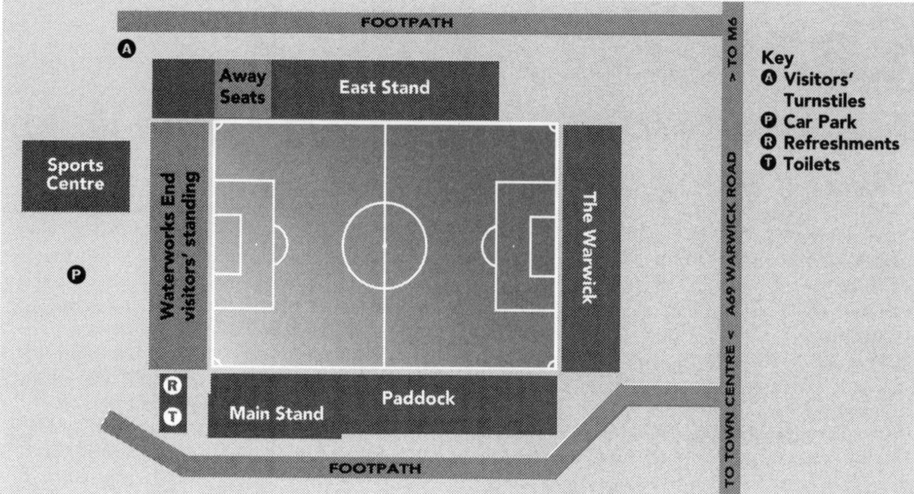

the night before, or the plumbing is too narrow!

Food and Drink: Fans like what they know, so viewed the 'Brunton Pasties' and 'Cumberland Pies' with some suspicion. Those who took the plunge with the Brunton Pasty (£1.15) found it 'pretty good', and 'more interesting than the usual football grub'. The more traditional Cornish Pasty (£1.15) 'filled a hole', while the meat-and-potato pie (£1.15) was 'almost delicious!' The tea (50p) and coffee (60p) were decent (27.9.97, 14.2.98).

PUB GUIDE

The Waterloo Aglionby (on the A69) (01225) 513 347
Greenalls (with Youngers). Traditional welcoming pub, with bar menu and sandwiches to order. Pool, darts. Families welcome. Large parties should book in advance. Open: 12-3, 6-11.
To get there: Exit M6 at junction 43 and follow Hexham signs – pub is on RHS.

The Green Bank London Road, Carleton (A6) (01228) 528 846
Scottish and Newcastle. Large, traditional pub with open fires – perfect for a cold Saturday in February! Bar meals served all day Saturday, 6-9 midweek. Pool, darts, TV. Families welcome. Open: all day.
To get there: Exit M6 at junction 42, and follow Carlisle signs onto A6. Pub is on RHS after 0.9 miles.

IN TOWN NEAR THE STATION:

The Friars Tavern (1) Devonshire Street (01228) 523 257
Whitbread. Friendly town pub, with big screen TV and a free jukebox! Bar meals served 11-2.30. Pool, darts. Families welcome. Open: all day.

The Howard Arms (2) Lowther Street (01228) 532 926
Theakstons. Recently refurbished and extended, but retaining a lot of character. Bar meals served 12-2. TV. Open: all day.

FOOD GUIDE

There is a fish and chip shop on Warwick Road, but it's not really within walking distance. For a wider choice, head into town. Those arriving by rail could try 'Mr Jingles' coffee shop, mentioned in the station directions.

LOCAL MEDIA

Local Radio: BBC Radio Cumbria 95.6 FM; CFM 96.4 FM.
Radio Phone-Ins: BBC Radio Cumbria, Saturdays 5-6, call (01228) 592 592.
Saturday Sports Paper: None.

MISCELLANEOUS

Safety Factor: Usually Carlisle is a very friendly place, but police advise visiting fans not to wear colours in the town centre.
Rivals: Er, none really, because of the distances involved. By the time fans arrive at Brunton Park, they're usually too tired to shout!
Fanzines: 'Land of Sheep and Glory', Tabrax, Wreay, Nr. Carlisle, Cumbria, CA4 0RL; 'Olga the Fox', 24A Wetheriggs Lane, Penrith, Cumbria, CA11 8PE; 'Hit the Bar', 14 Hartland Road, Friern Barnet, London N11 3JJ.
Unofficial Websites:
http://dspace.dial.pipex.com/a.woodcock/
http://www.kynson.demon.co.uk/
Reeves.is.offside.again/
http://www.fudge.force9.co.uk/
Tourist Information: (01228) 512 444.

C

Charlton Athletic

The Valley

Address: The Valley, Floyd Road, Charlton, London SE7 8BL
Telephone: Club (0181) 333 4000
Ticket Office (0181) 333 4010
ClubCall (0891) 121 146
Official Website: http://www.charlton-athletic.co.uk/

Climb up a Charlton Athletic floodlight – a long way up now, as this is after all a valley – and the most striking landmarks would be Canary Wharf, the Millennium Dome, Blackwall Tunnel and, closer to hand, the Thames Barrier and the never-ending roadwork that is the A206. South of the river it is, but The Valley is one of the easiest of all London grounds to find, only a few minutes' drive from the A102(M). Parking, however, is becoming extremely difficult. Travel by rail if possible, as the station's almost opposite the ground. Charlton is pure south-east London suburbia, with classic city pubs and takeaways, not to mention the 'FA Supermarket' and 'Totty' Chemists, within a 5-10 minute walk of the away turnstiles.

HOW TO GET THERE

BY CAR: There are two main routes to Charlton Athletic from the M25, via the A2 or the A20. The A2 is the quicker route, as the A20 runs through a more built-up area with several traffic lights. However, the A20 is the better choice for pubs and takeaways en route.

From All Main Routes (M25): Exit M25 at junction 2. At roundabout follow signs to London A2 onto the A2 dual carriageway westbound. Exit A2 after 11.6 miles (s/p Woolwich Ferry A206) and at roundabout turn right (s/p Woolwich Ferry A206, Charlton Athletic FC) onto the A206 Woolwich Road. (*)After 0.7 miles turn right, in front of the cream-and-red bricked 'Antigallican' pub (s/p Charlton Athletic FC, Charlton Station) into Charlton Church Lane. Take 2nd left into Floyd Road.

From M25 via the A20: Exit M25 at junction 3 (s/p London SE, Swanley) and at motorway roundabout follow signs to 'London A20' onto the A20 westbound. Follow 'Lee Green, Lewisham' signs for 8.7 miles, through several sets of lights to the first roundabout. Here, turn right (s/p S. Circular Road, Woolwich Ferry

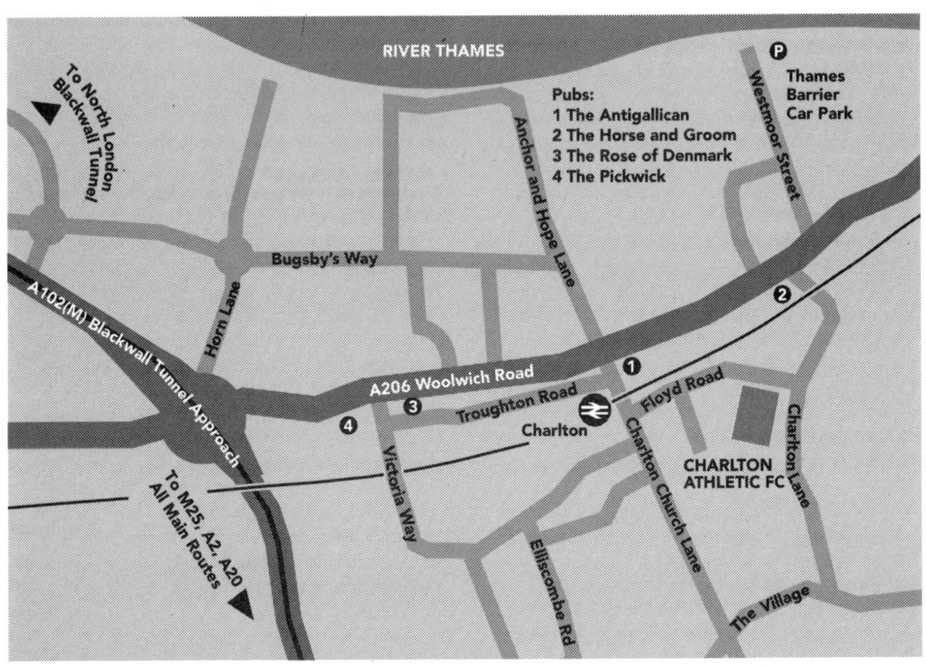

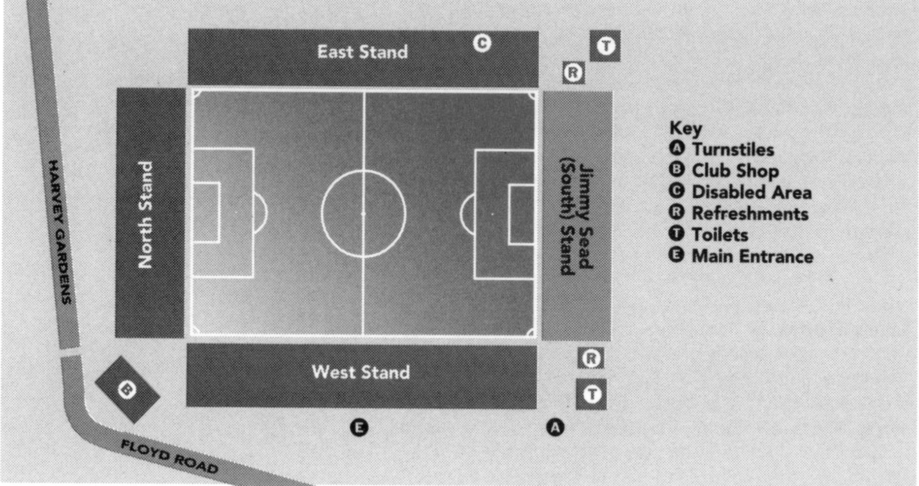

A205) onto Westhorne Avenue (the A205 South Circular). At roundabout after 0.4 miles take 2nd exit (s/p S. Circular Road, Woolwich Ferry) remaining on the A205. At junction/lights after 0.4 miles turn left (s/p Central London A2, Blackwall Tunnel) up onto the A2 (which becomes the A102(M)). Exit after 2.5 miles (s/p Woolwich Ferry A206) and at roundabout turn right (s/p Woolwich Ferry A206, Charlton Athletic FC) onto the A206 Woolwich Road. Then as From M25/A2(*).

From North London (for directions to the Blackwall Tunnel, see London Guide): Through Blackwall Tunnel and after 0.5 miles exit A102(M) (s/p Charlton Athletic Football Club, then Greenwich A2203). At roundabout after 0.2 miles, take 1st exit (s/p Woolwich Ferry, Plumstead A206) into Bugsby's Way. Go straight on at roundabout after 0.4 miles, remaining on Bugsby's Way, under railway bridge. At T-junction after 0.5 miles turn right (s/p Charlton Athletic Football Club, Woolwich Ferry A206) onto Anchor and Hope Lane. At crossroads by the 'Antigallican' pub, after 0.2 miles, go straight on into Charlton Church Lane, and 2nd left into Floyd Road.

FROM RAILWAY STATION (Charlton): Trains run from Charing Cross, London Bridge and Waterloo East. Two minute walk: turn right out of the station, and then first left into Floyd Road. At the 'Seabay Fish Bar' turn right to turnstiles.

Last Midweek Trains: Half-hourly service back to Charing Cross, last train 23.19.

BY BUS: Nos. 177 (Abbey Wood to Peckham) and 180 (Thamesmead East to Lewisham) run along Woolwich Road. Nos. 53 (Oxford Circus to Plumstead) and 54 (West Croydon to Woolwich) run along Charlton Road.

PARKING

The club reserves spaces at Fossdene School, an eight-minute walk from the ground. They cost £5 and should be booked in advance through the club. For everyone else, it's street parking. To deter people from parking in Charlton to visit the Millennium Dome, the council is planning to ban parking to the north-west of the ground, including Bugsby's Way and the nearby trading estate. This leaves the Thames Barrier car park (continue along the A206, past the 'Antigallican' and it's signposted left) and the streets to the north and east of the ground. Try around Charlton village and around Woolwich and Woolwich Common.

THE GROUND

For those who remember, or have seen photos of the overgrown Valley of the late 1980s, the ground is, well, a miracle. It was only through the never-say-die attitude of the club's supporters that Charlton Athletic returned to its true home in December 1992 after seven years in exile. Visiting fans approaching the Jimmy Seed Stand from the turnstiles can still see a reminder of the old Valley – a triangular section of ancient terracing between the refreshment kiosk and the path leading round the back of the stand. That said, The Valley – although neat and tidy – is not an architectural masterpiece, though it does retain a lot of character. Away fans are allocated all or part of the Jimmy Seed behind the goal, where the facilities are good. For those near the back, however, the view of the near touchline is obstructed, so supporters constantly stand up to see what's going on.

Total Capacity: 20,000. For away fans: at least 2,000.

Cost (97/98): Adults £13, concessions (OAPs, juniors, students) £9. Expect steep price rises for 1998/99.

Disabled Facilities: Space for about six supporters at the back of the East Stand. *Disabled Toilets:* Nearby. *Cost:* Free for disabled, concession price for helper. *Booking:* Essential. *Parking:* Limited availability, please book. *For the Blind:* 20 headphones with commentary, allowing supporters to sit where they like. Please book.
Visitors' Toilets: *Male:* 'Very nice and bright', said one fan after visiting the portakabins. 'You can see what you're doing.' *Female:* We are about to team two words that rarely go together in a football guidebook – 'hot' and 'water'. The female portakabins had hot water. It was welcome even on a scorchingly hot evening in August. NB These facilities were being rebuilt in 1998.
Food and Drink: Of the three types of pie, all at £1.55, visiting fans strongly recommended the steak-and-kidney. The chicken-and-mushroom pie had big bits of chicken but came in a foil bag complete with a trickle of water. The burgers (£2.10) were slated: 'I'm not convinced by it at all' was one rather cryptic comment. A grim faced supporter added that it was only the sugar that gave any flavour to the tea (70p), so stick with the excellent bovril (80p) (11.8.97, 1.11.97).

PUB GUIDE

All the pubs listed below are on the A206:
The Antigallican (1) 428 Woolwich Road (0181) 853 0143
Free House. The nearest pub to the ground, but there's room for all in a large club-like annex with big-screen TV. Sandwiches and pies. Darts. Families welcome. Darts, TV. Open: all day.
The Horse and Groom (2) 602 Woolwich Road/corner of Charlton Lane (0181) 858 0456
Scottish and Newcastle/Courage. A bright, traditional pub with pool table, darts and TV. Bar snacks and meals served 11-3. Families welcome. Open: all day.
The Rose of Denmark (3) 296 Woolwich Road (0181) 473 0038
Barter Inns. A locals pub with a big traditional bar area. Bar meals served 12-2. Darts, pool, TV. Open: all day.
Also recommended: **The Pickwick (4)**, 246 Woolwich Road (Courage). This is a large pub with big-screen TV and an extensive beer garden.

FOOD GUIDE

The 'Valley Café', by the railway station, serves a 'Saturday Special' (£2.50 including tea or coffee). Almost opposite is the ever-popular 'Kebab Express', and just round the corner in Floyd Road the 'Seabay Fish Bar' has cod at £2.20 and chips at 90p. Further up Charlton Church Lane is the 'Golden Fish Bar' and a Chinese restaurant. On the A206 Woolwich Road between the A102(M) and the 'Antigallican', is 'Chris's Fish Bar', offering barbecue chicken and ribs, and on the corner of Rainton Road, the 'York Café'. There's a large drive-through McDonalds on Bugsby's Way.

CHARLTON INTRODUCE NEW SCHEME TO INCREASE SIZE OF CROWDS ......
NO ONE ALLOWED IN UNDER 5' 4"
eagle

LOCAL MEDIA

Local Radio: Millennium Radio 106.8 FM; Capital Gold 1548 AM; GLR 94.9 FM
Radio Phone-ins: Millennium Radio, Sundays 7-8.30 pm, call (0181) 311 3111; Capital Gold, Saturdays 2-6.30, midweek 7-10 (or 7-8 if no match). Call on (0845) 35 60 7080.
Saturday Sports Paper: None.

MISCELLANEOUS

With its new fashionable Premier League status, Charlton Athletic commissioned a new club song, 'Down in The Valley', from the group 'Squeeze'. We asked at the club shop whether this had displaced Charlton's traditional favourite, Billy Cotton's 'Red, Red Robin'. The assistant replied, a little uneasily: 'No, well, of course not, it's just that, well, we wanted something a little more modern, more upmarket.' Charlton fans are adamant that the 'Red, Red Robin' must remain, and any mention of its abolition brings a torrent of complaints to the club and the local newspaper!
Safety Factor: Trouble is rare.
Rivals: The former website 'Let's all Laugh at Millwall' called the club's traditional London rivals 'the Soapdodgers', and 'The Spanners', the latter referring to an incident in the Millwall match at Reading in 1994/95.
Fanzine: 'Voice of the Valley' is turning from a fanzine to a club publication, though the editor plans to maintain it as a platform for the fans, critical or otherwise.
Unofficial Websites:
http://www.users.globalnet.co.uk/davelo/cafepage.htm
http://www.casc.org.uk/
Tourist Information: Greenwich (0181) 858 6376; Southwark (0171) 403 8299.

Chelsea

Stamford Bridge

Address: Stamford Bridge, London, SW6 1HS
Telephone: Club (0171) 385 5545
Chelsea Megastore (0171) 565 1490
Credit Card Hotline (0171) 386 7799
Ticket Information (0891) 121 011
ClubCall (0891) 121 159
Official Website:
http://www.chelseafc.co.uk/chelsea/

Enter through the sliding doors, up the escalator into the foyer, where everything smells of leather and polish, and sit back into one of the easy chairs for a mid-morning coffee. Yes, we are talking about Stamford Bridge. The Chelsea Village complex, with its restaurants, apartments and luxury 160-bedroom hotel is well and truly open. Rich football supporters, or those who want to splash out to dine in style, can eat at one of the four restaurants at the ground. And for everyone else, the choice along the nearby Fulham Road is huge, including classic takeaways, a popular Italian brasserie and an excellent vegetarian restaurant. The best way to reach Stamford Bridge is by tube, as the roads are heavily congested, especially at night, and parking is extremely difficult. Visiting supporters are best advised to drink en route.

HOW TO GET THERE

BY CAR: From All Main Routes, M25: Exit M25 at junction 15 (s/p M4 Heathrow, Terminals 1, 2 and 3, London (W)), onto the M4 eastbound. Remain on the M4, which becomes the A4, following signs to 'Central London' for 10.4 miles to Hogarth Roundabout. Here, take 2nd exit (s/p Central London, Hammersmith A4) remaining on the A4, passing the Griffin (Fullers) Brewery. At the Hammersmith Flyover junction after 1.1 miles, go straight on (s/p Central London A4, Olympia) onto flyover. Past 'Labatts Apollo' after 0.3 miles, and the boat-shaped 'Seagram' building after another 0.1 miles. After a further 0.7 miles, move into the right-hand lane and turn right at lights (no signpost, but it's by a Pricecheck on the left, and the 'Via Bar' on the right) into the B317 North End Road. Go straight on at the double mini-roundabout after 0.5 miles and after a further 0.5 miles, turn left at mini-roundabout by 'The George' pub into Fulham Broadway. (*)At junction/lights after 0.1 miles by the 'Jolly Bee' takeaway and the 'White Hart' turn left (s/p West End A4, Chelsea, South Kensington) into Fulham Road. Ground is on LHS after 0.2 miles.
From South (via Putney Bridge): For directions to Putney Bridge see London Guide: Over bridge, and after 0.1 miles go straight on at junction/lights by the 'Pharoah and Firkin' (s/p The West, West End). At roundabout after 0.1 miles, by 'Bowden Property Services' turn right (s/p West End A4, Fulham, Earls Court) into Fulham Road. At mini-roundabout after 0.7 miles, by 'The George' pub, go straight on (s/p West End A4, Chelsea, South Kensington) into Fulham Broadway. Then as From All Main Routes(*).

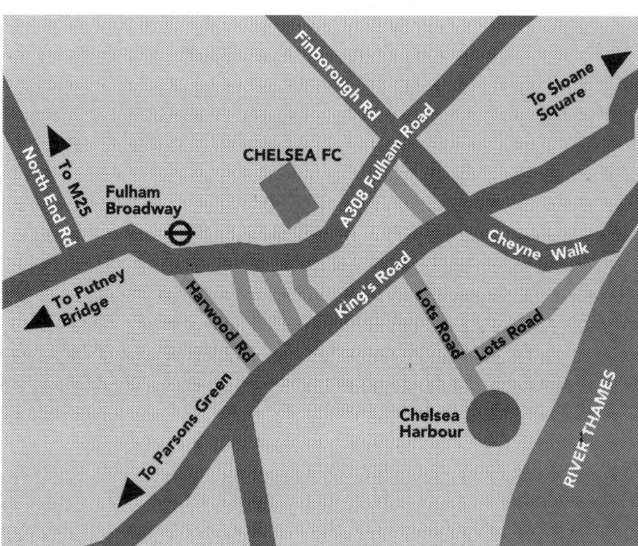

FROM UNDERGROUND STATION (Fulham Broadway, District Line, Zone 2): *By foot:* Turn left out of station along Fulham Road, and ground is on LHS after 0.2 miles.
Last Midweek Trains: See London Guide at front of book.
BY BUS: The nos. 14 (Putney to Tottenham Court Road) and 211 (Waterloo to Hammersmith) run along

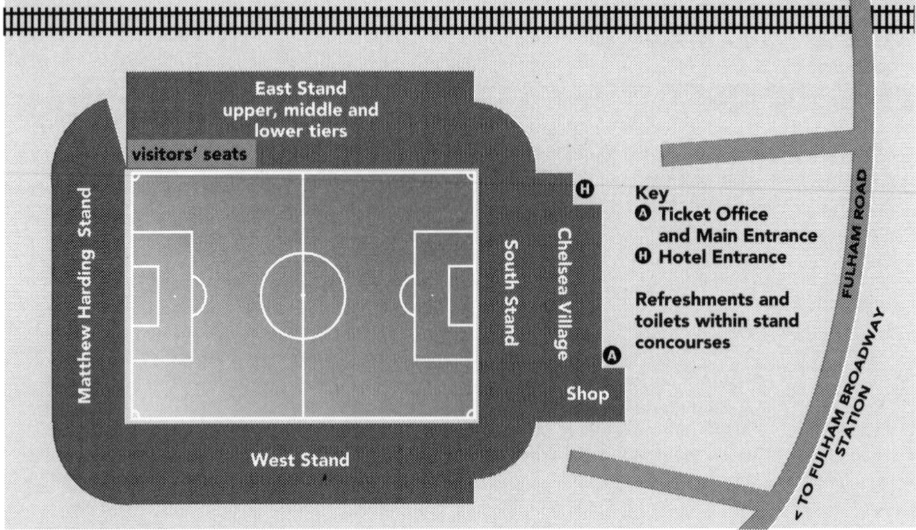

Fulham Road, while the nos. 28 (Golders Green to Wandsworth) and 391 (Richmond to Fulham Broadway) run along North End Road. Nos. 11 (from Liverpool Street) and 295 (Ladbrooke Grove to Clapham Junction) run along Harwood Road.

PARKING

The underground car park at the ground charges £15, and there's no access after 2 pm. The only alternative is street parking, though much of it is 'pay-and-display' or residents only. The best policy is to park the car on the outskirts of London and take the tube!

THE GROUND

A previous edition of this guidebook, written during the early stages of the ground's development, described Stamford Bridge as a 'right dog's dinner'. Today it's the dog's b******s, or nearly so! In total, £100 million has been spent on Stamford Bridge and the Chelsea Village complex and it shows. Both the North (Matthew Harding) and South Stands link round to the massive three-tier East Stand, though because of the piecemeal development, none of them match! A planning glitch has delayed the construction of the second tier of the West Stand, leaving supporters out in the rain and with the view from some seats badly obstructed by two temporary floodlight pylons. It's no use, by the way, buying one of the 30 apartments in Chelsea Village as a way to see the games, as no windows overlook the pitch!

Visiting fans are allocated either part of, or the whole of, the lower tier of the East Stand. The club no longer sells the back two or three rows, but the view from the rear sections is still poor.

Total Capacity: 35,250. For away fans: Either 1,600 or 3,200. Gates 4 and 6. For cup games, when away clubs claim their full allocation, visiting fans are allocated the 7,000 seats in the uncovered West Stand.

Cost (98/99): Adults £23, no concessions.

Disabled Facilities: Space for six visiting supporters in an enclosure shared with home fans in the East Stand. *Disabled Toilet:* Nearby. *Cost:* Category A game: £9 for disabled, £24 for helper. Category B game: £7 for disabled, £16 for helper. *Booking:* The six tickets are sent to the away club. *For the Blind:* No special facilities.

Programme: £2.50.

Visitors' Toilets: *Male:* Our researcher initially refused to go in, saying he didn't want his socks to get wet. 'A puddle even deeper than the one at Mansfield, but not as fast flowing', he said. The cubicles could have done with a spring clean too, but there was hot water ... though nothing to dry hands on. *Female:* The half-time queue was long, as there were only two main cubicles (both very narrow), plus one for the disabled. The water was hot, there was soap, and efficient hand-dryers.

Food and Drink: The pies (£2) were a success: 'It's chicken and mushroom', said one fan. 'And it's got chicken and mushroom in it ... you can't go wrong with that!' Another fan put Chelsea near the top of the 'pie list'. The chips (£1) were passable and the Kenco coffee (£1) was good. The cheeseburgers (£3) however were a disaster. 'It's c**p, cold and costly', said one fan, while another said it was the worst he'd ever had! (26.11.97)

PUB GUIDE

Visiting supporters are advised to stop for a drink well away from Stamford Bridge. Pubs near underground stations on the Circle and District lines are a good bet – see London Guide at the front of the book.

FOOD GUIDE

Stamford Bridge now boasts what must be the best (and most expensive) takeaway fish and chip outlet at any ground in the country. It's the takeaway section of the top-notch fish restaurant 'Fishnets', and for £5 fans receive a 5oz cod in homemade beer-batter with chips cooked in beef dripping. The restaurant itself is open on a matchday, with a two-course meal costing about £30 (book on (0171) 565 1430). Also at the ground, 'King's Brasserie' has a special matchday menu, two courses at £19.95, three at £22.50 (book on (0171) 565 1400). 'Arkles' claims to be 'London's Only Irish Fine Dining Restaurant'. Its matchday menu costs £21 or £25 for two courses. Book on (0171) 565 1420.

For those with a little less money to spare, the choice along Fulham Road is huge. The 'El Metro' Spanish Brasserie, visible from Fulham Broadway station, has a huge menu, including daily two-course specials for £6 (book on (0171) 384 1264). Turn right from Fulham Broadway station for a 'Perfect Pizza' and the 'Ruby in the Dust' café. The latter is described by the manager as 'funky, with a great eclectic choice of music.' To avoid the crowds, keep going along Fulham Road, heading away from the ground towards the junction with North End Road. Here, there's a 'Domino's Pizza', a Tapas Bar, a traditional fish and chip shop, several cafés and an excellent vegetarian restaurant called 'The Windmill'.

Opposite Fulham Broadway station is a very popular café/takeaway called 'Jolly Bee'. Turn left out of Fulham Broadway station, towards the ground, for a couple of classic football takeaways and cafes, the 'Stamford Bridge Café' and the 'Chelsea Kebab House'. 'The Lost Café' is more upmarket, with a good vegetarian selection. The 'Sundancer Gallery Café' is a bright art gallery/café with patisseries and sandwiches: try the 'Zola' sandwich: parma ham, smoked mozzarella and olive paste for £2.75.

LOCAL MEDIA

Local Radio: Capital Gold 1548 AM; GLR 94.9 FM; Radio Chelsea on 1494 AM broadcasts between 9-6 on Saturdays, and from 5.30-10 pm when there's an evening match.
Radio Phone-ins: Capital Gold, Sat 2-6.30, midweek 7-10 (or 7-8 if no match). Call on (0845) 35 60 7080.
Saturday Sports Paper: None.

MISCELLANEOUS

Safety Factor: Nothing serious in season 97/98. The supporters of foreign sides, in the European Cup Winners' Cup matches, caused the most problems!
Rivals: Tottenham, Manchester United and Arsenal.
Fanzines: 'Red Card', Email – Theredcard@msn.com; 'The Chelsea Independent', CISA, PO Box 4027, London, W9 3ZF.
Unofficial Websites:
'Chelsea Mania': http://www.chelseafans-no.com/
'CFC': http://www.btinternet.com/~alexc/chelsea.htm
'Blues Online': http://members.xoom.com/chelsea_fc/
'CFC Worship':
http://www.geocities.com/Colosseum/Field/5956/CFC_index.html
'Priesty's': http://www.geocities.com/Colosseum/2336/
http://www.geocities.com/Colosseum/Track/8534/index.html
'BluesNet': http://www.users.globalnet.co.uk/~davero/
Tourist Information: No local office.

Chester City

The Deva Stadium

Address: Deva Stadium, Bumpers Lane, Chester CH1 4LT
Telephone: Club (01244) 371 376 or 371 809
ClubCall (0891) 121 633

It doesn't sound very exotic ... 'turn left at the sign for the Household Waste Site'. Unfortunately those are the directions to the Deva Stadium. The ground's about 1.5 miles out of Chester, at the back of an industrial estate, with the Welsh border running straight across the pitch! For most fans, it's a drink and chip-free zone, so for sustenance either stop en route or head into the historic city centre, which has some truly excellent restaurants and pubs. Train travellers have a long walk, but the route takes in some of the best football-friendly hostelries.

HOW TO GET THERE

BY CAR: The ground and 'Sealand Industrial Estate', both on Bumpers Lane, are well signposted.
From All Main Routes, M6-M56: Follow the M56 to junction 16, where the motorway ends at a roundabout. Here, turn left (s/p North Wales, Queensferry A5117 A550) onto the A5117. At next roundabout after 0.6 miles (by Little Chef), turn left (s/p Chester A540) onto the A540. At next roundabout after 3.2 miles, take 3rd exit (s/p Queensferry A5480, Sealand Road Ind, Retail Parks) onto the Deva Link Road. At roundabout after 0.7 miles go straight on (s/p Sealand Industrial Estate). At crossroads by MFI Homeworks after 0.2 miles, go straight across into Bumpers Lane. Ground is on RHS after 0.6 miles.
From South (A483): Continue on A483 to roundabout at junction with the A55. Go straight across (s/p Chester A483). Follow signs to 'Chester A483' for 2.3 miles over three roundabouts and over River Dee. At next roundabout, by the statue, turn left (s/p Queensferry A483, Ellesmere Port) into Nicholas Street. After 0.2 miles, turn left at lights (s/p Queensferry A548, Sealand Road Industrial Parks) into Watergate Street, which becomes Sealand Road. After 0.9 miles, opposite Homebase, turn left (s/p Sealand Industrial Estate, Household Waste Site) into Bumpers Lane.
FROM RAILWAY STATION (Chester): About 2 miles. *By taxi:* up to £3.50. *By bus:* Take the Raillink bus to the bus station, then the no. 28 which runs along Sealand

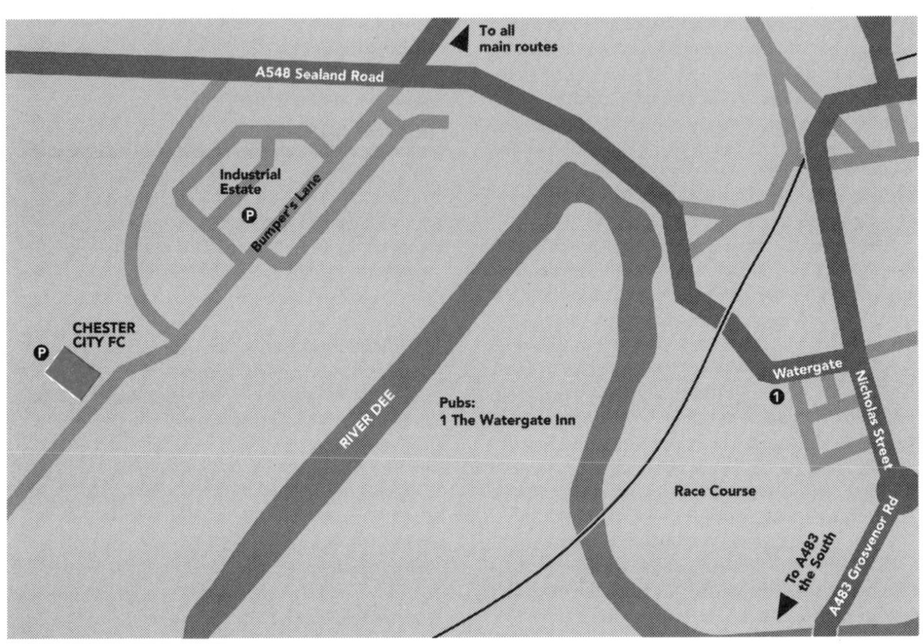

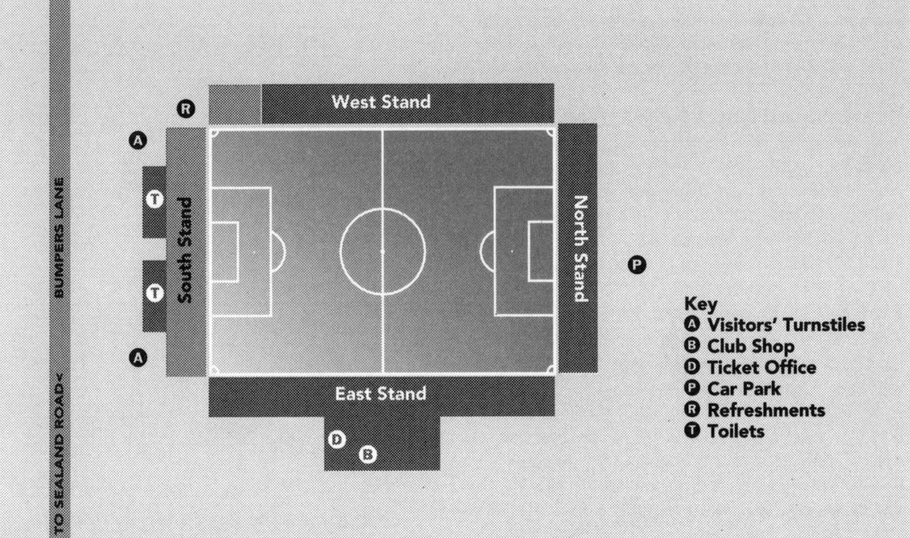

Road. *By foot:* Come out of the main exit opposite the 'Town Crier' and turn right into Station Road. Follow road round to left, between the 'Egerton Arms' and the 'Railway Inn'. At end of street, by 'Stanleys', go into underpass. In centre, take first exit towards tall black and white building. Take steps straight ahead (s/p Frodsham Street). Head towards the 'Oddfellows Arms', but before crossing bridge turn right into Gorse Stacks. Straight across crossroads by the 'Bull and Stirrup' into Canal Street, and under dual carriageway. At junction turn left, passing 'Telfords Warehouse' on RHS, and over canal. Where road divides, turn right into South View Road. At T-junction turn right into Sealand Road. The next left, after 0.5 miles, is Bumpers Lane.
Last Midweek Trains: Trains leave to Birmingham New Street via Crewe at 21.48 and 22.48; to Liverpool at 21.50 and 22.20; and to Manchester at 21.52 and 22.57.
BY BUS: The no. 28 runs from the bus station behind the town hall along Sealand Road. After the match, special buses take fans back to the city centre.

PARKING

There's a large, well-stewarded car park at the ground (£1.50), and a second access road has helped to alleviate the post-match gridlock. There's also street parking on the nearby industrial estate.

THE GROUND

The Rochdale fanzine 'Exceedingly Good Pies' once famously asked whether 'Deva' was Latin for 'breezeblock'. It's actually the Roman name for Chester and anyway, home fans have heard all the jokes before. As far as they're concerned, after two years of ground-sharing with Macclesfield, 1990-92, any stadium, anywhere, would do! Well, just about. Most agree that the ground, which is basically four shallow stands round a pitch, could at least be given more character, for example, by simply renaming the stands. The 6,000 capacity can be increased with second tiers should Chester gain promotion. One home fan muttered: 'Let's hope we go up soon, so we can knock the place down and start again!' Visiting supporters are allocated terracing behind the goal and seats in the West Stand. The view from both areas is good.
Total Capacity: 6,000. For away fans: Seating (West Stand) 600. Turnstile 7. Terrace (South Stand) 1,296. Turnstiles 8 and 9.
Cost (98/99): Seating £10, terrace £7.50. No concessions for away fans.
Disabled Facilities: Space for eight visiting fans at pitch level in front of the West Stand. *Disabled Toilet:* In West Stand. *Cost:* Free for disabled, £10 for helper. *Booking:* Advisable. *Parking:* Available, please book. *For the Blind:* Ten places with hospital radio commentary.
Programme: £1.50.
Visitors' Toilets: *Male:* Clean, with loads of loo paper, but never any paper towels. *Female:* Two cubicles, with everything in working order. A Mansfield fan commented on the 'strange U-shaped toilet seat arrangement.' One for the X-Files maybe.
Food and Drink: One fan said the tea (70p) 'tasted like it was brewed at one o'clock ... this morning!' The 'pastie' (£1.30) was a flat, stodgy lump of pastry but was actually quite tasty, while the meat-and-potato pie (£1.30) looked like a pie but wasn't tasty at all. The bovril (70p) was good (13.12.97, 7.2.98).

PUB GUIDE

A small number of admission tickets for the social club at the ground are sent in advance to the Away Supporters' Club.

The Wheatsheaf Parkgate Road (the A540, the main road into Chester from the M6-M56) (01244) 851 804

Whitbread/Brewers Fayre (with Boddingtons, Gold, and Flowers IPA). Large comfortable family-orientated pub. Full menu/children's menu, served 11.30 am-10 pm. Darts, TV, children's play area. Disabled facilities. Open: all day.

The Frog 164 Liverpool Road (01244) 373 719

Whitbread. Welcoming traditional pub serving the 'Classic Steaks' menu. Pool, darts, large TV. Families welcome. Open: all day.

To get there: At roundabout on A540, instead of turning onto the Deva Link Road, turn left (s/p Ellesmere Port A5480). Turn left at next roundabout (s/p Ellesmere Port A5116). Pub is on RHS after about 0.5 miles.

The Watergate Inn (1) 10 Watergate Square (01244) 323 779

Whitbread (and guest beers). Traditional-style pub, the nearest to the Deva, converted out of three cottages. Bar meals served 11-7. Families welcome. Pool, darts, TV. Open: all day.

There are also two great pubs en route from the railway station: **The Ship Victory,** at 47 George Street is a top-rate traditional ale house, renowned for its cask beers; **The Bull and Stirrup,** 8 Upper Northgate Street is a wonderfully football-friendly Greenalls pub serving both bar and restaurant meals.

FOR FAMILIES:

The Bache Miller's Kitchen, 76 Liverpool Road (Greenalls/Premier House), a classic Miller's Kitchen pub/restaurant on the same road as 'The Frog' (see directions above).

FOOD GUIDE

'Chester Retail Park' opposite the entrance to Bumpers Lane has a Pizza Hut and McDonalds. Otherwise, it's about a mile into town ... turn right out of Bumpers Lane and keep walking! One of the most popular restaurants is 'Fatty Arbuckles', near the cathedral, which promises 'the biggest portions in town.'

LOCAL MEDIA

Local Radio: BBC Radio Merseyside, 95.8 FM.

Radio Phone-Ins: BBC Radio Merseyside, 5.30-6, call (0151) 709 9333.

Saturday Sports Paper: The nearest is Liverpool's 'Football Echo', which makes occasional appearances in Chester newsagents.

'What odds do you think the bookies would give me for shooting in Wales, but scoring in England?'

MISCELLANEOUS

The club has been considering a new mascot, and has resurrected the idea of a seal (based on the club's former ground at Sealand Road). The only link with football is that a seal can balance a ball on its nose, which is beyond most players!

Safety Factor: A very safe place to visit. The only major problem in the past few seasons was at the FA Cup clash with Wrexham.

Rivals: 'The Welsh team' ... i.e., Wrexham, plus Macclesfield and Tranmere.

Fanzines: 'Hello Albert', St Michael's Vicarage, 96 Romsley Road, Bertley Green, Birmingham, B32 3PS; 'The Onion Bag', 65 Eaton Road, Chester, CH4 7EW.

Unofficial Websites:
http://www.chester-city.co.uk/
http://members.tripod.com/~chestercityfc/home.htm
http://www.sillysausage.demon.co.uk/

Tourist Information: (01244) 317 962.

Chesterfield

Saltergate

Address: Recreation Ground, Saltergate, Chesterfield, Derbyshire S40 4SX
Telephone: Club (01246) 209 765
Spireites Hotline (0891) 555 818

Chesterfield is rightly famous for its historic architecture. Firstly, of course, there's the crooked spire of St Mary's All Saints Church, a mathematical design error and a serious one at that. And then there's Saltergate. The two have a lot in common: not only did the spire, which dominates the skyline, give the football club its nickname, but both have character, look in dire need of repair, and are loved exactly as they are. No-one would dream of trying to untwist the spire, but Saltergate's days could well be numbered. The ground's at the top of a hill in a quiet residential area, with pubs, parking and the town centre all within easy ambling distance.

HOW TO GET THERE

BY CAR: From North, South, East (M1): Exit M1 at junction 29. At roundabout follow signs for 'Chesterfield A617, Matlock A632' onto the A617. At roundabout after 5 miles, take 2nd exit (s/p Town Centre, Bakewell A619). At roundabout after 0.3 miles, take 1st exit (s/p Bakewell A619, Buxton A6) onto the A619 Markham Road. At roundabout after 0.7 miles take 3rd exit, in front of KFC Express, into Foljambe Road.

From Sheffield (A61): At first roundabout on the outskirts of Chesterfield (just after Fiat garage) follow signs to 'Chesterfield North B6057' onto the B6057. At roundabout after 0.7 miles go straight on (s/p Town Centre B6057). At mini-roundabout after 0.9 miles turn sharp right (s/p Barlow B6051) into Newbold Road. Take 3rd turning on LHS (Cobden Road) to ground.

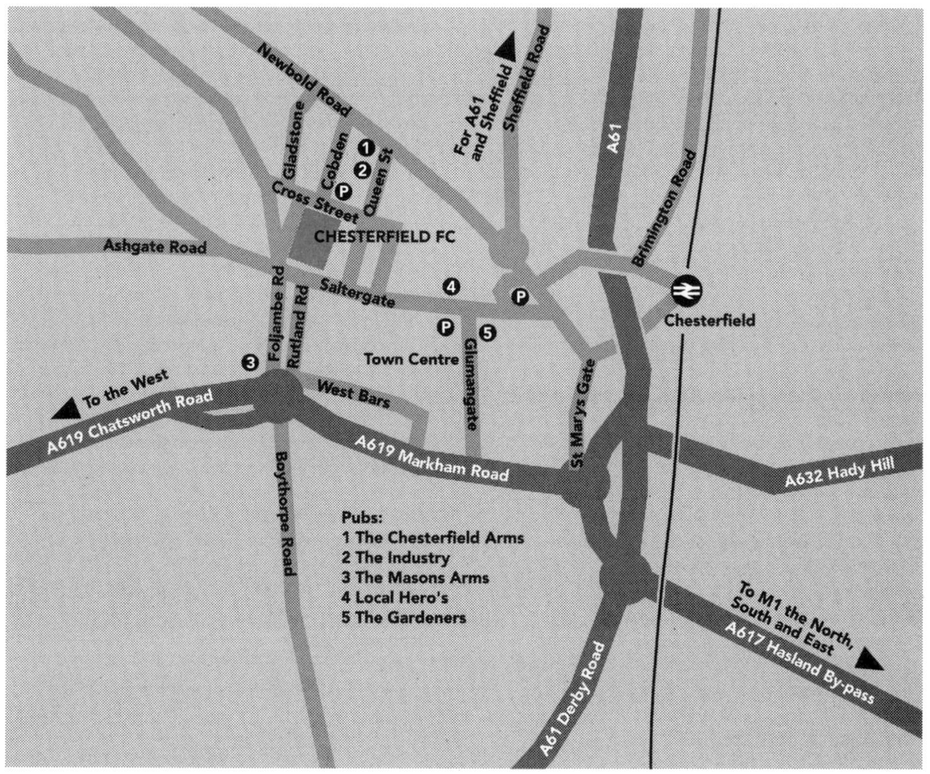

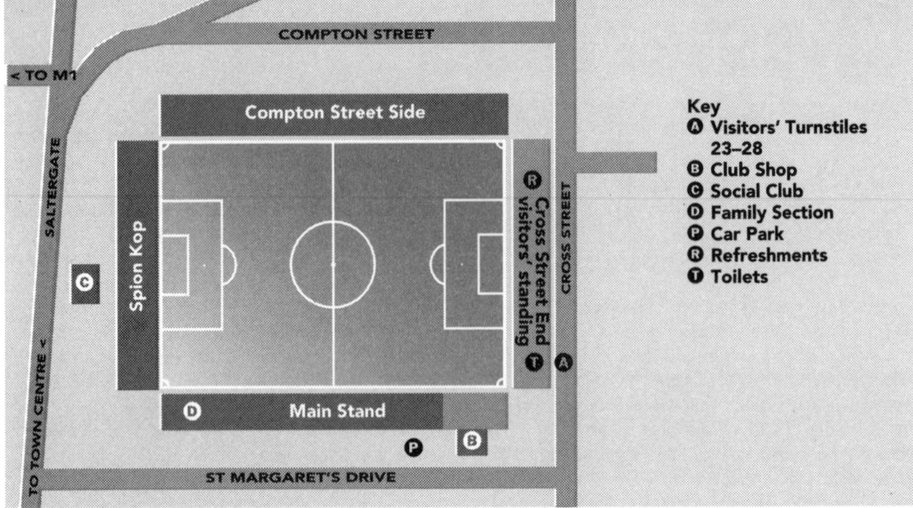

FROM RAILWAY STATION (Chesterfield): 0.75 miles. *By taxi:* £1.50-£2 depending on traffic. *By bus:* The no. 40 stops nearby on Compton Street. *By foot:* Head straight out of station, passing town map, and turn left into Corporation Street. Straight across crossroads, keeping the Chesterfield Hotel on the RHS, and over footbridge. Turn right at the Derbyshire Times (following pedestrian signpost to town centre). Cross Tapton Lane to large roundabout with car park. Here, head almost directly across the car park, passing Comet on the LHS, towards 'The Manhatten' pub. This is Saltergate. Ground is a 5-10 minute walk along Saltergate, on the RHS. *Last Midweek Trains:* The last trains are: to Sheffield at 00.37; to Derby at 23.03; and to Nottingham at 23.54. There are no connecting trains to London. Please double check on (0345) 484 950.

BY BUS: Nos. 4, 5, 6, 38 and 39 stop outside Manor College on Ashgate Road, a five minute walk.

PARKING

There are a number of choices:

a) Street parking is relatively easy. Try the roads off Cross Street and Ashgate Road.

b) On Ashgate Road, there's free parking at an old school, and a pay-and-display car park.

c) A school on Cross Street (opposite the visitors' turnstiles) has spaces for 400 cars (£1.50).

d) There's a large car park at the Town Hall. It's pay-and-display during the day, but free at night.

e) Other town centre car parks. Try the one in the large roundabout at the end of Saltergate. Car drivers should note that it's not possible to turn right at the top of Foljambe Road. So, on the A619 roundabout, instead of turning into Foljambe Road, take the next exit (s/p Municipal Offices) into Rutland Road. At the T-junction at top of hill turn right (s/p Through Traffic) into Saltergate. Town Hall car park is on the RHS.

THE GROUND

Football has been played at Saltergate for 125 years, and it remains one of the most traditional grounds in the country. The Main Stand still has wooden seating, visiting fans have the open terrace, and home fans shift from one end to the other at half-time, meeting and chatting to friends along the way. The club itself, however, is keen to relocate. It favours a move to Wheeldon Mill on the outskirts of town, while the District Council has put forward 'brown' land at the site of the old Avenue Coking Plant at Wingerworth, about three miles from Chesterfield on the A61 towards Derby.

The newly-formed 'Spireite Independent Fans Association' is pressing the club to redevelop Saltergate or, should a ground move prove unstoppable, to give preference to the Wingerworth site. Dave Radford of the defunct fanzine 'The Crooked Spireite' joked that at Wingerworth at least the club could save money by not installing floodlights: 'There's so much toxic waste there that the crowd will be glowing after 10 minutes!'

Total Capacity: 8,880. For away fans: Seating (Main Stand) 800, turnstiles 23-28 on Cross Street. Terrace 2,300, turnstiles 17-22 on Cross Street.

Cost (98/99): Seating £9.50, terrace £8.50. No concessions for away fans.

Disabled Facilities: Space for 20 under cover in front of the Main Stand. *Disabled Toilet:* Under the stand. *Cost:* Free for disabled, full price for helper. *Booking:* Advisable. *Parking:* Limited availability behind the Spion Kop. *For the Blind:* No special facilities.

Programme: £1.60.
Visitors' Toilets: *Male* (Main stand) A brick wall and a gutter, and mind your step or that won't be a rain puddle you're standing in. The pipes, conveniently positioned at head-height, were covered in furry material which appeared to have been collecting detritus for the last 20 years. A microbiologist would get very excited. *Female:* (Main Stand) The only reassurances were that the bin had been 'passed and inspected'.
Food and Drink: The steak-and-kidney pie (£1.50) was declared the 'pie of the season' by visiting Gillingham fans. The Cornish pasty (£1.50) was 'average, but nice and hot', while the expensive burgers (£2) 'did the job'. One taster recommended the beef drink, saying it had helped cure his bad flu-like symptoms! There was nothing for veggies except chocolate (4.11.97, 7.3.98).

PUB GUIDE

The Chesterfield Arms (1) 40 Newbold Road (corner of Queen Street) (01246) 275 421
Mansfield. Smart traditional pub with a warm, wood panelled lounge area, and public bar with pool table and TV. Sandwiches. Darts. Doorman on matchdays. Open: all day Saturday matchdays, from 6.30 pm for evening games.
The Industry (2) 49 Queen Street (next door to Chesterfield Arms) (01246) 271 606
John Smiths. A traditional friendly three-roomed pub, with TV, pool, darts and a separate area for children. Beer garden. Families welcome. Open: all day Friday-Sunday; from 7 pm for midweek games.
The Masons Arms (3) 3 Chatsworth Road (near Foljambe Road) (01246) 270 787
Kimberleys (a Nottingham Brewery, with Stones). Locals pub, with pool, darts, big-screen TV. Open: all day.
Local Hero's (4) 61 Saltergate (01246) 273 805
John Smiths (with Joshua Baileys on draft). Recently refurbished pub, with sports pictures and memorabilia – including of course Chesterfield's recent cup run – on the walls. Open: all day.
The Gardeners (5) Glumangate (off Saltergate) (01246) 201 619
Mansfield. Large smart modern pub, where the food, served 12-2, is highly recommended. Darts, 2 pool tables, TV. Open: all day.
Also recommended: **The Derby Tup** on the B6057 Sheffield Road, Whittington Moor (those coming in from Sheffield pass right by). It's a real-ale mecca with an excellent menu, including Giant Yorkshire Puddings.
Note that many of the pubs listed above run discos on weekend evenings.

'Is it the giant killing season already?'

FOOD GUIDE

The 'West Bars Fish Diner' and the 'West Bars Tandoori', are both highly recommended, and there's a KFC nearby. Both the A619 Chatsworth Road and the B6057 Sheffield Road are lined with takeaways.

LOCAL MEDIA

Local Radio: BBC Radio Sheffield 104.1 FM.
Radio Phone-ins: BBC Radio Sheffield 'Praise and Grumble', 5.05-6 pm Saturdays, call (0114) 268 2222.
Saturday Sports Paper: 'The Green' Un'.

MISCELLANEOUS

Preston fans awarded Chesterfield supporters the 'Chant of the Season' award in 97/98, for this effort as the third Spireite goal hit the back of the net: 'All quiet ... on the Preston front ...'.
Safety Factor: It's advisable not to wear colours when walking to the railway station or the town centre car parks.
Rivals: Chesterfield fans dislike Sheffield United, referring to its supporters as the 'Dee-Dahs'. A dislike of Mansfield dates back to the miners' strikes.
Fanzines: None.
Unofficial Websites: 'Aspire':
http://www.amazons.co.uk/spireites/
http://www/spireites.com/
http://www.fsa.org.uk/cfield.htm
Tourist Information: (01246) 207 777/8.

Colchester United

Layer Road

Address: Layer Road, Colchester, Essex, CO2 7JJ
Telephone: Club/Tickets (01206) 508 800
U's Line (0891) 737 300
Official Website: http://www.cufc.co.uk/

Colchester proudly claims to be Britain's 'Oldest Recorded Town'. Presumably a Roman noted: 'Couldn't find anywhere near the amphitheatre to park the chariot, view obscured by columna and a long queue for the vinum, glira (roast doormouse) with garum (rotting fish sauce).' The present-day British army has a garrison in Colchester too, right opposite Layer Road, where parking is strictly forbidden. It's street parking for all, so arrive early to avoid a long walk! Layer Road is about a mile to the south of the town centre, in a chippy and away-pub free zone, so make the most of any takeaways en route.

HOW TO GET THERE

BY CAR: From All Directions, A12: Exit A12 at signpost 'Colchester West, Halstead A1124'. At roundabout follow signs to 'Tollgate Retail and Business Park, Lexden, Mersea' into Essex Yeomanry Way. At Tollgate Roundabout after 0.3 miles, take 2nd exit (s/p Lexden, Mersea) into London Road. At lights after 0.8 miles, turn right (by NatWest Bank on LHS, s/p Mersea) into Straight Road. To double roundabout after 1.3 miles, by the 'Leather Bottle': turn left at the first, right at the second (s/p Mersea, Layer) into Gosbecks Road. At roundabout after 0.4 miles turn left (s/p Mersea B1025, Layer B1026). At double roundabout after 0.4 miles turn left (s/p Town Centre) into Layer Road – there's good parking along the main road here. Ground is on LHS after 0.9 miles.

FROM RAILWAY STATION (Colchester North): Two miles. *By taxi:* £3.50. *By bus:* Take any bus from the

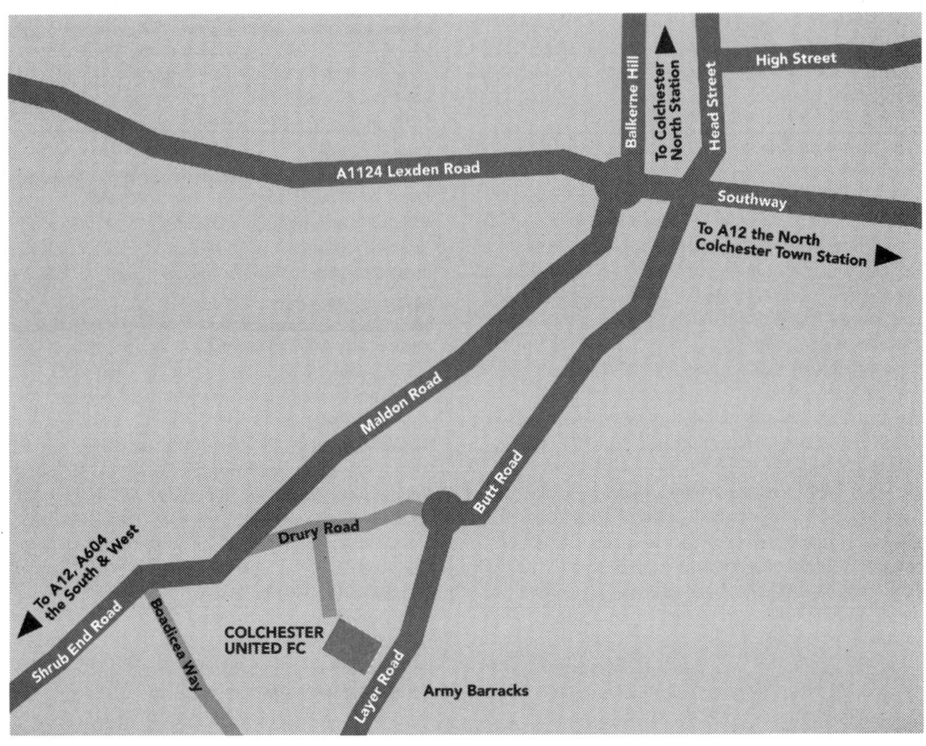

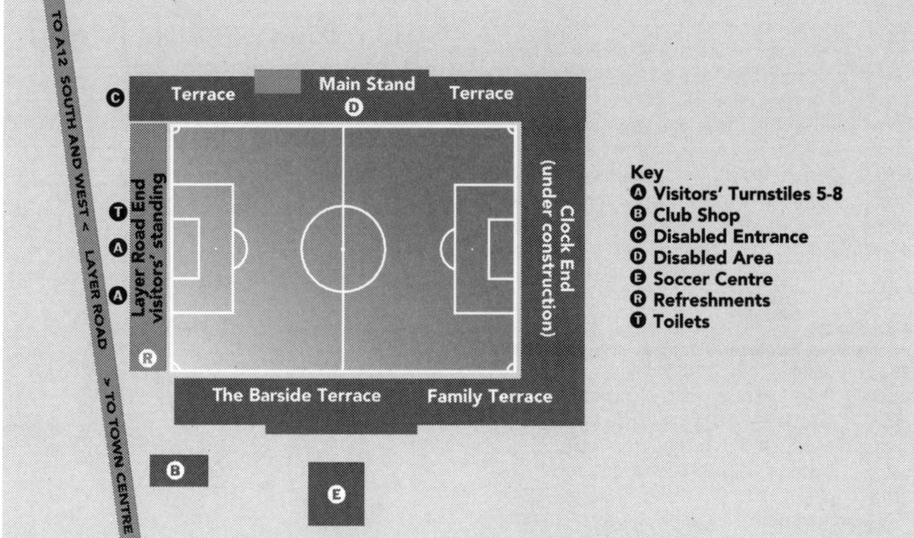

station to the first stop in the High Street. Walk back against the traffic flow and turn left at T-junction into Head Street. At crossroads turn into either St John's Street or Crouch Street for 'Eastern National' bus nos. 64 or 64A to the ground. *By foot:* Turn right out of station, down to main road, turn right. 2nd exit at roundabout (s/p Clacton A133) and 2nd exit at next roundabout (by 'The Albert' s/p Town Centre) into Station Road. Walk up hill, straight on at junction up North Hill and into Head Street. Take subway under the dual carriageway into Butt Road. At top of road, turn left by the 'Drury Arms' into Layer Road.

FROM RAILWAY STATION (Colchester Town, stopping trains from London, and on the Colchester North to Clacton line): 1.2 miles. *By foot:* Come out of station and take subway under roundabout. Take the third exit into Southway, the road to the left of the light-coloured 'Gala' building. Walk along Southway and turn left at lights into Butt Road. At top of road, turn left by the 'Drury Arms' into Layer Road. *Last Midweek Trains:* From Colchester North, trains run to London at 21.37, 21.51, 22.06, 22.29 and 23.07 and to Ipswich at 21.47 and 22.41. Please double-check on (0345) 484 950.

PARKING

It's street parking for all. The best area is around Shrub End Road, Maldon Road, Drury Road or Layer Road itself, particularly to the south of the ground. Don't park on the army housing estate.

THE GROUND

Okay, forget all those jibes about 'terraces built by the retreating Romans' and 'Boadicea used her chariot wheels to cut the grass', as Layer Road has had a facelift. A new 750-seater stand has been built at the Clock End, the Main Stand roof's been repainted, and new barriers constructed on the Barside. For away fans, however, little has changed. They're still housed behind the goal on a narrow, covered terrace, which is also relatively shallow. For the best view, arrive early and grab the front row. The queue for the refreshment kiosk is usually long, but worth it for the excellent tea and hot dogs!

Colchester United is actively looking for a site for a new stadium, and is in discussion with the local council and consultants from Alfred McAlpine. Few other details are yet available.

Total Capacity: 7,555. For away fans: Seating (Block E, Main Stand) 200. Turnstiles 9-14. Standing (Layer Road End) 1,200. Turnstiles 5-8. Away fans are also welcome in the Family Stand, through reciprocal arrangements with the away club. No tickets are available on the day.

Cost (98/99): Terrace: Adults £7, concessions (Juniors/OAPs) £4.50; Seating: £9/£6. Family Enclosure: Terrace: Adults £6, concessions £2.50; Seating £7/£3.50.

Disabled Facilities: Space for 10 wheelchairs in an enclosure at pitch level (Block A, Main Stand). *Disabled Toilet:* Behind Main Stand. *Cost:* £9 for disabled, free for a helper. *Booking:* Preferable. *Parking:* Only one space available. *For the Blind:* Two seats with hospital radio commentary.

Programme: £1.50.

Visitors' Toilets: *Male:* Know the expression, 'Room for a little 'un?' The answer here is 'No'! However, it was

very clean. *Female:* Just one cubicle, clean with a tiny sink and grafitti proclaiming that Doncaster Rovers were two up at half-time in season 93/94. It doesn't happen very often, so Rovers fans remember it well!

Food and Drink: Just hot dogs (£1) and burgers (£1.80), served from a tiny kiosk more suited to a Buckingham Palace guardsman! The burgers were 'all reet', but the hot dogs got rave reviews: 'Excellent, this is my third one', 'Better than Darlo's'. The tea (60p), with add-your-own-real-milk, was good and there was what one fan called 'Uri Geller bovril' ... so hot that the plastic stirrer-stick developed a definite kink! (21.10.97, 3.4.98).

PUB GUIDE

The Sun Lexden Road (01206) 574 327
Carlsberg-Tetley (with four real ales). Attractive pub in a 400-year-old building, and serving bar lunches. Pool room, TV, table football in beer garden. Families welcome. Open: all day weekends; from 5 pm for midweek games.

The Goat and Boot 70 East Hill (01206) 867 466
Greene King. Cosy, friendly pub in a 15th century building. Breakfast and bar snacks served 11-2. Pool table, darts, patio, TV. Open: all day weekends; from 6 pm for midweek games.

The Odd One Out 28 Mersea Road (off the roundabout by Colchester Town station) (01206) 578 140
Free House (with five guest beers, 50 malt whiskys and nine Irish whiskys). Small characterful real-ale house in an 18th century building. Beer garden. Open: all day weekends; from 4.30 pm for midweek games.

Also recommended: **The Albert,** Cowdray Avenue, near Colchester North station, a smart Whitbread-Beefeater, ideal for a family meal.

FOOD GUIDE

The only outlet near the ground is a corner shop selling sandwiches, crisps and the like, so for a greater choice, head into town. Butt Road has a Balti takeaway, while the High Street has the main chain restaurants. Those alighting at Colchester Town railway station can turn right into St Botolph's Street, which has a 'Southern Fried Chicken' (meals at £3); the 'Istanbul Delight' kebab house; and a café serving a three-course lunch for £4.45. Turn right at the end of the road into East Hill for the 'Food on the Hill' café-restaurant, with home-cooked meals from £2.50-£7; 'Pizza Galore' and the 'Sonali' Indian takeaway.

LOCAL MEDIA

Local Radio: SGR 96.1 FM; BBC Radio Essex 103.5, 95.3 FM, 1530 AM.

Radio Phone-Ins: BBC Radio Essex may do a phone-in during season 98/99, listen out for details.

LEFT RIGHT, LEFT RIGHT..
eagle

With the army barracks nearby, Colchester's pre-match warm up is a little unusual.

Saturday Sports Paper: None.

MISCELLANEOUS

Safety Factor: In 61 AD the away contingent (Boadicea United) burnt Colchester to a cinder. Things have been quieter recently, but visiting supporters should take care on derby days.

Rivals: Colchester swapped divisions with Southend, so again no league fixtures between the traditional rivals. Ipswich, Wycombe, Barnet and Gillingham also feature.

Fanzines: 'The Blue Eagle', 22 Silverdale Avenue, Westcliff, Essex, SS0 9BA.

Unofficial Websites:
TBE: http://wkweb5.cableinet.co.uk/skinners/
http://home1.swipnet.se/~w-16281/
Good Swedish site:
http://www.angelfire.com/ny/ColchesterUnited/

Tourist Information: (01206) 282 920.

Coventry City

Highfield Road

Address: Highfield Road Stadium, King Richard Street, Coventry, CV2 4FW
Telephone: Club (01203) 234 000
Ticket Office (01203) 234 020
Ticket Information Line (0891) 121 166
ClubCall (0891) 121 166
Official Website: http://www.ccfc.co.uk/

Coventry City's ground as a World Cup venue? Don't laugh ... the club has announced ambitious plans for a new £60 million, 40,000-seater stadium with retractable pitch and roof, to be built out near the M6. It would certainly be among the front runners, should England's bid to stage the 2006 World Cup prove successful. If all goes to plan, the new ground will be open for season 2001/02. The present ground, Highfield Road, is in a residential area about a mile from the centre of Coventry, and a real trek from the railway station. Finding a café and/or a drink is relatively easy, as there are two nearby local shopping areas: Far Gosford Street and Ball Hill.

HOW TO GET THERE

BY CAR: From North and East (M6): Exit M6 at junction 3 and at roundabout follow signs to 'Coventry, Holbrooks A444' onto the A444 dual carriageway. Follow 'City Centre A444' signs for 3.2 miles over four roundabouts to a 5th roundabout. Here, turn right (s/p Industrial Estate, Barras Heath Wholesale Market, Stoke, Football Stadium) into Waterman Road. At next roundabout after 0.2 miles turn left (s/p Football Stadium) into Swan Lane. At roundabout after 0.4 miles, take 2nd exit (no signpost) into Nicholls Street, which leads to the ground.

From South and East (M40): Exit M40 at junction 15 (s/p Warwick A429, Stratford, Coventry A46) and at roundabout follow signs to 'Coventry A46' onto the A46 northbound. At roundabout after 11.1 miles turn right (s/p Motorway M69, Leicester A46) onto the A4082 London Road. At roundabout after 0.4 miles, just past Safeways, turn left (s/p Seven Stars Ind. Estate, Stoke Plant B4110) into Humber Road. At roundabout after 1.3 miles turn right (s/p Rugby A428, Stoke), and then almost immediately left (no signpost) into Kingsway. At T-junction after 0.2 miles turn left (s/p City Centre A46, Nuneaton A444) onto Walsgrave Road, and then first right into Swan Lane to ground.

FROM RAILWAY STATION (Coventry): 1.5 miles. *By taxi:* £2.60. *By bus:* Nos. 17 and 27 run to the ground. *By foot:* A complicated route, partially signposted. Exit station and head towards the Station Pharmacy and Post Office, and turn right. Straight on at crossroads into Park

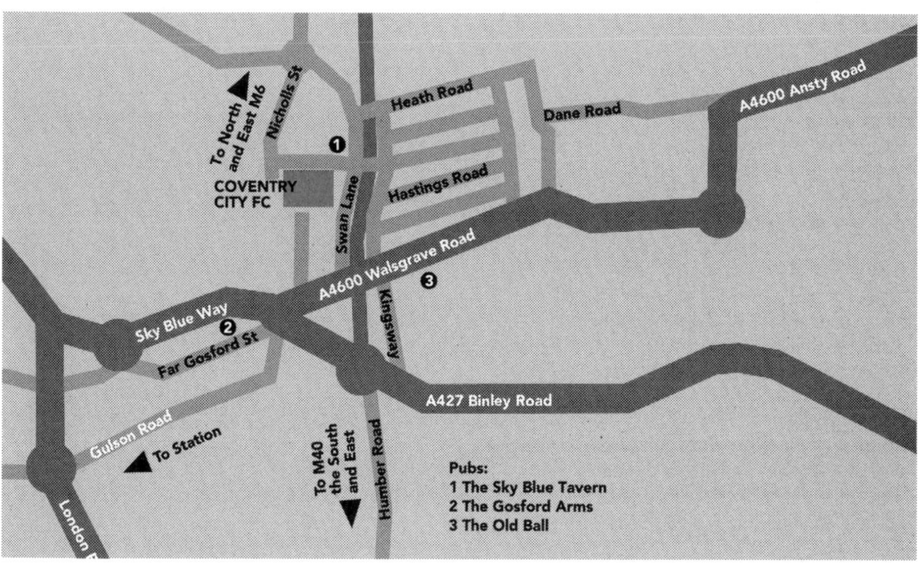

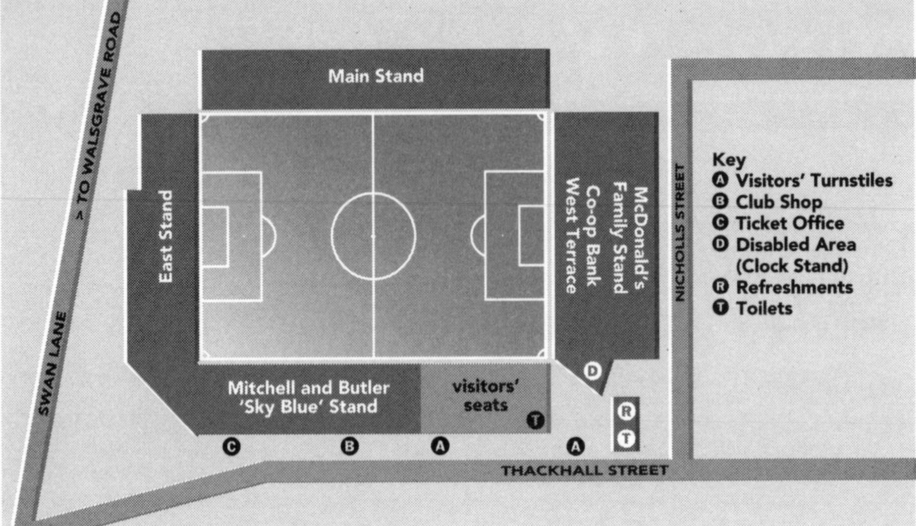

Road. At end of road, enter underpass, and in central area take 2nd exit. Follow signpost into Park Side (passing Cornercroft Engineering on the RHS) and then take first left by London Road Social Club into Paradise Street. At end of road, go left down ramp and right into underpass. Keep right, back under archway towards 'The Plough' pub. Turn left in front of pub, and then right into Gulson Road. At end of road walk diagonally right across park to Swan Lane.

Last Midweek Trains: Trains to London leave at 21.58 and 22.18; to Birmingham at 21.42, 22.00 and 22.04; and to Manchester, via Birmingham International and Crewe at 22.31. There are no trains to Peterborough, Doncaster or Newcastle after a midweek game. Please double-check on (0345) 484 950.

BY BUS: Nos. 7, 8, 32 and 33 run from Pool Meadow Bus Station along Walsgrave Road. The less frequent no. 31 runs from Trinity Street.

PARKING

There's a small shoppers' car park at Far Gosford, charging £1.60 for five hours (50p after 6 pm). Otherwise, it's street parking and not totally safe, so don't leave valuables in sight. Only the streets immediately around the ground are coned off. Try to the east of Highfield Road, eg. Hastings Road, Heath Road or Dane Road.

THE GROUND

For visiting fans, the most unusual feature of Highfield Road is the view! For a change, away supporters are housed in a side-stand, the Mitchell and Butlers, where the acoustics are excellent but the facilities generally crowded. Highfield Road is a smart, standard Premiership ground, with a total capacity of 23,600, deemed by many as simply too low to support a top-level team. A massive redevelopment of the ground is difficult, as it's hemmed in by terraced homes and roads on all sides. So, in November 1997 club chairman Bryan Richardson announced plans for a new super-stadium, to be built on land presently occupied by the Foleshill gasworks, out near the M6. The architects say they have studied, and improved on, the new ground at Vitesse Arnhem, to create a fully-enclosed stadium suitable for staging other sports, exhibitions and concerts, as well as football matches ... indeed, Mr Richardson has described it as the city's 'first landmark project since the building of the Cathedral'! There will be parking for 6,000 cars and hopefully a new railway station. Highfield Road is expected to be sold for housing.

Total Capacity: 23,627. For away fans: Seating (Mitchells and Butlers Stand) 4,148. Entrance via turnstiles in Thackhall Street.

Cost (98/99): Adults: £20. Concessions (juniors/OAPs £10), available on a reciprocal basis, must be bought in advance.

Disabled Facilities: Space for 24 visiting fans in a purpose-built stand between the away section and the Family Stand. *Disabled Toilet:* In stand. *Cost:* £5 for disabled, £11 for helper. *Booking:* Through the ticket office. *Parking:* Some space available, please book. *For the Blind:* 12 seats with headsets in the Clock Stand.

Programme: £2.

Visitors' Toilets: *Male:* NB, one block by the Family Stand, one under the stand. By the Family Stand, the facilities were clean and spacious, with hot and cold

'We've just had an argument and she's sent me to Coventry – suits me!'

water, mirrors, and stewards directing fans in and out! The ones under the stand can get very crowded.
Female: Clean, with 'decent washbasins' and plenty of loo paper and towels.
Food and Drink: A supporter described the chicken-and-mushroom pie (£1.55) as 'gloopy', meaning it was mostly sauce with 'nowhere near enough chicken.' The steak-and-kidney pies (£1.55) were edible but unspectacular, while the hot dogs (£2.10) were warmer before the match than at half-time. At £1, the coffee was 'reasonable' but the cola, in a large cup, cost an alarming £1.55 (29.4.98).

PUB GUIDE

The Sky Blue Tavern (1) Swan Lane (01203) 251 837
Mitchell & Butlers. Pub owned by Coventry City with separate rooms for home and away fans. TV. Entrance fee £1. Open: 12-4.30, 7-11; from 6 pm for midweek games.
The Gosford Arms (2) Far Gosford Street (01203) 632 943
Carlsberg-Tetley. Traditional local, which on matchdays, says the landlord, gets 'packed to the rafters.' Bar meals served 11-5. Pool, TV. Open: all day.
The Old Ball (3) 62 Walsgrave Road (01203) 459 016
Marstons. Traditional town pub with wooden floors and friendly matchday atmosphere. Large rolls/cobs at £3.20. Darts, table football and an L-shaped pool table. TV. Entrance fee £1. Open: all day.

FOR FAMILIES: There are a number of family pubs, including a Harvester, on the A4600, off junction 2 of the M6. To get to the ground, simply follow the A4600 into Walsgrave Road and past the 'Old Ball' pub, to the turning to Swan Lane.

FOOD GUIDE

For the best choice, head for Far Gosford Street (see map). 'Supermac's Pantry Store' sells Pukka Pies, as does the 'Devil's Kitchen' café and chip shop. Also serving takeaway food are the 'Coventry Fried Chicken' and the 'Kasra', which has pizza, burgers and vegetarian kebabs. For ethnic food, try the 'Gosford Massala' (Bangladeshi cuisine); the 'Quickstop Balti', or the 'Nawaz Balti' above the off-licence, serving good meals for about £5. The 'San Marco' Italian restaurant is more upmarket, with main meals costing about £10. Another area to try is round the 'Old Ball' pub, where there are a couple of cafés, a bakers, and two or three fish and chip shops.

LOCAL MEDIA

Local Radio: BBC Coventry and Warwickshire 94.8 FM; Mercia 97 FM; BBC Radio WM 95.6 FM.
Radio Phone-ins: BBC Coventry and Warwickshire, 1-2 pm, and to 6 pm, call (01203) 231 231; Radio WM, Friday evenings 7-9, until 6 pm on Saturdays and to 10 pm after midweek games, call (0121) 432 2000.
Saturday Sports Papers: The 'Coventry Pink', as well as the 'Sports Argus' and the 'Sporting Star'.

MISCELLANEOUS

Traditionally the team has run out to the vintage 'Sky Blue Song'. But for the last two years, it's been dumped in favour of ELO's 'Mr Blue Sky'. This has not found favour with all fans, especially as ELO are a 'Brummie group'. 'We'll never win anything again running out to that song', said one.
Safety Factor: Very few problems in 97/98.
Rivals: Coventry fans savour victories over Villa, but the dislike is not reciprocated. Leicester City, Derby County and Nottingham Forest, all now in the Premiership, are other big rivals.
Fanzines: 'Sent to Coventry', 17 Brewers Close, Binley, Coventry, CV3 2UP; 'In Dublin's Fair City', 33 Derby Road, Fallowfield, Manchester, M14 6UX.
Unofficial Websites:
http://www.netcomuk.co.uk/~cdwstc/ccfc/html
http://www.geocities.com/Colosseum/Loge/6594/
http://website.lineone.net/~stoned/
http://www.warwick.ac.uk/~cudbu/SkyBlue.html
Tourist Information: (01203) 832 303.

Crewe Alexandra

Gresty Road

Address: Gresty Road, Crewe, Cheshire, CW2 6EB
Telephone: Club (01270) 213 014
Ticket Line (01270) 252 610
ClubCall (0891) 121 647

Okay, it's time to forget all the corny puns about trains and railways. With the break-up of British Rail and the 'downsizing' of many of the new companies, fewer Crewe residents now work for the railway, and it's much less likely that the referee, linesman and the teams will be delayed by the wrong sort of leaves on the track! That said, the railway's not a bad means of transport to Crewe, as the station is just around the corner from Gresty Road. The town centre, on the other hand, is over a mile away, but few fans venture that far, preferring the numerous pubs and takeaways along the nearby Nantwich Road. The main problem for visiting supporters is actually gaining admittance to the 6,000-capacity Gresty Road, as – with the club in the First Division – most games are all-ticket.

HOW TO GET THERE

BY CAR: From North: Exit M6 at junction 17 (s/p A534 Congleton, Sandbach). At T-junction turn right (s/p Nantwich, Sandbach, Crewe) onto the A534. Follow signs to 'Crewe, Nantwich A534' through the village of Wheelock. At roundabout after Wheelock, turn right (s/p A534 Crewe, Nantwich). After 2.5 miles go straight on at roundabout (s/p Crewe Station). After a further 0.5 miles there are two roundabouts close together – go straight on at both (s/p Crewe Station) into Crewe Road. Straight over next roundabout (s/p Crewe Station) into Nantwich Road and over railway bridge. Pass station and turn first left into Gresty Road. The ground is ahead on the LHS.

From South and East: Exit M6 at junction 16 (s/p Stoke-on-Trent, Crewe A500, Nantwich). At motorway roundabout turn left (s/p Crewe A500, Nantwich). At roundabout after 2.2 miles turn right (s/p Crewe A5020). At next roundabout after 0.9 miles, turn left (s/p Crewe A5020). Follow signs to Crewe for 2.0 miles, over two roundabouts and through lights. Pass Brocklebank pub and Royal Mail building on LHS, then turn left at roundabout (s/p Nantwich A534, Crewe Station) into Nantwich Road and over railway bridge. Gresty Road is the first left after the station.

From West (from traffic lights at junction of A51 from Chester and A534 from Wrexham): Turn left if coming from Chester, or straight on if coming from Wrexham (s/p Crewe Station). Follow the signs to Crewe Station over three roundabouts, a distance of 5.9 miles, into Nantwich Road. Gresty Road is the turning

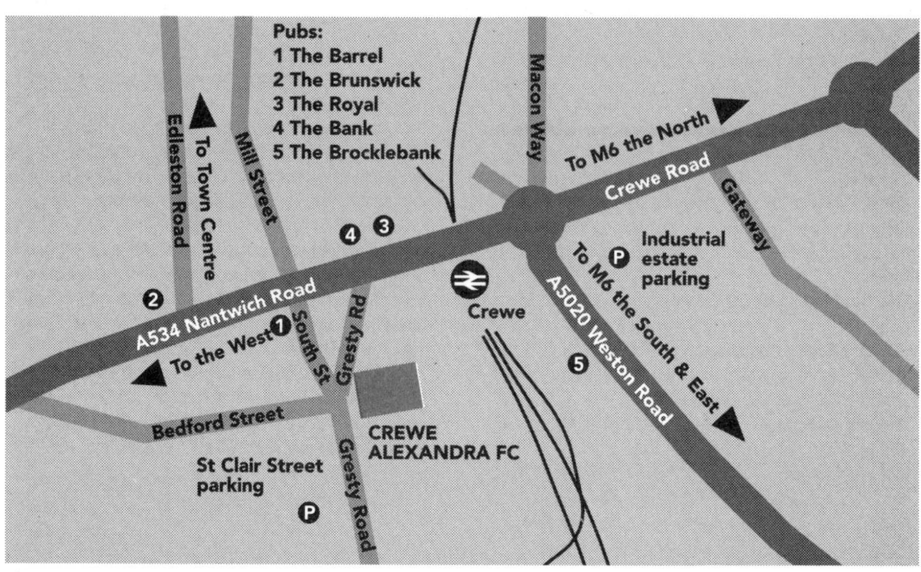

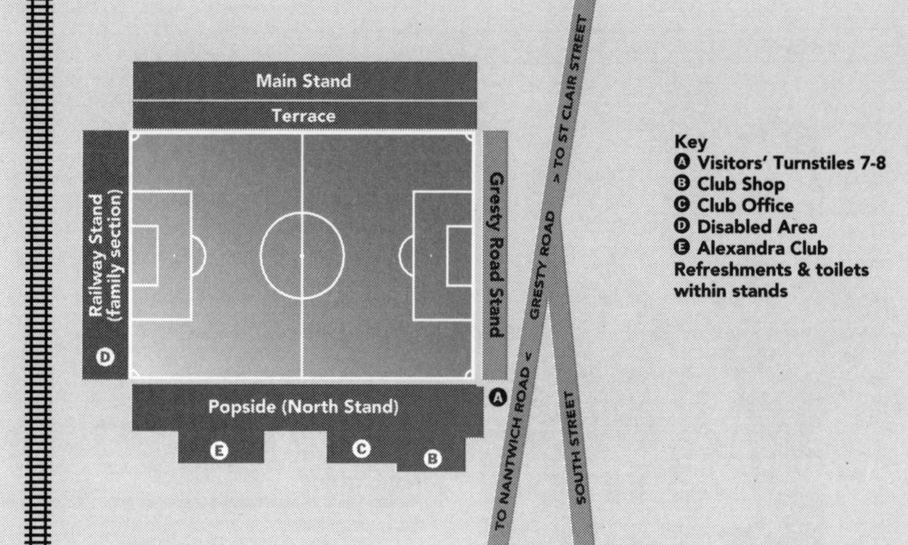

opposite the Royal Hotel, just before the station.
FROM RAILWAY STATION (Crewe): *By foot:* Turn left into Nantwich Road, then first left into Gresty Road. *Last Midweek Trains:* Trains leave to Birmingham New Street at 22.36, to Manchester Piccadilly at 23.36, to Preston at 23.50 and to Doncaster at 21.21. The last train to London, via Coventry, is at 21.03, and there are no connections to Newcastle. Please double-check on (0345) 484 950.
BY BUS: 'Arriva' bus nos. 4, 29, 39 and 44 all run near to Gresty Road.

PARKING

The best option is the industrial estate to the east of the A5020 Weston Road, opposite the Royal Mail sorting office. It's a 5-10 minute walk to the ground. Alternatively, there's a 500-600 stewarded car park in St Clair Street (£1). To get there, turn into Gresty Road and St Clair Street is the second turning on the right after the ground. There's also street parking around here, but the roads often get gridlocked before kick-off.

THE GROUND

During season 97/98, Crewe's first season in Division One, Gresty Road was simply bursting at the seams. As the team maintained its higher-level status with some ease, the club began to look at ways to expand Gresty Road, not that easy a task with roads and railway lines running along three sides of the ground. The plan now is to replace the old wooden Main Stand and Paddock with a 6,500 seater stand, almost doubling the ground's capacity overnight. However, not all of the finance is yet in place, and building work is unlikely to start in the near future. This leaves the ground with four low stands, with the Paddock as the only terrace, reserved for the home support. Away fans are housed in the Gresty Road Stand behind one of the goals, where the facilities are good. The view of play at the far end is not that great, but when the ball is in the near penalty area it's impossible to get much closer to the action anywhere in the league!
Total Capacity: 5,759. For away fans: 981.
Cost (98/99): Adults £13.50, concessions (OAPs £10.50, juniors £6) available on a reciprocal basis.
Disabled Facilities: Space for ten visiting supporters in an area at pitch level at the Gresty Road End. *Disabled Toilet:* At junction of the Gresty Road End and the Ringway Stand. *Cost:* Joint ticket for disabled and helper costs £10.50. *Booking:* Essential, through ticket office. *Parking:* Limited space available. Please contact Mr Cliff Simpson at the club. *For the Blind:* Ten seats in the Family Stand with hospital radio commentary.
Programme: £1.80.
Visitors' Toilets: *Male:* Smelt as clean as they looked, even at half-time. One enthusiastic fan said the hot air dryer worked 'beautifully'. The only gripe was that the queues were long. That said, the ramblings of the tannoy announcer, relayed by a loudspeaker in the toilet block, kept fans 'entertained'! *Female:* Well, female fans might as well stand up, grab a loudspeaker and yell: 'I'm off to the loo then', as the route to the facilities is right along the front of the away stand! Once there, though, visiting Charlton supporters tried to find a problem with locks, dryers or paper, but couldn't!
Food and Drink: 'Good value', 'faultless' and 'a pie eater's heaven' were three supporters' comments on the Crewe refreshments. The steak-and-kidney pie

'Every time you blow that whistle, a train pulls out of the station.'

(£1.30) was the tastiest, although it fell apart easily, making for messy eating! The cheese-and-onion pie (£1.30) was deemed unusual for having 'both cheese and onion in it!' Many fans went back for a second hot dog (£1.80), while the 'traditional pastie' (£1.30) was 'worth buying just for the pastry'. Tea, coffee and hot chocolate (all a bargain 60p) were more palatable than at most grounds where they cost twice as much (21.3.98 and 7.3.98).

PUB GUIDE

All local pubs are likely to shut after big matches (e.g., Port Vale, Sheffield United, Birmingham, Wolves and Sunderland).

The Barrel (1) 38 Nantwich Road (01270) 213 471
Tetley (with Kilkenny). Recently refurbished – 'now even more of an American-style bar' according to the landlord! Pool, big-screen TV. Families welcome. Open: all day from 12.

The Brunswick (2) 71 Nantwich Road (01270) 214 951
Whitbread (with Boddingtons, Trophy and one guest beer). Large and friendly pub, with an upstairs bar and big-screen TV, ideal for a pre-match drink. Pool. Open: all day, but may be shut right after the game.

The Royal (3) Nantwich Road (opposite junction of Gresty Road) (01270) 257 398
Free House, serving John Smiths, Websters, Beamish Red. Very popular on matchdays – bouncers on door. Sandwiches served before the match. TV. Open: all day.

The Bank (4) Nantwich Road (01270) 501 122
Banks's. Recently opened pub, already popular on matchdays. Reasonably priced meals served 12-2.30. Families welcome. TV. Beer garden. Open 12-3, 5-11.

FOR FAMILIES:

The Brocklebank (5) Weston Road (01270) 212 432
Whitbread/Brewer's Fayre. Large pub ideal for family meals, with extensive menu including children's options. Children's play area. Popular on matchdays – for some big games there are doormen who only let in families. Food served 11.30 am-10 pm. Open: all day.

The Old Manor Nantwich Road (01270) 662 326
Bass. Large, smart pub/restaurant. Good variety of meals, including children's menu. Separate building housing 'Deep Sea Den' play area with a slide, climbing area, games machines (entrance fee £1). Also outdoor play area and beer garden. Disabled facilities. Open: 12-11 (restaurant 12-9).

FOOD GUIDE

On Gresty Road itself is the 'Fish and Chip Stop', opposite the away turnstiles, which has been recommended over many years, and is therefore very popular. Nantwich Road offers an abundance of choice, including Chinese, kebab, burger and pizza takeaways. Crewe fans particularly recommend the 'Salt and Vinegar' chippie, on the corner of Mill Street and Nantwich Road, which is both a takeaway and restaurant.

LOCAL MEDIA

Local Radio: BBC Radio Stoke 94.6 FM; Signal Radio 96.4 and 102.6 FM.
Radio Phone-Ins: BBC Radio Stoke 'Praise or Grumble', Saturdays 5-6 pm. Call (01782) 208 008.
Saturday Sports Paper: The 'Green 'Un' (27p).

MISCELLANEOUS

Safety Factor: Gresty Road is a safe place to watch football. The police say that the biggest recent problem was against Kidderminster in the cup in 96/97.
Rivals: 'The Clayheads' from the Potteries: 'Joke City' and 'Port Fail'. The rivalry, particularly with Stoke, intensified in season 97/98, with Crewe in Division One.
Fanzine: None.
Unofficial Websites:
'Extravaganza': http://www.crewealex.u-net.com/
'Blue Moon Rising':
http://ourworld.compuserve.com/homepages/steelea/
Tourist Information: (01270) 610 983.

Crystal Palace

Selhurst Park

Address: Selhurst Park Stadium, London, SE25 6PU
Telephone: Club (0181) 768 6000
Ticket Office (0181) 771 8841
Selhurst Club Shop (0181) 768 6100
Croydon Club Shop (0181) 680 3468
ClubCall (0891) 400 333
Official Website: http://www.cpfc.co.uk

If aliens ever came to Earth and wanted to take back a 'classic south London suburb', they'd gouge out the square mile round Selhurst Park. Hurrah, say those who'd not miss the horrendous Saturday traffic jams, the annoying pay-and-display parking and the run-down shops of Thornton Heath High Street. Oh no, say the rest of us, as this can be a classic day out, with an excellent selection of friendly pubs and some top-rate chippies. And as suburbs go, South Norwood and Selhurst are pleasant enough, with neat terraced housing and well-kept blocks of flats. Selhurst Park is one of the most difficult clubs to reach by road, so the very best advice is – take the train.

HOW TO GET THERE

BY CAR: From South and West (M25): Exit M25 at junction 7 (s/p M23 Croydon, Gatwick), then follow signs to 'M23 Croydon' onto the M23. After 1.7 miles, the road becomes the A23 with two-way traffic, into the suburb of Hooley. Follow signs for 'Central London A23' for 8.5 miles (through the suburb of Coulsden, around the Purley Cross junction, along Purley Way, over a bridge, over a flyover, round a roundabout, past the Frank Watson Ford Garage) to an unsignposted T-junction by the Horseshoe pub where all traffic turns left. Here, keep in right-hand lane, following signs to 'Croydon A235' and passing the Plough and Harrow pub and the Bakers Oven, then turn left (no signpost) just after Barclays Bank and before Connells Estate Agents, into Brigstock Road. After 0.8 miles, by the clock tower and the Prince of Wales pub, follow the road round to the right into Thornton Heath High Street. At roundabout after 0.3 miles turn left (s/p Norwood B266, Crystal Palace) into Whitehorse Lane. Ground is on RHS after 0.3 miles.

From North and East (M25): Exit M25 at junction 4 (s/p Bromley A21, Orpington A224), and follow signs to Bromley A21 onto the A21. Follow signs to 'Croydon A232' for 4.7 miles over four roundabouts, to junction/lights by Chapter One Restaurant and Bar. Here, fork left (s/p Croydon, Sutton A232) onto the A232. Keep following 'Croydon A232' signs for a further 5.1 miles over three roundabouts to fourth roundabout by Trinity School. Here, turn right (s/p Croydon, Sutton

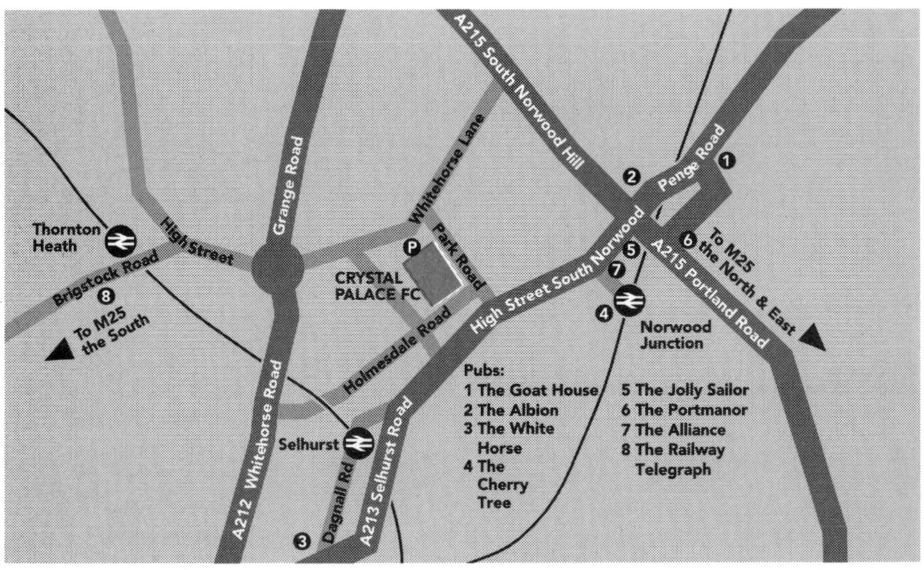

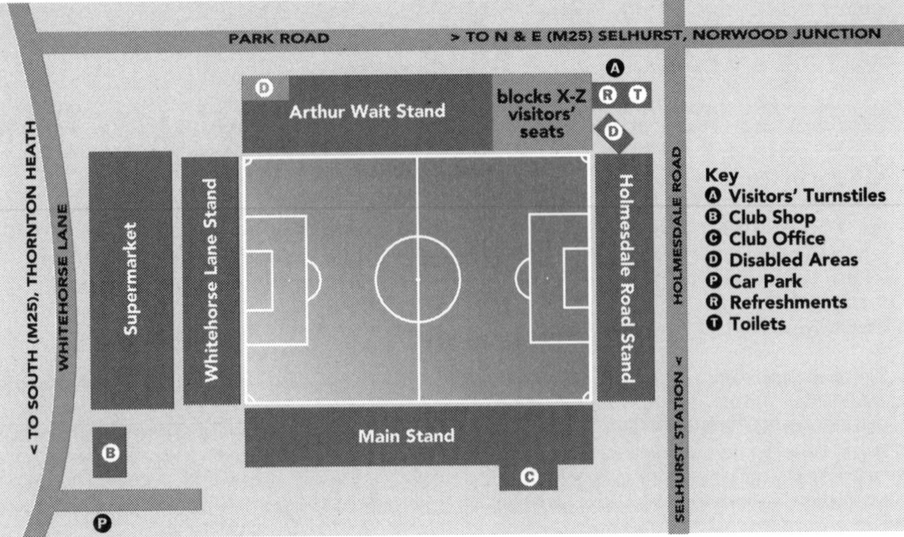

A232) onto the A215 Shirley Road. Straight over roundabout after 0.2 miles (s/p Norwood A215, Addiscombe (A222)) to T-junction after 0.6 miles in front of Ashburton Park. Here, turn right (s/p Beckenham A222, South Norwood) into Addiscombe Road. After 0.2 miles turn left (s/p South Norwood A215, Crystal Palace (A212)) into Spring Lane. At T-junction after 0.3 miles turn right (s/p Central London, South Norwood) into Portland Road. Straight on for 0.8 miles, passing the 'Portmanor' pub and under the railway, then turn left at lights/crossroads (s/p Croydon Town Centre, Selhurst A213) into South Norwood High Street. After 0.4 miles turn right at lights into Park Road.

FROM RAILWAY STATIONS: Trains to Thornton Heath and Selhurst run from Victoria, to Norwood Junction from Victoria and London Bridge. All are marked on the map.

Last Midweek Trains: Trains from Selhurst to London (via Thornton Heath) run until 23.18. Trains from South Norwood run until 23.23. Tip: If heading back to London, go to Selhurst Park station. The train fills up there, leaving little space for those waiting at Thornton Heath.

BY BUS: The main routes are the 68A, 75, 157, 196 plus nos. 50, 198, 412 and X68.

PARKING

The car park at the ground fills up quickly, so for most it's street parking. The best area is round Selhurst station (eg Edith Road and Dagnall Park). The roads in Thornton Heath are mostly pay-and-display. It's not expensive, but some allow only two hours' parking. After 5 pm, however, it's usually free.

THE GROUND

'If you sit in the Main Stand, Selhurst Park doesn't look bad at all!' said one Palace fan. In other words, the view would be of the excellent two-tier Holmesdale Road Stand, opened in 1995; the smaller Whitehorse Lane Stand with its executive boxes; and the much older Arthur Wait Stand. Palace fans have admired the new stadiums at Derby and Bolton ... 'clubs about our size' ... and feel that improvements at Selhurst are overdue. They don't have that long to wait, as the club is planning to replace the Main Stand in the summer of 1999. Away fans are allocated sections of the Arthur Wait Stand. The steps are shallow, so fans stand-sit-stand-sit every thirty seconds or so. If it's not raining, head for the seats near the front.

Total Capacity: 26,309. For away fans: 2,945 in blocks X-Z in the Arthur Wait Stand.

Cost (98/99): Adult £20, concessions (juniors/OAPs): £12. Fans have to buy their tickets first from the ticket office, and then queue again at Turnstile Block 4 to get in.

Disabled Facilities: Space for 15 visiting fans in Blocks R-S, half-way up the Arthur Wait Stand, plus extra space in the new Holmesdale Road Stand. *Disabled Toilet:* In both stands. *Cost:* Free for disabled, half-price for helper. *Booking:* Essential. *Parking:* In Sainsbury's car park, on first-come, first-served basis. *For the Blind:* 20 seats with hospital radio commentary.

Programme: £2.

Visitors' Toilets: *Male:* The sinks were dirty, but fans had seen a lot worse. *Female:* The smartest bits were the red louvered entry doors! After that it went downhill

... cold water, no soap, and lots of paper towels in the basins.

Food and Drink: Wow, excellent vegetarian food, including tasty cheese-and-onion and vegetarian pasties (£1.40). Overall the choice was good, with chips (£1, 'quite tasty'), burgers (£2 'cold, not nice'), pies (£1.40), sausage rolls (£1.20), and 'Britain's No 1 Hot Dog' (£2). Really? Yes, said some: 'tasty and well cooked'. No, said others: 'I'm sorry I bought it now. I wish I'd had the pie!' (8.11.97)

PUB GUIDE

The Goat House (1) 2 Penge Road (0181) 778 5752 Fullers. Large, super-football-friendly pub, with 'new low prices' on the beer and the bar meals, served all day. Big-screen TV, pool table, darts. Family room. Disabled facilities. Open: all day.

The Albion (2) 26 High Street (0181) 653 0558 Entrepreneur/Courage. Friendly traditional locals pub. Bar snacks served all day. Big-screen TV, pool, darts, patio. Families welcome. Open: all day.

The White Horse (3) 1 Selhurst Road, South Norwood (0181) 684 4498

Courage. Large traditional pub with a good family atmosphere. Full menu served 12-2. Big-screen TV, pool, beer garden, car park. Open: all day.

Also recommended: **The Cherry Trees (4),** an immensely popular Courage pub; **The Jolly Sailor (5),** a friendly Charringtons/Bass pub; **The Portmanor (6),** a Courage pub with an upstairs à la carte menu (call on (0181) 655 1308); **The Alliance (7)** a top-rate traditional Courage pub; **The Railway Telegraph (8)** 19 Brigstock Road, a highly recommended Youngs pub, serving French sticks/batches.

FOOD GUIDE

South Norwood and Thornton Heath high streets are lined with cafés and takeaways, so the following are just the highlights. On South Norwood High Street, near the station, is the recommended 'Norwood Fish and Chips'; and the Italian-run 'Piccolo' sandwich and pasta bar. On Thornton Heath High Street is a new café/takeaway called 'Bistro Laz', and the more traditional 'George's Palace', both offering all-day breakfasts. Near the ground in Whitehorse Lane is a new 'Doneagles' fish-and-chip restaurant and takeaway, and the ever-popular 'Lap Hing' takeaway. Fans arriving at Selhurst station should head for the excellent 'Tastys' by the station on Selhurst Road.

LOCAL MEDIA

Local Radio: Palace has its own matchday radio station on 1278 AM. Otherwise it's Capital Gold 1548 AM; GLR 94.9 FM; XFM 104.9.

Radio Phone-ins: Capital Gold, Saturdays 5-6.30 pm; midweek every night 7-8 or after live match

'I thought we had signed LOMBARDO...'

commentary. Call (0845) 35 60 70 80.

Saturday Sports Paper: None.

MISCELLANEOUS

One arrival in 1997 topped all others in the 'such a god can't possibly be playing for Palace' stakes: Lombardo. It gave rise to a new song, invented by the 'One More Point' team, to the tune of the 'Just One Cornetto' advert: 'Just one Lombardo, Give him to me, He's from Juventus, In Italy, He's got no hair, But we don't care, We've got Lombardo, From Italy.' It premiered to rapturous applause.

Safety Factor: Selhurst Park is generally safe and it's fine to wear colours outside the ground. Be more cautious at higher profile/derby matches.

Rivals: A 'One More Point' fanzine reader survey listed the club's rivals as Brighton, Manchester United and Millwall. There were no votes for Arsenal.

Fanzines: 'One More Point', 111G Selhurst Road, Selhurst, SE25 6LH; 'Palace Echo', PO Box 6172, London, SW11 2XP.

Unofficial Websites:
http://www.palace-eagles.com/
'SE25 Internet Fanzine':
http://members.tripod.com/~SE25/
'Tony's Web Pages':
http://www.netlink.co.uk/users/tonyd/cp_home.htm
'CP-FRIS': http://www.mite.net/rayb.cpfris/eagles/htm

Tourist Information: Croydon (0181) 253 1009.

D

Darlington

Feethams

Address:
Feethams Ground, Darlington DL1 5JB
Telephone: Club (01325) 465 097
Quaker Hotline (0891) 101 555
Official Website:
http://www.darlingtonfc.force9.co.uk

'Darlington is not your typical grim up-north place', said one Darlo fan, settling back happily in one of the many excellent town centre pubs. Indeed it's not. Although it's only fifteen minutes' drive from Middlesbrough, Darlington might as well be on another planet. It's a small market town, with many wide, tree-lined streets, cafés and sports-friendly hostelries. Feethams is just the other side of the inner ring road, next to the cricket ground. All in all, this is a classic lower division stress-free away trip: simply park up early, head into town for lunch and a leisurely pint, then amble back along the river, over the footbridge to the away turnstiles.

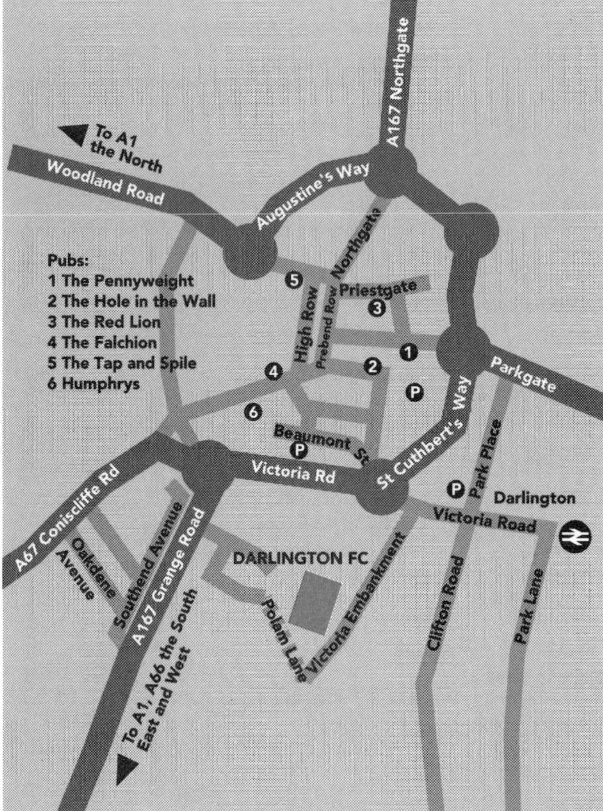

HOW TO GET THERE

BY CAR: From South (A1(M)): Exit A1(M) at junction 57 (s/p Darlington, Teesside A66(M)) onto the A66(M). At roundabout after 2.4 miles go straight on (s/p Darlington, Teesside A66), continuing on A66 and over River Tees. At next roundabout after 0.8 miles, by Nissan garage, take 2nd exit (s/p Darlington A167) into Grange Road. (*)At Grange Road Roundabout, by Safeway, after 1.1 miles turn right (s/p Durham A167, The North A1(M)), into Victoria Road. Down hill to 'Feethams Roundabout', where there's a choice for parking (see below).

From North (A1(M)): Exit A1(M) at junction 58 (s/p Corbridge, Darlington A68). At roundabout turn left (s/p Darlington A68). Follow signs to 'Darlington A68', and then 'Town Centre A68' for 2.8 miles over three roundabouts, and past the Memorial Hospital, to a mini-roundabout at the end of Woodland Road. Here, turn left (s/p A1(M), Durham A167) into St Augustines Way (the inner ring road). At next three roundabouts (the 'Northgate', 'Freeman's Place' and 'Parkgate' roundabouts), a total of 0.8 miles, follow signs to Northallerton A167. At 'Feethams Roundabout', there's a choice for parking (see below).

From East/Middlesbrough (A66): Keep on A66 to first roundabout. Here turn left (s/p The South A1(M), Scotch Corner A66, Darlington South), onto the A66 Darlington By-Pass. For the next 5.0 miles follow signs to 'The South A1(M), Scotch Corner', over two roundabouts, remaining on the A66. At third roundabout take 5th exit (s/p Darlington A167) into Grange Road. Then as From South (A1(M))(*).

FROM RAILWAY STATION: *By taxi:* It's such a short distance, taxis should

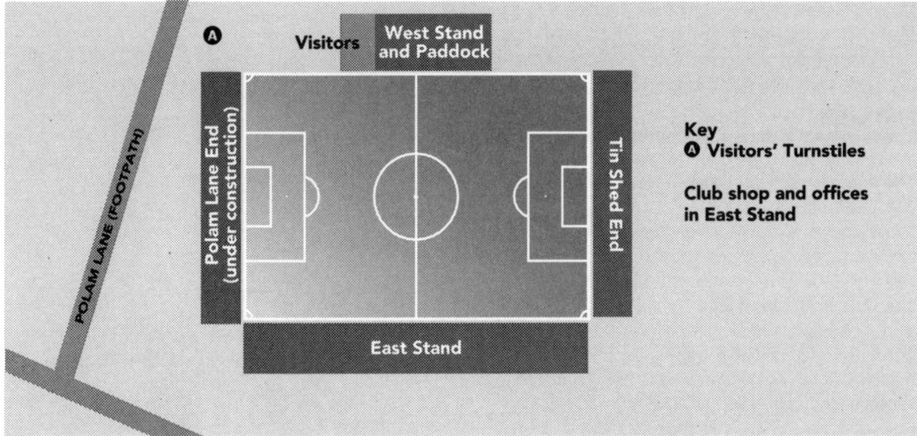

charge the minimum of £1. Ask to be dropped off at the end of Victoria Embankment. *By foot:* From platform, follow pedestrian signs to Feethams and Victoria Road through underpass into Victoria Road, passing Hogans on the LHS. At roundabout at end of Victoria Road, turn left into Victoria Embankment, which runs along River Skerne. The road ends after 0.2 miles at South Park. Here, turn right over footbridge to away turnstiles. *Last Midweek Trains:* The last train to London leaves at 21.07. However, there are trains to Newcastle at 21.26, 22.31 and 00.40, and to Manchester, at 22.10. Please double-check on (0345) 484 950.

BY BUS: NE Bus Company nos. X27, 29 and 74, and Stagecoach bus no. 23 run to the ground.

PARKING

There's street parking in the area of Southend Avenue and Oakdene Avenue (see map).

Other parking options are signposted off 'Feethams Roundabout'. The signpost 'Short Stay Car Parks' leads to the town centre car parks, immediately on the RHS. Both the 'Beaumont Street' car parks cost £2.40 for 4 hours, £3 for 5 hours. Both are free after 6 pm. The 'Long Stay' car parks are towards the station. There's a small, free car park on Victoria Road, and a bigger pay-and-display car park on Park Place. The car park at the station costs £2.

THE GROUND

The arrival of new Chief Executive and Darlo fan Mike Pedan in the summer of 1997 heralded a new era at Feethams. In autumn 1997, the old East Stand was demolished, and a new £2.2 million stand, seating 3,500, is nearing completion. It will contain a supporters' bar, a restaurant, conference facilities and nine executive boxes. The next stage, starting in the autumn of 1998, will see the demolition of the Polam Lane End (the South Terrace, which traditionally accommodated away fans) and the construction of a new covered terrace with space for 2,000 home supporters and 1,000 visitors. And yes, this does mean the demolition of the worst toilets in the football league! There are plans eventually to replace the West Stand, but the Tin Shed, a favourite home terrace, will remain sacrosanct.

While the Polam Lane End is rebuilt, away fans are to be accommodated in the West Stand and West Stand paddock.

Total Capacity: Between 5,000-6,000 while building work continues. When complete, 9,850. For away fans (until new Polam Lane Stand opens): 500 seats in West Stand, 150 standing in West Stand paddock.

Cost (97/98): Seating: Adult £11, concessions (juniors/OAPs) £6. Paddock: Adult £8, concessions £5.

Disabled Facilities: Details for season 98/99 have not been finalised, but fans are likely to be housed in the West Stand paddock. *Disabled Toilet:* Nearby. *Cost:* Free for disabled and helper. *Booking:* Essential, though there's rarely a problem. *Parking:* Not available, but can drop off. Please contact club in advance. *For the Blind:* Headsets with matchday commentary.

Programme: £1.50.

Visitors' Toilets: *Male:* Tantantara!! Yes, Darlo, after years of despair, have finally won something. The highly-coveted *Football Fans Guide* MATITLA! The Most Awful Toilet in the League Award. The competition was fierce but, you better believe it, there were no close rivals to this one. That said, Darlington FC, unappreciative lot as they are, are demolishing the lot in August 1998. *Female:* Sorry, but the worst female toilet award must go elsewhere as some spoil-sport had gone round and tarted them up. Soft loo paper, soap, working locks, no fun at all.

Food and Drink: Fans said the pie and peas (£1.50) were 'brilliant', 'spot on' and 'very hot'. One supporter

thought they were also very good value 'especially as they forgot to ask me for my money'. The tea (PG Tips, 50p) was excellent, the coffee (50p) wasn't, and the lemonade tasted like washing-up liquid (18.10.97).

PUB GUIDE

The best pubs are in the town centre:
The Pennyweight (1) Bakehouse Hill, Market Square (01325) 464 244.
Vaux (with six hand-pulled ales). Top-rate traditional town-centre pub. Full menu served 11.30-2. Families welcome. TV 'always with the football on'. Open: all day.
The Hole in the Wall (2) 14 Horsemarket (opposite the Pennyweight) (01325) 466 720
John Smiths. Classic traditional town centre pub with old pictures of local pubs on the walls. Thai food and more traditional bar food served 12-2. Darts, big-screen TV. Families welcome. Open: all day from 11.30.
The Red Lion (3) Priestgate (01325) 467 619
Whitbread (with Trophy, Boddingtons and 7 real ales). A highly recommended cosy traditional pub welcoming all footie fans. Bar meals and specials served 11.45-2.15. Big-screen TV. Function room available. Open: all day.
The Falchion (4) 8 Blackwellgate (01325) 462 541
Camerons. Traditional town centre pub, with – to quote the bar staff – 'the cheapest and best food in town'. Children's meals £1.50. TV. Open: all day.
The Tap and Spile (5) 99 Bondgate (01325) 361 346
Free House (with eight constantly changing real ales). Classic real-ale house in one of the oldest buildings in Darlington. Home-cooked food served 12-2. Big-screen TV, darts, traditional pub games, no-smoking room, function room. Families welcome. Open: all day.
Also recommended: **Humphrys (6),** 43 Blackwellgate, a large modern-style pub/bar serving Vaux beers and food (12-2.30).
FOR FAMILIES:
The Bit and Bridle Neasham Road (01325) 384 467
Allied Domecq (with Speckled Hen, Tetleys). Large smart new family pub in a semi-rural location. Comprehensive 'Big Steak Menu' and children's menu served 12-10 pm. TV (not Sky), baby-changing, disabled facilities, Wacky Warehouse. Open: all day.
To get there: From the A1(M), at the roundabout by the Nissan garage, instead of turning into Grange Road, take the 3rd exit, remaining on the A66 (s/p Neasham, Hurworth). At the next roundabout, turn right and the pub is on the RHS. From the A66, turn left off the 3rd roundabout.

FOOD GUIDE

The nearest outlets to Feethams are on Victoria Road. The cheerful 'Miller's Bakery', a favourite of the Darlo youth team, serves pasties and pies (45-55p) plus hot and cold sandwiches, jacket potatoes and salad boxes.

'The only crowd trouble at Darlington can be found up in the trees!'

The 'Victoria Road Fish Bar' has pies at 80p, burgers from 55p and 'cod bites and chips' for £1.50. On the junction with 'Feethams Roundabout' is 'Café 81', a popular eaterie serving a range of fry-ups.

In town, next to the 'Pennyweight', the attractive 'Bakehouse Coffee Shop' offers main meals at £4 and a good range of snacks. 'Crombies Café', round the corner on Church Row, has an all-day 'shoppers' special' (two courses for £3.50).

LOCAL MEDIA

Local Radio: Radio Cleveland 95 FM; Century Radio 100.7. 101.8, 96.2 and 96.4 FM; TFM 96.6 FM, 1170 AM; Alpha 103.2 FM.
Radio Phone-ins: Century Radio, Monday-Friday 6-7 pm. Call (0191) 477 2000.
Saturday Sports Paper: None.

MISCELLANEOUS

Safety Factor: The only problems during season 97/98 were at local derby games.
Rivals: Hartlepool, i.e. the 'Chimp Chokers' at the 'Victoria Funeral Park'.
Fanzines: 'Mission Impossible', PO Box 232, Darlington, DL3 7YQ - the most established fanzine, and a great read; 'Where's the Money Gone?', 34 East Green, West Auckland, Bishop Auckland, DL14 9HJ; 'Darlo, It's Just Like Watching Brazil', 23 Emley Moor Road, Darlington DL1 4QQ.
Unofficial Websites:
http://www.geocities.com/Colosseum/Track/3561/index.html
Tourist Information: (01325) 382 698.

Derby County

Pride Park

Address:
Pride Park Stadium, Derby DE24 8XL
Telephone: Club (01332) 202 202.
Ticketline (0891) 332 213
Corporate Enquiries (01332) 667 538/667 589
ClubCall (01332) 121 187
Official Website: http://www.dcfc.co.uk/

For years, the huge tract of land east of Derby city centre remained closed off, contaminated by chemicals and with the odd dodgy relic from its use as an army training ground. Now, after a major clear-up operation, a huge new development is underway, with Derby's 33,000-seater stadium as the centrepiece. In season 97/98, Pride Park was the only building in a vast, flat landscape: one fan wrote that supporters heading to the game looked 'like a trail of WWII refugees on the march.' The ground's no longer so isolated and there are plans for a leisure complex right alongside Pride Park, including a soccer centre and two food outlets. That's good news for supporters, as at present the nearest pubs and restaurants are well over a mile away! The car parks for visiting fans are away from the ground, so allow time for the bus ride or the walk.

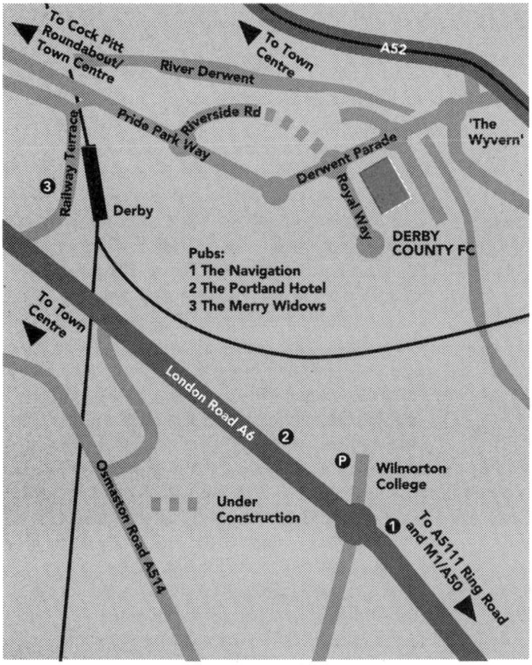

Pubs:
1 The Navigation
2 The Portland Hotel
3 The Merry Widows

HOW TO GET THERE

NB These road directions lead to one or both of the parking areas: on Megaloughton Lane and at Wilmorton College on the A6 London Road.

From M1 North and South, to both parking areas: Exit M1 at junction 25 (s/p Nottingham, Derby, Ilkeston A52) and follow signs to 'Derby A52' onto the A52.

a) To Megaloughton Lane parking: Exit M52 after 4.7 miles (s/p Spondon, Chaddesden). At roundabout take 2nd exit (n/s) into Megaloughton Lane.

b) To Wilmorton College parking: Exit M52 after 5.0 miles (s/p Ring Road A5111, Uttoxeter (A516), Burton A38) onto the A5111 Ring Road. At roundabout after 1.7 miles, by BP station, turn right (s/p City Centre A6) onto the A6 London Road. At roundabout after 1.1 miles turn right (s/p Derby Tertiary College, Wilmorton, Away Supporters) to the college.

From M1 North and South, to Wilmorton College Parking: Exit M1 at junction 24 onto the A50. Exit A50 at junction 2 (s/p Derby A6) onto new dual carriageway. (*) Exit dual carriageway after 0.3 miles (s/p Derby A6). Follow 'Derby A6' and 'City Centre A6' signs for 1.6 miles, over three roundabouts, to 4th roundabout by 'Li's Fish Bar'. Here turn left (s/p City Centre A6) onto the A6 London Road. At roundabout after 1.1 miles turn right (s/p Derby Tertiary College, Wilmorton, Away Supporters) to the college.

From South-West (A38): Exit A38 at signpost 'A50, M1 South, Uttoxeter, Stoke-on-Trent A50', and at roundabout turn right (s/p M1 South, Nottingham A50) onto the A50. Exit A50 at junction 2 after 7.2 miles (s/p Derby A6) onto new dual carriageway. Then as From M1 North and South, to Wilmorton College Parking(*).

From M6-A50 (Stoke-on-Trent): Remain on A50, which becomes the Derby Southern Bypass. Exit bypass (s/p Derby A6). Then as From M1 North and South, to Wilmorton College Parking(*).

FROM RAILWAY STATION (Derby Midland): *By taxi:* £3.50-£4. *By bus:* 'Arriva' special buses B1, B2 and B3 run to the ground at 2 pm. *By foot:* Turn right out of station into Railway Terrace. Towards end of road, with 'The

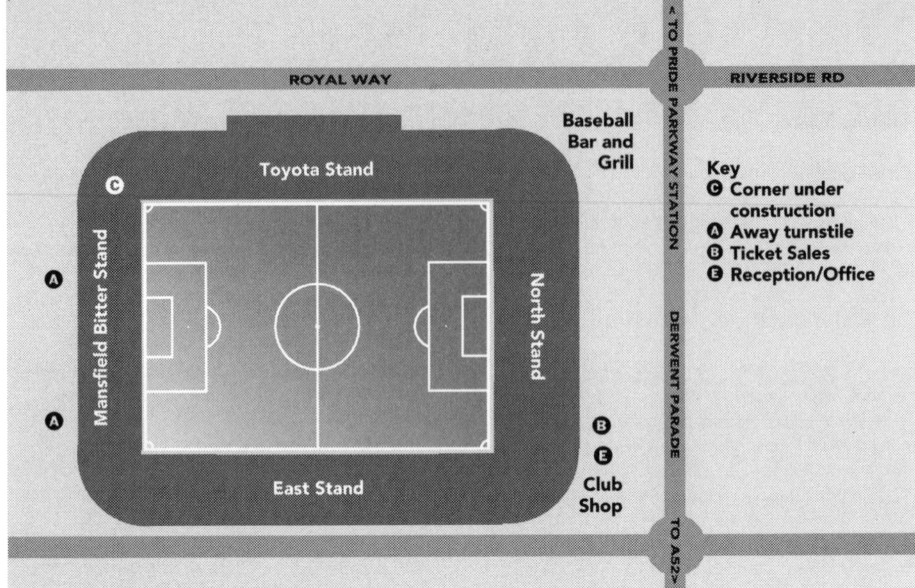

Brunswick' pub on the LHS, turn right into the white wooden passageway, and under the railway and road. Turn right following path and left or right around landscaping. The ground is visible from here.
Last Midweek Trains: There are no connections to London after a midweek game. However, the 21.52 from Derby arrives in Sheffield at 22.29, with connections to Manchester, Doncaster and Newcastle. Please double-check on (0345) 484 950.
BY BUS: Both 'Arriva' and 'Trent' buses run special services from the city centre and outlying areas of Derby. 'Trent' runs a shuttle service from the bus station.

PARKING

There are two recommended car parks for visiting fans: a 200-space Park-and-Ride scheme on Megaloughton Lane (£1), and a 600-space supervised car park at Wilmorton College (£3), from where it's a 12-15 minute walk to the ground. There's also a number of multi-storey car parks in the city centre. To get there, from the Wilburton College parking: continue on the A6 for a further 1.3 miles towards town, to major roundabout. Here, turn right (s/p Inner Ring Road, Chesterfield A61) onto the Inner Ring Road. The Eagle Centre parking is on the LHS after 0.1 miles, or continue to the Cock Pitt Roundabout after another 0.1 miles. A new multi-storey car park is under construction on the roundabout itself. For other city centre car parks, such as the 'Assembly Rooms' car park, turn left. Shuttle buses run from the bus station by the Cock Pitt Roundabout to the ground.

THE GROUND

Recipe for success: move to a new ground, buy Paolo Wanchope, and, of course, stay in the Premier League! The old Baseball Ground held fewer than 18,000. In 97/98, Derby County's first season at Pride Park, attendances averaged more than 27,000. The ground, built at a cost of around £24 million, was originally similar in design to The Riverside Stadium at Middlesbrough, with one main side-stand and the three others connected in a horseshoe. But, as at Middlesbrough, demand for tickets has been so high that the club moved quickly to increase capacity. The north-west corner was filled in by Christmas '97, with the south-west section under construction for season 98/99. Visiting fans are housed in the Mansfield Bitter Stand, behind-the-goal. The view is good, the legroom excellent and the pies are great. But the facilities – the concourses and the toilets – can be very crowded and were a mite disappointing.
Total Capacity: 33,500. For away fans: Up to 3,000.
Cost (98/99): Adults £19/£21, concessions £10/£11.
Disabled Facilities: Space for up to 30 visiting fans in the Mansfield Bitter Stand. *Disabled Toilets:* In all areas. *Cost:* Joint ticket for disabled and helper costs £15. *Booking:* Essential, call the club's Disabled Liaison Officer Ted Gascoyne on (01332) 667 531. *Parking:* Six spaces available for visiting fans. Otherwise, supporters can be dropped off at the ground. *For the Blind:* Headsets with loop system for matchday commentary.

Programme: £1.80.
Visitors' Toilets: *Male:* One fan wrote: 'A third division crowd could fit into one of these toilets. They've got the priorities right: they know that your average fan would rather p*** into a ditch than queue!' *Female:* Spacious, clean and the soap was made, so the sticker said, with 'natural coconut oil'. New grounds, don't you love 'em?
Food and Drink: The excellent hot pies (£1.50) were by far the best choice. The pasties (£1.50) were also good, but no-one liked the burgers (£2). The chips (£1.05) were crisp and very salty - 'to encourage you to drink more,' joked one Southampton supporter. The Kenco coffee (£1) was good, the Typhoo tea (90p) was hot, and the beer and lager were consumed in large quantities (13.9.97, 27.9.97, 8.2.98).

PUB GUIDE

By the Wilmorton College parking:
The Navigation (1) 805 London Road (01332) 576 941
Bass (with Caffreys, Worthington). Popular traditional pub, with a good matchday atmosphere. Sandwiches. Pool table, TV, darts, beer garden. Families welcome. Open: all day.
The Portland Hotel (2) 603 London Road (01332) 725 368
Scottish and Newcastle (with Old Speckled Hen). Friendly traditional pub with pool table, darts and TV. Bar snacks. Families welcome. No colours after the game please. Open: all day, Sundays 12-4, 7-10.30.
Opposite the station, try **The Merry Widows (3),** a small friendly pub with sporting prints on the walls.
There are two excellent pubs in the village of Spondon (see directions below). **The Prince of Wales** Chapel Street is a traditional Enterprise Inns pub, serving matchday sandwiches and operating a minibus service to the ground; **The White Swan** on Moor Street is a Tudor style Bass pub with an excellent lunch menu.

To get to Spondon: Exit M1 at junction 25 onto the A52, and exit A52 after 4.7 miles (s/p Spondon, Chaddesden). At roundabout take 1st exit (s/p Borrowash A6005, Spondon). At second mini-roundabout after 0.3 miles turn left into Willowcroft Road. At next mini-roundabout after 0.3 miles turn right into Sitwell Street. To the 'Prince of Wales', turn left in front of the 'White Swan'.

FOOD GUIDE

The only outlets within half-a-mile of Pride Park are a mobile burger bar under Pride Parkway on the way from the station, and a McDonalds on 'The Wyvern' retail park. Life for train travellers is a little easier, as opposite the station is a café called 'Caroline's Snackery and Take-Away' and the 'Station Fish Bar'.

Those travelling by car could stop off at the junction of the A5111 Ring Road and the A6. Here, try the highly

'Gary mate. Does it hurt – are you comfortable – do you need anything – can I have your season ticket?'

recommended 'Steve's Fish Bar', or 'Li's Fish Bar' just around the corner. Both serve Pukka pies. Almost next door is the 'Spice Hut' with pizzas, burgers, chicken and kebabs, but it doesn't open until 5.30 pm.

In the city centre, the Corn Market and St Peter's Street have a Deep Pan Pizza, a Pizza Hut and a McDonalds. Iron Gate towards the Cathedral has a new Pizza Express, a 'PJ Peppers' bistro (full menu from £3.55), a 'European Restaurant' (main courses about £10) and a 'Pasta Mania' (main courses £5.20).

LOCAL MEDIA

Local Radio: Ram 102.8 FM; Radio Derby 92.4, 95.3, 104.5 FM, 1116 AM; Trent FM 96.2.
Radio Phone-ins: Radio Derby, Mondays 6.05-7 pm, call (01332) 616 161.
Saturday Sports Paper: *The Derby Evening Telegraph* produces 'The Green 'Un'.

MISCELLANEOUS

Safety Factor: It's safe to wear colours except perhaps on high-profile matchdays.
Rivals: Derby fans in the pub after the game did a quick survey. Four disliked Nottingham Forest (the 'Red Dogs' or the 'Tree-huggers'), three came out against Leicester, and two against Sheffield Wednesday.
Fanzines: 'Hey Big Spender', 13 Walsham Court, Derby, DE21 4BS.
Unofficial Websites: 'RamsNet': http://easyweb-easynet.co.uk/~nickwheat/ramsnet.html
'DCFC Unofficial': http://user.aol.com/dcfcsite/dcfcsite/
http://users.aol.com/rammynet/ramstart.htm
http://www.baseley.demon.co.uk/derby/dcfcpage.html
http://www.cheme.cornell.edu/~jwillits/derby.html
Tourist Information: (01332) 255 802.

Everton

Goodison Park

Address: Goodison Park, Goodison Road, Liverpool L4 4EL
Telephone: Club (0151) 330 2200
Box Office (0151) 330 2300
Dial-A-Seat (0151) 471 8000
ClubCall (0891) 121 199
Official Website: http://195.44.47.16/

A trip to Goodison Park is ideal for the lazy! Fans can down a pint on one corner of the ground, buy a takeaway on the next, say a quick prayer at the church on the third and then amble through the turnstiles! Although the ground's a good two miles from Liverpool city centre, there's a busy shopping street nearby, a couple of pubs on Goodison Road itself, and some great chippies. Trouble at Goodison is rare, so the atmosphere is friendly. In fact for most visiting fans, the biggest headache of all is parking. For ease of mind, head for the official Stanley Park car park, or park well away from the ground.

HOW TO GET THERE

BY CAR: From South: Exit M6 at junction 21a (s/p M62 Liverpool, M57 Southport) and follow Liverpool signs onto the M62. After 10.7 miles, exit M62 at junction 6 (s/p A5080 Huyton, M57 Bootle, Southport and All Docks). At roundabout turn right (s/p M57, Southport, Prescot and Docks) onto the M57. After 5.6 miles, exit M57 at junction 4 (s/p Knowsley and Industrial Park, Bootle). At roundabout turn left (s/p Bootle, Liverpool A580) onto the A580. Pass Showcase Cinema on LHS after 1.8 miles. (*)After a further 1.9 miles, turn left (s/p Ring Road A5058, Widnes A561, Warrington) onto the A5058. At next major lights after 0.6 miles, turn right (s/p Anfield, Football Car Park, Liverpool FC, Everton FC) into Utting Avenue. After 0.7 miles, after railway bridge, turn right at crossroads/lights (opposite Hamilton House, s/p Football Car Park) into Priory Road. Car park is on LHS.
From North: Exit M6 at junction 23 (s/p Manchester,

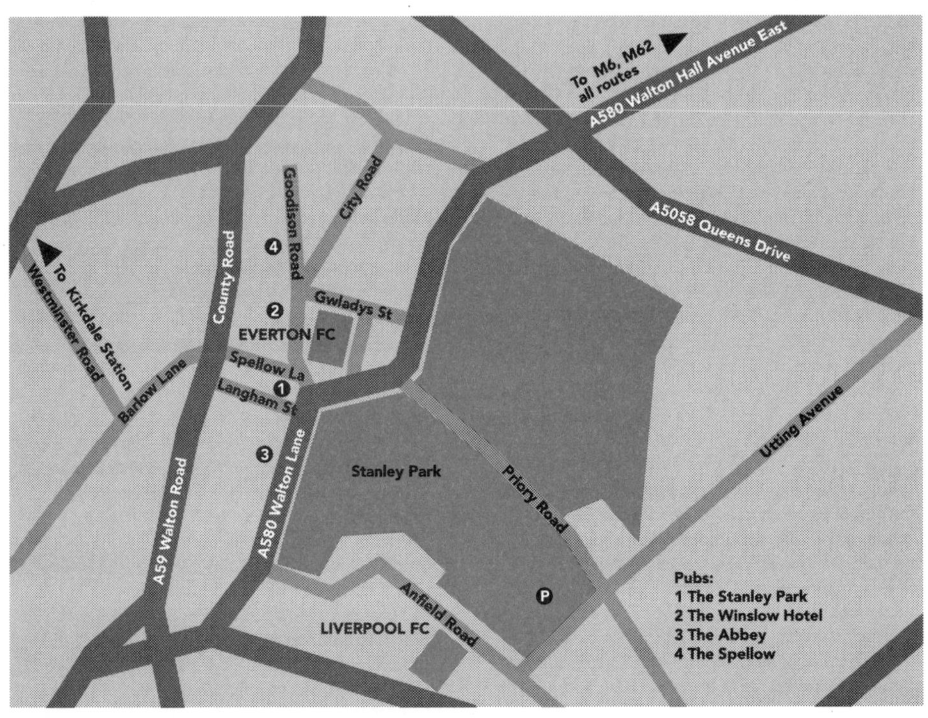

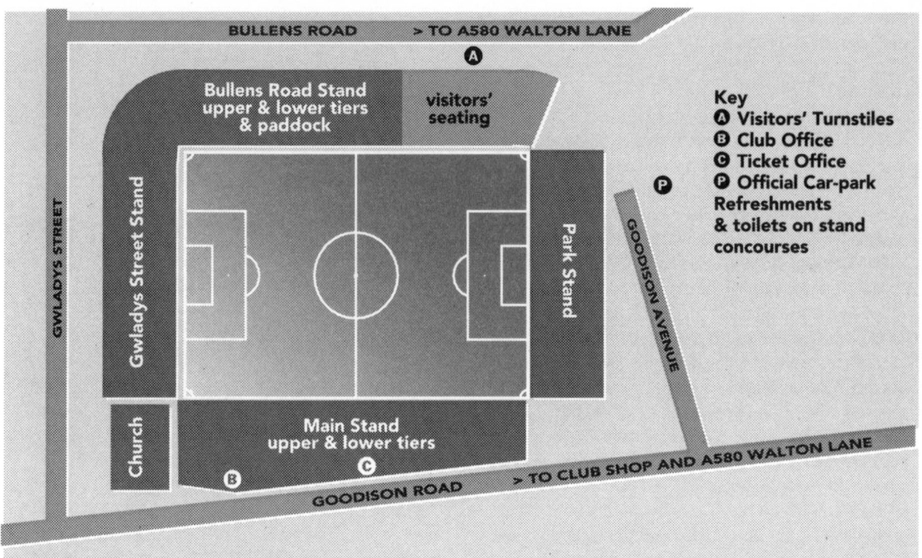

Liverpool A580). At roundabout follow signs to 'Liverpool A580' onto the A580 dual carriageway. After 10.1 miles, pass under the M57, and 1.4 miles further on pass the Showcase Cinema complex on LHS. Then as From South(*).

FROM RAILWAY STATION (Liverpool Lime Street): About 2.2 miles. *By taxi:* Up to £3.50. *By bus:* The no. 19 runs from Queen's Square, right opposite the station, along Walton Lane. It runs every ten minutes during the day, and every 20 minutes at night. Another good option is to switch to Liverpool Central station, a five minute walk away, and catch a Merseyrail Northern Line train to Kirkdale (see below). From the Liverpool Central platforms, turn left, and then right out of station to main road. Go straight on at pedestrian crossing, walking towards the pedestrianised town centre. Turn left by the large Wetherspoons pub on the corner, and past 'Yates Wine Lodge' on the RHS. At end of the road turn right, and the entrance to Liverpool Central station is on the LHS after about a hundred yards.

FROM RAILWAY STATION (Kirkdale, Merseyrail Northern Line): Trains from Liverpool Central run to Kirkdale (take any train with destination Ormskirk or Kirkby). Kirkdale station is 0.7 miles from Goodison. *By foot:* Up station steps and turn right. Straight across crossroads by the 'Melrose Abbey' pub into Westminster Road. After 0.4 miles, at T-junction in front of the 'Grand National' pub, turn left into Barlow Lane. At crossroads after 0.1 miles by the 'Royal Oak' go straight on (s/p Everton FC, Anfield Cemetery) into Spellow Lane.

Last Midweek Trains: From Liverpool Lime Street, trains run to Manchester Oxford Road at 21.52 and 21.55, and to Manchester Victoria at 22.20. The 22.52 goes on to Leeds. Connections to other routes are mainly from Manchester, and often entail taking the Metrolink to Piccadilly. There are no connecting trains to London after a midweek game. Please double-check on (0345) 484 950.

BY BUS: The no. 19 runs from the Queen's Square bus station along Walton Lane, while the no. 20 runs from St Thomas Street along Spellow Lane. The No. 68 from Bootle to Aigburth also runs close to Goodison.

PARKING

The road directions above lead to the best option, the Stanley Park car park. It has 1,000 spaces, costs £2 and is very secure. For those who don't know their way around, street parking is difficult, as many roads have 'residents-only' restrictions and the police tow illegally-parked cars. As in many inner-city areas, car crime is a problem, so don't leave valuables in view.

THE GROUND

To move or not to move, that's the zillion dollar question. The idea of a new stadium was first mooted by club chairman Peter Johnson in December 1996, and supporters soon divided into groups for and against. Those campaigning for a new stadium pointed out that Goodison, though admittedly majestic and much-loved, was no longer suitable for a Premiership club. The facilities were outdated, they said, and any redevelopment made difficult by the proximity of nearby housing. Supporters who opposed the ground move argued that it was possible to update Goodison, and

questioned how the building of a spectacular new stadium could be financed. The debate now appears to be on a backburner, with everyone more concerned about the team itself.

Goodison has been built, expanded, rebuilt, tinkered with and repainted over more than a hundred years. It was the first to have a two-tier stand, and then the first to build a three-tier. Therein lies much of the character of the ground and many of its problems: sections with excellent views (the new Park Stand, built in 1994 and seating 6,000), and stands with poor sightlines (the Bullens Road lower tier) ... areas with good facilities, and others where they're inadequate and overcrowded. Visitors are allocated part of the Bullens Road Stand. The paddock has plastic seating, while the lower tier has old wooden floors and seats, as well as a number of annoying pillars. The upper tier is by far the best option.

Total Capacity: 40,177. For away fans: 2,700.

Cost (98/99): Upper Tier: Adults £19, no concessions. Lower Tier/Paddock: Adults £17, OAPs (over 65s) £11, juniors £9. NB Don't buy tickets from touts, as they're often forgeries, so you'll pay a lot of money and not get to see the game.

Disabled Facilities: Space for 13 visiting supporters at the front of the Bullens Road Stand. *Disabled Toilet:* At end of stand. *Cost:* £18 for a joint ticket (disabled and helper). *Booking:* Through the away club. *Parking:* Limited availability in nearby streets and at the Stanley Park car park. *For the Blind:* Spaces in the Main Stand with commentary.

Programme: £2.

Visitors' Toilets: *Male:* Time to polish the elbows! There were two toilet blocks at each end of the concourse, but both were absolutely packed, with just one way in and out. *Female:* One fan, returning from an expedition to the ladies loo, said: 'They haven't touched those toilets since I was last here ... and that was for a match in the 1966 World Cup!'

Food and Drink: An excellent menu, including two varieties of soup (£1), mineral water (80p); Australian white wine (£1.60), wine gums (40p), vegetable pasties (£1.80), eclairs (£1.40), Everton mints (£1.40) and canned beer and lager for £1,80. Coventry fans found that much of it wasn't' actually available, while sausage rolls (not on the menu) were! The rolls, and the pies, were hot and tasty (10.5.98).

PUB GUIDE

The Arkles 77 Anfield Road (0151) 263 6419
Whitbread (with Boddingtons). This pub, the main away fans' pub listed under 'Liverpool', is also extremely popular for Everton games as well. Sandwiches, big screen TV. Open: all day.

The Stanley Park (1) Langham Street (0151) 284 9636
Carlsberg-Tetley. Large football-friendly pub close to the ground, so very popular on matchdays. Sandwiches. Families welcome. Pool, darts, TV. Open: all day.

'I think I realise why God gave us Scousers a sense of humour!'

The Winslow Hotel (2) 31 Goodison Road (0151) 286 3038
Whitbread. Large, traditional pub opposite the Main Stand. Regular promotions, including two shots for the price of one. Pool table (until pub gets too crowded), TV. Open: all day from 11.30.

The Abbey (3) 154 Walton Lane (off Tetlow Street) (0151) 207 0086
Carlsberg-Tetley (including Walker Bitter and Mild). A small traditional pub with an excellent beer selection. Sandwiches. Open: all day from 11.30.

Also recommended: **The Spellow (4),** 79 Goodison Road, a friendly family-orientated pub with a big-screen TV.

FOOD GUIDE

Right next to the ground on Goodison Road are the popular 'Goodison Supper Bar', which offers traditional fish and chips for £1.95, and 'Dino's', which does burgers and kebabs as well as pizzas for around £4. Nearby County Road, the main shopping street, offers more choice, including a McDonalds, a KFC, and the 'County Café' serving full meals such as sausages, chips, peas and gravy for £1.75. Those driving in from the motorways pass a McDonalds and an 'OK Diner' on the Showcase Cinema complex.

LOCAL MEDIA

Local Radio: BBC Radio Merseyside 95.8 FM; Radio City 96.7 FM; Radio Everton 1602 AM.
Radio Phone-Ins: BBC Radio Merseyside, from 5 pm, call (0151) 709 9333; Radio City, Saturdays 5-6 pm, call (0151) 472 0967.
Saturday Sports Paper: The pink 'Football Echo', available from around 5.30 pm.

MISCELLANEOUS

Safety Factor: No problems here, apart from the car crime.
Rivals: Just one name crops up – the team playing in red whose ground is a ten minute walk from Goodison. The Merseyside derby is one of the most eagerly awaited games of the season, though the intensity of competition on the pitch rarely leads to trouble off it. Other fans say Evertonians would like to cite Manchester United as a rival, but have to admit 'they're not that bothered about us ... we're simply not good enough!'
Fanzines: 'When Skies are Grey', PO Box 226, Liverpool, L69 7LE; 'Speke From the Harbour', 146 Woolton Road, Allerton, L19 5NH.
Unofficial Websites:
'Evertonia': http://www.evertonia.com/
'ToffeeWeb':
http://samson.hifm.no/~mep/everton/Welcome.html
'BlueView': http://www.blueview.com/
'Andrea's Site':
http://www.geocities.com/Colosseum/4422/efc.html
'Roundhouse': http://evertonfc.merseyworld.com/
Tourist Information: (0151) 709 3631.

E

Exeter City

St James Park

Address: St James Park, Exeter, EX4 6PX
Telephone: General Enquiries (01392) 254 073
Commercial Department (01392) 214 422
City ClubCall (0891) 121 634

Old Trafford it ain't, but for most Third Division supporters, the trip to St James Park, Exeter, is a highlight of the season. St James is a classic lower division ground just a few minutes' walk from the city centre and Cathedral. The pasties are good, the pubs are welcoming and the chances of getting thoroughly soaked are very high indeed! The only major drawback is that the ground is difficult to find, being a good four miles through the suburbs from the M5. It's surrounded by tall terraced town houses, whose residents insist – annoyingly! – on parking outside their homes, leaving few spaces for visiting football fans. Many Third Division supporters, accustomed to the Exeter trip, head straight to the city centre car parks, meandering over to St James Park after a good lunch and drink in town. For latecomers, there's an excellent fish and chip shop a few yards from the away turnstiles.

HOW TO GET THERE

BY CAR: From all Routes, M5: Exit M5 at junction 30 (s/p Dawlish, Exeter A379, Sidmouth, Exmouth A376), and at roundabout follow signs to 'Park and Ride, Middlemoor' into Sidmouth Road. At next roundabout after 0.1 miles, take 1st exit (s/p Bishops Court Quarry, Trading Estate, Middlemoor, Park and Ride) into continuation of Sidmouth Road. At roundabout after 0.7 miles, by Exeter Arms, take 3rd exit (s/p Honiton A30, then Pinhoe B3181, Broadclyst) onto Barton Hill/Ring Road. Down hill for 1.1 miles to T-junction/lights by Sainsburys. Here, turn left (s/p City Centre B3212) into Pinhoe Road B3212. Straight on for 1.8 miles, passing Bowling Green and Horse and Dray pubs, to roundabout by the Odeon. Take the 3rd exit (no s/p, but it's straight on past the Baker's Oven) into Old Tiverton Road. First left into St James' Road to ground.

FROM RAILWAY STATION: (a) From Exeter St Davids: 1.2 miles. There's an infrequent train service to St James Park, the station by the ground. *By taxi:* About £2.70. *By bus:* From the bus stop outside the station, take bus N to the High Street. From there, take bus C, E, F or P, along Old Tiverton Road. *By foot:* Head across car park towards Saab garage, and up path running between the garage and the houses, to the main road. Cross road, straight on into Howell Road. Straight over crossroads, past prison and Eagle Tavern to second crossroads. Turn left into Blackall Road, and right at T-junction into Pennsylvania Road. Take 1st left by letterbox into York Road, and 1st left into Well Street. First right into St James' Road.

(b) From Exeter Central: 0.6 miles. *By taxi:* About £2.50. *By foot:* Turn left, past the 'Copper Mine', to

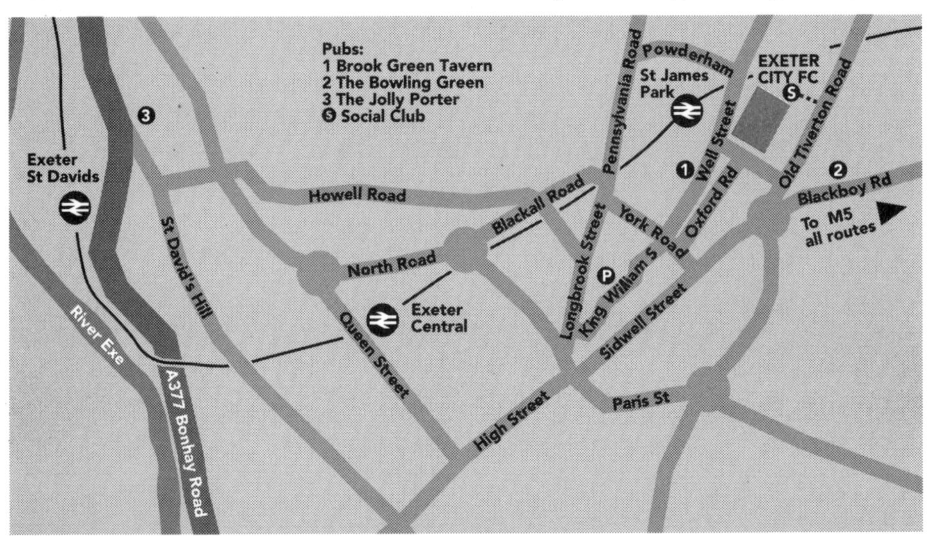

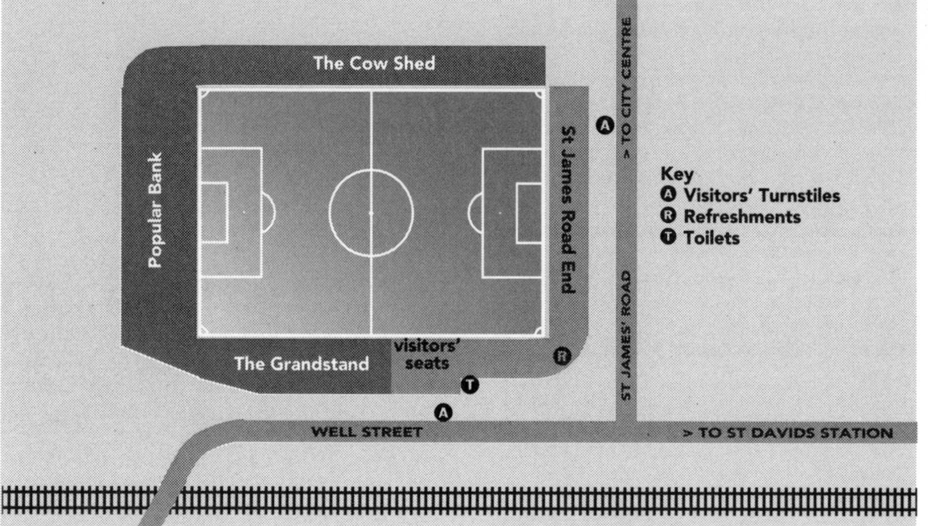

junction by C&As, and turn left along the pedestrianised High Street. At crossroads by Debenhams go straight on into Sidwell Street. Past Tescos, Odeon Cinema and KFC to roundabout. Keep on left-hand side of road and go straight on, passing the Bakers Oven on the LHS, into Old Tiverton Road. First left into St James' Road.
Last Midweek Trains: To London, the only choice is the overnight service. From St. David's this leaves at 01.25. No services to Cardiff from either station after 20.48. Please double-check on (0345) 484 950.
BY BUS: Stagecoach buses C, E, F or P run along Old Tiverton Road.

PARKING

Around the ground, it's street parking for all, though note that some roads are 'Residents Only'. Try the area between the Old Tiverton Road and Blackboy Road. Alternatively, St Sidwell's School in York Road has matchday parking for £1.50. The King William Street city centre car park, which is signposted off the roundabout at the end of Blackboy Road, has lots of space and is only a short walk from the ground. It charges £2 for 3-4 hours, and £3 for 4-5 hours.

THE GROUND

Three cheers for Exeter city council! Back in 1994, there was every chance that St James Park would be turned into a housing estate. But the council revoked the planning permission, bought the ground back and for a few spell-binding months in season 97/98 Exeter City stood on the verge of promotion. It was not to be, but fans found it a wonderful change to look for their team's position from the top of the table downwards rather than vice versa!

Rumours abound of redevelopment work, including the rebuilding of the Big Bank, but it's all long-term. As one fan said, the club's main plan appears to be 'muddling by'! The present St James Park is a ground of great character. The Cow Shed covered terrace stands on a raised grass bank; the Big Bank's one of the biggest terraces in the lower divisions, and the St James' Road End one of the smallest. The latter is the uncovered away terrace, opened only if a large number of fans is expected. Smaller contingents are allocated seats in the Grandstand, 'A' Block.

Total Capacity: 10,500. For away fans: Seating (Grandstand) 242. Terrace (St. James' Road End) 960.
Cost (98/99): Grandstand: Adult £10, concessions £7. Terrace: £8, with concessions, £5, available on a reciprocal basis.
Disabled Facilities: Space for 18 wheelchairs in the front row of the Grandstand. *Disabled Toilet:* There isn't one. *Cost:* Free for disabled and helper. *Booking:* Essential. *Parking:* None available. *For the Blind:* No special facilities.
Programme: £1.50 – and still excellent.
Visitors' Toilets (Grandstand): *Male:* The abiding memory is of water – lots of water. Water on the floor, on the steps, and flowing down into the concourse. *Female:* Shiver me timbers! Someone's ransacked an old sloop and used bits and pieces of it to build a toilet block at Exeter City. The wooden floor's painted bright blue, and the doors – secured with huge, ancient locks – are bright red. And in the wall, there's someone's front

door, with a silver postbox, and a no. 13 on it.

Food and Drink (Grandstand, shared with home supporters): Most fans chose the pasties (£1.25) and were well pleased. One ten-year-old was savouring every morsel and gave it a good nine-out-of-ten. It's probably a better choice than the bland burger (£1.75). 'What's the coffee [60p] like?', we asked one Exeter fan. 'Does it have coffee in it?' came the reply (17.1.98).

PUB GUIDE

Exeter City's social club, The Centre Spot, welcomes visiting supporters. It charges an entry fee of 50p, though supporters' club members and season ticket holders are admitted free.

The Brook Green Tavern (1) 31 Well Street (01392) 496 370
Whitbread. Friendly locals pub, with bar snacks served 11.30-1.30 (or until it gets too busy!).
Open: 11-3, 6-11.

The Victoria Union Road (01392) 254 176
Greenalls (with three hand-pulled guest ales). Large lively pub in a 19th century building retaining an 'olde worlde' feel. Full menu, including pizzas and Tex Mex dishes, served 12-2, 6-8. Pool table, 2 TVs. Disabled facilities. Open: all day.

The Bowling Green (2) Blackboy Road (01392) 422 527
Greenalls (with Bass, Wadsworth 6X and guest beers). It's designed to suit all tastes, with a games area, a lounge with armchairs and open fire, and a bar with wooden tables. Full menu served 12-2.30. Pool, table football, bar billiards, TV. Open: all day.

FOR FAMILIES:

The Jolly Porter (3)
St David's Hill (by Exeter St David's railway station) (01392) 254 848
Courage (with 2 guest beers). A CAMRA pub/restaurant of real character, with old newspaper cuttings on the walls, wooden floors and a library. Pizza/pasta menu/children's portions. Pool, bar billiards, table football, TV. Open: all day.

FOOD GUIDE

The best takeaway, and the one nearest the ground, is 'Kong's Chinese Takeaway and Fish Bar', on Old Tiverton Road, which – according to one local – serves 'the largest portion of chips south of Birmingham'. Chips cost 90p or £1.30, pasties £1 and peas 40p. For a wider choice, head up Sidwell Street towards the city centre. The 'Open Sesame' restaurant and takeaway has burger and chips for £2.30, as well as kebabs and sandwiches. Nearby are a KFC, a Spudulike, another kebab shop, the 'Curry 'N Hurry' Indian takeaway, and the recommended 'Raj India' takeaway. Pizza gourmets can find the Pizza Express by the Cathedral.

LOCAL MEDIA

Local Radio: BBC Radio Devon 95.8 FM; Gemini Radio 97 FM.

Radio Phone-ins: None.

Saturday Sports Paper: None.

MISCELLANEOUS

In their darkest hour, the penultimate game of season 96/97, Exeter City decided they needed supernatural inspiration. So Uri Geller, whose son supports the club, sent them crystals to bury behind each goal, and asked the local paper to print a large orange circle (orange being 'a mixture of physical red and spiritual yellow') for fans to take with them to the ground. Supporters had to concentrate on the circle, and the words written below: 'Believe, Trust Exeter Will Win'. The final score: Exeter City 1, Chester City 5.

Safety Factor: The bigger the crowd at St James, the greater the likelihood of trouble. That said, there was very little to worry about during season 97/98. The police advise fans to avoid the pubs in Sidwell Street after the match.

Rivals: Plymouth, Plymouth and er, Plymouth. Torquay doesn't really feature. Unsurprisingly, just as Plymouth fans have an aversion to anything red, Exeter fans avoid anything green. The local Safeways found that footie fans were pulling out twenty green baskets to get at a red one near the bottom!

Fanzines: None.

Unofficial Websites:
GreciaNet: http://ecfc.home.ml.org

Tourist Information: (01392) 265 700.

Fulham

Craven Cottage

Address: Craven Cottage, Stevenage Road, London SW6 6HH
Telephone: Club/Ticket Office (0171) 384 4700 ClubCall (0891) 440 044
Official Website: http://www.fulham-fc.co.uk/

There's one time every year that Craven Cottage is guaranteed TV coverage ... during the Boat Race! The ground's right on the north bank of the River Thames, with a park on one side and miles of smart residential streets to the east. It's picture-postcard stuff, but visiting fans be warned ... traffic in this part of London is usually at a complete standstill, and parking's reaching nightmare status. More supporters arrive late at this ground than at any other in the country! For those with lots of time, the choice for food and drink is fabulous, especially along Fulham Road and across the river in Putney.

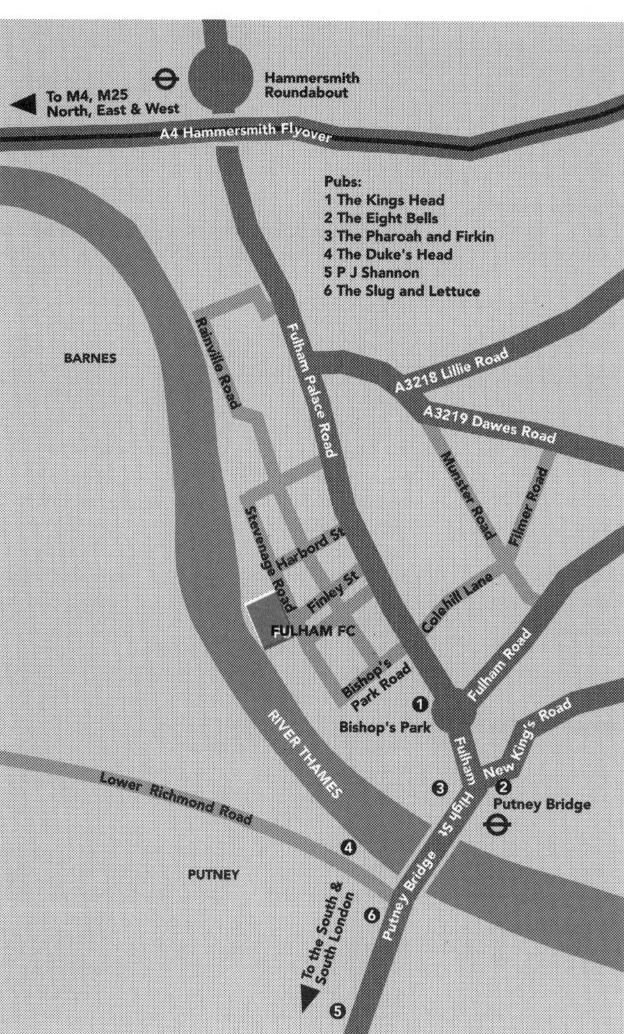

HOW TO GET THERE

NB Note that Stevenage Road is blocked close to the ground.

BY CAR: From North: Exit M25 at junction 15 (s/p M4 Heathrow, Terminals 1, 2 and 3, London (W)), onto the M4 eastbound. Remain on the M4, which becomes the A4, following signs to 'Central London' for 10.4 miles to Hogarth Roundabout. Here, take 2nd exit (s/p Central London, Hammersmith A4) remaining on the A4, passing the Griffin (Fullers) Brewery. At the Hammersmith Flyover junction after 1.1 miles, keep in left-hand lane and exit the A4 (s/p Hammersmith (A306, A315, A219)). Follow signs to Oxford (A40) for 0.3 miles to T-junction in front of Hays Accountancy Personnel. This is the Hammersmith Roundabout. Continue round roundabout for 0.3 miles to where road runs underneath and parallel to the A4, and turn left (s/p Alternative Route via Putney Bridge) into Fulham Palace Road. Go straight on for 1.2 miles, and turn right into Bishop's Park Road, which leads round to the ground.

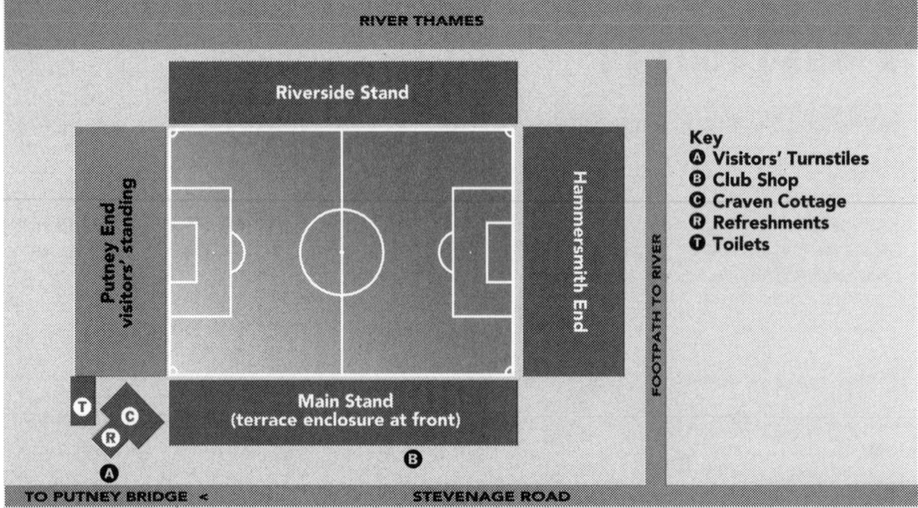

From South/South London, from Putney Bridge: (For directions to Putney Bridge, see London Guide.) Over bridge, and after 0.1 miles go straight on at junction/lights by the 'Pharoah and Firkin' (s/p The West, West End). At roundabout after 0.1 miles by the 'King's Head', go straight on (s/p The West A4, M4, West End A4, Oxford A40) into Fulham Palace Road. After 0.2 miles turn left into Bishop's Park Road to ground.

FROM UNDERGROUND STATION (Putney Bridge, District Line, Zone 3): Ten minute walk. *By foot:* Turn left out of station and right down Ranelagh Gardens. At end of road (i.e. before passing the 'Eight Bells' pub) turn left into Willow Bank and immediately right through the underpass into Bishop's Park. Walk along river bank to ground. NB The gardens are shut after evening games, when supporters have to walk via Fulham Palace Road.

BY BUS: The nos. 74 (from Baker Street Station to Roehampton), and 220 (from Harlesden to Wandsworth) both run along Fulham Palace Road.

PARKING

It's street parking for everyone, and the council has introduced pay-and-display parking on nearly all the residential streets in the borough. Round Craven Cottage, and on the streets to the east of Fulham Palace Road, it's mostly 60p per hour (free after 6.30 pm). There are traffic wardens out on matchdays, so watch out! Around Putney Bridge, a lot of the parking is for one hour only.

THE GROUND

'You can positively smell the jealousy wafting from this away end!' said one visiting supporter to Craven Cottage, surveying the smart new seating in the Riverside Stand, and the scaffolding surrounding the Stevenage Road Stand. Mr Al-Fayed has spent about £3 million simply to upgrade Craven Cottage, while plans for a new 26,000-seater stadium on the same site are drawn up. Fulham FC says that when construction work begins – and no date has yet been fixed – the club may well have to ground-share. But where? Fulham fans say 'anywhere but Stamford Bridge!' In the meantime, away fans are allocated the open Putney End. Part of it is sealed off because of subsidence, but the fences have been removed and the view is very good. The club apologises that no visitors' seating is available for season 1998/99.

Total Capacity: 19,215. For away fans: 4,000. Turnstiles 10-16 in Stevenage Road.

Cost (98/99): Adults £10, concessions £5.

Disabled Facilities: Space for about five visiting supporters in the disabled enclosure between the Riverside Stand and the Hammersmith End. *Disabled Toilets:* Nearby. *Cost:* Free for disabled, terrace price for helper. *Booking:* Essential. *Parking:* None available. *For the Blind:* No special facilities.

Programme: £2.

Visitors' Toilets: *Male:* The old open-plan portakabins have been replaced by six bottle-green individual Tardis-like constructions which, said one fan, 'are practising for Glastonbury!' A sign inside read: 'Not for use by more than 40 people per week', which 1,500+ visiting fans found rather amusing. *Female:* And the 'MIFTA' (Most Improved Footie Toilet Award') goes to ... Fulham! It's all

been repainted, with extra basins, soap and soft loo paper!

Food and Drink: Supporters found the food expensive (cheeseburgers £2.60, hot dogs £2.50) but the portions were generous. A Preston fan said his cheeseburger was 'hot, slightly undercooked but tasty, and so much of a mouthful even I admitted defeat!' The hot dog, with Frankfurter sausage, was delicious. Fulham also gave fans 'magic expanding cups': the drinks (coffee 80p, tea 70p) were so hot the containers buckled! (26.8.97, 21.11.97, 4.4.98, 7.4.98).

PUB GUIDE

With more supporters coming to watch Fulham, some of the traditional away fan drinking haunts have become home-only. More visiting fans are heading over Putney Bridge to Putney itself, so we're listing some of the most football-friendly pubs there as well:

NORTH OF THE RIVER:

The Kings Head (1) 4 Fulham High Street (0171) 736 1413

Punch Taverns. Renowned live-music venue undergoing extensive refurbishment in the summer of 1998. It's to have a new restaurant, conservatory and a 'tropical garden'! Traditional pub food served from 10. Two pool tables, big-screen TV. Open: all day.

The Eight Bells (2) 89 Fulham High Street (0171) 736 6307

Free House. Small attractive traditional pub, with wooden panels and high-backed benches. TV. Open: Saturday matchdays 11-3, 7-11; midweek all day.

Also recommended: **The Pharoah and Firkin (3),** 90 Fulham High Street, lets in small numbers of well-behaved supporters.

SOUTH OF THE RIVER:

The Duke's Head (4) 8 Lower Richmond Road (0181) 788 2552

Youngs. Wonderful traditional pub with large lounge area overlooking the river. Sandwiches. TV, table football. Families welcome. Open: all day.

P. Shannon and Sons (5) 46-48 Putney High Street (0181) 780 5437

Fullers. Popular friendly and very lively Irish theme pub, with wooden floors and lots of character. 'Irish-influenced' menu served all day. Big-screen TV. Families welcome/disabled facilities. Open: all day.

Also recommended: **The Slug and Lettuce (6),** 14 High Street. A smart lively pub with an extensive menu.

FOOD GUIDE

About the nearest eaterie to the ground is the 'ASK Pizza and Pasta' restaurant and takeaway, on Fulham Palace Road. Its pizzas cost from £3.80, and it's a firm favourite of the Fulham FC staff! Nearby is the 'Kelssy Fried Chicken', which one fan described as 'average'. Fulham High Street, towards Putney Bridge, has a better choice, including the highly-recommended 'Tastys'

café/takeaway on the corner of Fulham Road. Almost opposite is the smart 'Stravinskys' café/restaurant, with a 'brunch menu' and excellent cappuccino! By the tube station is the ever-popular chips-with-everything 'River Café', the much smaller 'Nancy's Café' (also a takeaway) and 'Ben's Bagels'.

Fulham Road has a Tapas restaurant called 'El Prado', the upmarket 'Pires Sandwich Bar' and a 'Pizza Express'. Putney High Street is the place for ethnic eating, with the 'Taboo' Turkish restaurant/takeaway, the French-style 'Café Tabac', 'La Mancha' tapas bar and restaurant and the 'Bar Iberica' offering breakfast for £5.95.

LOCAL MEDIA

Local Radio: Capital Gold 1548 AM; GLR 94.9 FM.

Radio Phone-ins: Capital Gold, Sat 2-6.30, midweek 7-10 (or 7-8 if no match). Call on (0845) 35 60 7080.

Saturday Sports Paper: None.

MISCELLANEOUS

Safety Factor: Some scuffles against Millwall, but generally no problems here.

Rivals: Brentford, Wimbledon, Northampton, Wycombe and Gillingham.

Fanzines: 'There's only one F in Fulham', 11 Johnson's Close, Carshalton, Surrey, SM5 2LU.

Unofficial Websites:
http://members.tripod.com/~cravencottage/index.html
http://members.tripod.com/~fulham_2/index.html
FulhamWeb: http://www.btinternet.com/~aredfern/
'Black and White Pages':
http://www.wilf.demon.co.uk/fulhamfc/ffc.html
'By the Riverside: http://home3.swipnet.se/~w-30830/

Tourist Information: No local office.

Gillingham

The Priestfield Stadium

Address: Priestfield Stadium, Redfern Avenue, Gillingham, Kent ME7 4DD
Telephone: Club (01634) 851 854/576 828
Commercial Hotline (01634) 851 462
ClubCall (0891) 332 211

For many years, so little changed at the Priestfield Stadium that Gills fans became immensely agitated if someone repainted the exit signs! Since 1995, when businessman Paul Scally saved the club from oblivion, life's been a positive rollercoaster ... with new signings, a new stand, new tea bars and a new sense of optimism! For the visiting fan, Gillingham itself – part of the Medway Towns – is not exactly a hot-bed of excitement, but life is easy enough. The High Street, with its pubs and restaurants, is only a few minutes' walk from the ground, and parking is no problem at all. Anyone wanting to make a day of it is perhaps best advised to head for Rochester, with its castle and pedestrianised High Street, or to Chatham with its new marina and museums.

HOW TO GET THERE

BY CAR: From all directions (M2): Exit M2 at junction 4 and at motorway roundabout follow signs to 'Gillingham A278' onto the A278. Stay on the A278 for 1.8 miles, over two roundabouts to a 3rd roundabout. Here, turn left (s/p Gillingham, Chatham A2) onto the A2. Straight on for 0.5 miles, over one roundabout, and then turn right at lights (s/p Strand Leisure Park/Riverside Country Park) into Woodlands Road. After 0.7 miles turn left (opposite Mayfair Cars) into Chicago Avenue. The floodlights are visible from here. Park this side of the ground for a quick(er) getaway. For the ground: At end of Chicago Avenue turn right and then abrupt left into Redfern Avenue.

FROM RAILWAY STATION (Gillingham): 5-10 minute walk. *By taxi:* £2.50 – ask for the turnstiles on Redfern Avenue. *By foot:* Turn left out of station and immediately left again (opposite Job Centre) onto Balmoral Road. Turn left after 0.4 miles into Gillingham Road, and then next right into Linden Road. At T-junction turn right into Redfern Avenue to the away turnstiles. *Last Midweek Trains:* Fast trains to London Victoria leave at 21.59 and 22.59. Stopping trains run at 22.10 and 23.10. For onward connections see London Guide at front of book. Please double-check on (0345) 484 950.

BY BUS: The nos. 101, 132, 136, 182 and 183 run from Chatham bus station at the Pentagon shopping centre to Gillingham town centre.

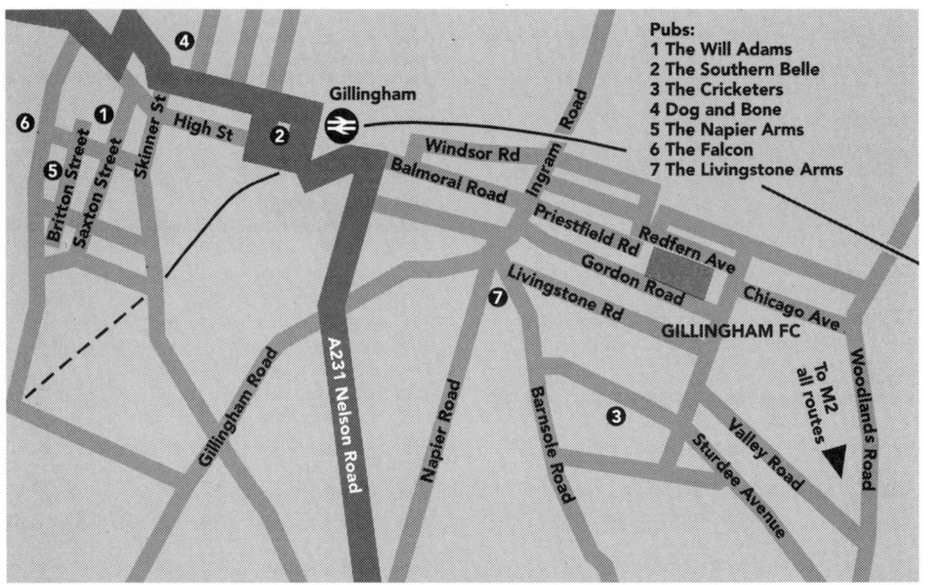

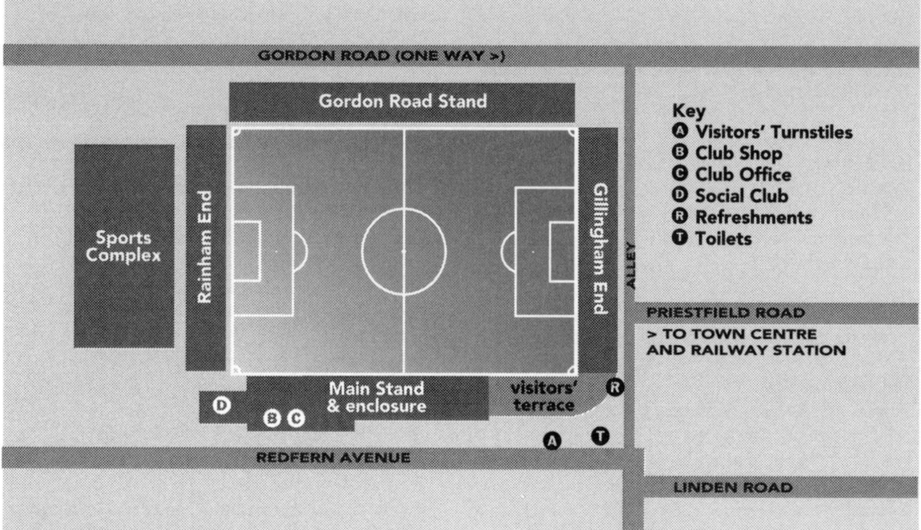

PARKING

It's street parking for all, and there are few restrictions. Early birds find spaces off Woodlands Road, or on Chicago Avenue, Livingstone Road and Sturdee Avenue. The public car park on Railway Street behind the station is only a 5-10 minute walk from the ground. To avoid some of the post-match gridlock, home fans advise visitors to park facing the way home, as turning round can take hours!

THE GROUND

After decades of planning and dreaming, Gillingham FC has finally built a new 2,500-seater stand on the Gordon Road side of Priestfield Stadium. The stand has yet to be named, and Gills fans have been asked for ideas. They live in hope that it won't end up as the 'Kool Yoghurt Stand', named after the club's sponsors! Future development plans include new stands to replace the covered Rainham End, presently the home terrace, and the Main Stand. Planning permission has already gone through, and work could begin in season 98/99, temporarily reducing the overall ground capacity. Away fans are unlikely to be affected. They will still be allocated the uncovered terrace in the corner next to the Main Stand. First the good news: the new floodlights mean less ducking and diving for a decent view. The bad news? The facilities are poor, and the wonderful old tea shed has been replaced by a mobile burger van.

In the long term, the club is looking to relocate to a new stadium, and a possible site has already been surveyed in Strood, to the west of Chatham and Rochester.

Total Capacity: 10,600. For away fans: Terrace (uncovered) 1,320. The capacity can be increased for exceptionally big games. Turnstiles 9-12 in Redfern Avenue. Away fans are also allocated seats in the Main Stand Enclosure.
Cost (98/99): Terrace: Adults £10, OAPs £8, juniors £5. Main Stand Enclosure: Adults £12, OAPs £10, juniors £7.
Disabled Facilities: Space for 20 supporters at pitch level by the Main Stand. It's uncovered, so bring waterproofs. *Disabled Toilet:* The men's toilet in the Main Stand, though not specifically for the disabled, can accommodate wheelchairs. The female disabled toilet is in the new Gordon Road Stand. *Cost:* Free for disabled, matchday prices for helper. *Booking:* Not required. *For the Blind:* Ask the club for details.
Programme: £1.60.
Visitors' Toilets: *Male:* One tiny sit-down jobbie for up to 1,200 people, plus a mouldy wall with a shallow gutter open to all the elements. Sinks? Pah! Soap? Pah! Running water? Hoho! *Female:* There is no sexual equality here ... the female loos get a roof! And why? Maybe rainwater is essential to keeping the male loos usable! The female loos are actually quite smart, but still lack sinks.
Food and Drink: Because of ground redevelopments, visiting fans were served by a van, which offered burgers (small £1.50, large £2.60) and cheeseburgers (small £2, large £2.80). Oh, and hot-dogs (£1.50). However, as the burgers were cooked on a grill with real onions, they were pretty good, though the bread was a bit stale. York fans noted that if they stirred the tea (65p) fast enough, the grease disappeared. There is no such thing

as a happy vegetarian at the Priestfield Stadium (8.11.97, 17.1.98, 24.2.98).

PUB GUIDE

The Will Adams (1) 73 Saxton Street (01643) 575 902
Free House (with London Pride and guests). A small friendly CAMRA pub, run by a football fan. Bar meals served 12-2. Families welcome. Pool, 'Kentish Doubles' dart board, TV, patio. Open: all day on matchdays.
The Southern Belle (2) 170 Gillingham High Street (01634) 280 699
Free House (with John Smiths, Websters Green Label, Pedigree and hand pumped Sussex). Small friendly locals pub, where the landlord is happy for fans to bring in their own takeaway food. Pool, darts. Open: all day.
The Cricketers (3) Sturdee Avenue (01634) 851 226
Scottish and Newcastle (with Courage Best, Directors and John Smiths). Large popular pub, refurbished with oak beams. Two pool tables, big-screen TV, beer garden and play area. Matchday sandwiches. Open: all day.
Dog and Bone (4) James Street (01634) 576 829
Free House (with guest ales). A newly refurbished family-run CAMRA pub with homely surroundings and restaurant. Beer garden, pool table. Open: all day.
The Napier Arms (5) 153 Britton Street (01634) 578 219
Free House/Courage (with two real ales). Cosy pub with traditional beamed ceilings and a larger games room. A plaque on the wall records its footballing history, as it was here that Brompton FC – later to become Gillingham FC – was founded. Sandwiches. Pool table, Darts, TV. Families welcome. Open: Friday-Saturday all day; from 5.30 for midweek games.
Also recommended: **The Falcon (6),** 95 Marlborough Road, a small traditional Courage pub serving bar meals 12-3; **United Services,** 27 Arden Street (Shepherd Neane), where bar snacks are served all day; **The Livingstone Arms (7),** Livingstone Circus (Courage).

FOOD GUIDE

Gillingham High Street, near the station, has a host of outlets, including two bakeries, a new café by 'The Britannia', a McDonalds and a Wimpy. For something different try 'Eel Pie Island', just past the junction with Skinner Street. Also recommended are the 'Central Chippy', by the 'Will Adams'; the 'Circus Fish Bar' on Livingstone Circus; and 'Sandhus' on Gordon Road, which sells 'cracking kebabs' (doner kebab, salad, sauces for £2). A bakery on Balmoral Road, just round the corner from the station, often has special offers on Saturdays.

LOCAL MEDIA

Local Radio: BBC Radio Kent 96.7 FM; Invicta FM 103.1 FM.
Radio Phone-ins: Invicta FM takes its sports coverage from Capital Gold, which has football phone-ins on Saturdays 5-6.30, midweek 7-8 (or to 10 pm if there's an evening game). Call (0845) 35 60 70 80.
Saturday Sports Paper: None.

MISCELLANEOUS

Chairman Paul Scally is good at PR. He toured the away terrace at Carlisle personally handing out free tickets for a forthcoming match at the Priestfield Stadium. One Gills fan pointed out, however, that nearly all the Gills fans who'd been mad enough to make such a long trip either preferred standing up or held season tickets in the Main Stand. The gesture was, however, greatly appreciated.
Safety Factor: For most of season 97/98, the Priestfield Stadium was trouble-free. Then, late in the season, a Fulham fan died in fighting outside the ground, near the alleyway which runs behind the Gillingham End. As a result, the police decided to close the alleyway on matchdays.
Rivals: Millwall and the south London clubs, though older Gillingham fans would list Swindon, following a couple of close-run promotion battles. A more recent contender is Brighton ... 'They slagged off our club and ground, and we were doing them a favour!'
Fanzines: 'Brian Moore's Head Looks Uncannily like London Planetarium', 11 Watts Avenue, Rochester, Kent, ME1 1RX. The name may change to 'Brian Moore's Head Looks Uncannily like the Millennium Dome'.
Unofficial Websites: 'Gills Online':
http://freespace.virgin.net/keith.pestell/Gillspage/gills/htm
'Football World':
http://ourworld.compuserve.com/homepages/gillsf.c/mainpage/htm
http://www.spods.dcs.kcl.ac.uk/~kennard/gills
Tourist Information: (01634) 843 666.

Grimsby Town

Blundell Park

Address: Blundell Park, Cleethorpes, North East Lincolnshire, DN35 7PY
Telephone: Club/Ticket Office (01472) 697 111
Grimsby Town ClubCall (0891) 555 855

Ah yes, the fish and chip special! Well, if you can't get a decent haddock fillet here, you might as well hit yourself over the head with the nearest bottle of ketchup. Grimsby is still a major importer and exporter of fish, even if the local trawlers no longer ply the North Atlantic, and there are several excellent chippies within easy walking distance of Blundell Park. And as this is Cleethorpes after all, many fans make a day of it, heading off to the seafront amusements and then into town for a slap-up lunch. The choice of recommended pubs, however, is severely limited – limited in fact to one, though it is extremely good. Parking is all on-street, but rarely a problem.

HOW TO GET THERE

BY CAR: All Main Routes, M180: Follow M180 to the 'Great Grimsby' sign. At the first roundabout, by the Haven pub after 1.1 miles, go straight on (s/p Docks, Cleethorpes A180). From here to Blundell Park, a distance of 2.7 miles, it's straight on all the way – simply follow signs to 'Cleethorpes A180' and 'Grimsby Town F.C.' The ground is behind the McDonalds.
The police recommend that fans approaching Grimsby on the A15 should continue to its junction with the M180, and then take the route above. Fans coming in on the A46 will find the route extremely well signposted 'Grimsby Town F.C.'
FROM RAILWAY STATION (Cleethorpes): About 1.0 mile: *By taxi:* £2. *By bus:* The nos. 45, 3F and 9X run along Grimsby Road. At night, there's also the 8X. *By*

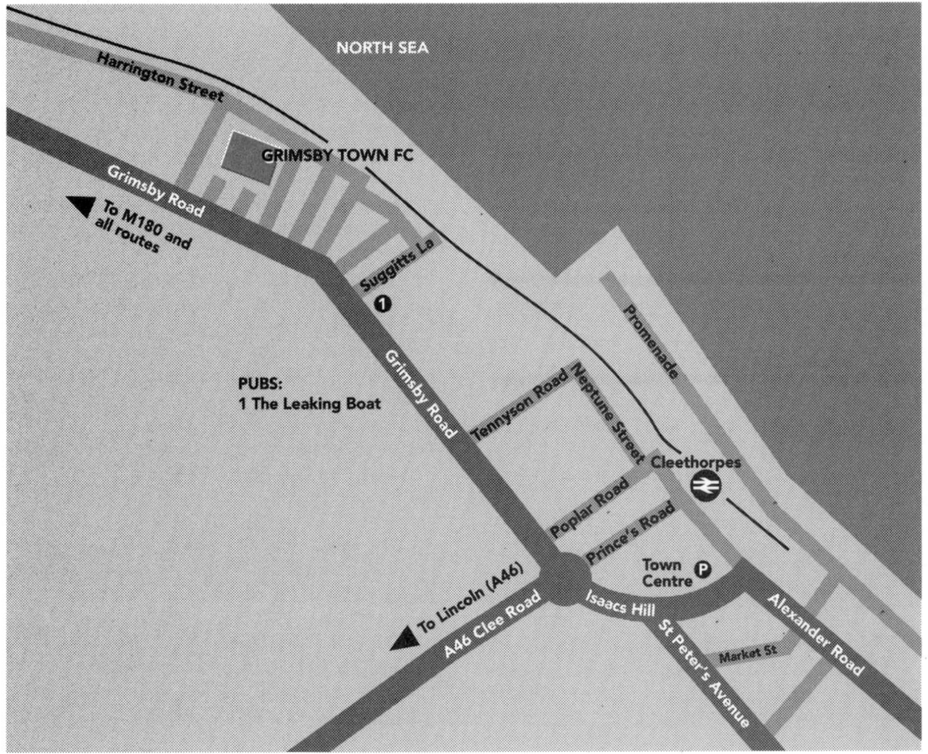

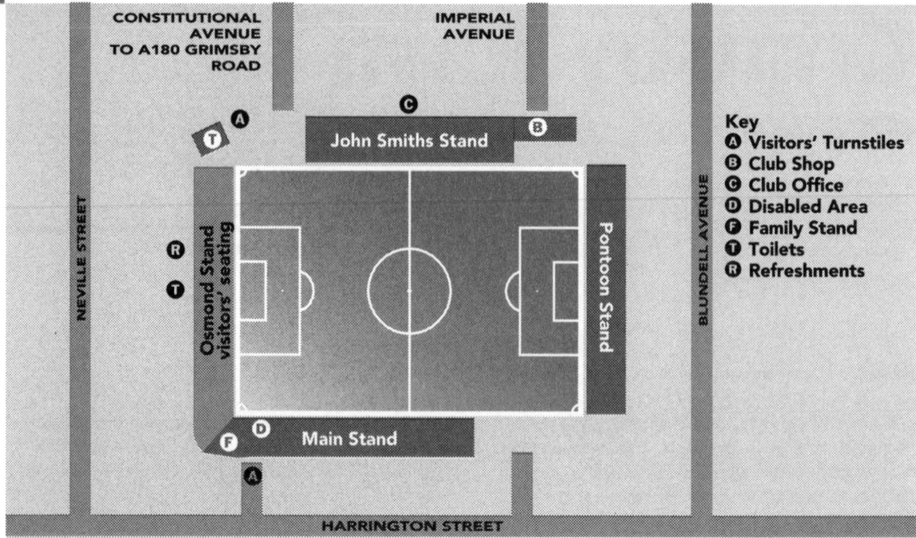

foot: Go through barriers at end of platform and turn right and right again, heading back along the railway line. Through station car park, towards 'Cleethorpes Station' sign, passing the 'No. 1' bar on the RHS. Past another car park on the LHS and take next left into Poplar Road. At T-junction turn right into Grimsby Road. Ground is on RHS after 0.7 miles. Note that New Clee station is now used only for local stopping trains.
Last Midweek Trains: The last train to anywhere leaves Cleethorpes at 21.16, so that's not much use! Please double-check on (0345) 484 950.
BY BUS: See above.

PARKING

It's street parking, but there are a lot of side-streets and few restrictions.

THE GROUND

Blundell Park is a draughty victim of the Taylor Report, with large gaps in three corners of the ground where old terracing has been removed. Local fans say the ground is 'just about adequate' and lament that the isolation of the main stands has killed off a lot of the old atmosphere: 'You don't even hear us sing: "Sing when we're fishing, we only sing when we're fishing" anymore!' said one. The most prominent feature of the ground is the John Smiths Stand, which rears high above its surroundings and affords an excellent view of the North Sea. When it was built 15 years ago, it was state-of-the-art, one of the very first to have executive boxes and restaurant facilities. But now it's now beginning to show its age.

The club is aware of the deficiencies, but is understandably reluctant to spend vast amounts of money upgrading Blundell Park while its application to build a new 15,000 seater stadium, on the M180 out-of-town, makes its laborious way through the local council.

Away fans in season 98/99 will continue to be housed in the covered Osmond Stand. Supporters need to choose their seats carefully, as there are two pillars towards the middle of the stand. The leg-room is surprisingly good, and the toilets unsurprisingly awful!
Total Capacity: 8,989, though the capacity can be increased for big matches with the construction of temporary seating in the corners. For away fans: 1,874. Turnstiles 5-14 in Constitutional Avenue and 15-18 in Harrington Street. Visiting fans are welcome in the Appleby Family Stand through reciprocal agreement. Please contact Gill Dobbs at the club.
Cost (98/99): Adult £13, concessions available through reciprocal agreement, Juniors £5, OAPs £7.
Disabled Facilities: Large enclosure in the NE corner of the Main Stand, and there's never any problem accommodating visiting fans. *Disabled Toilet:* In Main Stand. *Cost:* £5 for disabled, £6 for helper. *Booking:* Essential. *Parking:* None available. *For the Blind:* Eight seats available with hospital radio commentary. Cost £5.
Programme: £1.50.
Visitors' Toilets: *Male:* 'I had to wipe my feet on the way out', said one Chesterfield fan, and muttered something about bringing his wellies next time.
Female: This was definitely one for those hardy, seafaring types! The cistern was padlocked like Long

John Silver's sea-chest, while the sink had just cold water, no soap and no hand towels.

Food and Drink: Remember those scenes from 'Colditz' – or was it 'The Great Escape'? – when the captives try to make a teabag last several days, squeezing out every last drop of flavour? The tea at Grimsby (80p) was the colour of that last cuppa! 'All the other drinks are very nice' said a steward apologetically, and he was right! Fans loved the spicy sausage rolls (75p), but found they needed spoons to finish off the collapsing pies (£1.25). The steak-and-kidney version was particularly tasty (3.3.97).

PUB GUIDE

The local police strongly recommend that visiting fans stick to one pub, 'The Leaking Boot' about 0.4 miles to the south of Blundell Park.

The Leaking Boot (1) Grimsby Road (01472) 691 530
Wards/Vaux. Large pub with several bar areas and a family room with play area. It has a good menu, and offers fans two two-course meals for £5 (e.g. soup followed by haddock, chips and mushy peas). There's also a separate restaurant with à-la-carte menu. Pool, darts, TV. Open: midweek all day, Sat matchdays 11-4, 7-11.

FOOD GUIDE

For the connoisseur of the traditional English fish dinner, the Grimsby trip is a must. 'Hobson's' is the best choice near the ground, and was voted 'No. 1 Takeaway Award Winner for Grimsby and Cleethorpes' in 1996/97. It also has a restaurant. 'Best English Cod' costs £1.80, with chips at 69p. In town on St Peter's Avenue (see map) 'Suthies' won the 'No. 1 Takeaway Award' in 1993/94. It also has a restaurant, with haddock and chips at 2.30 and pies at 85p. Also on St Peter's Avenue is the 'Cloisters Café and Takeaway', an attractive shoppers' café with a children's menu.

The first turning left off St Peter's Avenue is Short Street, which leads to Market Street, where there's a cluster of restaurants and takeaways. These include 'Ernie Beckett's', which won that coveted 'No. 1 Takeaway Award' in 1995/96; 'Steel's Corner House', a highly-recommended restaurant, with a huge menu and children's meals; a Lebanese restaurant, a kebab house, a KFC, three Italian restaurants and a Wine Bar and Bistro.

Near the ground, as well as 'Hobson's', there's a fish-and-chip shop called 'Avon Fisheries' which specialises in filled Yorkshire puddings: e.g., sausage, mash, onions and gravy in a seven-inch Yorkshire pud for £1.70. Almost next door is 'The Picnic Basket', which offers hot sandwiches, pizzas, pastries and pies, while 'The Café', opposite, serves good-value meals. And of course there's a McDonalds right by Blundell Park.

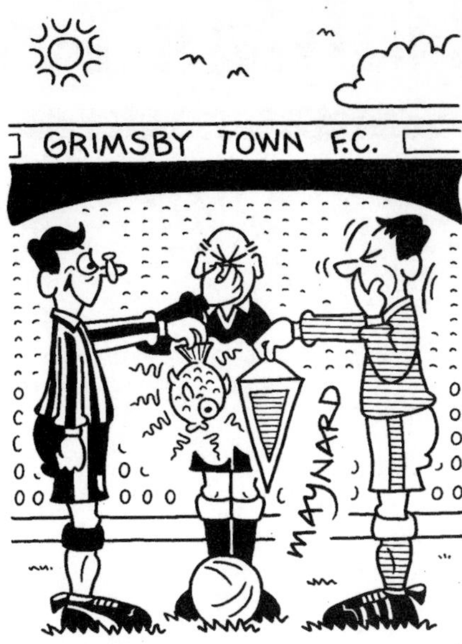

LOCAL MEDIA

Local Radio: BBC Radio Humberside 95.9 FM; Lincs FM 102.2 FM; Viking Radio 96.9 FM.

Radio Phone-ins: BBC Radio Humberside, Tuesdays 7-10 pm. Call (01482) 225 959.

Saturday Sports Paper: The 'Sports Telegraph'.

MISCELLANEOUS

Almost everyone in Grimsby either works in the fish trade, worked in the fish trade or knows someone who works or worked in the fish trade! So it's only appropriate that we report here on the Great Grimsby Fish Bribery Scandal. Grimsby fans and stewards relate that, until recent times, visiting teams and officials were given gift boxes of wet fish to take home. Many of the club's directors were in the fish business, and were most generous to-boot, seeing the gifts as a friendly gesture to honoured guests. The football powers-that-be, however, thought differently, believing the gifts could be seen as bribes to match officials. And that was the end of that.

Safety Factor: Until two or three years ago, Grimsby Town had a real hooligan problem, but it's almost all died away. Today, trouble is rare.

Rivals: Hull City and Scunthorpe United.

Fanzine: 'Sing When We're Fishing', 10 Glen Eldon Raod, St. Anne's, Lancashire, FY8 2AU.

Unofficial Websites:
http://www.gizmocat.demon.co.uk/gtfc/

Tourist Information: (01472) 342 422.

Halifax Town

The Shay

Address: Shay Grounds, Halifax HX1 2YS.
Telephone: Club (01422) 353 423
Shaymen Hotline (0891) 227 328
Official Website:
http://www.geocities.com/Colosseum/stadium/3043

Anyone driving over the M62 Pennine route at night cannot fail to admire the thousands upon thousands of lights carpeting the hills and valleys below – the West Yorkshire conurbation. Somewhere out there is Halifax. Yet the old textile town has retained its own separate identity, and its town centre is undergoing something of a regeneration. Believe it or not, just a few minutes' walk from the Shay, fans can feast on 'milano salami baguettes' followed by 'prune and almond frangipani!' Matchday parking's not a problem, but visiting supporters looking for a drink should stop en route.

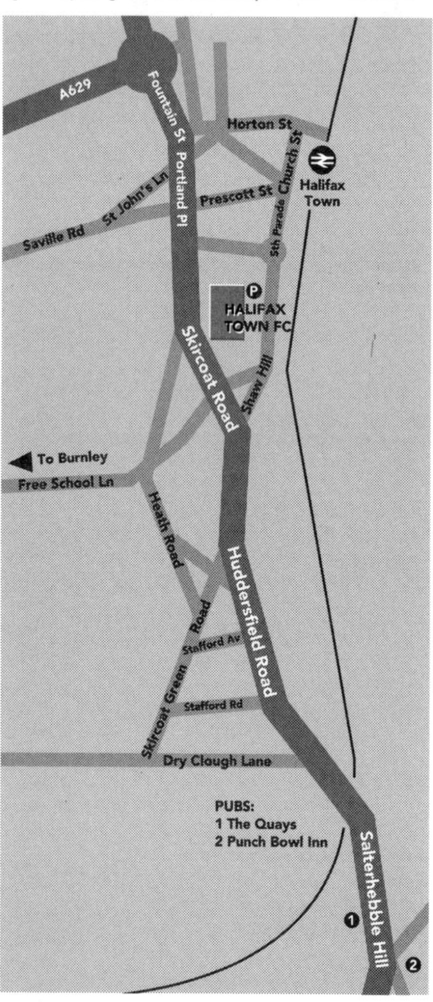

HOW TO GET THERE

BY CAR: All Main Routes, M62: Exit M62 at junction 24 (s/p A629 Huddersfield, Halifax). The sliproad descends to a dual carriageway and, after 0.5 miles, to a roundabout. Take 2nd exit (s/p Halifax A629, Eureka, Piece Hall) onto the A629 dual carriageway. Keep straight on following signs to 'Halifax A629', passing the Punch Bowl pub after 3.3 miles and The Quays pub after another 0.1 miles. Follow signs to Keighley A629, Town Centre for a further 0.9 miles, then take the right-hand filter at lights and turn right (s/p Town Centre East, Leeds (A58, M62), Bradford A6036, The Shay) into Shaw Hill. The ground is on LHS after 0.1 miles.
From Burnley (A646), From White Horse pub: At next junction after 0.2 miles go straight on (s/p Halifax A646, Leeds (A58, M62)). Past the Warley Springs Garage after 0.5 miles and The Peacock pub after a further 0.2 miles. After 0.9 miles, at next major junction/lights, get in right hand lane, following signs to 'Huddersfield A646 (A629), The Shay' into Skircoat Moor Road. At mini-roundabout after 0.2 miles turn left (s/p Royal Infirmary, Casualty) into Free School Lane. After 0.8 miles go straight on at crossroads (no s/p), remaining on Free School Lane. At lights/crossroads after 0.1 miles go straight on (no s/p) and at T-junction in front of Elmwood Garage turn left (no s/p) into Shaw Hill. Ground is on LHS after 0.1 miles.
From A65-A629 Carlisle/Keighley: It's a complicated route, as The Shay is on the other side of town, but thankfully it's well-signposted 'Huddersfield A629' throughout. The road skirts the town centre, taking in Broad Street and Cow Green, then turn right by the Victoria Theatre (s/p Huddersfield A629, Manchester M62) into Commercial Street. Straight on for 0.5 miles to junction/lights by HSS. Here, turn left (no s/p). At T-junction by Elmwood Garage turn left into Shaw Hill. Ground is on LHS after 0.1 miles.
FROM RAILWAY STATION (Halifax): 5-10 minute walk. Straight out of station to main road (Church Street) by the 'Imperial Crown', and turn left (pedestrian s/p

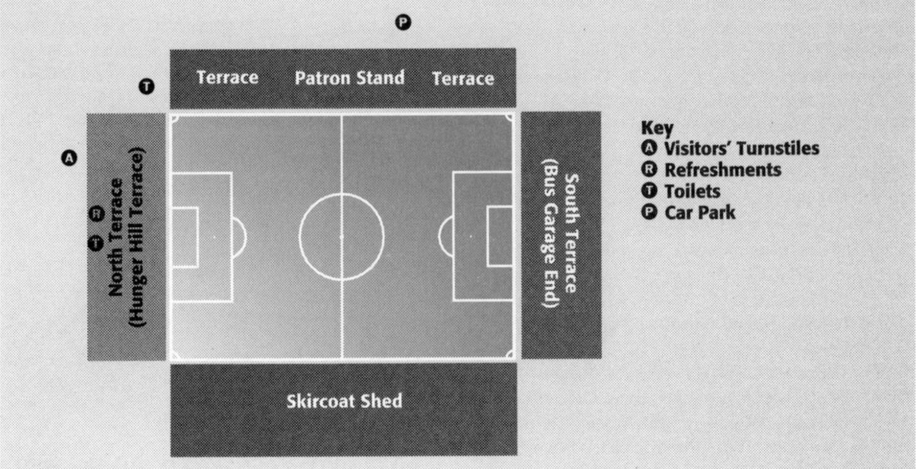

The Shay). At first mini-roundabout bear left (s/p Leeds, York) into South Parade. At next mini-roundabout by 'The Shay' pub turn right, up Hunger Hill, and then first left to the ground.
Last Midweek Trains: There are no trains to London after a midweek game. However, it's possible to get to Leeds (21.49), Manchester Victoria (22.07) and to Newcastle via York (22.25). Please double-check on (0345) 484 950.
BY BUS: Numerous buses run along Huddersfield Road, near the ground, including nos. 278, 279, 343, 344, 502, 503, 537, 538, 556 and 557.

PARKING

The car park at the ground (£2) is open to all, but fills up quickly. After that it's mainly street parking. The best roads to try are Free School Lane and Skircoat Green Road. The streets between the ground and the town centre are much narrower, with some parts designated 'Residents Only'. There's a small shoppers' car park on the corner of Union Street and Prescott Street. It costs £1.20 for three hours, and £1.60 for four hours (the maximum allowed).

THE GROUND

Gone is the delapidated Shay of old, with its speedway track and ancient terracing. In its place has come Super League rugby, an avalanche of money, two brand new behind-the-goal terraces and plans for further redevelopments. The first new terrace, housing 3,800, opened at the Hunger Hill (North) End in April 1998, and has been allocated to away supporters. The terrace is uncovered, but the facilities are good. A second new terrace, a mirror-image of the first, is being built at the Bus Garage (South) End. It's for home fans, and will house the new club shop. The club also proposes to move the pitch towards the Hunger Hill Terrace and the Skircoat Shed, which, until it is redeveloped itself, will leave the Patron Stand somewhat isolated. Once the ground is fully developed, the capacity will be in the region of 15,000.
Total Capacity: 11,000. For away fans: 3,800.
Cost (98/99): Adult £8, concessions (juniors/OAPs) £4, children under 12 £2.
Disabled Facilities: Space for 14 supporters in front of the Hunger Hill Terrace. *Disabled Toilet:* Nearby. *Cost:* £4 for disabled, matchday price for helper. *Booking:* Preferable. *Parking:* Available, please contact club in advance. *For the Blind:* Not yet known.
Programme: £1.50.
Visitors' Toilets: Halifax Town is moving away fans onto the Hunger Hill terrace for season 98/99, where the facilities are most acceptable.
Food and Drink: 'Your tea looks very nice', we said encouragingly to a home fan. 'It's coffee', he said brightly. His brew (60p) turned out to be good, but the tea (60p) was even better ... it came in its constituent parts (viz., cup, hot water, teabag, milk, sugar) and was excellent. So good in fact that we declare Halifax the winners of the coveted BAFTA (Best Away Football Tea Award). The pies (£1.20) – with a choice of mince or meat-and-potato – were also very tasty. Most fans, however, thought the boiled-meat burgers (£1.50) were ghastly (4.4.98).

PUB GUIDE

Most pubs near the ground are home only, and away fans are encouraged to stop at hostelries along the main A629 approach road:
The Quays (1) Salterhebble Hill, Huddersfield Road (01422) 347 700
Greenalls (with 7 hand-pulled ales). Spacious smart

family-orientated pub, with a large conservatory-style area overlooking the Calder-Hebble Navigation canal, and a separate family dining room. Full menu served all day from midday. Children's menu. TV. Disabled facilities and baby changing. Outdoor play area. Open: all day.

The Punch Bowl Inn (2) 389 Huddersfield Road, Salterhebble (01422) 366 937

Mansfield. Traditional two-roomed hostelry. Pool table, TV. Families welcome. Beer garden. Open: Fri-Sun all day, from 5 pm for midweek games.

'The Barge and Barrel' is a well-known real-ale pub in the town of Elland. Directions are given below, taking fans by other hostelries which might also be worth a try.

The Barge and Barrel Park Road, Elland (01422) 373 623

Free House. Spacious friendly traditional ale-house by the Calder and Hebble Navigation Canal. Good range of meals and snacks, including vegetarian selection, served 12-2.30, and (Tues, Wed, Fri and Saturday) 6-8 pm. Separate pool room. TV, darts. Families welcome, children's menu. Open: all day from 11.30.

How to get there: Exit the M62 onto the A629. Exit A629 after 1.3 miles (s/p Elland, Lowfields Business Park). At roundabout turn left (s/p Elland, Greetland B6114). At the next roundabout turn right, and follow the road round over the River Calder and right into Park Road.

FOOD GUIDE

Surprisingly, those approaching The Shay from the M62 along the A629 pass only one takeaway, the excellent Cantonese/Peking outlet called 'TinTin'. It's just after the Falcon pub on the LHS. However, the town centre has a great choice: try 'Elsie's' on New Road, which does a pie and peas special for £1.25; 'Pearson's' restaurant/takeaway on Union Street; or the 'Silver Spray' fish and chip shop on Clare Street. Locals recommend the 'Pride of Whitby' restaurant on the corner of Horton Street and Wards End – try the 'Whitby Whopper' haddock and chips for £5.25. There's also a Pizza Hut on Wards End. For a classic greasy spoon, head for the 'Yorkshire Fayre Cafe' on Westgate.

Piece Hall, on Westgate, is being developed as a market and craft centre, with lots of unusual little shops and cafés. Two mobile stalls are worth visiting: 'H. Walker Barbequed Chicken' offering hot chicken and turkey sandwiches with stuffing for £1.40; and the 'Rhine Sausage Company' which has, as the name implies, a range of sausages, as well as a 'Frickadelle Burger', made of Danish Pork, for £1.40. Of the cafés, try 'Croquembouche', which does an amazing array of fresh filled baguettes, and has a top quality patisserie. Nearby is 'Dunkers' Delight' with a range of American-style doughnuts (3 for £1).

"I'm sorry Mr Chairman, but my client won't accept anything less than 40 tins of 'Whiskas' per week!"

LOCAL MEDIA

Local Radio: Radio Leeds 92.4 FM, 107.9 Huddersfield FM.

Radio Phone-ins: Radio Leeds, Saturdays 5-6 pm, call (0113) 244 3222.

Saturday Sports Paper: The *Yorkshire Sport* produces a Saturday 'Pink'.

MISCELLANEOUS

Of all the great stories to come out of The Shay, perhaps the one about Benny the cat takes the biscuit. Back in season 1992/93 the club was so strapped for cash that the then-manager John McGrath sent a letter round all the companies he could think of, asking for a moggy-sponsor, as the club could no longer afford cat-food. Which is how Benny became to be sponsored by a London computer company. The same season, the manager contacted clubs with a list of all the players up for sale, and there at the bottom was, you guessed it, 'Benny the Cat'.

Safety Factor: Fans and police have difficulty remembering when there was last any safety problem at The Shay.

Rivals: The Supporters' Club, when asked to list their club's main rivals, simply chorused 'Burnley'.

Fanzine: 'Shaymen Down South', 175 Peartree Lane, Welwyn Garden City, Herts, AL7 3XL.

Unofficial Websites:

'Shaymen Online': http://www.shaymen.clara.net/
http://expage.com/page/Shaymen/

Tourist Information: (01422) 368 725.

Hartlepool United

Victoria Park

Address: Victoria Park, Clarence Road, Hartlepool, TS24 8BZ
Telephone: Club/Ticket Office (01429) 272 584

Major changes are underway at Hartlepool. The conversion of the old docks continues apace, with a marina complete with pubs and restaurants, a tall ships centre and a huge new shopping arcade. The old town too is undergoing a major facelift. The great news is that all these new facilities are within walking distance of Victoria Park, and there's parking right at the ground. Hartlepool fans have also been seeing some startling innovations at Victoria Park. The club now belongs to an Aberdeen-based oil company, which in turn is owned by a Norwegian oil magnate. And in season 97/98 the team was graced by a number of Norwegian internationals! The building work along the seafront has helped to cut out that mid-winter Arctic wind, but – as Third Division veterans will warn you – it's still a good idea to bring the warm mitts!

HOW TO GET THERE

BY CAR: From South: Exit A1 at junction 49 (s/p Thirsk A168, Teesside (A19)) onto the A19. Exit A19 after 37.7 miles (s/p Bishop Auckland, Motorway A1(M), Hartlepool A689). At roundabout turn right (s/p Hartlepool A689) onto the A689 dual carriageway. Follow 'Hartlepool A689' and 'Town Centre' signs for 6.4 miles, over four roundabouts, to major junction/lights by the Middleton Grange Shopping Centre and Wilkinsons. Here, go straight on (s/p The North, Sunderland, Durham A179 (A19)), and, just after the 'Hartlepool Mail' on the LHS, take left filter into Clarence Road. Ground is on LHS after about 200 yards.
From North (A19): Exit A19 at signpost Hartlepool A179, and at T-junction turn left onto the A179. Follow 'Hartlepool A179' signs for 3.0 miles over two roundabouts, to 3rd roundabout. Here turn right (s/p Town Centre, Docks A179) onto Easington Road. For next 1.5 miles, follow signs to 'Town Centre A179' over three roundabouts. At 4th roundabout after 0.5 miles, just after the snazzy blue-and-white railway bridge, turn right into new docks development. At next roundabout, after 0.5 miles, go straight on for the Jackson's Wharf parking. Minibuses/cars coming to Victoria Park from the North (A19) wanting to park at the ground should note that Clarence Road is one-way northbound. To get there: Follow directions as above, turning into Easington Road. At 2nd roundabout turn right into Raby Road. Go straight on through two sets of lights,

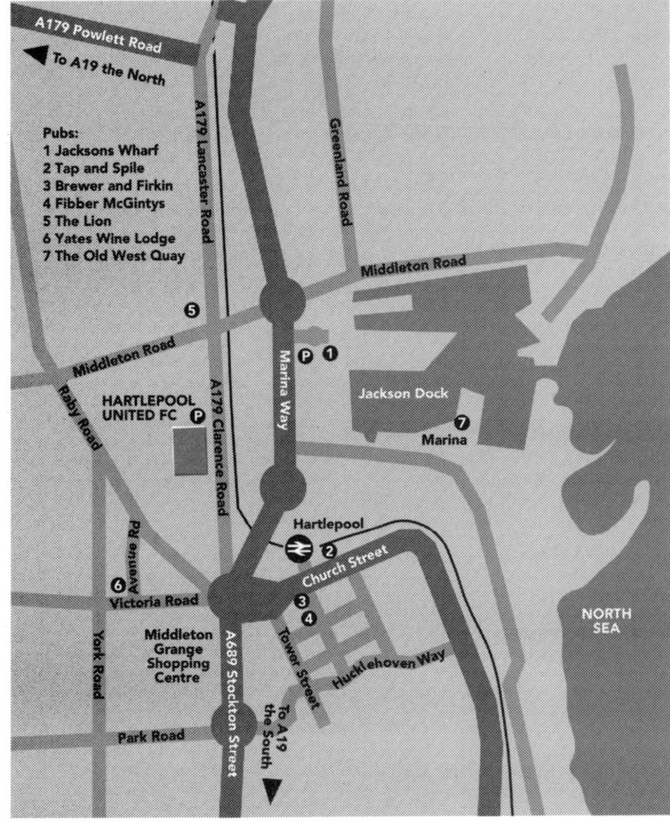

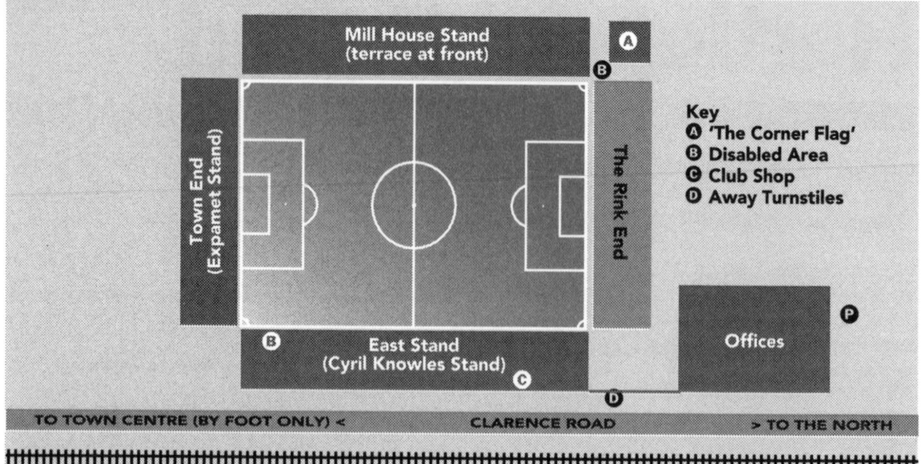

passing the Millhouse Centre on the LHS. Take 2nd left by new leisure park to ground.

FROM RAILWAY STATION (Hartlepool): About 0.3 miles. *By bus/taxi:* It's as quick to walk. *By foot:* Head straight out of the station, along Station Approach, to the main road (Church Street). Turn right towards church/art centre. Keep straight on, past church, to roundabout. The ground is visible from here.

Last Midweek Trains: The 'last train to anywhere' – to quote National Rail Enquiries – is at 21.02. Please double-check on (0345) 484 950.

BY BUS: Buses either run along Marina Way or along roads to the west of the ground (The Mill House). Running along Marina Way are services 7 and 7A, 3A, 4, 2 and 2A, and 14. The most frequent services to the Mill House are the 6 and 36. Other services include the nos. 1, 3 and 12.

PARKING

Free parking is available right by the ground, off Clarence Road. Alternatively, there's limited street parking, with early arrivals finding spaces in Raby Road. The new marina area, especially round Jackson's Wharf about five minutes' walk from Victoria Park, has loads of parking spaces right up to kick-off.

THE GROUND

Victoria Park is a smart, compact, ever-improving ground, the result of an ambitious board of directors keen for the club to rise through the divisions. It already has two all-seater stands – the Cyril Knowles Stand and the Rink End – and plans are afoot for a major redevelopment of the Mill House Stand. The idea is to build behind and underneath the stand, adding in executive boxes, lounges, a conference centre, gym and football school of excellence, at a cost of more than £1.5 million. Visiting fans are housed in the Rink End, named after a much-loved and long-since-demolished dance hall. The view is good, the acoustics better but the facilities a mite disappointing for a redeveloped stand.

Total Capacity: 7,271. For away fans: 741. Turnstiles 1 and 2 off Clarence Road.

Cost (98/99): Adults £11, concessions (juniors/OAPs) £8. Visiting fans are welcome in the Family Stand (part of the Cyril Knowles Stand) through prior arrangement. Cost: Adults £9, child £6.

Disabled Facilities: Space for ten visiting supporters in the Cyril Knowles Stand. *Disabled Toilet:* Behind disabled enclosure. *Cost:* £5 for disabled, £5 for helper. *Booking:* No. *Parking:* None available, though it's not usually difficult to find a space close by. *For the Blind:* No special facilities.

Programme: £1.50.

Visitors' Toilets: *Male:* Supporters found a small fault in one of the cubicles. However much liquid was added in the top of the bowl, the same amount emerged in a puddle at the bottom! Apart from that, the facilities were good for the division. *Female:* It doesn't bear thinking about: a metallic loo seat at frost-bitten Hartlepool! And don't leave the loo trip to the last minute, as there's just one cubicle.

Food and Drink: The FFG's favourite quote-master, Doncaster fan Ronnie, tasted the meat-and-potato pie (£1.40) and said: 'At first taste it appeared rather bland. But with the addition of tangy tomato sauce it then tasted like a bland pie with tangy tomato sauce on it'. So there you have it. Rotherham supporters, however, really liked them ... 'they looked and tasted lovely' said one. A

travelling tea expert assessed the Pools brew (60p): 'Yes, Assam with a hint of China. It would have been better with a teabag!' (24.1.98 and 28.2.98).

PUB GUIDE

Jackson's Wharf (1) The Highlight, Hartlepool Marina (01429) 862 963
Camerons. A top-rate new pub by the marina. Home-made bar meals served 12-2.30. Families welcome. Disabled facilities. Open: all day from 12.

The Tap and Spile (2) Church Street, near station (01429) 222 400
Century Inns (7 real ales). Warm, friendly traditional real-ale house, smartly done-out, all open plan on two floors. TV. Open: 12-3, 6-11.

The Brewer and Firkin (3) 2 Whitby Street (01429) 273 564
Whitbread (with real ale selection). Smart, traditional pub in 250-year-old building, winner of the town's best pub food award for the last two years. Meals, costing about £3, served 12-2. Pool, darts, big-screen TV. Families welcome. Open: all day Saturday, check with pub for midweek matchday opening times.

Fibber McGintys (4) Whitby Street (01429) 861 555
Free House. Popular Irish theme pub with wooden floors, tables and stools. Bar snacks served 12-3. Live music every night. Open: all day.

Also recommended: **The Lion (6),** 1 Lancaster Road, a small, traditional Whitbreads pub with pool table, darts, TV and car park; **Yates Wine Lodge (5),** a new pub on Victoria Road, with an excellent menu served 11-6.

FOR FAMILIES:
Two excellent choices: **The Old West Quay (7)** on Maritime Avenue is a large smart Brewers Fayre pub overlooking the marina, serving a full/children's menu from 11.30; **Owton Lodge,** on Stockton Road is on the route in From South. It's a Whitbread pub with everything for the footie family: an excellent menu, big-screen TV, 3 pool tables and outdoor and indoor play areas.

FOOD GUIDE

Church Street, the main road by the station, has the best selection. Try one of the following: the 'Romantic Palace' Chinese restaurant; 'The Bistro', a welcoming restaurant with a £6.95 set menu; 'Dillingers', a Cajun/Mexican bistro/restaurant, the favourite haunt of Emerson and Juninho during their Middlesbrough days; and the highly recommended 'Joe Rigatoni's'. On the corner of Station Approach is 'Beni's Fish and Chips', which serves pizzas, kebabs, chicken and burgers. By the church/art centre is the 'Al Syros', a friendly, beautifully decorated Mediterranean restaurant (average main meal price £9). There are also a couple of cafés in the Middleton Grange shopping centre to the south of Victoria Park.

New in the club shop "Supporter in a snowstorm."

LOCAL MEDIA

Local Radio: BBC Radio Cleveland 95 FM; Century Radio 100.7, 101.8, 96.2 and 96.4 FM; TFM 96.6 FM.
Radio Phone-ins: Century Radio, Monday-Friday 6-7 pm. Call (0191) 477 2000.
Saturday Sports Paper: 'The Mail Sports Special', produced by the *Hartlepool Mail.*

MISCELLANEOUS

It's not just the great illustrious teams which record their own songs. Back in the 1970s Hartlepool brought out a real belter, a 45 classic – and one of the FFG writers once had a copy. The words ran: 'Who put sugar in my tea, who put my boots away?/Once you win a game or two, they want you all to stay'. Our memories fail at this point ... More recently the club released another record called 'Up and Away'. But Pools fans are happier letting rip with their own version of the Rolf Harris classic 'Two Little Boys'.

Safety Factor: No problems here.
Rivals: The excellent fanzine 'Monkey Business' is particularly down on 'Dar-low', the 'lame old seadogs' at the 'Chip Pan Stadium', 'Piddlesbrough' (the 'smogmonsters') and 'Blunderland' at the 'Stadium of Blight'.
Fanzine: 'Monkey Business', 12 Swanage Grove, Hartlepool, Co. Durham, TS24 9RR.
Unofficial Websites:
'In the Net': http://www.geocities.com/Colosseum/Field/1490/
'Flying Pig': http://www.geocities.com/Colosseum/4221/
'Pools Statistics': http://www.stud.ifi.uio.no/~frodehe/Hartlepool/Pools.html
'Poolie Paradise': http://geocities.com/Colosseum/Sideline/6347/
Tourist Information: (01429) 266 522.

H

Huddersfield Town

The Alfred McAlpine Stadium

Address: The Alfred McAlpine Stadium, Huddersfield HD1 6PX
Telephone: Club (01484) 484 100
Ticket Office (01484) 424 123
Club Shop (01484) 484 144
ClubCall (0891) 121 635

The Alfred McAlpine Stadium is in a humdrum suburb just north of Huddersfield town centre, among a plethora of car showrooms, petrol stations and light industrial units. But there's absolutely nothing humdrum about the ground itself, with its huge high-tech blue roofs and white curved steelwork. And as it's on a slight rise, the stadium dominates its surroundings, giving a great view over the distant traditional houses and chimneys. Around the ground, eateries are few and far between, though it's only a ten minute walk to the town centre. Pubs are less of a problem, but parking can be, so allow a little more time to find a space.

HOW TO GET THERE

BY CAR: From South: Exit M1 at junction 38 (s/p Huddersfield A637). At motorway roundabout take second exit (s/p Huddersfield A637). Keep on the A637 for 6.1 miles, over one roundabout, to the Grange Moor Roundabout. Here, take first exit (s/p Huddersfield A642) onto the A642. At lights at the Waterloo Junction after 3.4 miles, by Cooke service station, go straight on (s/p Huddersfield A629, M62). After 1.7 miles, after passing through several sets of lights, turn right (by old church, now Aspley carpets, on LHS, s/p Leeds A62) into St Andrews Road. Pass 'The Aspley' pub on the LHS, and after 0.5 miles turn right at crossroads by Ford Cowie to ground.

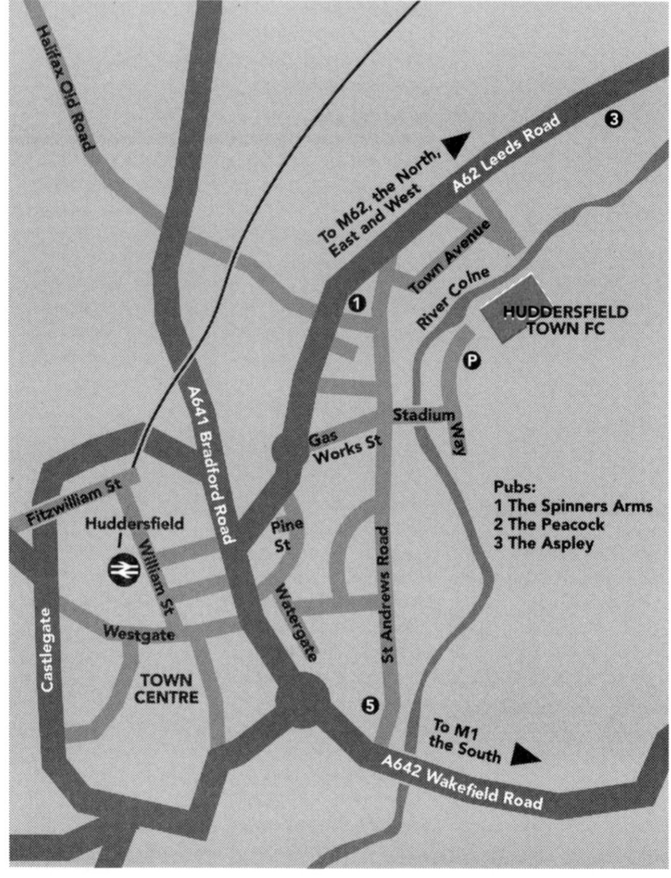

From North and East: Exit M62 at junction 25 (s/p Brighouse A644, Huddersfield (A62), also Alfred McAlpine Stadium). At motorway roundabout follow signs to 'Huddersfield East (A62), Dewsbury A644' onto the A644 Wakefield Road. At Cooper Bridge roundabout after 1.1 miles turn right (s/p Huddersfield A62). Follow 'Huddersfield A62' signs through several sets of lights for 2.9 miles and then turn left (s/p Sheffield A629, Wakefield A642, McAlpine Stadium) into St Andrews Road. At lights after 0.2 miles (by Ford Cowie) turn left to ground.

From West: Exit M62 at junction 24. At roundabout

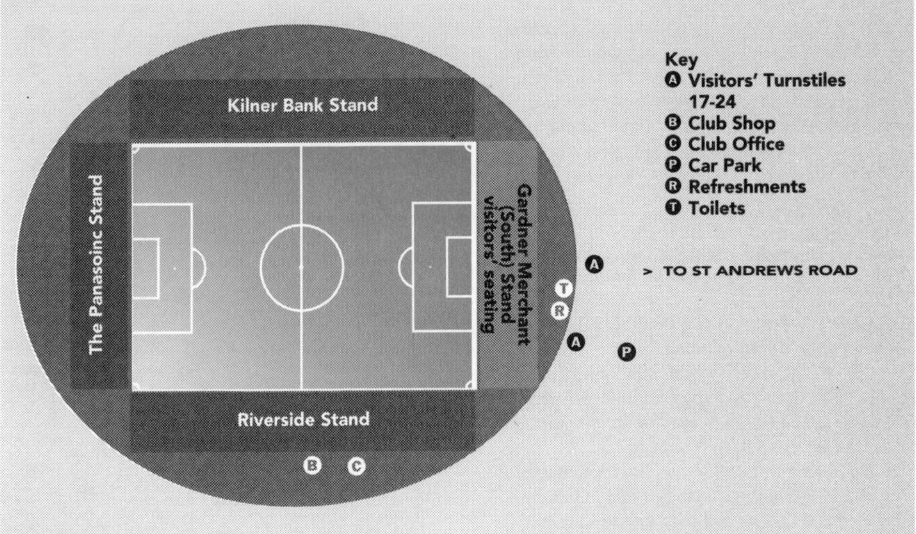

turn right, under the motorway. At roundabout after 0.2 miles, take 4th exit (s/p Huddersfield A629) onto the A629 Halifax Road. The ground is signposted from here (ie to end of the A629, left onto the Ring Road, second major exit onto the A62 Leeds Road).
NB: The above routes are designed for cars. Coach operators should check routes in advance with the police Football Liaison Officer on (01484) 436 654.
FROM RAILWAY STATION (Huddersfield): *By taxi:* £3. *By foot:* Bear left out of station past the George Hotel. Straight over crossroads into Northumberland Street. At end of street, go straight over major crossroads (s/p Leeds A62). At roundabout after 0.2 miles, just after 'Homestyle' bear right into Gas Works Street, passing the gas works and crossing canal. Straight on at crossroads by Ford Cowie to ground.
Last Midweek Trains: There are trains to Leeds at 23.52, to Liverpool at 22.13, Manchester Piccadilly at 23.59, to Newcastle at 22.25 and to Sheffield at 22.20. But there are no connecting trains to London. Please double-check on (0345) 484 950.
BY BUS: Special matchday buses, nos. 330 and 331, run from the bus station on Queensgate. Normal bus services to Leeds, nos. 201, 202, 203, 217, 218, 219, 220, 221 and 229 also run along Leeds Road.

PARKING

A lot of the parking at the ground is now reserved by season-ticket holders, but some spaces in the St Andrews Road car park are available to visiting fans on the day, cost £2. Otherwise there's a charity car park in Gas Works Street (£2) and a small multi-storey on Pine Street (40p/hour to 6 pm), which is signposted off the Leeds Road. Otherwise it's street parking. Car crime is a problem so keep valuables out of sight.

THE GROUND

Here's something unusual: a new stadium designed with imagination! The Alfred McAlpine Stadium, unlike many new grounds, does not consist of four 'box' stands arranged warehouse-style around the pitch. Since its construction in 1995 the ground has, however, suffered from the lack of a fourth side behind one goal. That stand, the Panasonic, is set to open for the start of the 1998/99 season, completing a fine modern sporting arena. Away supporters are housed in the Gardner Merchant Stand behind the goal, where the view and facilities are good.
Total Capacity: 24,000. For away fans: 4,000. Turnstiles 17 to 24.
Cost (98/99): Adults £12, concessions (under 16s and OAPs) £6.
Disabled Facilities: Space for 16 wheelchairs at the back of the South Stand, where the view is good. *Disabled Toilet:* In the same stand. *Cost:* £7 for disabled, £7 for helper. *Booking:* Essential. *Parking:* Available. *For the Blind:* Up to 26 spaces available in the lower tier of the Lawrence Batley Stand.
Programme: £1.80
Visitors' Toilets: *Male:* As one would expect from a nearly new stadium, the facilities were clean and spacious. However, fans were taken aback to find puddles on the floor before kick-off! *Female:* One of those annoying toilets where fans couldn't find anything to complain about!
Food and Drink: The 'Pie and Pint' counter had, as

the name suggests, Fosters and John Smiths at £1.90 a pint and Hollands Pies at £1.40. The meat-and-potato pie was tasty ('crusty pastry and a hot filling'), while the cheese-and-onion variety gave vegetarians something decent to munch on for a change. The 'Burger Bar', which didn't serve alcohol, was much less popular ... a pity, because the quarterpounder with cheese (£2.20) was good. Hot dogs (£2) and chips (£1) were also on sale (13.9.97, 28.3.98).

PUB GUIDE

The five pubs listed below are all on the A62 Leeds Road.

The Spinner's Arms (1) 100 Leeds Road (corner of Thistle Street) (01484) 421 062
Bass (with Millers). Friendly locals pub, immensely popular on matchdays so expect standing room only! Bar snacks served until pub becomes too crowded. Pool table. Disabled facilities. Open: all day.

The Woodman 862 Leeds Road, Bradley (between M62 and the ground) (01484) 531 993
Whitbread (with Trophy and guest beers). Large roadside pub, serving the 'Forrester's Feast' menu 12-2.30. Big screen TV, pool, table football, darts. Families welcome. Open: all day.

The Peacock Inn (2) 392 Leeds Road (opposite McDonalds) (01484) 427 637
Wards (with Samson, Lambtons, Double Max). Friendly, characterful pub in an old coach house. All-day breakfast served 8 am-12 noon, plus sandwiches 'until they're gone'! Pool table. Families welcome. Open: all day.

Also highly recommended: **The White Horse,** 761 Leeds Road, a recently-refurbished Free House with big-screen TV, and serving bar meals 12-3; **The Wise Owl** on Leeds Road, Deighton, a traditional Bass pub serving breakfast from 7.30 am, and bar snacks all day. It too has a big-screen TV.

FOR FAMILIES: A choice of two excellent pubs: **The Aspley (3)** on St Andrews Road is a large Whitbread/Brewer's Fayre pub, serving a full menu from 11.30; **The Old Corn Mill** on Wakefield Road (between M62 and the ground), a huge restaurant-pub-nightclub complex, with a bar and bistro. Carvery, full meals, snacks and sandwiches served Sat/Sun 12-3, midweek 12-2. Bistro Thurs-Sat evenings 6-10. Children's menu. Open: all day.

FOOD GUIDE

Immediately around the ground the only outlets are burger vans, offering the same fare as inside the away turnstiles. Along the Leeds Road there's a fish and chip shop (2.4 miles from the M62), a McDonalds, and the 'Taj Mahal Indian Food Takeaway'. In the town centre, head for the junction of John William Street and Kirkgate, where there's a McDonalds, a Pizza Hut, a 'Frankie and Benny's New York Italian Restaurant and

'There's one good thing about seats. At least we're miserable in comfort.'

Bar' and a recommended Tribells fish and chip shop/restaurant, also serving Holland's pasties. Also on John William Street is 'Sizzlers', with pizzas, kebabs and burgers, and 'Anaton's Restaurant', which serves full lunches such as meat-and-potato pie with veg for £4.30. For snacks try the 'Lions Coffee House' near the station.

LOCAL MEDIA

Local Radio: 107.9 Huddersfield FM; BBC Radio Leeds 92.4 FM; 96.3 Aire FM.
Radio Phone-Ins: Radio Leeds, Saturdays 5-6 pm, call (0113) 244 3222.
Saturday Sports Paper: None.

MISCELLANEOUS

Safety Factor: CCTV cameras cover the town centre, which has helped cut crime. That said, the small number of Huddersfield hooligans do congregate in town, so visiting fans should take great care walking from, and returning to, the railway station.
Rivals: Leeds United and Bradford City.
Fanzines: None.
Unofficial Websites:
http://home.clara.net/a.r.aedy/htfc/index.html
http://www.bogo.co.uk/richmills/index.htm
Tourist Information: (01484) 223 200.

Hull City

Boothferry Park

Address: Boothferry Park, Boothferry Road, Hull, East Yorkshire, HU4 6EU
Telephone: All enquiries (01482) 327 200

'The best bits of Hull are not near the football ground,' explained one local, extolling the virtues of the city as a thriving port and university town. True, but the area round Boothferry Park is pleasant enough: wide streets, parkland, semi-detached houses ... and a top class fish and chip shop. Finding the ground, which lies just a couple of miles from the main A63 approach road, is easy, and parking's a doddle. Moreover, there are three or four good pubs within easy walking distance. Those looking for a choice of food, however, will need a car ... and might like to try our 'Gourmet Tour' outlined below. For train travellers, it's a two-mile hike from the city centre, but with loads of food and drink possibilities en route.

HOW TO GET THERE

BY CAR: All Main Routes (M1-M62). At junction 38 of the M62 the motorway ends and the road becomes the A63. Exit A63 after 10 miles (s/p Humber Br. A15, Beverley A164, Costello Athletic Stadium, Hull City AFC). At roundabout after 0.5 miles take 2nd exit (s/p Humber Br. A15. Beverley A164) and go straight on at next roundabout after 0.3 miles (s/p Hessle A1105) onto Boothferry Road dual carriageway. (*)At next roundabout, by Total station after 1.1 miles, go straight on (s/p Hull A1105). At next roundabout after 1.5 miles, take 2nd exit (s/p Infirmary, University, Cottingham, also Boothferry Park), remaining on Boothferry Road. Ground is on RHS, behind Kwik Save, after 0.6 miles.

From South (from Humber Bridge – toll £2.10): At roundabout just after bridge turn right (s/p Hessle A1105) onto Boothferry Road dual carriageway. Then as From All Main Routes (*).

FROM RAILWAY STATION (Hull Paragon): 2 miles. *By taxi:* £3.40-£3.50. *By bus:* Stagecoach buses nos. 2 and 15 run along Anlaby Road to the ground, while the no. 1 runs along Hessle Road and North Road. The East Yorkshire Bus no. 66 runs along Anlaby Road every 15 minutes. *By foot:* Turn right along covered concourse (s/p Parcels Point) past Johnson's Heel Bars into courtyard. Turn right across car park, and then left down wide alleyway to main Anlaby Road, by the Prince Regent. Turn right ... and keep going! At roundabout after 0.6 miles go straight on (s/p Anlaby), over the flyover after 0.2 miles passing the Fisherman's Catch and The Parkers, and bear left at roundabout after 1.0 miles (s/p Leeds M62, Humber Bridge A15) and under bridge. Ground is on LHS after 0.2 miles.

Last Midweek Trains: Northbound routes are fine, as there's a train at 22.40 to Doncaster and a connecting train to Newcastle, arriving 01.14. Southbound is a bigger problem, as the last connecting train to London leaves at 20.06. Please double-check on (0345) 484 950.

BY BUS: As above.

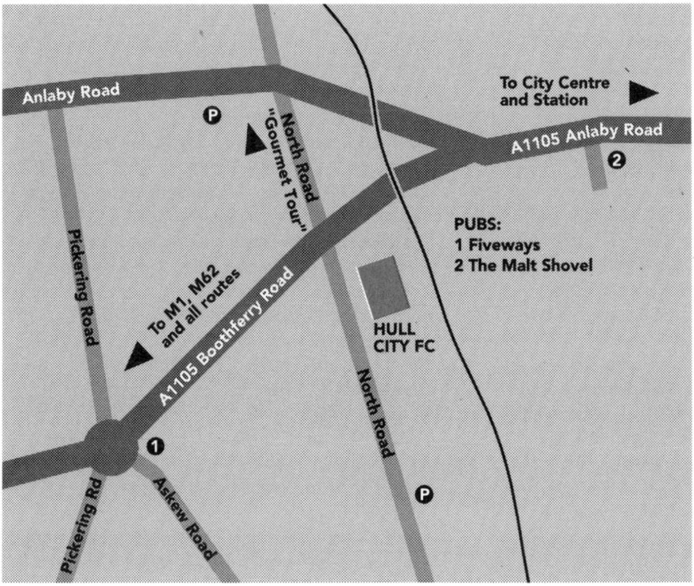

PARKING

Two schools, Eastfield Primary on Anlaby Road and Francis Askew Primary

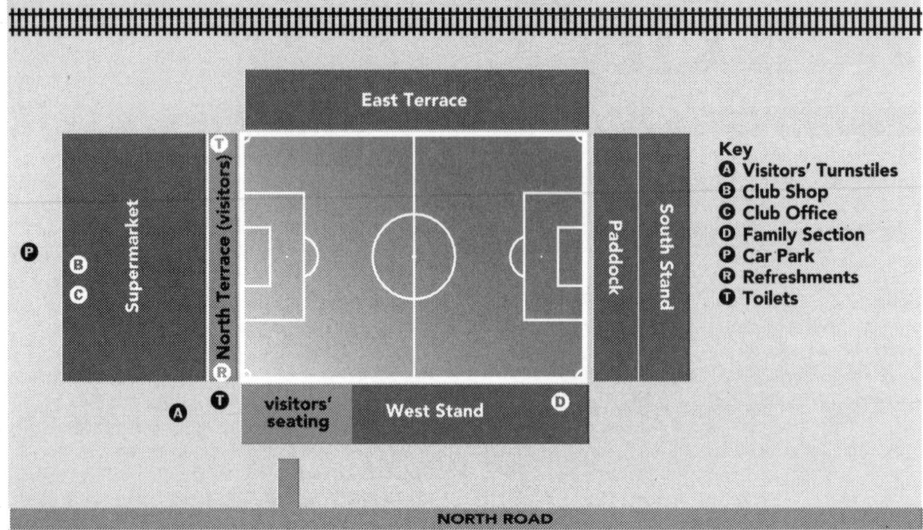

on North Road, provide parking on matchdays for £1.50. To get to Eastfield Primary: at last crossroads/lights before the ground, by the Cadbury newsagents, turn left (s/p Ring Road, University, Cottingham), into North Road. At next crossroads/lights turn left into Anlaby Road. Parking is on LHS. To get to Francis Askew school: At last crossroads before the ground, by the Cadbury newsagents, turn right (s/p Ring Road) into North Road. School is on LHS after 0.4 miles. Otherwise it's street parking. Many people park along Boothferry Road itself. Down sidestreets, don't try to squeeze between police parking cones just because other cars appear to have done so. Residents are allowed to park, football fans are not!

THE GROUND

'Hull Tiger Sharks,' says the telephonist to incoming callers to Hull City. No, not a new nickname, but a sign of the link between the football club and the rugby league team, both owned by tennis player-cum-multi-millionaire businessman David Lloyd. He came to Hull in the summer of 1997 with plans for a £20 million, 20,000-seater stadium and leisure complex, and went on to plough a small fortune into the clubs.

Money, however, does not necessarily buy success, and the spending at Boothferry Park came to an abrupt end a few months later, with Hull City near-bottom of the Third Division. And the plans for a new stadium – which involve the sale of Boothferry Park – have hit a brick wall. Mr Lloyd insists that he needs to buy Kwik Save, the supermarket at the ground, to make the site more attractive to buyers. But the supermarket is quoting too high a price.

And the view of the fans? 'When we see pigs fly by, we'll tell you about the new ground,' said one sceptical local. Many fear that Hull City will end up sharing the rugby league ground at the Boulevard, a move they suspect could be the beginning of the end for the football club.

Most agree however that Boothferry Park today, although much-loved and full of character, is a sad and sorry sight. It's not clear whether the huge East Terrace will be open at all in season 98/99, and plans to replace it with a new 5,000-seater stand have been shelved. Visiting fans are offered a narrow section of open terracing, and seats in the main West Stand. The view from the terrace is good, the pies are tasty, and the loos to be avoided at all costs.

Total Capacity: 13,552. For away fans: Terrace: 1,428, turnstiles 5-7. Seating: 530, turnstile 8.

Cost (98/99): Seating: Adult £11, concessions £5.50. Terrace: Adult £8, concessions £4.

Disabled Facilities: Space for 15 wheelchairs in the south-east corner. *Disabled Toilet:* Within disabled enclosure. *Cost:* Free for disabled, ground admission price for helper. *Booking:* Yes. *Parking:* Available, please book. *For the Blind:* Headphones in the West Stand for hospital radio commentary. Free admission.

Programme: £1.50.

Visitors' Toilets: *Male:* Yes, a front-runner – if not perhaps the overall winner – of the coveted MATITLA, the FFG's 'Most Awful Toilet in the League Award'. A truly stunning smell, and the filthiest cubicles ever seen – so bad in fact that our normally placid researcher launched into a stream of unprintable language. *Female:* 'Not brilliant', said one fan, adding that one of the doors

didn't shut. The sink was small, the soap was small, and the towels non-existent. No smells though.

Food and Drink: Fans liked the pies (£1.55) which – although deemed a tad expensive – were blisteringly hot and very tasty. One supporter said his pie was the best he'd had all season ... 'it's full of everything, it even had a bit of the programme in there!' The sausage rolls (£1.10) were also 'good and hot', as were the burgers (£2.10). Avoid the flat cola (£1.05) and try the bovril, described by one fan as, well, 'bovrilly' (29.11.97).

PUB GUIDE

Fiveways (1) 317 Boothferry Road (01482) 567 984
Bass. Top-rate football friendly pub, with excellent menu and big-screen TV. It has spacious traditional public and lounge bars, with pool table and darts. Bar meals, including giant filled Yorkshire puddings, platters and burgers, served 12-2.30, 5-7. Families welcome. Disabled facilities. Open: all day.

The Malt Shovel (2) 583 Anlaby Road (01482) 501 450
Vaux. Small friendly local set back in a row of shops. Bar lunches. TV, darts. Open: all day.

The Parkers 354 Anlaby Road (01482) 567 911
Bass. Traditional, quiet local with public bar with pool table, and cosy lounge bar. Large TV, beer garden. Sandwiches till they run out. Open: all day.
How to get there: From the ground, continue along Boothferry Road towards town, and at roundabout follow sign to 'City Centre' into Anlaby Road. Pub is on LHS after about 0.8 miles.

FOR FAMILIES:

Darleys 312 Boothferry Road. (01482) 643 121
Vaux (with Sampsons and guest beers). Large, smart pub/restaurant, ideal for a pre-match meal. Bar meals, with vegetarian options, served 12-2, full menu in restaurant. Family room. Public bar with TV, darts. Beer garden. Open: Sat/Sun all day; midweek 11-3, 5.30-11.

FOOD GUIDE

On the main route to the ground from the A63 is one of the best fish and chip shops in the area, 'Starfisher'. Visiting team coaches often stop here on the way home. Next door is a Chinese takeaway which opens at 5 pm.

The nearest outlets to Boothferry Park are on Anlaby Road. 'The Diner' is a small café/takeaway offering hot meals from £2.50. The nearby 'Golden Fisheries' has pies at 70p, while the 'Chicken George' next to the Malt Shovel pub does a spicy beanburger for £1.20 and chicken and chips for £1.80. Hull fans recommend the 'Tandoori Mahal' restaurant/takeaway. Further down Anlaby Road, on the LHS, is the recommended 'Izzy', with pizzas, kebabs, burgers and chicken meals. Almost next door is the excellent 'Shazan's', an Indian restaurant also serving pasta and pizza.

Supporters with a car might like to try our 'Gourmet Tour', compiled with the help of the Hull City Supporters Club. At the last crossroads before Boothferry Park, with the Cadbury's newsagents on the corner, turn left (s/p Ring Road, University, Cottingham) into North Road. At roundabout after 0.7 miles turn right (s/p off roundabout City Centre, Park and Ride) onto Spring Bank West. Immediately on the RHS is 'Pizza Peepers', which offers a varied menu including 'Spaghetti Pastaceria' for £3.30. Continue on Spring Bank West for 1.4 miles, passing a fish and chip shop and a couple of pubs, and turn left, by the Old Zoological Tom Cobleigh pub, into Prince's Avenue. This junction has a number of possibilities: the 'Asian Kitchen', the 'Spring Garden' Chinese takeaway, the 'Royal Tandoori', 'Las Vegas – English, Italian, American, Indian Food Continental Takeaway' and 'Chaplins Tex-Mex Vegetarian Restaurant'. After 0.5 miles, at the roundabout by the Queen's pub, turn right into Queens Road. At crossroad/lights after 0.3 miles turn right into Beverley Road. Straight on for 0.9 miles: here on the RHS is the 'Ferensway South' car park, ideal for those heading into the town centre. Otherwise, go straight on for 0.4 miles and turn right (s/p Infirmary, Anlaby) into Anlaby Road. From here, it's two miles straight on to the ground, passing the 'Kebab Barn', the recommended 'Fisherman's Catch' and all the outlets near the ground.

LOCAL MEDIA

Local Radio: BBC Radio Humberside 95.9 FM; Viking Radio 96.9 FM.

Radio Phone-ins: BBC Radio Humberside, Tuesdays 7-10 pm. Call (01482) 225 959.

Saturday Sports Paper: The 'Sports Mail'.

MISCELLANEOUS

Safety Factor: Although Hull City has a small hooligan following, there were few problems in season 97/98.

Rivals: Understandably, City fans don't like Hull Sharks, while among football teams, Grimsby are the obvious main rivals. 'Our fish shops fry fish much better than theirs', said one fan. 'And our water's nicer here too!' Scunthorpe, Scarborough and Doncaster (as in 'Thank God for ...') still feature as front-runners.

Fanzine: 'Amber Nectar', 12 Newington Avenue, Hull, HU4 6EP.

Unofficial Websites: http://www.hullcity.demon.co.uk

Tourist Information: (01482) 223 344.

I

Ipswich Town

Portman Road

Address: Portman Road, Ipswich, IP1 2DA
Telephone: Club (01473) 400 500
Ticket Office (01473) 400 555
Club Shop (01473) 400 501
Soccerline (0839) 664 488
Official Website: http://www.itfc.co.uk

Ipswich is a compact town, with a characterful, pedestrianised shopping centre and a series of excellent pubs and restaurants. No, we haven't been slipped a couple of hundred quid by Ipswich Borough Council! It's simply that all these amenities, plus the railway station, are but a short walk from Portman Road. Keep some coins to hand, however, for the pay-and-display car parks. However, times are a'changin' at Portman Road. A new leisure development is underway at nearby Cardinal Park, towards the railway station, with a multiplex cinema, bars and restaurants such as Brannigans and McDonalds. There are also proposals for further developments much nearer the ground, on land including the car park behind the 'Drum and Monkey' pub.

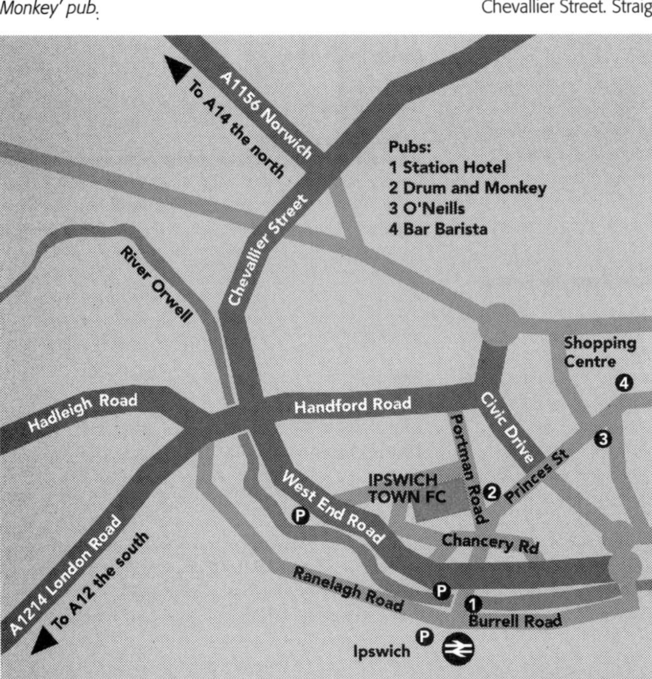

HOW TO GET THERE

BY CAR: From South (A12): The A12 leads to a major roundabout (by Tescos and Toys R Us) on Ipswich outskirts. Take 2nd exit (s/p Ipswich A1214, Hadleigh A1071, Football Ground) into London Road, passing Burger King on the LHS. Follow 'Ipswich A1214' signs for 2.4 miles, over roundabout and lights, to a major junction/lights at the bottom of hill. Go straight on (s/p Town Centre, Football Ground) and then, after a few yards at next lights, turn right (s/p Cliff Quay, Football Ground) into West End Road. The Princes Street car park is on the RHS after 0.5 miles. From here it's a five minute walk to the ground.

From North and West (A14): Two possibilities: a) Continue on A14 to junction with A12, and pick up route From South. b) Exit A14 at s/p 'Ipswich West and North A1156'. Follow 'Ipswich West and North' signs over two roundabouts into Bury Road, which becomes Norwich Road. After 1.7 miles, at double roundabout by Inkerman pub, turn right (s/p Colchester A12) into Chevallier Street. Straight on at crossroads after 0.3 miles (crossing Bramford Road). After 0.4 miles straight on at lights (s/p Cliff Quay, Football) into West End Road. The Princes Street car park is on the RHS after 0.5 miles.

FROM RAILWAY STATION (Ipswich): A five minute walk. Head straight out of station and pass to the left of the Station Hotel. Over bridge and two sets of lights into Princes Street. First left into Portman Road.

Last Midweek Trains: To London Liverpool Street 21.43 and 22.45. And that's about it, as there are no connecting trains either north or west. Please double-check on (0345) 484 950.

PARKING

Street parking is a real problem round Portman Road, so for peace of mind the best idea is to head for one of the many

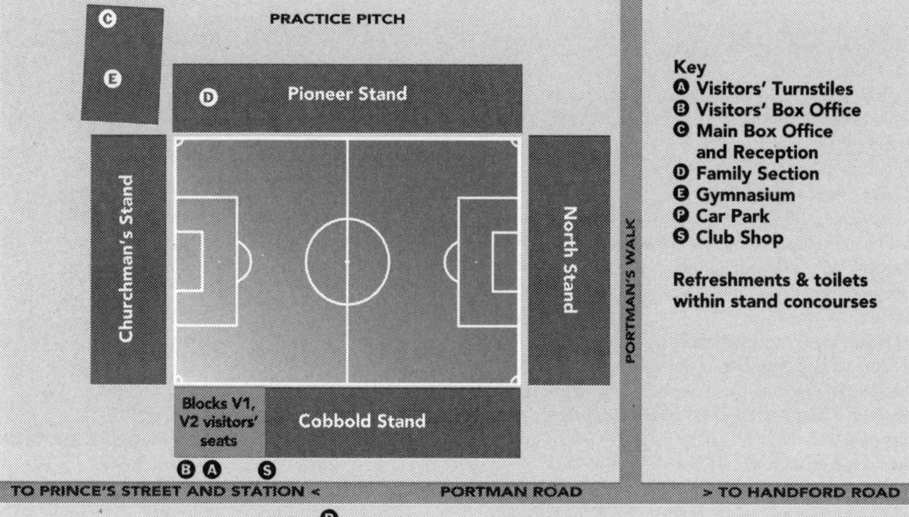

pay-and-display car parks. The Princes Street car park, mentioned above, is signposted off West End Road, and charges £1.80 for three hours, £2.70 all day and 60p all day Sunday. Ranelagh School in Paul's Road runs a matchday car park (£1), and there's pay-and-display parking at the railway station. There's also a huge car park in Portman Road itself (access via Handford Road). Visiting fans using this car park are advised not to leave anything in the car, including stickers from the local garage, which identify their home town.

THE GROUND

Portman Road is a ground with two impressive side stands, the Pioneer and the Cobbold, and two smaller, bland stands – the North and the Churchman's – behind each goal. The Pioneer Stand has three tiers, and four layers of advertisements, giving visiting fans, sitting opposite, plenty to read during half-time! The club is considering adding extra tiers onto the North and Churchman's Stands, although everything has first to be agreed with the council, which owns the ground. Visiting supporters are housed in a side section of the two-tiered Cobbold Stand, in blocks V1 and V2. The view is good, though the seats are rather cramped and the facilities overcrowded. This is caused by a narrow corridor linking blocks V1 and V2, which fills up with fans heading for the refreshment kiosk and queuing for the toilets.

Total Capacity: 22,600. For away fans: Seating (Blocks V1 and V2 of the Cobbold Stand) 1,700. There are new additional turnstiles for away fans, but supporters paying on the day should still buy tickets on arrival (i.e, before going to the pub/town), to avoid long queues nearer kick-off.

Cost (98/99): Adult £15, concessions £8.

Disabled Facilities: Space for 40 wheelchairs in the Pioneer Stand. *Disabled Toilet:* 'Within 25 yards,' says the club. *Cost:* Free for disabled, £12 for helper. *Booking:* Essential. *Parking:* Not available. *For the Blind:* 12 seats with plug-in headphones. Please ring club for details.

Programme: £1.80.

Visitors Toilets: *Male:* Fans admired the 'marbled effect' of the rusting metal, but stressed that it was all remarkably clean. *Female:* Ipswich Town, probably quite rightly, suspects that football fans retain that primordial urge to nick toilet rolls, because the loo paper in the ladies was firmly encased in solid plastic holders. It was all very smart, done out in blue, white and grey. The only downer was that the hot-air-dryer was a cold-air-dryer.

Food and Drink: The beef and onion pie (£1.55) was excellent, one of the best in the league ... 'made with proper animals' said one fan. Unfortunately the chicken-and-mushroom variety was not available, which left non-red-meat eaters with nothing except crisps and chocolate. Fans liked the burgers (£2.10) but thought them overpriced. The hot chocolate (£1) tasted of chlorine while supporters complained loudly about the 'TCP tea' (90p) (10.11.97).

PUB GUIDE

The Station Hotel (1) Burrell Road (opposite railway station) (01473) 620 664
Scottish and Newcastle (with Theakstons XB, Greene King IPA). Large, traditional wood-paneled pub, very football friendly and highly recommended. Sandwiches.

TV. Families welcome. Accommodation available. Open: all day.

The Drum and Monkey (2) Princes Street (01473) 253 025

Carlsberg-Tetley. Modern pub right by the ground. Very away-fan friendly – there's a big screen TV which shows videos of the away team! Basic front bar, but pleasant, large lounge bar at the rear. Bar food served 11-3. Open: all day.

The following pubs are in the town centre. To get there, walk along Princes Street passing the Drum and Monkey. At roundabout go into underpass, exiting at s/p 'Princes Street, Town Centre'. From here, follow signs for the Buttermarket.

O'Neills (3) 5 Princes Street (01473) 282 921

Bass (with Caffreys). Classic wooden-floored Irish theme bar. Friendly, welcoming atmosphere and helpful staff. Food (including Irish specials) served 12-7. Open: all day from 11.

Bar Barista (4) (formerly **The Wig and Pen**) 9 Buttermarket (01473) 219 376

Morland (with Old Speckled Hen and guests). Light, airy town centre pub, fun and full of character. Full and varied menu, with veggie options, served 11.30-8. Big-screen TV. Open: all day, closed Sundays.

FOOD GUIDE

A number of burger vans appear around the ground on matchdays, and that's about it in the immediate vicinity. However, it's only a few minutes walk into the town centre (see under pub guide above for route). Head for the Buttermarket and the Buttermarket Shopping Centre. McDonalds is on Tavern Street, which runs parallel to, and north of, the Buttermarket.

St Nicholas Street has a group of outlets, including 'Marno's', a busy and cheerful vegetarian restaurant open from 10.30-3.30 and on Saturday evenings. Nearby is the highly recommended 'Los Mexicanos', a Mexican restaurant where a main course costs about £7.50. To get to St Nicholas Street, head along Princes Street past the 'Drum and Monkey'. At the roundabout, turn right into Franciscan Way, then bear left into Cromwell Square. Left at the T-junction by the row of old houses into St Nicholas Street. For an excellent Indian restaurant called 'The Ghandi', turn right instead of left at the T-junction.

LOCAL MEDIA

Local Radio: BBC Radio Suffolk 103.9 FM (East Suffolk, Ipswich), 104.6 FM (West Suffolk); SGR FM 91.1.

Radio Phone-ins: BBC Radio Suffolk, 5.30 pm after the game. Call (01473) 212 121.

Saturday Sports Paper: 'The Green 'Un', 45p.

'The Gaffer wants you on. That's the fifth time we've hit the post!'

MISCELLANEOUS

Exorcisms of churches, haunted houses and spooky cellars we've heard of, but Ipswich Town must be the first to bring in a witch-doctor to lift the curse of a goalpost. Fans started noticing two years ago that the ball was hitting the North Stand goalpost, instead of the back of the net, at vital moments, such as play-off semi-finals, and, in 1998, the Coca-Cola Cup quarter-final against Chelsea, which Ipswich then lost on penalties. It got so bad that Ipswich fans started singing: 'Stand up if you hate the post'. So, in February 1998, the club brought in an anonymous witch-doctor, complete with leopard skin, who jumped around behind the goal chanting – according to the write-up in the *Ipswich Evening Star* – 'Pest of the Post/Repent of your sin/Each time we hit you/We never win. Listen to me/It's for your own good/If it happens again/You'll end up as firewood!'

Safety Factor: A safe ground to visit. The only major problems were when Norwich came to town.

Rivals: Norwich City. 'It's a county thing, Suffolk versus Norfolk,' explained one fan. Another said there's still a lot of resentment over the vast amount of coverage given to 'Norwich's one great season in Europe' (1993). Ipswich's glory year, 1981, when it won the UEFA Cup, was before the era of mass TV exposure.

Fanzines: 'Those Were The Days', PO Box 87, Ipswich, Suffolk, IP4 4JQ; 'Dribble', 63 Woodbridge Road, Ipswich, Suffolk, IP4 2EQ.

Unofficial Websites:

'Those Were the Days': http://www.twtd.co.uk/

'Virtual Reality': http://www.sys.uea.uk/recreation/sport/itfc/vrml/vrml/html

Tourist Information: (01473) 258 070.

Leeds United

Elland Road

Address: Elland Road, Leeds, LS11 0ES
Telephone: Club (0113) 226 6000
Ticket Office (0113) 226 1000
ClubCall (0891) 12 11 80
Leeds United Chat Forum (0930) 120 000
Official Website: http://www.lufc.co.uk

Anything Chelsea can do, Leeds can do better ... well, possibly! The club has plans to buy and redevelop land around Elland Road in a project which may turn the Blues' village green with envy! The idea is for a leisure extravaganza, including a 12,000 seater indoor arena, a 200-bedroom hotel, theme bars and restaurants. It'll certainly brighten up the rather nondescript Elland Road surroundings, presently made up of low industrial buildings, vast car parks and an elevated section of the M621. The ground's about 1.5 miles from the city centre, with few pubs or eateries nearby. However, connoisseurs of takeaway food are still in for a treat!

HOW TO GET THERE

BY CAR: From South and East (M1): Keep on M1 to the end of the motorway, junction 47. Here, keep in lane for Manchester M621, M62, onto the M621. Two choices from here:
a) To ground and parking: After 0.6 miles, exit M621 at junction 2 (s/p Morley A643, Elland Road). Take 1st exit at roundabout (s/p Morley A643, Elland Road, Beeston) onto Elland Road. Ground is on right, car parks 'A' and 'B' on the left.
b) For alternative away parking: After 1.2 miles, exit M621 at junction 1 (s/p Ring Road A6110, Dewsbury A653). At roundabout, turn right (s/p Ring Road A6110, Leeds A62) onto the A6110 Beeston Ring Road. (*)At first traffic lights turn right (s/p Leeds A62) into Gelderd Road. After 0.5 miles turn right (opposite HSS Hire Shop) into Low Fields Road.

From West and North-West: Exit M62 at junction 27 (s/p Leeds M621, Batley A62) onto the M621. Where road divides follow signs to 'Leeds M621'. After 3.0 miles exit M621 at junction 1 (s/p Leeds West A6110, Elland Road). Two choices from here:
a) To ground and parking: At roundabout, turn right (s/p Ring Road A6110, Wakefield A650, Dewsbury) onto the A6110 Beeston Ring Road. After 1.0 miles turn left at lights (s/p Elland Road) into Elland Road. Under railway bridge and ground is on left, car parks on the right, after 0.5 miles.
b) To alternative away parking: At roundabout turn left (s/p Leeds A6110) onto the A6110 Beeston Ring Road. Then as from South and East(*).

From North East (A1): Exit A1 at signpost 'Wetherby, Leeds A58'.

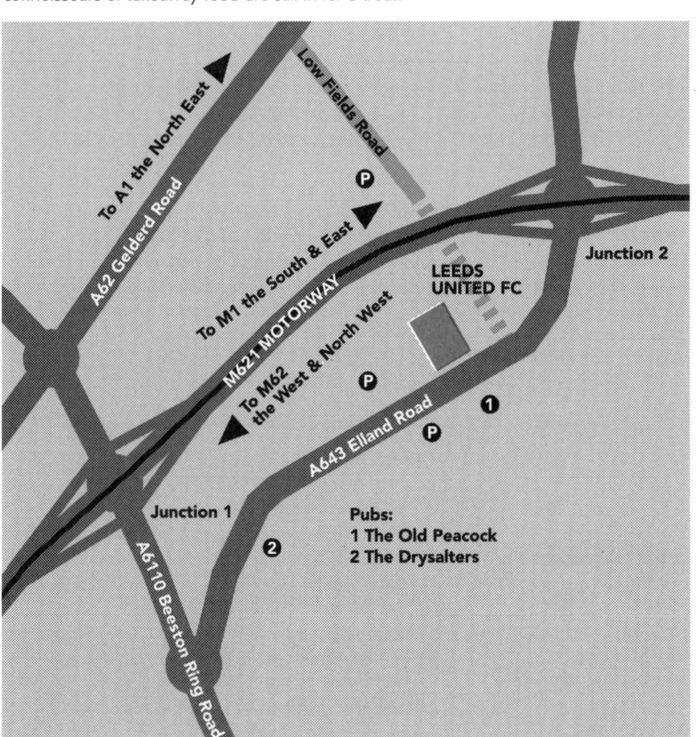

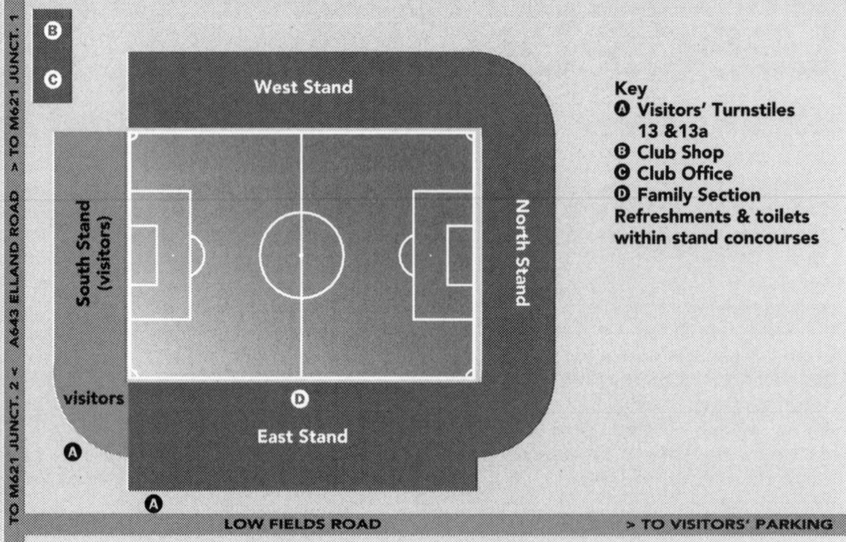

Follow Leeds A58 signs onto the A58. Go straight on for 7.7 miles, through villages of Bardsey and Scarcroft, to roundabout. Here turn left (s/p Ring Road A6120, The South A1) onto the Ring Road. At 2nd roundabout, after 1.7 miles, turn right (s/p City Centre A64) onto the A64 dual carriageway. Keep on A64, which becomes the A64(M), then the A58(M) for 5.6 miles. Get in left hand lane (s/p Motorways M621, M62, M1, Halifax A58), taking 1st exit at roundabout onto the A643. At next roundabout after 0.8 miles go straight on into Elland Road. Ground is on right, 'A' and 'B' car parks on the left.
FROM RAILWAY STATION (Leeds): 1.5 miles. *By taxi:* About £4-£4.50. *By bus:* 'First Leeds' runs special football buses from Neville Street, fare £1 return. For Neville Street, come straight out of the railway station, across the car park and down the steps. The buses are on the right under the railway bridge.
Last Midweek Trains: There are no trains to London or Birmingham after a midweek match. Trains to Doncaster leave at 21.44 and 22.39; to Manchester at 21.51, 22.59, 23.41 and 01.21; and to Sheffield and Nottingham at 21.46. Please double-check on (0345) 484 950.
BY BUS: See above.

PARKING:

The directions given above take visiting fans either to the visitors' car park at the ground (Car Park 'A', £2) or to Low Fields Road, which is a wide road on an industrial estate with loads of free parking. Home fans warn, however, that it's 'like the dodgems' at 4.45 pm. Further afield it's worth trying the Holbeck area, north-east of Elland Road, a ten minute walk or so. Home fans advise visitors to avoid the Heath Estate (over the road from the South Stand), which is patrolled by traffic wardens.

THE GROUND

As well as tabling plans for the huge leisure complex outlined above, the club proposes major work at Elland Road itself, already an impressive Euro '96 venue. It's bought back the stadium freehold from the city council (sold in 1985 to relieve financial concerns), and plans to build a second tier on the West Stand to bring the ground capacity up to 45,000. An enlarged West Stand would counterbalance the enormous East Stand, which opened in 1993 and seats 17,000. The ideas are still awaiting planning permission, and the residents of the nearby Heath Estate have voiced concerns, so the work is not expected to begin until 1999. Visiting fans are housed either in the South Stand or, if lower numbers are expected, in the South-East Corner. The corner section in particular is cramped, and fans have complained about having to 'cheer standing sideways' to celebrate a goal.
Total Capacity: 39,980. For away fans: Seating (SE Corner, upper tier) 1,600, turnstiles 13 and 13a; (South Stand) 3,300, turnstiles 14, 14a and 15. Visiting fans are welcome in the family stand (East Stand Lower Tier).
Cost (98/99): 'Standard' matches: Adults £20, concessions £14. 'Premier' matches: £23/£17. Family Stand: Adults £16.50, juniors £8. Concessions (juniors/OAPs/students) must be booked through the away club and are available on a reciprocal basis only. Take ID with you to the game.
Disabled Facilities: The disabled area, shared by home and away supporters, houses 110 wheelchairs,

and the facilities are excellent. *Disabled Toilet:* In all areas. *Cost:* Free for disabled, half-price for helper. *Booking:* One week in advance. *Parking:* Subject to availability. *For the Blind:* 52 seats with commentary in the South West Stand.

Programme: £2.

Visitors' Toilets: *Male:* One fan said: 'Not the best in the Premiership, but I can't find anything to complain about!' *Female:* The strange acoustics enabled fans to listen into the conversations going on in the gents next door. And no, we're not passing on any titbits!

Food and Drink: The food, served in plastic wrappers, was – said Villa fans – 'dry, but edible.' After a great deal of discussion, supporters decided that the meat-and-potato pie (£1.50) was slightly better than the Cornish Pasty (£1.50). Beer at £1.80 a pint, and expensive tea (£1), were also on sale (6.12.97, 14.2.98).

PUB GUIDE

The two pubs near the ground admit both home and away fans, but away fans can expect to be in the minority.

The Old Peacock (1) Elland Road (0113) 270 0759 Whitbread. Popular pub by the ground, with admittance at the doorman's discretion. Snacks served 12-2.30. Big-screen TV, beer garden. Parking available (£2). Open: all day.

The Drysalters (2) Elland Road (0113) 270 0229 Tetleys. Large attractive modern pub, serving home-cooked food from 12-2.30. Open: Saturdays 11.30-4, 7-11.30; midweek all day.

The two following pubs are a 15-20 minute walk from the ground:

The Wheatsheaf Gelderd Road (0113) 263 7070 Mansfield. Football-friendly pub with separate bar and lounge. Pool table, darts, TV. Pub food served weekends 12-3 and evenings on request. Open: all day.

The Pack Horse Inn Gelderd Road (0113) 263 8217 Bass (with Tetley). Traditional pub with beer garden, TV. Open: 11.30- 3, 5.30-11.

Good pub for those travelling from the south on the M1:

The Bay Horse Bradford Road, East Ardsley (just off junction 41 of the M1) (01924) 825 926.

Tetleys. Traditional village pub just a few hundred yards from the motorway (follow signs to Bradford A650). 'Big Steak Menu' served all day. TV, beer garden. Families welcome. Open: all day from 11.30.

FOOD GUIDE

The 'United Fisheries' on Elland Road is a traditional favourite: indeed, home fans joke that it often has longer queues than the ticket office! Almost next door is 'The Cracked Egg', serving excellent bacon 'sarnies' and mugs of coffee. And behind the East Stand is the wonderful 'Doreen's Café'. A little further away, there's a Burger King at the junction of Elland Road and the

A6110. Eight miles west of Leeds, in the village of Guiseley on the A56 (Leeds to Skipton road), there's the original and highly praised 'Harry Ramsdens'.

LOCAL MEDIA

Local Radio: Aire 96.3 FM; BBC Radio Leeds 92.4-95.3 FM

Radio Phone-ins: BBC Radio Leeds, Saturdays 5-6 pm, call (0113) 244 3222.

Saturday Sports Paper: *Yorkshire Sport* produces a Saturday 'pink'.

MISCELLANEOUS

Safety Factor: A few incidents in season 97/98 outside the ground and in the city centre.

Rivals: Manchester United, followed by Chelsea.

Fanzines: 'Square Ball', 47 Holborn Towers, Leeds, LS6 2QD; 'To 'Ell and Back', 7 Westminster Way, Ashby-de-la-Zouch, Leicestershire, LE65 2SX; 'The Hanging Sheep', 41 Woodhall Terrace, Thornbury, Bradford BD3 7BZ.; 'We Are Leeds', 4 Avenue Place, Harrogate, HG2 7PJ.

Unofficial Websites:

http://www.etrigan.demon.co.uk/leeds/
http://www.geocities.com/Colosseum/7523/
http://members.delphi.com/gaulll
http://www.geocities.com/Colosseum/Field/8651/lufc.html
http://www.hovington.demon.co.uk/
http://freespace.virgin.net/peter.jeffreys/index.htm

Tourist Information: (0113) 242 5242.

L

Leicester City

Filbert Street

Address: Filbert Street, Leicester LE2 7FL
Telephone: Club (0116) 291 5000
Ticket Office (0116) 291 5296
Ticket Sales (0116) 291 5232
ClubCall (0891) 121 185
Ticket Information (0891) 12 10 28
Official Website: http://www.lcfc.co.uk

'And on your left, for the third time, the magnificent city hall...' As many visitors have discovered, Leicester's one-way systems and narrow residential streets offer city tours, whether supporters want them or not! Filbert Street is in a residential area to the south, not far from the Tigers rugby ground. If the rugby team is playing at home on the same day, kick off times are usually staggered, but it still means that two sets of supporters are fighting for parking spaces and that elusive place near the bar! The city of Leicester is undergoing a major facelift, with trendy restaurants and wine bars springing up in the centre, and old factories around Filbert Street making way for modern housing and theme pubs. And the ground itself could also be moving ... to a new site just the other side of the river.

HOW TO GET THERE

BY CAR: From All Main Routes (M1): Exit M1 at junction 21 (s/p Coventry M69, Leicester A5460). At motorway roundabout turn right (s/p Leicester A5460). At next roundabout after 0.5 miles, take 2nd exit (s/p Leicester A5460) onto the Narborough Road dual carriageway. At lights after 2.3 miles, by Lloyds Bank, turn right (s/p City Centre S & E, Universities) into Upperton Road. Ground is down streets on the RHS after 0.4 miles.

From South and East (A1/A47): From village of Bushby, follow signs to City Centre and Central Ring Road for 3.0 miles, under bridge and past Burger King to roundabout. Here, take the 2nd exit (s/p Central Ring A594) onto Ring Road (St George's Way). Follow signs for 'Central Ring' for 0.7 miles to lights. Here, go straight on (n/s) crossing Regent Road. After 0.4 miles, all traffic turns left in front of the rugby ground. Immediately move into the inner (right-hand) lanes, and follow signs to 'Supermarket, Infirmary, Central Ring' to the right, and then right again, signposted 'City Stadium', passing the Mazda showroom. Then turn left (s/p City Stadium,

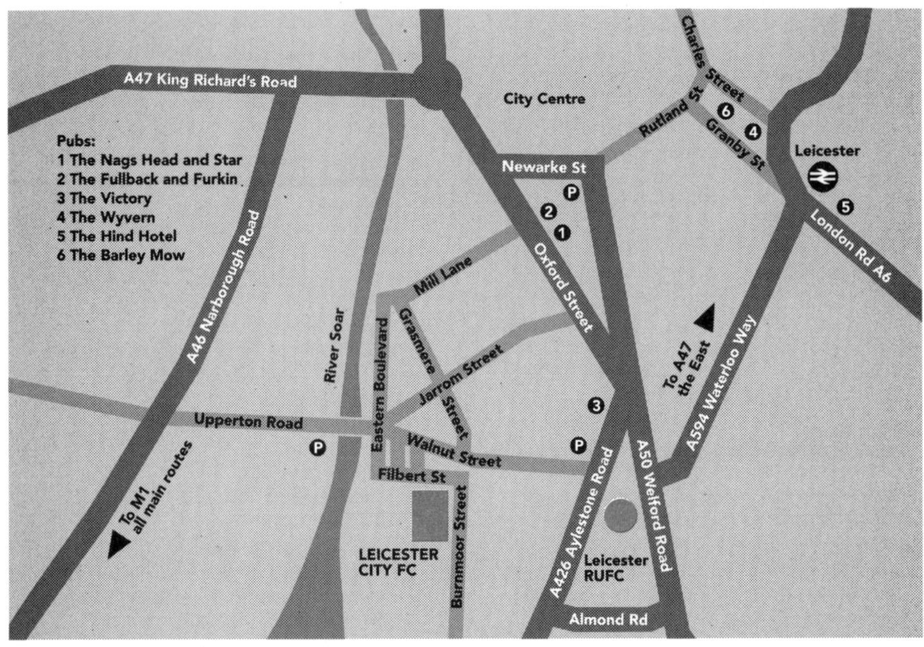

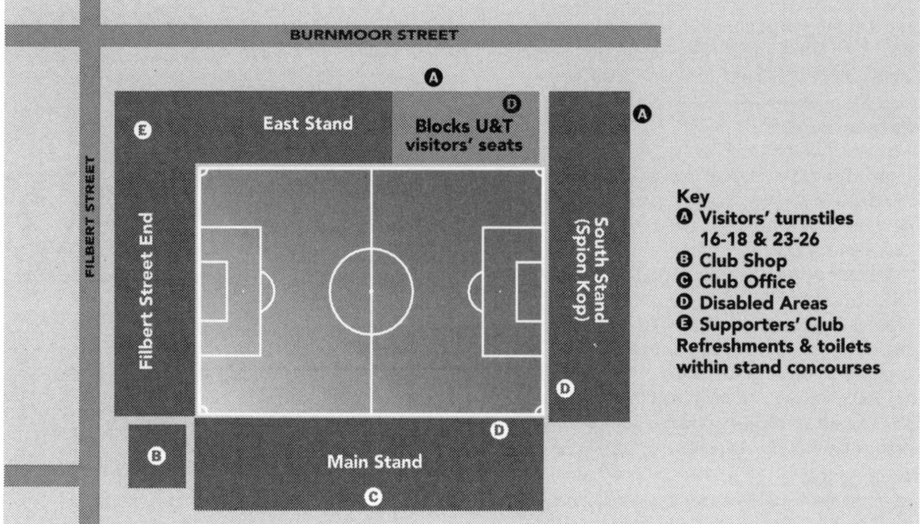

London M1) into Walnut Street. Ground is down streets on LHS after 0.2 miles.

FROM RAILWAY STATION (Leicester): About a mile. *By taxi:* £2.50-£3. *By bus:* No buses run directly to the ground. *By foot:* Cross the Ring Road/Waterloo Way towards the Royal and Sun Alliance Insurance building and turn left. Keep on pathway up and over hill (ie. don't cross footbridge). During the day, cut diagonally right across Nelson Mandela Park to junction of Walford Road and Aylestone Road and turn left (ie. around the corner by entrance to Granby Halls). Turn right in front of wall mural into Walnut Street. (After dark, avoid Nelson Mandela Park. Continue to T-junction and turn right instead.)

Last Midweek Trains: There are trains to London (22.00 direct or 22.29 via Coventry); to Sheffield (21.19, 23.23, with onward connections to Leeds); to Birmingham (22.07, 23.10, 00.10); to Manchester (21.19 via Sheffield or 22.29 via Nuneaton). Please double check on (0345) 484 950.

BY BUS: The nos. 52 (from the Clock Tower) and 170 (stand C29 on Charles Street) run along Walnut Street. Nos. 26, 37 and 38 run from the city centre along Welford Road (alight at Granby Halls). No. 20 runs down Narborough Road (alight at Upperton Junction).

PARKING

Car parks open up in and around Jarrom Street and Gateway Street, and at the rowing club by the river, opposite the ground off Upperton Road. There's a small car park signposted off Almond Road, while those stopping for a meal on the Freemen's Leisure Complex are welcome to leave their cars there. There's an NCP car park on Pelham Street, just north of the Royal Infirmary, and on Duke Street (turn left off Welford Road into Mill Street, right into Duke Street). Otherwise it's street parking. Those coming in from the A47 could try the roads either side of Waterloo Way (eg Lancaster Road), while those coming in from the M1 could try the streets to the west of the ground, off Narborough Road.

THE GROUND

Like at Luton, visiting supporters entering Filbert Street pass between and under terraced houses, which must be great fun for any local trying to sleep off a night-shift! The residents of Burnmoor Road and Filbert Street, which back onto the ground, oppose any large-scale ground redevelopment, which has left the capacity at 21,500. Nine-thousand are in just one stand, the impressive Carling (Main) Stand, opened in 1993. The other three sides are older and smaller. Visiting supporters are in the low, single-tier East Stand. The front row is below pitch level, so the stewards have to lie down on the perimeter track, while supporters further back contend with pillars and a low roof. With all these problems, the club has decided to build a new stadium at 'Bede Island South' only a couple of hundred yards away, on the opposite bank of the River Soar. If all goes to plan the club hopes the stadium, to seat 40,000, will be ready by season 1999/2000.

Total Capacity: 21,500. For away fans: 2,000, Blocks U and T of the East Stand. Block U use turnstiles 17 and 18, Block T 23-26.

Cost (98/99): Block U: Adults £18, concession £9. Block T: Adults £15, concessions £7.50.

Disabled Facilities: Space for 17 visiting supporters in

Block T of the East Stand. *Disabled Toilets:* Inside disabled entrance to Block T. *Cost:* Free for disabled, full price for helper. *Booking:* Please buy tickets through visiting club. *Parking:* Not available. *For the Blind:* Hospital radio commentary. Please book.

Programme: £2.

Visitors' Toilets: *Male:* The area was so small and cramped that Southampton fans felt right at home. *Female:* With only two loos, the queue was huge and slow. However, all the necessities of life were there, except for hot water.

Food and Drink: The steak-and-kidney pies (£1.60) were top-notch, though they collapsed quickly. One fan chose the chicken-and-mushroom version, which was so red hot he risked mouth blisters. Even so, he complimented its 'nice crisp pastry.' The hot dogs (£1.80) were 'spot on', while the cheese-and-potato slices (£1.60) made a nice change. The coffee (80p) was good (20.12.97, 14.4.98).

PUB GUIDE

Many pubs in Leicester prefer rugby fans, so it may be an idea to keep football colours out of sight.

Near the ground:

Nag's Head and Star (1) 72 Oxford Street (0116) 254 3335
Everards (with Old Original and Tiger). Traditional pub, recently refurbished and extended. Big-screen TVs. Bar meals served all day. Darts, pool. Open: all day.

Fullback and Firkin (2) 44 Oxford Street (0116) 254 1164
Allied Domecq (and guest). Large sports-orientated Firkin pub with wooden floors and lots of bric-a-brac. Bar billiards, 2 big-screen TVs, beer garden. Open: all day.

The Victory (3) 21 Aylestone Road (0116) 254 4105
Everards. Large traditional pub in listed building, refurbished in 1998. Fans admitted at doorman's discretion. Food served all day. Post-match opening decided by the landlord depending on the game.

Near the station, there are three good pubs to try: **The Wyvern (4)** on Granby Street is a Mansfield pub with two big-screen TVs and serving food from 12-2.30; **The Hind Hotel (5)** at 59 London Road (Allied Domecq) is a small friendly local with TV and pool table; **The Barley Mow (6)** at 93 Granby Street is a traditional real ale (Everards) pub, popular with students, serving snacks all day. It also has a large-screen TV.

Also recommended: On the Freemen's Leisure Complex, **The Counting House** at 40 Almond Road, a spacious, bright Kimberley Ales pub serving a football snack menu.

FOR FAMILIES:

Head for the excellent **Local Hero** at 84 Aylestone Road (the Freemen's Leisure Complex). It's a Tom Cobleigh pub serving hot baguettes.

'I wouldn't mind, but it's only the half-time entertainment!'

FOOD GUIDE

Near the ground, try 'The Shark' fish-and-chip shop on Walnut Street or the 'Wing Wah' Chinese/English takeaway on Grasmere Street. Also not far away is the 'Leicester City Fish and Chip Shop' on Aylestone Road near the rugby ground. For a wider choice head to Narborough Road, which home fans dub 'studentville' because of its many takeaways and cafés.

LOCAL MEDIA

Local Radio: BBC Radio Leicester 104.9 FM; Leicester Sound 105.4 FM.

Radio Phone-ins: Leicester Sound, 'Listener Line' pre/post match 2-6. Call (0116) 202 0222.

Saturday Sports Paper: *The Leicester Mercury* produces the 'Sporting Blue'.

MISCELLANEOUS

Safety Factor: Although some away fans still find visiting Filbert Street daunting, there was little trouble inside or outside the ground in season 97/98.

Rivals: Nottingham Forest, Derby, and to a lesser extent Coventry.

Fanzines: 'The Fox', PO Box 2, Cosby, Leicester LE9 1ZZ; 'When You're Smiling', Secular Hall, 75 Humberstone, Leicester, LE1; 'Where's the Money Gone?', PO Box 391, Leicester, LE5 0ZZ.

Unofficial Websites:
'ForFoxSake': http://www.forfoxsake.com/
http://homepages.webleicester.co.uk/steven/lcfc.htm
'Eurofox': http://www.bath.ac.uk/~ma6dlg/lcfc/
http://www.ratty.demon.co.uk/lcfc.htm (good links)

Tourist Information: (0116) 265 0555.

Leyton Orient

Brisbane Road

Address: Matchroom Stadium, Brisbane Road, Leyton, London, E10 5NE
Telephone: Club (0181) 926 1111
ClubCall (0891) 121 150
Official Website: ('OriNet')
http://www.matchroom.com/orient

'Leyton is all terraced streets with a football ground attached!' said one local. Fair enough, but those streets have lots of spaces for football supporters' cars, and a fair sprinkling of pubs and fish-and-chip shops too. Leyton is not the most beautiful of London suburbs, with its traffic-clogged High Road lined with downmarket shops, and a whopping great building site – the new M11 extension – cutting right through it. But it's lively enough on a matchday, and everything for the footie fan is close to hand. Well, except for a cash machine – the nearest is about a mile away in Bakers Arms.

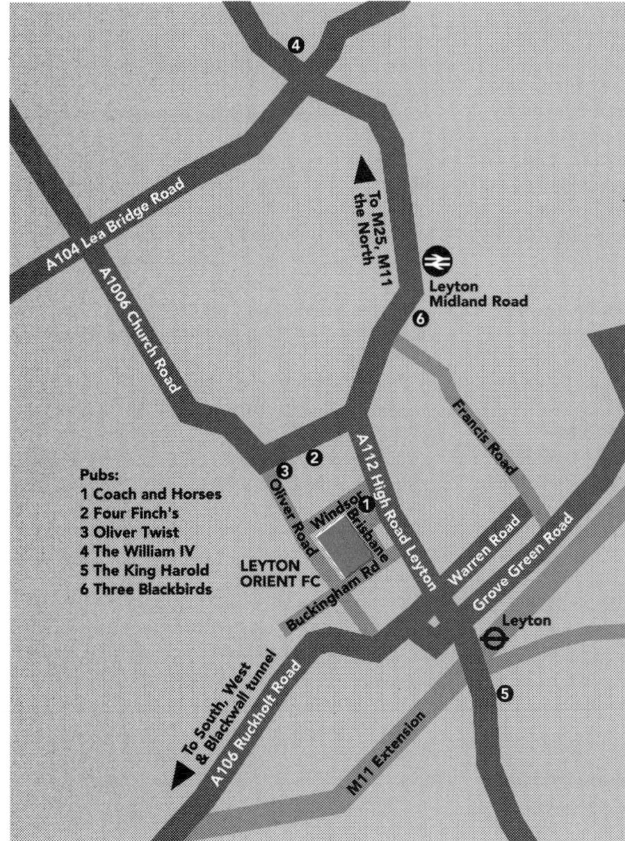

HOW TO GET THERE

BY CAR: From North: Exit M25 at junction 27 and follow signs to 'London (NE), M11' onto the M11 southbound. After 7.1 miles where the road divides, bear right (s/p A406 N. Circ. Rd West, London N and W) onto the North Circular Road. Keep in left hand lanes and take first exit after 0.6 miles (s/p Walthamstow and City A104, then Whipps Cross A104, West End (A503)). (*)At roundabout turn left (s/p Whipps Cross, Bakers Arms, Walthamstow A503) into Woodford New Road A104. At next roundabout (Whipps Cross) after 1.2 miles, take 2nd exit (s/p A104 Bakers Arms, Leyton) and follow road round to left, towards BP station, into Lea Bridge Road. After 0.5 miles, just after Esso station, turn left at lights (s/p Leyton, Stratford, then Leyton Leisure Lagoon) into Leyton Green Road. Filter left after 0.3 miles and turn left at T-junction into Leyton High Road. After 1.2 miles ground is down sidestreets on RHS.

From East (A12): NB The A12 west of the Gants Hill Roundabout was, at time of writing, one enormous roadwork. Until the M11 extension is finished, the following route is recommended: Continue on A12 under the M25. Stay on A12, following signs to 'Central London' and 'Gants Hill', for 9.3 miles to Gant's Hill Roundabout. Take 4th exit (s/p A1400 (A406) West End (A503)) onto Woodford Avenue A1400 dual carriageway. At next roundabout after 0.6 miles, by BP station, go straight on (s/p Woodford A1400). At next roundabout after 1.2 miles, go straight on (s/p A406, M11 West

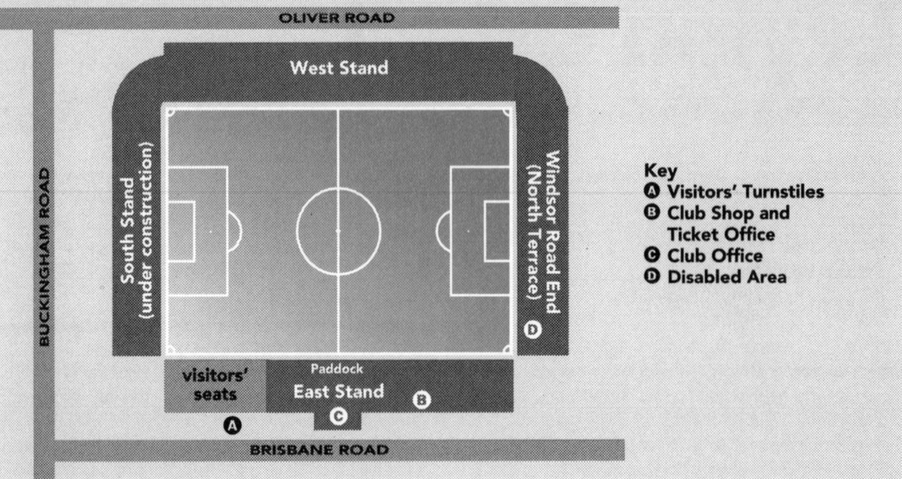

End A503) up onto the North Circular. Keep in left-hand lanes and take first exit (s/p Walthamstow and City A104, then Whipps Cross A104, West End (A503). Then as From North (*).

From South/South-East via Blackwall Tunnel. NB This route is likely to change when the new M11 extension opens: (For directions to Blackwall Tunnel, see London Guide.) Out of tunnel, continue on A102 following signs to 'Stratford, Dalston'. Remain on the A102/A106 for 4.2 miles, following signs for Leyton, passing New Spitalfields Market and over a bridge. At lights just after Venture Car Superstore, turn left into Oliver Road.

FROM UNDERGROUND STATION (Leyton, Central Line, Zone 3): Five minute walk. Turn right out of station into Leyton High Road. Take 7th turning on the LHS (Buckingham Road, just after Coronation Gardens) to away turnstiles.

FROM RAILWAY STATION: (Leyton Midland Road, line running from Barking to Gospel Oak): About 0.7 miles. *By taxi/bus:* Taxis are rare but numerous buses run along Leyton High Road. *By foot:* Down steps to road. Turn left to main road (Leyton High Road) and left again towards 'Three Blackbirds' pub. At the 'Lion and Key' pub bear left. Straight on to 'Coach and Horses' on RHS. Ground is down sidestreets on the right.

Last Midweek Trains: See London Guide at front of book.

BY BUS: Nos. 58, 69, 97 and 158 run along Leyton High Road.

PARKING

The car park at the ground (£3) will disappear once building work starts on the new South Stand. From then, it's street-parking for everyone. Oliver Road, Buckingham Road and Brisbane Road are best avoided as they are emergency access routes. The police say there is some car crime, so don't leave valuables in sight.

THE GROUND

Leyton Orient played seasons 96/97 and 97/98 at a three-sided ground, following the demolition of the old South Terrace. This left two cavernous side-stands – the East and the West – and the uncovered Windsor Road End, reserved for the home support. Away supporters have been switched from the South Terrace to a corner section of the East Stand and the Paddock terracing in front. Most visitors prefer the terrace, which means that those in the stand can usually pick and choose their seats to avoid the couple of large intrusive pillars.

The club hopes that building work on a new £4.5 million South Stand, to house 3,000 seats and – depending on various grants – a new community centre, club offices and creche. Much longer-term plans, and we're deep into wish-list territory here, involve demolishing the West Stand, and turning the pitch through ninety degrees.

Total Capacity: Just under 14,000. For away fans: Seating 932, Paddock 1,245.

Cost (98/99): Seating: Adult £12, concessions (OAPs, under 16s, students, unemployed) £8. Terrace: £10/£6. To encourage families to attend, if both parents attend the game with a junior, the second adult is admitted half price.

Disabled Facilities: Space for 15 wheelchairs in a disabled enclosure at the front of the North Terrace. *Disabled Toilet:* In East Stand. *Cost:* Free for disabled and helper. *Booking:* Please book through the Football in the Community Office, (0181) 556 5973. *Parking:* In

Buckingham Road, as directed by the police. *For the Blind:* No special facilities.

Programme: £1.50.

Visitors' Toilets: *Male:* Dingy but acceptable with a couple of clean(ish) sinks. *Female:* A large sign inside reads: 'Please leave this toilet as you would hope to find it'. For most people, this would mean bringing several cans of paint, a roll of plush carpet and some chintzy curtains, as the loos aren't anything like we'd like to find them! Joking apart, they actually weren't that bad, with soap, water and a working hot air dryer.

Food and Drink: Oh boy, oh boy, the catering's back to its excellent best. Comments on the burgers (£2) included: 'brilliant – this is the best Third Division catering', and 'moist and succulent, not burnt to a crisp like at other grounds'. The tea (50p) came complete with teabag while a carton of milk was available on the counter. Fantastic mama (5.9.97 and 28.12.97).

PUB GUIDE

Visitors are welcome in the Leyton Orient Supporters' Club at the ground (£1). The club has six real ales, and has a mention in the East London CAMRA. Arrive early though, as it's not that big. On the High Road, near the ground, is the ultra-friendly Bass pub, the **Coach and Horses (1)** Further from the ground are:

The Four Finch's (2) 50 Church Road (0181) 539 4213

Free House (with Caffreys and guest beer). Locals pub with big-screen TV and pool table. Full menu served 12-3. Darts, beer garden. Families welcome. Open: all day.

The Oliver Twist (3) 60 Church Road (0181) 558 1917

Whitbread. Recommended friendly local with TV, darts and beer garden. Snacks. Families welcome lunch-times. Open: all day.

The Birkbeck Tavern 45 Langthorne Road (0181) 539 2584

Scottish and Newcastle. Top-notch real-ale house, named as 'East London and City Pub of the Year 1996' by the local CAMRA branch. Sandwiches. Pool table, darts, large beer garden. Open: all day.

To get there: Turn left out of Leyton tube station, left down steps, left along Goodall Road, right at end into Langthorne Road.

Also recommended: **The William IV (4)** at 816 High Road, Baker's Arms, a free house with excellent food; **The King Harold (5),** at 116 High Road, a traditional sports-friendly pub with big-screen TV, pool table and bar snacks; **The Three Blackbirds (6),** at 640 High Road, near Leyton Midland station, a large characterful Scottish and Newcastle pub, with three pool tables, big-screen TV and excellent food served all day.

FOOD GUIDE

Of all the chippies down Leyton High Road, the locals recommend 'Nick's Café', near the junction with Osborne Road near the ground. Near the 'Coach and Horses' is the popular Atlanta Fish Bar, while the editor of the fanzine 'CheeryO's' recommends the 'Royal Café' for a quick, good value meal. Also between the ground and the tube station are a Pizza Hut takeaway and a fried chicken takeaway.

LOCAL MEDIA

Local Radio: XFM 104.9; Capital Gold 1548 AM; GLR 94.9 FM.

Radio Phone-ins: Capital Gold, Saturdays 5-6.30 pm; midweek every night 7-8 or after live match commentary. Call (0845) 35 60 70 80.

Saturday Sport Paper: None.

MISCELLANEOUS

If it isn't bad enough to concede a goal away from home, the tannoy announcer at Orient really rubs it in with a Continental-style shriek of 'Goooooooaaaaaaal'. It's so loud that, at its crescendo, the PA system cuts out. The club confirms that the tannoy announcer, Andrew Buonocore, is indeed of Italian origin. He always double-checks that the home goal is valid before launching into his vowels, to avoid an embarrassing 'Goooooooooo oo-oh s***'.

Safety Factor: No problems here.

Rivals: Orient does, after all, pride itself on being 'London's Family Club', and has no fierce rivalries.

Fanzines: 'CheeryO's', 10B Ingrebourne Gardens, Upminster, Essex, RM14 1BG, which has a new issue for every home match, 30p; 'The Orientear', 2 Chelmsford Court, Chelmsford Road, Southgate, London, N14 4JJ; 'All Aboard the Wagon Train', 10 St Margarets Road, Wanstead, London, E12 5DP.

Unofficial Websites: http://www.onet.clara.net http://www.web-orient.clara.net

Tourist Information: None.

L

Lincoln City

Sincil Bank

Address: Sincil Bank Stadium, Lincoln, LN5 8LD
Telephone: Club/Ticket Office (01522) 880 011
Impsline (0930) 555 900
Official Website:
http://isfa.com/server/web/Lincoln

The carved imp in Lincoln Cathedral, from which the football club derives its nickname, is ideally placed to keep an eye on its team's antics. The cathedral dominates the skyline for miles around – this is still fen country after all – and anyone perched on one of its pinnacles would have an uninterrupted view of the Sincil Bank pitch. Perhaps the imp could be asked to give semaphore directions to football fans trying to locate the football ground on foot or by car, as Sincil Bank is hidden behind serried ranks of terraced side streets. Finding the ground is the only problem for visitors, as parking's easy and there are pubs and takeaways galore along the High Street. The city centre is only ten minutes' walk away, so make a day of it!

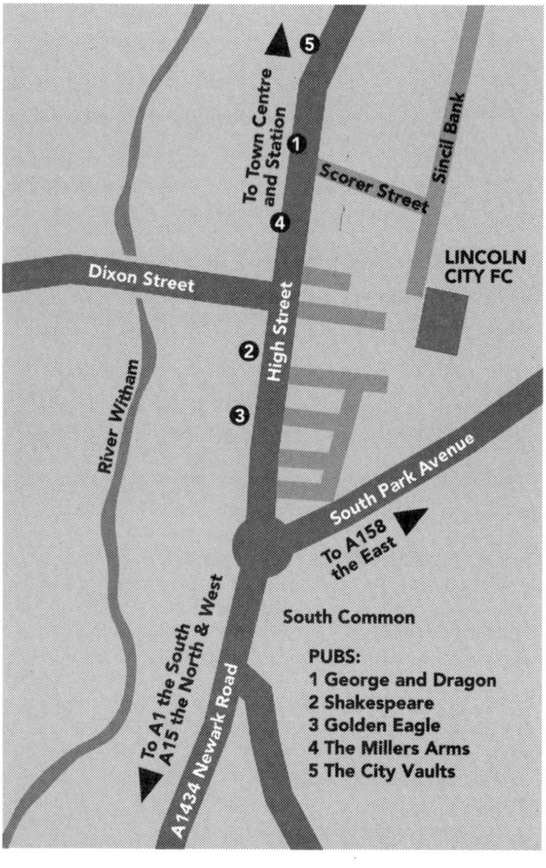

PUBS:
1 George and Dragon
2 Shakespeare
3 Golden Eagle
4 The Millers Arms
5 The City Vaults

HOW TO GET THERE

BY CAR: From South: Exit A1 at s/p 'Lincoln A46, Sleaford A17' onto the A46. At roundabout after 9.4 miles take 3rd exit (s/p Lincoln South A1434). Keep on A1434, following 'Lincoln and City Centre' signs for 4.3 miles. (*)Then get into inside lane (s/p City Centre, Worksop A57) and go straight on (1st exit) at roundabout into the High Street. (***)After 0.5 miles get in outside lane, and go straight on at lights (s/p City Centre, Worksop A57). After 0.1 miles turn right into Scorer Street.

From North: Exit A1(M) at the roundabout after the Fina and Shell garages (s/p Lincoln A57, E. Markham) onto the A57. At junction after 9.9 miles turn right (s/p Lincoln A57), remaining on the A57 which here runs alongside the Foss Dyke. At roundabout after 5.9 miles turn right (Lincoln South, Newark A46, Grantham A1) onto the A46. Straight on at roundabout after 1.8 miles. At next roundabout after 1.6 miles (by BP station) turn left (s/p Lincoln South B1190, Doddington Industrial Estate, Lincoln City FC Stadium) into Doddington Road. (**)Straight on for 2 miles to T-junction. Here, turn left (no signpost) onto Newark Road A1434. Keep on A1434 following Lincoln and City Centre signs. Then as From South (*). Tip: Have 20p ready for a small tollbridge en route.

From Scunthorpe (A15): At roundabout which forms the junction with the A46, take 3rd exit (s/p Lincoln Central and South, Newark A46). Stay on A46 for 5.0 miles, over two roundabouts. At 3rd roundabout turn left (s/p Lincoln South B1190, Doddington Industrial Estate, Lincoln City FC Stadium) into Doddington Road. Then as From North(**).

From East (A158): At roundabout which forms junction with A15, take 1st exit (s/p Lincoln, Sleaford A15) onto the A15. Follow Sleaford A15 signs for three miles, down steep

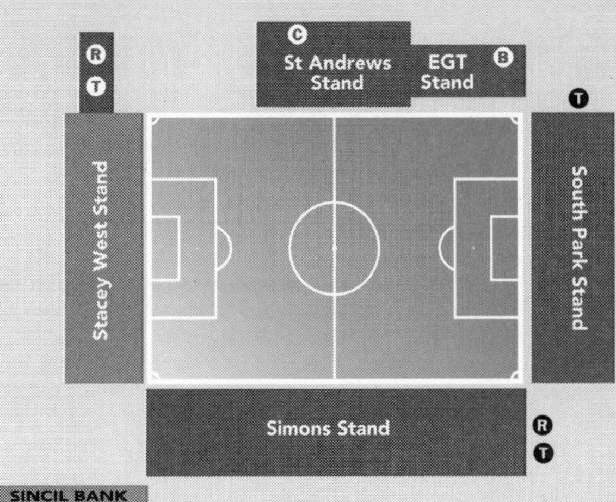

hill and over bridge. On the bridge, get into the right hand lane to turn right (s/p Sleaford A15, Grantham A607) onto South Park Avenue. At roundabout after 3.0 miles turn right (s/p City Centre, Worksop A57) into the High Street. Then as From South (***).

FROM RAILWAY STATION (Lincoln Central): 10-15 minute walk to ground. *By taxi:* £2.20-£2.40 depending on traffic. *By bus:* All the buses listed below run along the High Street. *By foot:* Turn left out of station and left again at the main road (the High Street), over the level crossing. Take the seventh turning on the LHS (Scorer Street), and first right into Sincil Bank.

Last Midweek Trains: There are no connecting trains to London after an evening game. There is, however, a train to Nottingham at 22.22. Please double-check on (0345) 484 950.

BY BUS: Bus nos. 4, 4a, 14, 24, 27, N1 and N2 all run along the High Street to 'South Park Circle' which is easy walking distance to Sincil Bank.

PARKING

There's a small car park at the ground (£2), though most supporters park in the sidestreets. The best bets are the roads to the west of the High Street, such as Boultham Avenue and Vernon Street. A little further away, there's additional car parking on South Common.

THE GROUND

Imps fans are justifiably proud of the revamped Sincil Bank ... 'only one or two lower division grounds, such as Notts County's, can compare with this', said one. Manchester City fans who visited in 1996 were startled to find a new 6,000-seater stand, and even more surprised that they were allocated a large section of it! 'Great little ground, grotty result' mumbled one afterwards. After more than ten years of building work, costing more than £3 million, Lincoln City has no plans for further redevelopments. With the capacity already above 10,000, there's no obvious need.

For season 98/99 the club has removed seating from the covered Stacey West stand and allocated the entire terrace to away supporters. No seating is available.

Total Capacity: 10,918. For away fans: Stacey West Stand 3,400.

Cost (98/99): Adult £13, concessions (juniors, OAPS, students) £8.

Disabled Facilities: Space for 20 in the Simons Stand. *Disabled Toilet:* Nearby. *Cost:* Free for disabled, full price for helper. *Booking:* Not necessary. *Parking:* A limited number of spaces available – please book. *For the Blind:* No special facilities.

Programme: £1.70.

Visitors' Toilets: (Simons Stand) *Male:* 'Clean enough' was the favoured lukewarm comment. Perhaps more was expected in a new stand, such as soap and hand-dryers. *Female:* Fans came in and sniffed the air – yep, an aroma of spicy sausage rolls. Of course, this was Team Lincoln, expect the unexpected. Everything was

clean, and there was hot and cold water plus, luxuries of luxuries, a plug.

Food and Drink: The hot dog (£1.20) 'didn't fit' said one fan, and our minds duly boggled. But no, he meant that the bread was a lot bigger than the sausage, though it was good nonetheless. Another found his burger (£1.50) was 'burnt to a crisp' which was fine because he 'liked them like that'. Others, however, did not. The tea (65p) no longer tasted of chlorine, but didn't taste of anything else either (4.10.97).

PUB GUIDE

The Supporters' Club at the ground, called the Centre Spot, welcomes all football fans (no charge) and, even better, sells 'Lincoln City's Legendary Pork Rolls'. Otherwise, there's a series of football friendly pubs along the High Street. However, some of them close on local derby matchdays.

The George and Dragon (1) 100 High Street (01522) 520 924
Free House (with Bass, Whitbread). Newly refurbished, but still, says the landlord 'a 100% boozer, very sporty and with lovely Guinness'. Visiting fans agreed. Bar snacks, including chip butties for 80p, served 11.30-2. Darts, pool, TV. Open: 11-3, 6-11.

The Shakespeare (2) 40 High Street (01522) 523 350
Scottish and Newcastle. A small, two-roomed friendly pub with TV, pool and beer garden. Open: Fri-Sun all day; midweek 11.30-3.30, 5-11.

The Golden Eagle (3) 21 High Street (01522) 521 058
Camra pub with 7 real ales, and very football friendly. Darts, TV, beer garden. Open: all day Friday-Sunday; midweek 11-3, 5.30-11.

The Millers Arms (4) 88 High Street (01522) 520 939
Scottish/Courage. Friendly, sports-orientated pub ... 'the best on the High Street' says the landlord. Don't be put off if the front room is busy – there's a larger room behind. Full menu and children's menu served 12-2. TV, pool, beer garden. Families welcome. Open: all day.

The City Vaults (5) Corner Alfred Street/High Street (01522) 521 035
Vaux. Choose between the busy wine bar fronting the High Street, or the traditional pub to the rear. The building dates from 1826, and was originally a police station. Its main claim to fame, however, is that Lawrence of Arabia reputedly spent the night in the cellars. Extensive menu served 12-2, 5-7: the 'Steak and Waggledance Casserole' at £3.50 sounds good! Darts, TV, pub games. Families welcome to 6 pm.
Open: all day.

O'Donoghues 173 High Street (01522) 541 943
Mansfield (with Guinness and Kilkenny). Friendly Irish theme pub where local shoppers heavily outnumber the Irish. Extensive 'Shoppers' Special' lunch menu served 11.30-2.30. TV, beer garden. Open: all day.

The following is a football-friendly pub on the A57, the route to Lincoln from The North A1(M):

The White Swan Main Street, Dunham on Trent (01777) 228 307
Mansfield. Highly recommended traditional two-roomed roadside pub, a great place to stop for a meal. Full menu served 12-2 and 7-9. Pool, darts, TV, beer garden. Open: Saturdays all day from 12; from 7 pm for midweek games, though the landlady says she may open earlier if supporters book in advance.

FOOD GUIDE

The nearest takeaway to Sincil Bank is 'The Fish Dish' on the corner of Cross Street and Scorer Street, which offers plaice and chips for £1.45 and also opens after the game. Nearby on the High Street are a Perfect Pizza, a KFC and another fish and chip shop. Visiting fans recommended the pie shop next to the Shakespeare pub. Towards town are a huge range of outlets, including a Balti House, a 'Sarnie Shack', and the Round House takeaway (opposite Argos) which sells chips for 65p. Opposite the station is the Sun Cafe, which offers an all day breakfast for £2.50 and hosts art exhibitions!

LOCAL MEDIA

Local Radio: BBC Radio Lincolnshire 94.9 FM; Lincs FM 102.2.

Radio Phone-ins: BBC Radio Lincolnshire, 5-6 pm. Call (01522) 511 052.

Saturday Sports Paper: The 'Sports Echo' arrives at about 5.45 pm.

MISCELLANEOUS

Safety Factor: No major problems, and it's safe to wear colours.

Rivals: Grimsby Town (usually with various references to smelly fish), Mansfield Town and Scunthorpe United.

Fanzine: 'The Deranged Ferret!', 185 Burton Road, Lincoln, LN1 3LT; 'The Yellow Belly', 6-8 Kenneth Street, Lincoln, LN1 3ED.

Unofficial Websites:
http://www.netlink/co.uk/users/impnet/
http://www.geocities.com/Collosseum/Arena/7742/lcfc menu.htm
http://www.demon.co.uk/elpasso/steve/ football/lcfc.htm

Tourist Information: (01522) 529 828.

Liverpool

Anfield

Address: Anfield, Anfield Road, Liverpool L4 0TH
Telephone: Club (0151) 263 2361
Ticket Office (0151) 260 8680
24 Hour Match Information (0151) 260 9999
Tickets (Credit Cards) (0151) 263 5727
ClubCall (0891) 121 184
Official Website: http://www.fa-carling.com/club/l.fc/

We were dead chuffed a couple of years ago when a film company phoned up asking us to recommend a football ground as the backdrop for an advert. They wanted somewhere with 'traditional gates, a traditional atmosphere and lots of supporters in colours in traditional streets.' Apart from suggesting they jump into a Lowry painting, our obvious first thought was Anfield. As at Highbury, the terraced streets are full of red-and-white ... scarves, shirts, flags, even the hot dog stalls are painted in the club's colours. And no club has gates to match those at Liverpool, dedicated to the legendary Bill Shankly. For visiting fans, parking is the biggest nightmare, and the nearest railway station is more than a mile away. On the other hand, the pubs, chippies and the locals are all pretty friendly.

HOW TO GET THERE

BY CAR: From South: Exit M6 at junction 21a (s/p M62 Liverpool, M57 Southport) and follow Liverpool signs onto the M62. After 10.7 miles, exit M62 at junction 6 (s/p A5080 Huyton, M57 Bootle, Southport and All Docks). At roundabout turn right (s/p M57, Southport, Prescot and Docks) onto the M57. After 5.6 miles, exit M57 at junction 4 (s/p Knowsley and Industrial Park, Bootle). At roundabout turn left (s/p Bootle, Liverpool A580) onto the A580. Pass Showcase Cinema on LHS after 1.8 miles. (*)After further 1.9 miles, turn left (s/p Ring Road A5058, Widnes A561, Warrington) onto the A5058. At next major lights after 0.6 miles, turn right (s/p Anfield, Football Car Park, Liverpool FC, Everton FC) into Utting Avenue. After 0.7 miles, after railway bridge, turn right at crossroads/lights (opposite Hamilton House, s/p Football Car Park) into Priory Road. The Stanley Park car park and the ground are on the LHS.

From North: Exit M6 at junction 23 (s/p Manchester, Liverpool A580). At roundabout follow signs to 'Liverpool A580' onto the A580 dual carriageway. After 10.1 miles, pass under the M57, and 1.4 miles further on pass the Showcase Cinema complex on LHS. Then as From South(*).

FROM RAILWAY STATIONS

a) From Liverpool Lime Street: About 2.2 miles. *By taxi:* Up to £3.50. *By bus:* Nos. 17, 17C, 17D or 217 run from Queen's Square bus station, by the railway station. Nos. 26 and 27 run from Paradise Street. Alternatively, walk to Liverpool Central Station and catch

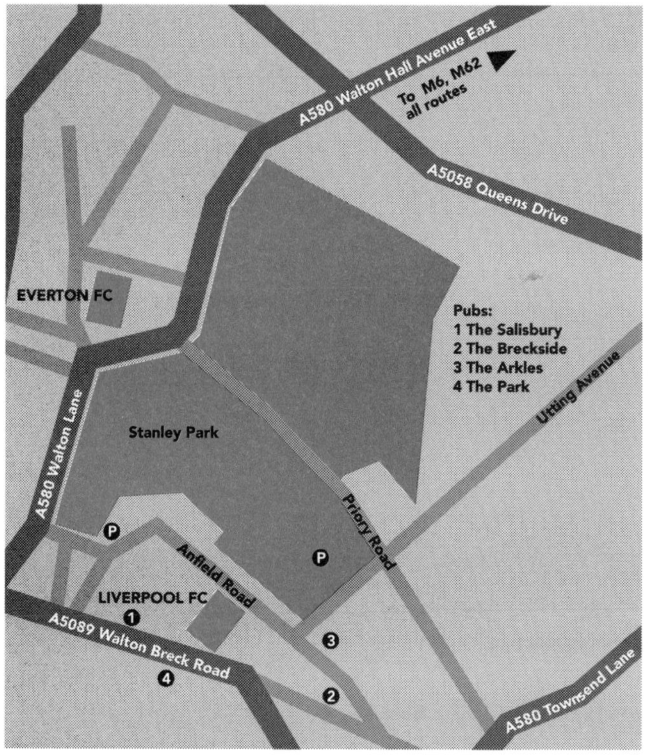

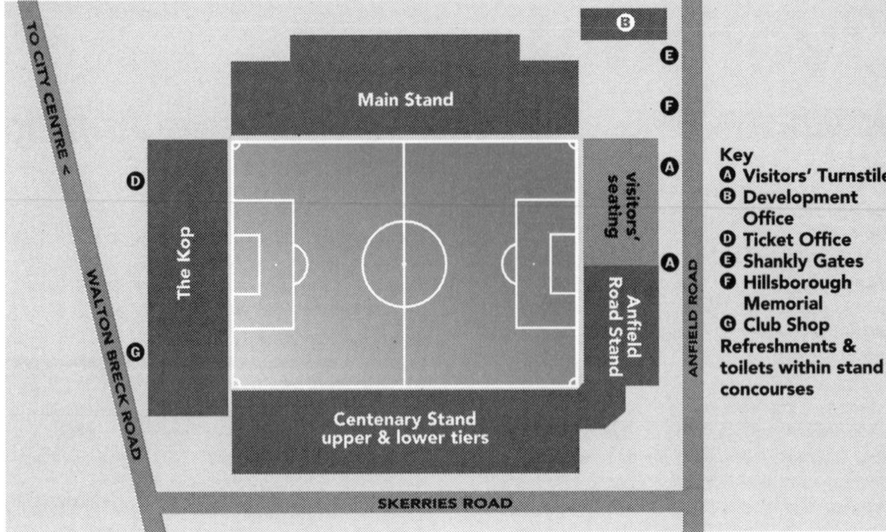

a Merseyrail Northern Line train to Sandhills. From the Liverpool Lime Street platforms, turn left, and then right out of station to main road. Go straight on at pedestrian crossing, walking towards the pedestrianised town centre. Turn left by the large Wetherspoons pub on the corner, and past 'Yates Wine Lodge' on the RHS. At end of the road turn right, and the entrance to Liverpool Central station is on the LHS after about a hundred yards.

b) From Sandhills: A walkable 1.3 miles. Come up path out of station and turn right along Sandhills Lane. At traffic lights continue up the hill on Lambeth Road, with the park on the RHS. Turn right before 'The Lambeth' pub, then after 100 yards turn left into Whittle Street. At main road (Kirkdale Road) turn left, then bear right and up the hill, following sign to 'St Helens A580'. Straight over lights then turn right (s/p Anfield) into Walton Breck Road. The ground is visible on the LHS after 0.4 miles.

Last Midweek Trains: From Liverpool Lime Street, trains run to Manchester Oxford Road at 21.52 and 21.55, and to Manchester Victoria at 22.20. The 22.52 goes on to Leeds. Connections to other routes are mainly from Manchester, and often entail taking the Metrolink to Piccadilly. There are no connecting trains to London after a midweek game. Please double-check on (0345) 484 950.

BY BUS: See above.

PARKING

There are usually spaces at the car park at Stanley Park, and at Anfield Comprehensive School on Priory Road. There's also a car park at Goodison (£3 – entrance off Bullens Road). For everyone else, it's street parking. The police enforce residents' parking schemes directly around the ground, so try further afield, eg, around Priory Road between Utting Avenue and Townsend Lane (the A580); around Goodison Park; or to the south of Townsend Lane. As at Goodison and many other inner-city areas, local youngsters approach drivers asking for money to 'mind the car'. The police advise fans to ignore them. For peace of mind however, you may wish to proffer £1. As car crime is also a problem, don't leave valuables in sight. If all this is daunting, consider leaving the car at a station along the Merseylink Northern Line (Ormskirk, Kirkby, Southport, Bootle) and taking the train to Sandhills.

THE GROUND

The completion of the second tier on the Anfield Road Stand brings to a close the latest redevelopment of this most famous of stadiums. The building work began in 1990, with the construction of a second tier on the Centenary Stand. In 1994, the famous Kop was closed and demolished, replaced with the single tier Kop Stand, complete with a McDonalds and a new club shop. The club then turned to the Anfield Road Stand, which houses both home and away fans. The view from some of the seats in the lower tier is poor, simply because they're right behind the goal, but those who like being close to the action will be in their element.

Total Capacity: 45,364. For away fans: Seating (Anfield Road Stand) 3,100. Turnstiles N, O and P.

Cost (97/98): Adults £18. Concessions: a joint ticket for an adult and child costs £27.

Disabled Facilities: Space for six visiting disabled

supporters in the Anfield Road Stand. *Disabled Toilet:* Nearby. *Cost:* £3 for disabled, full price for helper. *Booking:* Essential. *Parking:* None. *For the Blind:* Seats with headphones in the Anfield Road Stand. Please book.

Programme: £2.

Visitors' Toilets: *Male:* It was all rather cramped, as most fans didn't realise there were more toilet blocks further along, past the refreshment kiosk and the bookmakers. Everything was clean and prompted few complaints. Indeed, an Everton fan admitted it was all better than at Goodison! *Female:* Female fans found it highly amusing that, for a change, there were no queues for the ladies, and a right crush for the gents!

Food and Drink: Great stuff! The hot dogs (£2) were a popular choice, while the sausage roll (£1.10) was bigger than those described as 'jumbo' at other grounds. The steak-and-kidney pie (£1.30) fell apart easily but was delicious. Fans happily scoffed the rolls (£1.30) and the Eccles cakes (80p), washed down with tasty tea and coffee (£1). However, one fan muttered about having to remortgage his house for a coke (£1.30)! Carlsberg was also on sale at £1.80 a can (23.2.98, 13.4.98).

PUB GUIDE

The Salisbury (1) 121 Walton Breck Road (0151) 261 2741
Bass. Welcoming pub with large screen TV. Families welcome/disabled facilities. Bar snacks before the game. Open: all day from midday.

The Breckside (2) 377 Walton Breck Road (corner of Anfield Road) (0151) 287 1559
Carlsberg-Tetley (with the in-house Breckside Bitter). The pub's nicknamed 'the Flatiron' because of its triangular shape, and the landlord says it's 'the friendliest pub in Liverpool.' Sandwiches. TV. Open: all day from 11.30.

The Arkles (3) 77 Anfield Road (0151) 263 6419
Whitbread (with Boddingtons). Large modern colourful pub, formerly a hotel. Sandwiches, big screen TV. Open: all day.

Also recommended: **The Park (4),** 194 Walton Breck Road (Bass).

FOOD GUIDE

Walton Breck Road has a good choice of takeaways, including the 'Golden Dragon'; the 'Karaghi Kop' and, opposite the ground, the 'Moonlight Takeaway' offering 'Football Special Pizzas' for £3.40-£4.40. Nearby, the 'Kop Snack Bar' had fans queueing for the fish dinner at £2.70. Nearer the away end, on Anfield Road, is the 'Everpool Diner' with hot dogs for £1.50. There's a McDonalds in the Kop Stand, serving supporters inside and outside the ground. The Showcase Cinema complex on the A580 has a Deep Pan Pizza, a McDonalds and a KFC.

'EVERTONIAN?! – I thought the Dating Agency said ETONIAN!'

LOCAL MEDIA

Local Radio: BBC Radio Merseyside 95.8 FM; Radio City 96.7 FM.

Radio Phone-Ins: BBC Radio Merseyside, from 5 pm, call (0151) 709 9333; Radio City, Saturdays 5-6 pm, call (0151) 4720 967.

Saturday Sports Paper: The 'Football Echo' pink.

MISCELLANEOUS

Safety Factor: Few problems here, though tension can rise during games against Manchester United.

Rivals: Manchester United remains public enemy number one.

Fanzines: 'When Sunday Comes', 2 Maybury Court, Shaftesbury Road, Woking, Surrey, GU22 7DT; 'They all say our Days are Numbered', PO Box 31, Liverpool, L13 2HD; 'Another Wasted Corner', 89 Buckingham Road, Maghull, Merseyside, L31 7DW.

Best Unofficial Websites:
'JOW':
http://www.geocities.com/Colosseum/Loge/6460/
'This in Anfield': http://www.merseyworld.com/
'Anfield Forever': http://www.city.ac.uk/~bj105/lfc.html
http://geocities.com/Colosseum/Track/3780/
http://www.geocities.com/Colosseum/Field/3848/

Tourist Information: (0151) 709 3631.

L

Luton Town

Kenilworth Road

Address: Kenilworth Road Stadium, 1 Maple Road, Luton, Beds LU4 8AW
Telephone: Club (01582) 411 622
Ticket Office (01582) 416 976
ClubCall (0891) 121 123

Bring on the Kohlerdome....! That's the desperate cry from home and away fans alike. The club's been talking about moving to the out-of-town site since April 1995, as it's simply not possible to redevelop Kenilworth Road. The old ground, about half a mile west of the town centre, is hemmed in on three sides by terraced housing, so much so that the entrances to the away end cut under people's bedrooms! On matchdays, the police close the roads around the ground, and children from the local Asian community come pouring out to play cricket and football in the traffic-free streets. It's a pity more can't be enticed in to watch Luton Town. For footie fans, nearby Dunstable Road is the place for food, while the town centre and railway station are a 10-15 minute walk away. Parking is all on-street, so arrive early for the best places.

HOW TO GET THERE

BY CAR: From South (M1): Exit M1 at junction 10 (s/p A1081 Luton (S)). At motorway roundabout, turn right (s/p Luton South A1081) onto the A1081. After 0.5 miles, turn left at junction 10A (the next roundabout, s/p Stockwood County Park, Mossman Collection) into London Road. After 1.2 miles, turn left at roundabout (s/p Ring Road, Bedford A6, Dunstable A505) onto the Ring Road flyover. (*)Go straight on for 0.4 miles, and then, immediately before the roundabout, turn left into Dallow Road. After 0.4 miles turn right into Clifton Road. Ground is over bridge at end of road.

From North (M1): Exit M1 at junction 11. At roundabout turn left (s/p Luton A505) onto the A505 Dunstable Road. After 0.6 miles the road divides – bear right, following signs for the A505, remaining on

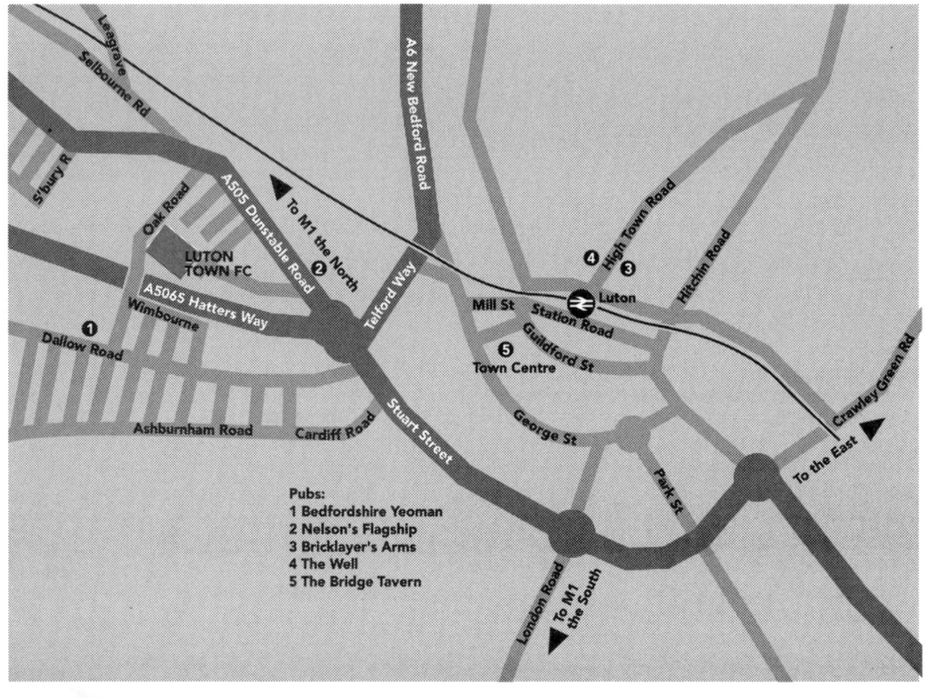

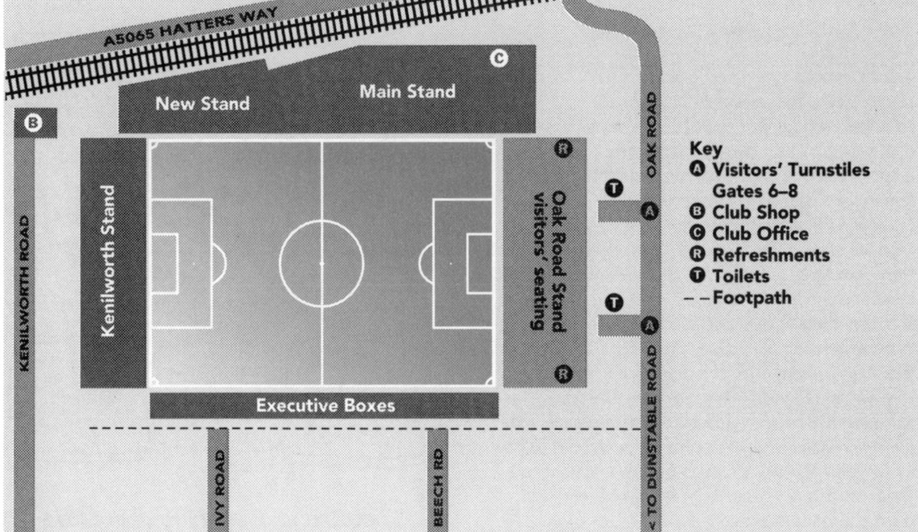

Dunstable Road. The A505 leads to the ground. At the Birchlink Gyratory after 1.7 miles, follow 'Town Centre A505' signs round small one-way system and ground is down streets on LHS.

From East (A505): At first roundabout on outskirts of Luton, go straight on (s/p Luton A505, Motorway M1) into Stopsley Way. At roundabout after 0.5 miles turn left (s/p Town Centre, Dunstable A505, M1) onto Vauxhall Way. At next roundabout after 0.7 miles, turn right (no s/p) into Crawley Green Road. Head down the hill for 1.0 miles to St Mary's Roundabout. Here, go straight across (s/p Dunstable A505, Bedford A6) onto Park Viaduct, and over flyover. Straight on at next roundabout (s/p Dunstable A505, Bedford A6). Then as From South(*).

FROM RAILWAY STATION (Luton): *By taxi:* £3. *By bus:* Nos. 31, 37, 38 and 61 run from Park Square or Upper George Street (by the Town Hall) along Dunstable Road. *By foot:* Follow signs to 'London Luton Airport, Railair Coach Link' down steps into Station Road, and turn right. Straight across Old Bedford Road into Mill Street, passing Job Centre on LHS. At T-junction by 'Pizza Palace' cross road and turn right. Follow road round, passing 'To Pigathaki' on LHS, and before the roundabout turn left through pedestrian area towards Sainsburys and the gents toilets. Turn left along dual carriageway and up pathway. Keep on path until there's a roundabout below. Bear right on walkway to central ironwork 'pagoda', and take first walkway down into Dunstable Road. First left to ground.

Last Midweek Trains: There are frequent trains to London Kings Cross Thameslink after a midweek game, until 00.16. There's a train to Leicester at 22.22 (with a connection to Birmingham). For many destinations, fans need to travel via London (see London Guide at front of book for onward connections). Please double check on (0345) 484 950.

BY BUS: In addition to those listed under 'From Railway Station', bus nos. 5, 15, 27 and 238 run from Manchester Street to Dunstable Road.

PARKING

It's street parking for all except honoured guests, but nearby roads have few restrictions. The local police, however, warn about car crime, and advise fans to park in the town centre, which is covered by CCTV.

THE GROUND

Kenilworth Road is a hotch-potch of stands, with one side simply a low row of executive boxes, which – say home fans – does absolutely nothing for the matchday atmosphere. One visiting supporter suggested that Luton Town could make a fortune renting the lot out to a double-glazing company, to display all its wares at once. Away fans are housed in the Oak Road Stand behind the goal, in seats bolted onto the old terrace. More than one visitor decided it was 'the worst away end in the history of the world' and yes, they had taken Mansfield's Field Mill into account! Fans start off by playing 'hunt the seat with a view', one without a pillar or part of the goal in the way. Then they discover the lack of legroom, and spend most of the match hunched sideways, moaning about the ticket prices.

So what's happened to the idea of a Kohlerdome, the 20,000-seater, £30 million stadium, named after the club chairman, to be built at junction 10 of the M1?

After many months, an announcement is imminent. Even if it gets the go ahead, however, it won't open until the year 2002!

Total Capacity: 9,970. For away fans (Oak Road Stand) 2,220. Turnstiles 6-8 on Oak Road.

Cost (98/99): Adults £13.50. Concessions (OAPs/juniors) £7. Concessions must be bought in advance from the away club. Some matches may be all-ticket. Check with away club for details.

Disabled Facilities: Space at pitch level in front of the Main Stand enclosure. *Disabled Toilet:* Nearby. *Cost:* Free for disabled, full price for helper. *Booking:* A month in advance. *For the Blind:* Hospital radio commentary is sometimes available. Please check with the club.

Programme: £1.60.

Visitors' Toilets: *Male:* 'Fascinating in a surreal sort of way,' wrote a Gills fan. 'They are in a house where the lounge should be. I imagine it reduced the value of the property!' All that said, the facilities were not half as bad as expected. *Female:* The soap was old and hard and there was no toilet paper, but it was well lit and the doors had working locks.

Food and Drink: Southend fans found the burgers (£1.70) tasty but overpriced. A group of hungry youngsters, scoffing burgers laden with mustard and ketchup, said they'd definitely buy more if they had the money. On the other hand, the hot dog (£1.50) was 'abysmal', cold with stale bread and no meaty taste at all. So go for the pies (£1.20), which were at least hot. The tea (80p) was good (18.8.97, 2.12.97, 31.1.98).

PUB GUIDE

WITHIN WALKING DISTANCE:

The Bedfordshire Yeoman (1) 214 Dallow Road (01582) 730 469
Greene King. Large pub, modern outside but more traditional inside, with pleasant lounge area. Pool, darts, TV, patio. Open: all day.

Nelson's Flagship (2) 2-5 Dunstable Road, Westside Centre (01582) 488 441
Whitbread. Popular modern-style pub, with anchors and oars decorating the walls. Bar snacks served from 1 pm, as well as West Indian cuisine such as curried goat, banana porridge and patties! Pool table, darts, TV. Open: all day from 11.30.

NEAR THE STATION:

The Bricklayers Arms (3) High Town Road (01582) 611 017
Free House. A great little pub in a 100-year-old listed building, renowned for its beers. Sandwiches. Darts, patio. Open: all day at weekends; from 5 pm for midweek games.

The Well (4) 5 High Town Road (01582) 618 811
Free House (with Whitbread). Traditional Irish bar with authentic sports memorabilia and farm equipment on the walls! Big-screen TV. Bar meals served all day.

'There's one good thing about lower crowds. Plenty of legroom!'

Families welcome. Open: all day from 12.

The Bridge Tavern (5) 95 Guildford Street (01582) 730 868
Whitbread. Large sporting pub, with two pool tables, big-screen TV. Open: all day.

FOOD GUIDE

Home fans highly recommend the takeaway 'Bluebird One' on the corner of Clifton Road and Wimborne Road. The chips are truly excellent. The nearby Dunstable Road is choc-a-bloc with takeaways, including a KFC.

LOCAL MEDIA

Local Radio: BBC Three Counties Radio 103.8 FM, 630 MW; Capital Gold 1548 AM.

Radio Phone-ins: Three Counties Radio, Friday evenings 6-7, Saturdays 2-2.30, 5-6 pm, call (0645) 455 555; Capital Gold, Saturdays 2-6.30, midweek 7-10 (or 7-8 if no match), call (0845) 35 60 70 80.

Saturday Sports Paper: None.

MISCELLANEOUS

Safety Factor: No problems ... except for some minor skirmishes when rivals Watford came to town in season 1997/98 and went 4-0 up in the first half hour.

Rivals: Watford. Only Watford.

Fanzines: 'Mad as a Hatter', 38 Twigden Court, Mount Pleasance Road, Luton LU3 2RL (60p plus postage).

Unofficial Websites: 'WHOSH': http://www.whosh.u-net.com/
'Hatters': http://www.btinternet.com/~ben.w/

Tourist Information: (01582) 401 579.

Macclesfield Town

Moss Rose

Address: Moss Rose Ground, London Road, Macclesfield, SK11 7SP
Telephone: Club (01625) 264 686
Blues Line (0930) 555 835
Official Website: http://www.mtfc.co.uk/

'The Silk Road' – the name conjures up images of Samarkand, epic journeys and adventure. The Silk Road which runs through Macclesfield lacks, well, all such excitement, but does highlight the town's history as a silk producing industrial centre. Nowadays Macclesfield is a small, quiet town on the edge of the Peak District, with the hills forming a picturesque backdrop for the out-of-town Moss Rose Ground. Yep, time to panic, train travellers ... 'out-of-town' does indeed mean a hike from the station, made a lot more bearable by the ten or so pubs en route. Parking at Moss Rose can be a problem, but the nearby pubs are extremely welcoming.

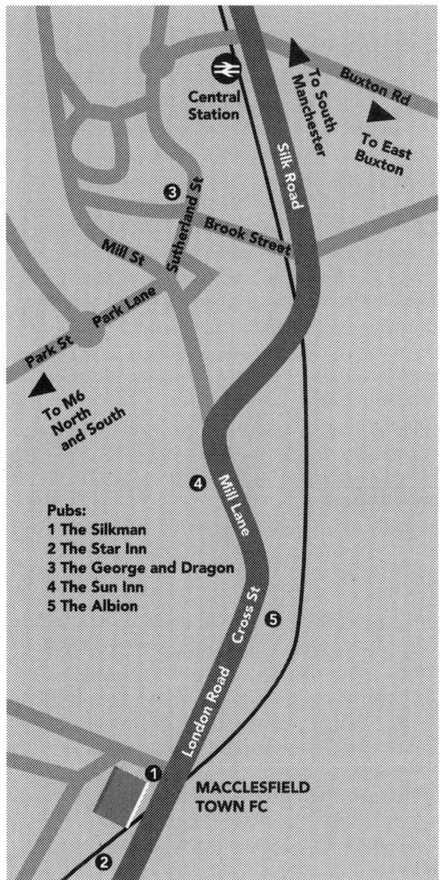

HOW TO GET THERE

BY CAR: From South (M6): Exit M6 at junction 17 (s/p Sandbach, Congleton A534). At T-junction turn right (s/p A534 Congleton) onto the A534. At T-junction in Congleton after 5.5 miles turn left (s/p Manchester A34, Town Centre), passing Waggon and Horses pub on LHS. At roundabout after 0.4 miles turn left (s/p Town Centre, Manchester A34, Macclesfield A536). Follow signs to 'Macclesfield A536' for a further 7.5 miles to crossroads/lights by the Flowerpot Inn. Here turn right into Park Lane (s/p Leek A523, Railway Station), down the hill. (*)From this point the ground is signposted either 'Leek A523' or 'Macclesfield Town FC'.

From North: Exit M6 at junction 19 (s/p Northwich, Knutsford, Macclesfield A556), and at roundabout turn right (s/p Knutsford, Northwich). At junction after 0.6 miles, turn left (s/p Macclesfield A5033 (A537)). At roundabout in Knutsford after 1.8 miles, by White Bear pub, turn right (s/p Stoke A50, Macclesfield A537), and then turn left after 0.4 miles, by Knutsford station (s/p Macclesfield A537) onto the A537. Continue on the A537 for 9.9 miles, through the villages of Ollerton and Chelford, over the Monk's Heath crossroads, to a roundabout by the Packhorse pub. Here, go straight on (s/p Macclesfield A537, Town Centre), and straight on for 1.0 miles, over an unsignposted roundabout, to 2nd roundabout. Here turn right (s/p Congleton A537, Birmingham M6) into Oxford Road. At crossroads after 0.7 miles, by the Flowerpot Inn, turn left (s/p Leek (A532) into Park Lane. Then as From South (M1)(*).

From North/South Manchester (A523) from junction with the A5091: Follow signs to 'Macclesfield A523' for 2.3 miles to the roundabout by Tescos. Here go straight on (s/p Leek A523, Macclesfield Town FC). From here follow signs to 'Leek A523' to ground.

From East (Buxton A537): Negotiate hairpins on descent from Peak District and pass Macclesfield town sign. After 0.9 miles go straight on at crossroads (no s/p) by Alldays store. At T-junction after 0.4 miles, just past Old Bull pub, turn left (s/p Leek A523, Congleton) onto The Silk Road. Follow signs to 'Leek A523' to ground.

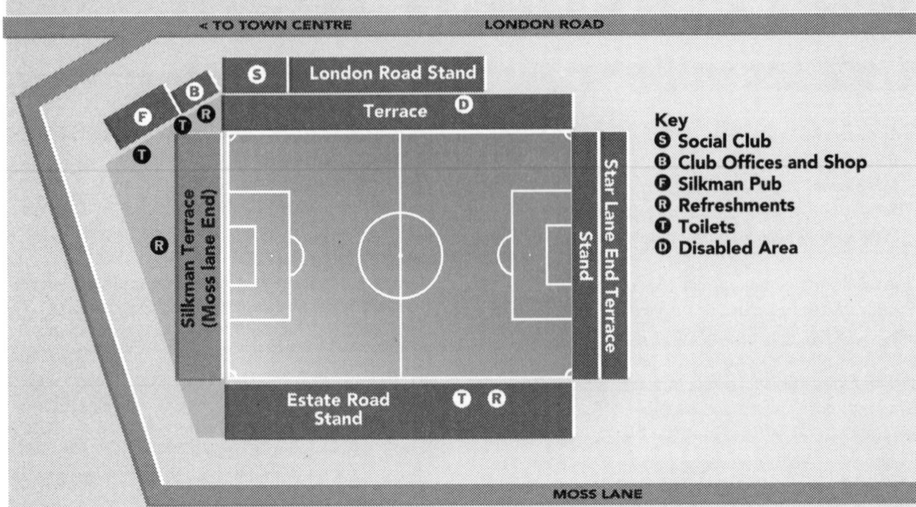

FROM RAILWAY STATION: 1.3 miles.
By taxi: About £3, plus an extra 20p per person. *By bus:* The bus station is opposite the railway station. The nos. 9 and 14 run to the ground (every 12 minutes during the day, every hour in the evening). *By foot:* Turn left out of station and down slope, turning left onto the main road (Sunderland Street) towards the George and Dragon. At end of road, by Topps Tiles, turn left and then right round war memorial square, towards Park Green Tandoori. Turn left into Mill Lane and at junction turn right (s/p Leek A523). This becomes Cross Street and then London Road.
Last Midweek Trains: The key train is the 22.05 to Stockport and Manchester Piccadilly. From these two stations there are links to Nottingham (arriving 01.31), Derby (01.55), Liverpool (00.13), Doncaster (23.48) and Newcastle (01.15). There are no connections to London. Please double-check on (0345) 484 950.
BY BUS: As above.

PARKING

Early birds get to park on London Road, although the section nearest Moss Rose is coned off. When it's not too wet, a local farmer opens up a large field opposite the ground (£1) which is very convenient. Nearby Ash Grove School on Belgrave Road also occasionally offers matchday parking (£1). The police advise visitors against parking in the housing estate to the west of the ground.

THE GROUND

'When Match of the Day films here', said one local proudly, 'they always start the camera shot on a close-up of that cottage up on the hills, and pull out to reveal the ground and everything'. Okay so it's rural, but the Moss Rose Ground – especially the Star Lane End with terracing above the seats – retains lots of character. It's a bit of a mish-mash, especially as the club's cost-conscious officials have travelled the north in search of bargains. The Ayresome Park auction provided the seats in the Star Lane End, put in to achieve the mandatory number to climb out of the Conference ... which is why they're red while Macc Town play in blue. More recently, the club bought more seats from Stoke's old Victoria Ground to replace sections of the Main Stand.

On gaining promotion to the Second Division, the club embarked on a series of ground improvements. The old Estate Road terrace is being replaced with a temporary, 1,700-seater stand, and there are plans to put a roof on the Silkman Terrace behind the goal, where away fans are housed.
Total Capacity: About 6,400. For away fans: Silkman Terrace 1,900. Visitors are sometimes admitted to the Main Stand by prior arrangement.
Cost (98/99): Adults £10, concessions (juniors/OAPs) £6.
Disabled Facilities: Visitors share the disabled area, which has space for 9 wheelchairs, at ground level in front of the London Road Stand. *Disabled Toilet:* A temporary structure nearby. *Cost:* Free for disabled and helper. *Parking:* Not available, but can drop off. *Booking:* Not necessary. *For the Blind:* No special facilities.
Programme: £1.50.
Visitors' Toilets: Good news folks. The club says they're being revamped for season 98/99.
Food and Drink: The chip butties (80p) and pizza (60p) were great, and a real change from the nosh

served up at most other grounds. However, most fans agreed with one supporter who said that the 'beefburger bap' (£1.20) was 'very not nice'. The tea (50p) was top-notch, possibly the best in the league, strong contender for a BAFTA (see Halifax). The club is putting in extra refreshment huts to reduce the queues (12.8.97, 23.8.97).

PUB GUIDE

The view from Macclesfield railway station, of five pubs and three takeaways, is an encouraging one. But be warned. Even though the town has loads of pubs, few are football-friendly. Only one near the station was keen on the idea of football fans, while others were downright antagonistic. One particularly wary pub on the outskirts of town came out with the quote of the season: 'We don't want to attract the wrong sort of family.' Hmmm. Pubs nearer the ground are more welcoming:

The Silkman (1) 159 London Road (01625) 614 766
Tetleys. Great football-friendly pub overlooking the ground – the landlord watches the game from the balcony. Bar food served from 12. Pool table, TV, patio. Families welcome. Open: Saturday matchdays 12-2.30; all day for midweek games.

The Star Inn/The Corner Post (2) 172 London Road (01625) 426 738
Marstons (Bitter and Pedigree). This pub is due to be demolished, and rebuilt as part of a scheme to improve access to the Moss. The name is expected to change to The Corner Post. However, it will remain football-friendly. Please phone for details.

The following three pubs are on the way from the station, Sunderland Street, Mill Lane or London Road:

The George and Dragon (3) 23 Sunderland Street (01625) 421 898
Robinsons. A local called it 'a proper pub', i.e. small, traditional and friendly. Sandwiches and pies (if you're early enough!). Pool, darts. Open: 11-5, 7-11; from 5.30 for midweek games.

The Sun Inn (4) 45 Mill Lane (01625) 610 436
Paramount/Free House (with hand-pulled real ales, Cains, Burtonwood and four guest beers). Bright, refurbished real ale house, based – says the landlord – on the idea of an old taproom. Bar snacks (sandwiches, pies, casseroles) served 12-2 (or later if there's still a demand). Pool, darts, TV in public bar, beer garden. Open: all day from 12.

The Albion (5) 6 London Road (01625) 425 339
Robinsons. A small traditional hostelry, described by the landlady as 'like a second home, a really friendly locals pub.' It has four small rooms, one housing the pool table. Darts, TV, beer garden. Families welcome in pool room. Disabled facilities. Open: all day.

FOR FAMILIES:

The following excellent pub is in the village of Henbury, on the route to Macclesfield From North (M6). It's on the RHS, nine miles from Knutsford:

The Blacksmith's Arms
Chelford Road, Henbury (the A537) (01626) 424 312
Greenalls (plus guest beer). Traditional-style family pub in semi-rural surroundings, and sports-friendly to-boot! From noon onwards it serves the 'Miller's Kitchen' menu (average main meal £5.75) and a children's menu from £2.25. TV, darts, beer garden, outdoor play area. Disabled facilities. Open: all day.

'I'll try the Earl Grey next, please Hives!'

FOOD GUIDE

The nearest takeaway to the ground is the highly recommended 'K & J Chippy' on London Road. It serves a huge platter of chips for 75p, and Hollands pies at 90p. Next door is the Rainbow Café, with a special breakfast at £3.30, but it shuts at 1 pm. Also nearby, the Golden Star Cantonese takeaway opens from 5.30 pm midweek. Near the station, local fans recommend the Waters Green Fish Bar, where one portion of chips (£1.10), they say, feeds a family of four. Sunderland Street also has a good selection of cafes and takeaways.

LOCAL MEDIA

Local Radio: Silk 106.9 FM; GMR 95.1 FM.
Radio Phone-ins: GMR, Saturday 1-3 pm, 5-6 pm, and after midweek games. Call (0161) 228 2255.
Saturday Sports Paper: None.

MISCELLANEOUS

Safety Factor: Macclesfield prides itself on being a family club and trouble is extremely rare.
Rivals: Altrincham, Yeovil and Stevenage ... 'but then everyone in the Conference dislikes Stevenage!'
Fanzine: 'Hang 'Em High', 62 Coare Street, Macclesfield, Cheshire, SK10 1DW.
Unofficial Websites: None.
Tourist Information: (01625) 504 114.

Manchester City

Maine Road

Address: Maine Road, Moss Side, Manchester M14 7WN
Telephone: Club (0161) 224 5000
Ticket Office (0161) 226 2224
TicketCall (0891) 121 591
ClubCall (0891) 121 191
City Store (0161) 232 1111
Official Website: http://www.mcfc.co.uk

An aerial view of Maine Road shows the ground in the middle of a triangle of terraced streets, with more terraced streets to either side, and, er, more terraced streets beyond. Oh, and a couple of parks! The ground's about two miles south of Manchester city centre, but without the rail and metro connections which have reached clubs such as Manchester United, Bury and Stockport. Those who choose instead to travel by car should note that, as in many inner-cities, this area of Moss Side does have car crime. However, the club has secured safe off-street parking for all, as long as drivers know where to look! Maine Road is also close to the suburb of Rusholme, where every other building is a curry house! Those who prefer less spicy footie favourites are also well catered-for, and there are a surprising number of friendly pubs within ambling distance.

HOW TO GET THERE

BY CAR: From South, M6: Exit M6 at junction 19 (s/p Manchester and Airport, Stockport A55, M56 East) and at roundabout turn right onto the A556. At the Bowdon Roundabout after 4.2 miles turn right (s/p Manchester M56) onto the M56. At junction 3 after 6.9 miles, where the road divides, go straight on (s/p

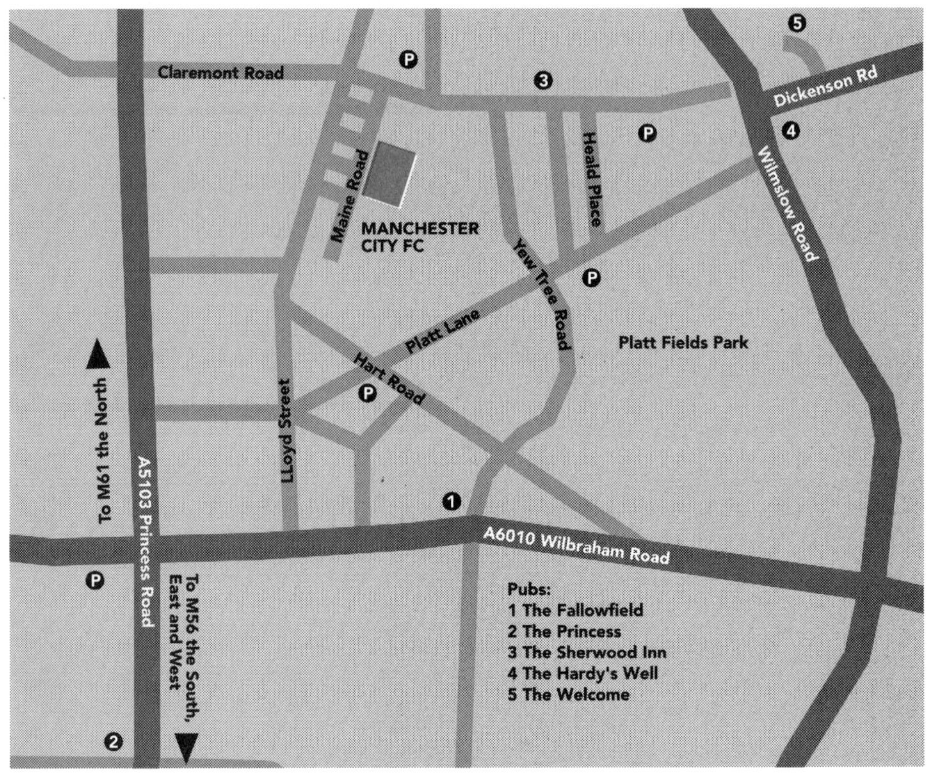

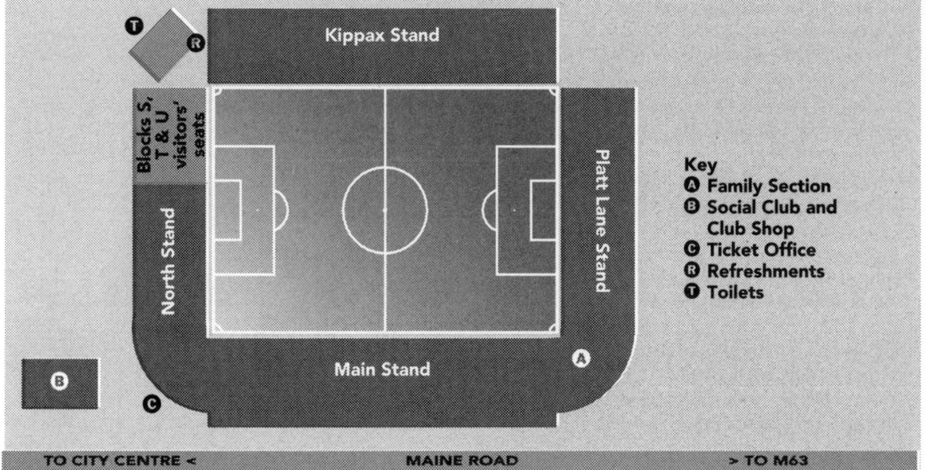

Altrincham, Congleton, Manchester A5103). At this point the road becomes the A5103 Princess Parkway. At next junction after 1.1 miles, go straight on (s/p City Centre A5103, Withington, Moss Side). (*)After 1.4 miles, get into right hand lane and turn right at lights (s/p Ashton-under-Lyne A6010, Sheffield A616, also MCFC, Princes Christian College) into Wilbraham Road. After 0.2 miles turn left (s/p MCFC) into Lloyd Street South. Maine Road is down the sidestreets on the RHS after 0.6 miles.

From North and East (M62 from Leeds): When the M60 eastern section is open, the quickest route will be to exit the M62 at junction 18 and head south on the M60 to Junction 5, turning right at the roundabout onto the A5103 Princess Road. Then as From South, M6(*). Until then, supporters should continue westbound on the M60, round the west of Manchester: As the M62 becomes the M60, follow signs to Stockport M60, remaining throughout on the M60. Exit M60 at junction 12 (s/p Warrington, Liverpool M62, Birmingham M6, M602 Salford). Keep in left hand lanes following 'Salford M602' signs, onto the M602. Go straight on for 5.7 miles, following signs to 'Manchester', and 'Manchester A57'. Immediately after underpass exit at signpost 'Chester A5103 (M56), Birmingham M6' (ie not going onto flyover). At roundabout take 3rd exit (s/p Chester M56, Hulme, Moss Side) onto Princess Road dual carriageway and under distinctive humped bridge. After 1.2 miles, turn left (n/s) into Claremont Road to ground.

FROM RAILWAY STATION (Manchester Piccadilly): About 2 miles. *By taxi:* £3-3.50. *By bus:* Turn right out of the station, down the hill, to a square called Piccadilly Gardens, the main bus station. From here, take the nos. 11, 41, 42, 43, 44 or 46 and ask to be dropped off at Platt Lane. Alternatively, take the nos. 101, 104, 105, 106, 108, 109 or the 110 and ask to be dropped off at the Princess Road Depot, which is a 10 minute walk from the ground. For further details call (0161) 228 7811.

Last Midweek Trains: From Manchester, trains leave to: York and Newcastle at 21.50; to Nottingham and Derby at 22.28; to Liverpool at 22.07, 23.12 and 23.15; to Leeds at 22.43, 23.50 and 01.50; to Birmingham at 21.40 (via Manchester Airport) and 22.33 (via Crewe). There is no service to London after a midweek game. Please double check on (0345) 484 950.

BY BUS: See above.

PARKING

Although street parking is an option, visiting fans are best advised to head to one of the many car parks, all within half a mile or so of Maine Road (see map). The Whalley Range High School offers 'protected parking' for £2. The Wilbraham High School on the junction of Hart Road and Platt Lane charges £1, while the Heald Place Primary School at the junction of Claremont Road and Heald Place charges £3. There are also 300 spaces at the Platt Lane Complex and the Hough End playing fields opposite 'The Princess' pub (£3).

THE GROUND

Maine Road is a schizophrenic mixture of stands, from different eras and attempts at redevelopment. Even though joined on three sides, each stand has a different style and character. The newest permanent addition, the 11,000 seater, three-tiered Kippax Stand, is huge and somewhat isolated, so home fans complain that any noise they generate simply dissipates up and out! In its shadow is a bank of seating in what home fans call 'Windy Corner'. It's a temporary uncovered stand providing overspill seating for 1,000 visiting fans. Most away fans, however, are housed in the single-tier North Stand behind the goal, where there's little legroom but

the view and the facilities are good.
Total Capacity: About 32,000. For away fans: (Blocks S, T, U and UU of the North Stand) 3,300. Block UU is the extra 1,000 seats in 'Windy Corner'. Turnstiles 42-46.
Cost (98/99): Adults £12, concessions £7. £1 reduction for seats in Block UU.
Disabled Facilities: Six spaces for away fans in the North Stand. *Disabled toilet:* By the turnstiles. *Cost:* Free for disabled, £5 for helper. *Booking:* Required. *Parking:* None available. *For the Blind:* 22 seats with commentary at the back of Block G of the Main Stand.
Programme: £1.80, sold inside the ground.
Visitors' Toilets: (North Stand): *Male:* There was plenty of room, and it was pretty clean. *Female:* Loads of cubicles, plus hand dryers and paper towels. However, it was all rather dirty.
Food and Drink: One fan complained that the meat-and-potato pie (£1.50) wasn't warm enough, but he ate it anyway as he'd already rejected a cold Cornish Pasty (£1.55) and couldn't bear to wait any longer. On Windy Corner, the queue was extremely slow moving, but the second the match restarted, the staff began closing the shutters, leaving fuming fans on the other side. In the end, one side did stay open to serve hot drinks, which were very good. Lager and bitter at £2 a pint, Guinness and cider at £3 and various shorts were also on sale (22.11.97, 13.4.98).

PUB GUIDE

Visiting supporters are welcome at Manchester City's training complex at Platt Lane, on the corner of Yew Tree Road. It serves Scottish and Newcastle beers and has a restaurant (please book for a pre-match meal). Families are welcome and there's a big-screen TV. Open 12-3 and from 7 pm. Tel: (0161) 257 0009.

The Fallowfield (1) 68 Wilbraham Road (0161) 224 1686
Free House/Greene King (with Wexford Cream Ale, Boddingtons). Large modern football-friendly pub, with plenty of big-screen TVs to build up the pre-match atmosphere. Food served 12-4, 6-10. Open: all day.

The Princess (2) 252 Mauldeth Road West, Chorton-cum-Hardy (0161) 860 7878
GRS (with Boddingtons, Murphys, Chesters). Huge detached building on the A56. Big-screen TV, lively music. Sandwiches if it's not too busy. Open: all day.

The Sherwood Inn (3) 417 Claremont Road (0161) 225 9176
Whitbread (with Boddingtons). Traditional local with big-screen TV, pool, darts. Open: all day.

Also recommended: **The Hardy's Well (4)** at 257 Wilmslow Road, a large modern-style Bass pub, serving a special football menu; **The Welcome (5),** 2 Hythe Close (off Dickenson Road), a friendly no-frills Greenalls pub.

'Of course I can prove my loyalty – here's my Manchester City season ticket!'

FOOD GUIDE

Home fans recommend the mobile van at the back of the Kippax for 'lovely' griddled sausages and burgers, and 'The City Chippy' on Claremont Road. The 'Blue Moon Chippy' on Maine Road and 'The Claremont Chippy', near the junction of Claremont Road and Princess Road, were both doing a roaring trade. Nearby is 'Willie's Café', serving big mugs of tea, plus fish-and-chips at £2.20 and pies at 90p. Rusholme, especially Wilmslow Road, is the place for a curry.

LOCAL MEDIA

Local Radio: GMR 95.1 FM; Piccadilly Radio 103 FM
Radio Phone-ins: GMR, Saturdays 1-3, 5-7 and after midweek games. Call (0161) 228 2255; Piccadilly Radio, Saturdays 5-6, call (0161) 288 1152.
Saturday Sports Paper: 'The Pink'.

MISCELLANEOUS

Safety Factor: Because of congestion outside the North Stand, the police advise visitors to wait in the ground for a few minutes to let the area clear. Don't wear colours in the town centre.
Rivals: It'll always be Manchester United.
Fanzines: 'King of the Kippax', 25 Holdenbrook Close, Leigh, Greater Manchester, WN7 2HL; 'Bert Trautmann's Helmet', 217 Dumers Lane, Radcliffe, Manchester, M26 2GE; 'The Fightback', c/o 2 Old Hall, Gatley, SK8 4BE.
Unofficial Websites: http://www.mancity.net/
http://www.geocities.com/Colosseum/Field/3084/
http://www.service.uit.no/mancity/
Tourist Information: (0161) 234 3157/3158.

Manchester United

Old Trafford

Address: Old Trafford Stadium, Sir Matt Busby Way, Manchester, M16 0RA
Telephone: Club (0161) 872 1661/930 1968
Ticket Information (0161) 872 0199
Megastore (0161) 848 8181
Mail Order Hotline (0161) 877 9777
ClubCall (0891) 121 161
Official Website: http://www.sky.co.uk/manu/

Love 'em or hate 'em, there's something special about a trip to Old Trafford. Simply stated, everything seems bigger and brighter ... for a start, where else would souvenir sellers offer 75 different types of badge just for the home club? Sir Matt Busby Way is closed to traffic before the game, and it simply swarms with supporters, mostly sporting red-and-white and not all speaking English! Until recently, the outside of Old Trafford was a bit of a let-down, but today the huge triple-tier North Stand towers over the surrounding area, with the bright neon lettering 'Manchester United' visible for miles around. Many of the old industrial complexes to the north and west of the ground have been demolished to make way for high-tech skyscrapers, apartment blocks, pubs and restaurants, many within walking distance of Old Trafford. For football fans, the new roads have made life a lot easier, parking's a doddle and there's a railway station at the ground.

HOW TO GET THERE

BY CAR: NB Sir Matt Busby Way is closed to through traffic 2 to 3 hours before each match.
From North/All away coaches: Exit M60 at junction 9 (s/p A5081 Trafford Park, Stretford). At roundabout take 1st exit (s/p Trafford Park A5081) onto Parkway. At Parkway Circle roundabout after 0.9 miles take 3rd exit (s/p Manchester A5081, also The Village, Wharfside, Old Trafford), onto Ashburton Road East. At Village Circle roundabout after 0.8 miles go straight on (s/p Manchester A5081, Old Trafford). The main car parks are signposted left, along Elevator Road, after 0.2 miles. To the ground, go straight on instead and ground is on RHS.
From South: Exit M6 at junction 19 (s/p Manchester and Airport, Stockport A55, M56 East) and at roundabout turn right onto the A556. At the Bowdon Roundabout after 4.2 miles turn right (s/p Manchester M56) onto the M56. Exit M56 after 8.1 miles (s/p Stretford, Leeds, Bolton, Preston M60), onto the M60. After 2.2 miles, exit M60 at junction 7 (s/p Altrincham, Stretford A56). At T-junction turn right (s/p Stretford A56). At roundabout after 0.4 miles, follow signs to 'Manchester, Salford, Trafford Park' onto the A56 Chester Road. Go straight on at lights after 0.8 miles (s/p Manchester A56, Salford A5063 and Old Trafford Football Ground). Sir Matt Busby Way is on the LHS after 0.8 miles, by the Rallye Sports Centre.

To get to the Talbot Road parking areas: Exit M60 as above, turning right at the T-junction and over the roundabout into Chester Road. After 0.8 miles turn right (s/p Old Trafford

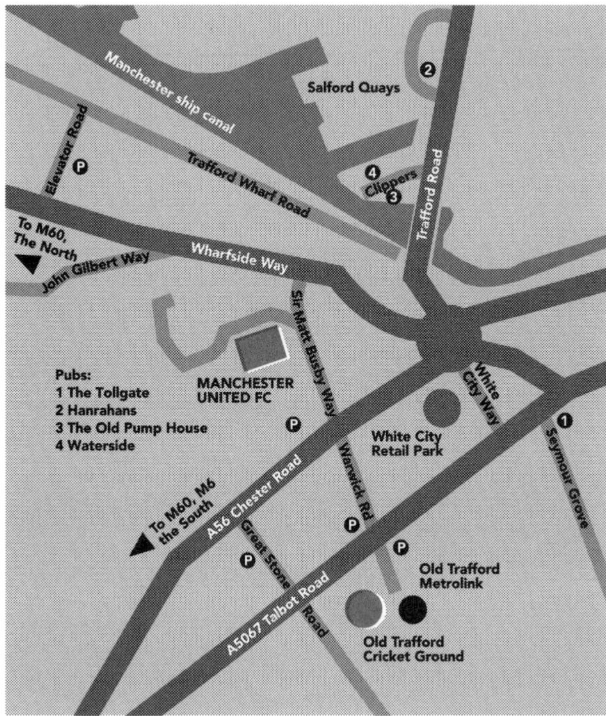

M

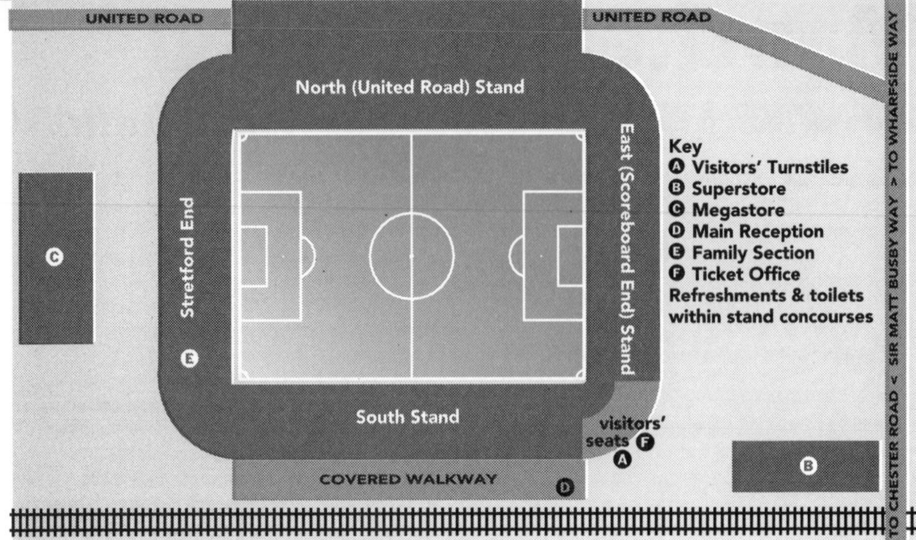

Cricket Ground) into Talbot Road (for parking details, see below).

There is an alternative route to Old Trafford. At the Bowdon Roundabout, instead of turning right onto the M56, go straight on (s/p Altrincham A56) onto the A56. There are lots of pubs and restaurants along the route. Simple follow the A56 for 8.0 miles, where it passes under the M60 at junction 7.

FROM METROLINK STATION (Old Trafford): 0.5 miles. *By foot:* Exit station into Warwick Road, passing the cricket ground on the LHS, and the Kelloggs building on the right. Straight over lights after 0.2 miles, and straight over crossroads by Old Trafford pub after 0.2 miles into Sir Matt Busby Way. There's another station, **Trafford Bar,** at the junction of Talbot Road and Seymour Grove, which is a good stop for those heading for 'The Tollgate' pub or the restaurants at the White City Retail Park.

NB: Overland trains from Piccadilly and Manchester Oxford Road stop on matchdays at Old Trafford Football Ground itself. However, large groups of away fans are sometimes not allowed on board.

Last Midweek Trains: From Manchester Piccadilly, a train to York and Newcastle leaves at 21.50, to York at 22.47, and to Nottingham and Derby at 22.28. There are no connecting trains to London after a midweek game. Please double-check on (0345) 484 950.

BY BUS: The nos. 252-257 inclusive, plus the 17, 114 and 236 run from Manchester Piccadilly to Old Trafford.

PARKING

For secure parking, try one of the following:

a) The large official car and coach park on Elevator Road.

b) A car park, charging £3, on John Gilbert Way.

c) Various car parks along Talbot Road. The best are at the Norweb building, the Town Hall and at Old Trafford Cricket Ground.

d) Schools and colleges, such as Stretford High School on Great Stone Road and the North Trafford College of Education on Talbot Road open their car parks on matchdays.

For street parking, try the roads off Trafford Park Road, which leads off the Village Circle roundabout. Don't park on Trafford Park Road itself, which has double yellow lines. Just because other supporters are taking the risk, it doesn't mean that traffic wardens aren't around.

THE GROUND

Old Trafford holds more than 55,000 people. Yet the club could fill the stadium three or four times over. In 97/98 Manchester United became the first Premiership club to attract more than a million people to watch its home games in one season, with capacity crowds for every single match. Those who did obtain a ticket were rarely disappointed. The ground is fully enclosed, with executive boxes on all sides, and excellent views for all. The gigantic North Stand, which on its own seats more than 25,000, is so tall that the match tickets warn about vertigo and the number of steps to climb! And so great is the demand for tickets that the club's already considering ways to increase the ground capacity even further. Away fans are allocated a corner section in the upper tier of the East Stand. The pies are good and fans were mightily impressed by the automatic lights in the loos! A visiting Everton fan wrote: 'I'd love to report on how bad the place was, but it really was excellent all round.'

Total Capacity: 55,000. For away fans (East Stand Upper) up to 3,000. Entrance E30.

Cost (98/99): Adults £20, concessions (OAPs, juniors) £10.

Disabled Facilities: Space for seven visiting fans for League games, and 11 for Cup games, in a raised area in the South-East corner. *Disabled Toilet:* Nearby. *Cost:* Free for disabled and helper. *Booking:* Essential, through the away club. *Parking:* Available in car park off Sir Matt Busby Way – please book through Manchester United. *For the Blind:* Away fans can apply for one of forty positions with commentary on headphones. However, those with matchday tickets can just as easily bring their own radios and listen to full match commentary on Manchester United Radio (details below).

Programme: £2.

Visitors' Toilets: *Male:* Extremely smart, plus a sign reminding supporters to 'Please adjust your dress before leaving.' Right on, say all female fans sick of males emerging still zipping themselves up! *Female:* It could only happen at Man U ... a light which switches on automatically when supporters come in. The grey tiles were real, the flooring was a smart red-and-grey design, the hot tap ran hot, the hand-dryer worked and there was a free banana on one of the shelves. Great stuff.

Food and Drink: 'The hotness is overpowering. I can't hold it,' said one Wimbledon fan, wishing he'd brought his woolly mitts to hold his pie (£1.20). Once they cooled down, the meat-and-potato pies were extremely good – one supporter gave it a straight ten-out-of-ten. The steak and kidney variety was popular too. The cheese pie (£1.10) was good value but was runny and bland. And the lager? Oh dear! It was canned, and one comment summed up many: 'It's s****, the worst lager in the country' (28.3.98).

PUB GUIDE

The Tollgate (1) Seymour Grove, Old Trafford (0161) 873 8213
Banks's. Smart friendly pub, with a full-size stagecoach mounted in an alcove! Bar snacks, such as pie and chips, served til they run out. Big-screen TV, darts, patio. Families welcome. Disabled facilities. Open: all day from 11.30.

The Throstles Nest 122 Seymour Grove, a 15-minute walk to the ground (0161) 860 5595
Whitbread. Large traditional pub, and an excellent place for a pre-match meal. Full menu, including a big breakfast for £4.25 and a 10oz steak meal for £4.95,

'Look at it this way Sir, at least your driving licence will be taking three points away from Old Trafford!'

served 12-3. In the evening there's a shorter menu, with soup, chilli etc. Large parties should pre-book food orders. Big-screen TV, pool table, car park. Families welcome up to 7 pm. Open: all day.

Hanrahans (2) Merchants Quay, Trafford Road (0161) 876 7463
Whitbread. An upmarket modern-style bar/restaurant, with high ceilings and wooden floors, and very popular on matchdays. Hot roast beef or pork sandwiches (£3.75) served in the bar area until they run out. The restaurant serves many of the favourites, such as pies, sausage casserole, steak sandwiches, steaks, burgers and pasta dishes – please book. TV, patio. Disabled facilities. Open: all day.

The following pubs are for Manchester United fans only, and are highly recommended.

The Old Pump House at Salford Quay (3)
3 Clippers Quay, Salford Quay (0161) 877 5982
Wolverhampton and Dudley (Banks's). Bright, classy renovation of an old dockyard building. Full bar menu served 12-2. TV, patio by dock. Families welcome. Open: Monday-Friday, non-matchday Saturday all day from 12, Saturday matchday 12-3, 5.30-11.

Waterside (4) Clippers Quay, Salford Quay (0161) 873 1921
Bass. Bright, modern bar/restaurant serving a 'Steak Menu'. Open: all day from 12.

FOOD GUIDE

Numerous mobile burger vans have set up shop along Sir Matt Busby Way and Wharfside Way. Apart from those, the nearest outlets to Old Trafford are the chippies on the corner of Chester Road and Sir Matt Busby Way. The 'Warwick Café', which has a series of counters, offers 'chicken and mush' for £1, burgers for £1.70 and chips for £1. 'The Red Devils' and 'Lou Macari's' have the same menu, with Hollands pies at £1 and cod-and-chips for £2.80. The United Chip Shop also has kebabs from £2.50, pizza, barbecue chicken and jacket potatoes. Further down Chester Road is an 'Oriental Express' takeaway, the 'Chester Road Chippy', a 'Peter Pan Pizza' and the 'Winner' Chinese takeaway.

On the White City Retail Park there's a Pizza Hut and a huge new fish-and-chip restaurant/takeaway called 'Busters'. In its restaurant, a meal of cod, chips, peas, bread and butter costs £4.95, and there's a children's menu too.

On the same retail park as Hanrahans, on Merchant's Quay, is a 'Frankie and Benny's New York Italian Restaurant and Bar', an American diner called 'Fatty Arbuckles' and a Mexican restaurant called 'Chiquito'. On Salford Road itself is a drive-thru Burger King and, by the turning to Merchant's Quay, a 'Starvin' Marvins'.

LOCAL MEDIA

Local Radio: 'Manchester United Radio' (matchday broadcasting) 1413 AM; The club is also running its own TV channel on satellite and cable; GMR 95.1 FM; Piccadilly Radio 1152 AM.
Radio Phone-ins: GMR, Saturdays 1-3 and 5-7, and after midweek games. Call (0161) 228 2255; Piccadilly Radio, Saturdays 5-6, call (0161) 288 1152.
Saturday Sports Paper: *The Manchester Evening News* produces the 'Manchester Pink'.

MISCELLANEOUS

Safety Factor: Old Trafford is one of the safest grounds in the country. However, Leeds and Manchester fans clashed outside the ground in season 97/98, so the obvious message is to take more care on derby days.
Rivals: Andy Mitten, editor of the excellent fanzine 'United We Stand', says that some United fans like seeing arch-enemies Manchester City drop down the divisions, while others miss the old derby games. Apart from the Blues, the main rivals remain Liverpool and Leeds. However, Andy says so many opposition fans join in the 'we hate Man U' chants, United fans have developed a siege mentality.
Fanzines: 'United We Stand', PO Box 45, Manchester, M41 1GQ; 'Red News', PO Box 384, London, WC1N 3RJ; 'Red Attitude', PO Box 83 SWDO, Old Trafford, Manchester, M15 5NJ.

Unofficial Websites:
'Red Devils': http://ireland.iol.ie/~mmurphy/
'MUFC': http://mufc.simplenet/com/
'Totally Red': http://hjem.get2net.dk/mufc/
'MUFC': http://www.angelfire.com/ga/sameersoccer/
'Red Café': http://www.iol.ie/redcafe/
'Red Now, Red Forever':
http://www.geocities.com/Colosseum/Field/3883
'Surf.to/ManU':
http://www.dcus.demon.co.uk/manu/main/html
Tourist Information: (0161) 234 3157/3158.

Mansfield Town

Field Mill

Address: Field Mill Ground, Quarry Lane, Mansfield, Notts NG18 5DA
Telephone: Club (01623) 623 567
ClubCall (0891) 121 311

The bulldozers are coming! Finally, after years of delays, financial setbacks and planning enquiries, Field Mill is being redeveloped. And it needed it! Ah, many a happy hour we've spent on that open terrace in the cutting winds, sleet and Nottinghamshire drizzle, tucking into those excellent pies. Mansfield is a small town, which means that the vital ingredients of a decent day out – the railway station, car parks, pubs, food – are all within reasonable walking distance.

HOW TO GET THERE

BY CAR: From South (M1): Exit M1 at junction 27 (s/p Mansfield A608). At roundabout take 3rd exit (s/p Hucknall, Mansfield A608) onto the A608. Go straight over two roundabouts, following signs to 'Mansfield A611' and at the third turn left (s/p Mansfield A611) onto the A611. Continue through countryside and suburbs for 3.8 miles to lights at T-junction. Here, turn left (s/p A611 Mansfield) onto the A60 Nottingham Road. Past the 'Trading Post' pub on the LHS after 0.1 miles, and between 'The Talbot' and 'The Plough' after 0.7 miles. (*)Past KFC on LHS and straight through 2nd set of lights (s/p Ring Road, Town Centre). At next lights, (by church) turn left into Quarry Lane.

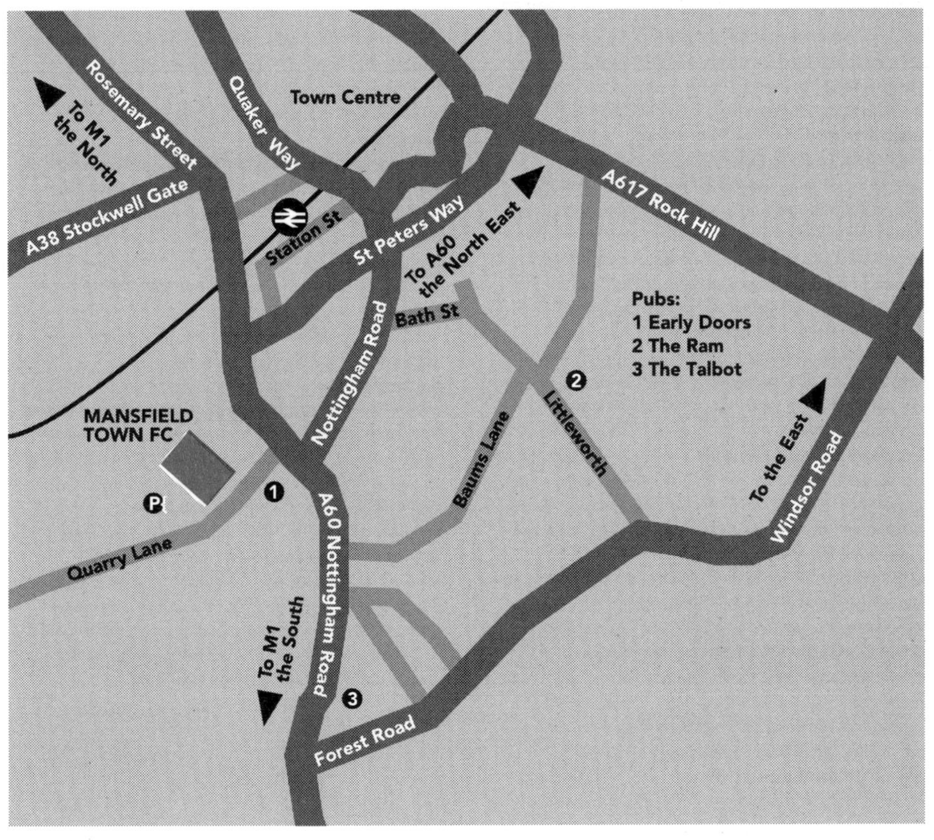

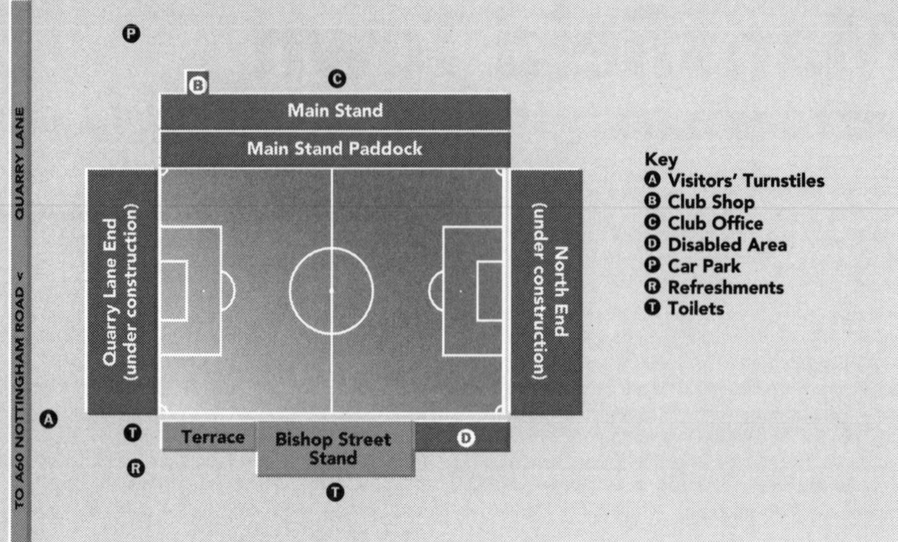

From North (M1): Exit M1 at junction 29. Take 2nd exit at roundabout (s/p Mansfield A617) onto the A617. At roundabout after 3.4 miles, take 3rd exit (s/p Mansfield A617). After 2.7 miles, just past the 'Pheasant Inn', turn right at lights (s/p M1 South, Derby A38) into Rosemary Street. Go straight on, passing the bus station and Tescos, under the railway bridge and over crossroads (s/p M1 South, Nottingham A60). At next lights, with the church on the LHS, turn right into Quarry Lane.

From South-East (A1-A617, from junction with B6020 in Rainworth): Stay on A617 for 3.0 miles to lights by 'The Reindeer' pub. Here, turn left (s/p Nottingham B6030 (A60)) into Windsor Road. At T-junction after 1.1 miles, turn right (s/p Town Centre A60) onto the A60 Nottingham Road. Go straight on, passing between 'The Talbot' and 'The Plough' pubs. Then as From South(*).

From North-East (A1-A60): Past sign for 'Mansfield Woodhouse'. Go straight on for 2.4 miles to lights. Here, turn left (s/p M1 South, Nottingham A60) into St Peters Way. Straight over crossroads after 0.3 miles (s/p Town Centre) and left at lights after 0.2 miles (s/p South M1, Nottingham A60) into Nottingham Road. After 0.3 miles turn right (s/p M1 North, Derby A38), and 1st left into Quarry Lane.

FROM RAILWAY STATION: Ten minute walk. Exit platform following signs to Stockwell Gate and Bus Station, down steps. Turn left along dual carriageway. Straight on at lights, continuing along Portland Street. Turn right at lights (by church) into Quarry Lane.

Last Midweek Trains: The last train from Mansfield is the 21:45 to Nottingham, arriving 22.18. From Nottingham there are connections to: Birmingham (23.09), Leeds (22.27, with a change of station at Newark), Derby (22.58) and Sheffield (23.57). Please double-check on (0345) 484 950.

BY BUS: Nos. 63 and X2 run along Nottingham Road.

PARKING

Space at the club car park (£1.50) will be reduced during the rebuilding work, and many fans will have to look elsewhere. There's street parking down Quarry Lane towards 'The Lord Byron' pub, and on various streets off Baums Lane. If other members of the family prefer movies to football, there's a car park at the Multiplex Cinema behind Safeways, just off the Nottingham Road south of Field Mill.

THE GROUND

After several false starts and many dashed hopes, the club has at last started work on a £5 million redevelopment of Field Mill. The idea is to replace both the Quarry Lane and North End terraces with 2,250-seater stands by July 1999. In the summer of 1999 work should start on the West Main Stand. The framework of the stand is to be kept, but the internal fabric replaced with 5,500 seats, executive boxes and other facilities such as a restaurant and shops. While all this is going on, visiting fans will be housed on the Bishop Street side of the ground, where there's a covered stand with backless plastic seats, and a section of open terracing.

Total Capacity: 5,289. For away fans: Bishop Street Stand: Seating 564, Standing 517.

Cost (98/99): Seating: Adults £10, concessions £5.

Standing: £8/£3.
Disabled Facilities: Room for 40 disabled supporters and their helpers in a covered enclosure by the Bishop Street Stand. *Disabled Toilet:* Nearby. *Cost:* Free for disabled, £5 for helper. *Booking:* Not necessary. *Parking:* In the club car park. *For the Blind:* No special facilities.
Programme: £1.50.
Visitors' Toilets: The loos at the Quarry Lane End were certainly vying hard for the MATITLA (see Darlington). However, the facilities in the Bishop Street Stand, where visiting fans are to be housed from August 1998, are marginally better.
Food and Drink: The pies (£1.40) were, said one fan, 'very burn-tongueish', so much so that a couple of other supporters, picking their pies off a tray, simply dropped them with a strangled 'Eeeyaaarh!' Generally, however, the pies were a very popular choice: one supporter was too busy munching to comment, simply giving a hearty thumbs-up between bites. Fans were impressed with the pasties (£1.30), which came wrapped in a serviette. The kiosk also stocked that great old footie favourite, guaranteed to bring back childhood memories, the Waggon Wheel (30p) (5.9.97, 29.11.97).

PUB GUIDE

Early Doors (1) Nottingham Road (01623) 421 687
Free House. Large popular modern pub overlooking a lake. Doorman on matchdays. Food served all day, Tex-Mex resturant. TV, patio. Families welcome/disabled facilities. Open: all day.
The Lord Byron Quarry Lane (01623) 621 933
Enterprise Inns (with Stones, Boddingtons, and guest beers). Welcoming sports-orientated pub with large lounge and separate TV and pool rooms. Darts. Sandwiches. Open: all day.
To get there: Turn right out of the club car park and it's a five minute walk along Quarry Lane.
The Ram (2) Littleworth (01623) 656 071
Mansfield (with Old Bailey). Smart football-friendly pub, with a warm comfortable lounge, and public bar with darts, pool, and a big-screen TV. Sandwiches. The landlady extends a warm welcome to 'genuine fans', and allows customers to leave their cars in the pub car park and walk to the ground. Open: all day.
The Talbot (3) 151 Nottingham Road (01623) 623 357
Greenalls. Smart family-orientated pub serving the 'Ale 'n Hearty' menu (with giant toad-in-hole for £3.95, spicy bean-and mango burger £1.75) from 12-2, 6-9. TV. Open: Saturdays all day; from 5 pm for midweek games.
FOR FAMILIES:
The Trading Post (formerly The Rushley)
Nottingham Road (01623) 629 657
Mansfield. Large smart 'Wild West' theme pub with an excellent menu (fish and chips £3.95, spitroast chicken £4.95), served all day from 11.30. 'Fort Adventure' play area and beer garden. Disabled facilities. Open: all day.

'These goal celebrations are getting ridiculous!'

FOOD GUIDE

On Nottingham Road near 'The Talbot' pub there's a fish-and-chip shop and a Chinese takeaway, while the retail park has a KFC and McDonalds. Otherwise it's a short walk to the town centre.

LOCAL MEDIA

Local Radio: BBC Radio Nottingham 95.5, 103.8 FM; Trent FM 96.2 FM and 999 AM.
Radio Phone-ins: BBC Radio Nottingham, Saturdays 5-6, call (0115) 934 3434; Trent FM is planning a phone-in, listen out for details.
Saturday Sports Paper: The *Nottingham Evening Post* publishes the 'Football Post'.

MISCELLANEOUS

Safety Factor: A safe place to visit.
Rivals: While the rest of the country enjoyed Chesterfield's 1996/97 cup run, Mansfield fans seethed. Steve Hartshorn of 'Follow the Yellow Brick Road' adds to the rivals' list: 'Any Yorkshire or Lincolnshire clubs and the big-headed supporters of the Nottingham sides'
Fanzines: 'Follow the Yellow Brick Road' 14 Coniston Road, Kirkby-in-Ashfield, Nottinghamshire, NG17 7PH.
Unofficial Websites:
http://www.geocities.com/Colosseum/Field/7145/
http://web.jet.es/roe/ssib/index.htm
Tourist Information: No local office.

M

Middlesbrough

The Cellnet Riverside Stadium

Address: Cellnet Riverside Stadium, Middlesbrough, TS3 6RS
Telephone: Club (01642) 877 700
Ticket Office (01642) 877 745
Shop (01642) 877 720
Boro Livewire (0891) 424 200

The Cellnet Riverside Stadium has, over the last three seasons, become a major landmark in north Middlesbrough. This is for two main reasons: firstly it's a spectacular building, a mass of grey and white steelwork just north of the main A66 through town. Secondly, and more to the point perhaps, it's the ONLY building of note in the entire area. The stadium was constructed on reclaimed industrial land next to the River Tees, but since then the rest of the huge site has remained undeveloped: no multiplex cinemas, no pubs, no nothing. Not even a supporters' car park. Hence football fans have to look further afield for a meal and a pint, but thankfully the town centre is only a ten minute walk from the ground.

HOW TO GET THERE

BY CAR/PARKING: As there is no parking at the ground, these road directions take supporters to parking areas within easy walking distance of the Riverside.

From South (A19): Exit A1(M) at signpost 'Thirsk A168, Teesside A19' onto the A19 dual carriageway. Exit A19 after 31.9 miles (s/p Middlesbrough, Stockton, Darlington A66). Almost immediately, the road divides: bear right (s/p Middlesbrough A66) onto the A66. (*)As there's no car park at the ground for visiting fans, start thinking about parking from here. The options are:
a) Take 2nd exit from the A66 after 1.1 miles (s/p M'bro Centre, St. Hildas A178, also Hill Street Centre and Brentnall). At roundabout turn right (s/p Other Car Parks, M'bro Centre). There's a Sainsburys on the left – the pay-and-display parking (Denmark Street) is not just for the superstore, and is a good option. Alternatively, go straight on at the crossroads/lights, and at the next lights turn left (s/p Brentnall). The Brentnall car park is ahead of you. Turn right in front of it to the car park entrance. The top two floors of the multi-storey are for cheaper, long-term parking (£1.50 all day). To get to the ground from here, head through the bus station to Corporation Road, and turn right. Keep going to the end of the road by car parks. Cross road at lights and go straight on: the underpass to the ground is visible from here.
b) Take 2nd exit from the A66 as above. At the roundabout turn left (s/p St. Hildas, Riverside Park). Go

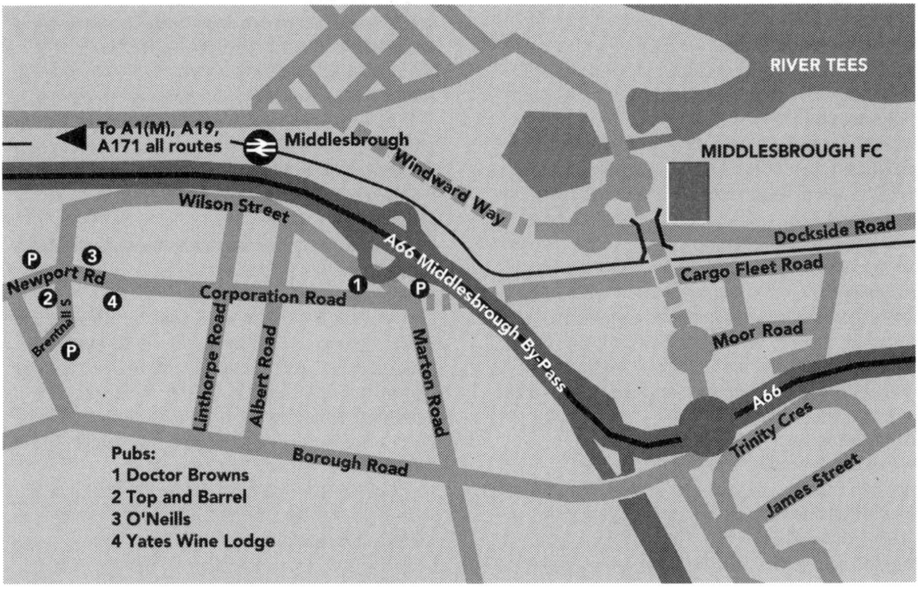

Pubs:
1 Doctor Browns
2 Top and Barrel
3 O'Neills
4 Yates Wine Lodge

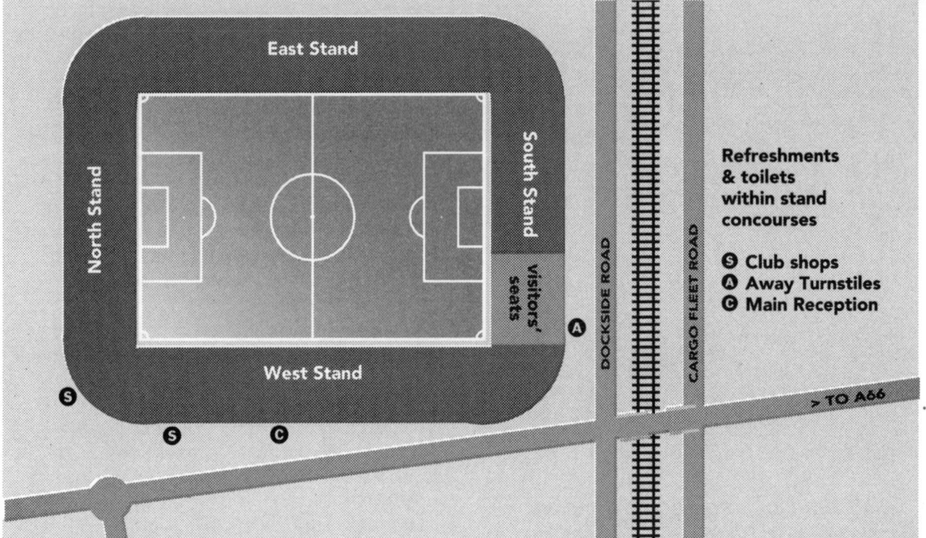

straight on through lights into North Road. At the crossroads/lights by the station turn left (s/p Transporter Bridge) into Queens Square, which leads to Cleveland Street. There's street parking on the roads off to the right.
c) Take the 3rd exit off the A66 (s/p Middlesbrough Centre, Short Stay, Long Stay Parking). At the roundabout, take 2nd exit (s/p Long Stay parking). There are two large car parks here, and a short-cut to the ground through an underpass at the end of Cargo Fleet Road.
From North (A19): Exit A19 at signpost 'Middlesbro. A66' onto the A66. Then as From South(*).
FROM RAILWAY STATION (Middlesbrough): 0.75 miles. *By foot:* Come down steps from platform and turn left, taking the back exit from the station (ie not via the ticket office). Turn right, and head straight across crossroads towards the Bridge pub in Bridge Street East. After about 0.2 miles, turn right into Windward Way. The ground is clearly visible from here.
Last Midweek Trains: It's not possible to reach either London or Doncaster after a midweek game. However the 21.42 has links, via Darlington, with Newcastle, Leeds and Manchester. Please double-check on (0345) 484 950.
BY BUS: Nos. 36, 37 and 38 run from the bus station to North Ormesby, from where there's an underpass to the ground.

THE GROUND

The average attendance at Ayresome Park was 18,000 so Middlesbrough, when designing the Riverside Stadium, naturally assumed that a 30,000 capacity would be ample. Wrong! Such was the attraction of the new ground and the club's big-name signings that by season 97/98 the Riverside all season-ticket for home fans, with many left disappointed. So in the summer of 1998, the corners of the ground were filled in to create a further 4,600 seats. The development also includes a spacious new club shop, an extended ticket office, two hospitality restaurants and six extra executive boxes. With the new corner stands, the Riverside became a fully-enclosed stadium, which is likely to further improve the already-cracking matchday atmosphere. And as final proof of the club's go-ahead image, Middlesbrough FC has become the first in the country to sell wine in the concourses!

Away fans are allocated a section of the South Stand behind the goal. The view is excellent, and there's ample leg room. However, many visiting supporters found the other facilities a tad disappointing.
Total Capacity: 35,000. For away fans (South Stand): From 1,031 to 2,775. Turnstiles 75-79.
Cost (97/98): Adult £17, concessions (Juniors/OAPs) £10.
Disabled Facilities: Space for 12 wheelchairs and 12 helpers halfway up the South Stand, so the view is good. *Disabled Toilet:* Nearby. *Cost:* Joint ticket at £17 covers disabled and helper. *Booking:* Essential. *Parking:* None available, but can drop off on Dockside Road. *For the Blind:* Headphones with commentary are available, please book via the Commercial Department.
Programme: £2.
Visitors' Toilets: *Male:* One fan summed up the frustration: 'I couldn't get in, then I couldn't get out. They're far too small, the worst in the league!' Others,

Bob suddenly realised he'd pulled on his brother's shirt by mistake!

already riled, went on to complain that the tap water was so hot, fans could make cups of tea with it!

Female: In contrast, no problems here. Stunningly, there was a cleaner at work, and she said she always came back at half-time too.

Food and Drink: The pies (£1.20) went down a treat, nice 'n hot. The Kenco coffee was very strong, and came in large cups. The bitter (£1.80) had 'no great taste', but fans liked the lager (£1.90) ... one said his pint was the best he'd ever had at a football ground. Unfortunately no-one was sipping the wine (£2.40) and the kiosk had run out of sausage rolls (£1) (5.10.97).

PUB GUIDE

Doctor Browns (1) 135 Corporation Road (01642) 213 213

Century Inns (with Black Sheep, Bass, Caffreys, guest beers). Newly renovated, traditional pub with great food, good beer and a superb pre-match atmosphere. Home-made 'Boro Pie' (mince or steak) with chips and peas (£2.95) plus a range of hot and cold sandwiches served 11.30-5. Big-screen TV, patio. Families weclome/disabled facilities. Open: all day from 11.30.

The Tap and Barrel (2) 86 Newport Road (opposite Sainsburys) (01642) 219 995

Century Inns (with Black Sheep, Jennings and 8 guest beers). Excellent friendly pub of real character, featured in the good beer guides. Full menu served 12-2. TV (not Sky). Families welcome. Open: all day from 11.30.

O'Neills (3) 69 Newport Road (01642) 499 050

Bass Taverns. Smart Irish theme pub, with wooden floors, friendly atmosphere and 'excellent Guinness and Caffreys', says the landlord. Bar food served 12-7. TV, beer garden. Disabled facilities. Open: all day.

Yates Wine Lodge (4) 16-18 Newport Road (01642) 243 764

Yates (with Scottish and Newcastle, Bass and Whitbread). Large, smart pub on two floors. Varied menu, served 11-6 (Sundays 12-6). Families welcome. Disabled facilities. Open: all day.

Those travelling to Middlesbrough on the A19 from the south pass the highly recommended pub called **The Black Swan** (on the Black Swan Crossroads, 22 miles from the A1). It's a Whitbread pub, with Black Sheep and Boddingtons, full of sporting memorabilia, and serving good food from 12-3.

FOOD GUIDE

The town centre is within easy walking distance of the Riverside, and close to most of the parking areas. The best roads to try are Corporation Road and Linthorpe Road. Fans walking from the Brentnall Street car park, at the west end of Corporation Road, have a great choice, including 'Grubbs Diner', which offers a 99p 'shoppers' special' and children's meals from 95p; the more upmarket 'Brambles Coffee Shop'; 'Brunches Café' which has salad platters from £2.95; and 'Bodega', which serves quiche and jacket potatoes. Linthorpe Road, which crosses Corporation Road, has a Burger King, McDonalds and Pizza Hut.

LOCAL MEDIA

Local Radio: BBC Radio Cleveland 95 FM; TFM 96.6 FM; Century Radio 100.7. Middlesbrough FC has been the first club in the country to launch its own cable TV programme, Boro TV.

Radio Phone-ins: Century Radio, Monday-Friday 6-7 pm. Call (0191) 477 2000.

Saturday Sports Paper: *The Middlesbrough Evening Gazette* produces the pink 'Gazette Sports'.

MISCELLANEOUS

Safety Factor: Middlesbrough FC has become much more family-orientated in recent years. However, take more care for derby games, and don't leave club colours on display in the car.

Rivals: Newcastle and Sunderland running neck-and-neck, with Leeds United coming in close behind.

Fanzines: 'Fly Me to the Moon', Unit 7 Brentnall Centre, Brentnall Street, Middlesbrough, TS1 5AP.

Unofficial Websites: 'Fly Me to the Moon':
http://www.hk.super.net/~tlloyd/personal/FMTTM/html
http://www.skwalker.demon.co.uk/mfc.htm
http://www.geocities/com/Colloseum/1088/
http://www.geocities/com/Colosseum/Track/9561/

Tourist Information: (01642) 243 425.

Millwall

The Den

Address: The Den, Zampa Road, London, SE16 3LN
Telephone: Club (0171) 232 1222
Ticket Office (0171) 231 9999
Club Shop (0171) 231 9845
ClubCall (0891) 400 300
Official Website: http://www.millwallfc.co.uk/

Millwall FC may not have won much on the field recently, but they attracted plaudits on two fronts from visiting football fans: for the impressive stadium with its excellent views, and – unusually for London – for stocking Pukka Pies. Getting to the ground is no great problem, with many visitors travelling by overland train to South Bermondsey or by underground to Surrey Quays. Yet few fans would list the Millwall game as a favourite day out. It's mainly down to the Den's South London surroundings: railway bridges, council flats, gas works, industrial units, breakers yards and a large rubbish incinerator. Parking is not a problem, but as one visiting supporter remarked dryly: 'Check how many wheels are left before you drive off!' Visiting supporters tend to drink well away from the ground, but the cafés along Rotherhithe New Road are certainly worth a visit.

HOW TO GET THERE

BY CAR: From North, West and East (from Blackwall Tunnel): For directions to Blackwall Tunnel see London Guide. From tunnel: Stay on the A102(M) for 1.9 miles, then exit at signpost 'Central London A2'. At roundabout turn right (s/p Central London) onto the A2 Shooters Hill. (*)Go straight on for 2.2 miles, following signs to Deptford and New Cross. After passing Greenwich Magistrates Court on the RHS and going under a railway bridge, take the right-hand filter and turn right into Deptford Church Street (no signpost). Straight on for 0.4 miles, over a roundabout, to T-junction. Here, turn left (s/p Bermondsey, Rotherhithe Tunnel, Tower Bridge) into the A200 Evelyn Street. Straight on for 0.8 miles, passing the Marmara Restaurant and the KFC on the LHS and going over a bridge, then turn left (before the Shell station on the RHS) into Grinstead Road. Follow road round for 0.8 miles through railway arches, over a mini-roundabout to a T-junction (there are pedestrian short-cuts to the ground from this area). Here, turn right into Ilderton Road (s/p Lewisham Lions Centre), and right again after 0.1 miles to ground.
From South (M25): Exit M25 at junction 2 (s/p

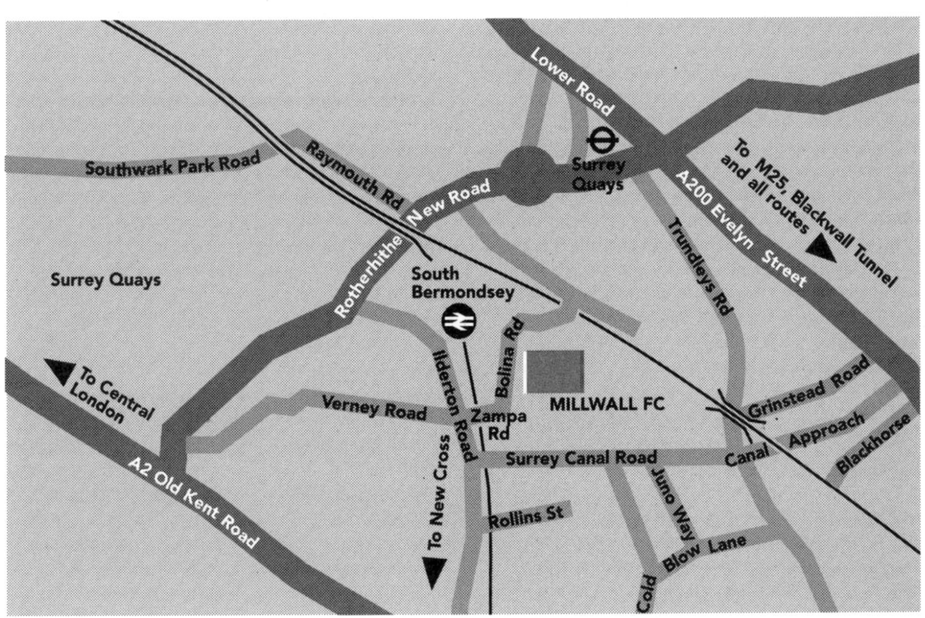

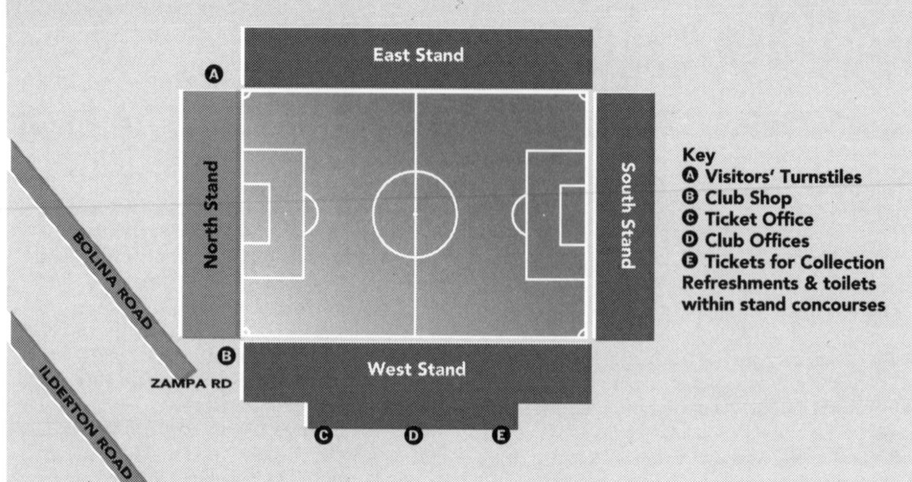

London A2, Dartford A225). Keep left where road divides (s/p London SE A2) onto the A2 dual carriageway. Exit A2 after 10.3 miles (s/p Central London A2). At roundabout turn left (s/p Central London A2) onto the A2 Shooters Hill. Then as From North, West and East(*).

FROM UNDERGROUND STATION (Surrey Quays, East London Line, Zone 2): Yes, the station's reopened. *By foot:* 5-10 minutes. Take left-hand exit out of station and turn left along Rotherhithe Old Road, against the traffic flow, passing 'Super Noodle' Chinese takeaway on the LHS. At T-junction after 0.1 miles, by 'Auto Screen', turn right into Rotherhithe New Road. Go straight on for 0.3 miles, crossing roundabout towards 'Carpet Warehouse' and under railway arches, past the 'Sunshine Café' and 'Bermondsey Trading Estate', under another railway bridge and then turn left (s/p South Bermondsey Station, Car Pound) into Ilderton Road. After 0.25 miles turn left into Zampa Road to ground.

FROM RAILWAY STATIONS:

a) South Bermondsey (trains from Victoria and London Bridge): By foot: 3 minutes. Head down the path at the end of the platform. Where the path divides, fork left (s/p Ilderton Road, Millwall FC). At main road (Ilderton Road), turn left again to ground.

b) New Cross (Hayes-London Bridge) 1.5 miles to ground, and New Cross Gate (East Croydon-London Bridge) 1.3 miles to ground: *By tube:* both stations are one stop, on the East London underground line, to Surrey Quays. *By foot:* Turn right out of stations into New Cross Road. Keep right where the road divides, walking against the traffic flow. After about 0.4 miles, just after passing a BP station on the LHS and going under a railway bridge, turn right by the Canterbury Arms into Ilderton Road. Turn right after 0.5 miles into Zampa Road to ground.

Last Midweek Trains: All lines run a frequent service back to London. For onward connections see London Guide at front of book.

BY BUS: The following buses run along the Old Kent Road: nos. 21 (Moorgate to Foots Cray), 53 (Oxford Circus to Plumstead) and the 78 (Shoreditch to Peckham Rye). The P11 (Waterloo to Peckham) runs along Rotherhithe New Road, while the P13 goes from Streatham to Surrey Quays via Ilderton Road. Several buses stop at Surrey Quays: the 188 from Euston, the 199 from Elephant and Castle, and the 47 from Shoreditch via Liverpool Street.

PARKING

At present it's street parking for everyone. The club car park on Juno Way is shut, even though it's signposted 'Stadium Parking' off Surrey Canal Road. However, it's not a bad idea to follow that signpost, as Juno Way, Cold Blow Lane and the other roads around the site of the old ground, are good for street parking. Other roads to try are Rollins Street and Hatcham Road. Millwall FC is actively looking for a new car park site, so it's worth giving them a quick call to see if anything's been lined up.

THE GROUND

The Den is a top-class stadium, with excellent facilities, wonderful sight-lines and good legroom, but it's rarely more than half-full. This is its major drawback. When the Den is packed, the atmosphere is excellent. But even the most ardent Millwall fans can do little to gee up the team if large sections of the stands, including the away end, are empty. The Den comprises four separate stands, each with a lower tier almost half the size of the

upper. The concourses are wide, with TVs, American-style food kiosks and excellent British-style pies! For the Second Division, this is paradise! Away fans are allocated the North Stand behind the goal, and usually only the top tier is opened.
Total Capacity: 19,253. For away fans: 4,382. Turnstiles 31-36.
Cost (98/99): Adult £11, concessions (OAPs/juniors) £6.
Disabled Facilities: Space for 50 away fans in an area about half-way up the West Stand, where the view is excellent. *Disabled Toilet:* 17 available. *Cost:* Free for disabled, £10 for helper. *Booking:* Not necessary. *Parking:* 10 bays available – please book. *For the Blind:* Two headsets available allowing supporters to sit where they wish. Please book.
Programme: £1.80.
Visitors' Toilets: *Male:* 'Palatial, fantastic,' said one supporter, impressed at the lack of graffiti, the dry floors and the working doors! *Female:* The walls are what Laura Ashley would term 'duck-egg blue', very soothing if 4-0 down at half-time. However, there was no loo paper and the hand-dryer didn't work. Lots of space though, and hooks on the walls.
Food and Drink: Pies! In the south! And good ones too! Millwall are serving Pukka Pies (£1.60): 'Very good, very hot but not too hot, edible hot, with lots of meat,' said one ecstatic supporter. The chips were the thin variety, like McDonalds, hot and tasty. The 'double burgers' (£2.80) were rather bland: 'It's got ketchup and it needs it', was one comment. The tea (80p) was bitter and flat, the coffee (90p) strong, the lager (£2.10) 'nice and fresh' and the beer (£2.10) 'like vinegar' (1.10.97, 7.3.98).

PUB GUIDE

Many of the pubs around The Den are 'home only' and most visiting fans either drink inside the ground or stop en route.

FOOD GUIDE

The nearest takeaway to The Den is 'Moby Dick's' on Ilderton Road near Rollins Street, which serves Peter's Pies. Next door is the 'Ilderton Café'. On Ilderton Road to the north of the ground, at the junction with Rotherhithe New Road, is a row of shops including a Baker's Oven and a Chinese takeaway. On Rotherhithe New Road, towards Surrey Quays station, is the excellent 'Sunshine Café': it's smarter than most and serves some healthier options such as omelettes (£1.50), and home-made lasagne (£2.90). Nearby is the 'Victory Fish Bar', open all day, and the 'Lions Den Café', which shuts at 4 pm. At the junction of Rotherhithe New Road and Lower Road, near Surrey Quays, is the friendly and popular 'Docklands Café', which has a huge breakfast menu, as well as full meals and toasties, all home-made.

However, it shuts at 6 pm. Lower Road, just round the corner, has a wider takeaway choice.

LOCAL MEDIA

Local Radio: Capital Gold 1548 AM; GLR 94.9 FM; XFM 104.9.
Radio Phone-ins: Capital Gold, Saturdays 5-6.30 pm, midweek every night 7-8 or after live match commentary. Call (0845) 35 60 70 80.
Saturday Sports Paper: None.

MISCELLANEOUS

Safety Factor: Crowd trouble inside The Den is non-existent. Outside it's rare, and almost all arrests are for drunken, rather than violent behaviour. That said, the police still warn that there is always 'the potential for violence' outside The Den. They advise covering up club colours and to avoid parking on the Silwood Estate.
Rivals: West Ham and Crystal Palace are Millwall's traditional rivals, but George Craig of the excellent fanzine 'No-one Likes Us', says only half-jokingly, that Gillingham and Fulham are now more realistic adversaries.
Fanzines: 'No-one Likes Us', 30 Wendover Road, Bromley, Kent, BR2 9JX; 'The Lion Roars', TLR Towers, No 12, 157-159 Boundfield Road, Catford, London, SE6 1PE; 'Tales from Senegal Fields', 85 Lower Road, Maidstone, Kent ME15 7RH.
Unofficial Websites: 'We are Millwall': http://freespace.virgin.net/angela.grice/millwall.html 'House of Fun': http:///www.hof.org.uk/ http://home3.swipnet.se/~w-32587/index.htm
Tourist Information: Greenwich (0181) 858 6376.

N

Newcastle United

St James' Park

Address: St. James' Park, Newcastle-upon-Tyne, NE1 4ST
Telephone: Club: (0191) 201 8400
Ticket Office (0191) 261 1571
Club Shop (0191) 201 8426
ClubCall (0891) 121 190
Official Website: http://www.newcastle-utd.co.uk/nufc

Somewhere on each approach road to the city must be a big neon sign saying: all Newcastle males over the age of six months must now don a Newcastle United football shirt, no exceptions! They're everywhere, and certainly add to the matchday atmosphere. St James' Park is right in the city centre, which can make parking a problem, but is great for pubs, restaurants, takeaways and shopping. It's also near the city's mini-'Chinatown' area, with two excellent little restaurants opposite the ground. Just what the doctor ordered after that long drive north!

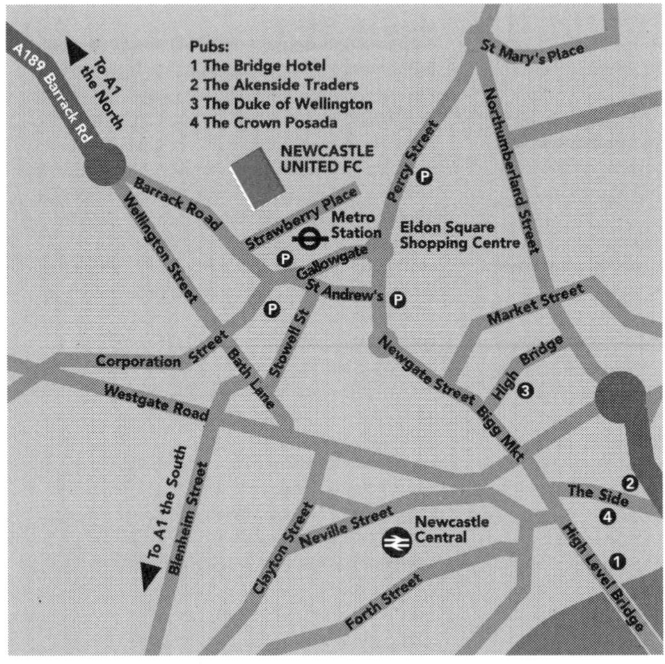

HOW TO GET THERE

BY CAR: From A1(M): At junction 65, where the road divides, keep left (s/p A1 Gateshead, Newcastle) onto the A1. Exit A1 after 4.8 miles (s/p Gateshead, Newcastle Centre (A184)). Follow signs to 'Newcastle A189' for 1.4 miles, keeping in right-hand lanes onto and over the Redheugh Bridge. At lights at end of bridge after 0.8 miles, go straight on (s/p City (North), Ashington A189) into Blenheim Street. Go straight on for 0.4 miles, over two sets of lights, to T-junction by 'Big Luke's Texas Restaurant'. Here, turn left (s/p Ashington A189, Morpeth A1) into Bath Lane. To ground and city centre car parks, turn right after 0.1 miles by 'National Tyre and Autocare' into Corporation Street. To the Barrack Road parking, and the 'Leazes Inn', go straight on instead. At roundabout after 0.3 miles, by the 'Black Bull' pub, take 2nd exit (s/p City West and North A189) into Barrack Road. The 'Leazes Inn' is on the RHS after 0.4 miles.

From North: Exit A1 at s/p 'Jedburgh A696, City (Centre) A167'. At roundabout turn left (s/p City (Centre) A167) onto A167 Ponteland Road. Go straight on for 1.2 miles, over three roundabouts and following signs to 'City Centre', to a fourth roundabout. Here turn left (s/p City Centre A167, Ashington) onto the A167 Jedburgh Road. Exit A167 after 0.6 miles (s/p City (West), City (North) A187, Ashington A189). Turn right at first roundabout (s/p West Central Route, City (West) A189) and straight on at the second (s/p City (West), Gateshead via Redheugh Bridge) onto the A189 Grandstand Road. After 0.2 miles all traffic turns left (s/p City Centre) onto the A189 Ponteland Road. Keep straight on 0.6 miles, over the Fenham Hall junction and over lights by BBC North, into Barrack Road, a good area for parking. For the ground and city centre car parks, keep on Barrack Road,

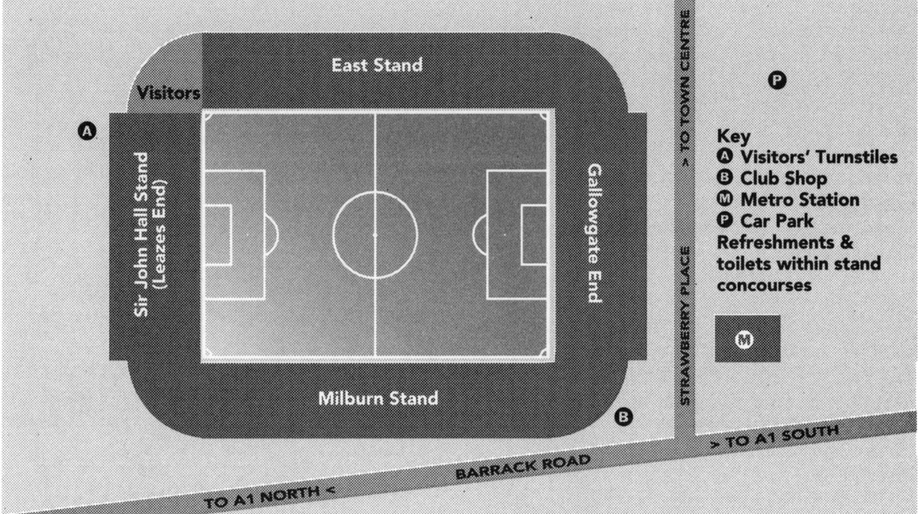

taking first exit at roundabout by the 'Black Bull' pub. NB The A189 Redheugh Bridge-Barrack Road-Grandstand Road is being widened to create a new 'West Central Route' through the city, so allow extra time for roadworks.

FROM METRO STATION: St James' metro station is right by the ground, though home fans suggest that it's often quicker to walk from 'Monument' station.

FROM RAILWAY STATION: 0.5 miles. *By taxi:* £3-£3.10. *By foot:* Cross road towards the 'Baker's Oven' and turn right along Central Street. Turn left just after the County Hotel into Grainger Street and then left again into Westgate Road. After about 0.15 miles turn right (s/p Ring Road South and East) into Bath Lane, towards National Tyres. Ground is on RHS. NB for safety reasons avoid the short cut from the station along a narrow alley called Pink Lane.

Last Midweek Trains: There are no trains to either London or Sheffield after a midweek game. It is possible to reach York and Leeds on the 22.43. Please double-check on (0345) 484 950.

BY BUS: Catch one of the many buses to 'Gallowgate'.

PARKING

The St. James' and Corporation Street open-air car parks near the ground are a good option, charging 40p an hour up to 6.30 pm, but do fill up early. Another good option is the multi-storey Greenmarket car park, which is well-signposted from Corporation Street and charges £3.60 for 3 hours and £4.80 for 4 hours parking. However, nearby roads are jammed after the match, so expect a slow getaway. Otherwise it's street parking. A good area to try is along Barrack Road, and on the streets off Stanhope Street.

THE GROUND

Take a Newcastle fan from the spring of 1992 and deposit him in today's St James' Park and he simply wouldn't recognise the place. Sir John Hall's millions have transformed the ground into a mightily-impressive 32,800-seater stadium ... and there are now plans to add extra tiers on the Sir John Hall and Milburn Stands, at a cost of £42 million, to increase that capacity to 51,000. The ground will be, says the club's literature, 'the Rolls Royce of football stadiums', and the extra seating will certainly be welcomed by the many thousands on the waiting list for season-tickets. At the time of writing, however, the plans were still subject to approval by the Deputy Prime Minister, John Prescott. Visiting fans are housed in the NE corner of the Sir John Hall Stand, where the view is excellent.

Total Capacity: 36,824. For away fans: 1,861.

Cost (97/98): Adults £21, concessions (juniors/OAPs) £13.

Disabled Facilities: Visiting fans are allocated about 13 spaces in the Sir John Hall Stand. *Disabled Toilet:* In Stand. *Cost:* Half price for disabled, full price for helper. *Booking:* Essential. *For the Blind:* Spaces available.

Programme: £2.

Visitors' Toilets: *Male:* Clean and spacious, though one fan said 'I wouldn't eat in them!' *Female:* Hot water, bars of soap, a dinky push-flush thingamajig, paper towels and a waste bin. And a strange mirror which looked like it had been left out in a fierce sandstorm.

Food and Drink: The mince pie (£1.30) was by far the best bet. We found a real connoisseur, who said: 'Yes, it feels quite warm, looks pleasant, it's appealing to the eye. Indeed, that is a good pie.' The cheese and

onion pasty (£1.30) was a 'hot air, cheese and onion pasty' – in other words it took three bites to get into the middle. It was good, however, which is more than could be said for the burgers (£1.90). The coffee (Kenco 90p) and the hot chocolate (90p) were excellent, but the tea was – according to one fan – 'like water that's been inside a radiator for three years and about as warm!' Beer and lager are also on sale (24.9.97, 18.3.98).

PUB GUIDE

The Leazes Inn Barrack Road (0191) 221 1588
Sherwood Inns (with Flowers, Boddingtons, Castle Eden and guest). Large smart family-orientated pub with everything for the footie fan: big-screen TV, two pool tables, two snooker tables, darts, table football and full menu (served 12-2.30 and 5-9). Children's menu/Outdoor play area, large car park. Open: all day.

The Bridge Hotel (1) Castle Garth (by High Level Bridge) (0191) 232 6400
Fitzgerald (with Black Sheep, John Smith, Boddingtons, Bass, Theakston XB). Highly recommended family-orientated pub, newly renovated and extended, with views over the river. Excellent menu, with full meals at £3.99, served 11.30-2 (Sundays to 2.30). 2 TVs, terrace/beer garden. Open: all day from 11.30.

The Akenside Traders (2) The Side (0191) 269 3011
Bass (with guest beer). Spacious smart modern-style city centre bar. Bar meals served to 2.30, snacks to 5. Two big-screen TVs. Disabled facilities. Open: all day.

The Duke of Wellington (3) High Bridge (0191) 261 8852
Tetleys (with guest real ales). Popular friendly real-ale house, full of character. Sandwiches and bar meals. TV. Open: all day.

Also recommended: **The Crown Posada (4)**, The Side, a renowned real-ale house. And for great pre-match atmosphere, neutrals might like to visit the Toon Army pubs **The Strawberry** on Strawberry Place and **Rosie's Bar** and **The Newcastle Arms,** both on St Andrew's Street.

FOOD GUIDE

For that Chinese food, try 'Charlie's' and 'Wok This Way' on Gallowgate, which both offer 'eat as much as you can' buffets for about £4.50. For top-class sandwiches and salads try 'Gourmet Grub' on Leazes Crescent. On St Andrew's Street near 'Rosie's Bar' is the 'Butter Fingers' takeaway, with pies, quiche and sandwiches. For classic takeaway fare head for Newgate Street and the Bigg Market, where there's a Wimpys and McDonalds, as well as two classy sandwich bars 'Frenchies' and 'Alexander's Deli'.

'Gerroff! It's my turn for the season ticket!'

LOCAL MEDIA

Local Radio: 'Magpie Radio' broadcasts on 1413 AM; Metro Radio 97.1 and 103 FM, 1152 MW; BBC Radio Newcastle 104.4 FM, 1458 MW.
Radio Phone-ins: Metro Radio, Saturdays 5-6 pm, call (0191) 488 3188; Radio Newcastle, Saturdays 11.15-noon, call (0191) 232 6565.
Saturday Sports Paper: 'The Football Pink'.

MISCELLANEOUS

Safety Factor: The police advise visiting fans to cover colours after the match, and at night to avoid the pubs around the railway station.
Rivals: Geographically it's Sunderland and Middlesbrough. But Mark Jensen of the excellent fanzine 'The Mag' says Manchester United took over the No.1 spot in season 95/96.
Fanzines: 'The Mag', 1st Floor, 3, St James Street, Newcastle-upon-Tyne, NE1 4NF; 'The Number Nine', 27 Laburnum Avenue, Heworth, Gateshead, NE10 8HH; 'Talk of the Tyne', 49 Valley View, Sacriston, Co. Durham, DH7 6NX.
Unofficial Websites:
'The Mag': http://www.THEMAG.co.uk
http://www.swan.co.uk/TOTT/current.htm
'Niall MacKenzie's Site': http://www.nufc.com/
'Magpies Zone': http://geocities.com/Colosseum/Stadium/6778/index.html
http://www.geocities.com/Colosseum/4764/
Tourist Information: (0191) 261 0610.

Northampton Town

Sixfields Stadium

Address: Sixfields Stadium, Upton Way, Northampton, NN5 5QA
Telephone: Club Office (01604) 757 773
Box Office (01604) 588 338
Cobblers ClubCall (0930) 555 970

In the spring of 1994, Northampton Town FC was stagnating at the bottom of Division Three and playing at a much-loved but very-grotty ground in front of a couple of thousand diehards. In mid-1998, the team was riding high in Division Two and drawing crowds of more than 6,000. Much of the club's success can be attributed directly to its move, in 1994, to the out-of-town Sixfields Stadium. The area is now a fully developed leisure complex, with pubs, restaurants and a cinema. It sounds like the makings of a good day out, but not all of these facilities welcome away supporters. The ground is easy to find by road, though leaving the car park after the game is more troublesome!

HOW TO GET THERE

BY CAR: The ground is well-signposted 'Sixfields Leisure'. Check whether Northampton Rugby Club is playing at home. If so, add 15 minutes to your journey time.

From South: Exit M1 at junction 15a (s/p Northampton (N), Oxford A43, Services). Follow signs to 'Northampton A43' for 1.3 miles, over three roundabouts, to fourth roundabout. Here, go straight on (s/p Coventry A45, Market Harborough A508, Sixfields Leisure). At next roundabout, on Upton Way, turn right into Sixfields complex.

From North: Exit M1 at junction 16 (s/p Northampton A45). At motorway roundabout turn left (s/p Northampton A45) onto the A45 dual carriageway. Follow Northampton A45 signs for 3.4 miles, passing The Turnpike Beefeater on LHS, to 2nd roundabout by MGM cinema. For away parking, turn right (s/p Ring Road, M1 South, A45) and then left at next roundabout into Sixfields complex.

From East (A14): Exit A14 at junction 13 (s/p Wellingborough, Northampton A45, Peterborough A605). Follow Northampton A45 signs for 17 miles to Great Billing interchange. Go straight on (s/p Town Centre, Coventry A45). You will pass a sign saying 'for Sixfields leisure follow A45'. Take this advice, as the A45 leads to the ground, 7.8 miles away.

FROM RAILWAY STATION (Northampton): 1.5 miles. *By taxi:* £3-£3.50. *By bus:* nos. 27 and 28 run to the Sixfields complex. *By foot:* Cross car park and up steps to main road. Turn right towards Esso garage, over bridge, passing Shell garage and 'Thomas A Becket' pub. After 0.4 miles, where road divides, bear left (s/p Motorway M1, Rugby, Coventry A45) into Weedon Road. Past rugby ground on LHS and 'Big Hand Mo's' pub on RHS, and straight over roundabout by Rover garage (s/p Coventry). Turn left at next roundabout into the Sixfields complex.

Last Midweek Trains: There are trains to London (22.04) and to Birmingham and Wolverhampton at 22.09 and 23.30. There are no connections to Newcastle. Please double-check on (0345) 484 950.

BY BUS: As well as those mentioned in the station details, bus no. 100 runs from the old County Ground to Sixfields and back.

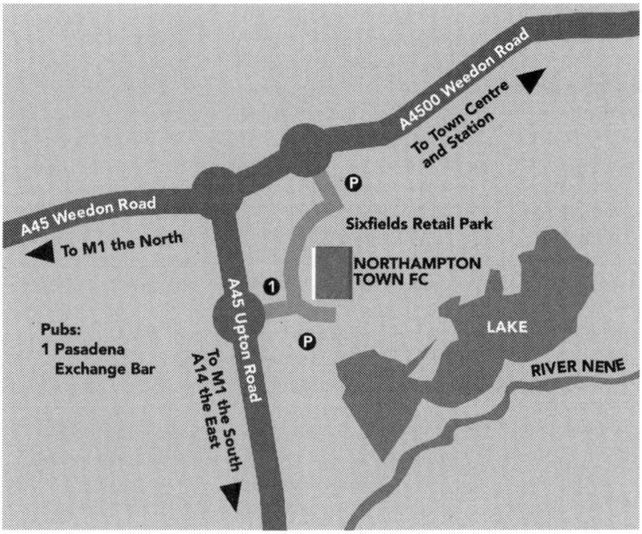

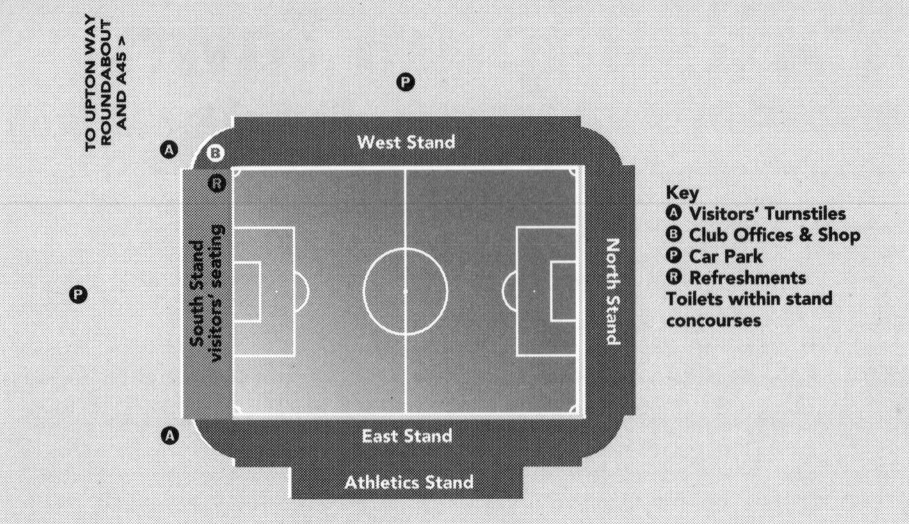

PARKING

Parking is not as easy as it looks. The cinema and all the new restaurants on the Sixfields complex have severely reduced the number of available car parking spaces. A park-and-ride scheme into town has added to the congestion. The police advise visiting fans against following the example of home supporters and parking on nearby industrial estates or at Sainsburys, as wheel-clamping is widespread, and there is some car crime. The key is to arrive early at the designated away parking, and be prepared for a long wait to get out again after the game. Sit back and savour the victory/equaliser/stonking defeat.

THE GROUND

'I can't remember if I'm at Chester, Walsall or Northampton', remarked one visiting fan. For many, this sums up Sixfields, a classic from the warehouse school of stadium design. That criticism aside, the ground is smart and neat, and it's a safe and friendly place to watch football. In addition, the disabled facilities are superb. There is potential to increase the capacity, which may soon be necessary with the club's fortunes on the pitch most definitely on the up. However, as fanzine editor Rob Marshall says, 'the money just isn't there.' Visiting fans are usually housed in the South Stand. The view from most seats is good, but it's worth avoiding the first couple of rows as fans amble back and forth to the loos and refreshment kiosks. Some supporters behind the goals found the net a serious obstruction.

Total Capacity: 7,653. For away fans: Seating (South Stand) 944, turnstiles 3 and 4. A further 423 seats can be made available in the East Stand, turnstiles 1 and 2, for large away followings.

Cost (98/99): Adults (South Stand) £10.50, concessions £7.50. Visiting fans have to buy their tickets from a kiosk, as there's no cash payment at turnstiles.

Disabled Facilities: Space for 155 wheelchairs plus helpers in all four stands, plus the back row of the East Stand reached by lift. *Disabled Toilets:* In NW, NE and SE corners, and in the East Stand. *Cost:* £5 for disabled, £5 for a helper. *Parking:* 30 spaces available. *Booking:* Preferable. *For the Blind:* Headsets available, please book.

Programme: £1.50.

Visitors Toilets: *Male:* A visiting Gillingham fan described the Northampton loos as having the 'post-modern brutalist unfinished look', viz, breezeblocks! However, York fans found them to be remarkably clean, with 'hand dryers which actually dried hands'. The main problem was that the facilities were too small to cope with large crowds, and the queue sometimes stretched back the length of the pitch. *Female:* Two cubicles, so again there can be quite a long queue at half time. Apart from that, the facilities are excellent. One fan wrote: 'Warm, clean, with water, soap, toilet rolls, seats, locks, lights, doors ... most unusual!'

Food and Drink: A visiting Preston fan wrote: 'If Egon Ronay doesn't include the food bar in the away enclosure at Northampton in next year's 'Good Food Guide' then it's a travesty of justice'. He was particularly taken with the Cornish pasty (£1.40), 'crispy, hot and full of taste', and the coffee (80p), 'delightful, without doubt the best of the season.' The flip side of this is that the kiosk often runs out of food early, leaving just the

rather small sausage rolls and hot dogs (both £1.40) (17.1.98, 18.10.97, 21.10.97).

PUB GUIDE

Most of the pubs on the Sixfields site are 'home only', but visiting fans are welcome in the:

Pasadena Exchange Bar and Diner (1) Nene Park, off Upton Way (by away parking) (01604) 589 456
Morland (with Calders Bitter). Large American-style bar/restaurant, with a classic menu of burgers, chicken, ribs and Mexican dishes. Families welcome/disabled facilities. 2 TVs. Open: all day from midday.

IN TOWN:

The Old Black Lion Black Lion Hill (by railway station) (01604) 639 472
Free House (Pedigree, Websters, Directors, Natterjack (from the local Frog Island brewery) and 2 guest beers). Top-rate traditional friendly pub in an 11th century building. Bar meals (including vegetarian options) served 11-3. Families welcome. Pool, darts and the unique Northamptonshire skittles game, TV, patio. Open: all day.
To get there, from station: walk up to main road, turn left, straight across traffic lights and pub is on RHS.

FOR FAMILIES:

The Cromwell Cottage High Street, Kislingbury (01604) 830 288
Whitbread/Brewer's Fayre (Boddingtons, Flowers and one guest ale). Country pub in an idyllic village setting, next to a little bridge over a river. Extensive menu served 12-10 pm, children's menu. Children's room with Lego table. Darts. Disabled facilities. Open: all day.
To get there: It's off the A45 between the ground and junction 16 of the M1. Follow signs to Kislingbury from roundabout.

FOOD GUIDE

The Sixfields complex has a Deep Pan Pizza, McDonalds, Burger King and a Bella Pasta. In addition, there's a Little Chef, just by the complex on the A45.
Otherwise, follow signs to the town centre (passing a McDonalds on RHS) along the Weedon Road for 0.7 miles, where there's a row of shops and takeaways, including the highly-recommended 'Golden Chicken' chinese takeaway/fish and chips. One northern fan insisted that his chips and mushy peas (£1.25) were the best he'd EVER had. The jovial proprietor asks large groups to phone their orders through in advance on (01604) 581 209. It's open from 11.30-2 pm, and from 4.30 pm. Nearby are: an Indian Brasserie; the 'China Cottage' Peking/Cantonese takeaway (open from 5 pm); and the 'Rainbow' fish and chip takeaway, open all day from 11.30. The latter does pies from £1.50 and chips from 80p. From here, it's worth ambling across the road to admire the amazing architecture at the rugby ground.

LOCAL MEDIA

Local Radio: BBC Radio Northampton 104.2 and 103.6 FM.
Radio Phone-Ins: None
Saturday Sports Paper: None, although the Coventry Pink sometimes appears locally, stretching its coverage to Northampton and Kettering.

MISCELLANEOUS

Safety Factor: The Sixfields site is a safe place to visit, although Millwall fans caused problems in season 97/98.
Rivals: Peterborough remains in that coveted 'most disliked' spot, way ahead of any other rivals. Fulham replaced Barnet at No.2 in season 97/98, after claiming that the Cobblers' long ball game disrupted their 'purist' approach. In other words, Northampton always beat them!
Fanzines: 'What a Load of Cobblers', 123 Draycott Road, Sawley, Nottinghamshire, NG10 3BX.
Unofficial Websites: WALOC: http://www.users.globalnet.co.uk/~waloc
http://web.ukonline.co.uk/ntfc
'Cobblers Heaven': http://freespace.virgin.net/robert.dunkley/welcome.html
http://www.cs.nott.ac.uk/~sjl95m/football.html
Tourist Information: (01604) 622 677.

N

Norwich City

Carrow Road

Address: Carrow Road, Norwich, NR1 1JE
Telephone: Club (01603) 760 760
Box Office (01603) 761 661
ClubCall (0891) 12 11 44
Official Website: http://www.ecn.co.uk/ncfc/

A trip to Norwich? Here's a suggested checklist: tickets, copy of the 'FFG', scarf, bibs, silver knife and fork and maybe a spoon for those little fruit pastries for afters. Well, if Delia Smith's on the board of directors, football fans should expect the best! If they did, they'd have been disappointed in season 97/98. But new caterers were in place for August 1998, and meals in the executive areas are to be prepared by the former chef at Chequers, the country home of the Prime Minister! Let's hope it all lives up to expectations, as the choice of eateries around Carrow Road is limited. However, there's an excellent pub nearby, and the car parks, railway station and historic city centre are all within easy walking distance.

HOW TO GET THERE

BY CAR: NB The ground is well signposted. From West (A47): At roundabout forming junction with roads to Ringland and Easton, Marlingford, go straight on (s/p Norwich E, Great Yarmouth A47). The A47 becomes the Norwich Southern Bypass. Stay on A47 for 10.3 miles, exiting at s/p Lowestoft A146, Trowse (also football ground). (*)At lights turn left (s/p Norwich A146). At T-junction after 0.7 miles, turn right (s/p Ring Road, City Centre A1054). At roundabout after 0.3 miles take 1st exit for County Hall car park, 2nd exit (s/p Ring Road, City Centre) for ground. To ground: keep in RH lane and after 0.2 miles turn right (s/p Ring Road A47) into King Street. After 0.2 miles the road bends to right (s/p Ring Road A47), over river, straight on at lights and ground is on RHS after 0.1 miles.

From South (A11): Keep on A11 and at roundabout follow signs for 'Norwich E, Great Yarmouth' onto the A47. After 4.8 miles exit at s/p 'Lowestoft A146, Trowse'. Then as From West.

From Ipswich (A140): At roundabout take 3rd exit (s/p Norwich E, Great Yarmouth A47, football ground) onto the A47. After 2.1 miles, exit A47 (s/p Lowestoft A146, Trowse). Then as From West.

Tip: If lost follow signs to, or ask directions to, County Hall or Colman's Mustard factory. Both are near the ground.

FROM RAILWAY STATION (Norwich): A ten minute walk. *By taxi:* About £2.50. *By foot:* Head across car park to main road by 'Sasse's Restaurant'. Turn sharp left along Riverside, with river on RHS. At lights turn left into Carrow Road.

BY BUS: No buses run to, or near the ground, and the main bus companies say it's quicker to walk from the city centre and the railway station.

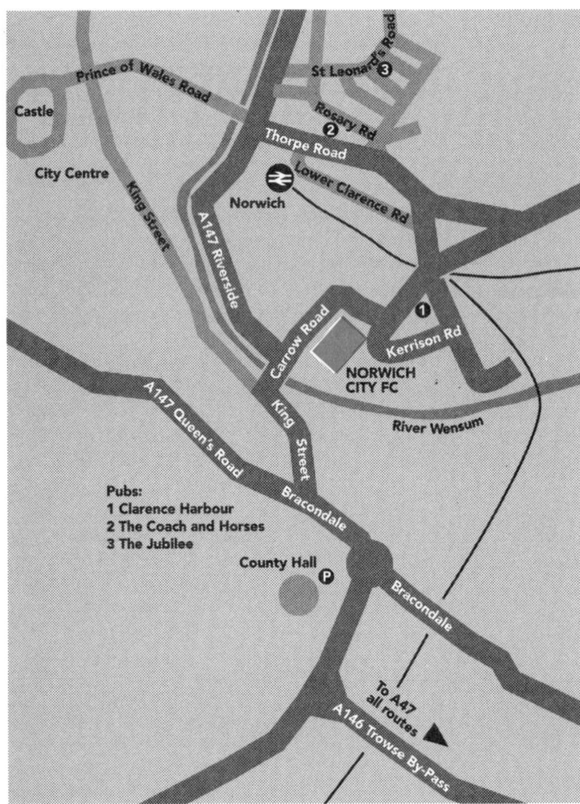

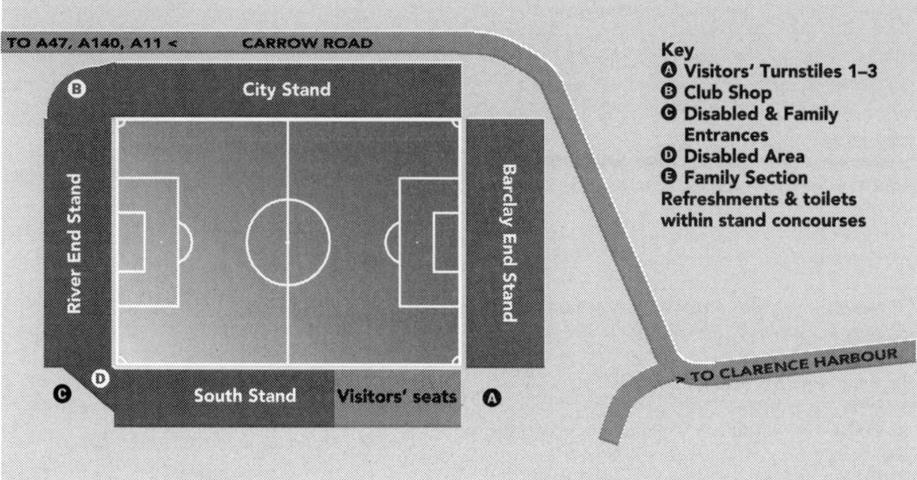

PARKING

Note that the Riverside car park of previous seasons is no longer available. Instead, try one of the following:
a) The away coaches parking area is in Lower Clarence Road, and there's space for cars too. It costs £2 for cars and £10 for coaches.
b) County Hall, signposted on the way to the ground – a 10 minute walk to Carrow Road. This is a very popular car park as it has loads of space. There's a short-cut to Bracondale and the ground.
c) The Park and Ride car park in Kerrison Road, right next to the ground. In season 97/98 it cost £1.70 which included a bus ticket to the city centre. Unfortunately football fans parking here must still pay this even if they are staying at the ground. NB The council was, at time of writing, still negotiating for the continued use of this car park. Check with them on (01603) 212 420.

THE GROUND

Carrow Road isn't an overwhelming stadium, compared for example, with the Reebok or the Stadium of Light, but it's a perfect home for a club the size of Norwich. The modern stands at each end are impressive, with two tiers of green and yellow seating and executive boxes. Home fans say the facilities in the Barclay End in particular are excellent. The Barclay Enders do their best to create an atmosphere, as difficult as that is in all-seater stadia, and often strike up a good singing contest with the visitors sitting in the South Stand. This, unsurprisingly, is the unmodernised side of the ground, and the view from some seats is obscured by pillars. To be fair, those tickets are marked 'restricted view' ... Ipswich fans swear this is because you can see the pitch (haha!). As Norwich City's a bit cash-strapped, plans to redevelop the South Stand have been put on the back burner.

Total Capacity: 21,994. For away fans: It's flexible, up to 2,300 in Blocks F, G, H and J of the South Stand.

Cost (98/99): Category A matches: Adults £18, concessions (under 16s, over 60s) £11. Category B matches: Adults £12, concessions £7. Category C matches: Adults £5, concessions £1.

Disabled Facilities: Norwich City sends tickets for the disabled to the away club, and does its best to accommodate all. The disabled area, between the South Stand and the River End, is shared with the home support. *Disabled Toilet:* Nearby. *Cost:* Free for disabled, concession price for helper. *Booking:* Through away club. *Parking:* Very limited. Please contact Norwich City for details. *For the Blind:* Commentary available in the disabled area.

Programme: £1.80.

Visitors' Toilets: *Male:* Basic, but clean and tidy. And small! So avoid the half-time rush. Two seasons ago the 'FFG' complained there was nowhere for fans to dry their hands. There still isn't. *Female:* 'It had a mirror, and it wasn't broken!,' said an excited Bury fan. All of life's other essentials were there and in good working order. 'Eight out of ten,' commented another supporter – praise indeed.

Food and Drink: We'll start with the good news: the Cornish pasty (£1.20) was generally deemed 'delicious', with a quality mince filling, and was very good value too. However all this meant nothing to one Bury supporter as he washed his pasty down with a small cup of coke which cost 85p. 'The price is disgusting – and you can quote me on that!', he said. His friend tackled the

mince-and-onion-pie (£1.50 with 10p extra for sauce) and soon renamed it 'a gravy pie – it's too runny'. The coffee (50p) was 'nothing special' either. And now for the even better news: as mentioned above, new caterers (with a good reputation) are taking over for season 98/99 (26.9.97, 1.11.97).

PUB GUIDE

The Clarence Harbour (1) 81 Carrow Road (01603) 442 459
Free House (with eight real ales). This wonderfully football-friendly pub has been completely renovated in traditional style, with a new restaurant area, a pool room and three big-screen TVs. Extensive menu served 12-3 and every evening except Sunday 6-9. Families welcome. Open: all day.

The Coach and Horses (2) 82 Thorpe Road (01603) 477 077
Free House with own brewery and usually 4 or 5 guest beers. A highly recommended, smart real-ale house, with wooden floors and a wonderful menu (served 12-9). It's got a new chef, and the Specials Board is particularly good. Darts, TV, front patio. Open: all day.

The Jubilee (3) 26 St Leonard's Road (01603) 618 734
Free House with ten real ales. An excellent, characterful real-ale house just off Thorpe Road. Football snack menu (ie jumbo sausage, chilli etc). Games room with pool table. Conservatory, beer garden, TV. Open: all day.

FOOD GUIDE

Supporters recommended the fish and chip shop opposite the South Stand, and the burger bar on the corner by the visitors' turnstiles. Near the station (on Thorpe Road) is a pizza restaurant and takeaway, which also does fish and chips. The Kabin Snack Bar, opposite the station by the river, does a large range of sandwiches and breakfasts ... the bacon sandwich (90p) was tasty. Fans walking into town pass a KFC and a 'Domino's Pizza' on Prince of Wales Road, along with other various snack bars and cafés. Vegetarians and vegans could try the excellent 'Tree House' restaurant at 14-16 Dove Street.

'The Floating Restaurant' is a converted barge moored on Corporation Wharf, Riverside. It specialises in seafood, but the menu caters for all, including children, and it's only a five minute walk from the ground. On Fridays and Saturdays it's advisable to book on (01603) 611 129.

LOCAL MEDIA

Local Radio: BBC Radio Norfolk 95.1 and 104.4 FM, 655 and 873 MW.

Radio Phone-ins: Occasional phone-ins on Radio Norfolk.

'He's been taking advice from Delia Smith again – simmering gently for 20 minutes before being brought to the boil!'

Saturday Sports Paper: The 'Pink 'Un', produced by Eastern Counties Newspapers.

MISCELLANEOUS

The summer of 1997 saw 'fashion' become a buzz word at Carrow Road, with City's new kit, designed by Bruce Oldfield, unveiled on the catwalk! However some City fans remain sceptical, bemoaning the disappearance of the traditional green shorts from the Norwich strip, which is now all yellow. Maybe the club's sponsorship deal with the local mustard factory might have had something to do with it!

Safety Factor: Season 1996/97 saw a few minor incidents when Ipswich visited, but generally Carrow Road is a safe ground to visit.

Rivals: East Anglian rivals Ipswich Town: 'the team that's going nowhere ... again'. Norwich fans love the play-offs. Not because Norwich ever participates, mind you, but because Ipswich Town always gets knocked out.

Fanzines: 'Man United are on the Tele Again!', 77 Pennyroyal, Old Catton, Norwich NR6 6JH; 'Cheep Shot', 17 Southerwood, Catton, Norwich, Norfolk, NR6 6JN; 'Ferry 'Cross the Wensum', 56 Quebec Road, Thorpe Hamlet, Norwich, NR1 4HZ (occasional only).

Unofficial Websites: 'Capital Canaries':
http://www.petch.ncmail.com/nclasc
http://www.geocities.com/Colosseum/Sideline/5992/index.htm
'Unofficial': http://www.ncfc.norwich.com/
http://www.users.zetnet.co.uk/ncfc/

Tourist Information: (01603) 666 071.

Nottingham

The grounds of Notts County and Nottingham Forest are on opposite sides of the River Trent. Hence the road directions, and other information, are almost the same for both clubs. The road routes are proscribed by the police and unfortunately are rather complex:

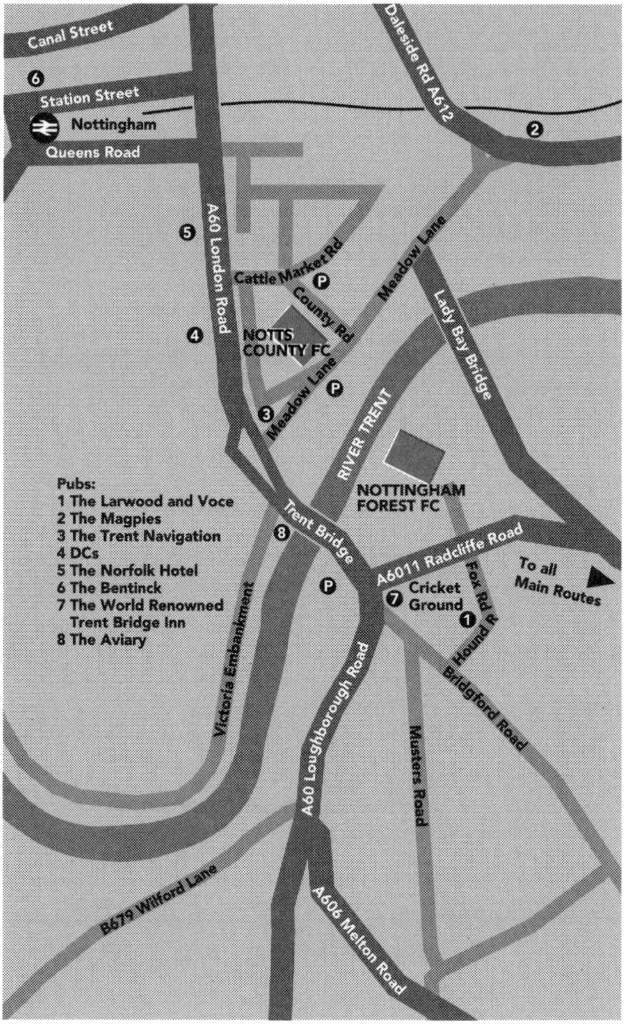

Pubs:
1 The Larwood and Voce
2 The Magpies
3 The Trent Navigation
4 DCs
5 The Norfolk Hotel
6 The Bentinck
7 The World Renowned Trent Bridge Inn
8 The Aviary

HOW TO GET THERE

BY CAR: From North (M1): Exit M1 at junction 26 (s/p Nottingham, Ilkeston A610). For the next 2.8 miles stay on the A610, following signs to 'Nottingham A610', to major junction. Here turn right (s/p Ring Road, Derby (A52), Birmingham A453, Football and Cricket Traffic) onto the A6514 Western Boulevard/Ring Road. Follow Ring Road/Ring Road South and Football Traffic signs for 3 miles, over two roundabouts, through underpass and onto flyover. Here, keep straight on, following signs to 'The South M1, Grantham, Birmingham A453'. (*)After 0.7 miles where road divides, keep in left-hand lanes (s/p Grantham A52, Melton A606, Football Traffic) onto the A52. (**)Keep on the A52, following signs to 'Grantham A52', for 5.5 miles over two roundabouts to third roundabout. Here turn left (s/p Nottingham A6011) onto the A6011. (***)Immediately get in right hand lanes (s/p Nottingham A6011) and over flyover. After a further 0.9 miles the road divides: To the City Ground, keep left (s/p Nottingham via Trent Bridge) into Radcliffe Road. For Meadow Lane: Bear right (s/p Nottingham A6011, Colwick) over the Lady Bay Bridge. At T-junction after 0.5 miles turn left (s/p M1, Birmingham A543, Derby A52) into Meadow Lane.

From Derby A52: At roundabout, junction with M1, go straight on (s/p Nottingham A52). Follow signs for Nottingham A52 for 5.2 miles to roundabout. Here, turn right (s/p Ring Road, Grantham A52) onto A6514 Western Boulevard/Ring Road, and over flyover. Then as from North (M1)(*).

From South (M1): Exit M1 at junction 24 (s/p A453 Nottingham S), and at motorway roundabout turn right (s/p

Nottingham South A453), towards power station. At roundabout after 0.6 miles go straight on (s/p Nottingham A453 and W. Bridgford). After 1.2 miles exit A453 (s/p Grantham A52, Newark A46, Melton A606 – ie not going over the flyover). At roundabout after 0.3 miles turn left (s/p Grantham A52, Melton A606). At mini-roundabout after 0.3 miles, turn right (s/p Grantham A52, Melton A606, also Football and Cricket Traffic) onto the A52. Then as from North (M1)(**).

From South A1: Exit at s/p Grantham, Nottingham, A52. At T-junction turn left (s/p Nottingham A52) onto the A52. At roundabout by Shell Station after 13.2 miles, take 2nd exit (s/p M1, Nottingham A52), remaining on the A52. At roundabout after 5.6 miles go straight on (s/p Nottingham A6011) onto the A6011. Then as From North (M1)(***).

From North A1: Exit A1 at junction with A46 (s/p Newark, Lincoln). Follow signs to A46 Newark for about 13.5 miles to roundabout with Shell station, the junction with A52. Here, take 4th exit (s/p M1, Nottingham A52), remaining on the A52. At roundabout after 5.6 miles go straight on (s/p Nottingham A6011) onto the A6011. Then as From North (M1)(***).

SHORT CUT TO PARKING

For a neat short cut to the parking along Victoria Embankment:

From North (M1): After flyover three miles from the junction of the A610 and the A6541, exit the A52 (s/p City Centre A453, Park and Ride, Industrial Estates). At roundabout turn left (s/p City Centre A453) onto Queen's Drive. (*)Straight on for 1.8 miles, passing Harry Ramsdens, then turn right (s/p Meadows Area). At roundabout after 0.3 miles, go almost all way round, then branch off through elaborate gates into Victoria Embankment. From here it's 1.2 miles to 'The Aviary' pub by the Trent Bridge, and there's parking all the way.

From South (M1): Follow the main road directions 'From South M1' above, but instead of exiting the A453, continue straight on over the flyover (s/p Nottingham A453, Derby A52). Keep in left-hand lanes and after 0.7 miles take first exit (s/p City Centre A453, Queen's Drive Ind. Estate) into Queen's Drive. Then from (*) in previous paragraph.

FROM RAILWAY STATION (Nottingham): *By bus:* See below. *By foot:* Turn left out of station along covered walkway and turn left into Queen's Road. At T-junction/lights turn right into London Road (s/p Loughborough A60, Grantham A52). From here,

a) To Meadow Lane: take 1st left into Cattle Market Road (s/p Nottingham Racecourse) to away turnstiles.

b) To the City Ground: Continue along London Road and over Trent Bridge. Either turn left along pathway by river, and round Trent End to away turnstiles, or take 2nd left (main road s/p Nottingham Tollerton Aerodrome) into Radcliffe Road. Past row of shops, and left into Colwick Road. First right to club car park.

BY BUS: Buses run from the Broadmarsh Centre: To get there, turn right out of the railway station to the T-junction with Canal Street, and it's directly ahead. Buses now have names instead of numbers: take the 'Keyworth Connection', 'Cotgrave Connection' or 'Rushcliffe Line' (L1, L2, L3, L4). After the match 'Football Specials' run back to the city centre.

PUB GUIDE

The Larwood and Voce (1) Fox Road (0115) 981 0392
Scottish and Newcastle. Immensely popular large, smart modern pub next door to the cricket ground. Bar snacks served 12-2 Saturdays, 5-7 midweek. TV, table football. Disabled facilities. Open: 11-2.30, 5-11.30.

The Magpies (2) Meadow Lane (0115) 911 8877
Scottish and Newcastle. Traditional locals pub with pool table and darts, and lots of football memorabilia on the walls. Daily lunch specials. Open: all day.

DC's (4) 152 London Road (0115) 986 6881
Free House (Mansfield, Worthington, John Smiths Smooth). Traditional locals pub. Sandwiches. Open: all day from 12 (from 11 for early kick-offs).

The Fellows, Morton and Clayton Brewhouse Company 54 Canal Street (0115) 950 6795
Free House. Top rate real-ale house with low ceilings, wooden floors and alcoves. Fifty-seater restaurant, please book. Families welcome. TV. Open: all day.

The VAT and Fiddle (formerly **The Tom Hoskins**) 12-14 Queen's Bridge Road (near railway station). (0115) 985 0611
Tynemill (with 10 real ales). The landlord says this is a 'real ale drinkers pub - no gimmicks'. Snacks served 12-3, 5-8. Open: all day.

Also recommended: **The Norfolk Hotel (5)** 68 London Road (Newcastle Brewery), a locals pub with pool table and TV; **The Bentinck Hotel (6),** Station Street (opposite station), a small Bass hotel-pub serving basket meals all day.

Last Midweek Trains: Trains leave to London St. Pancras at 21.33; to Birmingham at 21.49; to Coventry at 21.52; to Newcastle (via Newark North) at 21.25; to Leeds (switching stations in Newark) at 22.27; to Manchester Piccadilly (via Nuneaton) at 21.52; to Sheffield at 23.57. Please double-check on (0345) 484 950.

LOCAL MEDIA

Radio: BBC Radio Nottingham 95.5, 103.8 FM; Trent FM 96.2 FM and 999 AM; Century 106 FM.

Radio Phone-ins: BBC Radio Nottingham, Saturdays 5-6, call (0115) 934 3434; Trent FM is planning a phone-in, listen out for details.

Saturday Sports Paper: The *Nottingham Evening Post* publishes the 'Football Post'.

Tourist Information: (0115) 915 5330.

Nottingham Forest

The City Ground

Address: City Ground, Nottingham NG2 5FJ
Telephone: Club (0115) 982 4444
Ticket Office (0115) 982 4445
Credit Card Hotline (0115) 971 8181
ClubCall (0891) 121 174
Official Website: http:/www.nottinghamforest.co.uk

'Nottingham has everything', said one happy resident. 'And it's central too', meaning that Nottingham-based football supporters have less far to travel to away games. It's certainly a sports fan's paradise, with two football grounds, racing, international cricket, tennis and water sports, and an excellent city centre with one of the highest ratios of pubs per square mile outside London. The City Ground is about a mile from the centre, on the east bank of the River Trent, with its own selection of welcoming hostelries, including one at the nearby County Cricket Ground. For latecomers, parking can be a problem, but finding fast food certainly is not.

HOW TO GET THERE

BY CAR: See 'Nottingham' chapter.
FROM RAILWAY STATION: About 1.0 miles. *By taxi:* about £2.75-3.00. *By foot:* See 'Nottingham' chapter.
BY BUS: See 'Nottingham' chapter.

PARKING

For off-street parking try the County Hall (£3) between the river and the A60 Loughborough Road, or the Victoria Embankment (£2.50, see 'short cut' road directions in the 'Nottingham' chapter). Early arrivals find spaces in Musters Road or in Fox Road and Hound Road by the cricket ground. A small number of cars can park at the Elf Garage in Trent Boulevard (£5) and there's street parking in the same area. It's also worth looking on the other side of the river, around Notts County's ground (see 'Notts County' entry). Don't park illegally, or your car could be towed.

THE GROUND

The City Ground occupies one of the most dramatic locations of any League ground, right on the bank of the River Trent, with the two-tier Trent End rising high over the water. The stand, which seats 7,000, is the club's pride and joy, though many fans still lament the loss of the old shed terrace. 'It's a bit clinical', said one fan, 'and the acoustics are poor.' Almost as impressive is the Executive Stand, also two-tier and seating more than 9,000. Visiting fans are allocated the lower tier of the Bridgford End, and happily prove that the acoustics there are excellent ... so much so that home fans have been campaigning to switch ends! The view is good, though fans still stand up to see the action at the far end. The oldest section of the ground is the Main Stand, which is slated for a £12 million redevelopment, though no firm date for the work has yet been set.
Total Capacity: 31,000. For away fans: (Bridgford Stand, Lower Tier) 3,000-5,000. Turnstiles 49-54.
Cost (98/99): 'AA' matches: Adults £25, concessions £12.50. 'A' matches: £22/£12. 'B' matches: £20/£10. Concessions on a reciprocal basis only.
Disabled Facilities: Space for 22 visiting supporters in the front row of the Bridgford Stand Lower Tier. *Disabled Toilets:* At least one in every stand. *Cost:* Free for disabled, full price for helper. *Booking:* Advisable. *Parking:* Limited availability in the Executive Stand car park. *For the Blind:* 40 seats with plug-in earphones for full match commentary.
Programme: £1.60.
Visitors' Toilets: *Male:* Nothing to complain about here, except for the lack of hot water. *Female:* ER-style surgical wash basins, unpainted brick walls and soap which looked like it had been kicked around the floor ... yes, we're definitely at a football ground! But it was all clean and spacious, with the softest toilet paper in Britain.
Food and Drink: The cheese-and-onion pasty (£1.50) was described as 'beaut', while others recommended the 'pies in the blue tins'. All were red hot. The burgers (£1.90), however, were a bit of a disaster, thin and burnt, and so many supporters complained that the kiosk stopped selling them fifteen minutes before kick-off! Few liked the chips, described as 'pretty sad', while the bovril (£1) was 'not as good as at Doncaster Rovers' (27.8.97).

PUB GUIDE

See 'Nottingham' chapter.

FOOD GUIDE

The café on Trent Bridge itself, by the path which leads down along the river, is very popular. Locals also recommend the 'Bridgford Restaurant' in a row of shops on Radcliffe Road, and 'Papas' for burgers, kebabs, jacket potatoes and pizza. Further along Radcliffe Road is a McDonalds. For a good curry, try the 'Pink City Balti Palace' on London Road just the other side of the Trent Bridge. Many mobile burger vans also turn up for Forest games.

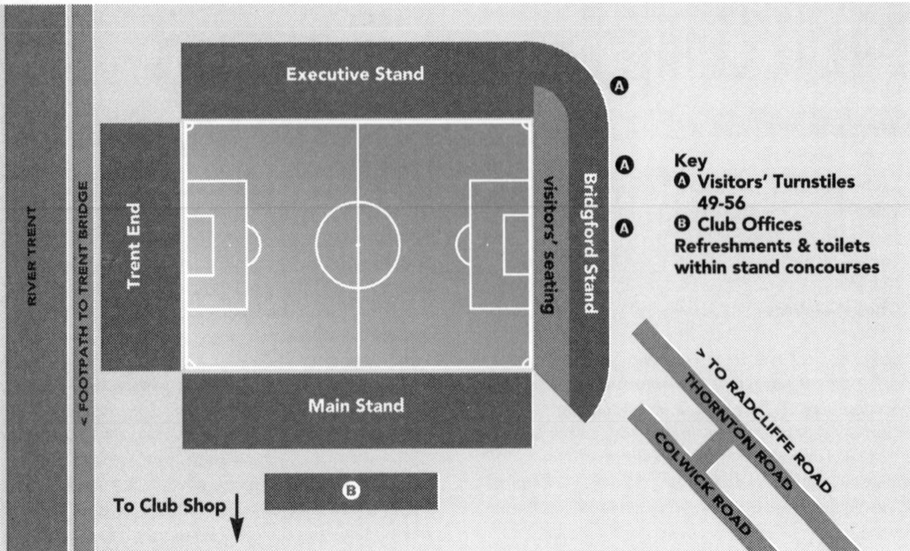

MISCELLANEOUS

Safety Factor: Forest does have a small hooligan element, so take the normal precautions. That said, there haven't been any problems for ages.
Rivals: Locally it's Leicester and Derby, and the power failure at Pride Park early in season 97/98 caused some merriment ... up went the chant at the City Ground: 'Four-one and the light's still on....'

'Firstly, the good news is that you'll be celebrating promotion again in two years time...'

Fanzines: 'Forest Forever', 69 Fernleigh Avenue, Mapperley, Nottingham, NG3 6FN; 'The Tricky Tree', 149 Blake Road, West Bridgford, Nottingham, NG2 5LA.
Unofficial Websites:
'Grezza's':
http://www.geocities.com/Colosseum/Sideline/5335/
'The Magical Forest':
http://users.aol.com/AFBryant1.nfwingp.htm
'Forest 79 Online': http://surf.to.nottingham-forest
'Garibaldi Reds':
http://www.nott.ac.uk/~ccznffc.NFFC.html
'Shiney Red Balls':
http://www.geocities.com/Colosseum/Field/2228/hello.html
http://www.the-eye.com/nffc.htm

Notts County

Meadow Lane

Address: Meadow Lane Stadium, Nottingham NG2 3HJ
Telephone: Club (0115) 952 9000
Ticket Office (0115) 955 7210
County Clubline (0891) 888 684
Official Website: http://www.nottscounty.co.uk

In England and Wales, are there two league grounds as close to one another as Forest and County? The City Ground dominates the east side of the River Trent, while Meadow Lane, opposite, remains out of the limelight, tucked away behind factories and warehouses. Older County fans will happily reminisce about the days when Notts were the city's top team ... but they are going back to the good ol' days of Tommy Lawton and Co! Meadow Lane, with its 20,000 capacity, was certainly built with a return to the big time in mind. And all those nearby warehouses are handy for football fans, as they provide lots of cheap parking.

HOW TO GET THERE

BY CAR: See 'Nottingham' chapter.
FROM RAILWAY STATION: *By taxi:* £2.50-2.75. For other directions see 'Nottingham' chapter.

PARKING

On Meadow Lane, there's the Cattle Market car park (£1.50), a car park opposite the club shop (£2), and parking in the forecourt of 'Stephen Jenkins Bedrooms' (£2). Another option is to try the industrial estate on Daleside Road by the Lady Bay Bridge. Alternatively there's usually plenty of space (£2.50) along the Victoria Embankment (to get there, see the 'short cut to parking' section in the 'Nottingham' chapter). Or try parking on the opposite side of the river, around the City Ground.

THE GROUND

Notts fans see Meadow Lane as the 'Wembley of the Lower Divisions', and few would disagree. There's a downside, however, as many visiting teams view the game as a big fixture and rise to the occasion. Forest fans refer to their near-neighbour as 'Lego Lane', alluding to the way three of the stands were constructed, for just £8 million, in the 1992 close season. But they also admit it was an impressive transformation of an ancient traditional shed-style ground into a 20,000 all-seater with modern facilities. Wind-swept terraces have been replaced by smart comfortable stands, and in another quality move a new pitch was added in the summer of 1998. Visiting fans are housed in the Kop Stand, which has good views, reasonable legroom and excellent pies.

Total Capacity: 20,300. For away fans: (Kop Stand) 5,438. Turnstiles 32-41. A further 1,281 seats can be made available in the Jimmy Sirrel Stand.
Cost (98/99): Adult £11, concessions (Juniors/OAPs) £5.50. Concessions available on a reciprocal basis.
Disabled Facilities: Ample space for visiting supporters at pitch level in front of the Family Stand. *Disabled Toilet:* In the concourses of the Family and Pavis stands, and on the corner between the Sirrel and Family Stands. *Cost:* Free for wheelchair disabled, full price for helper. *Booking:* Preferable. *Parking:* Some available - please book. *For the Blind:* Seating at the back of the Pavis Stand, with the hospital radio broadcasters.
Programme: £1.50.
Visitors' Toilets: *Male:* Three clean cubicles and several clean sinks ... no-one could use them as there was no running water! *Female:* Oh Gawd, those thin grey loo seats ... uncomfortable or what!
Food and Drink: Notts County's pies (£1.40) are legendary, and rightly so! A Cambridge fan said of the steak-and-kidney variety: 'Very good, hot, meaty. I've had pies all over Britain, and this is the best!' Supporters were less keen on the burgers ... 'beefburger? It's more like a bread burger', though the hot-dogs (£1.70) did have 'some detectable meat' in them. The coffee (95p) was so large the spoon didn't reach the bottom (25.10.98).

PUB GUIDE

Also see the 'Nottingham' chapter for other excellent hostelries, **The Larwood and Voce (1), Fellows, Morton and Clayton, Vat and Fiddle, The Magpies (2)** and **DCs (4)**.
The World Renowned Trent Bridge Inn (7)
2 Radcliffe Road (0115) 982 2786
Ansells (with Burton, Pedigree, Tetley). Imposing listed 1832 building next to the cricket ground, but with a modern, young decor and atmosphere inside. Two large screen TVs. Families welcome. Open: 12-3, 6-11.
The Trent Navigation (3) Meadow Lane (0115) 952 0333
John Smiths (plus guest beer). Traditional-style pub by the canal. Bar snacks served all day. Pool, darts, TV. Disabled facilities. Parking £1.50. Open: all day.

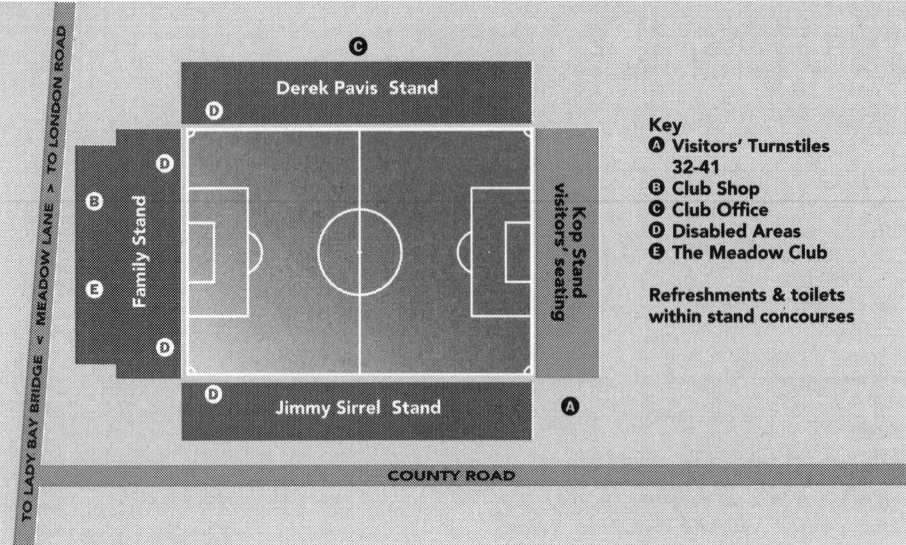

The Aviary (8) Trent Bridge (0115) 986 1830 Whitbread. Large, modern-style pub with great views over the river. Pub meals and sandwiches served 12-2.30, 5.30-9. Open: all day.

FOOD GUIDE

The fish-and-chip shop, 'Amigos' on Meadow Lane, towards 'The Magpies' is not too popular, so County supporters tend to 'cross the dreaded water' to the takeaways near Forest's ground on Radcliffe Road. The café just the other side of Trent Bridge is very popular. Locals recommend the 'Bridgford Restaurant' in a row of shops on the left-hand-side of Radcliffe Road, and 'Papas' for burgers and kebabs. A little further along, there's a McDonalds. For a good curry, try the 'Pink City Balti Palace' on London Road near the Trent Bridge.

MISCELLANEOUS

Back to that age-old question: 'What's the difference between a Forest and a County supporter?' Here are some thoughts from Ivan 'Bart' Bainbridge of the County fanzine 'No More Pie in the Sky': 'I've always supported the underdog, and I like the fact that I know everyone on the away terrace. County also has an older support ... Forest fans are all Billy Boy Racer types, Steve and Sharon'. The song 'I had a wheelbarrow and the wheel fell off' is still a big County favourite, but there's a County-are-winning version now too, with 'Sweet Chariot' becoming 'Sweet Wheelbarrow' - it rhymes better too!

Safety Factor: No trouble now for quite a few seasons.

Rivals: Nottingham Forest, although it is not reciprocated.

Fanzines: 'No More Pie in the Sky', 37 Whittier Road, Sneinton, Nottingham, NG2 2AT; 'The Pie', c/o 9 Yew Tree Close, Radcliffe on Trent, Nottingham, NG12 2AZ; 'Piefect Day', 7 Loughborough Road, Burton-on-the-Wolds, Loughborough, Leics, LE12 5AF.

Unofficial Websites:
'MagpieNet': http://home.sol.no/~benn/magpienet/
http://www.ntu.ac.uk/staff.baylidj/ncfc.htm

'Going up?'

Oldham Athletic

Boundary Park

Address: Boundary Park, Oldham, OL1 2PA.
Telephone: Club (0161) 624 4972
Fax (0161) 627 5915
Latics Clubcall (0891) 12 11 42
Latics Ticket Call (0891) 12 15 82
Official Website: http://www.u-net.com/latics/

'Meat pie, sausage roll, come on Oldham give us a goal.' Now there's a rousing football ditty. Visiting fans, given the choice, would come up with something along the lines of: 'Searing wind, always sleeting, come on Oldham, switch on the heating.' Indeed, rumour has it that one evening in 1990 Ipswich fans had to be rescued from the old open terrace and treated for hypothermia. The problem is that the ground's high up, surrounded mainly by parkland and car parks ... i.e. no barriers between it and the Pennines, and from there out to the Arctic! To be fair, the stands now have side panels which provide some protection. Apart from the cold, visitors encounter few problems at Boundary Park. The ground's easy to find – a couple of minutes' drive from the motorway – and the nearby pubs are welcoming.

HOW TO GET THERE

BY CAR: All Routes: Exit M62 at junction 20 (s/p Ashton, Rochdale, Oldham A627(M)). At roundabout follow signs to 'Ashton, Oldham, Manchester A627(M)' onto the A627M. After 0.5 miles, where the road divides, keep right (s/p Manchester East A663, Oldham, Ashton A627). After 1.4 miles exit A627(M) (s/p Oldham, Ashton A627). At the roundabout(**), take the 1st exit following signs for Oldham Athletic FC (also s/p Royton A663, Rochdale A671) onto Broadway. Take first right turn, after 0.4 miles, into Hilbre Avenue, which leads to the car park.

FROM RAILWAY STATION (Oldham Werneth): 1.1 miles. *By taxi:* There don't tend to be any. *By bus:* The no. 420 runs along Featherstall Road – but only once an hour. *By foot:* Walk up pathway to main road (Featherstall Road South). Cross the road and turn right, and go straight on for 0.3 miles, passing several curry houses. Cross straight over roundabout (by new Tescos) to next roundabout. Here, take pedestrian subway. In the centre turn left where the path divides, through tunnel, left up the steps towards the telephone kiosk, and left into Maygate towards 'The Spinners Arms'. Straight over crossroads. Follow road round to the right, passing the Health Authority building on LHS. The road becomes more of a rutted track (Westhulme Avenue). Straight on for about 0.2 miles to ground.

Last Midweek Trains: Trains to Manchester run at 21.57 and 22.27. For onward connections see 'Manchester City' entry. Please double check on (0345) 484 950.

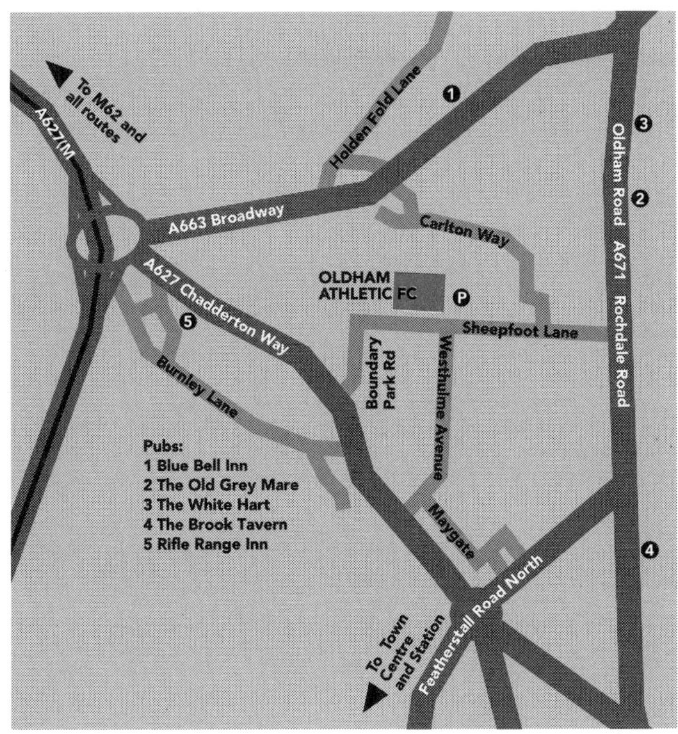

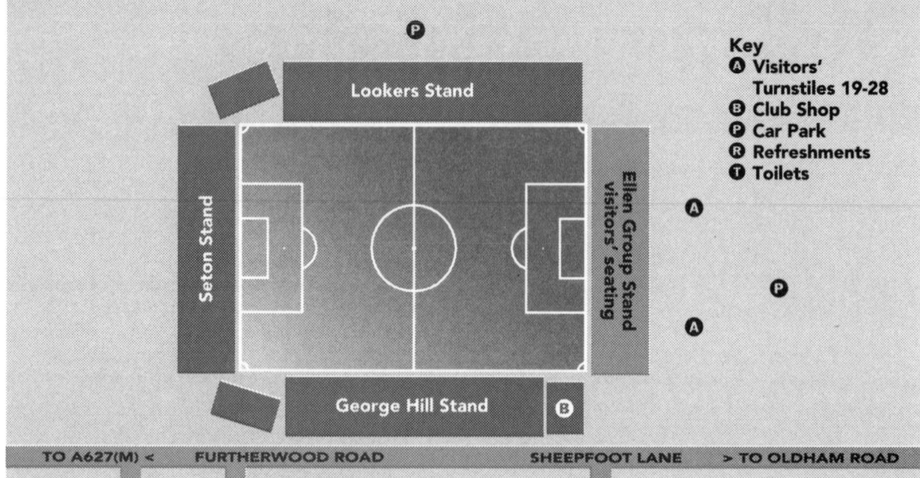

BY BUS: The nos. 182 and 413 run from Oldham town centre to the Oldham Road, while the nos. 406 and 418 run from Oldham town centre along Chadderton Way. The 409 from Oldham town centre to Rochdale, and the 400 from Stockport to Bolton also run along Oldham Road.

PARKING

Somewhere, not all that far from Boundary Park, must be a large factory churning out traffic cones ... because there's flippin' hundreds of them on Oldham streets on matchdays! It's probably easiest to use one of the large car parks at the ground (£1). However, cars are packed in nose-to-tail, so don't bank on a swift getaway. Alternatively, the 'Blue Bell' pub has parking for £2. The police advise fans not to park at Elk Mill Business Park, as the clampers are waiting to pounce.

THE GROUND

Plans are underway for one of the closest ground moves of all time ... just a few yards into the park next door! With the working title 'Sports Park 2000', the idea is to build a three-sided 15,000-seater stadium on the site of an existing sports centre. The possibility would remain, Huddersfield-style, for a fourth side to increase the capacity to 25,000. The council has already granted planning permission, but nearby residents – including the 'Clayton Fields Action Group' – are vociferously against. They point out that the park is land left to the people of Oldham, and should remain as it is.

For next season at least, therefore, Oldham Athletic remains at Boundary Park. It's now all-seater, though in many places the seats were simply grafted onto the existing terrace. Amazingly, visiting supporters are housed in the best stand of all, the Ellen Group Stand – it's the only one without stanchions, and the facilities are good.

Total Capacity: 13,700. For away fans: Seating: 1,670 to 4,660. Turnstiles 19-22 (plus 23-28).

Cost (98/99): Adults £12, concessions (Juniors/OAPs) £5.

Disabled Facilities: Space for 40 wheelchairs in the Ellen Group Stand. *Disabled Toilet:* Two nearby. *Cost:* Free for disabled, matchday prices for helper. *Booking:* Yes. *Parking:* Available directly behind the Ellen Group Stand. Please book. *For the Blind:* No special facilities.

Programme: £1.60.

Visitors' Toilets: *Male:* The three-star variety – clean, good quality, nothing flash. One satisfied fan said: 'Well impressed with them bogs – they're well clean.' *Female:* Smart, with all amenities. The two hand-dryers were a sight for sore eyes for fans nursing frostbitten hands.

Food and Drink: Opinions varied widely. Luton supporters described the meat-and-potato pies (£1.55) as 'much better and larger than expected', and the steak-and-kidney ones as 'better than most'. Gillingham fans said the meat-and-potato pies were overcooked, and filled with something resembling pulped baby food. A couple of them took their pies, with a large bite out of each, back to the kiosk, and got a refund and an apology! The burgers (£2.10) came with those weird dried onions. However, the tea (70p) was 'purfect' and there was a cheese-and-onion pasty (£1.50) for vegetarians. The club is employing a new catering company in 1998/99 (7.11.97, 17.1.98).

O

PUB GUIDE

The Blue Bell Inn (1) Broadway, Royton (0161) 652 0772
JW Lees/Tennants: An extremely football friendly pub, highly recommended by the parking attendants! It's large, with a choice of lively bar area with pool table and big screen TV, or a quieter lounge. Reasonably priced bar food, including scampi and chips for £2.95 and 'chip muffin' for £1.50. Beer garden. Families welcome. Open: all day from 11.30.

The Old Grey Mare (2) 331 Oldham Road, Royton (0161) 624 2719
Greenalls (with Boddingtons). Large, smart modern pub, serving bar meals 12-2.30, 5-7. Darts, big-screen TV. Families welcome. Open: all day from 11:30.

The White Hart (3) Oldham Road, Royton (0161) 624 8167
Courage. Very attractive, spacious pub with separate dining area. Excellent choice of food served 12-2.30. Families welcome. Darts. Open all day from 12.

The Brook Tavern (4) 260 Rochdale Road (0161) 628 3896
Greenalls (with Boddingtons). Large modern family-orientated pub, and also very safe as the police usually park opposite! Pool, snooker, darts, big-screen TV. Open: all day from 11:30.

The Rifle Range Inn (5) 372 Burnley Lane, Chadderton (0161) 626 5543
JW Lees. A pub converted from four cottages and retaining a homely feel – and there was indeed a First World War rifle range nearby. Bar meals, including vegetarian options, served 12-3. Families welcome. Pool, darts, TV, beer garden. Open: all day.
How to get there: At roundabout marked (**) in road directions, take third exit (s/p Manchester A663), and turn first left off the slip road, and first left again to pub.
Also recommended: **The Greyhound,** No 1 Elly Clough, Holden Fold, Royton. This is a cosy, traditional JW Lees pub, with a sun-trap beer garden.
To get there: At roundabout marked (**) in road directions, take first exit onto Broadway. Take 2nd turning on LHS after 0.3 miles into Netherhey Lane. This becomes Holden Fold Lane – pub is in valley.

FOOD GUIDE

There are two chippies on Oldham Road, opposite the 'Save' petrol station. The popular 'Ree Ming' sells Hollands pies (77p-82p), cheeseburgers for £1 and fish from £1.35. The 'Sun Hing' has pies (75p-83p), fish at £1.30 and chips at 75p. Featherstall Road North, the route from the railway station, has a series of good Indian restaurants and takeaways, including the 'Balti House' which does takeaways from 11am to midnight. There's a McDonalds and KFC on the A627(M) roundabout. Home fans recommend Yorkshire Road (in the town centre) for fans 'looking for a smarter pub'.

'They say our ground is renowned for the icy wind and driving rain off the Pennines – but I think it's quite mild for July!'

LOCAL MEDIA

Local Radio: GMR 95.1 FM; Piccadilly Radio 1152 AM; Key 103 FM.
Radio Phone-ins: GMR, Saturdays 1-3 and 5-7, and after midweek games. Call (0161) 228 2255; Piccadilly Radio, Saturdays 5-6, call (0161) 288 1152.
Saturday Sports Paper: The *Manchester Evening News* produces the 'Manchester Pink' which includes coverage of Oldham.

MISCELLANEOUS

Safety Factor: No problems here.
Rivals: The editor of 'Beyond the Boundary' said: 'There aren't any in this division, but if we keep playing like we are, it will soon be Rochdale!' In the meantime, the main rivals remain Bolton Wanderers, Manchester United and, as an afterthought, Blackburn.
Fanzines: 'Beyond the Boundary', 17 Saville St, St Catherines, Lincoln, LN5 8NH.
Unofficial Websites:
'Beyond the Boundary':
http://www.homeusers.prestel.co.uk/oasia/index.htm
Tourist Information: (0161) 627 1024.

Oxford United

The Manor Ground

Address: The Manor Ground, Headington, Oxford OX3 7SR
Telephone: (01865) 761 503
Clubline (0891) 440 055
Official Website: http://www.oufc.co.uk/

Oxford United FC starts season 98/99 with one-and-a-half grounds: its traditional home in the lively suburb of Headington, and its new out-of-town stadium which stands, half-complete and slowly decaying, about four miles to the south-east at Minchery Farm. Work began on the new ground in August 1996, and three stands quickly began to take shape ... before the money ran out. The club hopes construction work can restart soon, with a few matches played at the new ground towards the end of season 98/99. Minchery Farm is on the edge of town, in an area called Blackbird Leys, sandwiched between large new housing estates and the Oxford Science Park. There's one pub nearby and no chippy in sight. Footie fans are eyeing the development – a remoter version of the Britannia Stadium or Pride Park – with some trepidation. For a traditional day-out, with good beer and a fish-and-chip lunch, the Manor Ground wins by a mile. Parking is usually not a huge problem either, but come dressed for downpours on the open away terrace.

Most of the information here is for The Manor Ground. However, at the end we've also included road directions to, and a map of, Minchery Farm.

HOW TO GET THERE

To The Manor Ground: NB: Roundabouts in Oxford have names, which appear on the signs, and they are used in the directions below.

BY CAR: From East (including London): Exit M40 at junction 8 (s/p A40 Cheltenham, Oxford) onto the A40 dual carriageway. Straight on for 6.0 miles to Headington Roundabout. Here, go straight on (2nd exit, s/p City Centre) onto the A420 London Road. Ground is on RHS after 0.8 miles.

From North: Exit M40 at junction 9 (s/p Bicester, Aylesbury A41, Oxford A34). At roundabout, take 3rd exit (s/p Oxford, Newbury A34) onto the A34 dual carriageway. After 6.0 miles, exit A34 at the Peartree Interchange (s/p Oxford, Evesham A44). (*)At the roundabout take 1st exit (s/p Ring Road, Oxford A44) onto the Woodstock Road dual carriageway, and at the Wolvercote Roundabout after 0.4 miles take 2nd exit (s/p Ring Road, London A40) onto the A40 Northern By-Pass. At Headington Roundabout after 4.0 miles, turn right (s/p City Centre) onto the A420 London Road. Ground is on RHS after 0.8 miles.

From West (A420, junction with A34): At roundabout, turn left (s/p Ring Road, The North A34, The West A40). After 2.8 miles, exit A34 at Peartree Interchange (s/p Ring Road, Oxford, Evesham A44, London A40). Then as from North(*).

From South: Exit M4 at junction 13 and follow 'Oxford

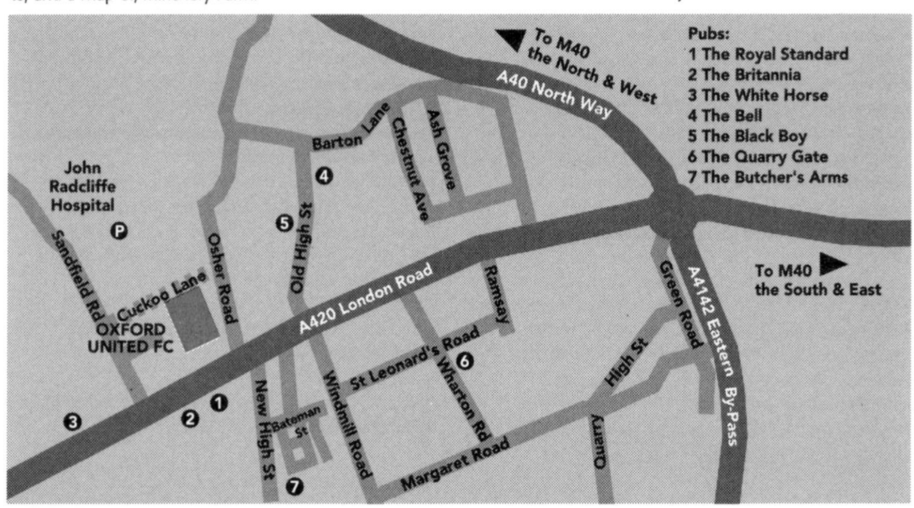

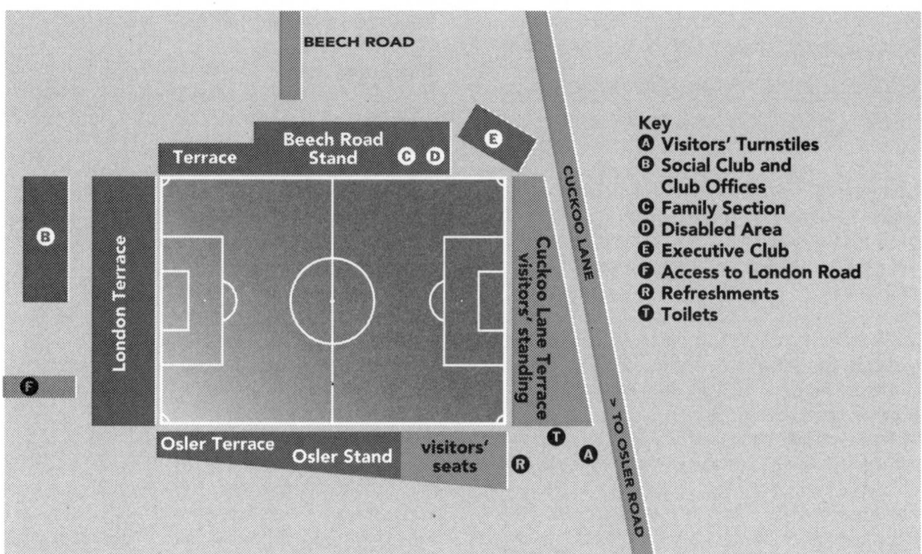

A34' signs onto the A34. Exit A34 after 21.2 miles at the Hinksey Hill Interchange (s/p Ring Road, Oxford A4144). At roundabout turn right (s/p Ring Road, Oxford A4144) onto the Ring Road. From here, it's signposted Ring Road or London A40 all the way to the Headington Roundabout, a distance of 5.2 miles. At Headington Roundabout, turn left (s/p City Centre). Ground is on RHS after 0.8 miles.

FROM RAILWAY STATION (Oxford): The station is on the opposite side of town, more than two miles from The Manor. *By taxi:* £4.50-5.50. *By bus:* No. 22 runs from the station to the ground via Queen Street every half hour until 7 pm. Alternatively, it's a five-minute walk to Cornmarket Street (left along Park End Street, left into Worcester Street, right into George Street, right into Cornmarket Street) from where the buses listed below run to the ground.

Last Midweek Trains: Trains to London Paddington run at 22.15, 22.24, 22.38, 23.15 and 00.20. It's not possible to reach destinations on the Coventry/ Birmingham/Manchester line, as the last train is at 19.23. Please double check on (0345) 484 950.

BY BUS: The following buses run from The Cornmarket (outside Boots) to the ground: nos. 2, 2a, 2b, 7, 7a, 7b.

PARKING

It's mostly street parking but note that police tow-away vans are constantly on the prowl. Some of the best areas to try are: around St Leonard's Road and Wharton Road; the Old High Street, which also has some pay-and-display; and Chestnut Avenue, from where there's a short-cut to the ground through Bury Knowle Park (though it shuts at 7.30 pm). Oxford United leases 200 spaces in the John Radcliffe Hospital car park, which are usually available on the day.

THE GROUND

The sign by the half-built Minchery Farm ground reads: '15,000 capacity, 30 executive boxes, an executive lounge, extensive supporters' club facilities, 1,950 car park spaces, opening 1997.' And, in 1998, what is there exactly? Two stands with internal staircases but no seats, a skeleton structure of another side stand, a lot of weeds and some dumped rubbish. Work at the site halted after just four months when a financial backer pulled out and the club was unable to meet the first £5 million payment to builders Taylor Woodrow. Oxford United FC remains committed to a ground move, pointing out that it's the only way for the club to survive in the higher divisions. However, time is not on its side. By August 1999, all the club's remaining terraces – and there are a lot of them – must close. So, if Minchery Farm is not ready, the club needs to build temporary seating at The Manor, or face a dramatic cut in capacity. Some fans, including Paul Beevers, editor of the fanzine 'Rage On', fear the worst: a ground-share with Reading or Wycombe.

While the club tries to solve the financial conundrum, the team continues to play at the Manor Ground, a motley collection of stands and terraces, all different shapes and sizes, built piecemeal over fifty years. Visiting fans are allocated the large uncovered Cuckoo Lane Terrace, and a small section of seating in the corner of the Osler Stand. The view from the terrace is partially

obscured by fencing and a CCTV camera, and overall facilities are poor. 'Back to the 80s!' commented one visitor glumly.

Total Capacity: 9,572. For away fans: Seating (Cuckoo Lane East) 434. Turnstile 5. An extra 108 seats can be made available in Cuckoo Lane West for big matches. Standing (uncovered) 2,107. Turnstiles 6-8.

Cost (98/99): Seating: Adults £14, concessions £9.50. Terrace: £11/£6.50.

Disabled Facilities: Area for 25 supporters, slightly raised from ground level, in front of the Manor Club, where the view is not good. *Disabled Toilet:* Nearby. *Cost:* £5.50 (concessions £3.25) for disabled, full price for helper. *Booking:* Yes. *Parking:* Limited availability for Orange Badge Holders in Beech Road, on a first-come, first-served basis. *For the Blind:* No special facilities.

Programme: £1.50.

Visitors' Toilets: *Male:* 'It's a cave,' one voice echoed out. Birmingham fans complained it was dingy and dark, which made aiming difficult ... though it was in such a state most concluded that it didn't matter. *Female:* Trying to invoke humour in the face of adversity, a Birmingham fan said: 'I'm glad I didn't dress up for this.' The building was best described as a spider shed ... a corrugated roof and flooded floors with loos that didn't flush. However, if there's ever an auction of Manor Road artifacts, our choice would definitely be the wonderful wooden loo-paper-dispenser!

Food and Drink: A survey in 'Rage On' found that only 23% of Oxford supporters thought The Manor Ground food was 'all right'. The rest thought it was worse! Visiting supporters were annoyed by having to queue twice, once for the food, once for hot drinks. The pasties (£1.30) were hot and spicy, while the hot-dog-with-brown sauce (£1.80) was tasty but expensive. One fan gave his burger 'one-out-of-ten and that's generous', even though it was freshly cooked. It arrived without onions but with plenty of extra grease. The Klix coffee (90p) was 'passable' (17.2.98, 25.4.98).

PUB GUIDE

Away supporters are usually welcome in the Supporters' Club for an entrance fee of £1. It's Carlsberg-Tetley/Youngers, and can get very crowded.

The two pubs opposite the main entrance to The Manor, **The Royal Standard (1)** (Morrells) and **The Britannia (2)** (Benskins/Tetley), are football-friendly, serve food, and are very popular. A little further from the ground, try:

The White Horse (3) 1 London Road (01865) 762 447
Whitbread/Morrells. Huge pub, with wooden floors, traditional décor and a friendly atmosphere. Large menu (chilli £5.25, vegetable stir fry £5.25) and a family dining area. Disabled facilities. Pool table, bar billiards, large car park. Open: all day.

The Quarry Gate (6) 19 Wharton Road (01865) 762 593
Courage (with unusual guest beers). Traditional locals pub with separate bar and lounge areas. Sandwiches. Pool table, darts, beer garden. Open: Saturday all day; from 5 pm for evening games.

The Butcher's Arms (7) 5 Wilberforce Street (01865) 761 252
Fullers (with four real ales). Small pub with one long bar area, wooden floors and benches, featured in the 1998 *Good Beer Guide.* It's sports-mad, with loads of football memorabilia. Excellent beer garden. Open: Friday-Sunday all day; from 5.30 pm for midweek games.

The following pubs are in the Old High Street, an attractive backwater with narrow windy streets and a village atmosphere, all less than ten minutes' walk from The Manor:

The Black Boy (5) 91 Old High Street (01865) 763 234
Morrells (with Graduate, Varsity, Mild, Best plus guest beers). Traditional real-ale pub on the village crossroads. Sandwiches (50p). Pool table, darts, TV, beer garden with children's play area. Open: Saturday all day; from 6 pm for evening games.

The Bell (4) 72 Old High Street (01865) 761 594
Carlsberg-Tetley. A traditional local village pub, recently refurbished. Sandwiches. Pool table, TV. Open: Saturday all day; from 5.30 pm for midweek games. NB There's a short cut to the ground from the back door.

FOOD GUIDE

Home fans recommend two fish-and-chip shops on London Road: 'Smarts Takeaway', a café with cod and chips at £2.95, Pukka pies £1.35, and a kiddies special of sausage, chips and a drink for £1.50; and the 'Mediterranean' fish-and-chip shop (doner kebab £2.75, cod and chips £2.90). The 'Chef's Pantry' bakery/Deli, also on London Road, offers something a little different, such as Jamaican patties, chicken beef or excellent salt fish. The 'Oxford Kebab House' is quite upmarket, with chargrilled burgers and kebabs (£3.20 or £4). Those with time for a proper sit-down meal could try the chic 'Café Francais' or 'Café Noir'. London Road also has a 'Domino's Pizza' and, on the Headington Roundabout, a McDonalds in a half-timbered house! On the Old High Street, 'The Croissant Café' serves bacon baps at £1.50.

LOCAL MEDIA

Local Radio: BBC Thames Valley 95.2 FM; Fox FM 102.6.

Radio Phone-ins: BBC Thames Valley, Saturdays 5-7, call (01865) 311 111; Fox FM, Saturdays 5-6, call (01865) 871 026.

Saturday Sports Paper: None.

MISCELLANEOUS

We've heard of some bizarre half-time entertainment, but this is surreal! For the last two seasons, Oxford United has staged 'dizzy' penalty shoot-outs. Local celebrities were spun around before attempting a 20-yard run-up and penalty attempt. Most were unable to run more than a few feet before falling in a heap.
Safety Factor: Trouble at the ground is rare.
Rivals: Most venom is reserved for local rivals Swindon. But some fans dislike Wolves, because of 'their assumption that they have a divine right to be in the Premiership just because they have a good ground.'
Fanzines: 'Rage On', 17 Foster Road, Abingdon, Oxon, OX14 1YN; 'Yellow Fever', Flat 6, .126 Long Acre, London WC2E 9PE.
Unofficial Websites:
'Steve Merritt':
http://members.aol.com/SteMerritt/Main.html
'Ox Tales': http://www.oxtales.com/
'Mark Sennett:
http://www.geocities.com/Colosseum/Bleachers/5382/
Tourist Information: (01865) 726 871.

Minchery Farm

HOW TO GET THERE

From South/M4: Exit M4 at junction 13 and follow 'Oxford A34' signs onto the A34. Exit A34 after 21.2 miles at the Hinksey Hill Interchange (s/p Ring Road, Oxford A4144). At roundabout turn right (s/p Ring Road, Oxford A4144) onto the Ring Road. (*)Straight over the Kennington Roundabout (s/p Ring Road) after 0.4 miles, and then take 3rd exit at the Heyford Hill Roundabout after 0.8 miles (s/p Reading A4074, Henley A4130), onto the A4074 Sandford Link Road. Exit A4074 after 0.6 miles (s/p Cowley, Watlington B480, also Oxford Science Park). Follow signs to 'Cowley, Watlington' for 0.5 miles to ground.
From North: Exit M40 at junction 9 (s/p Bicester, Aylesbury A41, Oxford A34). At roundabout follow 'Oxford, Newbury A34' signs onto the A34. Exit A34 after 11.6 miles at the Hinksey Hill Interchange (s/p Ring Road A423). At roundabout turn left (s/p Ring Road A423, London A40, M40) onto the Ring Road. Then as From South/M4(*)
From East/London: Exit M40 at junction 8 (s/p A40 Cheltenham, Oxford). Go straight on for 6.0 miles to Headington Roundabout. Here, turn left (s/p Science Park, Cowley) onto the A4142 dual carriageway. After 2.1 miles exit A4142 at the Cowley Junction (s/p Watlington B480, Oxford Business Park), and at roundabout turn left (s/p Watlington, Blackbird Leys B480) onto the B480 and under railway bridge. At roundabout after 0.9 miles turn right (s/p Reading A4074) into Grenoble Road. Follow signs to 'Reading, Oxford A4074, for 1.3 miles, over three roundabouts, to ground.
Tip: If lost, follow signs to Oxford Science Park, which is on the same industrial development as the new ground.

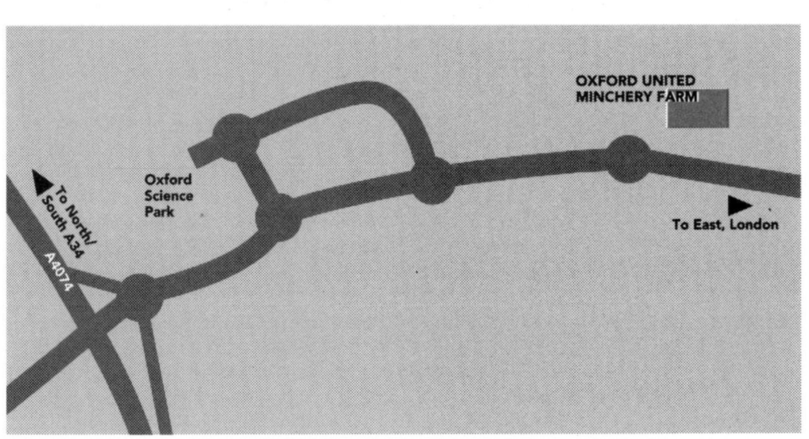

P

Peterborough United

London Road

Address: London Road Ground, London Road, Peterborough, PE2 8AL
Telephone: Club (01733) 563 947
Commercial (01733) 569 760
ClubCall (0891) 121 654
Official Website: http://come.to.PUFC

The location of Peterborough's ground, just outside the city centre, makes this one of the least stressful footie days ever. There's a large car park nearby, a couple of friendly pubs about sixty seconds' staggering distance away, and the railway station's not that far either. The club's owned by Peter Boizot, former chief of Pizza Express. However, traditional pie-loving fans needn't worry, as the catering hasn't gone Italian ... yet!

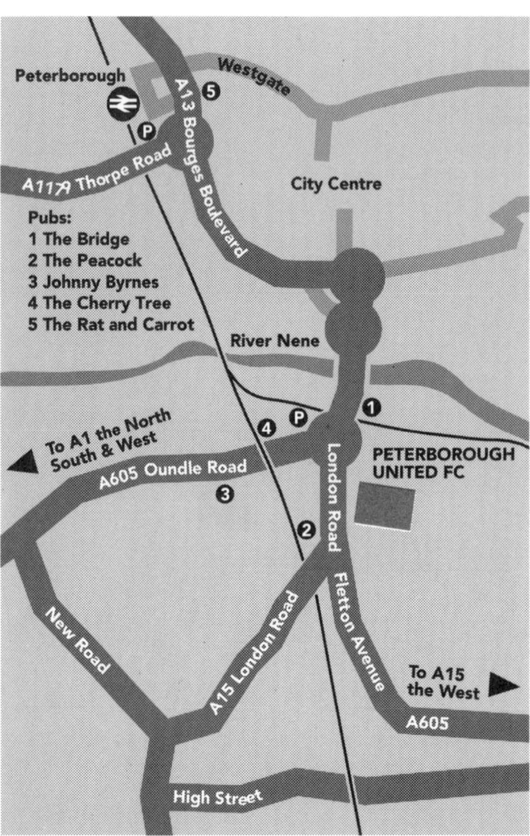

HOW TO GET THERE

BY CAR: From South (A1): There are roadworks on this route, which means some details may change, but it's well-signposted 'Football Car Parks': 2.1 miles after the Norman Cross junction, exit A1 (s/p Peterborough A1139, Northampton, Oundle A605). Follow signs to 'Peterborough A1139' onto the A1139 Fletton Parkway. Exit Fletton Parkway at junction 3 (s/p City Centre, Sleaford A15). At roundabout turn left (s/p City Centre A1260) onto the A1260 Nene Parkway. Take 1st exit after 0.2 miles (s/p Woodston Industry, Orton Longueville) and at roundabout turn right (s/p Woodston Industry) into Morley Way. At next roundabout after 0.4 miles, turn left (s/p Woodston, Orton Longueville) into Shrewsbury Avenue. At T-junction after 0.6 miles by Longueville Autos, turn right (n/s) into the A605 Oundle Road. The Football Car Park is on the LHS after 1.0 miles.

From North (A1): Exit A1 at signpost 'Leicester, Peterborough North A47'. Turn left at T-junction onto the A47. Exit A47 after 5.3 miles, at junction 15 (s/p City Centre, Orton A1260, Football Car Parks). At roundabout turn right (s/p City Centre) onto the A1260 Nene Parkway. Exit Nene Parkway after 1.1 miles (s/p Nene Park, Orton Longueville). At mini-roundabout by the 'Gordon Arms' turn left (n/s) onto the A605 Oundle Road. The Football Car Park is on the LHS after 1.5 miles.

From North A15 (junction with B1443): Straight across roundabout (s/p Peterborough, Wisbech A15). At roundabout after 0.7 miles, take 1st exit (s/p Peterborough (E) A15) onto the Glinton by-pass. At roundabouts 22, 21 and 20, follow signs to 'Wisbech A47', and at roundabout no. 8 take the 3rd exit (s/p City Centre, London A1) onto A1139. (*)After 3.5 miles, exit A1139 (s/p Whittlesey A603, Yaxley and Football Ground). From here follow signs for Football Ground to junction with A15 (opposite 'The Peacock'), and turn right into London Road.

From East (A47): Pass through the village of Eye following signs to Peterborough A47. At roundabout, turn left (s/p Peterborough (E) A1139, London A1) and at next roundabout turn right (s/p All Other Routes). At roundabout

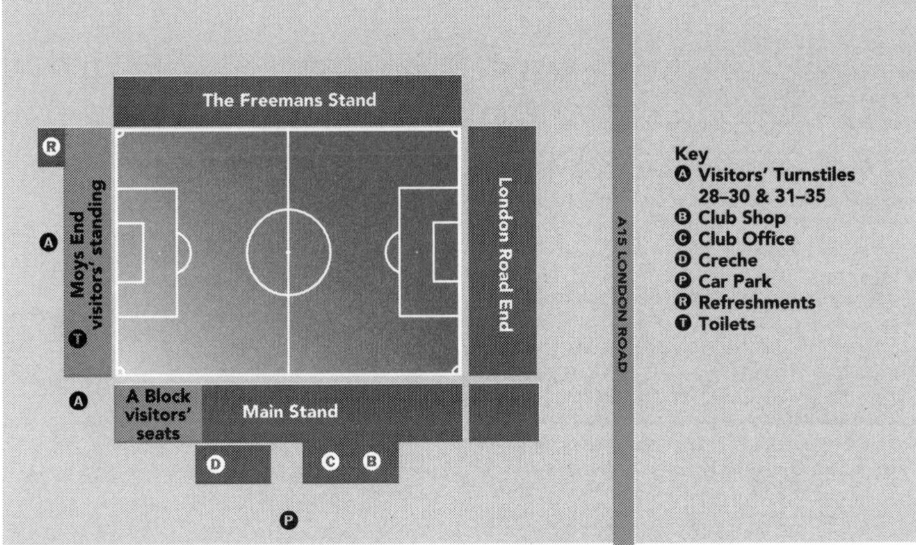

no. 8 take 2nd exit (s/p City Centre, London A1). Then as From North(*).

FROM RAILWAY STATION: (Peterborough): About 0.75 miles. *By taxi:* £2. *By bus:* No buses run from the station itself, but the bus station is just across Bourges Boulevard. Turn right out of station and then left, and take footbridge over main road to bus station (see below for bus details). *By foot:* Turn right out of station and into the long-stay car park. Under railway bridge, and there's a 'Serviceman' workshop on LHS. Immediately after the workshop walk up path or steps to the main road (Bourges Boulevard). Turn right, passing Evening Telegraph building on LHS and then Asda to the right. Turn right by 'Next' into pedestrian shopping area (Bridge Street) and straight on over river and mini-roundabout. Ground is on LHS.

Last Midweek Trains: Trains run to London at 21.47, 22.15 and 22.54, and to Newcastle at 22.44. Please double-check on (0345) 484 95.

BY BUS: From the bus station next to the Queensgate shopping centre, buses 13 and 14 run from Bay 3 along London Road every ten minutes up to 7 pm. From then on, it's the no. 53, also from Bay 3.

PARKING

There's parking at the ground, but it's usually full by 2 pm. The police advise visiting fans to park in the Fair Meadow carpark on Oundle Road. The entrance is easy to spot, right next to the 'Cherry Tree' pub. It's run by the council and costs £1.50. Some street parking is also available.

THE GROUND

How would you describe the ground, we asked a Peterborough fan. 'Half empty!', he replied. This is no reflection on the Peterborough support, simply that the Freeman's Stand, which opened in 1996 with 5,700 seats, has given the club a lot of spare capacity. The stand itself is – to quote the same fan – 'brilliant', but all the spare seats have affected the atmosphere. The rest of London Road is traditional, with spacious, covered terraces behind each goal. One of them, the Moys End, is allocated to away fans, plus seating in Block A of the Main Stand. The terracing is quite shallow, but just a couple of hundred travelling fans can create a right cacophony thanks to the cavernous roof.

Chairman Peter Boizot has plans to buy the shops near the ground to give the club frontage along the main London Road. If the sale goes ahead, the club will demolish the shops (including the takeaways, sob), build new club offices and a large club shop.

Total Capacity: 15,675. For away fans: Seating 875. Terrace 2,500.

Cost (98/99): Adults: Main Stand £9, concessions (juniors/OAPs) £3. Terrace £7, no concessions.

Disabled Facilities: Room for 30 supporters in the London Road End and the Freeman's Family Stand. *Disabled Toilet:* Nearby. *Cost:* £7 for disabled, £7 for helper. *Booking:* Essential. *Parking:* Limited parking available, please book. *For the Blind:* No special facilities.

Programme: £1.50.

Visitors Toilets: *Male:* 'A wall and a gutter, what more do you want?' said one fan. The facilities were basic, but the wall and the gutter looked clean enough!

Female: Two cubicles, which met the expectations of Leyton Orient fans. The bent coat hanger from 1995 had been replaced with a proper chain!

Food and Drink: Hungry supporters found the beef-and-onion pie (£1.50) 'very hot' and 'delicious'. The beefburger (£1.80) and cheeseburger (£2) were edible, but could have been warmer, and there were no onions. Another fan was more impressed with his cup ('doesn't burn your fingers!') than the tea (70p) inside it. The coffee and tomato soup (70p each) were good (20.9.97, 2.12.97).

PUB GUIDE

The Bridge (1) London Road (01733) 312 192
Trent Taverns. A spacious, newly-renovated football-friendly pub. Sandwiches. Pool table, TV. The landlord stresses that the pub is away fans only. On police advice, it sometimes shuts on big derby matchdays. Open: Sat. matchdays 11-3; from 6 for evening games.

The Peacock (2) London Road (01733) 66293
Free House (with John Smiths, Theakston XB, Banks). Traditional family pub with large lounge and public bar, almost opposite the ground. Doorman on match-days. Two pool tables, table football, TV. Open: all day.

Johnny Byrnes (3) 72 Oundle Road (01733) 348 563
Free House. 'Respectable' fans allowed into this very friendly pub, decorated with Irish road signs and paintings of racehorses. Families welcome. Sandwiches. Pool, darts, two TVs, beer garden. Open: all day.

The Cherry Tree (4) 9-11 Oundle Road (01733) 703 495
Carlsberg-Tetley. Small traditional pub with wooden flooring and open (gas) fires, recently refurbished. Hot meals and snacks. Pool, darts, table football, TV. Open: weekends all day; from 6 for midweek games.

The Rat and Carrot (5) 90 Westgate (01733) 561 288
Greene King. This traditional pub is a firm favourite of the local bikers, but it's very football-friendly on a matchday and great fun too. Full menu served 12-3, 5-8. Big-screen TV, pool, car park. Open: all day.

FOR FAMILIES:

The Botolph Arms 465 Oundle Road, Orton Longueville (for those coming from A1 South and North, it's on the LHS just after junction of the A1260 and Oundle Road) (01733) 234 170
Samuel Smiths. Smart pub/restaurant in 150-year-old building, which has retained a traditional feel. Bar menu and à-la-carte restaurant. Small family room with TV, outdoor play area. Open: all day.

FOOD GUIDE

The mobile burger stall on the corner of the ground's car park is still a matchday favourite: the hot dog (£1.50) was delicious. Outside the ground on the London Road

'I haven't kidnapped her for the club's commercial interest. I'm trying to lure David Beckham!'

is a row of shops including the 'Turkish Delight' kebab shop, 'Gino's Dial-a-Pizza', the 'Lucky House' Chinese takeaway and 'Foley's Fish and Chips'. Opposite is a KFC. Near the 'Johnny Byrne's' pub are two takeaways: 'Woodston Fish and Chips' and 'Ming Gardens'.

LOCAL MEDIA

Local Radio: BBC Radio Cambridgeshire 95.7 FM, 1026 MW.

Radio Phone-Ins: Radio Cambridgeshire, Saturdays 5.30-6pm, call (01223) 252 000.

Saturday Sports Paper: None.

MISCELLANEOUS

Safety Factor: London Road is generally a safe ground to visit, and the police have a good reputation. Isolated trouble sometimes flares when local teams such as Cambridge, Lincoln and Colchester are in town. Brighton and Hull caused problems in season 97/98.

Rivals: For younger fans, it's Cambridge United at their ground the Shabby Stadium. Older fans dislike Northampton Town, and from the days of dizzier league positions Leicester City!

Fanzine: None.

Unofficial Websites: 'Posh Out West':
http://freespace.virgin.net/mickbratley/POW/posh.htm
http://freespace.virgin.net/s.brewer/football001.htm
http://www.geocities.com/Colosseum/Loge/4439/

Tourist Information: (01733) 452 336.

Plymouth Argyle

Home Park

Address: Home Park Stadium, Plymouth, PL2 3DQ
Telephone: Club (01752) 562 561
Pilgrim Shop (01752) 558 292
Pilgrimline (0839) 442 270

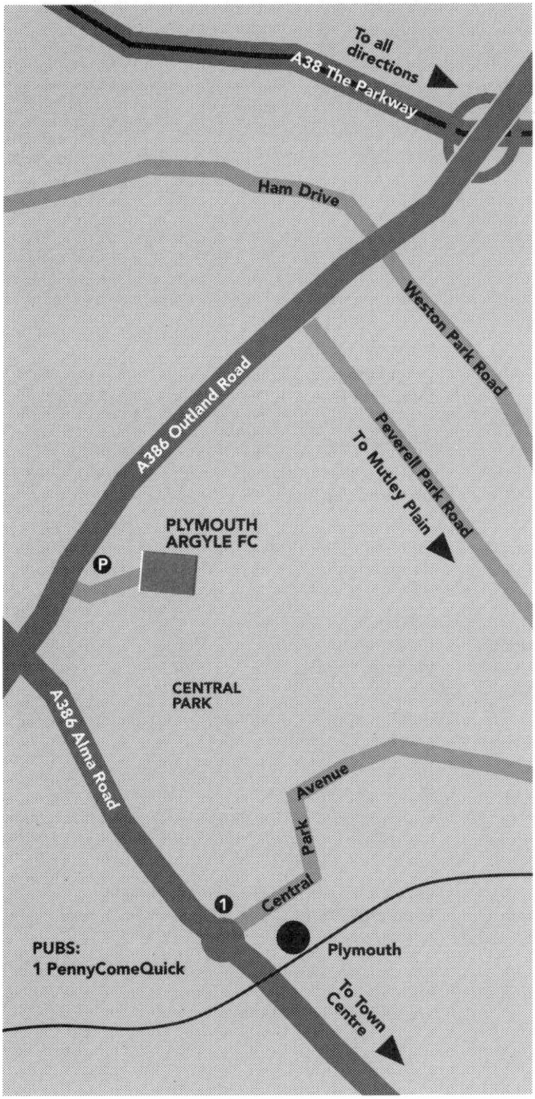

To all directions
A38 The Parkway
Ham Drive
Weston Park Road
A386 Outland Road
Peverell Park Road
To Mutley Plain
PLYMOUTH ARGYLE FC
CENTRAL PARK
A386 Alma Road
Avenue
Park
Central
Plymouth
To Town Centre
PUBS:
1 PennyComeQuick

Saturday morning, 5 am, and on comes the radio alarm. Yep, it's either Plymouth or Carlisle away! Yet the great thing about both journeys is that the grounds are dead easy to find – in Plymouth's case, a few minutes' drive from the main A38 through town. Parking's a synch too, though take a good book for the wait to get out after the match. The big downside of the Plymouth trip is that nearby pubs – such as they are – have decided on an 'away-fan-free zone' which means a bit of a slog to the nearest watering hole. And of course, the seafront is nearly a mile away. Argyle had a difficult time, both on and off the pitch, in season 97/98 but they must be doing something right ... the seagulls perched on the Mayflower Stand always seem to be facing the field of play!

HOW TO GET THERE

BY CAR (From All Directions): Keep on the A38 passing 'Plymouth: Spirit of Discovery' sign. At the Marsh Mills junction keep straight on, continuing on the A38 (s/p A38 West, also Home Park, Plymouth Argyle, Cornwall, Liskeard A38). After a further 2.4 miles exit A38 at the Manadon junction (s/p Home Park, Plymouth Argyle, Manadon, Tavistock, City Centre A386). At roundabout take 2nd exit (s/p City Centre A386, Torpoint A374, also Home Park) onto Outland Road A386. The ground and car parking are on the LHS after 1.1 miles.

FROM RAILWAY STATION (Plymouth): About 0.8 miles, partly uphill. *By taxi:* £3.80 plus 10p per person. *By bus:* All the buses listed below run past the railway station. *By foot:* Turn right out of station, and right again (s/p Home Park, Plymouth Argyle) downhill towards and then under the railway bridge painted with an ivy design. At roundabout go straight on (s/p Saltash A388) into Alma Road passing the PennyComeQuick pub on the RHS. After 0.3 miles turn right (s/p Plymouth Argyle) through Central Park – the ground is visible from here. *Last Midweek Trains:* The only choice is the overnight sleeper.

BY BUS: The Plymouth City buses nos. 29, 43 and 43B run from the city centre to the Mile House bus depot (on the corner of Outland Road and Alma Road). Western National buses

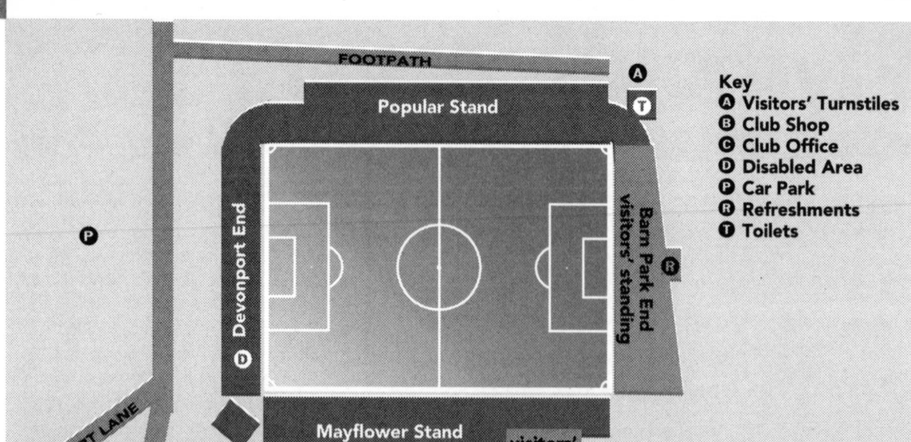

nos. 1, 2, 13, 14 and 81 run from Royal Parade in the city centre to the Mile House depot, while the no. 86 bus to Tavistock runs from the Bretonside bus station along Outland Road, passing the ground.

PARKING

There's a 900-space free car park at the ground. Cars are parked nose-to-tail so only the car at the front of the queue gets to leave early. For the rest, expect up to a 20 minute wait. Alternatively, park at the Plymouth Sports Club, signposted left just before the ground, opposite the Esso station. It charges £1 (for charity) and promises a quicker getaway.

THE GROUND

Home Park remains one of the largest traditional football grounds in the English leagues, with old-style floodlights, the wonderful Leitch-designed Mayflower Stand, a hotch-potch of other stands, open and covered terraces and prehistoric toilets! All super stuff for the lovers of football history, but a headache for Argyle which has to pay for the endless repair work.

Two years ago Argyle announced gradiose plans for a 23,000-seater stadium alongside the existing ground in Central Park. At the time of writing, all the plans were on hold, as Chairman Dan McCauley put the club – which has debts of £2.6 million – up for sale.

In the midst of all this, away fans continue to be housed on the large, open Barn Park Terrace where the loos are primitive and the pasties are luscious. The wonderful warning signs 'Ten Steps Start Here' remain, as does fencing at the front of the terrace. However, the terrace is rarely full enough for anyone's view to be obstructed. Seating is also available for visitors in the Mayflower Stand.

Total Capacity: 19,600. For away fans: Seating (Mayflower Stand) 180. Main Entrance Turnstiles. Terrace (Barn Park End) 2,640. Turnstiles 35-38.

Cost: (98/99): Seating: Adult £12-£13, concessions £10-£11. Terrace: Adult £7.50-£8.50. No concessions.

Disabled Facilities: Places available in the Devonport End. *Disabled Toilet:* Nearby. *Cost:* Free for disabled, helper £7.50-£8.50. *Booking:* Essential, please call Cath Watkins at the club. *Parking:* Available, please book. *For the Blind:* 12 places available in the Grandstand with hospital radio commentary.

Programme: £1.50.

Visitors' Toilets: *Male:* 'Quite clean for walls', said one fan. Er, that's it folks, four walls, painted in black and white. In reply to the question: 'Was there anything unusual in the gents?' another fan said: 'Yes, toilet paper!' *Female:* Whey-hey, those ancient wooden loo seats have gone, replaced by yer standard pea-green coloured plastic. No more splinters in painful places. The notice 'Warning: Please Pull Chains Carefully' caused some amusement ('pull the other one, haha') because there weren't any chains – just bits of string!

Food and Drink: The 'local pasties' (£1.25) were, said one happy fan 'excellent as always – for marks out of ten, I'd give it 15', to which his mate promptly replied 'I thought that was the number you'd eaten'. A York fan simply described his pasty as 'superb'. The hot dog (£1) actually was hot, with lots of onions, and the tea (60p) was excellent (15.11.97, 14.2.98).

PUB GUIDE

The PennyComeQuick (1) Central Park Avenue (on the PennyComeQuick roundabout) (01752) 661 412 Ansells (with Bass and Dartmoor). Welcoming and very football-friendly pub about ten minutes' walk from the ground. Excellent pasties (£1). Pool, darts, big screen TV. Open: all day.

The following pub is in Mutley Plain. For directions on how to get there, see under Food Guide below:

The Hyde Park 88 Mutley Plain (01752) 662 302 Ansells (with Tetley, Dartmoor real ales). Large traditional pub, popular and sports-friendly. Large selection of bar meals served 12-2. Pool, 2 TVs including big-screen. Open: all day.

The following pub is in Stoke village, about one mile from Home Park. For directions on how to get there, see under Food Guide below:

The Stoke Inn 43 Devonport Road (01752) 561 084 Bass. Cosy, one-roomed 'Community Pub', described by the landlord as 'the best in the village'. Darts, TV (not Sky), beer garden. Open: all day Friday-Sunday; midweek 11-3, 7-11.

FOR FAMILIES:

The Marsh Mills Beefeater and Travel Inn

300 Plymouth Road, on the Marsh Mills junction, by the A38 (01752) 600660. Whitbread (with selection of cask ales). Large, smart Beefeater pub/restaurant with the usual extensive menus. Disabled facilities. Open all day.

FOOD GUIDE

The only food available near the ground is from the mobile burger bars. The Pennycomequick pub does a good pasty, but otherwise supporters have to travel about a mile from the ground. Try the following:

a. Mutley Plain: It's a shopping street with a number of pubs, including the Hyde Park listed above, and a good choice of takeaways and restaurants, including Perfect and Domino's Pizza, a KFC, fish and chips and a bakery. To get there: Exit the A38 as in the road directions above, but take the 1st exit at the roundabout (s/p Mutley B3250), up past the Shell garage. Go straight on, following signs to the City Centre for 1.2 miles, until the Hyde Park pub appears on the RHS. Parking is signposted.

b. Stoke Village, a Plymouth suburb a short drive from Home Park. The 'Stoke 'n Chips' takeaway near the Pear Tree pub is recommended by the locals, while 'Jumbo's Amusements Cafe' round the corner has an all day breakfast for £2.95.

To get there: Continue along Outland Road, passing Home Park on the LHS. At the two sets of lights after 0.4 miles keep in the left-hand lanes following signs to Torpoint A374 into Milehouse Road. Stoke Village is a further 0.5 miles along this road.

LOCAL MEDIA

Local Radio: BC Radio Devon 103.4 FM, 855 MW; Plymouth Sound 1152 MW.

Radio Phone-ins: None.

Saturday Sports Paper: None.

MISCELLANEOUS

If visiting fans think the occasional early start to an away game is a real drag, spare a thought for the Cornwall-based Argyle supporters. It's a case of 'anything you can do, we got up earlier' ... the Cornish supporters' coach left Penzance at 3 am for the Carlisle trip. Older supporters from the pre-motorway era top that with tales of leaving Cornwall at 5 pm on the Friday, overnighting in Plymouth, and not getting home until 2 pm on the Sunday afternoon. 'You got used to it', said one fan nonchalantly.

Safety Factor: Plymouth Argyle does unfortunately have a small hooligan following, which appears on derby days and for other high profile matches.

Rivals: Exeter City. 'Don't even think about wearing a red coat to a Plymouth game', said one local.

Fanzines: 'Rub of the Greens', 14 Craven Way, Bristol, BS15 5DR; 'Hoof', 32 Trevorth Road, Falmouth, Cornwall, TR11 2JS.

Unofficial Websites:

'Green Army': http://www.argyle.org.uk/

Tourist Information: (01752) 264 849.

P

Portsmouth

Fratton Park

Address: Fratton Park, Frogmore Road, Portsmouth PO4 8RA
Telephone:
Main Office (01705) 731 204
Box Office (01705) 618 777/750 825
Pompey Socccer Line (0891) 121 182
Official Website: http://www.pompeyfc.co.uk

Portsmouth is famous for its naval dockyards. But the biggest vessels most visiting fans see are the little yachts moored either side of the A2030! Fratton Park is well to the east of the docks, in a residential part of Southsea, and there are some interesting houses to look out for. Near Christmas, the garden of a terraced home on Velder Avenue had a snowman, fairy lights in the trees and a huge Santa's sleigh, complete with reindeer, on top of the porch. And a sunny scene with palm trees has been painted onto one of the homes backing onto the away end! As becomes a navy town, Portsmouth has a host of pubs, but finding a takeaway is not so easy. Parking is mostly on-street, so arrive early to reserve the best places.

HOW TO GET THERE

BY CAR: From North: Continue on A3(M) to 'end of motorway' signs (following s/p Portsmouth, Southampton M27). The road bends to the right (otherwise it would fall into the sea) and joins the A27. Exit A27 after 0.7 miles (s/p Southsea A2030). At roundabout turn left (s/p Milton, Eastney, Southsea) onto the A2030. (*)Straight on for 3.0 miles to roundabout by ground - the floodlights are clearly visible along the route.
From West: Continue to end of M27, and take next exit (s/p Southsea A2030). At roundabout turn right (3rd exit, s/p Milton, Eastney, Southsea) onto the A2030. Then as from North(*).
From East: Continue on A27 past junction with A3(M). Take next exit (s/p Southsea A2030). At roundabout turn left (s/p Milton, Eastney, Southsea) onto the A2030. Then as from North(*).
FROM RAILWAY STATION (Fratton): 0.6 miles. *By taxi:* £1.80-£2. *By bus:* Nos. 13 and 18 run along Goldsmith Avenue and are so regular the bus company jokes 'we're sick of the sight of them!' *By foot:* Walk up

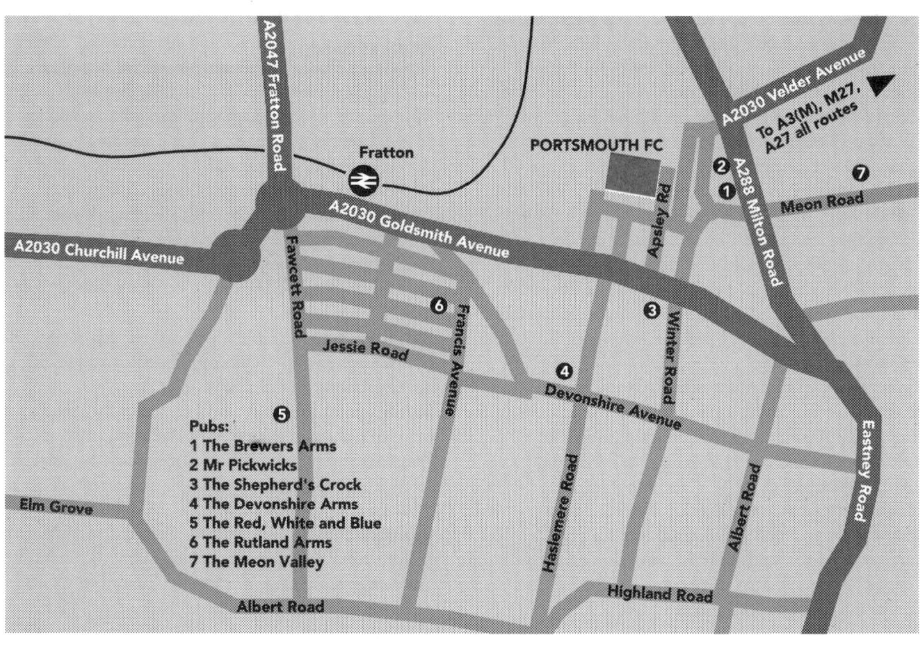

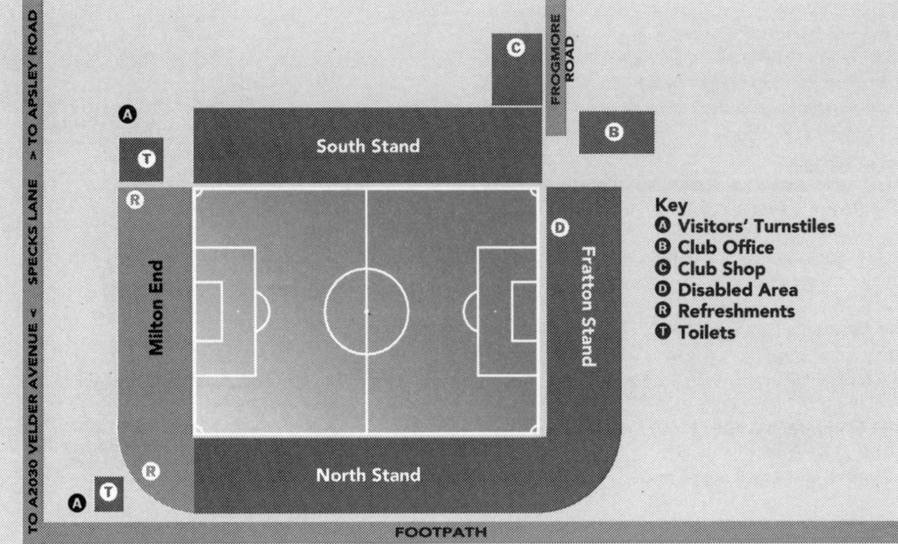

to footbridge and turn left. At main road (opposite 'The Railway Café') turn left. After 0.5 miles take 3rd residential road on left (Apsley Road), straight across crossroads to away turnstiles.

Last Midweek Trains: The last and only train to Waterloo after a midweek game is at 22.26. Please double check on (0345) 484 950.

BY BUS: See above.

PARKING:

There's a car park (£2.50) off Goldsmith Avenue, but apart from that it's street parking for all. Steer clear of the roads directly around the ground as they are sprinkled with no waiting cones. Fans coming in on the A2030 could park up en route. Try the roads around the 'Good Companion' pub, such as Warren Avenue or Moorings Way. To the south of the ground, try Haslemere Road or head down Goldsmith Avenue towards the railway station and park on the roads on the LHS. The roads are narrow but there are no parking restrictions.

THE GROUND

Fratton Park has suffered perhaps more than any ground in the post-Taylor Report era. When plans for a ground move fell through in 1995, the club faced the embarrassment of having to fence off acres of terracing or add in temporary seating. Pride was salvaged in October 1997 with the opening of the new 4,600-seater Fratton Stand. The colours in the seating show Pompey legend Jimmy Dickinson, and most noise, including the never-ending 'Play Up Pompey', rings out from this stand. Away fans are opposite, on a bank of temporary, uncovered seating at the Milton End, shivering in the wind and drizzle swirling off the English Channel. Great stuff. The facilities however, have had an overhaul, and the pies aren't bad! Portsmouth FC has plans to roof the Milton End, and to add extra seating elsewhere, but no work is likely until the ownership of the club is resolved.

Total Capacity: 19,214. For away fans: Milton End (uncovered seating) from 1,175 to 3,121.

Cost (98/99): Adults £12, concessions £6.

Disabled Facilities: Space for up to five visiting supporters at pitch level in the new Fratton Stand. Entrance via Frogmore Road. *Disabled Toilet:* In the SW corner nearby. Two more are planned when the area at the back of the stand is completed. *Cost:* £12 for joint ticket for disabled and helper. *Booking:* Required – contact Mr Watson at the club. *Parking:* None available. *For the Blind:* No special facilities, but the club will try to find seating near the commentary box. Contact Mr Watson at the club for details.

Programme: £2.

Visitors' Toilets: *Male:* 'It's not just a wall any more,' said one surprised fan. 'It's got porcelain facilities, two cubicles and it's quite clean!' *Female:* A recent lick of paint in the obligatory blue and white and a new wooden ceiling has cheered the loos up no end. Fans also admired the traffic cone. Yes, the traffic cone! No, we don't know why it was there.

Food and Drink: Burgers were a popular choice at £2, but the hot dog (£2) was not: 'It's horrible. I'm only eating it because I'm hungry,' said a Charlton fan. The pies (£1.50) and pasties (£1.50) were the best value.

'Quite a nice pie, that,' said one satisfied customer. You know that guy on the TV advertising wood-seal, which 'does exactly what it says on the tin.' Well, that tin contains the Portsmouth tea (80p). Nice and strong it is, protecting fans against that cutting sea air! (6.12.97, 20.12.97 and 4.4.98)

PUB GUIDE

The Brewers Arms (1) 170 Milton Road (01705) 785 335.
Gales. A pub with loads of character and close to the away turnstiles to-boot, so it's very popular. Sandwiches. Pool table, darts, beer garden. Open: 11-3, 6-11.
Mr Pickwicks (2) Milton Road (01705) 833600
Free House. Large football-friendly pub with bicycles on the ceiling! Pub food served12-2.30. Pool table, TV. Families welcome. Open: 11-3, 6-11.
The Shepherd's Crook (3) 107 Goldsmith Avenue (01705) 825 906
Whitbread. A real football pub this, with lots of momentoes on the walls. Sandwiches. Pool table, darts, big screen TV. Open: all day.
The Devonshire Arms (4) 29 Devonshire Avenue (01705) 825 190
Whitbread. Sports-friendly pub frequented, so the story goes, by a mischievous ghost! Sandwiches. Big screen TV. Open: all day.
Also recommended: **The Red, White and Blue (5),** at 150 Fawcett Road, a wonderful Gales pub; **The Rutland Arms (6)** 205 Francis Avenue (01705) 737 886, a traditional Whitbread pub with an amazing array of bric-a-brac; **The Meon Valley (7)** at 77 Meon Road, a locals Whitbread pub with pool table and TV.
FOR FAMILIES:
The Good Companion 2 Eastern Road, Milton (01705) 825 206
Whitbread (with Flowers and guests). Large smart pub, with separate children's play area. Full restaurant menu served Monday-Saturday 11-9.30, Sundays 12-10.30. Disabled facilities. Pool table, darts. Open: all day.

FOOD GUIDE

The nearest takeaway is the aptly named 'Fish and Chips' on Winter Road, near the junction with Liss Road. It has cod, haddock or plaice from £1.90, black pudding (55p) and 'pea fritters' (40p). Nearby is 'Butlers Bakery', which has pasties, sausage rolls and pies, which can be heated up. There's also a newsagents and a little supermarket. At the junction of Priory Crescent and Milton Road is a 'Happy Shopper' with pre-packed pies and sausage rolls. 'The Railway Café'/takeaway, opposite the station on Goldsmith Avenue, has a vegetarian breakfast at £2.50, as well as the usual carnivore fry-ups. Those with transport and a map could seek out Eastney Road and Albert Road, which have a wider selection of pubs and takeaways.

'A word of advice – don't upset the mascot!'

LOCAL MEDIA

Radio: BBC Radio Solent 96.1 FM, 999 MW; Ocean FM 96.7, 97.5; Capital Gold 1170 AM.
Radio Phone-ins: Radio Solent, Saturday pre-match 1.10-2.30, call (01703) 631 316; Capital Gold, Saturdays 2-6.30, midweek 7-10 (7-8 if no match), call (0845) 35 60 70 80.
Saturday Sports Paper: *The Sports Echo* produces a Saturday pink.

MISCELLANEOUS

The 'FFG' is proud to announce that we have the answer to the question that's been on everybody's lips for months. Just what happened to that eight-foot tall blow-up model of El-Tel? It's up for sale, with the proceeds, said one fan tongue-in-cheek, going to the players' wage fund!
Safety Factor: The most highly publicised incident at Fratton Park in season 97/98 was the away fan's attack on a linesman. A full report was commissioned and the club was not found at fault.
Rivals: Southampton, and it's reciprocated too.
Fanzines: 'Blue and Wight', 38 Rowen Court, Southsea, PO4 8UZ; 'January 3, 88', PO Box 63, Gosport, Hants PO12 3QR; 'Pisces', PO Box 88, Southsea, Hants, PO5 3PH; 'True Blue' (Portsmouth Supporters Club Magazine), Victory Business Centre, Victory House, Somers Road North, Portsmouth, Hampshire, PO1 1PJ.
Unofficial Websites:
http://www.mech.port.ac.uk/staffp/pb/pfc.html
http://homepages.newnet.co.uk/pompey
Tourist Information: (01705) 826 722.

Port Vale

Vale Park

Address: Vale Park, Hamil Road, Burslem, Stoke-on-Trent ST6 1AW
Telephone: Club (01782) 814 134
Club Shop (01782) 833 545
ClubCall (0891) 121 636
Official Website: http://www.port-vale.co.uk/

'Vale Park' has been aptly named. True, the only 'vale' is a little valley behind the nearby supermarket. But parks, both the grassy and tarmaced variety, are abundant. Opposite Port Vale's ground is Burslem Park, with its formal gardens, and on the other side are the open playing fields of Bycars Park. The club also has a large car park, as does the supermarket, both of which are available to visiting fans. The ground's only a five minute walk from Burslem town centre, but supporters don't even have to stagger that far for a friendly pub, an excellent chippy and a shop selling the local speciality, oatcakes.

HOW TO GET THERE

BY CAR: The police and the club direct away fans on the following route. On the map it's clearly not the shortest route, but it's well signposted and avoids the traffic congestion in Burslem.

From South: Exit M6 at junction 15 (s/p Stoke-on-Trent, Newcastle A500). At roundabout follow signs to 'Stoke-on-Trent A500, Stone A34' onto the A500 dual carriageway. At roundabout after 2.9 miles, and at the next roundabout after a further 0.5 miles, go straight on (s/p M6 North, Nantwich A500). After a further 0.9 miles exit A500 (s/p Newcastle-under-Lyme, City Centre, Leek A53). At roundabout turn right (s/p Leek A53, Stoke-on-Trent) into Etruria Way. (*)Where the road divides after 0.4 miles keep right (s/p Leek A53, Warrington A50, Port Vale FC) over flyover. From here, it's well signposted 'Port Vale FC' to the ground, a distance of 3.8 miles.

From North: Exit M6 at junction 16 (s/p Newcastle-under-Lyme, Stoke-on-Trent North). At roundabout turn left (s/p Newcastle-under-Lyme, Stoke-on-Trent A500), onto the A500. Exit A500 after 7.0 miles at signpost 'Leek A53, Stoke-on-Trent', into Etruria Way. Then as From South(*).

FROM RAILWAY STATION:

a) Stoke: 3.0 miles. *By taxi:* £5-£6. *By bus:* No. 24 runs to Burslem.

b) Longport: 1.3 miles. *By foot:* Come straight out of the station, passing the 'Railway Inn' on LHS. At T-junction turn left, passing between the 'Pack Horse' and the 'Duke of Bridgewater', and over the bridge. At roundabout turn right (s/p City Centre A50, Burslem)

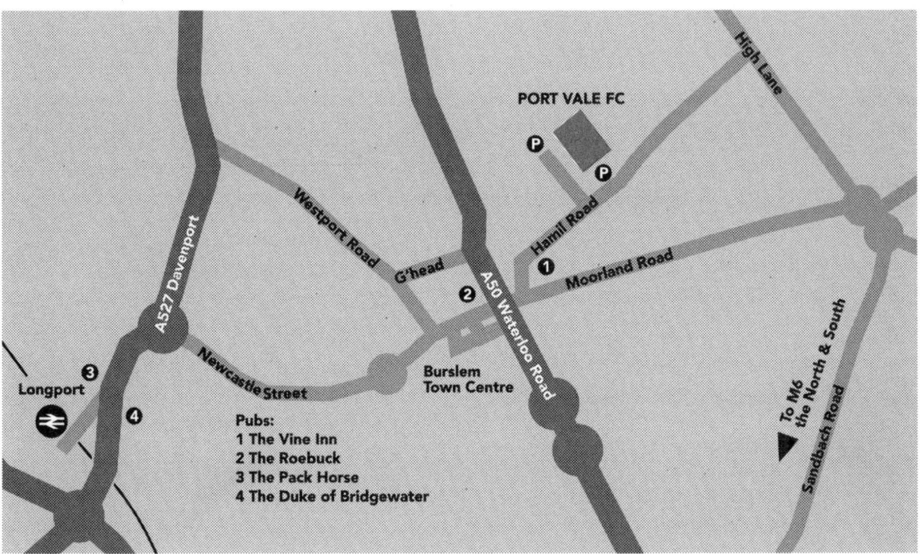

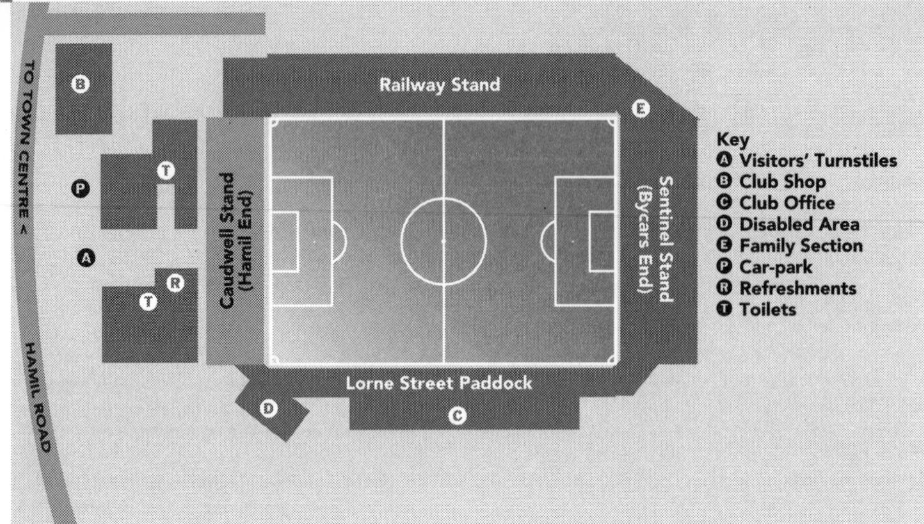

into Newcastle Street. At mini-roundabout by Kwik Save go straight on (s/p Warrington A50, Congleton A527). Go straight on through two sets of lights (s/p Leek A53, Smallthorne) passing the 'Post Office Vaults' on the RHS. After a few hundred yards, just past pedestrian lights, turn left into Hamil Road, passing 'The Vine Inn' on the RHS. Ground is on LHS, after 0.2 miles.
Last Midweek Trains: The last train from Longport to Stoke leaves at 21.41, arriving 21.47. From Stoke, there are no trains to London after an evening game. However, the 21.45 to Stockport has onward connections to Nottingham, Derby, Doncaster and Newcastle. The only later train is the 23.07 to Stafford and Manchester. Please double-check on (0345) 484 950.
BY BUS: As well as the no. 24 listed above, 'PMT' buses nos. 22, 27 and 29 run from the top of Piccadilly in Hanley to Burslem town centre.

PARKING

The car park at the ground costs £4, but expect gridlock after the game. The supermarket next door offers parking for £2, refundable against purchases at the store ... one of those roast chickens, for example (see 'Food Guide'). The best area for street parking is to the north, in the sidestreets off Hamil Road and High Lane.

THE GROUND

Three sides of Vale Park have been covered and seated since 1995, which left just the Lorne Street side as open terracing, with a dinky 300 seater executive stand on top. No more! Work has already begun to build a new 5,000-seater Lorne Street Stand, complete with 50 executive boxes and a restaurant. The stand should be complete by the beginning of 1999. Away fans in the Hamil End are unaffected by the building work. The view from most seats is good, though there are four slender posts. All the facilities were rebuilt in 1995, with a spacious covered concourse and some of the best loos in the Nationwide!
Total Capacity: 17,656 (with closure of the 4,700 Lorne Street Terrace). For away fans (Hamil End) 4,550. Turnstiles 1-8. Visiting families are welcome in the Family Enclosure. Turnstiles 21-24.
Cost (98/99): Adults £15, concessions (juniors/OAPs) £11.
Disabled Facilities: The disabled area between the Lorne Street Paddock and the Hamil End remains open until January 1999, when the disabled facilities are being moved to the new Lorne Street Stand. *Cost:* £5 for disabled, £6 for helper. *Booking:* Well in advance. *Parking:* Available. *For the Blind:* Headsets in the Specialist Stand with hospital radio commentary.
Programme: £1.80.
Visitors Toilets': *Male:* Top rate facilities here. Stockport fans were amazed to find loo rolls in the cubicles, even at half-time. We asked if there was 'anything unusual', and the answer came back: 'No graffiti!' *Female:* Probably the best in town!
Food and Drink: The filling of the meat-and-potato pie (£1.50) was a white mush with flecks of black pepper, but even so it was warm and reasonably tasty. A Sunderland fan said of the hot dog (£1.60): 'Dog good, buns dry!' The coffee (60p) was like 'white hot water' (25.8.97, 9.9.97).

PUB GUIDE

The Vine Inn (1) Hamil Road (01782) 813 983
Free House (with 4 guest ales). Small, friendly pub just round the corner from the ground. Doormen allow in 'respectable' supporters. Sandwiches. TV, darts. Open: all day Friday/Saturday; from 6 pm for midweek games.

The Roebuck (2) Wedgwood Place, Burslem (01782) 837 568
Scottish and Newcastle. Traditional, immensely popular town centre pub. Snacks and full meals available all day. Pool, darts, TV. Doormen on matchdays. Open: Saturdays 12-2.30, 7-11; from 5 pm for midweek games.

FOR FAMILIES:

The Pack Horse (3) Station Street, Longport (01782) 577 322
Pub Estates (with seven guest ales). Very smart pub, recently refurbished. Full menu served 12-2, 7-10. Beer garden, function room. Open: 11-4, 7-11.

The Duke of Bridgewater (4) 1 Station Street, Longport (01782) 811 290
Enterprise Inns (with Bass and Worthington). Pub in an 18th-century building, with a beer garden by the canal. Bar snacks served all day. Pool, TV. Open: all day.

FOOD GUIDE

Right by Vale Park is the 'Discount Giant' supermarket, which offers various pies and pasties at 49p, spring rolls, and whole roast chickens! To the east of the ground on Hamil Road, is the 'Hamil Oatcakes Snacks', which serves the local speciality, oat pancakes with savoury fillings, such as cheese (52p) or bacon and egg (85p). On nearby May Street is the highly recommended 'May Street Chippy' with chilli and chips at £1.98 and pies at 86p. On Moorland Road to the west of the ground, opposite 'The Vine', is the 'What's Cooking' café, with a tasty all-day breakfast for £1.75. In the town centre, there's a KFC and, opposite, 'Burslem Kebab House'. Queen Street has a good selection: 'O'Reilly's Sandwich Emporium'; the 'Javz Eastern Grill', with a variety of takeaways including pizzas at £4; and 'Wright's Pies', offering pies, peas and gravy for a tasty £1.45, as well as tea (30p) and coffee (35p). On Sandbach Road on the main road route to Vale Park (see above), there's the 'Captain Kook's' traditional fish and chip restaurant, with a huge range of good-value meals and snacks.

LOCAL MEDIA

Local Radio: BBC Radio Stoke 94.6 and 104.1 FM; Signal Radio 102.6 FM.
Radio Phone-ins: BBC Radio Stoke 'Praise or Grumble', Saturdays 5-6 pm, call (01782) 208 008.
Saturday Sports Paper: The 'Green 'Un', produced by the *Evening Sentinel*, available from about 6 pm.

Potteries road rage.

MISCELLANEOUS

Safety Factor: No major trouble in season 97/98, though Manchester City fans were 'lively'.
Rivals: Vale fans watched the descent of Stoke City into the Second Division with undisguised glee.
Fanzines: 'Vale Park Beano', PO Box 485, Kidsgrove, Stoke-on-Trent, Staffordshire, ST7 3BZ.
Unofficial Websites:
'ValeWeb':
http://web.dcs.hull.ac.uk/people/pjp/PortVale/PortVale.html
'Only One Vale Fan in Bristol':
http://ourworld.compuserve.com/homepages/rob_fielding/frame.htm
Tourist Information: (01782) 284 600.

P

Preston North End

Deepdale

Address: Deepdale, Sir Tom Finney Way, Preston PR1 6RU
Telephone: Main Office (01772) 902 020
Ticket Office (01772) 902 000
ClubCall (0891) 660 220
Official Website: http://www.prestonnorthend.co.uk

The team may be in the Second Division, but two sides of Deepdale have been promoted into the Premier League! The two new stands, named after the legendary players Tom Finney and Bill Shankly, rise high above the houses and parks of the north Preston suburbs. Perhaps the club could put some flashing lights on those pinnacles of white steelwork, to guide in visiting fans at night! Preston is the county town of Lancashire, and as such is well served by road and rail links. However the ground is a trek from the railway station. The good news is that the local pubs are welcoming and the ultra-lazy can down a pint in the Legends bar right behind the Tom Finney Stand. Parking is usually no problem, as there are loads of sidestreets.

HOW TO GET THERE

BY CAR: From North, South and East: Exit M6 at junction 31. At roundabout take 1st exit (s/p Preston A59) onto the A59. At mini-roundabout after 1.0 miles, by the Hesketh Arms, take 2nd exit (s/p Ring Road, Blackpool A583, Football Ground), onto the Blackpool Road A5085. Straight on for 1.2 miles, then filter left before lights (s/p Town Centre, Football Ground) into Deepdale Road. Ground is on LHS.
From West: Exit M55 at junction 1 (s/p Preston, Garstang) and at roundabout turn right (s/p Preston A6) onto the A6 Garstang Road. Straight on for 2.0 miles through two sets of traffic lights, signposted 'Town Centre', then 'Blackburn, Clitheroe, M6 North', to a 3rd set of lights. Here, turn left (s/p Ring Road, Blackburn, Clitheroe A59, Deepdale Retail Park) onto Blackpool Road. At next lights after 0.7 miles, turn right (s/p Chorley A6) onto Deepdale Road. Ground is on LHS.
FROM RAILWAY STATION (Preston): About 1.6 miles. *By taxi:* £2.70. *By bus:* All buses at the railway station go to the bus station. From there, bus nos. 5, 6 and 19 run along Deepdale Road. The no. 19 has the most frequent service. *By foot:* Come out of station and turn left in front of the Fishergate Centre, passing 'The Railway' pub. Turn right at T-junction. The main road bends to the left and becomes Corporation Street ... don't go along it. Instead continue straight on into Fishergate, which after 0.75 miles becomes Church Street. At junction with A6, go straight on into the continuation of Church Street. Where road divides keep left into Deepdale Road. Ground is on RHS after 0.75 miles.
Last Midweek Trains: No trains run to either Nottingham or London after a midweek match. However, there's a train to Manchester Oxford Road at 22.01, and to Manchester Piccadilly at

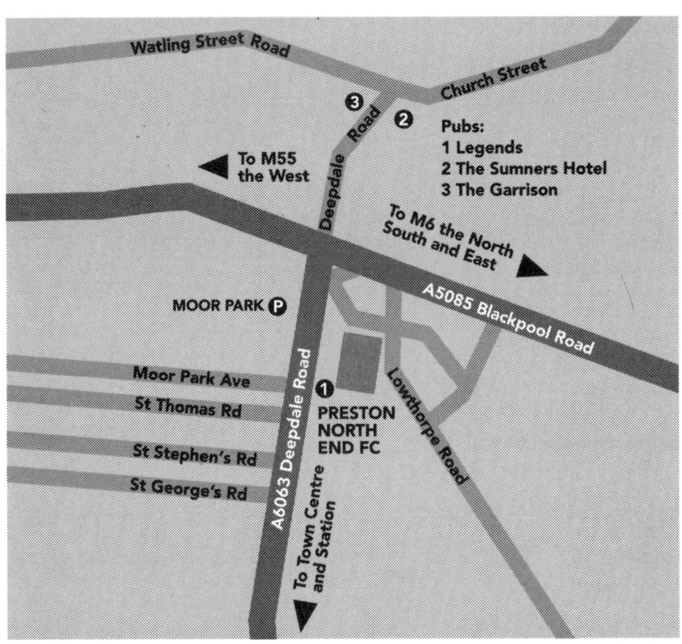

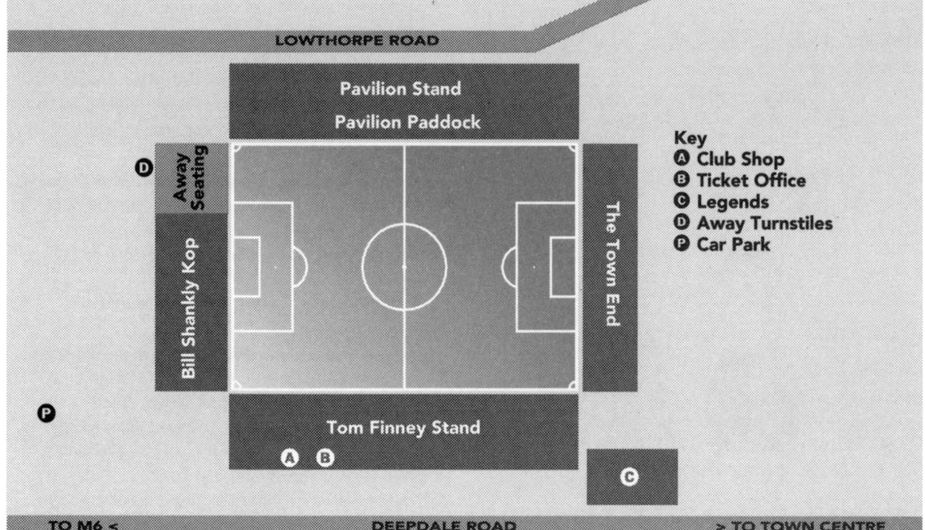

22.23, from where there's a connecting train to Sheffield (00.19). The last Leeds train is at 21.23. Please double-check on (0345) 484 950.

BY BUS: See above.

PARKING

The club hopes to provide some parking for visiting fans behind the new Bill Shankly Stand. Alternatively, local schools such as the ones in Moor Park Avenue and St Stephen's Road, off Deepdale Road, offer safe parking for £2. There's plenty of street parking around the ground, although steer clear of Lowthorpe Road, Hollins Road, Parkside and St Stephen's Road, which are emergency access routes. Cars parked in these roads will be towed away.

THE GROUND

For decades Deepdale was a huge traditional northern ground, steeped in footballing history, with some really ancient silverware (FA Cup 1889 and 1938, League Champions 1889 and 1890) gracing the trophy cabinet. With massive financial backing from local company Baxi, the club has been taken off the shelf and given a good dusting! The ancient West Stand was demolished in 1996, replaced by the 8,000-seater Tom Finney Stand, recognised nationwide for the depiction of the great man's face in the seating. Next to go was the Kop, a terrace since 1921. That's now the 6,000-seater Bill Shankly Kop, named after the man who played more than 300 matches for North End, and went on, of course, to become one of Liverpool's most successful managers. Away fans are being allocated part of this new stand, to make up perhaps for the grotty conditions they've endured for the last four years or so! Future development plans include the replacement of the Pavilion Stand and Paddock with a new 8,000-seater stand, but that work will go ahead only if Preston reaches Division One.

Total Capacity: 21,500. For away fans: Up to 6,000.

Cost (98/99): Adults £13, concessions £8.

Disabled Facilities: All are accommodated in the Sir Tom Finney Stand, with 100 spaces at pitch level and 10 more on an elevated platform. *Disabled Toilet:* Nearby. *Cost:* £6 for disabled, £6 for helper. *Booking:* Yes. *Parking:* Available. *For the Blind:* Match commentaries are available. Please book.

Programme: £1.80.

Visitors' Toilets: As away fans are being moved to the Bill Shankly Stand, we've said goodbye to the Mesolithic-style brick walls and cramped portakabins which served as the loo facilities in the Pavilion Paddock. One feature of the male loos will, however, be sorely missed: that conveniently placed window which gave a view of the action in the near goalmouth.

Food and Drink: Visiting fans will be in the new Bill Shankly Kop from season 98/99, and the club is also launching a new in-house catering company. However, it says it's to serve the same pies, which is excellent news. Fans in 97/98 said they were among the season's best, and many went back for seconds and thirds (10.1.98, 21.2.98).

PUB GUIDE

Legends (1) At the Ground, Deepdale Road (01772) 653 548

Free House/Whitbread. It's a nightclub which on

"Seeing as we once had Beckham on loan, the next one should be called 'The Spice Rack'!"

matchdays opens up one large room, with eating areas, welcoming home and away supporters. Bar snacks served 12-3, 9.30-2 am. Families welcome before the game. Open Saturday matchdays 12-3, 9-2.30 am.

The Sumners Hotel (2) Corner of Watling Street Road/Deepdale Road (01772) 705 626
Boddingtons (with guest beers). A large, modern pub with bar and quieter 'sit-down' area, although both get packed on matchdays. Full menu served 12-7. Large-screen TVs, pool, darts, beer garden. Open: all day from 11.

The Garrison (3) 193 Watling Street Road (01772) 794 470
Scottish and Newcastle (with Theakstons). A more traditional locals pub opposite the Sumners. Bar food served 12-9.30. Families welcome. Pool, big-screen TV. Open: all day.

The Hesketh Arms Corner of Blackpool Road and New Hall Lane (on way to ground from M6) (01772) 791 972
Scottish and Newcastle. Large and welcoming pub, a favourite matchday venue. Large range of meals served all day. Pool, darts, big-screen TV, car park. Families welcome. Coaches and large parties must book in advance. Open: all day.

FOOD GUIDE

The nearest outlet to the ground is the excellent 'Clare's Pantry', on the corner of Deepdale Road and St Stephen's Road, open every matchday from 8 am-3 pm. It offers locally-made pies, with a serving of pie, peas and gravy costing £1.35. Further along Deepdale Road towards town are: 'Romero Pizza/Kebabs/Burgers', 'Barbara's Buttie Bar' on the corner of St Gregory's Road, and a shop called 'Pizza Pie'. Those coming in from the M6 along Blackpool Road pass 'Tasty Fried Chicken', and a traditional chippy called 'Mel's Plaice'. A 'Big Steak' pub was being built on Deepdale Retail Park in 1998.

LOCAL MEDIA

Local Radio: BBC Radio Lancashire 103.9 FM; Red Rose Radio 999 AM.
Radio Phone-ins: BBC Radio Lancashire, Saturdays 6-7 pm, call (01254) 583 583.
Saturday Sports Paper: 'The Manchester Pink'.

MISCELLANEOUS

Now here's a mascot with some real character: the Deepdale Duck. Brian Ellis, Sports Editor of the *Lancashire Evening Post*, has observed the duck's antics over the seasons, and relates how it once clambered into the stand, threw all his notes into the air, and chucked the radio reporter's clipboard down the steps. The Duck enjoys sitting in the opposition dug-out, legs crossed, and warming up with the visiting players. Not all take too kindly to this, and the Duck's been told to tone it down a bit. As Mr Ellis says: 'His wings have been clipped!'

Safety Factor: Very little trouble, though derby days can be tense. Visiting supporters should steer clear of the Friargate area in town, while those walking from the station should avoid Meadow Street, ie. sticking to the route outlined in the directions above.

Rivals: Public enemy no. 1 is, of course, Blackpool – and it's reciprocated! Burnley retains second place. Preston supporters also dislike the 'part-time, glory-seeking fans' of Blackburn Rovers.

Fanzines: 'Pie Muncher' has ceased publication, but is coming out under a new title shortly. The club is to print and distribute the fanzine, but the editors say they will maintain their independence.

Unofficial Websites:
Unofficial: http://www.g4vaj.demon.co.uk/pnefc/
'Supporters' Club/Pie Muncher':
http://www.pylonvu.demon.co.uk/pneosco.html
'Homepage': http://freespace.virgin.net/paul.billington/PNEWeb_HomePage.htm
'Dave's Page: http://www.dpne.demon.co.uk/

Tourist Information: (01228) 512 444.

Queens Park Rangers

Loftus Road

Address: South Africa Road, Shepherd's Bush, London W12 7PA
Telephone: Club (0181) 743 0262
Box Office (0181) 740 2575
24-Hour Box Office Information (0181) 740 0503
ClubCall (0891) 121 162
Official Website: http://www.qpr.co.uk/

If Old Trafford has warehouses and Spotland has parks, Loftus Road has 1930s tower blocks. And they don't like football fans either ... every matchday, up go the barricades to stop any illegal car parking! Take the hint, and if possible travel by tube. This Shepherd's Bush/White City area of west London is a cultural melting pot, as reflected in the street names and the multitude of accents. It also means there's a good choice of ethnic food, especially round Shepherd's Bush Green – about half a mile to the south – where most supporters head for pre-match amusement. Mayfair it's not, but it does has everything from 'The House of Pies' to a Polish delicatessen.

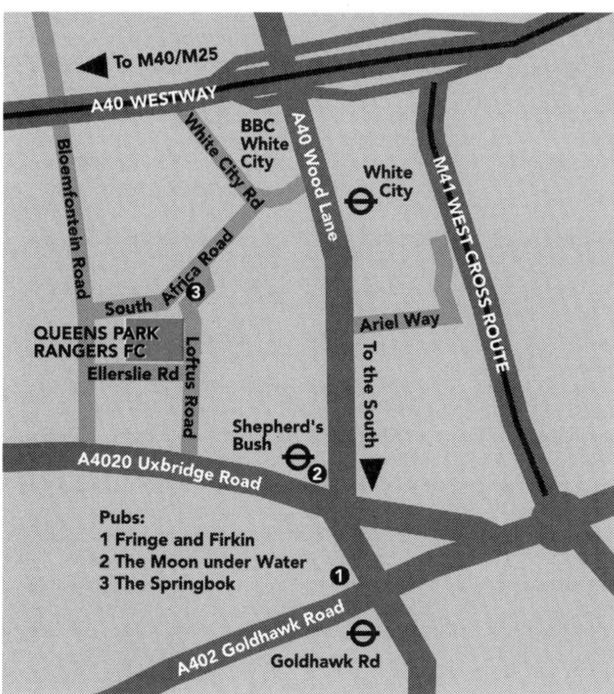

HOW TO GET THERE

NB: The M40 into London becomes the A40 Western Avenue. Although it's a dual carriageway, the road is often heavily congested, especially in the evening. Allow plenty of time. South Africa Road is usually blocked before the match.

BY CAR: From West (M40): Keep on M40 over the M25. Exit A40 after 14.1 miles (s/p White City A40, Harlesden A404).(*) At T-junction/lights turn right (s/p White City, Shepherd's Bush) onto Wood Lane and under the A40. At next lights, just past the BBC's White City complex on the RHS, turn right (n/s) into South Africa Road. Ground is on LHS after 0.3 miles.

From West (M4): Exit M4 at junction 4b (s/p Watford, M1, M40, Heathrow Terminal 4), and stay in lane for 'Watford M1, Oxford M40' onto the M25. Exit M25 after 4.8 miles (s/p M40(E), Uxbridge, London (W)) onto the M40 eastbound (which becomes the A40 Western Avenue). Exit A40 after 13.9 miles (s/p White City A40, Harlesden A404). Then as From West A40 (*).

From South: (From Hammersmith Roundabout, see London Guide for directions to roundabout). Take 2nd exit (n/s), passing Lloyds Bank on LHS, into Shepherd's Bush Road. After 0.7 miles, go straight on at lights at Shepherds Bush Green (s/p Central London A40, Oxford A40). Pass the 'Fringe and Firkin' on the LHS and go straight through next lights (s/p Oxford, White City A40) into Wood Lane. After 0.5 miles, after passing the BBC Television Centre on LHS, turn left at lights by Esso Station (n/s) into South Africa Road. Ground is on LHS after 0.3 miles.

FROM UNDERGROUND STATIONS:

a) Shepherd's Bush (Hammersmith and City Line, Zone 2 (NB Not the Central Line station!): Turn right out of station into Uxbridge Road. Those with tickets for the Upper Tier of the School End should turn right down Loftus Road (the turning after about 0.2 miles, opposite Zain Textiles), and then first left into Ellerslie Road. Those with tickets for the Lower Tier

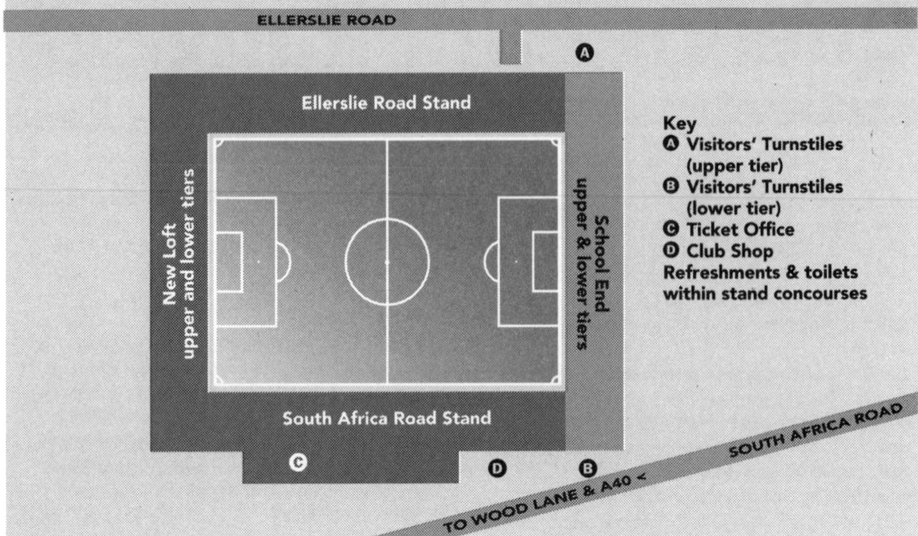

should continue along Uxbridge Road for a further 0.15 miles, turning right at the first set of lights into Bloemfontein Road (s/p Evangelical Church). Take the 3rd right turn into South Africa Road.
b) White City (Central Line, Zone 2): Cross road in front of station and turn right. Take next left into South Africa Road and ground is on LHS after 0.3 miles.
Last Midweek Trains: See 'London Guide' at front of book.
BY BUS: The 293 (Hammersmith to North Acton), 72 (Roehampton to East Acton), 95 (Southall to Shepherd's Bush) and 220 (Harlesden to Wandsworth) all stop near the ground.

PARKING

Cars and parking in London are never an ideal combination. Many of the streets around the ground are coned off, including South Africa Road and Bloemfontein Road, and others are reserved for residents, who are mightily territorial. There is some street parking for early arrivals, but don't use the apartment block car parks, where cars are regularly clamped. There's street parking to the north of the A40 flyover; in the Flowers Estate, west of Bloemfontein Road; south of Uxbridge Road; and in the Ariel Way industrial estate. To get to Ariel Way from A40: instead of turning into South Africa Road, go straight through lights, passing White City tube station on LHS, under railway bridge and take next left. Keep valuables out of sight at all times: thieves have been known to break the windows of cars waiting at traffic lights to steal handbags, mobile phones and the like.

THE GROUND

One headline you'll never see is: 'QPR announces major redevelopment of Loftus Road'. For one thing, the club calls the ground 'The Rangers Stadium', and more to the point, there's simply no room. The stadium is small, compact and intimate: indeed, it's such a squeeze that the front rows of supporters are only a couple of yards from the touchline. It all makes for a good matchday atmosphere (assuming enough supporters have turned up), but does mean that some seats have a restricted view. This applies to the School End, where visitors are housed: in the Upper Tier, those not in the front two rows or so have to stand up to see the near goal-line! If fewer than 1,500 travelling fans are expected, only the lower tier is opened. QPR has spent a lot of money improving the facilities, though the concourses still get very crowded.

The club obviously aims to return to the Premiership. But to do that at Loftus Road, with its limited capacity and gate receipts, would be very difficult. A site for a new stadium has been earmarked near the A4 in Uxbridge in the west London suburbs. As yet, however, no definite date has been set for work to begin.
Total Capacity: 19,143. For away fans: School End 3,873. Entrance to Upper Tier via Ellerslie Road, for Lower Tier via South Africa Road.
Cost (98/99): School End Lower Tier: Category 'A' matches £18, category 'B' matches £16. Upper Tier: 'A' matches £16, 'B' matches £14. Concessions half-price.
Disabled Facilities: Space for 13 visiting supporters in the Ellerslie Road Stand. *Disabled Toilet:* In X Block, Ellerslie Road Stand. *Cost:* Free for disabled and helper.

'What I like about Loftus Road is, how close you feel to the action!'

Booking: Essential. *Parking:* Street parking in Ellerslie Road for those with disabled stickers. *For the Blind:* Seats with commentary in X Block, Ellerslie Road Stand.
Programme: £2.
Visitors' Toilets: Fantastic! Birmingham, Bury and Sheffield United fans thought they were among the best in the division. *Male:* Clean, with sink, soap, hand-dryers, cubicles and mirrors. *Female:* Four star, and snazzy too, with the walls decorated in huge blue-and-white hoops! Smart department store style doors, dinky sinks, hot water and a mirror that made everyone look ten years older!
Food and Drink: The hot dogs (£1.80) were disappointing: 'Poor bread, poor sausage, poor ketchup,' said one dissatisfied customer. The meat pies (£1.70) looked like they'd been stored on a hot plate, which had made the pastry soggy. Fans also complained that they 'weren't very chunky.' The hot drinks, however, were good. One fan said the tea (90p) was 'probably the best ever, for the snack-pack variety', while the hot chocolate (90p) was 'excellent – it almost tastes of chocolate!' Vegetable pies (£1.70) were also on sale (1.11.97, 25.2.98, 3.5.98).

PUB GUIDE

The Fringe and Firkin (1) (formerly 'The Bush') 2 Goldhawk Road (0181) 749 9861
Firkin beers, with a mini-brewery on the premises. Large welcoming pub with wooden benches, with the Bush Theatre upstairs. So in any one evening customers can include footie fans, happy Australians and groups discussing the merits of the latest French play. Sandwiches (£2.50). Big-screen TV. Open: all day.
Moon on the Green (2) 172-174 Uxbridge Road (0181) 749 5709
JD Weatherspoons (with Theakstons Best, IPA, Directors and Sundance). Classic smart town pub, with a non-smoking/dining area downstairs. Full menu, snacks and vegetarian options served 11-10. Football fans welcome, but not in football shirts. Open: all day.
The Springbok (3) South Africa Road (0181) 735 0882
Labatts. A large modern-style pub with open-plan bar, right by the ground. Sandwiches and pies (£1.50). TV, patio. Open: all day.

FOOD GUIDE

The 'First Choice' takeaway by the Springbok pub on South Africa Road is popular, especially as it's the only option near the ground. A local said the chips (80p) were better after the match (maybe it depends on the result)! Around Shepherd's Bush Green there's a Burger King and a McDonalds, while Goldhawk Road has a Pizza Hut. Uxbridge Road has traditional outlets such as 'Domino's Pizza', 'The House of Pies' and a KFC, plus a choice of Caribbean, Greek, Indian, Mediterranean, Thai and Nepalese takeaways and restaurants, as well as that Polish Delicatessen. For upmarket cuisine try: 'Edwards' (formerly the 'Beaumont Arms'), a wine bar on the junction of Wood Lane and Uxbridge Road; and 'Albertines Wine Bar' on Wood Lane, which has an excellent vegetarian menu. It opens before evening games.

LOCAL MEDIA

Radio: Capital Gold 1548 AM; GLR 94.9 FM.
Radio Phone-ins: Capital Gold, Saturdays 2-6.30, midweek 7-10 (or 7-8 if no match). Call on (0845) 35 60 7080.
Saturday Paper: None.

MISCELLANEOUS

Safety Factor: Few problems.
Rivals: Traditionally Chelsea. Watford come in a poor second ... 'just when we're in the same division ... otherwise they don't bother us.'
Fanzines: 'In the Loft', 24 Woodham Road, Catford, London, SE6 2SD; 'A Kick Up The R's', Beech Lodge, Hollinwood, Whixall, Whitchurch, Shropshire, SY13 3NL.
Unofficial Website: http://www.qpr.org/
Tourist Information: No local office.

R

Reading

Madejski Stadium

Address: Madejski Stadium, Bennet Road, Reading, Berkshire RG2 0FL
Telephone:
Club/Ticket Office (0118) 968 1000
ClubCall (0891) 121 000
Official Website: http://www.readingfc.co.uk/

From the makers of the 'Reebok Stadium' comes the latest release, the 'Madejski Stadium', a fully enclosed 24,200 all-seater ground with hotel and conference facilities just five minutes' drive from the M4. It's visible from the motorway, but don't be lulled into a false sense of security. Until the new A33 relief road is opened some time in 1999, access is expected to be a nightmare. And as for getting out again ... well, take a good book and a thermos flask! The Madejski Stadium has been built on the site of an old rubbish tip, in an area earmarked for further business and retail park development. Parking should not be a great problem, and there are a couple of good takeaways on the nearby Basingstoke Road. Finding a good football-friendly pub, which isn't already up to the rafters with happy football fans, is going to be a bit more difficult.

HOW TO GET THERE

BY CAR: From all directions, M4: Exit M4 at junction 11 (s/p Reading Cen. And S., Basingstoke A33). At roundabout follow signs to 'Reading A33' onto the A33 Basingstoke Road. At first roundabout after 0.5 miles, by 'The Chippy' and the Forte Post House, go straight on. At lights after 0.4 miles, turn left into Bennet Road. From here, follow the stadium signs. Until the A33 relief road is built, all car traffic has to enter and exit via Bennet Road ... aaarrrggghh!
FROM RAILWAY STATION (Reading Central): About 3 miles. *By taxi:* £5-£6. *By bus:* Shuttle buses take fans to the stadium.
Last Midweek Trains: Trains to London Paddington run at 21.34, 21.30, 22.00, 22.20, 22.39 up to 23.38. There's a train to Cardiff and Swansea at 22.25 and to Cardiff at 01.22. Please double-check on (0345) 484 950.
BY BUS: Visiting fans are welcome on the shuttle buses, which run from the town centre and points throughout Reading. Bus lanes ensure a quick getaway too. Contact Reading Buses for details on (0118) 959 4000.

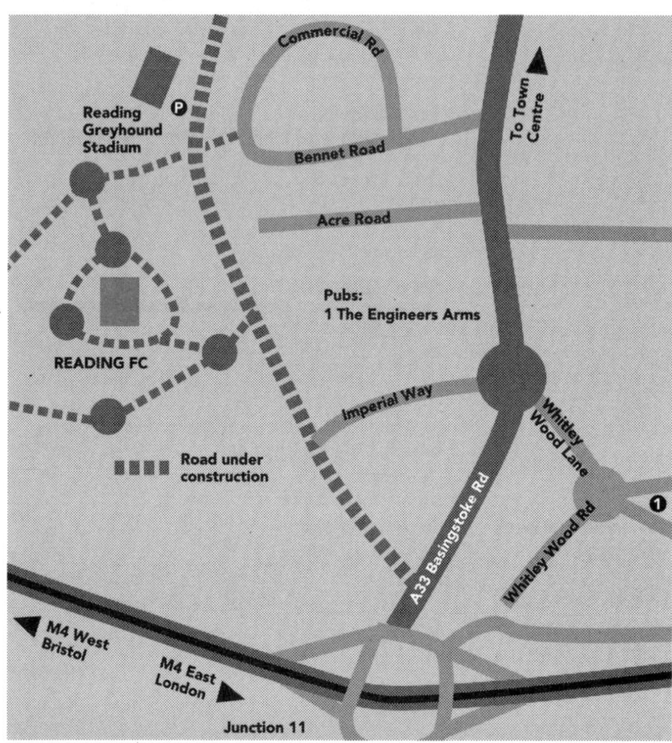

PARKING

For season 98/99, the club has 1,800 car parking spaces, of which 700 are reserved. The Reading Greyhound Stadium, a few minutes' walk away, has an extra 500 spaces, and there's street parking in the nearby industrial estate. It's hoped that some of the industrial units will also open their car parks, for a fee of course. The club is planning to set up some park-and-ride schemes

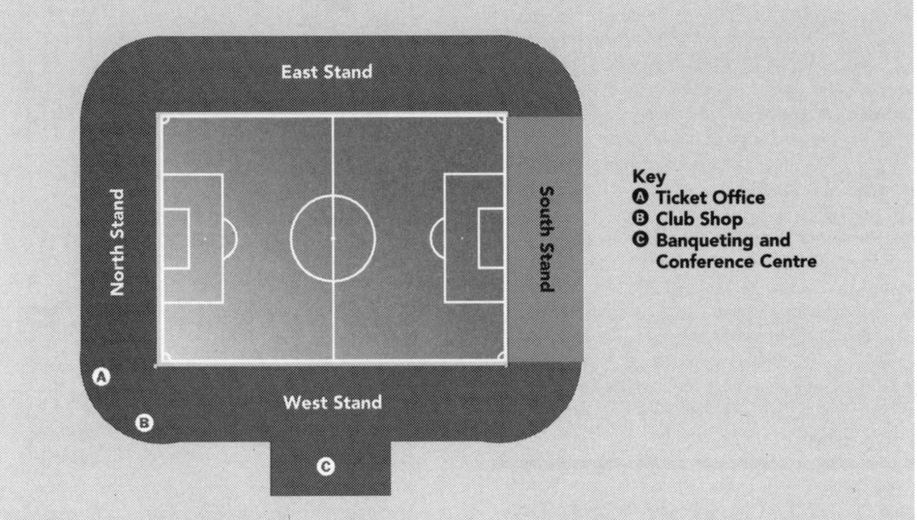

at nearby schools. A large number of the car parking spaces at the ground will be lost in season 99/2000 as the council, bizarrely, plans to run a Saturday shoppers park-and-ride scheme from one of the car parks.

THE GROUND

A large number of lower division clubs must be hoping that Reading Chairman John Madejski, who's put £10 million of his own money into the club's new ground, has a brother looking for a new investment! The outside of the ground is all blue-and-white, with a bright yellow extension (the conference centre) to match the bright green in the envious eyes of many a visiting supporter! The stadium is fully enclosed, with all sides one-tier except for the two-tier, 12,000-seater West Stand, which houses the hospitality suites, the club shop and ticket office, a restaurant, conference centre and the family enclosure. It's all state-of-the-art, with unimpaired views from all seats, and the roof angled to prevent the sun from shining into the eyes of the assembled masses. Look out for the 'Wall of Fame', with bricks inscribed, for a fee, with fan names and dedications. Away fans are housed behind the goal in the South Stand.

Total Capacity: 24,200. For away fans: 4,000. Gates 9-10.

Cost (98/99): Adults £14, concessions (under 16s, over 65s) £8.

Disabled Facilities: 28 spaces available half way up the South Stand, where the view should be excellent. *Disabled Toilets:* Nearby. *Cost:* A joint ticket for disabled and helper costs £6 if bought in advance, £7 on the day. *Booking:* Not necessary. *Parking:* Possibly at the ground, on a first-come, first-served basis. Contact club for details. *For the Blind:* 12 seats in the West Stand with hospital radio commentary.

Programme: £2.

Food and Drink: The new caterers are promising 'traditional football fare but of a higher standard', plus some more innovative dishes such as stir-fries, casseroles, and Mexican and Italian themes, 'depending on the fitting-out of the concourses'. But will it be available in the away end? ... the six billion dollar question.

PUB GUIDE

The Engineers Arms (1) Whitley Wood Lane (0118) 987 2539
Morrells (with John Smiths, Courage). A large sports-friendly traditional 'community pub', serving home-cooked bar food all day. Separate pool room, darts, big-screen TV, beer garden. Families welcome. Open: all day.

Another pub on the Basingstoke Road is the 'Four Horseshoes', but the landlord might be moving on, and the pub turned into a restaurant. However, it's worth checking if it's still there, as it's large and football friendly:

The Four Horseshoes 177 Basingstoke Road (0118) 987 1604
Spring Inns (with London Pride, John Smiths Smooth). Huge detached traditional pub with two pool tables, darts, TV and a large car park. Bar food. Open: all day weekends and on midweek matchdays.
How to get there: continue along the A33 north of the ground, to where the main route turns left. Go straight on instead (s/p Local Traffic) and the pub is on the RHS.

Another idea is to try out the pubs to the south of the M4. At junction 11, take the A33 southbound (instead of heading north to the Madejski Stadium). At the first roundabout, turn left (s/p Three Mile Cross, Spencers Wood), and simply follow the road round. There are two or three traditional village pubs on this road, but they are unlikely to welcome large groups of lads in colours. A right turn at the roundabout (s/p Burghfield) leads to the village of Grazeley and beyond.

FOR FAMILIES:

The Harvester pub on Basingstoke Road, about 0.3 miles north of the ground, says it won't allow in anyone wearing football colours. That said, it's still a good choice for food. It has a pub menu with sandwiches from £2.60 and all the classic favourites 'in a basket'. There's a restaurant with a huge menu – steaks, grills, chicken and the like, with an average meal costing about £8. The children's menu has meals from £1.45.

FOOD GUIDE

Those approaching the Madejski Stadium from the M4 pass a 'Little Chef' on the right-hand-side. Further north along Basingstoke Road are three takeaways: 'The Chippy' on the first roundabout, the 'Seagull Fish Bar' just north of the Bennet Road junction, and 'Lam's' Chinese takeaway. 'The Chippy' is one of the best chip shops in the region, and sells Wrights Pies too! The 'Seagull Fish Bar' has Pukka Pies, haddock at £2.20, and burgers at £1.80, and specialises in milkshakes! Next door, the 'Londis' store has sandwiches as well as pies and pasties, which can be heated up. For another option, at junction 11 of the M4, head southbound on the A33 dual carriageway for 0.8 miles to a service station with an 'M's Diner'. Note, however, that to turn round, cars have to drive three miles further south to the first roundabout.

LOCAL MEDIA

Local Radio: Thames Valley FM 95.2 FM; Classic Gold 1215 MW.

Radio Phone-ins: BBC Thames Valley, Saturdays 5-7, call (01865) 311 111; Classic Gold, Saturdays 5-6, call (0118) 928 2828.

Saturday Sports Paper: None.

MISCELLANEOUS

Kingsley Royal, Reading's lion mascot, had a fine old time during half-time in the club's Coca Cola Cup quarter-final against Middlesbrough. 'Hob Nob Anyone!' reported that he kicked Middlesbrough's own lion, Roary, up the rear end 'because it was there', and incited the crowd into anti-northern-lion chants. He also squared up to Wolfie, the Wolves furry friend. Finding an appropriate punishment was difficult as 'pulling a rival's tail' doesn't appear to be covered by FIFA regulations.

The Nightmare on Elm Park ... is over!

Safety Factor: There was very little trouble at Elm Park in season 97/98.

Rivals: Swindon Town, Oxford and any club associated with Mark McGhee. Some Reading fans are boycotting Goodyear Tyres 'because it's easier than boycotting Walker's Crisps!'

Fanzines: 'Heaven Eleven', PO Box 2120, Reading, RG1 8YR; 'The Whiff', PO Box 2607, Reading, RG1 8XU.

Unofficial Websites:

'Hob Nob Anyone?': http://www.i-way.co.uk/~readingfc/

'Royal Web':

http://www.geocities.com/Colosseum/Field/1200/royal.htm

Tourist Information: (0118) 956 6226.

Rochdale

Spotland

Address: Spotland, Rochdale, OL11 5DS
Telephone: Club/Ticket Office (01706) 644 648
Commercial/Club Shop (01706) 647 521
Dale Newsline (0891) 555 858
Official Website: http://www.rochdale-football-club.co.uk

Whereas Old Trafford has warehouses, Rochdale – lying on the southern edge of the Pennines – has trees and parks. Spotland overlooks one of them, Denehurst Park, and a golf course. For the visiting football fan, life is just hunky-dory. Parking's easy, there's an excellent fish and chip shop right opposite the away turnstiles and a pub just along the road. And the club's still serving those excellent pies. Only train travellers encounter any problems, as the station is a good 30 minute walk away in the town centre.

HOW TO GET THERE

BY CAR: From All Main Directions, M62: Exit M62 at junction 20 (s/p Rochdale, Oldham, A627(M)). At roundabout turn left (s/p Rochdale A627(M)) onto the A627(M). At next roundabout, by Homeworld, after 0.9 miles, turn left (s/p Bury A644 (A58)) into Edinburgh Way. At next roundabout after 0.4 miles, take 2nd exit (s/p Blackburn B6452, also Spotland Stadium) into Roch Valley Way, passing the Clog and Shawl pub on the LHS. At crossroads by the Cemetery pub after 0.9 miles go straight on (s/p Spotland Stadium) into Sandy Lane. Ground is on RHS after 0.5 miles.

From North (M65-A56-A680 Rochdale Road): Continue on A680 into the Rochdale suburb of Norden, to double mini-roundabout by the Turf Tavern. Go straight on at both, and straight on for a further 0.7 miles, passing the Lancashire Lass and Star Inn pubs, to crossroads/lights. Here, turn right (s/p Bury (B6452), Manchester (M62)) into Sandy Lane. Take 1st left into Willbutts Lane.

FROM RAILWAY STATION: Rochdale, about 1.4 miles. *By taxi:* About £3. *By bus:* Take the nos. 443, 444 and 445 from the town centre bus station. Only the no. 444 runs in the evening. *By foot:* The route below goes through a small park, so after nightfall it's advisable to stick to the main roads, as outlined in the alternative version (b).

a) Take second left turn off the roundabout in front of the station, into Lower Tweedale Street. Take the 3rd right, by the Queen's pub, into Milkstone Road. Cross main road (Drake Street) straight into Church Stile. At T-junction in front of church, turn left, and where road bends round to left, continue straight on towards school sign into Sparrow Hill. Past the Broadfield Hotel to end of road. Turn left into park, bear right along path and right again down to the main road. Cross road and turn left in front of Asda into Dane Street. Keep on main road, which becomes Mellor Street, for 0.6 miles, to mini-roundabout. Here go straight on (2nd exit, s/p Blackburn A680) into Spotland Road. At next roundabout by the After Eight restaurant turn left (s/p Blackburn A680) up into Edenfield Road. 2nd left into Willbutts Lane to away turnstiles.

b) For evening games: Follow route above down Milkstone Road. Instead of going straight across into Church Stile, turn left, down to T-junction with dual

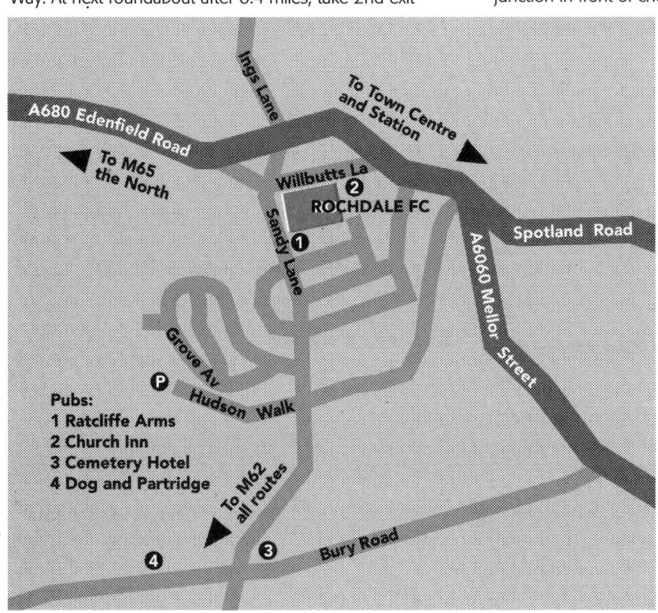

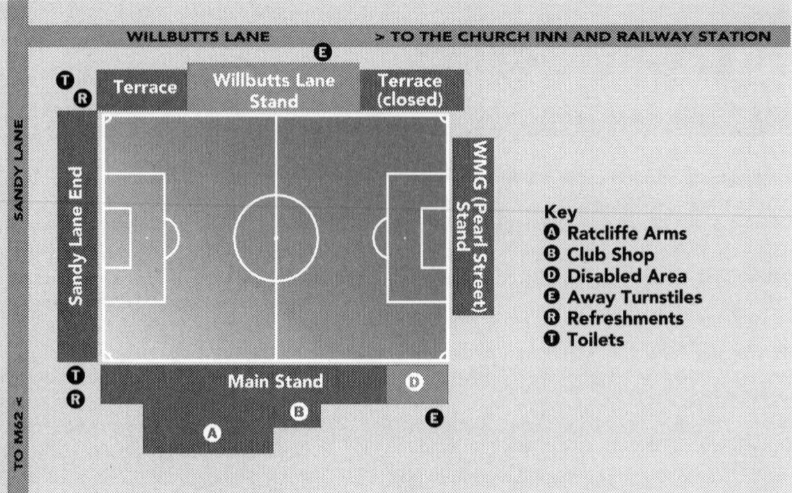

carriageway. Here turn right (s/p Halifax, Blackburn A677) into Manchester Road. At next main junction, by Asda, turn left into Dane Street. Then as above.
Last Midweek Trains: The last train to Manchester leaves at 23.46. Trains from Manchester run to York and Newcastle at 21.50, to York at 22.47, and to Nottingham and Derby at 22.28. It's not possible to get to London after a midweek game. Please double-check on (0345) 484 950.
BY BUS: See above.

PARKING

Early arrivals can park on nearby streets though the police advise fans against parking to the west of Sandy Lane. The club has a large car park behind the WMG Stand, open to all (£2). Alternatively, the church on Willbutts Lane opens its car park for church funds. There's free parking a little further from Spotland (about 0.3 miles) at Oulder Hill School, at the end of Hudson's Walk, off Sandy Lane. For those approaching Spotland from the M62, it's signposted left 'Oulder Hill Leisure Complex', about 0.2 miles from the crossroads by the Cemetery pub.

THE GROUND

The new 2,700 all-seater WMG stand opened at the Pearl Street end of Spotland in October 1997, marking the latest stage in the complete redevelopment of the ground. The stand, which cost £900,000, brought the ground capacity to over 9,000. The Main Stand was redeveloped in 1992, complete with executive boxes, bars and a restaurant, and the Sandy Lane End has also been revamped. This leaves one remaining undeveloped side, the Willbutts Lane Stand, which unsurprisingly houses away supporters. However, the terrace is covered, and the allocation is generous. Seats are also available in Block A of the Main Stand. The club has plans to rebuild the Willbutts Lane Stand, possibly in season 1999/2000.
Total Capacity: 9,096. For away fans: Terrace 2,500, seating 250. Turnstiles (terrace) 13-15 in Willbutts Lane.
Cost (98/99): Willbutts Lane: Adults £8, no concessions. Main Stand: Adults £10, concessions £5. Visiting fans are welcome in the Family Stand: Adult £8, first two accompanying children £1 each. Tickets from ticket office, no cash on the gate.
Disabled Facilities: Visiting supporters can choose whether to sit with away fans in the Main Stand, or in the new disabled area in the WMG Stand. About 14 places are available. *Disabled Toilet:* In both stands. *Cost:* Free for disabled, £8 for helper. *Booking:* Preferable. *Parking:* Available, please book. *For the Blind:* Six seats with hospital radio commentary.
Programme: £1.50.
Visitors' Toilets: *Male:* Geared towards a large but unhygienic crowd. In other words, lots of troughs, but no sink. All reasonably clean though. *Female:* Bring a torch, and a bar of soap! At least there is a sink, unlike in the gents, and plenty of loo roll!
Food and Drink: Rochdale is a prime example of a club concentrating on what it does best: serving excellent pies (£1.20). The steak pie had plenty of gravy, and one taster said: 'It's made a seven-out-of-ten as I've just found a piece of steak'. Others were more generous, describing their pies as 'excellent'. The meat-and-potato was just as good: 'Very nice, with pepper, crusty ... though a bit expensive!' To complete a meat-eater's delight, the bovril (70p) was also good. For vegetarians? Crisps at 30p (28.3.98)

PUB GUIDE

Visiting fans are welcome in the new Rochdale social club called Studds, under the WMG Stand. It serves food, has two TVs, and opens at midday on Saturdays, and from 6 pm for midweek matches.

The Ratcliffe Arms (1) In club car park (01706) 861 440
JW Lees. Club-style pub at the ground. Bar snacks served from 12. Pool, darts, TV. Children welcome on matchdays. Disabled facilities. Open: all day from 11.30.

The Church Inn (2) Willbutts Lane (01706) 639 879
John Smiths (with Websters). Friendly traditional three-roomed pub with separate pool and darts rooms. Bar snacks served all day. TV, beer garden. Families welcome. Open: Sat/Sun all day from 12, from 5 pm for midweek games.

The Cemetery Hotel (3) 470 Bury Road (01706) 645 635
Free House (range of cask-conditioned ales). Don't be put off by the name as this is an excellent, characterful pub with good home-made food, from toasties to 12oz. Sirloin steaks, served 12-2.30. TV, darts. Families welcome. Open: all day from 12.

The Dog and Partridge (4) 520 Bury Road (01706) 648 073
Whitbread (wide selection of real ales). Top-rate traditional pub highly recommended by all. Excellent menu including steak-and-kidney pudding, wild mushroom lasagne and Thai red chicken curry. Pool, big-screen TV, patio. Families welcome/children's menu. Open: all day from 12.

The Clog and Shawl
23 Roch Valley Way (en route from M62) (01706) 649 355
Whitbread. Traditional locals pub with darts, TV and pool table. Meals served from 12-5 weekends, 12-3, 5-7 midweek. Families welcome. Open: all day from 12.
Also recommended: **The Citizens,** 110 Drake Street (near the station). An attractive Vaux pub with an excellent range of home-made bar food.

FOOD GUIDE

The highly recommended 'Fish and Chips' takeaway in Willbutts Lane has fish and chips at £1.65, chips and curry at £1 and pies at 75p. There's a Chinese/English takeaway, the 'Fortune City', on the way to the ground from the M62, on Greave Avenue, off Spotland Road, signposted 'Shopping Precinct'.

On the Bury Road, opposite the Dog and Partridge pub, is the fun new 'Indigo Café', open from 10-5.30. It has sandwiches (£1.75), speciality sandwiches (£2.10), and a range of jacket potatoes. From 7 pm it becomes a restaurant with a more extensive menu. Almost next door is 'Young's Fish Bar', also recommended, with fish at £1.35, chips at 75p and pies at 78p.

"Once upon a time, many years ago..."

LOCAL MEDIA

Local Radio: GMR 95.1 FM.
Radio Phone-ins: GMR, Saturdays 1-3 and 5-7, and after midweek games. Call (0161) 228 2255.
Saturday Sports Paper: The 'Manchester Pink'.

MISCELLANEOUS

Rochdale FC, nicknamed 'Dale', shares Spotland with the rugby league team, the Rochdale Hornets. So why exactly does it have a dragon as a mascot? Apparently mascot costumes are expensive, and Rochdale couldn't afford one ... until the marketing manager heard of a company who used a dragon costume in its advertising campaigns. He asked to borrow it for the club, and very popular it's proved too!

Believe it or not, bearing in mind that Dale haven't won promotion for 29 years, there is a Manchester United season ticket holder who remains a loyal Rochdale supporter. He loans out the season ticket, and follows Dale everywhere. 'It's more of a community here,' he explained. 'At United I was just a number, at Rochdale I'm an individual, and everybody knows each other'.

Safety Factor: Rochdale fans have difficulty remembering when there was last trouble at Spotland.
Rivals: Bury, Burnley plus a strong dislike of Manchester United fans.
Fanzine: 'Exceedingly Good Pies', temporarily dormant but hopefully to be revived in season 98/99. No current address available.
Unofficial Websites:
http://www.rafc.demon.co.uk/pages/rafc.html
Tourist Information: (01706) 356 592.

R

Rotherham United

Millmoor

Address: Millmoor, Masbrough Street, Rotherham, South Yorkshire S60 1HR
Telephone: Club (01709) 512 434
Commercial Department/Club Shop
(01709) 512 760
Chatterbox Line (0891) 121 637
Official Website: http://www.rotherhamufc.u-net.com/

Even the slowest of trainspotters can hardly miss the locomotives by Millmoor – they're stacked on the scrapyard which virtually surrounds the ground. Unsurprisingly, scrap metal is a bit of a taboo subject with Millers fans, who admit to the surreal fear that the yard will one day engulf the ground! Millmoor's just off the Rotherham ring road, ten minutes from town and the railway station and – more to the point – about thirty seconds from the first of several excellent pubs. Note that the club is proud to serve Eric Twigg's Pukka Pies, so arrive early before everyone else eats them up.

HOW TO GET THERE

BY CAR: From North and West (M1): Exit M1 at junction 34 (s/p Sheffield (Meadowhall), Rotherham A6109) and at roundabout take 2nd exit (s/p Rotherham A6109) into Meadow Bank Road. At lights after 1.4 miles (by 'The Wilton' pub) turn right (n/s) into Kimberworth Road. At T-junction after 0.4 miles turn left over bridge to ground.

Alternative route from North and West via A629: (passing by 'The Effingham Arms' and 'The Drawbridge'). Exit M1 at junction 35 and at motorway roundabout turn left (s/p Rotherham A629) onto the A629 Upper Wortley Road. Follow signs to Rotherham A629 for 4.0 miles (passing the 'The Effingham Arms' at 1.8 miles, and 'The Drawbridge' at 2.5 miles) to the College Road Roundabout. Here turn right (s/p M1 South, M18, Sheffield A630) onto Centenary Way. At the Masbrough Roundabout, turn right to Millmoor (s/p Masbrough), or follow signs to the Visitors' Parking.

From South (M1): Exit M1 at junction 33 (s/p Sheffield Centre, Rotherham A630). At motorway roundabout turn right (s/p Rotherham A630) onto The Rotherway. At first roundabout after 0.4 miles turn left (s/p Rotherham A630) onto West Bawtry Road. (*)At Canklow Roundabout after 0.7 miles turn right (s/p Rotherham A630), and go straight on at the Ickles Roundabout after 1.1 miles (s/p Doncaster A630, Barnsley) and over River Don. At Masbrough Roundabout after 0.4 miles turn left to ground (s/p Masbrough, Public Weighbridge), or go right round roundabout for Visitors' Parking.

From South and East (M18): Exit M18 at junction 1 (s/p Rotherham A631). Follow signs to Sheffield A631 for 4.4 miles, over the Wickersley, Brecks and Worrygoose Roundabouts to the Rotherway Roundabout. Here go straight on (s/p Rotherham A630) onto West Bawtry Road. Then as From South (M1)(*).

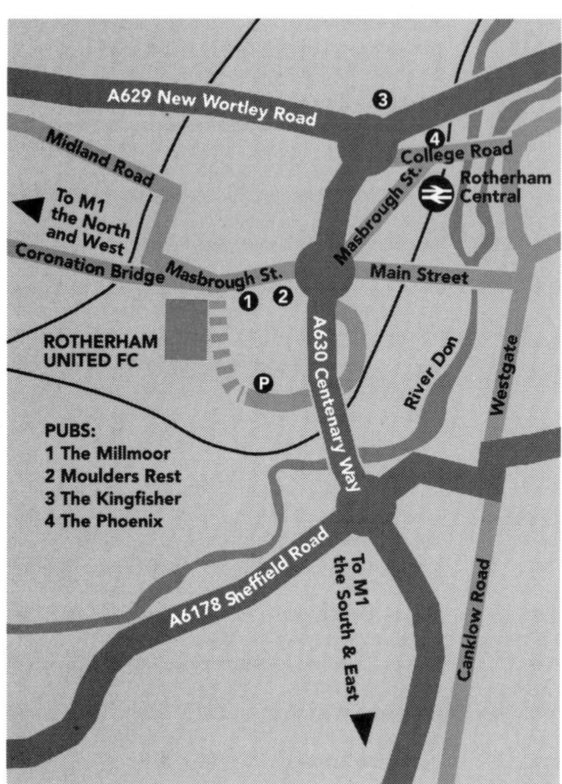

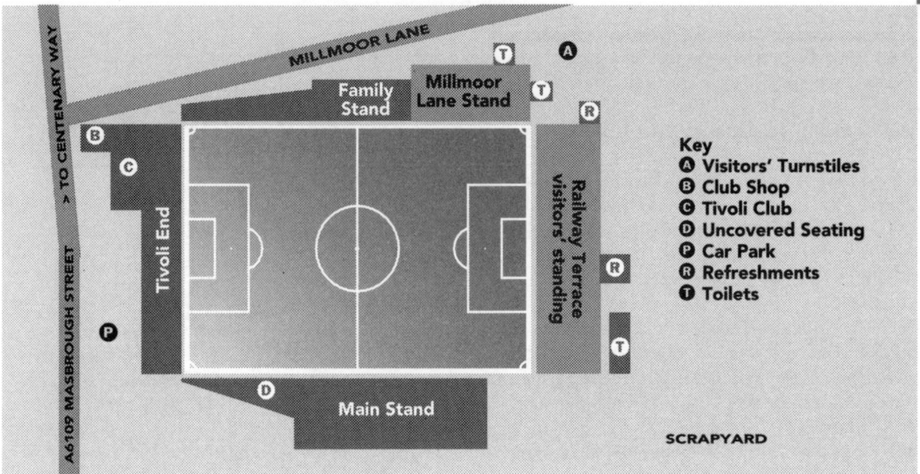

FROM RAILWAY STATION (Rotherham Central): 0.5 miles to ground. *By foot:* Turn left out of station into College Road. After about 30 yards turn left again into Masbrough Street (no signpost, but head past Bar Refrigeration). At end of street, by 'The Traveller's Rest' pub, go into subway, straight across centre area and up stairs on left into the continuation of Masbrough Street to ground.

Last Midweek Trains: To London: 21.11 (via Doncaster). To Newcastle: 21.36 (but with 2 hour wait at Doncaster). Frequent service to Sheffield. Please double-check on (0345) 484 950.

BY BUS: The following buses run past the ground: the 137 and 138 (to Kimberworth and Meadowhall), the 602 (to Meadowhall) and the X78.

PARKING

The main (free) car park for away fans is signposted off the Masbrough Roundabout. Those approaching from the south have to drive right round the roundabout, heading back up Centenary Way. The car park is informal – simply park where you see the other parked cars. There's a small car park by the Phoenix pub in College Street, 50p all day, and limited street parking.

THE GROUND

Millers fans continue to live in hope of ground improvements or a new stadium, but all such plans appear to be on hold. In the meantime, Millmoor is a Mecca for traditionalists, with a Main Stand, some open seating, covered terracing behind both goals, perfect pies and terrible toilets. 'A nice compact ground,' said one Rotherham supporter. 'But a bit grim!' Away fans have a large covered terrace and a little stand to themselves. Take some thermal gloves – not for the cold weather, but as protection against the heat of the stupendous Millmoor pies. 'We warm them up in a blast furnace,' say the locals. 'By 3 pm the mercury's bubbling.' They also warn visitors against taking the top off any pies during play, as the steam disrupts the match!

Total Capacity: 11,533. For away supporters: Standing (Railway Terrace, covered) 3,125. Turnstiles 31-37. Seating (Millmoor Lane Stand) 1,094. Turnstiles 29-30.

Cost (97/98): Railway Terrace: Adults £7.50, Juniors/OAPs £5. Millmoor Lane Stand: Adults £10, Juniors/OAPs £6.50. NB Concessions are available on a reciprocal basis only – i.e., if the away club also offers concessions to visiting fans. Visiting fans can also use the Family Stand, where a joint adult/child admittance costs £9. OAPs and extra children pay £5.50.

Disabled Facilities: Space for 13 supporters in the Millmoor Lane Stand. *Disabled Toilet:* Nearby. *Cost:* Free for disabled, £5 for helper. *Booking:* Essential. *Parking:* Available. *For the Blind:* No special facilities.

Programme: £1.50.

Visitors' Toilets: *Male:* One visiting fan wrote, cryptically: 'Ideal facilities for football traditionalists ... painted in club colours too'. Roughly translated, a running gutter, no sinks, no cubicles, and a smell so intense that if it were manufactured by Iraq it would be subject to at least 25 UN disarmament resolutions. A leading contender for the MATITLA (see under Darlington). *Female:* Two years ago the *Football Fans Guide* noted there were no locks on the loo doors. Now there are locks, but they don't work. Progress of sorts!

Food and Drink: One comment summed up the rest: 'I've never had a better pie'. Now that's a satisfied customer. The only complaint about the 'Eric Twigg Pukka Pies' (several varieties at £1.25) was that they were almost too hot, and that there weren't enough of them. The pasties (also £1.25) were not as good as the pies but still gained an eight-out-of-ten (12.8.97).

PUB GUIDE

The Tivoli Club at the ground generally welcomes visiting supporters, and there are a number of pubs within an easy ten-minute walk:

The Millmoor (1) Masbrough Street (01709) 512 123
Stones. This is the place, says the landlord, for 'a good drink in a friendly atmosphere'. Away fans are welcome in a large clubroom upstairs. Sandwiches and hot pies. Pool, darts, TV. Families welcome. Open: 12-4, 5-11.30.

Moulders Rest (2) Masbrough Street (01709) 560 095
Free House. Traditional family local, and long-time favourite of home and visiting supporters. Food available weekdays only. Free pool table, darts, TV, beer garden. Families welcome. Open: 12-4, 7-11 (from 6 pm for evening games).

The Kingfisher (3) 17 Mary Street (01709) 838 422
Old Mill (traditional beers). Another favourite, with top-quality beers and a friendly (and peaceful!) atmosphere. Limited menu, though the pie-and-peas are always popular. Parties should pre-book. Darts, beer garden, TV (not Sky). Children welcome to 9 pm. Open: all day.

The Drawbridge Wortley Road (on Alternative Route via A629) (01709) 557 701
Bass (with Stones, Caffreys). A large locals pub with, says the landlord 'friendly staff and good service'. Bar food 12-7. For midweek games, there's a restaurant downstairs where families are welcome, open 5-9.30. Pool, darts, big-screen TV, patio. Open: all day from 12.

Also recommended: **The Phoenix (4),** 1 College Road (near station). It's a Free House with tiled floors and conservatory-style furniture, pool table and TV.

FOR FAMILIES:
All the pubs listed below have children's menus. The Sir Jack and the Brecks Beefeater are on the road route in From South and East M18:

Sir Jack Bawtry Road, Bramley (couple of hundred yards from M18) (01709) 530 306
Tom Cobbleigh PLC. Huge new family pub with full menu (main courses from about £5) served 12-9.30. Children's play barn (£1 per hour). Disabled facilities, baby-changing. Open: all day.

The Brecks Beefeater (and Travel Inn)
Bawtry Road (by the Brecks Roundabout) (01709) 543 216
Whitbread. Popular Beefeater restaurant. Varied menu, all very good value too, say the staff! Darts, TV. Disabled facilities. Open: all day from 11.30 (restaurant from 12).

'The Effingham Arms' is on the road route in From M1 (Alternative Route via A629):

The Effingham Arms Upper Wortley Road (01709) 382 094
Tetleys. Bright, welcoming 'real family pub', with Big Steak menu served 12-9.45. Disabled facilities. Open: all day.

'What are YOU looking at – I came back, didn't I?'

FOOD GUIDE

There's now a good range of cheap food near Millmoor. The 'Millmoor Café', opposite the ground, offers the usual menu including a chip butty for £1, while the nearby 'Ehsan Balti House' has fish and chips for £2.50. A new café/takeaway, 'Reo's', has opened on Masbrough Street between 'The Millmoor' pub and 'The Moulder's Rest', and is highly recommended by local supporters. It too has a good menu, but many opt for the pasty, peas and drink for an all-in price of £1.50.

LOCAL MEDIA

Local Radio: BBC Radio Sheffield 88.6 FM, 94.7 FM and 104.1 FM; Hallam FM 97.4 and 103.4 FM.
Radio Phone-ins: BBC Radio Sheffield, 'Praise or Grumble', 5 pm. Call (0114) 268 2222.
Saturday Sports Paper: 'The Green 'Un'.

MISCELLANEOUS

Safety Factor: No major problems here.
Rivals: Many Rotherham residents support Sheffield Wednesday and United, returning to Millmoor when the Millers have a good season. So Rotherham fans, unsurprisingly, dislike both clubs.
Fanzines: 'Moulin Rouge', 178 Greatwood Avenue, Skipton, North Yorkshire, BD23 2SQ.
Unofficial Websites:
http://www2.krisalis.co.uk/wwwneil/index.html
Tourist Information: (01709) 823 611.

Scarborough

The McCain Stadium

Address: The McCain Stadium, Seamer Road, Scarborough, YO12 4HF
Telephone: Club/Ticket Information (01723) 375 094
ClubCall (0891) 121 650
Official Website: http://www.yorkshirecoast.co.uk/scarbrofc

Milano, Roma, Spaghetti, Scarborough ... Scarborough? Yep, the Italian flag flies high at the McCain Stadium and the team's resplendent in the Italian national colours of red, white and green. It's all due to new kit sponsors/manufacturers Errea. Don't laugh, it's a lucrative deal! The McCain Stadium – or the McStad as it's known locally – is easy to find, on the main A64 in from the south, set among the DIY stores and car showrooms on the edge of town. The coast, town centre and railway station are over a mile away, but there are excellent pubs and takeaways along the route.

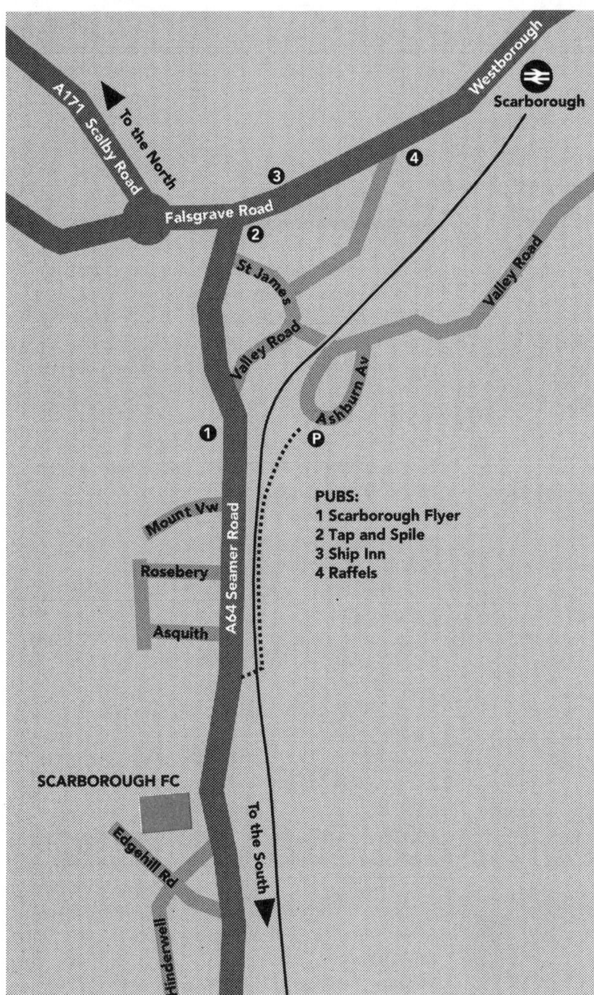

HOW TO GET THERE

BY CAR: From South and West (A64): Exit A1(M) at s/p 'Leeds, York A64'. Stay on A64 bypassing York, through the villages of Rillington, Sherburn and Ganton (all of which have pubs and takeaways). At roundabout after 51 miles (by Springwood Oak caravan tour park) turn left (s/p Scarborough A64, Seamer). At next two roundabouts, after 2.8 miles and 0.7 miles, follow signs to 'Scarborough A64'. At next roundabout after 1.3 miles go straight on (s/p Town Centre A64, Whitby A171) into Seamer Road. Ground is on LHS after 0.2 miles.
From North (A171 from Whitby): Keep on A171 to the Scalby village sign. Pass the Rosette Inn on RHS after 0.8 miles, and then follow signs to 'Town Centre A171' for a further 1.9 miles over traffic lights and roundabout to second roundabout. Here turn left (s/p Town Centre A171, York A64) into Falsgrave Road. Get in right-hand lane and after 0.1 miles turn right at lights (s/p York A64, Bridlington A165) into Seamer Road. The ground is on the RHS after 0.7 miles.
FROM RAILWAY STATION (Scarborough): 1.2 miles, mainly uphill. *By taxi:* £2.60 plus 10p per person. *By bus:* During the day the no. 17 runs every 15 minutes to the ground. After 6 pm it runs every hour,

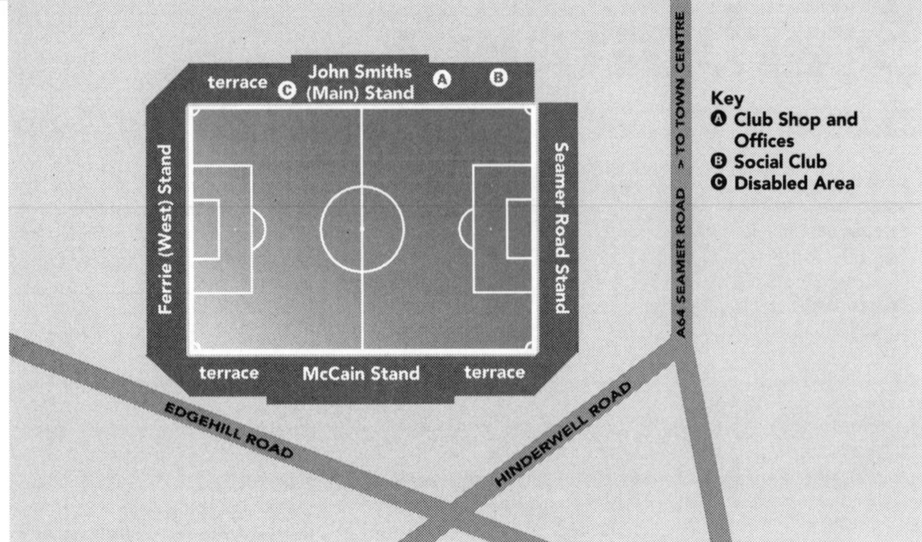

at one-minute past. It's the no. 7 on the way back. *By foot:* Turn left out of station into Falsgrave Road, passing the Victoria Hotel on RHS. At traffic lights after 0.5 miles turn left (s/p York A64) into Seamer Road. The ground is on RHS after 0.7 miles.

Last Midweek Trains: The last train to York is at 21.42. From here there are connections to Leeds (arriving 23.33) and Newcastle (arriving 01.15 but after a two hour wait at York!). There are no connections to London. Please double-check on (0345) 484 950.

BY BUS: See above.

PARKING

The choice is very limited, especially as the police strongly advise visiting fans not to park on streets near the ground. The best bet, therefore, is the Weaponness Valley Road coach and car park. To get there:

a) From South: Continue on Seamer Road past the ground for a further 0.5 miles to lights. Here turn right (s/p Town Centre, Bridlington A160, Coach and Car Park) into Valley Road. Go under railway bridge then turn right (s/p Coach and Car Park) into Ashburn Road.

b) From North: Turn right, as in main road directions above, into Seamer Road. After 0.2 miles turn left (s/p Town Centre, Coach and Car Park, Park and Ride) into St James Road. At T-junction turn right into Londesborough Road and follow signs to 'Town Centre, Coach and Car Park' under the railway bridge. Turn right (s/p Coach and Car Park) into Ashburn Road.

There's a short cut from the car park to the ground. Head away from the entrance up towards the railway line, and turn left along the path by the tracks. Turn right through underpass, and then left into Seamer Road.

THE GROUND

The McStad is now a neat, smart little ground, very much the envy of many a lower division supporter. It's the result of several years' upgrading work, which saw new 1,300-seater stands behind each goal, built at a cost of £1 million, including money raised by the supporters themselves. A lot of character has been retained – helped by the ground's location at the foot of the North York Moors – but without the nightmarish conditions of yesteryear! Visiting fans have benefited from the changes too. The view, from the West Stand behind the goal, is good and facilities generally excellent. Another innovation in 1998 was the re-introduction of terracing for away supporters: however, the price for both seating and standing remains the same.

The club has long-term plans for further ground improvements, mainly dependent on the team gaining promotion. A more bizarre proposal is to erect a huge board between the Main and West Stands, to stop people (including those banned from the ground) watching the game for free from the grassy bank behind.

Total Capacity: 5,538. For away fans: Seating 1,350, standing 688. Turnstiles 1-5 in Edgehill Road.

Cost (98/99): West Stand and Terrace: Adult £10.50, concessions (OAPs/juniors) £6.50.

Disabled Facilities: Space for 20 visiting supporters to the side of the Main Stand. *Disabled Toilet:* Nearby. *Cost:* Free for disabled, full price for helper. *Booking:* Not required. *Parking:* Available, but must be booked in advance. *For the Blind:* No special facilities.

Programme: £1.50.

Visitors' Toilets: *Male:* 'Smart with a few fag ends'

was one description, but fans were generally well impressed. *Female:* Ooo-er, pink and beige brickwork, posh eh? AND seven cubicles, a peg on the wall, hot water and automatic dryers. The Ritz of the lower divisions – puts some Premier clubs to shame, this.
Food and Drink: The pasties were the best bet at £1, though fans considered the steak-and-kidney pies (also at £1) good value, despite their tendency to collapse. The server stirred the tomato soup (70p) most assiduously, but most of it was still left in a greasy lump at the bottom of the cup (9.8.97).

PUB GUIDE

The supporters' club at the ground, which serves John Smiths, admits visiting supporters, entry fee 50p. The next nearest watering hole is the Scarborough Flyer. The other three pubs listed below are all on Falsgrave Road, just a few minutes' drive from the ground towards town:
The Scarborough Flyer (1) Seamer Road (01723) 374 845
Bass. Traditional local with, as it's by the railway line, pictures of trains on the walls. Sandwiches. Pool, TV, darts, beer garden. Families welcome. Open: Saturdays all day from 12; from 4 pm for evening games.
The Tap and Spile (2) Corner of Seamer Road and Falsgrave Road (01723) 363 837
Century Inns (real ales, with 9 guest bitters and 2 guest scrumpy ciders). Excellent traditional ale-house with exposed brickwork and stone floors. Bar meals served Saturdays 11.30-4.30. Darts, TV, beer garden, traditional pub games. Families welcome, separate no-smoking room. Open: all day.
The Ship Inn (3) 71 Falsgrave Road (01723) 508 931
Bass (with cask ales). One-roomed, traditional pub with a good matchday atmosphere, where the food's particularly popular. It serves the Top 20 menu, with all meals at £2.99, from 12-2 and (on Friday, Saturday and Sunday) 5-7. Darts, TV, beer garden, car park at front. Families welcome. Open: all day from 12.
Raffels (4) Falsgrave Road (junction Belgrave Crescent) (01723) 377 859
John Smiths (with Theakstons XB and Directors). Large detached pub/restaurant described by the landlord as 'a classy establishment, welcoming all, with good food, good beer and a good atmosphere'. It's certainly popular. Good menu, from burgers to full three-course meals. Families welcome to 9 pm. Open: all day from 11.45.

FOOD GUIDE

The takeaway in Hinderwell Road has reopened and is the only option near the ground. The fanzine recommends two fish and chip shops on Falsgrave Road, on the way from the station: 'Alleyways' opposite The Ship pub, which does cheap specials, ideal for kids; and 'Mannings' by the Tap and Spile, used by visiting

'They must be Scarborough fans.'

teams for their evening takeaway. There are pizza restaurants and cafés in the same area. In the town centre, very near the railway station, try 'Mother Hubbards' in Westborough, which again won the local 'Fish and Chip Shop of the Year Award'. However, it's more of a restaurant than a takeaway, with haddock and chips costing £3.25.

LOCAL MEDIA

Local Radio: Yorkshire Coast Radio 96.2 FM; BBC Radio York 95.5 FM.
Radio Phone-ins: BBC Radio York, 5-5.30 pm, call (01904) 641 641.
Saturday Sports Paper: None.

MISCELLANEOUS

One of the most misspelt place names in Britain must be 'Middlesbrough'. Not so for Scarborough fans for whom it's a touchy subject. They say Middlesbrough has no claim to the nickname 'Boro' because the town lacks that vital extra 'o'. However, it must be admitted that 'Come on You Bro' lacks a certain something. The fanzine 'The Seadog Bites Back' has been running a campaign for Scarborough to adopt the nickname 'The Seadogs', and the idea's already proving popular. A quick word while we're here about that seagull mascot – why does it have half a duck-billed platypus hanging off its rear end?
Safety Factor: No problems here.
Rivals: York City, 'the worst team in North Yorkshire'.
Fanzines: 'The Seadog Bites Back!', 59 Scalby Road, Scarborough, YO12 5QL.
Unofficial Websites:
http://www.snaiton.demon.co.uk
http://www/angelfire.com/sc/seadogonline
Tourist Information: (01723) 373 333.

S

Scunthorpe United

Glanford Park

Address: Glanford Park, Doncaster Road
Scunthorpe, North Lincolnshire, DN15 8TD
Telephone: Club (01724) 848 077
ClubCall (0891) 121 652
Official Website: 'The Iron World':
http://freespace.virgin.net/su.fc/

Many visiting supporters must leave Scunthorpe with completely the wrong impression! Glanford Park is right on the edge of town, in what estate agents would describe as 'semi-rural surroundings', pleasant but not spectacular. The huge steelworks are on the other side, out of sight over a hill to the east – though at least three plumes of smoke are usually visible on the horizon. Glanford Park is just off the M181, which makes it one of the easiest grounds to find in the entire world. Parking is easy too. From then on, however, life gets more difficult: the choice of food and drink near the ground is limited, and without a car it's a right trek into town.

HOW TO GET THERE

BY CAR: All routes: Exit M180 at junction 3 onto the M181 (s/p Scunthorpe West and Centre M181). After 2.6 miles, at end of motorway, take 3rd exit at roundabout (s/p Scunthorpe A18). The ground is on the RHS a matter of yards from the roundabout.
FROM RAILWAY STATION: 1.9 miles. *By taxi:* About £3. *By bus:* Buses run from John Street. Turn right out of station along Station Road, and take fifth turning on the LHS (Cole Street). John Street is the third turning on the right. Nos. 335 and 341 run though the housing estate to the east of Glanford Park. Ask the driver to tell you the best place to get off. *On foot:* Turn left along main road (s/p Glanford Park). Straight over crossroads/lights into Church Lane, passing a large church on the RHS and then the General Hospital after 0.5 miles. At T-junction after a further 0.3 miles turn right (no s/p) into Kingsway. At Berkeley Roundabout after 0.6 miles take 2nd exit (s/p Doncaster A18 (M180), Goole A186) into Doncaster Road. The ground is on LHS after 0.4 miles.
Last Midweek Trains: There are no connecting trains to London after a night match. The last train to Newcastle leaves at 22.21, via Doncaster, arriving Newcastle at 01.14. Please double-check on (0345) 484 950.
BY BUS: See above.

PARKING

There's parking for 600 cars at the ground (£1), though expect a wait of up to 20 minutes to get out again. Street parking is very limited.

THE GROUND

The surroundings might be rural, but Scunthorpe and Steel go together like, er ... Swindon and Roundabouts, Blackpool and Rollercoasters, Rochdale and Pies, etc, etc. Huge lettering on the North Stand at Glanford Park reads 'British Steel: Scunthorpe Works, Home of Quality', while the opposite stand, where away supporters are housed, is sponsored by the local works Caparo Merchant Bar. Glanford Park was opened in August 1988, when Scunny became the first league team since

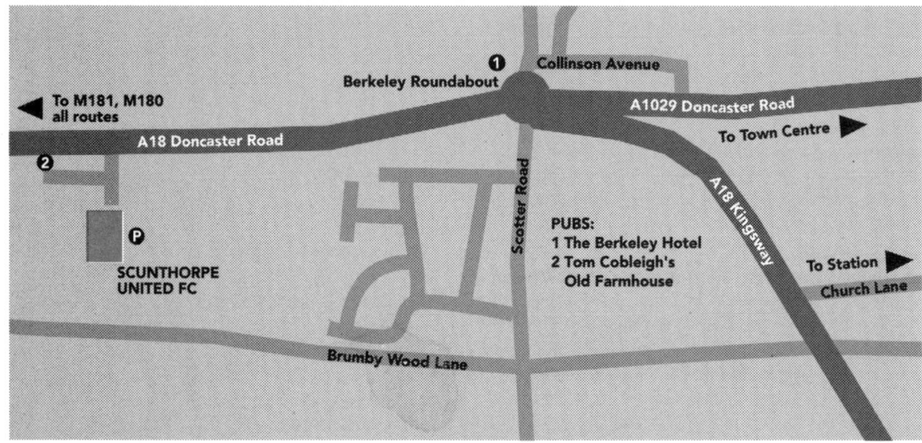

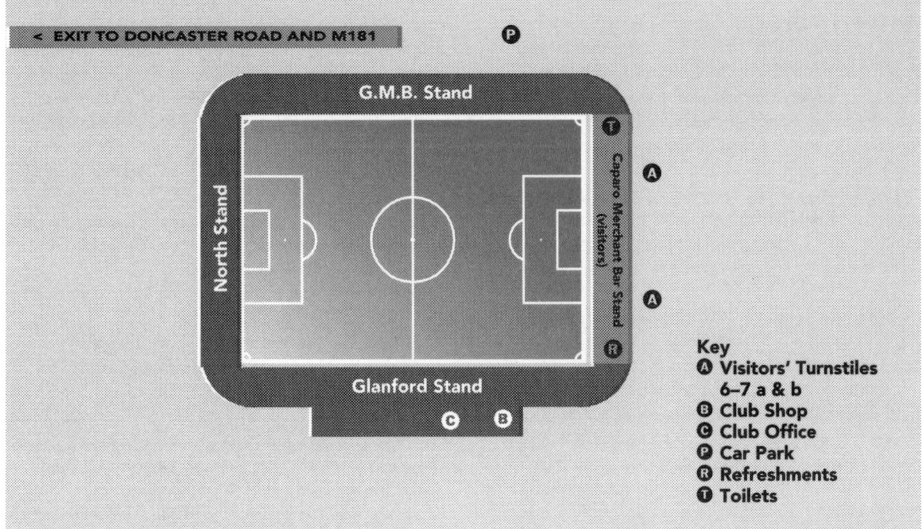

the 1950s to move to a new stadium. For the £2 million it cost to build, it's a valiant effort, but even Iron fans call it 'the tin stadium'. The ground's fully enclosed, which helps the atmosphere, with seating on three sides, terracing for home fans in the North Stand (or 'Donny Road End') and pillars for everyone. The seating in the away end was a late addition, which means that those heading to the snack bars or the loos walk along the front, blocking the view for those in the first few rows. Further back, however, the view is good. The facilities, too, are more than acceptable.

Mention Scunny's former home, the Old Show Ground, and a dreamy look comes over the faces of Third Division fans. 'Now that was a football ground!' they say. 'Was' being the key word really as it's now, sadly, a Safeways. A Scunny fan, Chris Vaughan, wrote a few weeks after the Old Show Ground closed: 'No more shall I enter by turnstile/That stadium where heroes were made/To climb in anticipation/The steps so long ago laid/No more will United's great heroes/Display their wide range of styles/But Brownsword, Thomas and Cammack/Will haunt the supermarket aisles!'

Total Capacity: 9,183. For away fans (Caparo Merchant Bar Stand) 1,643. Turnstiles 6a, 6b, 7a and 7b.

Cost (98/99): Adults £10, children/OAPs £5.50. The SUFC Executive Package is available to visiting fans. It costs £22.50 for a three-course meal, executive seating and access to bars before, during and after the game.

Disabled Facilities: Space for 16 wheelchairs in front of the G.M.B. Stand. *Disabled Toilet:* In G.M.B. Stand. *Cost:* Free for disabled, full price for helper. *Booking:* Advisable. *Parking:* Available. *For the Blind:* Six sets of earphones available in the G.M.B. Stand, linked to hospital radio broadcasts. Please book.

Programme: £1.50.

Visitors' Toilets: *Male:* No more scuzzy Scunny! Clean cubicles, loo paper, locks that worked, sinks, towels – everything except soap. *Female:* 'The cleanest ever!' said one surprised Doncaster follower, though she added, with the suspicion ingrained into the Third Division supporter ... 'Maybe we caught them on a good day'.

Food and Drink: The pie (£1.30) came with a fork (wow!) and was 'not bad – though it could do with more filling', while the pasties (£1.30) and sausage rolls (£1) were 'tasty'. For vegetarians there were cheese-and-onion pies. Fans were impressed with the excellent 'Kenco Silver Seal' coffee (90p), but thought the hot chocolate was a 'bit watery'. Not everyone was happy, however. One tomato-ketchup-less Donny fan had peered into the home end: 'It's an oasis of condiments in there', he raged. 'This away end is a disgrace to the catering services of north Lincolnshire' (13.9.97, 16.9.97).

PUB GUIDE

The Parkinson Arms Mary Street (01724) 844 382
Whitbread. Large friendly – and trendy – pub done out in traditional style, particularly popular on a Saturday night! Basket meals served all day. Big screen TV, pool table. Open: all day from 12.
To get there from Berkeley Roundabout: Take exit signposted 'Town Centre'. At traffic lights after 0.9 miles by the Post Office and the Royal Hotel, turn right (n/s)

into Exeter Road. First left into Mary Street.

The Honest Lawyer ,70 Oswald Road (01724) 849 906 Free House (with 7 ever-changing guest real ales). Cosy real-ale pub of real character, with antique nick-nacks on the walls. Upstairs seating area, all wood paneling and wooden benches, with TV (not Sky). Sandwiches served all day. Families welcome upstairs. Open: all day from 12.

To get there from Berkeley Roundabout: Take the exit signposted 'Town Centre'. At crossroads/lights by 'The Britannia' after 1.2 miles turn right (s/p Grimsby, Gainsborough A159) into Oswald Road. The pub is on LHS after 0.2 miles.

Also highly recommended: **The Berkeley Hotel (1),** Doncaster Road (Sam Smiths, on the Berkeley Roundabout).

The following two pubs are in the village of Gunness. To get there: At the roundabout at the end of the M181, instead of turning right to Glanford Park, turn left (s/p Doncaster A18). Keep on the main road – the Jolly Sailor is on the LHS after 1.2 miles, and the Ironstone Wharf Inn is 0.3 miles round the corner on the RHS.

The Jolly Sailor Doncaster Road, Gunness (01724) 782 423 John Smiths. Popular, cosy village pub. Bar snacks. Pool, darts, TV. All well-behaved fans welcome. Open: all day.

The Ironstone Wharf Inn Station Road, Gunness (01724) 782 486

John Smiths. The ultimate old-style village local, complete with a small sweet/cigarette stall! Small lounge area and public bar with darts and TV. Bar snacks, and full meals at £3.25 – 'anything you want', says the landlord, and that includes rabbit stew. Breakfast from 8 am, meals until 8 pm. Families welcome. Open: all day.

FOR FAMILIES:

The first major development of the sites next to, and opposite, Glanford Park is:

Tom Cobleigh's Old Farmhouse (2) Doncaster Road (01724) 276 376

Tom Cobleigh (with Boddingtons, Waddington's Draught, Pedigree and 3 guest ales). Large new pub, very welcoming and excellent for families. Full menu (including beefburger and chips for £3.95) served 12-9.30. Children's menu. Playbarn (£1 per hour). Disabled facilities and baby-changing. Open: all day. NB The pub charges £1 for parking, redeemable at the bar.

FOOD GUIDE

The nearest takeaway to Glanford Park is the 'Moon Palace', near the Berkeley Roundabout, but it doesn't open until 5.30 pm. It does Chinese and English food, including sausage and chips for £2.90. For a wider choice, take the exit at the Berkeley Roundabout signposted 'Town Centre', and continue straight on for another mile. On the RHS there's a row of shops, including a KFC, three Chinese takeaways/restaurants, an Indian restaurant, and two highly recommended fish and chip shops. The first is 'Atlantis Fish and Chips', which is proud of all its awards as best Scunthorpe chippie. It does a fish and chip lunch special for just £1, as well as burgers for 75p and pies for £1.25. The nearby 'Hungry Fisherman' offers haddock and chips for £2.75 and pie and chips for £2.65. It also has a bar and restaurant, advertising children's main courses for £1.75.

LOCAL MEDIA

Local Radio: BBC Radio Humberside 95.9 FM; Lincs FM 102.2 FM; Viking Radio 96.9 FM.

Radio Phone-ins: BBC Radio Humberside, Tuesdays 7-10 pm. Call (01482) 225 959.

Saturday Sports Paper: The 'Sports Telegraph', which covers Scunthorpe and Grimsby, arrives in Scunthorpe at about 5.45 pm.

MISCELLANEOUS

The *Football Fan's Guide* is always interested in the weird and wonderful, and this was a great story. 'Everyone seemed friendly,' wrote one Everton fan of his trip to Scunthorpe for a Coca Cola tie in September 1997. 'But the two young female Scunthorpe fans who ran towards the Everton end without clothes were perhaps being a little too friendly.' Apparently the ref didn't even halt the game ... now that's concentration! But really, streakers? At Scunthorpe? Now Lord's or Wimbledon Centre Court we can understand, but Glanford Park? However, it's not a new phenomenon. Scunny fans say the first streaker at Glanford Park was in a pre-season friendly against Clydebank a couple of years back. To the disappointment of (most) fans, this one was male.

Safety Factor: Another first for Scunthorpe. During and after the FA Cup match against Ilkeston in 1997, the police used CS gas to disperse fighting fans – the first time it had ever been used at a football ground. However, the rival supporters were those of Nottingham Forest and Derby County, who'd come along to support Ilkeston. Scunthorpe fans were not involved and Glanford Park is generally a very safe ground to visit.

Rivals: An Iron fan listed: Grimsby ('Codheads'), Doncaster ('because they always do well at our place. Always!'), Hull and Lincoln ('the sort of timid rivalry you can live with').

Fanzine: 'Son of a Referee', 40 Victoria Road, First Floor Flat, Ashby, Scunthorpe, North Lincolnshire, DN16 2SA.

Unofficial Websites:

http://www.personal.ksu.edu/~njh/sufc/

Tourist Information: No office in Scunthorpe.

Sheffield United

Bramall Lane

Address: Bramall Lane, Sheffield, S2 4SU
Telephone: Club (0114) 221 5757
Ticket Information (0114) 221 1889
Shop (0114) 221 3132
ClubCall (0891) 888 650
Official Website: http://www.sufc.co.uk

Sheffield, as the locals always tell you, is a great place to live – not too big, not too small and with the Pennines only a short drive away. 'It's the largest village in England', said one supporter. 'People even say thank-you to bus drivers!' At present the area round Bramall Lane is flat and unremarkable – mostly student housing and industrial units – interspersed, thankfully, with a number of pubs and takeaways. However, there are ambitious redevelopment plans, both for the football stadium and the surrounding area, which will make Bramall Lane even more of a landmark. The city centre and the station are less than ten minutes' walk away, but matchday parking remains a bit of a pain.

HOW TO GET THERE

BY CAR: From All Main Routes (M1): Exit M1 at junction 33 (s/p Sheffield (Centre), Rotherham A630). At roundabout follow signs to 'Sheffield Centre A630' onto the A630 dual carriageway. At Victoria Quays Roundabout after 5.3 miles keep in lane for 'City Centre A61'. At Park Square roundabout after 0.2 miles take 3rd exit (s/p Ring Road, Chesterfield A61) into Sheaf Street. After passing railway station on LHS, get in middle lane for Sheaf Square roundabout. Take 1st exit (s/p Ring Road, Chesterfield A61, Bramall Lane) and then keep in right-hand lane, turning right at the lights (s/p Ring Road, Bakewell A621, also The Leadmill) into Shoreham Street. Straight through first set of lights (s/p Ring Road, Bramall Lane) and straight on at the next. Ground is on RHS after 0.1 miles (away turnstiles on opposite side of ground).

From Chesterfield (A61): At first roundabout on edge of Sheffield go straight on (s/p Sheffield A61, Lowedges) and straight on at Meadowhead Roundabout (s/p City Centre A61). Keep on A61 for a further 3.0 miles – down a long hill, through the suburb of Woodseats, past Bridge Inn on RHS and over river bridge. At lights by Rawson Bathrooms, bear right (no s/p) into Queens Road. Keep in left hand lane and after a couple of hundred yards turn left just after Earl of Arundel and Surrey pub (s/p City Centre A621, Barnsley A61). The road immediately divides: the left fork (up towards J.E James cycle shop) is Bramall Lane.

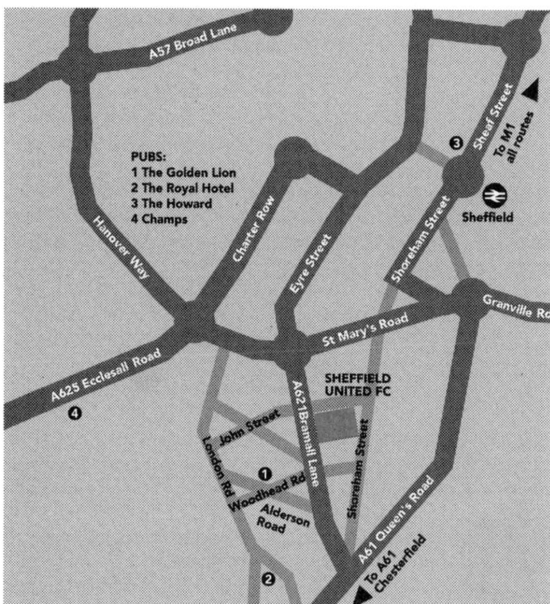

FROM RAILWAY STATION: About 0.5 miles. *By bus:* It's quicker to walk. *By foot:* Bear left to roundabout, and take first exit. Where road divides turn right (s/p Ring Road, Bakewell A621, Leadmill) into Shoreham Street. Straight over two sets of lights and ground is on RHS.

Last Midweek Trains: To London (via Doncaster) 21.32. To Newcastle (via Doncaster) 23.09. Please double-check on (0345) 484 950.

BY BUS: Buses 13, 15, 16, 18, 252 and 253 run from Arundel Gate (opposite the Crucible Theatre) while the no. 39 runs from the bus station.

BY SUPERTRAM: Two lines, the Blue and the Purple, run to Granville Road, about three minutes walk from Bramall Lane.

PARKING

Street parking is about the only option, so try to arrive early for the best spots. Despite extra

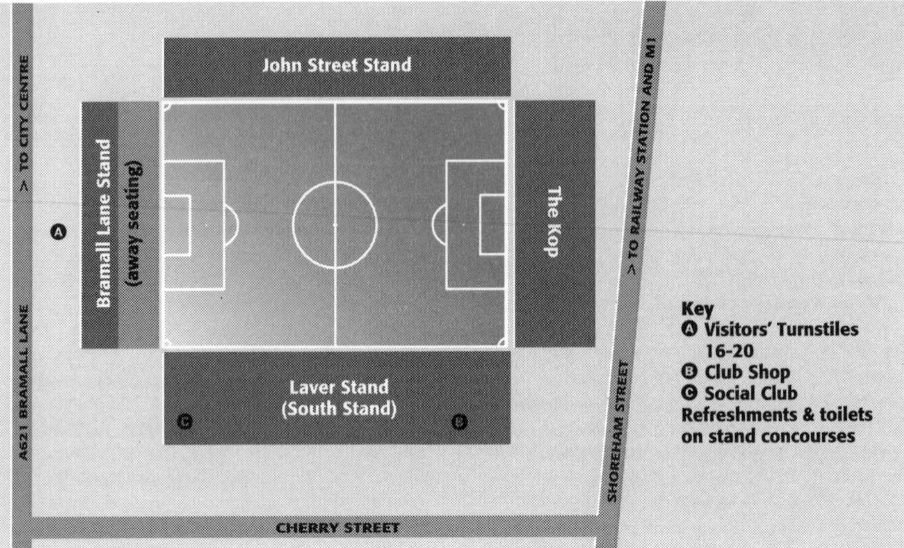

police patrols on matchdays, there is still some car crime so don't leave valuables in sight and remove all away-team insignia.

THE GROUND

The new John Street Stand was opened in October 1996 with great fanfare and a huge sigh of relief from Unitedites. Overnight Bramall Lane became a four-sided ground once more, with 30,000 seats and a lot of the old atmosphere. It appears this was just the start of the building work. United, in association with the city council and the local community, has announced plans for a 'Blades Leisure Park' to 'propel the club, the facilities, the image and experience of visiting the Bramall Lane area into the 21st century'. The stadium capacity will be increased to 35,000 by the infilling of the corners and additional low-level seating, while a hundred-bed hotel, linked to a 'sky deck viewing platform over the football ground' will rise from the south-west corner. Other developments include a new club megastore and museum, housing and new shopping and leisure complexes.

Away fans have been moved from the top to the bottom tier of the Bramall Lane Stand, though the view remains good. When a lot of visiting fans are expected, the club can also make the upper tier available. There's a betting kiosk inside the stand. The unreserved seating for home fans in the top tier of the Bramall Lane Stand has proved popular with Unitedites, who are now campaigning to take over the entire stand, with visitors moved to the sides. No final decision on such a change has, however, yet been made.

Total Capacity: 30,000. For away fans: Seating (lower tier, Bramall Lane): 2,663. Additional upper tier seating: 2,700. Turnstiles in Bramall Lane.

Cost (98/99): Adult £11, concessions (under 16s and OAPs) £7. Concessions for students available if bought in advance through the visiting club.

Programme: £1.50.

Disabled Facilities: Space for 6-10 disabled supporters, plus their helpers, in the John Street Stand Family Enclosure. *Disabled Toilet:* Two available nearby. *Cost:* Free for both wheelchair and ambulant disabled, £5 for helper. *Booking:* Essential – please call Daniel Oldfield at the club on (0114) 221 5757. *Parking:* Available, but booking essential. *For the Blind:* Hospital radio commentary in the Laver Stand. Booking essential.

Visitors' Toilets: *Male:* Our researcher had visited the John Street toilets the previous season, which he described as 'palatial, immaculate, with taps you can see your face in'. The Bramall Lane Stand loos didn't quite match up especially as by half-time there were no loo rolls or paper towels. All acceptably clean, however. *Female:* Strange to go in the loos and immediately think of jelly and blancmange – it was the combination of the red doors and sugar-pink walls! Again, all very acceptable, though those trendy aircraft-style loos are a mite uncomfortable.

Food and Drink: What a great idea – boy meets girl at Bramall Lane, magnificent last-minute winner caps a cracking cup-tie, and boy plucks up courage to invite girl back into the stand for another cup of Gold Blend coffee. Well, if they sell the stuff at the ground – and very nice it is too (80p) – why not film the advertisement there? It might deflect attention away from the big-bun-little-meat burgers (£2.10) and the fact that the kiosks ran out of onions, cheese and sauce! Sunderland fans liked the hot dogs (£2.10) but Ipswich fans described the pies (£1.55) as 'crisp pastry filled with a cold, grey sludge' (10.8.97, 3.2.98).

PUB GUIDE

The Golden Lion (1) 69 Alderson Road. (0114) 258 1640.
Free House. Small fan-friendly traditional pub, which – says the landlord – 'concentrates on good beers'. It's very popular, so does fill up quickly. Sandwiches. TV. Families welcome. Open: 11.30-3.30; from 5.30 for midweek games.
The Royal Hotel (2) London Road. (0114) 250 6910
Bass. Enormous pub run by a football fan, and with a good matchday atmosphere. Bar snacks served 12.-2.30 and after the match until 8 pm. There's also a restaurant. Pool table, snooker, big-screen TV. Families welcome. Open: all day.
The Howard (3) 57 Howard Street (opposite station). (0114) 278 0183
Mansfield Brewery. Large, busy, traditional city centre pub, all dark wood and red velvet seats. Breakfast served from 8 am, lunches 11-4. Pool table, big-screen TV. Disabled facilities. There are doormen from 2-4 on matchdays, and away fans are usually admitted. However, entry may be restricted when there's a big game. Open: Sat matchdays 11-3, 7-11; midweek all day.
Champs (4) 315-319 Ecclesall Road, about 0.75 miles from Bramall Lane. (0114) 266 6333.
Free House (with frequent special promotions). Large smart 'Sports Bar', full of sporting memorabilia. Meals and snacks available all day from 12. Families welcome/children's menu. 44 TVs! Open: all day from 11.30.

FOOD GUIDE

There's no need to wander too far afield for sustenance here. Unusually, local fans recommend a mobile burger van – the one which parks outside the John Street Stand'. Also right by the ground, try the 'Shoreham Fisheries, on Shoreham Street – 'absolutely fabulous food' said one Unitedite and indeed there are usually hordes of fans outside tucking into chips and mushy peas (£95p-£1.10) or chilli and chips (£1). 'Pee Bees' also on Shoreham Street, towards the city centre, offers sandwiches, pies (80p) and chip butties (70p). London Road has loads of takeaways, and is best known for its Chinese and Indian restaurants – though visiting fans are advised against wearing colours in the area. Ecclesall Road – about half a mile from Bramall Lane – has a wider variety, such as Café Rouge, Pizza Hut and KFC.

'To hell with Majorca. We can come here for a fortnight!'

LOCAL MEDIA

Local Radio: BBC Radio Sheffield FM 88.6, 104.1, 94.7; Hallam FM 97.4 and 103.4 FM.
Radio Phone-Ins: BBC Radio Sheffield, 'Praise or Grumble' 5 pm. Call (0114) 268 2222; Hallam FM, Saturdays 5-6 pm and after midweek games to 10 pm. Call (0114) 285 2050.
Saturday Sports Paper: The 'Green 'Un', produced by the *Sheffield Star*, arrives in shops from 6 pm.

MISCELLANEOUS

Safety Factor: Bramall Lane is a very safe ground to visit, though it's a good idea to cover club colours along London Road.
Rivals: The 'Red and White Wizaaaard' lists: 'That shower on the other side of town (Sheffield Wednesday), and 'that horrible lot at the end of the M1' (Leeds).
Fanzines: 'Flashing Blade', 4 Cross Myrtle Road, Sheffield, S2 3EL; 'The Greasy Chip Buttie', 48 Grove Avenue, Hemsworth, West Yorkshire, WF9 4JB; 'The Red and White Wizaaaard' (published by the Blades Independent Fans Association), PO Box 111, Sheffield, S8 7YU.
Unofficial Websites:
http://www.shef.ac.uk/city/blades/
BIFA: http://pine.shu.ac.uk/~cmssa/bifa.html.
Tourist Information: (0114) 273 4672.

S

Sheffield Wednesday

Hillsborough

Address: Hillsborough, Sheffield S6 1SW
Telephone: Club (0114) 221 2121
Ticket Office (0114) 221 2400
The Owls Superstore (0114) 221 2345
ClubCall (0891) 121 186
Official Website: http://www.swfc.co.uk

When Sheffield Wednesday moved to its present site in 1899, it was into a rural area well outside the furthest north Sheffield suburb. Now of course, Sheffield has engulfed the ground, bringing with it terraced houses, industrial estates, the Supertram and three excellent fish and chip shops. Hillsborough, especially for night games, has a genuine old-style atmosphere: hundreds of fans trundling up and down Penistone Road, going in and out of the corner newsagents, carrying programmes, burgers and bags of chips. If visiting fans complain about anything, it's about the matchday traffic jams and parking problems. And the good points? Excellent pubs, good pies and a great view of the game.

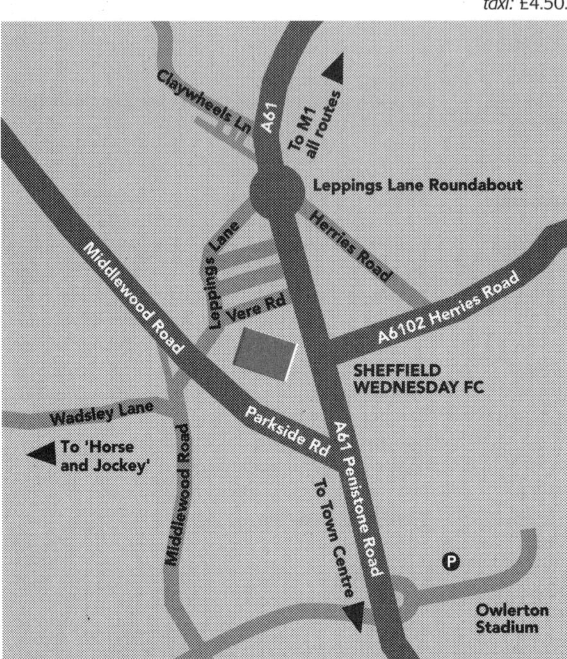

HOW TO GET THERE

For big games, allow lots of extra time for pre-match traffic and to find a parking space.

BY CAR: From North: Exit M1 at junction 36 (s/p Barnsley (South) A61). At roundabout turn right (s/p Sheffield A61) onto the A61 dual carriageway. At roundabout after 0.9 miles, go straight on (s/p Sheffield North A61). (*)From here, signs to 'Sheffield North' and 'City Centre A61' lead directly to the ground, a distance of 5.6 miles. The route passes the Norfolk Arms after 3.4 miles, the Red Lion after 3.6 miles and the White Horse after 5.1 miles. The road leads to a roundabout (the Leppings Lane Roundabout) at the bottom of hill, by an Esso station. It forms the junction of the A61, Penistone Road and Leppings Lane.

From South: Exit M1 at junction 35A (s/p Manchester A616), and at roundabout follow signs to Manchester A616 onto the A616. At roundabout (by McDonalds) after 1.2 miles, take 1st exit (s/p Sheffield North A61) onto the A61. Then as From North(*).

FROM RAILWAY STATION (Sheffield): 3.5 miles. *By taxi:* £4.50. *By bus:* Special buses run from Flat Street, next to the Pond Street Interchange. The Interchange entrance is opposite the station. Normal bus service nos. 43, 53, 74, 77, and 80 run along Penistone Road; nos. 57, 66, 67, 85 and 86 go via Middlewood. Mainline Buses usually park outside the visitors' end after the match to take fans back to the station.

Last Midweek Trains: To London (via Doncaster) 21.32; to Leeds 23.14 (not Friday); to Newcastle (via Doncaster) 23.09. Please double-check on (0345) 484 950. On Saturdays, the police often escort the buses from Hillsborough to the railway station so London-based supporters can catch the 17.25.

BY BUS: As above.

BY SUPERTRAM: The Yellow line, from Meadowhall to Middlewood via the city centre, runs past the top of Hillsborough. Ask for the Leppings Lane stop. There are also connections from the railway station.

PARKING

There's a large car park at the Owlerton greyhound stadium, a 8-10 minute walk

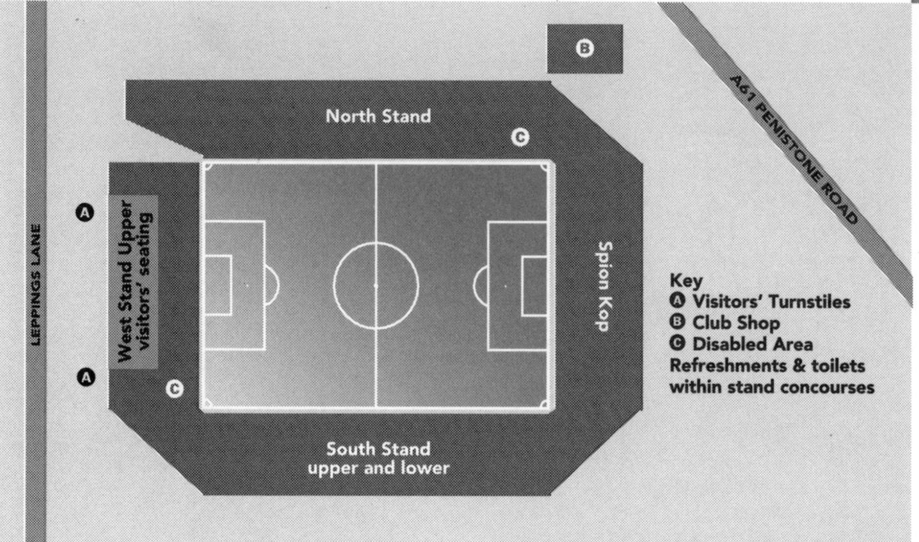

from the ground. To get there: from the Leppings Lane Roundabout by the ground, go straight on (s/p City Centre A61, Owlerton, Hillsborough), and the stadium is on the LHS after 0.6 miles (s/p Barnsley A61, Manchester A628). Alternatively, loop all the way round the Leppings Lane Roundabout and head back up the A61. Turn left almost immediately (s/p Clay Wheels) into Beeley Wood Road, which leads into Clay Wheels Lane. Cars park along here, and there's a secure car park at the site of an old brewery, on the RHS after 0.4 miles.

For bigger games, the police contact local schools and other institutions to ask them to open their car parks for matchday parking, eg. the Chaucer School, on the A61 just before 'The White Horse'.

THE GROUND

Hillsborough is one of Britain's top football stadiums, and was rightly chosen as a venue for Euro 96. However, because it was developed piecemeal, it has four individual stands, all impressive but somewhat cavernous. Wednesdayites say a lot of atmosphere was lost when the ground was converted to all-seater, and – to make matters worse – it's often only two-thirds full. That said, the ground has retained some character, including an intricate gable, designed by the great football architect Archibald Leitch, which adorns the top of the South Stand. The River Don flows behind this stand, and before the match many supporters gather on the outer concourse, drinking their coffee and staring into the murky water. Visiting fans are housed in the top tier of the West Stand, where the view is excellent.

Total Capacity: 40,000. For away fans: West Stand Upper 3,800.

Cost (97/98): Adult: £18, £15 or £13 depending on match category. Concessions (juniors/OAPs): £12, £10 or £9. Turnstiles 11-13 and 20-23.

Disabled Facilities: Space for six visiting supporters in the West Stand Lower. *Disabled Toilet:* Nearby. *Cost:* Free for disabled and helper. *Booking:* Essential. *Parking:* Subject to availability. *For the Blind:* Headphones with commentary available throughout the stadium.

Programme: £2.

Visitors' Toilets: *Male:* If the All-Yorkshire Curry-Eating Champions are at the match, expect big trouble. Yep, just one cubicle! Both it, and the other facilities, were very clean, however. *Female:* Very old-fashioned, with a bizarre colour scheme: rust on the floors, blue and primrose on the walls.

Food and Drink: Blackburn fans really liked the pies (£1.60). One said: 'Absolutely brilliant, superb. I might even go for another one in a minute.' He'd also liked the hot dog with onions (£1.70). The only criticism was about the lack of choice (pies, pasties or hot dogs), and the price of the Kenco coffee (£1.10) (26.1.98).

PUB GUIDE

Most of the pubs near Hillsborough are home fans only, so visitors have to venture a little further afield. These first three pubs are on the main A61 into Sheffield from the M1:

The Norfolk Arms Grenoside (on A61) (0114) 245 4153

Wards (with Vaux). Cosy, one-roomed pub, with a good selection of hot bar meals served 12-2.15 (not Sundays, sandwiches only if very busy). TV. Families welcome lunch-times. Open: all day.

The Red Lion 95 Penistone Road, Grenoside (on A61, opposite UK petrol station) (0114) 246 0084
Whitbread (with Pedigree, Boddingtons and Trophy). Large pub in a 16th century listed building, with smart lounge/restaurant and a more traditional tap room with TV. Full menu served 12-10 pm. Families welcome/children's menu. Open: all day.
The White Horse 104 Halifax Road (on A61) (0114) 231 1434
Tetley. Large Mr Q's theme pub, so the emphasis is on snooker and pool. Very football friendly, with big-screen TV. Bar snacks served all day. Open: all day.
'The Fox' is on a side road off the A61, 0.2 miles further down the hill from 'The White Horse'. Turn right at lights just before the railway bridge into Foxhill Road. Pub is on RHS after 0.6 miles. Easy walk to ground, steep hill back.
The Fox Foxhill Road (0114) 231 1346
Whitbread (plus Magnet). Large, traditional pub with smart lounge and smaller tap room with pool table. TV, darts. Families welcome. Large car park. Open: all day.
The Horse and Jockey Wadsley Lane (top end, junction with Worrall Lane, 0.75 miles from ground) (0114) 234 8440
Whitbread (selection of traditional ales). Attractive pub in a 100-year-old building – and retaining almost a country feel. Sandwiches. Pool, darts, TV. Families welcome. Open: all day.
Champs on Ecclesall Road near Bramall Lane welcomes all football fans. It's a very popular 'sports bar' full of memorabilia, with a restaurant open all day from 12.

FOOD GUIDE

Those approaching Hillsborough from the M1 pass several eateries, including a McDonalds on the Wentworth Industrial Park. By 'The White Horse' is a row of shops including a fish and chip shop called 'Today's Catch', and 'The Pork Shop', serving a Sheffield speciality, hot pork sandwiches with stuffing and crackling for £1.05. For a wider choice, head for the shopping street at Middlewood (signposted from around Hillsborough) which runs along the top of Leppings Lane. It has another 'Today's Catch', another 'Pork Shop', a 'Proud Potato', 'Perfect Pizza', a KFC, Chinese and Indian takeaways and a bakers selling pies.

Around the ground are three good takeaways: The 'Hoong Too' on the corner of Penistone Road and Vere Road; 'Mitchells', on the corner of Leppings Lane and Bickerton Road; and 'Four Lanes' at the top of Leppings Lane (corner Middlewood Road).

LOCAL MEDIA

Local Radio: BBC Radio Sheffield FM 88.6, 104.1, 94.7; Hallam FM 97.4 and 103.4 FM.
Radio Phone-ins: BBC Radio Sheffield, 'Praise or Grumble', from 5 pm, call (0114) 268 2222;
Hallam FM, Saturdays 5-6, and after midweek games to 10 pm, call (0114) 285 2050.
Saturday Sports Paper: The excellent 'Green 'Un'.

MISCELLANEOUS

Safety Factor: Trouble at Hillsborough is rare.
Rivals: Sheffield United. Graham Lightfoot, editor of the excellent fanzine 'Spitting Feathers' says that, as a child, he was told never to eat streaky bacon because of the red and white stripes ... and he still doesn't!
Fanzines: 'Spitting Feathers', PO Box 97, Sheffield, S10 1YD; 'War of the Monster Trucks', 79 Beechwood Road, Sheffield, S6 4LQ.
Unofficial Websites:
SWFC:
http://www.dcs.shef.ac.uk/~u6dbg/wedframe.htm
Barmy Army:
http://www.geocities.com/Colosseum/2938/
Owls@Sheffield:
http://www.shef.ac.uk/students/fr/fra95eth/
OwlsNet: http://www.sheffwed.net.au/index.html
Tourist Information: (0114) 273 4671/2.

Shrewsbury Town

Gay Meadow

Address: Gay Meadow, Shrewsbury, SY2 6AB
Telephone: Club/Ticket Information (01743) 360 111
Town Talk (0891) 121 194
Official Website: http://www.Shrewsburytown.co.uk

The sign at Arsenal boasts: 'Highbury – the Home of Football'. The town of Shrewsbury sends out tourist information headlined: 'Shrewsbury – The Home of Brother Cadfael'. The famous fictitious monk lived, according to the medieval mystery books, at Shrewsbury Abbey, just opposite Gay Meadow, and his beloved gardens may perhaps have stood under the present-day football turf. Footie may not be the main focus of the town's tourist officials, but for the visiting supporter this is usually one of the season's highlights. Gay Meadow lays claim to the most picturesque location in the league, right on the bank of the River Severn. And it's only a short walk from the old town centre, with its touristy shops, pubs and cafés. There's ample parking, and a number of friendly pubs nearby.

HOW TO GET THERE

BY CAR: From West (A5): Keep on A5 as it bypasses Shrewsbury, to the roundabout which forms the junction with the A49/A5112. Take 1st exit (s/p Shrewsbury A5112) into Hereford Road. Straight on at Hereford Road Roundabout after 0.3 miles (s/p Meole Brace, Town Centre). At Meole Brace Roundabout after 0.4 miles and at the Sutton Park Roundabout after a further 0.7 miles follow signs to 'Town Centre' and 'Monkmoor A5112'. At Reabrook Roundabout after 0.4 miles take 3rd exit (s/p Football Ground, Abbey, Shrewsbury Quest) into Hancock Way. At Column Roundabout after 0.3 miles take 1st exit (s/p Football Ground, Abbey, Shrewsbury Quest) into Abbey Foregate. (*)The Abbey Foregate parking is on the LHS after 0.6 miles. For the ground and the away parking there, go straight on to next roundabout. Here, follow signs to the 'Town Centre' under the railway bridge. Then move into right hand lanes, following signs (on the road) for Other Traffic, and then Shrewsbury Quest. Move back into the left hand lanes, and turn left in front of the 'Balti Bazar' – i.e. before passing under the elaborate railway bridge.

From East (M54): Follow M54 to its end, where it becomes the A5. After 6.6 miles go straight on at roundabout (s/p North Wales, Shrewsbury A5) keeping on the A5. At next roundabout after 1.2 miles, take 4th exit (s/p Shrewsbury A5064) onto the A5064 London Road. At Column Roundabout after 1.1 miles take 3rd exit (s/p Football Ground, Abbey, Shrewsbury Quest) into Abbey Foregate. Then as From West (*).

From North (A53,A49): At roundabout which forms junction of A53 and A49, follow signs to 'Shrewsbury A5112' into Battlefield Road. Go straight on for 1.6 miles to the Heathgates Roundabout. Here, take 2nd exit (s/p Monkmoor A5112, Ludlow A49 and Football Ground) into Telford Way. From here the ground is well signposted, bringing traffic into Abbey Foregate. Then as From West(*).

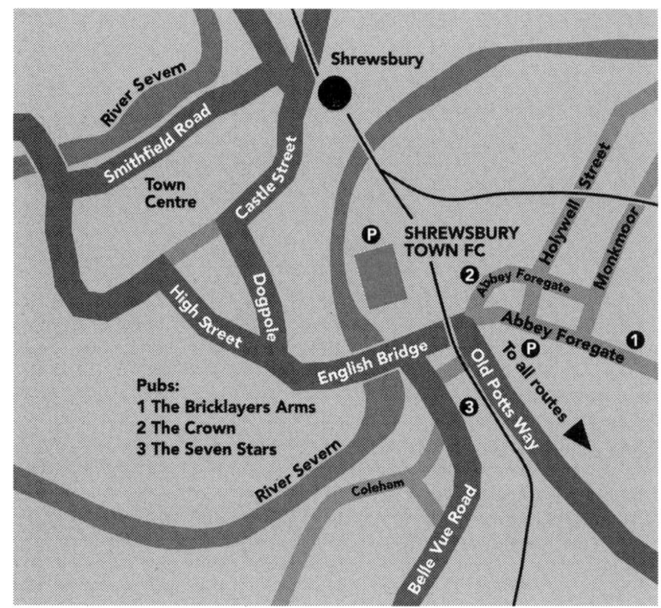

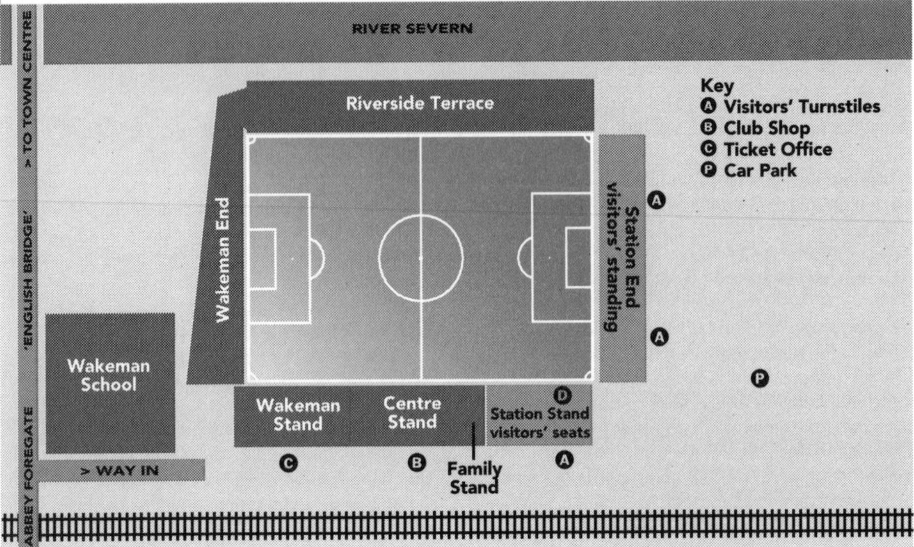

Tip: If lost, follow signs to The Shrewsbury Quest or Shrewsbury Abbey, which are both close to the ground.

FROM RAILWAY STATION (Shrewsbury): Short walk over bridge or 0.7 miles through town. *By taxi:* £2. *By foot:* The back route to the ground, avoiding the town centre, has reopened. The ground is visible from the platform: head over the railway bridge then bear right down to the ground.

Last Midweek Trains: There are no connecting trains to London after an evening match. However trains run to Crewe (23.32) and Birmingham (21.57). Please double-check on (0345) 484 950.

BY BUS: The best buses from the town centre are nos. 1 and 11. However minibus numbers 8, 16, 19, 21 and 26 also run to the ground.

PARKING

There's a car park (£2) for visiting supporters at the ground. Alternatively try the large pay-and-display car park by Shrewsbury Abbey, almost opposite Gay Meadow (70p up to 6.30 pm, free thereafter). There's also street parking in the areas round Holywell Street and Monkmoor Road.

THE GROUND

Gay Meadow is nearing its sell-by date, and fast. The club is well aware that improvements need to be made, and are keen to make them, but finances remain tight. A council covenant on the ground, stipulating its use as a sporting venue only, prevents the club from raising money by other means (e.g. car boot sales, fund-raising events). So improvements in 1998 were restricted to the upgrading of terracing, ready for the addition of seating by the 1999 deadline.

All that aside, Gay Meadow is a well-kept, characterful ground, with covered or uncovered terracing on three sides. Visiting fans are allocated the Station End terracing, which is partially covered, and seats in the Main Stand. Don't expect the Ritz.

Total Capacity: 8,000. For away fans: Seating (Station Stand) 500. Turnstiles 13-14. Terrace (Station End) 1,500. Turnstiles 15-17.

Cost (98/99): Seating: Adults £10, concessions (juniors/OAPs) £7. Terrace £8/£5. Concessions for students on production of student cards.

Disabled Facilities: Space for six away fans in the corner of the Station Stand. *Disabled Toilet:* In the home disabled area only. *Cost:* Free for disabled, £5 for helper. *Booking:* Helpful, but not essential. Call Mike Ashton at Shrewsbury Town on (01743) 356 316. *Parking:* Available. *For the Blind:* No special facilities.

Programme: £1.50.

Visitors' Toilets: *Male:* And for today's modern football supporter we have ... one wall and two cubicles. *Female:* The toilets were reasonably clean and the sink was very clean, but there were no dryers — okay in August, but not so grand in mid-February.

Food and Drink: A strange sound emanated from near the snack bar ... slap,slap,slap,slap. Ghostly flagellating monks perhaps?! No, away fans chucking their red-hot pasties (£1.55) from hand to hand. When they did cool down they were pretty good, with meat and 'a pea'. The sausage rolls (£1.10) had 'heavenly pastry' but fans thought them — and the burgers at £2.10 — a bit expensive (9.8.97, 4.10.97).

PUB GUIDE

The police advise visiting fans to avoid the town centre. Nearer the ground, try:

The Bricklayers Arms (1) Abbey Foregate (01743) 235 779
Bass (with Caffreys). Traditional newly-refurbished local, voted 'Sports Pub of Britain 1995'. Sandwiches. Pool, darts, TV, beer garden. Families welcome before match. Open: all day from 11.30.

The Crown (2) Abbey Foregate (01743) 242 972
Bass (with guest beer). Popular two-roomed pub. A doorman on matchdays allows in well-behaved home and away fans. Families welcome. Full bar menu served 11.30-1.30 (or until it gets too busy). Darts, TV, beer garden. Open: all day.

The Heathgates Whitchurch Road (by Heathgates roundabout on route in From North) (01743) 344 752
Bass. Large newly-refurbished and particularly sports-friendly pub, with separate pool room. Families welcome. Bar meals and snacks, plus children's menu. Big-screen TV, darts, bar games. Disabled facilities. Open: all day.

The following football-friendly pub is in Coleham, a few minutes' walk from the ground. There are other good pubs nearby, but they don't welcome groups of football supporters, or football colours.

The Seven Stars (3) Old Coleham Head (01743) 352 108
Free House (with real ales, Bass). Small, extremely friendly locals pub, where clog dancers regularly go to practise! Families welcome. Separate pool room. Darts, TV. Open: all day from midday.
How to get there: At roundabout by ground, follow signs to Belle Vue into Coleham Head. Pub is on LHS.

FOR FAMILIES:

The White Horse 7 Wenlock Road (on Column Roundabout) (01743) 356 339
Ansells (with Tetleys). Highly recommended 'Big Steak' pub/restaurant within walking distance of the ground. Large smart lounge bar/restaurant area, plus separate public bar with TV. Full menu plus bar meals served 12-10 pm. Children's menu, vegetarian options. Darts, two pool tables, patio. Disabled facilities.

For a quiet drink, try the **Nag's Head** pub in Wyle Cop in town. It's a lovely traditional pub in a 14th century building, and very family-orientated.

FOOD GUIDE

Abbey Foregate, around 'The Crown' pub, is a little community in itself, with several takeaways including the 'Abbey Fish' Restaurant (cod £1.75, chips from 75p), a little supermarket, a newsagents, a bank and a bookies. Home supporters recommend 'The Dropped Scone', a small café/takeaway, for cheap classics, such as the all day breakfast for £2 and the hot dogs at £1. The café

also serves full meals for around £3.50. The 'Balti Bazar', right by the entrance to Gay Meadow, is a 'Master Chef, Roll of Honour' – or so says the certificate on the door – so it should be good. A little further from the ground, by the 'White Horse' pub, is another fish and chip shop called 'The Shire Fryer'. It has fish for £1.80 and pies for £1.20.

LOCAL MEDIA

Local Radio: BBC Radio Shropshire 95/96 FM, 756 and 1584 MW; Beacon Radio 103.1 FM.
Radio Phone-ins: BBC Radio Shropshire takes calls if there's a big talking point. Call (01743) 248 321; Beacon Radio has a phone-in from 5-6 pm on Saturdays. Call (01743) 244 295.
Saturday Sports Paper: The Sporting Star, known as the 'Pink 'Un', produced in Wolverhampton, arrives in Shrewsbury at about 6.30 pm.

MISCELLANEOUS:

Safety Factor: Inside the ground there's been no trouble for years, and most matches are 'police-free'. All hooligans have been banned. However, Shrewsbury does have a small idiot following, which usually keeps to the town centre.
Rivals: Wrexham and Walsall, and anyone who mistakenly believes Shrewsbury to be in Wales.
Fanzines: 'A Large Scotch', 15 York Road, Harlescott Grange, Shrewsbury, WY1 3RD; 'The Mighty Shrew', 17 Priory Ridge, Shrewsbury, Shropshire, SY3 9EH.
Unofficial Websites: None.
Tourist Information: (01743) 350 761.

Southampton

The Dell

Address: The Dell, Milton Road, Southampton SO15 2XH
Telephone: Club (01703) 220 505
Ticket Office (01703) 228 575
ClubCall (0891) 121 178
Official Websites: http://www.soton.ac.uk/~saints/
http://www.saintsfc.co.uk/index.htm

Visiting supporters hoping for a glimpse of the sea, sand and inflatable banana boats will be truly disappointed. The Dell is about a mile north of the docks and the city centre, in a pretty smart area of town next to Hampshire County Cricket Ground. In fact, it's so well tucked away in detached-house-and-nice-garden suburbia that it's quite possible to drive straight past and miss it. Locating a decent pub is not a problem, but finding a parking space is. If you want to know what several thousand sets of teeth all grinding at once actually sounds like, just stand outside The Dell at 2.55 pm when the latecomers try to find a space within a one-mile radius.

HOW TO GET THERE

BY CAR: From North (M3): Continue to end of M3, exiting at signpost 'M27 West, Southampton Docks'. After 0.8 miles, where road divides, bear left (s/p A33 Southampton) onto the A33. Straight over first roundabout (s/p Southampton A33, then City Centre, The Docks). At 2nd roundabout after 0.8 miles, take 1st exit (s/p City Centre, Docks A33) into Bassett Avenue, which becomes The Avenue. (*)After 1.3 miles, just after 'The Cowherds' on RHS, turn right before lights (s/p County Cricket and Dell Football) into Northlands Road. The T-junction at the end of the road is right by the away turnstiles.

From East: Exit M27 at junction 5 (s/p Southampton Airport, Eastleigh A335). Turn left at roundabout (s/p Southampton A335) onto the A335. At 2nd set of lights, go straight on (s/p Swaythling, University) into High Road. After 0.2 miles where road divides (in front of McDonalds), turn right (s/p General Western) onto A35 Burgess Road. At lights after 1.2 miles, turn left (s/p City Centre A33) onto The Avenue. Then as From North(*).

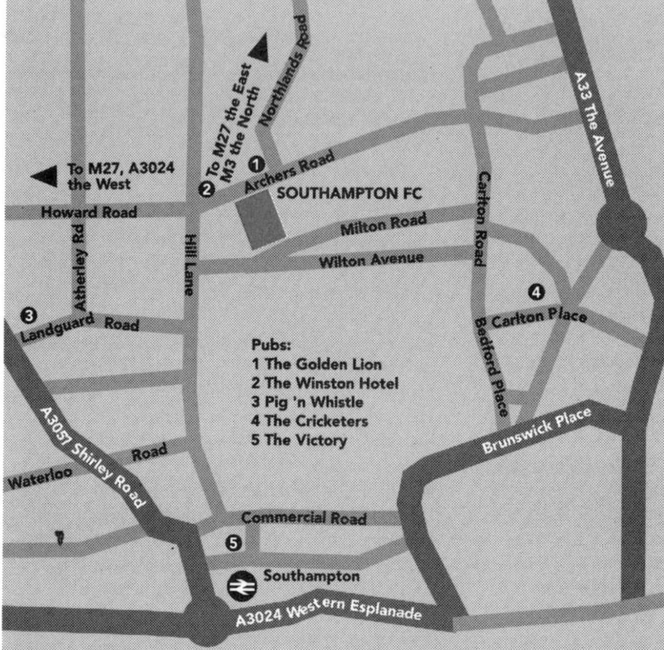

From West: Exit M27 at junction 3 (s/p M271 Southampton and Docks). Turn right at roundabout (s/p Southampton, the Docks) onto the M271. At roundabout after 1.6 miles, turn left (s/p Southampton, The Docks A35) onto the A35. Straight on over flyover (s/p City Centre A3024), and after 1.3 miles turn left (just after 'The Sailors Return' pub on LHS, s/p Shirley, Portswood) into Paynes Road. Straight over two crossroads into Archers Road.

FROM RAILWAY STATION (Southampton Central): 0.7 miles. *By taxi:* Between £2.50 -£3 (but after the game it can be quicker to walk). *By bus:* No. 25 runs along Hill Lane. *By foot:* Exit station onto Brook Road

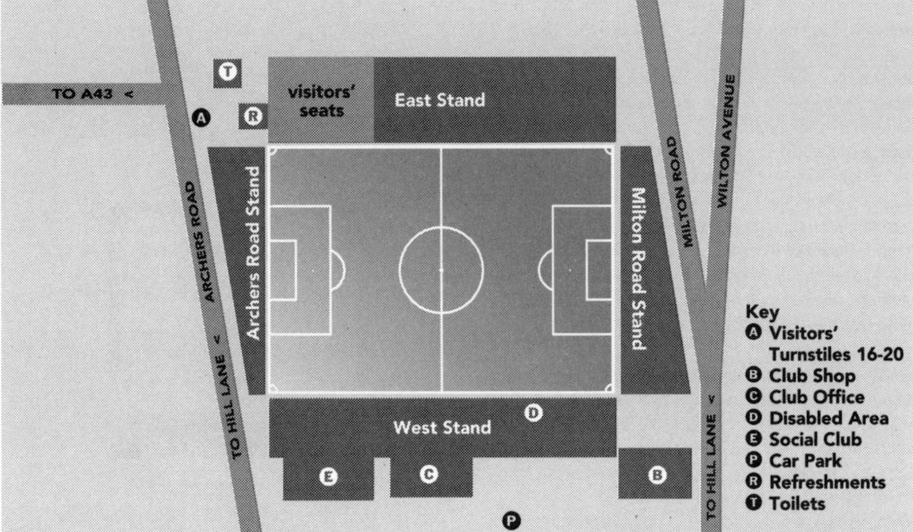

(opposite 'The Victory'), turn right and then left into Wyndham Place. Past bus stops, and turn left at T-junction into Commercial Road. Right at lights into Hill Lane. After 0.4 miles (by 'The Winston' pub) turn right into Archers Road. Away turnstiles are on RHS after 0.1 miles.

Last Midweek Trains: The last train to London is the 22.50 to Waterloo (arriving 01.02). Please double-check on (0345) 484 950.

BY BUS: In addition to the no. 25 listed above, the no. 5 runs from the city centre via Bedford Place to the ground.

PARKING

Yoho, this is where the fun really starts! Many streets around the ground have two-hour-only and residents-only parking restrictions. However, the good news is that a number of off-street car parks have opened recently, on Hill Lane, Archers Road and Howard Road, charging £2-£3. However, the spaces fill up early (by 1.30 pm in some cases) so latecomers will still have problems.

THE GROUND

Southampton FC continues, as ever, to try to escape the sardine-like qualities of The Dell. Its 15,000-capacity is simply too low, leaving fans locked out and the club lacking the revenue to compete with the Premiership big-boys. Relocation plans have been bogged down for years, and the club's original proposals, for a 25,000 all-seater stadium at Stoneham, near junction 5 of the M27, are likely to be rejected. The club is now considering another site, at St Mary's next to the River Itchen. Interestingly enough, St Mary's Church was where the club was originally founded, hence the nickname the 'Saints'. The proposed stadium would have 33-35,000 seats, but no associated leisure and retail developments which probably held up the Stoneham site. There's a railway line close by and the unusual possibility of reaching the ground by boat. Home fans, initially disappointed over the Stoneham debacle, feel this is the best option, as the site is in an existing community, with lots of pubs and chippies nearby.

Back at The Dell, seating for away fans is tucked away in the corner of the two-tier East Stand, close to the pitch and to the home fans in the Archers Road End. This makes for an interesting and high-spirited exchange of views (hmmmm!). The front rows get wet and the back rows contend with pillars, whilst in the upper tier fans have to lean over to see throw-ins directly below.

Total Capacity: 15,300. For away fans: Seating (East Stand) 1,500. Turnstiles 16-18 (for lower tier), 19-20 (upper tier). Access via Archers Road.

Cost (98/99): Upper tier £20, lower tier £18. No concessions for away fans.

Disabled Facilities: Space for 16 in the lower tier of the West Stand. *Disabled Toilet:* Up ramp, under Milton Wing. *Cost:* Free for disabled, £10 for helper. *Booking:* Essential, please call (01703) 667 547. *Parking:* The local disabled organisation has an arrangement with a school – call above number for details. *For the Blind:* 10 seats immediately behind the dugout, with hospital radio commentary.

Programme: £2.

Visitors' Toilets: *Male:* There were two options: the 'pick a wall variety' which fans said was 'one of the worst

football toilets ever!' or an unbelievably small cubicle opposite. There was an unofficial third option, as some fans decided that the gents were so bad, they'd use the ladies instead! *Female:* The queue was huge outside, because there was only room for one inside. 'Disgusting, but usable', said one fan.
Food and Drink: The refreshment kiosk is right by the loos so take care when choosing a half-time queue. The steak-and-kidney pie (£1.55) was, said a Villa fan (warming up for the great pie debate) 'okay, but it's not that hot, therefore it is not a good pie.' The tea (70p) was, said another supporter, 'strong with a strange aftertaste, not that it's a bad thing, mind.' Best of all it came with a lid (18.4.98).

PUB GUIDE

NB: Members of Independent Supporters' Clubs are welcome at the Maple Leaf Club, 16-22 The Polygon, Southampton (01703) 390 881.
The Golden Lion (1) (formerly 'The Gateway')
82 Northlands Road (01703) 224 517
Whitbread. Large traditional pub with two resident ghosts! Hot roast beef sandwiches (£2) and chips (£1). Giant-screen TV, pool table, beer garden. Families welcome. Open: all day.
The Winston Hotel (2) 51 Archers Road (01703) 224 404
Free House (Courage plus real ales). Large detached hotel/pub serving bar food 11-2.30. Families welcome. Two pool tables, TV, beer garden. Open: all day.
The Pig N' Whistle (3) 108 Shirley Road (01703) 322 259
Whitbread (with guests). Smart traditional locals pub. Bar snacks. Pool table, darts, TV, beer garden. Open: Saturday all day; from 6 pm for midweek games.
The Waterloo Arms 101 Waterloo Road (01703) 220 022
Hopback Brewery (including Summer Lightning). A locals' pub, but beer-connoisseurs travel from miles around to sample the brew. Speciality sausages in a roll £2. Large beer garden. Families welcome. Open: all day from 12.
The Bellemoor 250 Hill Lane (15-20 minute walk to ground) (01703) 771 495
Scottish and Newcastle. Smart pub serving an excellent menu. Families welcome. Open: all day from 11.30.
Also recommended: **The Cricketers (4)** 34 Carlton Place, a small Scottish and Newcastle pub serving a full menu all day; **The Victory (5)** in Brook Road near the station, a modern-style pub serving matchday food such as bangers and mash for £3.95.
FOR FAMILIES:
The Bassett 111 Burgess Road (not within walking distance) (01703) 790 604
Whitbreads/Brewers Fayre (with Boddingtons, Flowers IPA). Large, smart pub/restaurant with 'Charlie Chalk Fun

GARY'S REBELLING AGAINST THIS ALL-SEATER NONSENSE.
SFC
eagle

Factory'. Disabled facilities. Open: all day (restaurant 11.30-10).

FOOD GUIDE

For choice, head straight to Bedford Place (see map). It has numerous takeaways; a vegetarian bistro (with a £3 all day breakfast); a 'Fatty Arbuckles'; and the 'Apollo Café' (try the 'Football Fry-Up' at £3). Nearer the ground, home fans recommend two fish-and-chip shops on Shirley Road – 'Pete's' and 'Chippy Chips', near the junction with Payne Road. There's also a café serving all-day breakfasts from £1.50. Of the mobile burger vans around the ground home fans recommend 'Russells Burger Bar' behind Milton Road.

LOCAL MEDIA

Local Radio: BBC Radio Solent 96.1 FM, MW 999; Ocean FM 96.7, 97.5; Capital Gold 1557 AM.
Radio phone-ins: Radio Solent, Saturday pre-match phone-in, 1.10 to 2.30. Call (01703) 631 316; Capital Gold, Saturdays 2-6.30, midweek 7-10 (7-8 if no match). Call on (0845) 35 60 70 80.
Saturday Sports Paper: A Saturday 'Sports Echo' pink.

MISCELLANEOUS

Safety Factor: No trouble in season 97/98.
Rivals: Still Portsmouth.
Fanzines: 'The Ugly Inside', PO Box 67, Hedge End, Southampton, SO30 4ZF; 'Red Stripe', PO Box 72, Salisbury, Wiltshire, SP2 8RD.
Unofficial Websites:
'Marching In': http://www.saintsfans.com/marchingin/
'The Ugly Inside' is setting up a new site 1998/99.
Tourist Information: (01703) 221 106.

Southend United

Roots Hall

Address: Roots Hall, Victoria Avenue, Southend-on-Sea, Essex SS2 6NQ
Telephone: Club (01702) 304 050
Ticket Office (01702) 304 090
Shop (01702) 601 351/304 140
Soccerline (0839) 664 444
Infoline (0839) 664 443

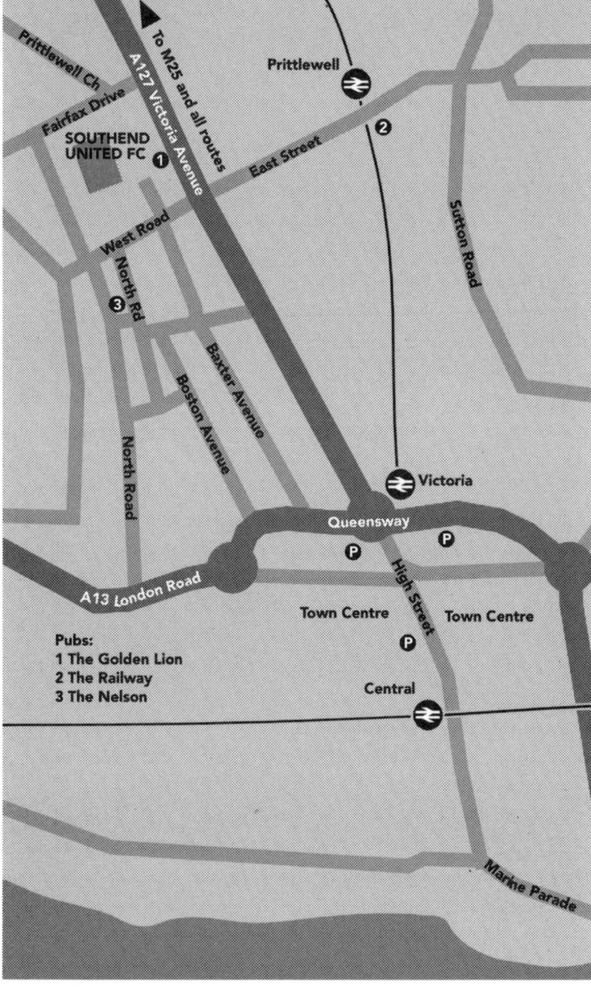

Take the brain of an average sort of footie fan and feed in the following images: funfair, ferris wheel, beach, drink. Yes indeed-ee, many supporters head straight to Southend seafront (or 'Thames-Estuary-front' as it should perhaps be known) to join the day-trippers and the stag-nighters to have a 'jolly good time'. What the heck, make a day of it! Southend may not be everyone's cup of char, but there's plenty to keep the family entertained. Although it doesn't have a tower, Southend is proud of its 19th century pier, the longest pleasure pier in the world, and its jellied eels! Roots Hall is in a much more sedate residential part of town, about a mile and a half inland. It does pitch in, however, with its share of shops, welcoming pubs, and an excellent chippie.

HOW TO GET THERE

BY CAR: From North and West: Exit M25 at Junction 29 (s/p Romford, Basildon, Southend A127). At motorway roundabout turn left (s/p Basildon, Southend A127) onto the A127. (*)Straight on for about 19 miles. At roundabout by the 'Strawberry Fields' pub and Tesco's, turn right (s/p Central Southend) continuing on the A127. At next roundabout after 0.4 miles turn right (s/p Town Centre) into Victoria Avenue. Roots Hall is on the RHS after 0.6 miles.

From South: Exit M25 at junction 30 (s/p Thurrock Lakeside, Tilbury A13 East). At roundabout turn right (s/p Grays, Tilbury A13, Thurrock A125) onto the A13. At Saddlers Farm roundabout after 13.8 miles turn left (s/p Chelmsford, A130, Southend A127). Follow Chelmsford/Southend signs for 2.9 miles, over two mini-roundabouts, to a third main roundabout. Here, turn right (s/p Southend A127) onto the A127. Then as From North and West (*)(it's 6.6 miles from here to the Victoria Avenue roundabout).

FROM RAILWAY STATIONS: There

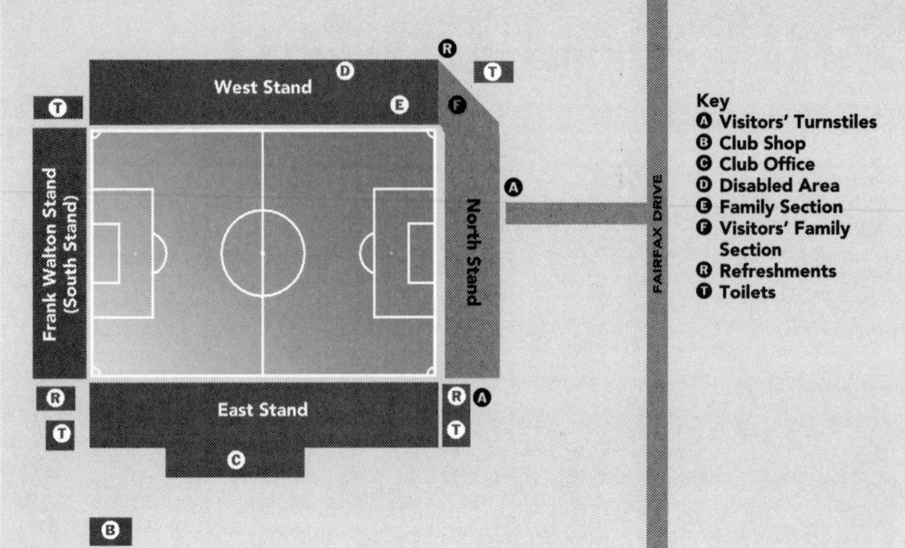

are three stations in Southend. Prittlewell and Southend Victoria are on the Liverpool Street line while Southend Central, the station nearest the shops and seafront, is on the Fenchurch Street line. *By taxi:* From Victoria £2.50, from Southend Central £3. Most taxis charge 20p per additional passenger.

Prittlewell is the nearest station to Roots Hall, a five-minute walk or so. *By foot:* Bear left out of the station and up to the main road (viz. East Street, the road with 'The Railway' pub on it). Turn right, and then right again at the crossroads into Victoria Avenue. For the away turnstiles, turn left along Fairfax Drive.

Last Midweek Trains: Fast trains from Southend Central to London run at 21.45, 22.15, 22.45 and 23.15. Trains from Southend Victoria to London run at 21.50, 22.10, 22.30 and 23.00. Please double-check on (0345) 484 950.

BY BUS: Plenty of buses run regularly from the town centre, along Victoria Avenue, to Roots Hall, including nos. 7, 8, 9, 15, 16, 20, 25, and 33.

PARKING

It's street parking, but as Roots Hall is in a residential area, it's not usually too difficult to find a space. Try along Prittlewell Chase or the sidestreets around West Avenue. Illegally parked cars will be towed away.

THE GROUND

Roots Hall has, throughout its history, been a hotch-potch, the best the club could manage on available finances. In 1955 it was a new hotch-potch. Today it's a much older hotch-potch, with – in many places – seats bolted onto terracing to conform with all-seater stipulations. There's been a lot of speculation about a possible ground move, but as yet nothing concrete. The newest part of Roots Hall is the narrow two-tier South Stand, built on what was left of the old South Bank terrace after a large chunk was sold for housing. Away fans are in one of the oldest sections, the North Stand. The acoustics are great, but a large fence and several pillars can obscure the view, and the front few rows are below pitch level.

Total Capacity: 12,435. For away fans: about 3,500. Turnstiles 13-20 and/or 20A, 20B.

Cost (98/99): Adults: £10. Concessions are available on a reciprocal basis. Some tickets are sold with 'Fence View' stamped on them.

Disabled Facilities: 20 spaces at the back of the West Stand, so the view is good. Entrance from Shakespeare Drive. *Disabled Toilet:* Next to the bar in the West Stand. *Cost:* £5 for disabled, £10 (concessions £5) for helper. *Booking:* Essential, through the Ticket Office. *For the Blind:* Seats and commentary in the East Stand. Blind supporter free, half-price for helper.

Programme: £1.60.

Visitors' Toilets: *Male:* Fans went on a loo comparison project and came out in favour of those in the NE corner, which had cubicles and a sink. The smell in the NW loo block was, well, 'powerful'. *Female:* Both the NE and NW blocks were clean, but only the ones in the NW had lights, locks and a usable mirror. Lighting is vital, because the female toilets often contain males fed up with queuing next door!

Food and Drink: The main problem was simply

getting served, so head for the refreshment area in the NE corner, where the queues moved pretty quickly. It has a small sit-down café too. Fans appreciated the pies (£1.60 – 'unusual for the south'), but most tried the 'pretty decent' burgers (£1.90) (8.11.97, 21.3.98, 13.4.98).

PUB GUIDE

The Golden Lion (1) 289 Victoria Avenue (01702) 347737
Taylor-Walker (with Burton, Kilkenny). Popular, welcoming pub – arrive early to avoid the rush! Sandwiches 11-3. Two pool tables, TV. Families welcome. Doorman on matchdays. Open: weekends 11-3, 7-11; midweek all day.
The Railway (2) 108 East Street, Prittlewell (near Prittlewell station) (01702) 616 214
Scottish and Newcastle. Large pub attracting both sets of supporters. Full bar menu (including 8oz steak £2.99, breakfast £1.49) served all day. Pool table. Open: all day.
The Nelson Hotel (3) North Road, Prittlewell (01702) 436 329
Bass (with real ales and keg beer). Traditional, football-friendly hostelry. Pool table, darts. Sandwiches. Families welcome, marquee for children. Open: all day.
The Bell Prince Avenue, Prittlewell (A127) (01702) 351 331
Allied Domecq (with Tetley, Kilkenny). Large traditional-style locals pub, serving snacks 12-2 (except Sunday). Two pool tables, TV. Open: all day.
Footie fans are attracted to Southend seafront like bees to a honey pot, but should note that some pubs display 'no football colours' signs. Two of the best seafront hostelries are the **Cornocopia** (Free House), reputedly the smallest pub in Essex, and **The Falcon** (Ridleys). Supporters looking for a more traditional pre-match drink could stop off at Old Leigh, a fishing village in the western suburbs. The best two pubs here are: **The Crooked Billet** at 51 High Street, an Allied Leisure pub (with several regional guest beers), housed in a wonderful sixteenth-century building. It serves a full bar menu 12-2:30; **The Smack Inn** at 7 High Street, a Scottish and Newcastle pub with a selection of real ales. It's a large, traditional pub, full of character, serving meals all day. Allow 25 minutes to get from Old Leigh to Roots Hall by car or take the train from Old Leigh station.

FOOD GUIDE

'The Fish House' on the corner of East Street and Victoria Avenue is one of the best in town, while West Street and Victoria Avenue have a series of takeaways, including Chinese, pizza, kebabs and sandwich bars. The town centre is about half a mile away: continue past Roots Hall on the A127 to a main roundabout. The shopping precinct is straight ahead. Families might enjoy

SOUTHEND
IS SO BRACING...
eagle

a visit to the 'Kursaal' on the seafront. It's a new indoor entertainment centre, with ten-pin bowling, restaurants and live music.

LOCAL MEDIA

Local Radio: BBC Essex 95.3 FM, 765 MW; Essex Radio 102.6 & 96.3 FM; The Breeze 1359 and 1431 AM.
Radio Phone-ins: None.
Saturday Sports Paper: None.

MISCELLANEOUS

Safety Factor: Trouble is rare.
Rivals: In the lower divisions, it's Colchester. A more long-standing rival is West Ham, the nearest 'big' club. Many former Londoners, now resident in Southend, still travel to Upton Park, much to the annoyance of Southend supporters ... hence the chant: 'We're not Cockneys, we're Southenders'.
Fanzines: 'Shrimp Season', 289 Avon Road, Chelmsford, Essex, CM1 2LB; 'What's the Story, Southend Glory', PO Box 1930, Leigh-on-Sea, Essex, SS9 1TN.
Unofficial Websites: http://www.shrimp.force9.co.uk/
http:www//thurgood.force9.co.uk/
http://homepages.enterprise.net/tonycowell/sufc/
http://www.ucl.ac.uk/~ucesbco/sufc.html
http://www.alcatraz.demon.co.uk/
Tourist Information: (01702) 215 120.

Stockport County

Edgeley Park

Address: Edgeley Park, Hardcastle Road, Edgeley, Stockport, Cheshire SK3 9DD
Telephone: Ticket Information (0161) 286 8888
County ClubCall (0891) 121 638
Official Website:
http://www.stockportmbc.gov.uk/county/

Maybe we're just slow to adapt, but it still looks to us like the league tables HAVE been printed upside-down. Only a few years ago Stockport was worried about a haemorrhage of fans to Manchester City! Stockport is a town in its own right, just south of the M60 which encircles Manchester, and only a short drive from the foot of the Peak District. For visiting fans, parking is usually the main problem, and – with the increased gates at Edgeley Park – the local pubs do fill up early. The ground's just across the road from a small but busy shopping street, which is full of cafés and takeaways.

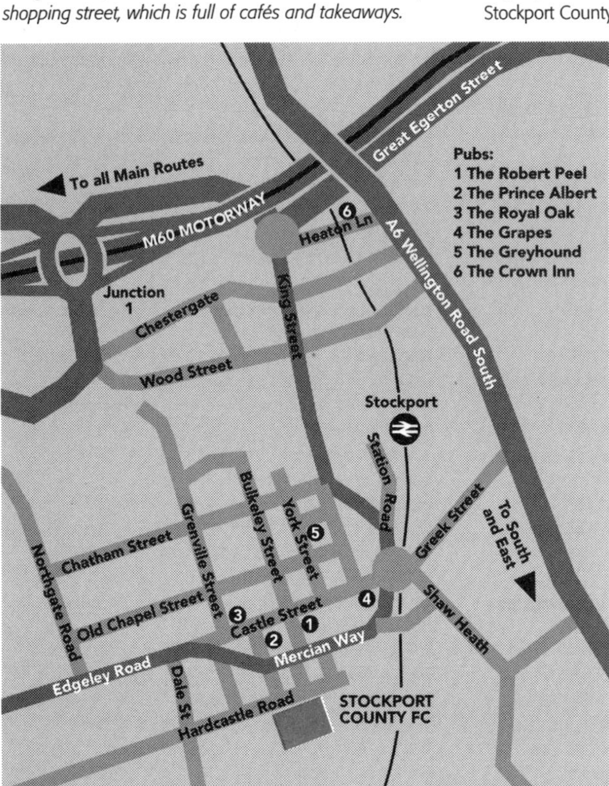

HOW TO GET THERE

BY CAR: From South, M6: Exit M6 at junction 19 (s/p Manchester and Airport, Stockport A55, M56 East) and at roundabout turn right onto the A556. At the Bowdon Roundabout after 4.2 miles turn right (s/p Manchester M56) onto the M56. Exit M56 after 6.9 miles (s/p Stockport M60, Sheffield M67) onto the M60. Exit M60 at Junction 1, after 2.4 miles (s/p Stockport Town Centre). (*)At roundabout, follow signs to Cheadle A560, also Stockport County FC, into Hollywood Way. Go straight on at the first lights, and turn right at the next (s/p Cheadle A560, Stockport County FC) onto the A560, towards 'Ye Olde Woolpack' pub. After 1.1 miles, turn left (no signpost, by 'The Farmers' Arms' and 'Friar Tuck's') onto the B5465 Edgeley Road. After 1.0 miles, turn right at lights (s/p Stockport County FC, St. Mark's Church) into Dale Street to ground.

From North (M62 from Leeds): When the M60 eastern section is open, the quickest route will be to exit the M62 at junction 18 and head south on the M60 to Junction 1 (s/p Stockport West), then as above(*). Until then, supporters should continue westbound on the M60, round the west of Manchester to Junction 1.

From South and East (A6/A523) over Peak District, directions from the junction of the two roads, at the 'Rising Sun' pub: Follow signs to 'Stockport A6', then 'Manchester A6'. After 2.8 miles, by the 'Nelson Tavern' and with the town hall (a big white building) ahead on the RHS, turn left (s/p Cheadle A560, Stockport County FC) into Greek Street. At roundabout after 0.3 miles take 2nd exit (s/p Cheadle A5465) onto Mercian Way (dual carriageway). Take the 2nd left turn into Caroline Street to ground.

FROM RAILWAY STATION (Stockport): About half a mile. *By taxi:* As quick to walk. *By foot:* Down steps and turn left along tunnel (ie. away from the booking office and the

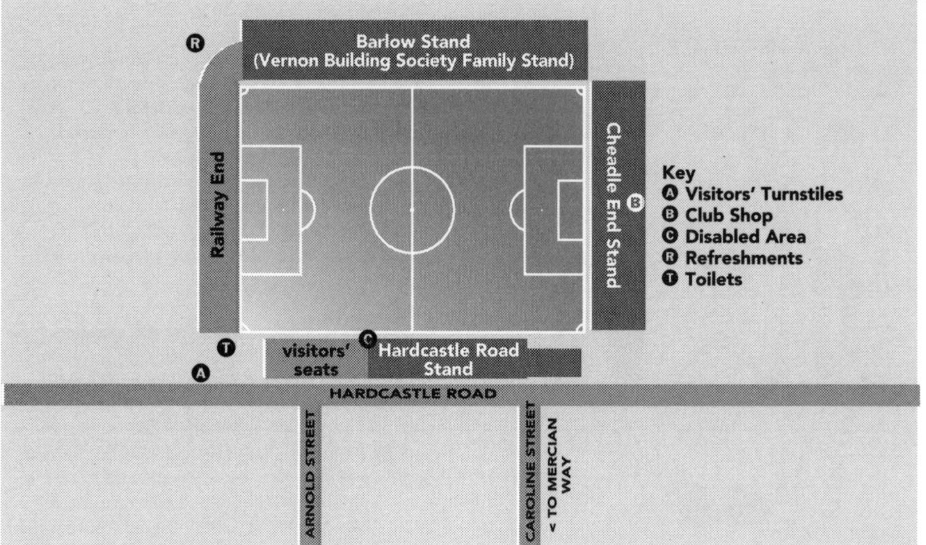

main exit). Walk up the cobbled Station Road and turn left onto Shaw Heath. Cross the main road and at roundabout take the exit signposted 'Cheadle A5464' into Mercian Way. The floodlights are visible from here. *Last Midweek Trains:* Frequent service to Manchester Piccadilly up and beyond midnight. From Manchester, trains leave to: York and Newcastle 21.50; to Nottingham and Derby at 22.28; to Liverpool at 22.07, 23.12 and 23.15; to Leeds at 22.43, 23.50 and 1.50; to Birmingham at 21.40 (via Manchester airport) and 22.33 (via Crewe). There is no service to London after a midweek game. Please double check on (0345) 484 950.

BY BUS: The no. 192 runs from Piccadilly Gardens in Manchester city centre, to Greek Street.

PARKING

Those who arrive early can park in the council car parks off Mercian Way (50p). Otherwise it's street parking. Parking is severely restricted around the ground, but the streets to the north of Edgeley Road are fine. Those approaching from the M60 (using the directions above) should continue past the turning to Dale Street, and take the next left, into Grenville Street.

THE GROUND

Looking back a decade, the rise and rise of Stockport County and Edgeley Park is dramatic. In the late 1980s, the team was in the Third Division and the Cheadle End was nothing but a small pile of rubble. Now the Cheadle End is the club's pride and joy, seating 5,000 and popular with Stockport fans. The two side stands are all-seater, leaving the open Railway End as the only remaining terrace. This houses the visiting support, who breathed a collective sigh of relief when the club opened new catering and toilet facilities in March 1998. Visitors are also allocated seats, either in the Hardcastle Road Stand or the Vernon Building Society Stand, which still has a few annoying pillars. The club has plans to build a new stand at the Railway End, to match the Cheadle End opposite and to raise the total capacity to 15,000. To do this, however, it has to buy land behind the terrace, presently occupied by a private social club.

Total Capacity: About 11,600. For away fans: allocations depend on the expected size of the away contingent: Terrace: 2,050. Seating (Block F, Hardcastle Road Stand) 255. Turnstiles 7 and 8; or (Vernon Building Society Family Stand) 897. Turnstiles 20-25.

Cost (98/99): Terrace: Adults £13. Seating: Vernon Building Society Stand £15. Hardcastle Road Stand £15. Concessions (OAP's £8, Juniors £6, all areas) are available on a reciprocal basis.

Disabled Facilities: Space for 12 supporters in an area raised above pitch level to one side of the Hardcastle Road Stand, in front of the seating for away fans. The view is good, but bring waterproofs. *Disabled Toilet:* Nearby. *Cost:* Free for disabled, full price for helper. *Booking:* Required for free admission and 'big games'. *For the Blind:* Four walkman-style headsets. Please contact Steve Bellis at the club on (0161) 286 8888.

Programme: £1.80.

Visitors' Toilets: *Male:* Crewe fans, more used to the horrors of lower division facilities, marveled at the 'electric hand dryers', while Forest fans, accustomed to Premier League luxury, were much more blasé: 'the

'Do you remember when they told us we were mental for supporting County?'

usual new football style – serviceable, hygienic stainless steel.' *Female:* Forest supporters were pleased to see plenty of cubicles, hand dryers, and 'sparkling clean basins', but were taken aback by the empty barrels on the lock fittings. The ever-caring bunch suggested a whip-round to send Stockport County the estimated £5 for the bolts.

Food and Drink: Jacket potatoes! With cheese (£1.50)! For a football ground, this is a culinary masterpiece. It's even nutritional. The pies (£1.20) weren't bad either, but the hot dogs and burgers (£1.50) were just 'edible'. Forest fans raved about the hot chocolate (50p), which came in a large cup, but said the tea (50p) was nothing special (28.3.98, 18.4.98).

PUB GUIDE

The closest pubs are on Castle Street, the local shopping area. However, for high profile games it's sometimes a better idea for away fans to look a little further afield.

Sir Robert Peel (1) 83 Castle Street (0161) 477 3424
Greenalls (with Stones Bitter). Traditional pub with separate welcoming lounge bar and games room with pool, darts and TV. Food served 11.30-2. Families welcome. Beer garden. Open: all day.

Prince Albert (2) 107 Castle Street (0161) 374 3113
Wilsons (with John Smiths). A cosy traditional pub, with one small room and a great atmosphere. Bar snacks. Families welcome. Pool, TV. Open: all day.

The Royal Oak (3) 124 Castle Street (0161) 477 7159
Wilsons. A small traditional pub, a great matchday favourite. TV, darts. Open: all day.
Also recommended: **The Grapes Hotel (4),** 1 Castle Street (Robinsons), described by locals as a 'good working man's pub'; **The Greyhound (5),** 27 Bowden Street, a small Boddingtons pub with a lively matchday atmosphere; **The Crown Inn (6),** 154 Heaton Lane (under viaduct on exit from Junction 1 of M60, 15 minute walk to ground), a real ale haven with TV and pool table.

FOOD GUIDE

Castle Street has a good range of outlets. For traditional fish-and-chips (eat-in and takeaway) try 'The Friary', which has cod and haddock at £1.55, and steak pie and chips for £1.65. The 'Castle Pizza House' has pizzas from £2.70 and 'giant hot dogs' at £1.90. 'Sivoris Café' displays a sticker which reads: 'Stockport County FC Do it for 90 Minutes', and also serves full breakfasts for £2.20. There are also two bakeries, a Balti house, a Chinese takeaway and the 'Edgeley Kebab House'. For a full lunch, try 'Giovanni's Ristorante/Pizzeria' with prices starting from £4.50. It opens from 12-2, and from 6 pm.

LOCAL MEDIA

Local Radio: GMR 95.1 FM; Piccadilly Radio 1152 AM.
Radio Phone-ins: GMR, Saturdays 1-3, 5-7 and after midweek games. Call (0161) 228 2255; Piccadilly Radio, Saturdays 5-6, call (0161) 288 1152.
Saturday Sports Papers: *The Manchester Evening News* produces 'The Pink'.

MISCELLANEOUS

'Vernon the Bear', one of our great favourites. He used to dance around in a flea bitten bear suit, described by one fan as 'the first one he came across in the joke shop.' That is, until the club realised what a superstar they had in the making and splashed out on a brand new outfit complete with furry football boots. He's worth the ticket price all on his own!
Safety Factor: Few problems here.
Rivals: Dave Espley of 'The Tea Party' explains that County don't have any 'official' rivals. Despite the large number of Manchester City shirts paraded around Stockport streets, relations between the two clubs have traditionally been good.
Fanzines: 'The Tea Party', c/o 3 Dunlin Close, Offerton, Stockport, Cheshire, SK2 5UF.
Unofficial Websites:
http://www.isfa.com/server/web/stockport/main.html
http://www.geocities.com/Colosseum/Sideline/4117.index.html
http://www.mawhite.dircon.co.uk
Tourist Information: (0161) 474 3320.

Stoke City

Address: Britannia Stadium, Stanley Matthews Way, Stoke on Trent ST4 4EG
Telephone: Club (01782) 592 222
Ticket Office (01782) 592 200
Club Shop (01782) 592 244
ClubCall (0891) 121 040

Stoke City moved from the much-loved Victoria Ground to the much-admired Britannia Stadium during the summer of 1997. The old and the new are less than a mile apart, separated by the River Trent and two dual carriageways, but the stadium design and surroundings couldn't be more different. The Britannia Stadium – which dominates the skyline on the western approaches to the town – is the first and only development on a huge reclaimed industrial site at Sideway, formerly the Hem Heath Colliery. Other leisure facilities are planned, but until then there's not a chip to be had for a good half-mile in any direction. So either eat and drink in the ground, or stop en route. The club says there is no parking for visiting fans at the ground, so the road directions below lead to alternative parking.

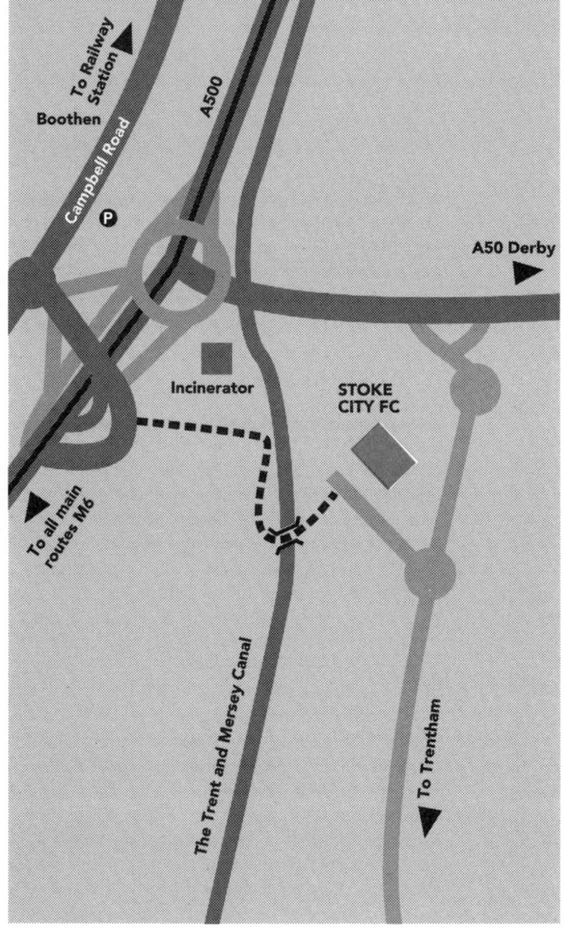

HOW TO GET THERE

BY CAR: From North, South and West: Exit M6 at junction 15. At motorway roundabout go straight on (s/p Uttoxeter, Stoke-on-Trent A500, Stone A34). As there's no parking at the ground, decide here whether to head for the Great Fenton Business Park or the Bookers car park.
a) to Great Fenton Business Park: Take 2nd exit off the A500 after 1.6 miles (the Sideway Junction, s/p Uttoxeter, Derby A50). Where the road divides, keep right, following signs to the A50. At roundabout turn right onto the A50 dual carriageway. Take 1st exit (the Heron Cross Junction) after 0.7 miles, and at roundabout turn left into Burton Road. At crossroads after 0.1 miles turn left into Grove Road. The business park is on the RHS. It's a ten-minute walk to the ground, and the club says there will be signposts.
b) To Bookers car park: Take 2nd exit off the A500 after 1.6 miles (the Sideway Junction, s/p Uttoxeter, Derby A50, also Campbell Road, Michelin). Keep in left-hand lanes where the road divides (s/p Fenton, Longton). At top of road all traffic turns left. At roundabout after 0.2 miles turn right, and the Booker Cash and Carry is on the RHS.
From North-East: The best route is M1-A38-A50 as follows. Exit M1 at junction 28 (s/p Derby A38, Matlock A615) and at roundabout follow signs to 'Derby A38' onto the A38. At the Little Eaton Roundabout after 13.5 follow signs to 'The Ring Road, Burton A38', and at the next two roundabouts, after 2.8 miles and 0.7 miles, follow signs to 'The South M1', remaining on the A38. After 0.5

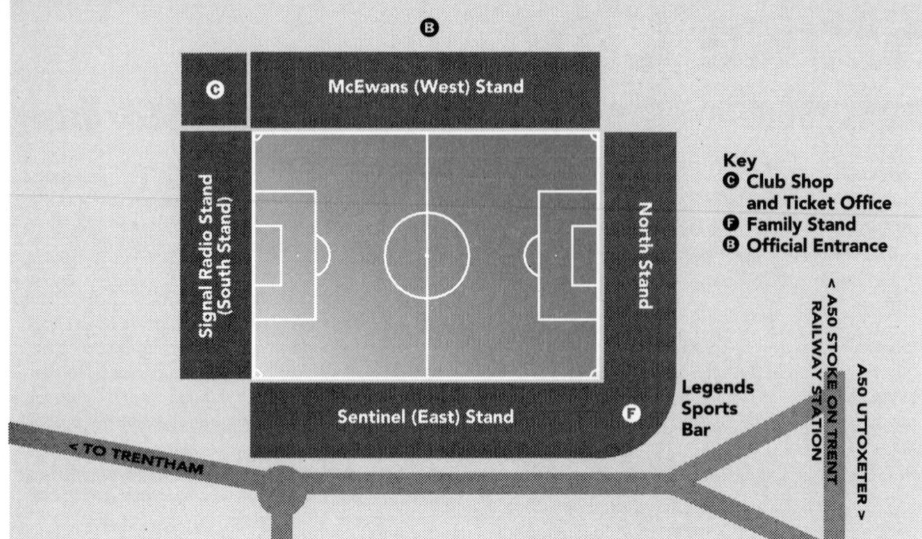

miles exit A38 (s/p Stoke on Trent, Uttoxeter A516 (A50)) onto the A516. At double roundabout after 4.5 miles follow signs to 'Stoke on Trent A50' onto the A50. Remain on the A50 for 22.5 miles into the outskirts of Stoke (note the strict speed limits here) and through road tunnel. Exit A50 after a further 2.3 miles at the Heron Cross Junction. Go straight on at the 1st roundabout, and turn right at the 2nd into Burton Road. Then as From North, South and West(*).

FROM RAILWAY STATION (Stoke-on-Trent): 2 miles. When a large number of visiting supporters is expected, shuttle buses run from the railway station. *By taxi:* £5. *By bus:* Special matchday buses run from Glebe Street (see below). *By foot:* Turn right out of station to traffic lights by the Roebuck Hotel. Here, turn sharp right into Glebe Street, under low bridge and across the A500. At T-junction turn left (s/p Kingsway Civic Centre) remaining on Glebe Street (buses to the ground run from here). At end of street do a 'dogleg' left then right into Lonsdale Road. At crossroads go straight on (s/p Recreation Centre) into Campbell Road. At end of road after 0.9 miles turn left (s/p Uttoxeter A50, Incinerator). At next roundabout, follow signs to incinerator, and then take footpath between the high wire fences running towards the canal, which leads to the ground.

Last Midweek Trains: There are no trains to London after an evening game. However, the 21.45 to Stockport has onward connections to Nottingham, Derby, Doncaster and Newcastle. Please double-check on (0345) 484 950.

BY BUS: Special matchday buses run from Glebe Street in Stoke village; from Stand A in the Strand in Longton; and from the bus stations in Hanley and Newcastle.

PARKING

There are few, if any, parking spaces at the ground for visiting fans, who are advised to head for the car parks at the Great Fenton Business Park or at the Booker Cash and Carry. Directions to both are given above. The Michelin car park is closing, and street parking around the site of the old Victoria Ground is now strictly 'residents only'.

THE GROUND

It's amazing how quickly a new ground becomes home: ten minutes or so into a match in December, the refreshment kiosk staff were serving the last latecomers when a cheer went up. 'Oh dear, one-nil to Crewe', said a tea-lady, instinctively recognising the sound of an away goal (they were quite common in 97/98!). Stoke fans think the new stadium is superb, and say that the atmosphere – given a decent crowd – is better than at the Victoria. The design of the Britannia, which cost £14.7 million, is reminiscent of the original Riverside Stadium, though the Sentinel and South Stands are not joined into a horseshoe, leaving away fans well segregated. Visiting supporters, behind the goal, have an excellent view, lots of legroom, and concourse facilities which even include a pay-phone!

The executive facilities are state-of-the-art: there are 24 suites, each with its own private outside balcony. And for those who have a head for heights, there are 26 'Sky Boxes' at the top of the Main Stand, affording great

views of the pitch and the surrounding countryside.
Total Capacity: 28,000. For away fans: 4,964.
Cost (98/99): Adults £14, concessions (juniors/OAPs) £8. Concessions are available on a reciprocal basis, and may have to be bought in advance. Please check with the visiting club.
Disabled Facilities: ... are excellent. There are a total of 164 places, with 30 reserved for visiting fans half-way up the South Stand, so the view is good. *Disabled Toilet:* Nearby. *Cost:* Free for disabled, matchday price for helper. *Booking:* Essential. *Parking:* Available, near visiting turnstiles. Please book. *For the Blind:* The club is installing headphones for season 98/99.
Programme: £1.80.
Visitors' Toilets: *Male:* 'Functional, crowded – not as good as at other new grounds', summed up the general opinion. *Female:* Sad, isn't it, when one stops to admire a large flip-top rubbish bin! Maybe it's the rarity value. Anyhow, there was one in the loos at Stoke, along with all the other necessities of life.
Food and Drink: The longer the game went on, the less the fans liked the pies (£1.50) and no, the visiting team wasn't losing. Before kick-off both the meat-and-potato and the steak-and-kidney versions were 'excellent', 'very good and hot – this is my third!' By the end of half-time, one comment summed up several: 'Premier ground, cold non-league pies!' Both the bitter (£1.90) and the lager (£2) were ice-cold. For vegetarians there was excellent coffee (£1) and ghastly tea (90p). Full marks, however, for the friendly serving staff (13.12.97).

PUB GUIDE

With the ground relocation, the pubs which used to welcome away supporters were flooded with home fans, and the local police now advise visitors to drink inside the stadium, or to stop well away from town. The pubs listed below are all in the village of Stone, which is well signposted from the M6 and Sideway area. Within Stone itself, the main road makes a complete circle. The 'Crown and Anchor' is on this circle, while the 'Royal Exchange' is a few yards off it (follow signs to Leek A520).

The Crown and Anchor 1 Station Road (01785) 285 401
Bass. A listed building with wooden floors and panels, now a Bass 'ale shrine' catering for the younger market – though all are made welcome. Bar snacks served all day (except Sun/Mon). Darts, pool, 2 big-screen TVs. Open: all day.

The Royal Exchange 26 Radford Street. (01785) 615 415
Banks's (with Morrell's Graduate and Varsity). It's the busiest pub in town, says the landlord, and it certainly has a lot to attract the football fan – 8 TVs, pool, darts, table football, a video jukebox, linked driving machines and a cosy real fire. Open: all day.

FOOD GUIDE

There's absolutely nothing near the Britannia, so think ahead! Burger bars park in the Campbell Road area, and some of the fish and chip shops on Campbell Road are still operating. Near the Plough Motel is 'Hopwood's Takeaway Sandwich and Snack Bar', and there's a takeaway near the junction of Campbell Road and Selwyn Street. Those visiting the village of Stone should head for 'Millies' on Radford Street, near the 'Royal Exchange'. It sells Wrights pies, and sandwiches for £1.

LOCAL MEDIA

Local Radio: Local Radio: BBC Radio Stoke 94.6 and 104.1 FM; Signal Radio 102.6 FM.
Radio Phone-ins: BBC Radio Stoke, Saturdays 5-6 pm. Call (01782) 208 008.
Saturday Sports Paper: The 'Green 'Un'.

MISCELLANEOUS

Stoke City finally have a new mascot. A hippo. And why? Well, everyone at the club spent hours trying to think of a mascot to reflect the city of Stoke. The suggestion of a 'Peter Potter' was met with some bewilderment. So what better than a hippoPOTamus? And very popular it is too!
Safety Factor: New stadium, old habits! Stoke City has retained its hooligan contingent, and there has been trouble outside the ground on big matchdays.
Rivals: Neighbours 'The Fail', noted say Stoke fans, for 'their 100 years of total non-achievement'. Other clubs, in descending order of dislike, are Wolves, Birmingham and Stockport.
Fanzine: 'The Oatcake', PO Box 276, Stoke-on-Trent, Staffs, ST4 7SQ. New issue every matchday.
Unofficial Websites: 'The Oakcake' fanzine site:
http://www.fenetre.co.uk/~oatcake/
http://www.geocities.com/Yosemite/9185/
Tourist Information: (01782) 284 600.

Sunderland

Stadium of Light

Address:
Sunderland Stadium of Light, Sunderland, SR5 1SU
Telephone: Club (0191) 551 5000
Ticket Office 90191) 551 5151
Ticketmaster (0990) 862 015
ClubCall (0891) 121 140
Official Website: http://www.sunderland-afc.com/

Striker Niall Quinn said on national radio: 'Sunderland has one of the very best stadiums in the country, on a par perhaps with Old Trafford'. Most Sunderland supporters, and visitors, would agree. From the outside the ground is impressive enough, but inside? It's magnificent. And the old Roker Roar has moved the half-mile down the road to the Stadium of Light, and if anything has intensified. Sunderland's new ground is on the site of the old Wearmouth Colliery, overlooking the river and the bridge to town. Parking at the stadium is limited, but the club has set up an efficient park-and-ride. Finding an away-friendly pub is not as easy as at Roker, and the pie shops are not as good. So make the most of the excellent 'Joan's Café' right by the ground.

HOW TO GET THERE

BY CAR: From South: Exit A1(M) at signpost 'Thirsk A168, Teesside A19' onto the A19 dual carriageway. Exit A19 after about 51 miles, after crossing River Wear (s/p Gateshead, Newcastle West, Sunderland North A1231). At roundabout turn right (s/p Sunderland A1231) onto the A1231 Wessington Way. (*)Go straight on at Ferryboat Lane Roundabout after 0.2 miles (s/p City Centre A1231, Sunderland Enterprise Park). At the next three roundabouts ('Enterprise 1, 2 and 3'), there are signposts to the matchday park-and-ride. To the ground, continue straight on at all three roundabouts (s/p City Centre A1231) to fourth roundabout/junction(**). Here, go straight on (s/p Roker B1289) into Queens Road. Turn right at next roundabout, after 0.9 miles, to ground.

From North: Exit A1 at s/p 'Sunderland A1231, Non-motorway traffic'. At roundabout after 0.4 miles turn left (s/p Washington, Sunderland A1231). At next roundabout after 1.0 mile go straight on (s/p Sunderland A1231) onto the Eastern Highway. At next roundabout, the junction with the A19, go straight on (s/p Sunderland A1231) onto Wessington Way. Then as From South(*).

To Sunderland city centre parking: At roundabout marked (**) above, turn right (s/p Sunderland City Centre A1231), onto and over the Queen Alexandra Bridge. At roundabout just after bridge turn left (s/p City Centre A1231, Wearmouth Bridge). At next two roundabouts, after 0.4 and 0.2 miles, follow 'City Centre' signs. At next two roundabouts follow signs to 'South Shields A1018' into St Mary's Way. The St Mary's car park is signposted on the left after 0.1 miles. To the ground, walk over the Wearmouth Bridge.

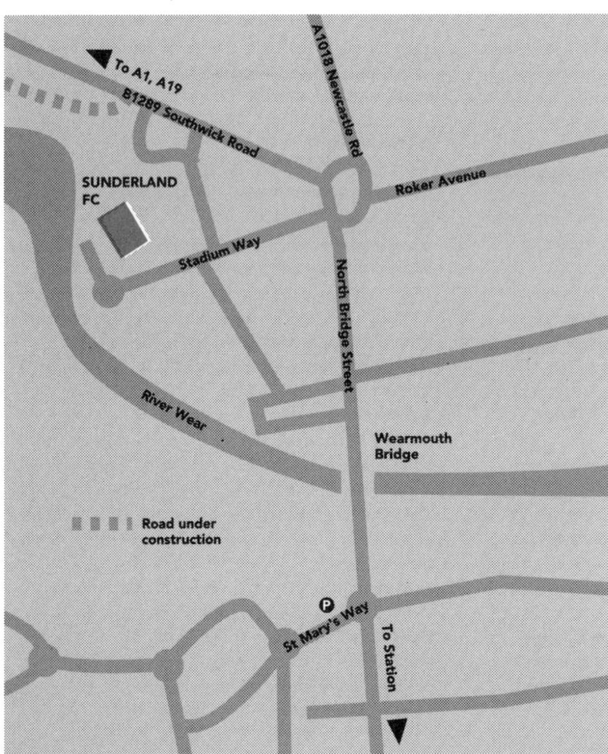

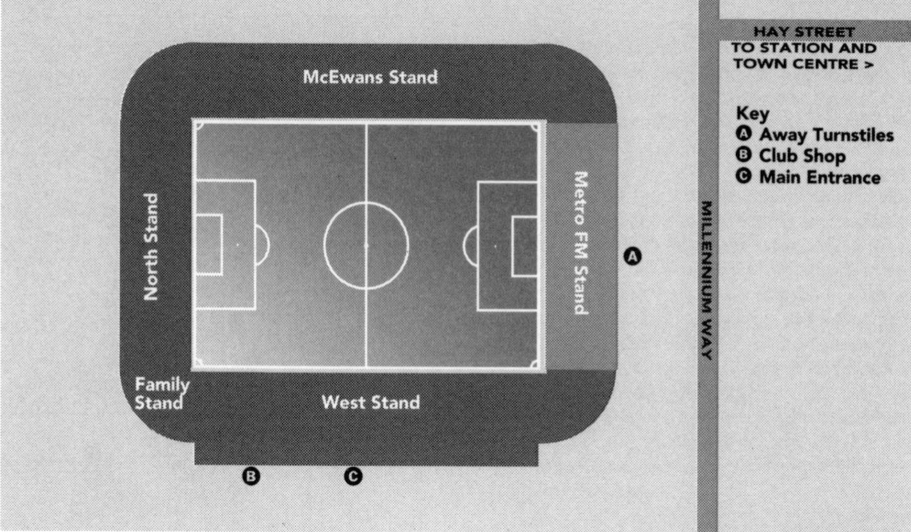

FROM RAILWAY STATION (Sunderland, 10-15 minute walk): *By taxi:* Not always available. *By bus:* 'Stagecoach Busways' buses leave from Fawcett Street, in front of Wilson's. The nos. 27, 28 and 29 run across Wearmouth Bridge, stopping at the Wheatsheaf pub, from where it's a short walk to the ground. 'Go Ahead Northern' bus nos. 131 and 538 run to the ground from the Park Lane Bus Station next to the Civic Centre. *By foot:* Come out of station towards William Hill and the Alliance and Leicester Building Society. Turn left towards Wilkinsons, and left again at crossroads by Regency Windows (s/p Tourist Information) into Fawcett Street. Keep straight on, passing the AA and Woolworths to crossroads by 'Tucci'. Here head straight on towards and over Wearmouth Bridge. Take 2nd left turn after the bridge, just before the museum, into Sheepfolds North, and first right into Hay Street to ground.
Last Midweek Trains: Trains to Newcastle run up to 23.30. However, there are no connecting trains, after an evening match, to Doncaster, Sheffield, Liverpool or London.
BY BUS: See above.

PARKING

The majority of the 1,200 parking spaces at the ground are allocated to season-ticket holders, but some are available if booked in advance through the Ticket Office. Many fans use the park-and-ride scheme, which is well signposted off the A1231. Leave plenty of time as the buses get caught in matchday traffic before and after the game.

There is also some street parking. Many Sunderland fans park around the site of the old Roker Park, or on the streets off Newcastle Road. For away fans, however, this means wading through the pre-match traffic on the A1231 past the ground. There are multi-storey car parks in Sunderland city centre. One of the best, and the most secure, is the one on St Mary's Way, though it's not open on Sundays. To get there, see road directions above. The car park has 475 spaces, and costs 70p per hour (or a one-off payment of £1 after 6 pm). If this car park is full, others are well signposted.

THE GROUND

The best way to view the Stadium of Light is at night, when red and white lights are shone vertically up through the mass of steel roof supports, and the main West Stand is floodlit. In daylight it's not as impressive perhaps as the Reebok, principally because the first 20 or so rows of seats are set below ground level. The ground, built at a cost of £18 million, is completely enclosed, and with capacity crowds towards the end of season 97/98, the atmosphere was superb. The West Stand houses the club shop and the main executive facilities, including a restaurant overlooking the river. Visiting fans are allocated sections of the South (Metro FM) Stand. The facilities are good, and the concourses less crowded than at other new grounds. For everyone, the view and the legroom is excellent.

The old Roker Park, alas, is no more. It's been demolished and turned into a housing estate.
Total Capacity: 41,590. For away fans: 1,100, 3,200 or 6,000. Turnstiles: Usually 57-61.
Cost (97/98): Adult £15. Concessions available on a reciprocal basis, and must be bought through the away club.

Disabled Facilities: Space for up to 58 visiting supporters in various locations around the ground. *Disabled Toilets:* In all stands. *Cost:* £8 for disabled, £10 for helper. *Booking:* Essential. *Parking:* Available at the stadium – please book through the Ticket Office. *For the Blind:* The club provides Sony Walkmen for local radio match commentary in the South Stand.
Programme: £1.70.
Toilets: *Male:* Imagine the scene: the fourth Sunderland goal hits the back of the net, and a disgruntled visiting fan goes into a whirlwind of frustrated anger. He wreaks his terrible revenge by ... filling every sink up to the brim with water. The Phantom Port Vale Sink-Filler strikes again! That apart, the loos were spacious and clean. *Female:* Remember Crazyfoam? What great stuff it was – and now it's available in the soap dispensers at the Stadium of Light.
Food and Drink: Fans loved the meat-and-potato pasty (£1.50): 'nice, hot, lots of black pepper'. The mince-and-onion pie had a tendency to disintegrate, leaving fans grappling with a lukewarm soggy mess. For vegetarians, there were cheese pasties, which were great hot and awful cold. The lager (£2) was 'excellent', as was the bovril (31.1.98).

PUB GUIDE

For visiting fans, the choice is very limited. The friendly pubs around the site of the now-demolished Roker Park are still a good option, including the old favourite:
The New Derby Roker Baths Road (0191) 548 6263
Whitbread. Large, popular modern-style pub with two pool tables and big-screen TV. Bar lunches unless it's too busy, but snacks such as chip butties always laid on. Families welcome. Open: all day.
FOR FAMILIES:
The Wessington Wessington Way (the A1231, near A19 junction) (0191) 548 9384
Whitbread/Brewers Fayre. Pub-restaurant and proud winners of the 'Tommy's Parent-Friendly Campaign' award 97/98. Full menu served 11.30 am-10pm/ children's menu. Outdoor play area and Charlie Chalk indoor play area. Disabled facilities. Open: all day.

FOOD GUIDE

The best option at the ground is 'Joan's Café'. It does all the classics, including a huge fry-up called the 'Belly Buster' for £1.99. On North Bridge Street, by the Wearmouth Bridge, is a café/takeaway called the 'Red 'N' White', plus a Balti restaurant and takeaway. North of the ground, home fans recommend the 'Crozier Street Fish Bar', Crozier Street being a turning off the Newcastle Road, about five minutes' walk from the ground.

Those parking up in the park-and-ride on Sunderland Enterprise Park should look out for 'Quincey's', a friendly American-style diner on Timber Beech Road.

'I know that the atmosphere is worth a goal start, but that's ridiculous!'

LOCAL MEDIA

Local Radio: Sun 103.4 FM; Metro Radio 97.1 and 103 FM, 1152 MW; BBC Radio Newcastle 94.5 FM, 1458 MW.
Radio Phone-ins: Sun FM, Saturdays 5-6 pm, call (0191) 567 3344; Metro Radio, Saturdays 5-6 pm, call (0191) 488 3188; Radio Newcastle, Saturdays 11.15-noon, call (0191) 232 6565.
Saturday Sports Paper: *The Sunderland Echo* produces the pink 'Sports Echo'.

MISCELLANEOUS

Safety Factor: On derby days, the police advise fans to get into the ground early to avoid any possible crowd trouble. Don't wear club colours in the town centre.
Rivals: It will always and forever be Newcastle United.
Fanzines: 'A Love Supreme', 1 Hodgson's Buildings, Stadium Way, Monkwearmouth, Sunderland, SR5 1BT; 'It's the Hope I Can't Stand', PO Box 16335, London, SW1A 1ZG.
Unofficial Websites:
'A Love Supreme': http://www.als.sunderland.com/
http://dspace.dial.pipex.com/hope/html/ithics/html
http//members.aol.com/ftmexec/f-start.htm
http://ourworld.compuserve.com/homepages/kmaw/
Tourist Information: (0191) 565 0990.

Swansea City

Vetch Field

Address: Vetch Field, Swansea SA1 3SU
Telephone: Club (01792) 474 114
Commercial/Club Shop (01792) 462 584
ClubCall (0891) 121 639

A friend once likened Swansea to San Francisco. Okay, laugh away! He actually meant that both cities are on the coast and have steep hills. Yes, the resemblance stops there but Swansea, after all, is much less likely to suffer a devastating earthquake! The Vetch is just a few hundred yards from a sandy beach, and the beautiful Gower Peninsula is a short drive away. Indeed, the area's so nice, no Swansea resident ever wants to leave. Much of this is lost on visiting football supporters, especially those who travel by coach or train and who miss out on the sea views. It's a shame, as the city's worth a full day out, and – with tension between rival fans decreasing – many more pubs are opening their doors to visiting supporters.

HOW TO GET THERE

BY CAR: From all directions: Exit M4 at junction 42 (s/p Swansea A483) onto the A483 Fabian Way. Go straight on for 4.6 miles to major junction/lights by the River Tawe. Here, get into the left-hand lane, marked 'City and Docks' and go straight on (s/p Gower A4067, City Centre, Mumbles). From here to the ground, simply keep in this same lane, following signs to Mumbles, The Gower, County Hall and Marina, for 0.8 miles. For the parking at the County Hall, turn left (s/p County Hall and Marina) into Bathurst Street.

FROM RAILWAY STATION (Swansea): About one mile to ground. *By taxi:* About £2.30. *By bus:* Most Swansea buses run to and from the Quadrant Centre, which is a 5-10 minute walk from the away turnstiles. *By foot:* Come out of station and cross main road, heading into Alexandra Road towards the large red-bricked building. At first crossroads/lights after about 0.1 miles

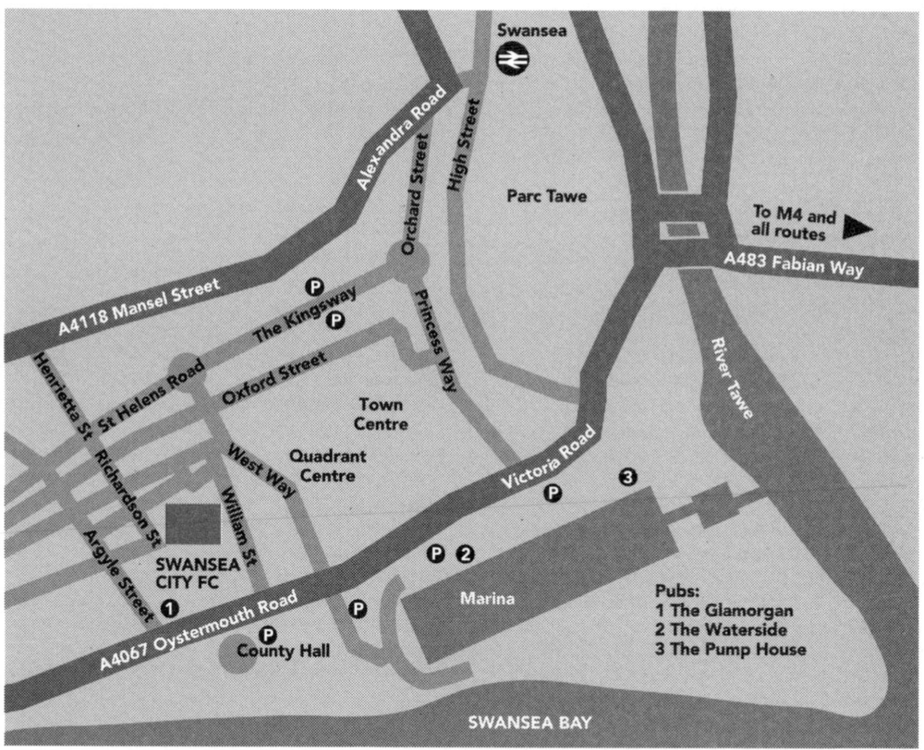

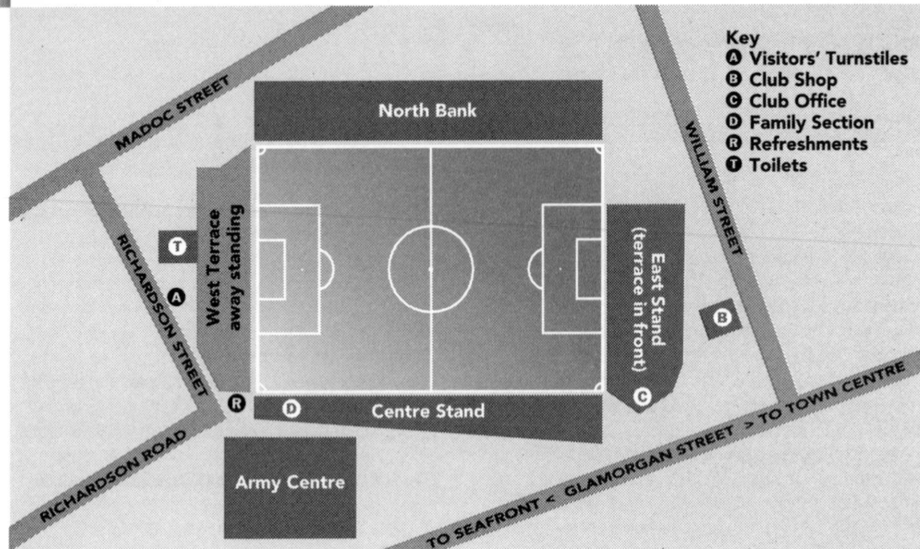

turn left (s/p City Centre) into Orchard Street. At first roundabout after 0.1 miles, by NCP car park and Wimpy, turn right (s/p Kingsway MSCP) into Kingsway, passing Shaws the Drapers on the LHS. At roundabout after 0.3 miles, go straight on towards 'Chick King' into St Helens Road. Turn left at 'M and P Cycles' after 0.2 miles into Richardson Street to away turnstiles.

Last Midweek Trains: The last train to Cardiff is at 22.24, with connections to Hereford. There are no trains to London after a midweek game. Please double-check on (0345) 484 950.

BY BUS: As above.

PARKING

Street parking is available in the maze of roads around the ground and further along Oystermouth Road towards the cricket and rugby ground. However, many of the roads near The Vetch are one-way, and some are blocked at one end. A better idea is to leave the car in the County Hall car park (see map). It costs £1.50 all day. There's a huge pay-and-display car park (£1.75 all day) near the County Hall, on the other side of Bathurst Street.

THE GROUND

In February 1998, the owners of Swansea City – Silver Shield Group PLC – announced plans to move the club to a new 25,000-seater stadium at Morfa, about two miles north-east of the city centre. They say the stadium and the associated leisure complex – to include shops, restaurants and a hotel – will cost about £75 million, and should be open in August 1999. It will, they say, be modeled on Sunderland's Stadium of Light and Stoke's Britannia Stadium, and may be shared with a top-class rugby league side. Most Swansea fans agree that a move from the much-loved but dilapidated Vetch Field is inevitable. So season 98/99 could well be the last at the old ground. For visiting fans, this is probably no great loss, as the facilities are poor, and the view from the terrace obstructed by fencing.

Total Capacity: 12,000. For away fans: 1,200. Visiting families are welcome in the Jewson (Family) Stand but must book in advance. All seating areas are unsegregated.

Cost (98/99): Terrace: Adults: £8, no concessions. Family Stand: Adult £11, with one child £15, with two children £17, extra children £4.

Disabled Facilities: Room for about three visiting fans in a shelter at pitch level in front of the Centre Stand. *Disabled Toilet:* None. *Cost:* Free for disabled, £7.50 for helper (OAPs £5.50). *Booking:* Essential. *Parking:* None available. *For the Blind:* No special facilities.

Programme: £1.50.

Visitors' Toilets: *Male:* 'What is there then?' we asked. 'Nothing' came the reply. 'Just three walls and a little grate.' And natural air conditioning and ventilation (ie no roof). *Female:* In the end, it was no contest. The female MATITLA (Most Awful Toilet in the League Award) goes to Swansea City. Neither loo was flushing, one door wouldn't shut and both cubicles stank. But it was the large puddle, littered with coke cans and sweet wrappers, which really clinched it.

Food and Drink: For food, the choice was between hot dogs (£1.20) and 'Corned Beef and Potato Puff Pasties' (£1) served in their cellophane wrappers. Fans were ordering up to four hot dogs each, even though they weren't overkeen on them. 'We're just greedy sods,' explained one. The pasties were very hot, and were generally given the thumbs up. The coffee was Gold Blend (good), the crisps were Walkers (good) and the Snickers bars cost 75p! 'I thought Dick Turpin had reappeared!' exclaimed a Doncaster fan. The old jokes are the best ones, right? (25.4.98).

PUB GUIDE

The Glamorgan (1) 88 Argyle Street (01792) 455 120
Mercury Taverns (with Marstons and Banks). Small welcoming traditional pub, with a good menu served 12-2.30 (or to 3 if it's busy). Darts, TV. Families with older children welcome. Open: all day.

The Fisherman and Firkin 400 Oystermouth Road (01792) 652 610
Firkin. The landlord describes it as a 'down-to-earth Firkin pub': large, with wooden floors and a big central bar area. Full menu served 12-3, 6-8. Hot and cold baps available all day. Darts, table football, big-screen TV, linked racing car machine. Families welcome. Disabled facilities. Open: all day from 12.

FOR FAMILIES:

The Waterside (2) 18 Anchor Court, Swansea Marina (01792) 648 555
Bass. A European café-style bar/restaurant, with great views over the marina. Snack menu (BLTs, chilli etc)/children's menu. Disabled facilities. Open: all day from 12.

The Pump House (3) Pump House Quay, Swansea Marina (01792) 651 080
Whitbread/Beefeater (with cask conditioned ales). Large new family pub next to the marina lock gates. Lunchtime bar meals. Please book for the restaurant. Children's menu. Open: all day from 11.30.

FOOD GUIDE

The fish and chip shop in Argyle Street rarely opens. Nearby St Helens Road has a couple of attractive café/takeaways including 'Snack Attack' on the corner of Richardson Street. It offers bacon, eggs, beans and chips for £1.99. Further towards town, there's a cluster of takeaways at the junction of Kingsway and St Helens Road, including a 'Macari's' restaurant/takeaway. Kingsway itself has a Pizza Hut and a McDonalds, while The Quadrant Shopping Centre on West Way has a café called 'The Gallery', which has excellent coffee. The more adventurous could visit Swansea market to stock up with seafood to take home, including Gower cockles and the local speciality 'Laver Bread'.

LOCAL MEDIA

Local Radio: Swansea Sound 1170 MW; Sound Wave 96.4 FM; BBC Radio Wales 882 MW.
Radio Phone-ins: Swansea Sound, Sundays 10-11 am, call (01792) 893 031.
Saturday Sports Paper: *The South Wales Evening Post* brings out a Saturday results paper, the 'Sporting Post'.

'I'm just going to the gents!'

MISCELLANEOUS

Swansea 'Jacks'? Why the nickname? Apparently it dates from the 1930s, and a little black labrador called Jack. The courageous canine – even though totally unqualified with absolutely no life-saving certificates – used to leap into the sea to haul out those in danger. There's a monument to him on the seafront opposite the rugby ground.

Safety Factor: Safety problems eased in season 97/98, and both Cardiff and Swansea fans were allowed to attend derby games – though only on presentation of a special voucher for travel on official coaches. However, Swansea City still has a small but significant hooligan following, and for bigger games, the police put up barriers to keep visiting fans towards the seafront and home fans inland.

Rivals: The rivalry with Cardiff extends beyond football, into business, media coverage, the Welsh Parliament and government grants. Swansea residents feel that Cardiff grabs nearly all the resources, and all of the attention. 'And another problem is that we don't mix', said a Swans supporter. 'The distance between the towns is just too big. It's like Rangers and Celtic'. Swansea fans actually like Wrexham, as they have something in common – a dislike of Cardiff.

Fanzines: 'Jackanory', PO Box 372, Swansea, SA1 6YY.

Unofficial Websites:
http://www2.prestel.co.uk/gmartin/index.html
http://ourworld.compuserve.com/homepages/slrnet
http://www.btinternet.com/~mdnet/scfc/

Tourist Information: (01792) 468 321.

S

Swindon Town

County Ground

Address: The County Ground, County Road, Swindon, Wiltshire, SN1 2ED
Telephone: Club (01793) 430 430
Ticket office (01793) 529 000
ClubCall (0891) 121 640
Club Shop (01793) 423 030

The name 'Swindon' is not exactly one to get the heart a-racing. Indeed, the town's image is one of roundabouts, housing estates and industrial developments, but there are also lots of plus points. The town's surrounded by beautiful countryside, such as the Cotswolds and the Wiltshire Downs, while – more importantly for the football fan perhaps – there are some excellent pubs to discover, some within walking distance of the County Ground. Until recently, the townsfolk were wary of football supporters, but times are changing, with more and more hostelries opening their doors on matchdays. Parking's also become much easier. In other words, this can be an unexpectedly good day out!

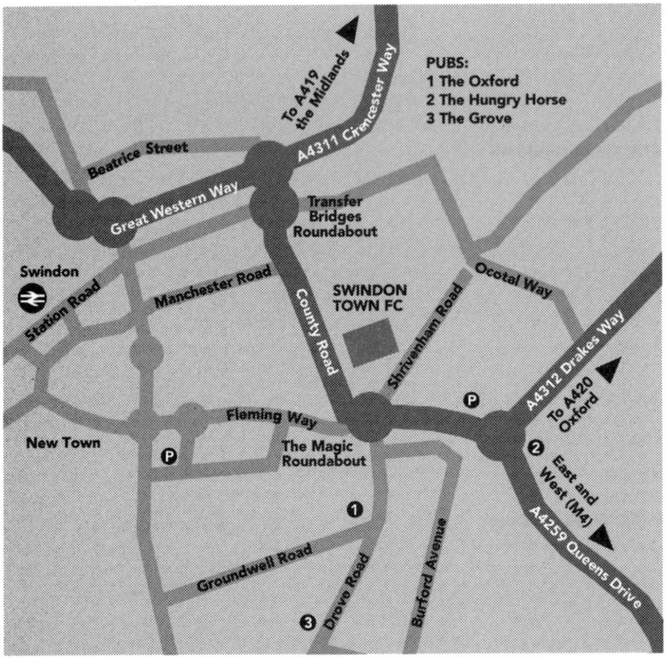

HOW TO GET THERE

BY CAR: With all its roundabouts, Swindon is a confusing town. Thankfully the County Ground is well signposted, and still has traditional floodlights. A major feature near the ground is a complex junction, comprising a maze of mini-roundabouts, called the Magic Roundabout. This is an important junction for visitors – from here, roads lead to the ground itself, the town centre parking, the Old Town, and 'The Oxford', 'The Grove' and 'The Hungry Horse' pubs.

From East and West, M4: Exit M4 at junction 15 (s/p Marlborough A346, Swindon A419). Follow Swindon signs for 1.9 miles to the Coate Roundabout, and then 'Football Traffic' and 'County Ground' signs to the ground, a further 1.8 miles. At the Magic Roundabout take first exit to 'The Oxford' pub, second exit for town centre parking, or turn back along Queens Drive to the school parking and 'The Hungry Horse' pub.

From the Midlands (A419): Exit A419 at the Turnpike Roundabout. At next roundabout turn right (s/p Swindon Centre) into Cricklade Road. At Moonrakers Roundabout after 1.4 miles, go straight on (s/p Headlands, Swindon Centre A4311). Follow Swindon Centre signs for another 1.3 miles, over three roundabouts, to the double roundabout called Transfer Bridges. At the first roundabout turn left (s/p County Ground, Swindon Centre) under railway bridge, and at the second take the second exit (s/p County Ground, Swindon Centre) into County Road. The ground is on the LHS after about 0.2 miles.

From Oxford (A420): Continue on A420 to the Gablecross Roundabout. Here, go straight on (s/p Swindon, Motorway M4, A420). At the White Hart Roundabout after 0.2 miles, take 3rd exit (s/p Swindon A4312) into Oxford Road. Go straight on, following signs for Swindon Centre A4312, for 2.0 miles, over the

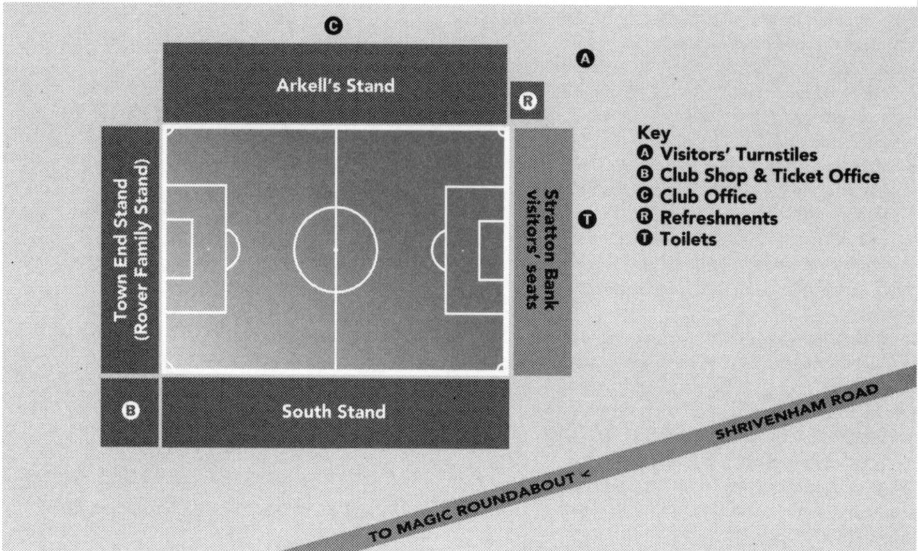

Lady Margaret and Greenbridge Roundabouts to a third roundabout. Here turn right (s/p County Ground, Walcott West, Swindon Centre). The floodlights, and the Magic Roundabout, are visible from here.

FROM RAILWAY STATION (Swindon): 0.6 miles. *By taxi:* £3.20. *By bus:* Buses run from Fleming Way, a short walk from the railway station (see below). *By foot:* Straight out of station, and head between the 'Flag and Whistle' and Queens Tap pubs. At next junction, turn left (s/p Country Ground) into Manchester Road. Go straight on at mini-roundabout after 0.1 miles, passing a fish-and-chip shop on the LHS. At mini-roundabout after 0.4 miles turn right (s/p Ring Road, Marlborough A345, Country Ground) into County Road. Ground is on LHS after 0.1 miles.

Last Midweek Trains: To London: 22.34. To Cardiff: 22.57.

BY BUS: From Fleming Way, nos.1 and 1a run from Bus Stop Q, the 13 and 15 from Bus Stop S.

PARKING

Early arrivals can still find street parking in Shrivenham Road or the sidestreets off Drove Road. There's well-signposted matchday parking at St Joseph's RC Comprehensive near the Drove Roundabout (£2 for school funds), and at the County Cricket Ground (entrance off County Road, £2). The town centre multi-storeys are also nearby: from the Magic Roundabout, follow signs to 'Swindon Centre and Parking' into Fleming Way. Long-stay parking is signposted left after 0.3 miles, by Halfords. It costs £1.40 for four hours, or just 50p in the evenings.

The Nationwide Building Society offers a park-and-ride from its premises, Nationwide House, in Piper's Way (50p bus fare). To get there, from route in from M4: turn left at the Coate Roundabout. Turn left at third (Piper's) Roundabout into Piper's Way.

THE GROUND

'From the sublime to the ridiculous' – an excellent expression to describe the County Ground. The South Stand, built in 1994, is the sublime, described by one Swindon fan as 'absolutely superb'. Opposite is the large, rather cavernous Arkell's Stand, where the view is still excellent. Further down the scale is the Town End, the covered stand for home supporters – 'primative at best' say the locals. Which leaves the 'grumpy little Stratton Bank'. This is the ridiculous bit: it's an open stand allocated, surprise, surprise, to away fans, who frazzle in the sun and sit, hunched and bedraggled, in the frequent Wiltshire downpours.

To be fair, the club has made strenuous efforts to improve the lot of the visiting fan. It's applied several times, without success, for planning permission to redevelop the Stratton Bank and then, on rainy days, opened a section of the covered Arkell's Stand for the away support. However, the local police have now decided against allowing visitors in the Arkell's Stand because of segregation problems, unless a particularly large away contingent is expected.

Total Capacity: 15,780. For away fans: Seating (Stratton Bank) 1,600.

Cost (98/99): Adults £14. Concessions (juniors, OAPs, students and for the unemployed), must be bought in advance through the away club.

Disabled Facilities: Four spaces for visiting supporters

at the front of the Arkell's Stand. *Disabled Toilet:* Nearby. *Cost:* Joint ticket for disabled and helper costs £5.50. *Parking:* Spaces in club car park, available on first-come first-served basis. *Booking:* Essential. *For the Blind:* Six seats with commentary in the Arkell's Stand.

Programme: £1.80.

Visitors' Toilets (Arkell's Stand): *Male:* The sinks were spotless AFTER half-time which meant either a) they had been cleaned or b) had not been used by the visiting support. *Female:* All was fine though a bit old-fashioned, but what WAS that weird-looking contraption high up on the wall? Some ancient boiler, perhaps?

Food and Drink: Who better to taste the Swindon snacks than the players from the America Omni touring football team? 'Not bad!', said one. 'American burgers are much better of course, but these are pretty good compared with the rest we've tasted in Britain'. Which is, we suppose, the definition of a back-handed compliment. Everyone appreciated the free biscuits which came with the expensive, but tasty, coffee (£1) (11.10.97, 28.12.97).

PUB GUIDE

There are four areas to try:

NEAR THE GROUND:

The Oxford (1) Drove Road (01793) 431 496
Whitbread. Large traditional pub with a great pre-match atmosphere. Snacks served 12-2.30. Pool table, darts, big-screen TV. Families welcome. Open: all day.

The Hungry Horse (2) (formerly The Bulldog) Queens Drive (01793) 533 455
Greene King. Large smart family pub with separate restaurant area and pub/drinking room with darts and big-screen TV. Full restaurant/childrens' menu. Open: all day.

ON THE ROAD ROUTES TO THE GROUND:

The Moonrakers Cricklade Road (on Moonrakers Roundabout) (01793) 721 017
Arkells. Large friendly sports-orientated pub, on route from The Midlands. Pool, darts, TV. Lunchtime rolls. Families welcome. Open: all day.

Also recommended: **The Bakers Arms,** 121 Beechcroft Road (Arkells), a pub 2.2 miles from the ground, but worth searching out. To get there: From Transfer Bridges roundabout (see map) follow signs to Cirencester to the Moonrakers Roundabout. Turn right and pub is on LHS after 0.5 miles.

IN THE OLD TOWN:

Two possibilities here: **The Royal Oak,** on the corner of Newport Street and Devizes Road, a Courage pub with big-screen TV; **The Steam Railway Co,** (Greenalls) on Newport Street, for excellent lunches. To get to the Old Town: From the Magic Roundabout, follow signs to Wroughton and Devizes into Drove Road, and then signs to the Old Town into Newport Street..

The roundabouts are confusing, but at least the ground is well signposted!

IN THE NEW TOWN:

The Savoy at 38 Regent Street, a huge Weatherspoons pub in a converted cinema, proud to be in the 'Good Beer' guide; **The Footplate and Firkin** at 25 Bridge Street, a classic, sports-friendly Firkin pub, with big-screen TV, table football and an excellent menu.

FOR FAMILIES:

The Grove (3), a Whitbread/Beefeater on Drove Road, accepts advance bookings from families for its restaurant. Please call (01793) 521 028.

FOOD GUIDE

The choice near the ground is limited to a Burger King on the Magic Roundabout, and a fish-and-chip/Chinese takeaway. On Manchester Road towards the railway station are another couple of takeaways, but the café on the junction of Manchester Road and County Road has closed down.

LOCAL MEDIA

Local Radio: GWR 97.2, 102.2 FM, 1161 MW; BBC Wiltshire Sound 103.6, 103.5, 104.3 and 104.9 FM.

Radio Phone-ins: None.

Saturday Sports Paper: None.

MISCELLANEOUS

Safety Factor: Trouble is rare.

Rivals: The main rival by far is 'Poxford'.

Fanzines: None.

Unofficial Websites:
http://www.swindon-fc.demon.co.uk/
http://geocities.com/Colosseum/Track/7215/index.html
http://members.aol.com/jspen26237/swindon.html

Tourist Information: (01793) 530 328.

Torquay United

Plainmoor

Address: Plainmoor Ground, Torquay,
Devon TQ1 3PS
Telephone: Club/Ticket Office (01803) 328 666
Fax (01803) 323 976

At half-time, try playing 'I-Spy' from the away terrace. Possible subjects are: a house window stacked with cuddly toys, four palm trees, five seagulls and a supermarket trolley piled with paint. As one local said: 'This is a holiday resort which happens to have a football team in it!' And that's the all-pervading feeling – that everyone's out to have a good time. Plainmoor is about a mile up (and it's a steep 'up' too) from the seafront, surrounded by a maze of terraced sidestreets. Many of the houses are painted in the soft pastels so typical of west country seaside resorts, and the street parking is very safe. No need to wander far here, as there's an excellent social club/pub at the ground, and a shopping street nearby. The railway station, however, is a right trek so many fans divert to the 'arcs' (the amusement arcades) and harbour-front before taking a taxi to the ground.

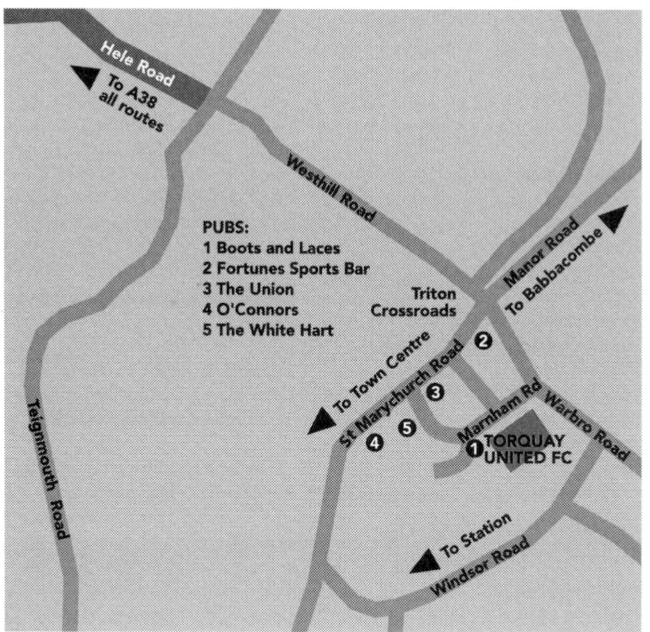

HOW TO GET THERE

There's a crossroads near Plainmoor, by a company called Triton, which is a key junction for giving road directions. For simplicity, we've called it the 'Triton Crossroads', as marked on the map.

BY CAR: From North and East: Exit A38 onto the A380 (s/p Torquay A380). Over River Teign after 9.1 miles, to Penn Inn roundabout (which has a Beefeater pub and McDonalds on it) after a further 1.1 miles. Here, go straight on (s/p Torquay A380, Kingkerswell) into Torquay Road. After 3.0 miles, after passing through village of Kingkerswell, take 1st exit at next roundabout (s/p Torquay A3022, Teignmouth B3199) onto the A3022 Riviera Way. After 1.0 miles, in front of Texaco garage, turn left (s/p Teignmouth B3199, St Marychurch, Babbacombe, Plainmoor TUFC) into Hele Road. (*)From here to the 'Triton Crossroads' the ground is signposted, a distance of 1.2 miles. Go straight across the 'Triton Crossroads' into Warbro Road to ground, or turn right into St Marychurch Road, which is a local shopping street with pubs and takeaways.

From South-West (i.e. Plymouth): Exit A38 at Marley Head junction (s/p Paignton A385). Follow Paignton A385 signs for 11.0 miles, through Dartington and Totnes, over River Dart and into the Borough of Torbay to crossroads/traffic lights (the junction with the Ring Road). Here turn left (s/p Ring Road, Exeter, A380, also Marldon, Torquay) onto the Ring Road. Straight on for 3.3 miles, over the Churscombe and Preston Down roundabouts (both s/p Torquay A3022) to the Gallows Gate roundabout. Here, turn right (s/p Shiphay, Abbotskerswell) into Marldon Road. At T-junction after 1.7 miles turn left (s/p Exeter A380) into Newton Road. At junction after 0.3 miles, just after Texaco petrol station, turn right (s/p Teignmouth A3199, Plainmoor TUFC). Then as From North and East (*).

FROM RAILWAY STATION (Torquay): About 2.2 miles, mainly uphill. *By taxi:* £4 plus 10p

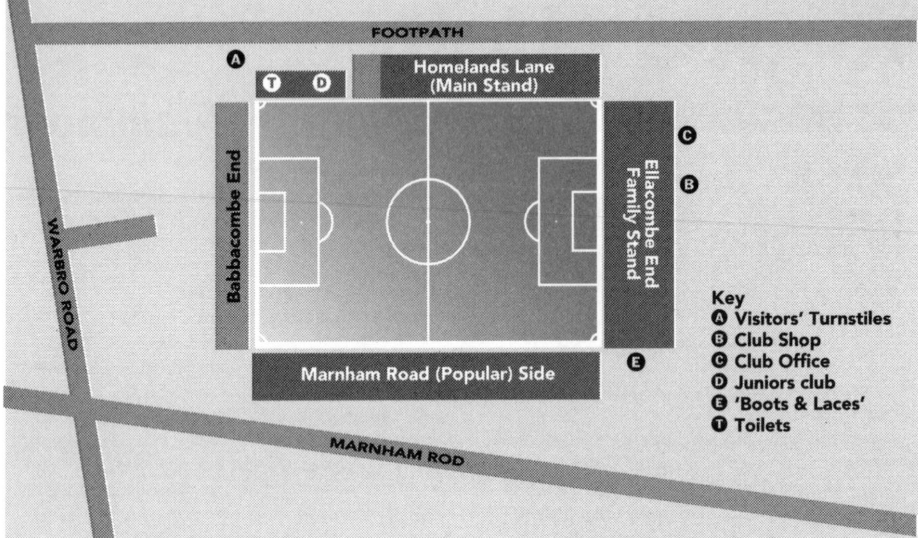

per person. *By bus:* Frequent service. Take the no. 12 to Cary Parade in the town centre, and change to the no. 34 to Plainmoor.
Last Midweek Trains: No trains to either Bristol or London after evening games. On a Saturday, the last train to London is at 18.31 (changing at Newton Abbot). Please double-check on (0345) 484 950.
BY BUS: As above.

PARKING

Street parking only. The roads immediately around the ground are coned off, but otherwise there are no restrictions.

THE GROUND

The many good points about Plainmoor make the Torquay trip one of the best of the year. The ground is neat and tidy, the pricing is more than reasonable, and the excellent social club welcomes visiting fans both before and after the match. The downside is that the away terrace, behind the goal, is uncovered, and it always seems to be either blisteringly hot or sub-zero with easterly winds straight off the sea! Home fans enjoy better facilities, especially those in the Ellacombe End Family Stand who disappear at half time for a drink in the warm, cosy Boots and Laces pub. Never mind, the pasties on the away end are still excellent!
Total Capacity: 6,003. For away fans: Seating 196, terrace 808. Turnstiles 11 and 12.
Cost (98/99): Terrace: £8 Adults, OAP's/Students £5, Under 16's £4. Seating: £9/£6/£4.
Disabled Facilities: Space for 15 visiting supporters in the Family Stand. *Disabled Toilet:* Nearby. *Cost:* Free for disabled, £5 for helper. *Booking:* Yes. *Parking:* None available. *For the Blind:* Space for 15 people in the Main Stand. Please book.
Programme: £1.50.
Visitors' Toilets: *Male:* One sniff was enough. Our loo-checker decided to wait until he got to the pub after the game. However, this was right at the end of the match, and earlier in the season, Ipswich fans had found the facilities to be 'generally okay'. *Female:* No smell, but not much else either. On the walls, Burnley fans had recorded their away attendance and Macc Town had made their first entry into the graffiti stakes.
Food and Drink: Fans liked both the pasties (£1.30) and the sausage rolls (£1 – 'real sausage, very nice') but gave a definite thumbs-down to the hot-dogs (£1). One fan said the pasty was so big he couldn't eat it all, but the hot-dog had 'nothing to it'. The coffee (60p) was tasteless (23.9.97 and 7.3.98).

PUB GUIDE

Boots and Laces (1) Marnham Road (at the ground) (01803) 327 532
Carlsberg-Tetley. This is Torquay United's own pub, and most welcoming it is too. It's large and modern, with a family area, big-screen TV and upstairs restaurant. Bar snacks also available. Darts, pool table. Disabled facilities. Open: Fri/Sat 11am-midnight; midweek all day.
Fortunes Sports Bar (2) 187 St Marychurch Road (01803) 326 272
Free House. A spacious 'sports bar', with big screen TV. 'We're the cheapest pub in the Bay!' declares the landlord, and in addition he puts out free food (sandwiches, chicken, chips etc). Darts, pool, 4 other

TVs. Open: all day.

The Union (3) 127 St Marychurch Road (01803) 328 356

Courage. Local high street pub, welcoming a good mix of supporters. Separate games area with pool and darts. TV. Bar snacks. Open: all day.

O'Connors Irish Bar (4) 133 St Marychurch Road (01803) 328 271

Free House. Popular Irish theme pub, but as the landlord says, 'the only Irish thing is the name and some of the paraphernalia'. Bar snacks, darts, two skittle alleys, two pool tables, separate family room. Open: all day.

Also recommended: **The White Hart,** 58 St Edmunds Road. A locals Courage pub with 'fine ales and good service', according to the landlord.

A LITTLE FURTHER AWAY:

The Old Brewery Lower Ellacombe Church Road (01803) 213 336

Free House. A pub full of character and, though under new management, still very football-friendly. Snacks and sandwiches. Snooker room, pool, skittle alley, darts, big-screen TV, disabled facilities and a large children's room. Open: all day.

To get there: Go straight across the 'Triton Crossroads' into Warbro Road. At T-junction with Reddenhill Road turn right, then take first left into Windsor Road (s/p Central Area). Take 1st right (s/p Central Area) into Ellacombe Church Road, and then 1st left into Lower Ellacombe Church Road.

IN BABBACOMBE:

On Babbacombe Road are two wonderful pubs, both highly recommended: **The Dog and Duck** at 70 Babbacombe Road is a Free House owned by former player John Turner, who used to run the 'Old Brewery'. He's still providing free food (chicken, ribs etc) after the game, and there's a pool table, skittle alley, darts, bar snacks and big-screen TV; **The Masons Arms** at 110 Babbacombe Road is a traditional sports-friendly Greenalls pub serving an extensive, good-value menu.

FOR FAMILIES:

The Old Coach House 86 Babbacombe Downs Road, Babbacombe is a large popular family pub/restaurant in an old coaching inn; **The Willow Tree** is a new pub on the main route to Plainmoor from the North and East. Follow the road directions from the Penn Inn Roundabout, but after 3.5 miles filter left (s/p Willows Superstores, County Court) into Browns Bridge Road. Straight on at 1st roundabout, and pub is on LHS by Marks and Spencer. It's an Allied Domecq pub with a 'Wacky Warehouse', and an extensive menu served all day to 10 pm.

FOOD GUIDE

For fast food, supporters need wander no further than nearby St Marychurch Road. Locals recommend both the Plainmoor Bakery and the Plainmoor Fish Bar. The

nearby Riviera Takeaway, which opens at 5.30 pm, has an extensive menu with pizzas, kebabs, burgers, lasagne and moussaka. For a good sit-down fry-up, the fanzine 'Bamber's Right Foot' recommends the Anchor Café, just past O'Connors pub.

In Babbacombe there are two fish and chip shops vying for awards: 'Drakes Celebrated Fish and Chips' and 'David Hanburys', which was voted the South-West '1997 Fish and Chip Shop of the Year'.

Fleet Street, down by the harbour, has the usual chains, such as Wimpy, Pizza Hut and KFC. The staff at Torquay United recommend 'Options' for those preferring the healthy alternative to burger-and-chips. A new Pizza Express has opened on the harbour front.

LOCAL MEDIA

Local Radio: BBC Radio Devon, 103.4 FM; Gemini Radio 954 and 666 MW.

Radio Phone-ins: None.

Saturday Sports Paper: None.

MISCELLANEOUS

Safety Factor:. If there is any bother at Torquay, it's at matches against Exeter or Cardiff.

Rivals: 'Plymuff Argoool' fans dislike Exeter, and Exeter fans dislike Plymouth, which leaves Torquay feeling a little left out.

Fanzine: 'Bamber's Right Foot', PO Box 77, Torquay, Devon, TQ2 5YR.

Unofficial Websites:

'Gull's Net': http://www.mervo.com/torquay-united/
http://www.angelfire.com/oh/tufc/index.html
http://www.stix.demon.co.uk/tufc/cover.htm

Tourist Information: (01803) 297 428.

T

Tottenham Hotspur

White Hart Lane

Address: 748 High Road, Tottenham, London, N17 OAP
Telephone: Club (0181) 365 5000
Ticket Office (0181) 365 5050
Non-Members Tickets (0171) 420 0234
Spurs Line (0891) 335 555
Spurs Shop (0181) 365 5042
Mail Order (0181) 808 5959
Official Website: http://www.spurs.co.uk

One day an unsuspecting football fan on his way to Spurs will buy a bag of chips, and a thousand lights will flash, sirens wail and a scantily clad female will emerge to present a prize for 'the 30 billionth chip bought on Tottenham High Road'. The great thing about multi-cultural Haringey is that there's a little more variety among the takeaways: try Caribbean, Turkish, Greek or Italian food, all within a hundred yards. The shops and cafés may be downmarket, but many of the pubs are first-rate, and football friendly to-boot. Unusually for north London, there's no nearby tube station, but the overland rail and bus services are good. Those travelling by car should allow lots of extra time to negotiate the London traffic jams and to find a parking space.

HOW TO GET THERE

BY CAR: From North, West and East (M25). The quickest route by far is M11-A406 as follows: Exit M25 at junction 27 and follow signs to 'London (NE), M11' onto the M11 southbound. After 7.1 miles where the motorway ends and the road divides, bear right (s/p A406 N. Circ. Rd West, London N and W) onto the North Circular Road. Exit North Circular Road after 3.9 miles at the 'Kenning Hall' junction (s/p Tottenham, Brimsdown A1055). (*)At junction after 0.3 miles turn right (s/p Brimsdown, Tottenham A1055) into Montagu Road. Straight on at lights after 0.2 miles (s/p Picketts

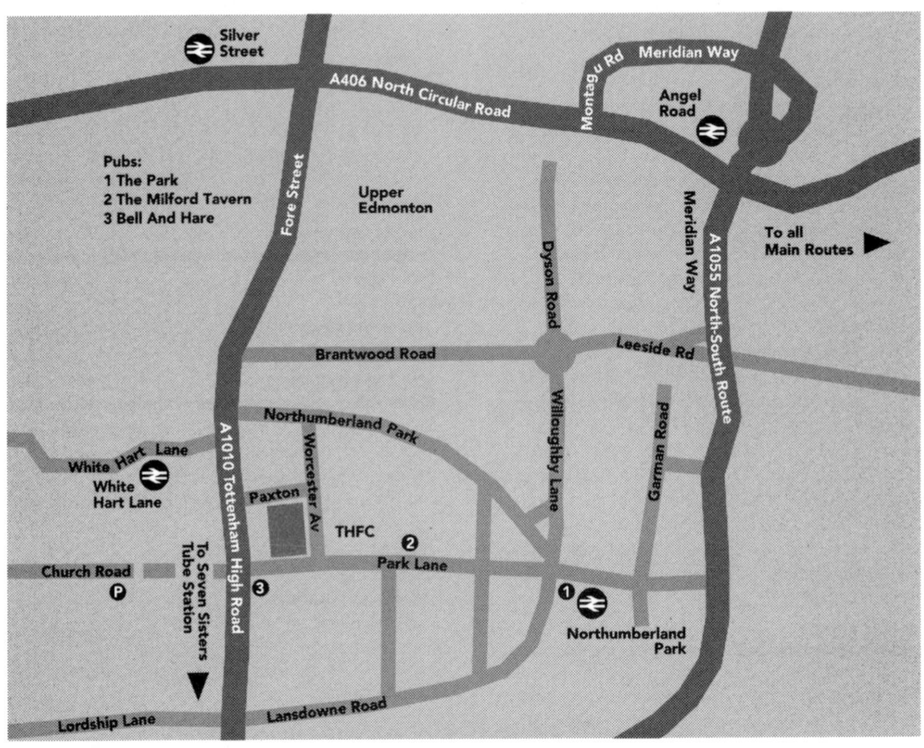

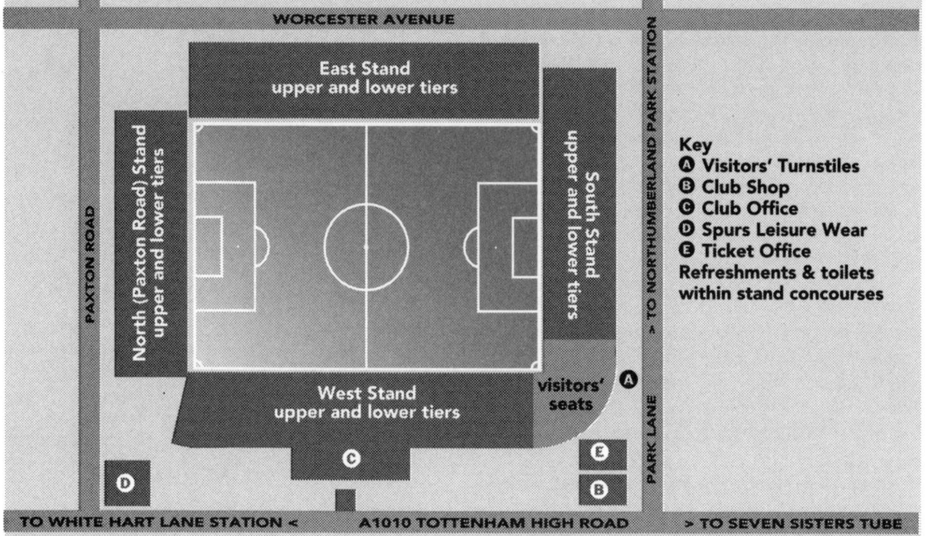

Lock, Ponders End A1055) into Meridian Way, passing Angel Road station on the LHS. Go straight on at roundabout after 0.3 miles (s/p Tottenham A1055). Straight on for 0.4 miles, under the North Circular and passing Tescos on the LHS, then filter right at lights (s/p Brantwood Road Industry) into Leeside Road and over bridge. Straight on at mini-roundabout into Brantwood Road. At T-junction after 0.6 miles opposite Sainsburys turn left into Tottenham High Road. Ground is on LHS after 0.2 miles.

From South (M25): Approaching the Dartford Tunnel, keep in the left-hand lanes (s/p Dagenham A13). Go through tunnel and exit M25 after 0.8 miles at junction 31 (s/p Dagenham, Services, A13 West), and turn left at roundabout (s/p London, Rainham A13) onto the A13. Exit A13 after 10.1 miles (s/p North Circular A406, The North (A1, M1)), and at roundabout turn right onto the A406 North Circular Road. Exit North Circular after 9.4 miles at the 'Kenning Hall' junction (s/p Tottenham, Brimsdown A1055). Then as From North and West(*). NB Away coaches should drop supporters off at the Bell and Hare pub on the High Road by the ground, and then drive via Lansdowne Road, Shelbourne Road and Willoughby Road into West Road. At half-time they will be escorted by the police to Worcester Avenue.

FROM UNDERGROUND STATION (Seven Sisters, Victoria Line Zone 3): 1.5 miles to ground, ie a good 30 minute walk. The quickest way to White Hart Lane is to switch to the overland railway line. Simply follow the signs to 'Main Line Station'. Trains run every 20 minutes or so, and it's usually just one stop. *By taxi:* About £3. *By bus:* Nos. 149, 259 and 279 run along Tottenham High Road. *By foot:* Follow signs to 'Way Out and High Street'. Past ticket office and turn left, following signs to High Street West. It's then straight on for 1.5 miles to the ground.

FROM RAILWAY STATIONS:

a) White Hart Lane (on the Liverpool Street-Hertford East line): Five minute walk to ground. Come down the steps and turn right along White Hart Lane, crossing Love Lane. At T-junction turn right into Tottenham High Road.

b) Northumberland Park (stopping train from Liverpool Street to Bishop's Stortford and Stansted Airport): Ten minute walk. Down steps to Park Avenue Road, by the excellent 'Seastar' takeaway, and turn left. Cross the main road (Shelbourne Road) into Park Lane. The ground is visible from here.

Last Midweek Trains: From White Hart Lane, trains run to Liverpool Street at 29, 44 and 59 minutes past the hour until 23.44. The last train to Hertford East, via Cheshunt, is at 23.16. From Northumberland Park, trains run to Liverpool Street at 22.22 and 23.22, and to Stansted at 22.16 and 22.22. For season 97/98 Network South East ran a special matchday service on this line – call its customer services line (0345) 818 919 for more information. For connecting trains from London, see London Guide at front of this book.

BY BUS: Nos. 149, 259 and 279 run along Tottenham High Road. The 171A diverts down Lansdowne Road to Northumberland Park railway station, while the W3 runs from Northumberland Park Station along White Hart Lane to Finsbury Park. Note, however, that the buses can get caught in matchday traffic, and sometimes it's quicker to walk.

PARKING

On the map, it looks like street parking won't be a problem. However, the council trundles round on matchdays flipping over a series of signs, imposing parking restrictions on most of the nearby roads. The best areas to try are to the east of the ground, as far out as Sedge Road and Graham Road towards the A1055. To the west of the ground, Bull Lane and Queen Street are emergency access roads, but it's worth trying the sidestreets. Various schools and offices open up to provide matchday parking, but some are very expensive. About the nearest is at the Gibson Business Centre (£10), at the junction of White Hart Lane and Tottenham High Street, while a small car park on Church Road charges £8. Those who can find their way from The Roundway to the other side of the Church Road barrier can park at a school for £5.

THE GROUND

The appearance and the atmosphere of White Hart Lane improved dramatically with the opening of the second tier of the North Stand, which now seats 10,000. The ground is an impressive modern Premiership venue, but traditionalists maintain it's not a patch on the old White Hart Lane, with its huge terraces, roof gables, the ever-popular Shelf and the cracking atmosphere of yesteryear. Visiting fans are housed in the South Stand behind the goal. The legroom is good, and the view at the back much better than at nearby rivals Arsenal. On cold days, those on the back row turn round and look enviously into a warm glass-fronted executive area behind! Huge video screens are mounted on the top of both the North and South Stands, and many fans find themselves watching the game on the TV – old habits, one assumes! Some think they're great, some find them distracting. Others have suggested that Spurs screen 'Gone with the Wind' instead of the football, so all family members have something to watch!

Total Capacity: 36,000. For away fans: from 2,200 to 4,000 depending on whether it's a league or cup game. It's very unusual, however, for the whole stand to be allocated to the visiting support.

Cost (97/98): South Stand Upper Tier – 'Premier' games £25, standard games £22. Lower Tier – 'Premier' games £21, standard games £18. No concessions for away fans.

Disabled Facilities: Up to seven spaces in an area at pitch level, shared with home fans, in front of the South Stand. *Disabled Toilet:* Nearby. *Cost:* Free for disabled, matchday price for helper. *Booking:* Tottenham Hotspur sends tickets to the away club, which deals with bookings. *Parking:* None at ground. *For the Blind:* Headsets provided so fans can sit where they wish. Please book.

Programme: £2.

'So, Tracy from Tottenham, you've picked Harry from Highbury... ...slide back the screen.'

Visitors' Toilets: *Male:* Fans wondered whether the loos from the old stand had been carefully dismantled, put into storage, then put back into the brand new concourses! 'Very old-fashioned looking and quite dirty', said one fan. The sinks were clean enough, however, with soap and working hand-dryers. *Female:* Why are the ladies loos at White Hart Lane like those of a World War II submarine? Answer: the loo seats are constantly warm! Honest, the history books say that submarine loos were in constant use ... so it is at Spurs, though once desperate fans did get inside, the facilities were good.

Food and Drink: At least Spurs were offering something a little different, such as a 'chicken sandwich', complete with salad, for £2.20. Most fans found it tasty and pricey! The 'fries' (£1) were also good, as were the hot dogs (£2). One supporter had put so much mustard on his dog that no-one could understand how he could eat it. 'Easy', he said. 'I'm alcoholically overwhelmed!' The spicy beanburgers (£2) were surprisingly bland. And, of course, Spurs couldn't please everyone: 'I could really do with a pie', sighed one supporter. Beer and lager are usually on sale (13.4.98).

PUB GUIDE

The Beehive Stoneleigh Road (0181) 808 3567
Courage. Traditional pub in a 400-year-old building, and wonderfully sports-friendly. The pub is proud of its menu, offering fish-and-chips, pies, burgers, lasagne etc., all day. Big-screen TV, 2 pool tables, darts, beer garden. Families welcome/disabled facilities. Open: all day.

The Park (1) 220 Park Lane (0181) 808 3391
Whitbread (with Boddingtons). Smart, comfortable pub

with separate games room and an excellent beer garden. Full bar menu served unless it's too busy. Darts, 3 pool tables, table football. Families welcome. Open: all day.

The Milford Tavern (2) 159 Park Lane. (0181) 801 2778

Courage. Traditional locals pub which, in the late 19th century, served as Tottenham Hotspur's changing rooms. Pool table, darts, TV. Open: all day.

The Elbow Room 503-505 High Road (0181) 801 8769

JD Weatherspoon (with Sundance). Small but friendly Weatherspoons pub, serving full menu (til it gets too busy!). Over 18s only admitted. Open: all day.

Also highly recommended: Two small, country-style pubs, both Free Houses, in Scotland Green, **The Two Brewers,** stocking mainly Courage beers and with a wonderful beer garden; and **The Victoria,** with pool table and table football.

NB A large new Weatherspoons pub is opening in 1998 north of the ground, on the corner of the High Road and Claremont Street.

FOR FAMILIES:

The Bell and Hare (3) 724 Tottenham High Road, corner Park Lane (0181) 808 3657

Whitbread (with Flowers). Comfortable traditional town pub, with lots of dark wood panelling and a bright back room overlooking the beer garden. Hot dogs, pool table, darts, TV. Note that the doormen ONLY allow in family groups. Open: Saturdays 11-3, 4.45-11; from 5 pm for midweek games.

FOOD GUIDE

Supporters walking along the High Road pass a takeaway or café every twenty seconds or so. Near the ground, home fans recommend the 'Hotspur Restaurant' which has a breakfast special at £2.99 as well as omlettes, salads and sandwiches. Both the 'King Neptune' (pies £1.30, chips from 90p), and the 'Coral Bay Fish Bar' (cod from £1.95, chips 70p) have long queues – always a good sign! 'Mick's Grill' offers all-day breakfasts from £3.25, as well as full meals and sandwiches. Further down the high road is the 'Ukay Turkish Cuisine', and the Caribbean takeaway 'Peppers and Spice'. Towards Seven Sisters, try the 'Tottenham Beigel Bakery' (beigels 80p, pasties 90p), and for a proper sit-down meal, head to the 'San Marco' family-run Italian restaurant, right by Bruce Grove railway station. A meal with wine costs about £12. Please book on (0181) 808 9494.

Near 'The Park' pub and Northumberland Park railway station is the truly excellent 'Seastar Fish Bar'. It has cod at £2.50, chips at 80p, kebabs from £2.30 and a wonderful spicy beanburger at £1.50.

LOCAL MEDIA

Local Radio: Capital Gold 1548 AM; GLR 94.9 FM; XFM 104.9.

Radio Phone-ins: Capital Gold, Saturdays 5-6.30 pm; midweek every night 7-8 or after live match commentary. Call (0845) 35 60 70 80.

Saturday Sports Paper: None.

MISCELLANEOUS

Safety Factor: Few problems here.

Rivals: Er, Arsenal ... and any London club doing well such as Chelsea and West Ham. Plus any club which knocks Tottenham out of the cup. And any club Teddy Sheringham plays for!

Fanzines: 'Cock-a-Doodle-Doo', PO Box 6979, London, N5 1JQ; 'The Circumcised Cockerel', no address given.

Unofficial Websites:

'748 High Road':
http://home.sol.no/~hlindas/mspurs.htm

'SpursWeb': http://members.aol.com/neilv1/

'White Hart Site':
http://www.xpress.se/~ssab0019/index.html

'Darren's THFC Page':
http://www2.fortunecity.com/wembley/whitehart/15/index.htm

Tourist Information: None nearby.

Tranmere Rovers

Prenton Park

Address: Prenton Park, Prenton Road West, Birkenhead, Wirral L42 9PN
Telephone: Club (0151) 608 4194
Ticket Office (0151) 609 0137
Club Shop (0151) 608 0438
ClubCall (0891) 121 646
Official Website:
http://www.merseyworld.com/rovers

'Tranmere Rovers, the Pride of Merseyside'. Of course some might beg to differ, and a game at Prenton Park may not be the overpowering football experience of Anfield and Goodison Park on the other side of the river. But a trip to Tranmere Rovers is almost hassle-free, especially as car crime is rare, and match tickets readily available! Birkenhead is a quiet, suburban area, within easy commuting distance (via the Mersey Tunnel) of Liverpool. Prenton Park is near a motorway, but a mile from the nearest station. There are several good eateries on one road near the ground, and the nearest pint is within a few yards of the away turnstiles.

HOW TO GET THERE

BY CAR: From South and East: Exit M53 at junction 3 (s/p Birkenhead A552). At roundabout turn right (s/p Birkenhead, Liverpool and Tunnels A552) onto the A552. (*)After 1.1 miles, just after the Esso garage on the LHS and by the 'Halfway House' pub, turn right (s/p B5151 Clatterbridge, then Higher Bebington) into Storeton Road. Take 1st left into Woodchurch Lane to ground.

From Birkenhead Tunnel (£1 toll): Out of tunnel, bear right and then left, following signs for 'A552, Tranmere Rovers FC, Heswall, Prenton'. After 0.5 miles, go straight on at lights along Borough Road. Follow signs to 'Motorway M53, Clatterbridge, Heswall' for 0.9 miles to third set of lights. Here, bear left (s/p Clatterbridge, Bebington B5151, Tranmere Rovers FC), remaining on Borough Road. Ground is on RHS after 0.2 miles.

From Wallasey Tunnel (£1 toll): From tunnel follow signs to join the M53. After approximately 4 miles, exit motorway at junction 3 (s/p Birkenhead A552). At roundabout take first exit (s/p Birkenhead A552, Liverpool and Tunnels A552), onto the A552. Then as From South and East(*).

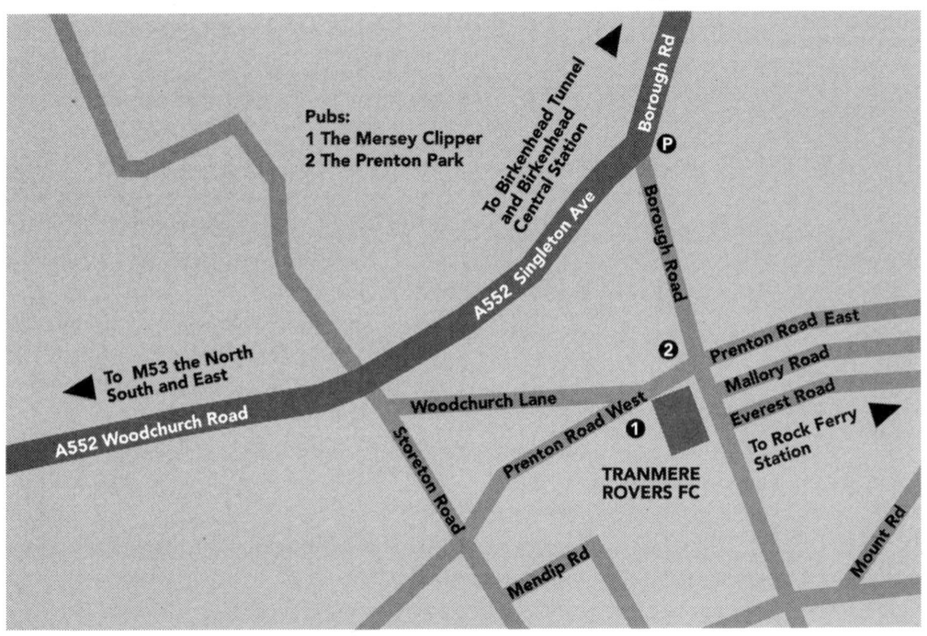

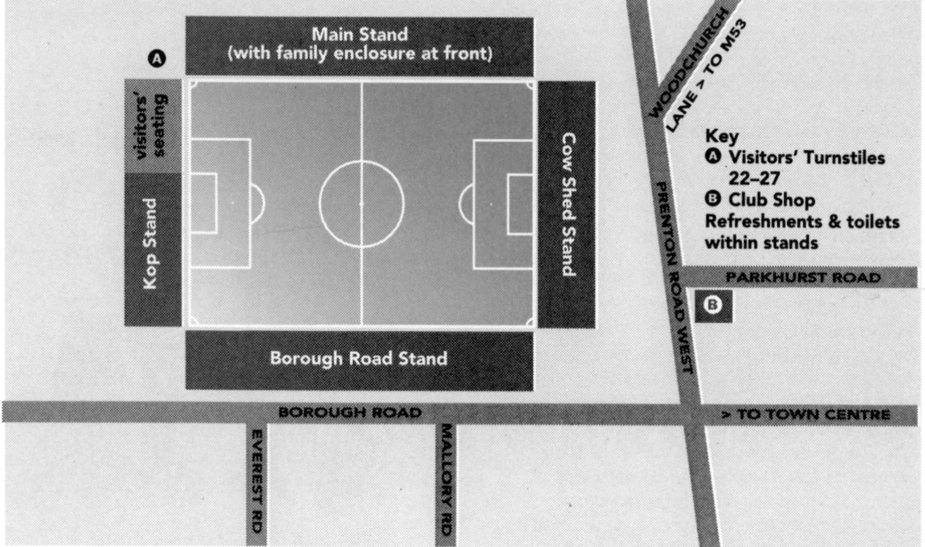

FROM RAILWAY STATIONS: The following stations are on the Wirral Line, which can be reached via Liverpool Lime Street or Chester.
a) Birkenhead Central: 1.3 miles. *By taxi:* About £2. *By bus:* Nos. 42, 64 and 177. *By foot:* Come out of station to the huge roundabout with the clock tower. Bear left, following signs to Heswall, Clatterbridge into Borough Road. Where road divides after 1.1 miles, bear left (s/p Clatterbridge, Bebington B5151, Tranmere Rovers FC). Ground is on RHS after 0.2 miles.
b) Rock Ferry Station: 1.1 miles. *By bus:* None. *By taxi:* £1.60-£1.80. *By foot:* Up steps to main road and turn right onto Bedford Road. Straight on at crossroads after 0.2 miles into Bedford Avenue. At roundabout after 0.2 miles, turn right into Bebington Road. At big roundabout after 0.3 miles, take the 2nd left turn (before the St Catherine's Hospital sign) into Everest Road to ground.
c) Hamilton Square Station: This is the best station for those who want to travel to Prenton Park by bus. Turn sharp left, then right into Bridge Street, and take bus nos. 3, 3b, 64, 70, 71 or 72. Most stop on Singleton Avenue (ask for the 'Wirral Tech' stop).
d) Conway Park (trains from Liverpool to New Brighton or West Kirby): The railway station is near a new bus station. Most of the buses mentioned above stop here, plus the no. 170 which runs to the ground.
Last Midweek Trains: From Birkenhead Central, trains run to Liverpool at 22.06, 22.21, 22.36, 22.51 and 2306. The journey takes five minutes. To Chester, trains run at 22.14 and 22.44, and take 30 minutes. For last trains from Chester see Chester City chapter, and from Liverpool Lime Street see Liverpool chapter.

BY BUS: Bus nos. 42, 64 and 177 run from the centre of Birkenhead to the ground. Nos. 3, 3b, 70, 71 and 72 stop on Singleton Avenue (ask for the 'Wirral Tech' stop), a 5-10 minute walk from the ground.

PARKING

The car park at the ground charges £3.50, entrance off Prenton Road West, but fills up early. The Shaftesbury Boys Club next door has parking on grass, so it can only be used in better weather. Otherwise, it's street parking, which isn't easy because of residents-only parking schemes. Try around Prenton Road East and Mount Road, towards Rock Ferry station.

THE GROUND

In 1994, Tranmere Rovers 'did a Notts County' ... in other words, in the space of a few months, the club demolished and then rebuilt, three sides of the ground. Down came the Kop (the home terrace), the Borough Road Stand and the covered Cowshed. In their place rose three new stands, including the towering Kop Stand, seating 5,823. The Main Stand, built in 1968, now looks outdated but, with the club strapped for finance, it's unlikely to be redeveloped in the near future. Although the old-style ground was much-loved, Rovers fans knew that redevelopment was vital ... for a start, every time the ball hit one of the old stands, the supporters underneath were showered with rust! Visiting fans are allocated part of, or all of, the Kop Stand behind the goal, where the view and the acoustics are excellent.
Total Capacity: 16,792. For away fans: Up to 5,823 seats in the Kop Stand, depending on size of away contingent. Turnstiles 22-27.

Cost (98/99): Adults: £10, £12 or £14, depending on match category. Concessions (£7) are available on a reciprocal basis.
Disabled Facilities: Space for 28 wheelchairs at pitch level in the Main Stand Paddock (at the front of the family enclosure). *Disabled Toilet:* Nearby. *Cost:* Free for disabled, full price for a helper. *Booking:* Essential. *Parking:* Available. *For the Blind:* Headphones with commentary available in the Main Stand. Please book via the Ticket Office.
Programme: £1.40.
Visitors' Toilets: *Male:* Sunderland had brought a huge following, and at half-time, both they and the toilet facilities were bursting at the seams! *Female:* All the essentials were there and in working order, and the missing seat from 1996 had been replaced.
Food and Drink: One supporter described the hot dog (£2) as 'good value, with lots of good onions in a fresh bun.' The cheeseburger (£2.20) was also above average. The main complaint was about the lack of variety: no pies, pasties and certainly no vegetarian options. The tea (70p) had scarcely improved from earlier seasons, but the coffee (70p) was good (3.4.98).

PUB GUIDE

Few fans venture further than these two excellent watering holes by the ground:
The Mersey Clipper (1) 17 Prenton Road West (0151) 608 3446
Greenalls (with Stones Bitter). Immensely popular friendly pub, with a great matchday atmosphere. It serves the 'Ale 'n Hearty' menu, with vegetarian options and separate children's menu, 12-2.30, 5-8.30. Family room and dining area. Big-screen TVs. Open: all day.
The Prenton Park (2) Borough Road (0151) 608 3852
Whitbread. Large, friendly traditional pub with two pool tables, darts and big-screen TV. Families welcome/disabled facilities. Open: all day.

FOOD GUIDE

Those looking for takeaway have a good choice on Borough Road. Just along from the 'Prenton Park' pub is the excellent 'Eastern Delight', serving Chinese dishes (£3.50-£4) and southern fried chicken and chips for £2.20. The 'Wirral Takeaway' offers large burgers at £2.70 and pies from 55p, while 'The Breaktime Café' serves good value meals including an all-in breakfast for either £2.75 (small) or £3.50 (large). Woodchurch Lane is home to a Balti house, a café, and the upmarket 'Villa Venezia' restaurant, opposite the ground on Prenton Road West.

LOCAL MEDIA

Local Radio: BBC Radio Merseyside 95.8 FM; Radio City 96.7 FM; MFM (Wirral) 97.1 FM.

'He only asked if you support Liverpool or Everton!'

Radio Phone-Ins: BBC Radio Merseyside, from 5 pm, call (0151) 709 9333; Radio City, Saturdays 5-6 pm, call (0151) 4720 967.
Saturday Sports Paper: The 'Football Echo', which appears around Merseyside from 5.30 pm.

MISCELLANEOUS

Safety Factor: The only problems in season 97/98 were with Stoke City fans.
Rivals: Locally, Tranmere find themselves in a strange situation, as they are two divisions above Chester City, but still not up there with Liverpool and Everton. Many fans cheered the relegation of Bolton 'up and down' Wanderers in 1997/98, as they're something of an old enemy and the nearest thing Rovers get to a true 'local' rival. Tranmere supporters were also cheering, throughout season 97/98, for Everton's drop to the First Division. However, Everton yet again avoided their first ever 'dreaded derby match with Tranmere'.
Fanzines: 'Give Us An R', 5 Rockybank Road, Birkenhead, Merseyside, L42 7LB.
Unofficial Websites:
http://www.demon.co.uk/trfc.htm
http://homepages.which.net/~barbara.jones/tranmere.html
http://www.mersinet.co.uk/deadlysub/
http://www.users.globalnet.co.uk/~johnbn/tranmere.htm
http://www.geocities.com/Colosseum/Sideline/6625/
Tourist Information: (0151) 647 6780.

Walsall

The Bescot Stadium

Address: Bescot Stadium, Bescot Crescent, Walsall WS1 4SA
Telephone: Club (01922) 622 791
Club Shop (01922) 631 072
Saddlers Hotline (0891) 555 800
Official Website: http://www.saddlers.co.uk

'Duerr's Marmalades Beat the M6 Jams', says the huge advertising hoarding on top of the Bescot Stadium. It's a clever slogan, because the advert is clearly visible from the M6, and the motorway at this point is one of the most congested in Europe! Football fans should take heed, and allow lots of extra travelling time, especially if coming from the south for an evening game. The ground, on a new retail/leisure development, is just a few minutes' drive from the motorway and there's a railway station next door. Parking is easy. However, apart from a McDonalds on the retail park, the nearest takeaways and pubs are a good ten minute walk away.

HOW TO GET THERE

BY CAR: From South and West: Keep on M5 past junction 1 to where the road divides. Bear right (s/p The North West, Walsall, Wolverhampton M6). After 1.6 miles the road joins the M6. Exit at next junction (junction 9, s/p A461 Wednesbury). At roundabout turn right (s/p Walsall A461). (*)After 0.1 miles, keep right where road divides (s/p Ring Road A4148 and Bescot Stadium) into Wallows Lane, through traffic lights, over bridge, and right at the lights into Bescot Crescent.
From North and East: Exit M6 at junction 9 (s/p A461 Wednesbury) and at roundabout follow sign to Walsall A461. Then as From South and West(*).
Alternative route From East (M6): A particularly good route for evening games. Exit M6 at junction 7 (s/p Birmingham N, Walsall A34). Keep in lane marked 'Walsall A34', taking the third exit from the roundabout onto the A34. After 0.9 miles turn left just after 'The Bell' into Walstead Road (s/p Bescot Football Stadium, Bescot Station and Tame Bridge). After 1.4 miles go straight on at crossroads (junction of Walstead Road and West Bromwich Road) into Walstead Road West, and away parking is on RHS after 0.5 miles.
FROM RAILWAY STATION (Bescot Stadium): Opposite the ground but no Sunday Service.
Last Midweek Trains: Trains run to Birmingham New Street at 21.51 and 22.51. From Birmingham New Street, trains to London run at 21.55, 22.50 and 23.09; to Manchester/Leeds at 22.01 and 23.30; to Derby and Sheffield at 22.25; and to Bristol at 22.27 and 23.00. Please double-check on (0345) 484 950.
BY BUS: Bus nos. 401, 402 and 405 run from Walsall town centre along Bescot Crescent. A 'Pete's Travel' bus no. 637 runs from Bradford Place in the town centre along Broadway West.

PARKING

The away car park is well signposted off Bescot Crescent and charges £2. The parking at the stadium is covered by CCTV, and so is protected from car crime. Opposite is the Bescot Stadium station car park (£1). For street parking, try the sidestreets off Broadway West.

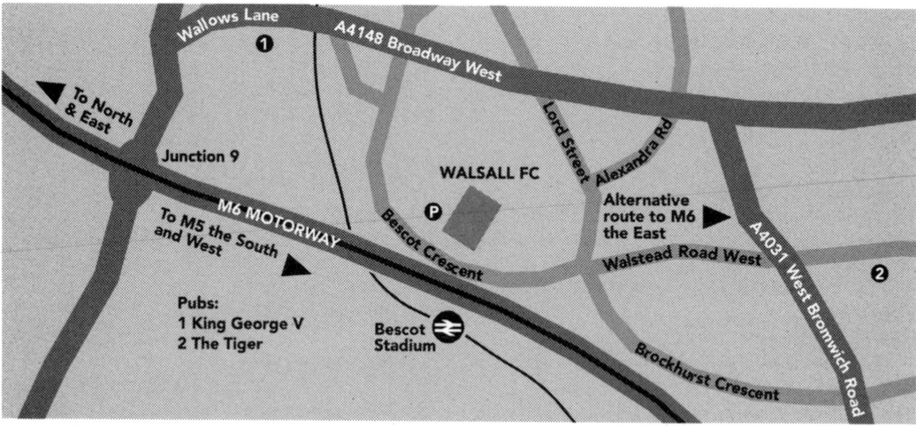

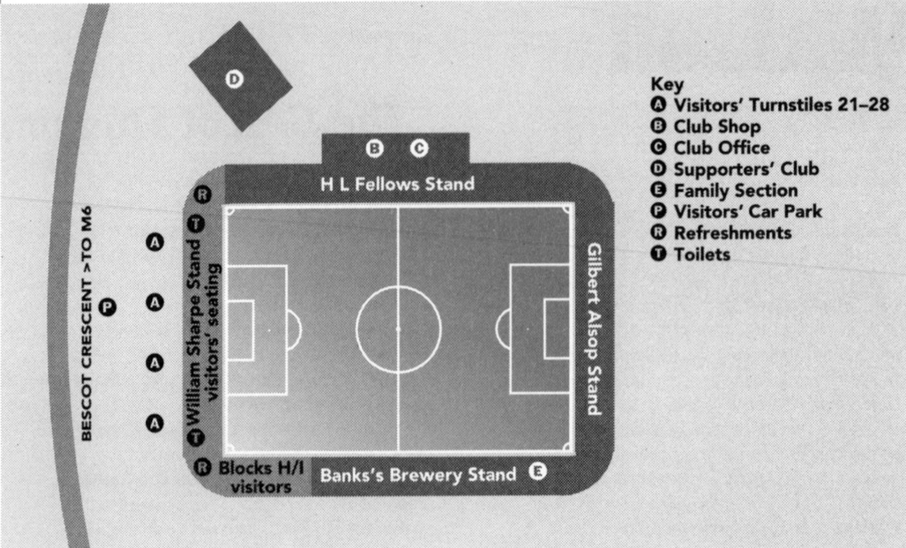

THE GROUND

Walsall FC moved from the classic, traditional Fellows Park – now a Morrisons supermarket – to Bescot Stadium, about half a mile to the south, in 1990. The stadium design, all grey cladding, red seats and crush barriers, is disappointing. The ground is fully enclosed, which obviously helps the atmosphere, but the stands are much of a muchness, and all have pillars. That said, the view from the William Sharp Stand behind the goal, where visiting fans are housed, is still pretty good. The facilities are basic but clean, and Walsall's Balti pies are rapidly becoming the stuff of legend.

Total Capacity: 9,000. For away fans (Seating, William Sharp Stand): 2,000. Turnstiles 21-28.

Cost (98/99): Adults £12, concessions (juniors and OAPs) £8.

Disabled Facilities: Space for 16 supporters in the Banks's Brewery Stand. *Disabled Toilet:* By the disabled supporters' entrance. *Cost:* Free for disabled and helper. *Booking:* Essential. *Parking:* Available outside the Banks's Brewery Stand, please book. *For the Blind:* No special facilities.

Programme: £1.80.

Visitors' Toilets: *Male:* No frills, clean but cramped, creating long queues at half-time. The cubicles had toilet paper, but no hand-dryers or towels. *Female:* One fan simply described the ladies' loos as 'full!' The locks had been mended, and Preston supporters said 'nothing too horrific was lurking in there.'

Food and Drink: Balti pies (£1.40), what a great idea! One visiting fan said they were 'possibly the tastiest thing ever found in the Second Division.' Fans also liked the hot dogs (£1.70), and the 'good, hot filling' of the steak-and-kidney pies (£1.30). The generous portions of chips (£1) tasted slightly undercooked. The cheeseburger looked good value and meaty, but was served stone cold ... the unmelted square of cheese resembled orange plastic. The tea (60p) was very strong, and not recommended, but the coffee and bovril (60p) were good (31.1.98, 31.3.98).

PUB GUIDE

King George V (1) Wallows Lane (opposite Morrisons) (01922) 626 130
Courage (with Theakstons, XB, guest ales and Highgate Bitter at £1 a pint). A large, friendly pub with lounge, family room and tap room. Darts, pool, TV, beer garden. Open: all day.

The Tiger (2) Walstead Road (01922) 704 931
Bass (with Cask Mild). Large traditional pub with an excellent matchday atmosphere. It serves the 'Top 20' menu – all the classic favourites – Monday-Friday 12-2, Saturday 11.30-1.30, 6-8. Families welcome/children's menu. Pool, darts, big-screen TV. Beer garden with children's play area and, in good weather, a bouncy castle. Open Friday-Saturday all day; from 5 pm for midweek games.

The following two pubs are on the A34 Birmingham Road, the route from junction 7 of the M6 (see road directions above):

The Bell (0121) 357 7461. Bass Taverns (with Worthingtons). Large, country-style pub which serves an excellent menu 12-9 pm. Families welcome/children's menu. TV, beer garden. Open: all day from 12.

The Beacon/Harvester (0121) 357 2567. Bass

The man who exited the M6 in time for the game.

(with Highgate Dark, Brew XI). Smart and spacious roadside pub with extensive menu and generous portions. Disabled facilities. Open: all day.

FOOD GUIDE

On Bescot Crescent itself, there's a McDonalds on the Broadwalk Retail Park, and a chip van parked near the ground. Those travelling via the A34 could try the 'L&S Middleton' fish and chip shop at the crossroads of Walstead Road and West Bromwich Road, open all day, serving Pukka Pies at £1.25 and kebabs at £1.70. By the King George V pub is 'Andy's Fish Bar', also serving Pukka Pies, and fish and chips from £1.15. Morrison's supermarket, opposite, has a café.

LOCAL MEDIA

Local Radio: BBC Radio WM 95.6 FM; Capital Gold 1152 AM.
Radio Phone-ins: Radio WM, Friday evenings 7-9, 5-6 pm on Saturdays and to 10 pm after midweek Capital Gold 1152 AM Saturday 5-6.30 pm; midweek every night 7-8, or after live match commentary. Call (0845) 35 60 70 80.
Saturday Sports Paper: 'The Sports Argus' (33p), which covers all teams, from the Premiership to the local clubs, plus the Wolverhampton-based 'Sporting Star'. Both go on sale at about 5.30 pm.

MISCELLANEOUS

Safety Factor: Very safe: in season 97/98, only one fan was arrested for disorder.
Rivals: Wolves and Aston Villa, but it's unreciprocated. In fact, supporters of some of the bigger local sides pick Walsall as their favourite second team, which annoys Saddlers fans no end. Of the lower division teams, there's rivalry with Shrewsbury Town and Crewe. Peterborough United became 'disflavour of the month' after Barry Fry bought a couple of Walsall players.
Fanzines: None.
Unofficial Websites:
'Unofficial': http://www.steveroy.com/walsall/
'Totally Unofficial':
http://ds.dial.pipex.com/totally.walsall.fc/index1.htm
'Guide': http://www.cpmiller.demon.co.uk/
Tourist Information: No local office.

Watford

Vicarage Road

Address: Vicarage Road Stadium, Watford, Herts WD1 8ER
Telephone: Club (01923) 496 000
Ticket Office (01923) 496 010
Hornets Shop (01923) 496 005
ClubCall (0891) 104 104
Official Website: http://www.watfordfc.com

American razzmatazz has come to Vicarage Road. Firstly the team gallops out to motivational tunes such as the Star Wars theme and Snap's 'I've Got the Power'. Then Harry the Hornet, a fab mascot if ever we saw one, zooms out to the sound of ZZ Top. This doesn't suit everyone of course. 'It is', said one traditionalist, 'loud and in yer face.' Finding the town of Watford is not a problem, as it's close to London, the M1 and the M25. Locating Vicarage Road, half a mile or so west of the town centre, is a little more tricky as there are no obvious straightforward routes. Visiting supporters are now being advised to park in the town centre or off Vicarage Road, which are both fine for pubs and takeaways.

HOW TO GET THERE

BY CAR: From All Directions, M1: Exit M1 at junction 5. At motorway roundabout follow signs to 'Watford Town Centre A4008' onto the Stephenson Way dual carriageway. After 0.6 miles take slip road (s/p Watford Town Centre, Bushey, Oxhey A4008) to bypass roundabout. At Waterfields roundabout after 0.9 miles go straight on (s/p Watford Town Centre) onto Beechen Grove. After 0.2 miles, by 'Trewins', all traffic turns left (s/p Ring Road A411) onto the Ring Road. Keep in lane for 'Ring Road, West Watford' and after 0.4 miles turn left (s/p Hospital Watford General, West Watford, Northwood) into Vicarage Road. After 0.1 miles all traffic turns left into Merton Road. Immediately get into the right-hand lanes and turn right (s/p Rickmansworth, West Watford A4145) into Farraline Road. Immediately get into the left-hand lane and turn left (s/p Rickmansworth, West Watford A4145, Watford General) into Vicarage Road to ground. Tip: If lost pick up signs to Watford General Hospital, which is right next to the ground in Vicarage Road.

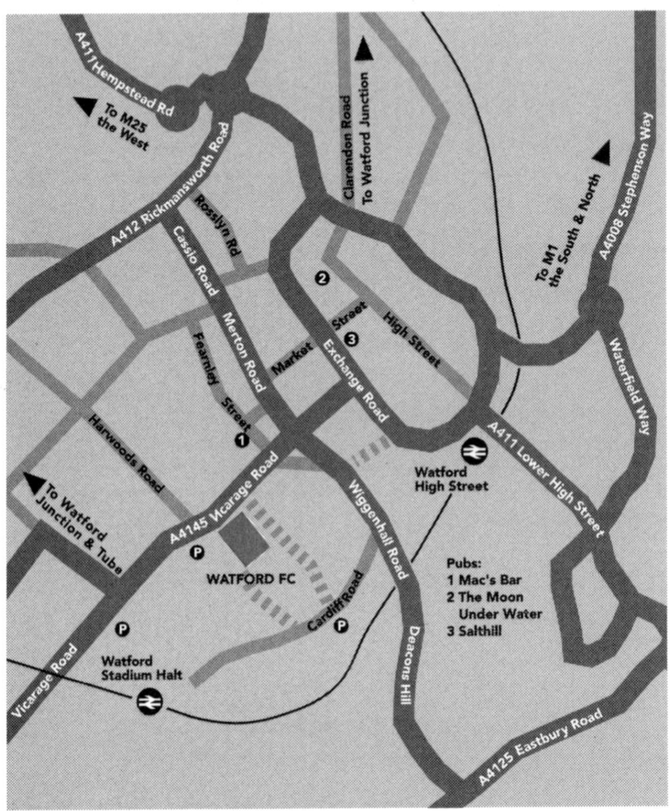

FROM RAILWAY STATIONS:

a) Watford Junction: 1.2 miles. *By train:* Local trains to Watford High Street Station run every 20 minutes, £1.20 return. *By taxi:* About £3. *By bus:* No. 11 runs hourly to Vicarage Road. *By foot:* Follow pedestrian signs down Clarendon Road. After 0.4 miles, head straight over lights (s/p Service Road A)

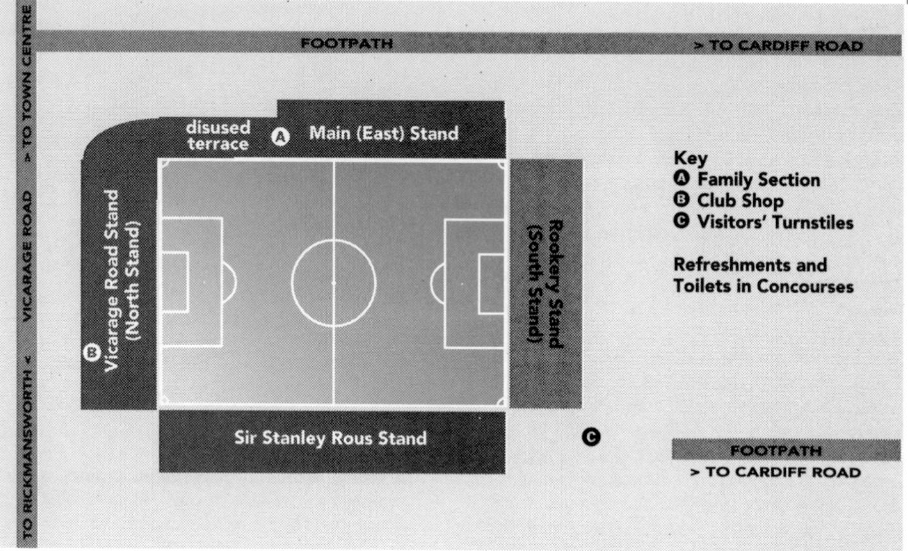

passing the theatre on LHS. At T-junction by the Cheltenham and Gloucester, turn left into the High Street. Turn right in front of the NatWest Bank into Market Street. Straight over crossroads by Hay Rood Catholic Church (s/p Vicarage Road Stadium), remaining on Market Street, and at T-junction by 'Ebb Tide Restaurant Fish 'N' Chips' turn left into Merton Road. Cross road at pedestrian crossing into the Vicarage Road Precinct. Straight over crossroads by the 'Joy Garden' Chinese takeaway into Vicarage Road to ground.
b) Watford High Street station (stopping train from Euston to Watford Junction): 15 minute walk. *By foot:* Turn left out of station and left along main road, passing 'Watford Springs'. Keep on footpath, and go straight on at crossroads. Past school on LHS and turn left into wide alleyway just before first detached house. Right into Wiggenhall Road, left into Farraline Road, and left again into Vicarage Road.
Last Midweek Trains: Trains run from Watford Junction to Euston at 21.33, 22.13, 22.30, 23.31 and 00.41. From Watford High Street, there are frequent services to Watford Junction. To Euston, trains leave at 21.35, 22.05, 22.35 and 23.09. Please double-check on (0345) 484 950.

FROM UNDERGROUND STATION (Watford, Metropolitan Line, in what London Underground describes as 'Beyond the Zones'!): 1.0 mile. *By taxi:* £2.50-£3. *By foot:* Turn right out of station and right again round station building. Down steps by taxi kiosk and turn right through car park into Station Approach. After 0.6 miles cross main road into Hagden Lane, and then branch left into Queens Avenue. Straight on at junction, and road becomes Vicarage Road.

BY BUS: Nos. 7, 10 and 11 run from Market Street in the town centre to Vicarage Road.

PARKING

Visiting fans are now being directed to park in the town centre multi-storeys, or in the official and unofficial car parks off Vicarage Road. The town centre car parks charge £2 for four hours, 50p after 7 pm. However, finding a space could be a big problem at Christmas, when football fans and shoppers are both out in force! The parking on Vicarage Road is at the Watford Grammar School for Girls (£2 blocked in, £3 not blocked in!), at the Laurence Haines School, and in Willow Lane by the General Hospital. Street parking is very limited indeed. One of the best areas to try is south of the ground, on Eastbury Road or the streets off Deacons Hill.

THE GROUND

Vicarage Road is shared by Watford FC and Saracens RUFC, but even so, from season 98/99 no-one should be complaining about the state of the pitch. The two clubs have spent £700,000 on installing a new 'hi-tech playing surface and undersoil heating system'. Three sides of Vicarage Road boast new stands, lavishly decorated in Watford's traditional colours of yellow and red. The fourth side holds the Main Stand and the last remaining sections of closed-off terracing. The club has plans to redevelop the Main Stand at some stage, and home fans will be glad to see the back of it. One supporter said: 'Main Stand! The name's a joke – it's that shed over there.' The newest of the three modern stands is the Rookery, or South Stand, opened in 1995

and seating 7,000. Surprisingly, this is where away fans are generally housed: the view is good, as is the legroom, and the facilities are top-class.

Total Capacity: 22,000. For away fans: Up to 6,936.

Cost (98/99): Adults £14. Concessions £10, must be bought in advance through the away club.

Disabled Facilities: Space for 24 in the Rookery Stand. *Disabled Toilet:* Nearby. *Cost:* £6 for disabled, full price for helper. *Booking:* Not necessary. *Parking:* None. *For the Blind:* 24 seats with headphones and match commentary in the East Stand, Block E. No charge.

Programme: £2.

Visitors' Toilets: *Male:* Here's a novelty ... the floor was dry! *Female:* Fans stopped to admire the cattle-feeding trough, and then discovered with some relief that this was actually the sink. It was all clean and modern, with those narrow loo seats which leave neat lines on one's rear end!

Food and Drink: The hot dogs (£2) were a popular option with Bristol Rovers fans, who found them 'satisfying'. Wycombe fans weren't so keen (one threw his away), but youngsters thought they were great. The pies (£1.50) went down a treat, and supporters marveled at the cheese and salad baguettes (£2.30). A Gills fans said they were 'crusty and quite generous too ... amazing, whatever next?' (7.9.97, 9.2.98, 28.2.98).

PUB GUIDE

NEAR THE GROUND:

Mac's Bar (1) 14 Fearnley Street (01923) 225 766
Carlsberg/Tetley. Small, traditional locals pub, mighty popular on matchdays. Sandwiches. Pool table, darts, TV, beer garden. Open: all day.

IN THE TOWN CENTRE:

The Moon Under the Water (2) 44 High Street (01923) 223 559
JD Weatherspoons. Large smart city centre pub, serving a full menu 11-10, Sundays 12-9.30. Doormen for big matches. No under-18s. Open: all day.

Salthill (formerly the Rose and Crown) (3) 9 Market Street (01923) 219 616
Lees (with Caffreys and Worthingtons). A large building, described by the landlord as a 'traditional drinking pub'. Bar snacks and sandwiches served 12-7. Pool table, large screen TV, darts. Open: all day.

NEAR WATFORD JUNCTION:

The Nascot Arms 11 Stamford Road (01923) 231 336.
Greene King. A traditional favourite, serving bar meals 12-3 and 5.30-8.30. Big-screen TV. Open: all day. To get there: turn right out of station along Station Road. Cross dual-carriageway into Langley Road, and take first left.

Also recommended, out of town: **The Red Lion,** 50 High Street, Bushey. It's a wonderful traditional Bass pub, serving hot and cold bar snacks, 12-2 and 6.30-9.

'Oh sorry – I thought we were AWAY to Saracens!'

FOOD GUIDE

The nearest takeaway is 'Fry Day' on Vicarage Road, recommended by the home supporters. Almost opposite is 'Hot Bread' a real family bakers. There's a café/takeaway called 'Snack Bar' in the Vicarage Road Precinct, and the more upmarket 'Ebb Tide Restaurant Fish 'N' Chips' on the corner of Merton Road and Market Street. Market Street also has a 'Dial-a-Balti', two Tandooris and 'Jenny's Restaurant', a family café/restaurant open from 8.30 am to 9 pm. The High Street has a 'Roosters Chicken', a Pizza Hut and a Burger King.

LOCAL MEDIA

Local Radio: BBC Three Counties Radio 103.8 FM, 630 AM; Capital Gold 1548 AM.

Radio Phone-ins: Three Counties Radio, Saturdays 2-6.30 and midweek 7-10. Call (0645) 455 5555; Capital Gold, Saturdays 2-6.30, midweek 7-10 (or 7-8 if no match). Call (0845) 35 60 70 80.

Saturday Sports Papers: None.

MISCELLANEOUS

Safety Factor: It's been a quiet season.

Rivals: Luton Town, 'The Unmentionables' or 'The Insignificants'.

Fanzines: 'Clap Your Hands, Stamp Your Feet', 9 West Towers, Pinner, Middlesex HA5 1TZ; 'The Horn', 56 Park Lane, Victoria Mews, Newbury, Berks, RG14 1EN.

Unofficial Websites: 'wfc.net': http://www.wfc.net/
http://www.display.co.uk/watford/
http://www.kowalski.demon.co.uk/watford/
http://freespace.virgin.net/christina.demetriou/WatfordFC/ftybr.html

Tourist Information: No local office.

West Bromwich Albion

The Hawthorns

Address: Stadium: The Hawthorns, Halfords Lane, West Bromwich, West Midlands B71 4LF
Offices: The Tom Silk Building, Halfords Lane, West Bromwich, West Midlands B71 4BR
Telephone: Club (0121) 525 8888
Ticket Hotline (0121) 553 5472
Club Shop (0121) 525 2145
ClubCall (0891) 121 193
Official Website: http://www.wba.co.uk

Any decent book on urban planning should define 'ribbon development' as 'the A41 between the M5 and The Hawthorns football ground.' Here are the car showrooms, garages and industrial units so typical of big-city suburbs. The difference at West Brom, perhaps, is that behind the buildings, especially to the north, is open land, a golf course, cricket ground and a boating lake! Latecomers can have a fine old time exploring the area ... in a desperate search for a parking space! Indeed, more and more fans are parking on the other side of the M5, towards West Bromwich town centre, the best area for a drink and/or a meal. Life has become much easier for train travellers, however, with the opening of a station just to the south, appropriately called 'The Hawthorns', with good connections to Birmingham.

HOW TO GET THERE

BY CAR: From North, East and West: Exit M6 at junction 8 (s/p M5 The South West, Birmingham W & S) onto the M5. After 0.7 miles exit M5 at junction 1 (s/p A41 West Bromwich, Sandwell, Birmingham (NW)). For the ground, turn left at roundabout (s/p Birmingham A41) into Birmingham Road.
From South (M40): At junction 3a, the M40 ends and becomes the M42. Follow signs to 'M5 The South West, Birmingham S & W', remaining on the M42. After 11.7 miles, the M42 ends at junction 4a of the M5. Follow signs to 'M5, The North West, Birmingham W, N and Cent' onto the M5 northbound. After 13.9 miles, exit M5 at junction 1 (s/p A41 West Bromwich, Birmingham N and W). (*)At the roundabout, take the 4th exit (s/p Birmingham A41) into Birmingham Road to the ground.
From South West (M5): Exit M5 at junction 1 (s/p A41 West Bromwich, Birmingham N and W). Then as From South(*).

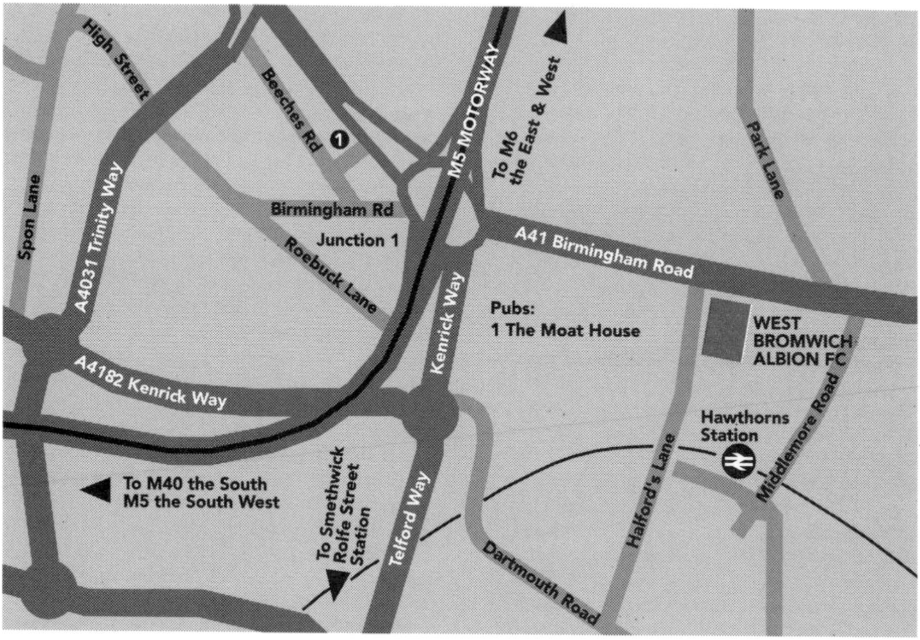

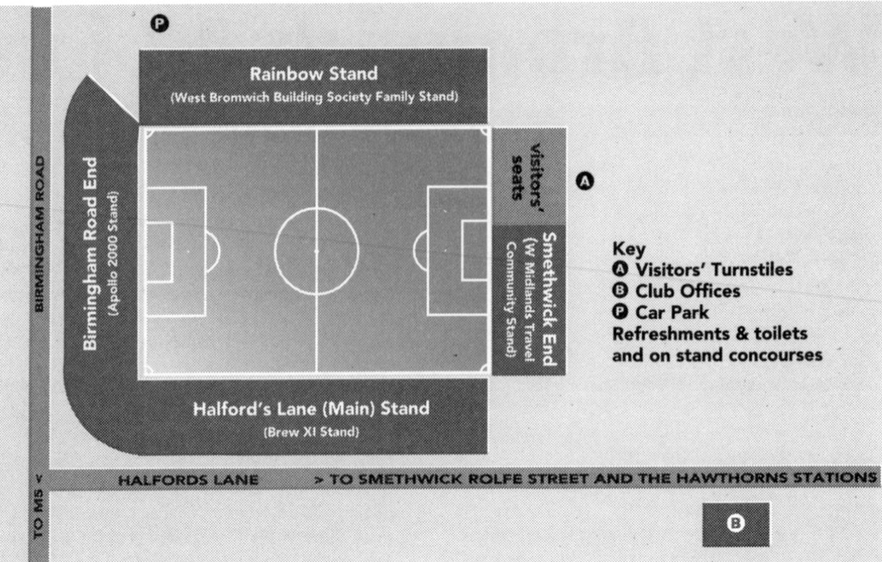

FROM RAILWAY STATIONS: a) Birmingham New Street. Either take a taxi (up to £7), or catch a local train to Smethwick Rolfe Street (see below). There are two other alternatives: walk across the Bull Ring to Moor Street station, from where trains run to The Hawthorns station; or head to Snow Hill station, from where the new Metro runs to The Hawthorns station.
b) The Hawthorns: just a few hundred yards from the ground (see map).
c) Smethwick Rolfe Street: 1.0 mile, mostly uphill. *By bus:* Bus no 450 runs every half hour to the ground. *By foot:* Turn right out of station and left into North Western Road. Straight on at traffic lights into Halfords Lane.
Last Midweek Trains: From The Hawthorns, trains run to Moor Street and Snow Hill in Birmingham city centre at 21.48 and 22.18. From Smethwick Rolfe Street, trains run to Birmingham New Street at 22.04 and 23.09.
BY BUS: Nos. 74, 78 and 79 run from Bull Street (off Corporation Street) in Birmingham city centre to the ground. Note that the buses don't give change.

PARKING

a) For those who arrive in plenty of time, the best bet is the club car park in Halfords Lane (£3). To get there is a little complicated because of matchday one-way systems: at the motorway roundabout, follow signs to 'A4182, Matchday Parking' into Kenrick Way. At next roundabout turn left into Dartmouth Road. After about half a mile turn left again into Halfords Lane. There's also a car park (£2.50) at The Hawthorns station, and in nearby side streets.
b) At the motorway roundabout follow signs to 'West Bromwich Town Centre' onto Birmingham Road, which becomes the High Street. There's street parking here, or continue along the High Street to where all traffic turns left. Keep in the right hand lanes, passing Safeways on the RHS, and park in one of the signposted town centre car parks. These car parks are free, though there are moves to impose charges. From here it's a good 1.5 miles to the ground. Catch bus no 74, or the Metro from the park opposite Safeway.
c) The Moat House, which has matchday car parking for £2, is also signposted off the M5 roundabout (see pub guide).

THE GROUND

'It's a big change from the old days!' said one impressed visiting supporter, admiring the new stands and upgraded facilities at The Hawthorns. He may well have been remembering the tiny, uncovered corner terrace and the portacabin loos, allocated to away fans while the two end stands were rebuilt in the mid-1990s. Thankfully, once the construction work was complete, visiting supporters were moved into one of those new stands, the Smethwick End, where the view is excellent and the concourses first-class. The two side stands at The Hawthorns are much older: the Main Stand, built in 1981, and the Rainbow Stand, dating back to the 1960s. The club has planning permission to demolish the Rainbow Stand and replace it with a 9,600-seater 'Corporate Stand'. The work is not expected to start during the 1998/99 season.
Total Capacity: 25,000. For away fans: Seating (Smethwick End) 2,000, 3,000 or 5,000, depending on the size of the away contingent. Turnstiles A1-5, B1-5.
Cost (98/99): Tickets bought in advance are: Adults

£13, concessions (juniors/OAPs) £7. Matchday prices: £14/£7.50.
Disabled Facilities: Space for up to 40 supporters at pitch-level in front of the away seating (Smethwick End). *Disabled Toilet:* Nearby. *Cost:* Free for disabled, full price for helper (again, tickets bought in advance have a £1 discount). *Booking:* Not vital, but it helps! *Parking:* None. *For the Blind:* Headphones with commentary in the Halfords Lane Stand. Please book.
Programme: £2.
Visitors' Toilets: *Male:* Excellent facilities, spacious, clean, with hot and cold water and mirrors. Almost as good as at home in fact. No scope for horror stories here then... *Female:* ...nor here!
Food and Drink: The Cornish pasty (£1.55) had plenty of tasty vegetables and mince, but was lukewarm. The steak-and-kidney and meat-and-potato pies (both £1.55), were hotter, but were, said one veteran pie-eater, pretty bland. He still went back for seconds though! Vegetarians were stuck with King Size Mars Bars (65p)! Both the tea (70p) and coffee (80p) were recommended more for their heating powers than for flavour (7.3.98).

PUB GUIDE

Most of the pubs near The Hawthorns operate membership schemes, leaving visiting supporters to wander further afield. The best bet is to head into West Bromwich town centre (signposted off the M5 junction 1 motorway roundabout). There are numerous pubs along this road, and its continuation past the shopping precinct. The local police are not keen on this book recommending any particular pubs, but point out that none of them have bad reputations. Another possibility is **The Moat House (1),** which is also signposted from the M5 motorway roundabout. Football supporters are welcome in the Chase Bar (Mitchells & Butlers), which has a big-screen TV and serves bar snacks.

FOOD GUIDE

The nearest outlet to the ground is the 'Grill House' on Birmingham Road, which serves good-price meals such as chicken and chips for 99p. West Bromwich High Street, signposted from the M5 motorway roundabout, has a series of takeaways, including 'The Fish Inn', near Florence Road, which has pies at £1.20 and kebabs at £1.25. The High Street leads to a large roundabout, in the middle of which is the pedestrianised shopping centre. Parking is to the north (ie continue round the roundabout past Safeways). The shopping centre has a 'Bakers Oven', the 'Chip King' café, the 'Pizza and Spice' takeaway (with Pukka pies and Balti dishes), a KFC, Pizza Hut and McDonalds.

LOCAL MEDIA

Local Radio: BBC Radio WM 95.6 FM;

Capital Gold 1152 AM.
Radio Phone-ins: Radio WM, Friday evenings 7-9, 5-6 pm on Saturdays and to 10 pm after midweek games, call (0121) 432 2000; Capital Gold 1152 AM, Saturday 5-6.30 pm. Midweek every night 7-8 or after live match commentary. Call (0845) 35 60 70 80.
Saturday Sports Paper: 'The Sports Argus' (33p), plus the Wolverhampton-based 'Sporting Star'.

MISCELLANEOUS

In the last edition of the *Football Fan's Guide,* we speculated on the origin of the Albion nickname 'The Baggies'. One suggestion was that, before the days of turnstiles, a man used to go through the crowd collecting money in a bag. But reader Mr C.M Taylor from Queensland wrote to say that his grandfather, who had trials for WBA around the turn of the century, was adamant that the nickname stuck because the team was the last in the league to 'give up wearing knickerbockers.'
Safety Factor: WBA has a hooligan following, but it seeks out other idiots, so genuine fans wanting to see the game are unlikely to run into any trouble.
Rivals: Albion fans in the pub debated for a good half an hour over who was the number one rival — Wolves or Villa! 'It often depends', said one, 'on where you live, who you work with, or who your friends or colleagues support!' Wolves seem to have pipped it in recent years, as they've been in the same division.
Fanzines: 'Grorty Dick', 34 Vicarage Road, Wednesbury, Staffs, DY10 9BA.
Unofficial Websites: http://www.baggies.com/
http://www.geocities.com/Colosseum/Park/1176
http://www.geocities.com/Colosseum/Track/4059/index.html
Tourist Information: (0121) 525 7366.

West Ham United

Upton Park

Address: Boleyn Ground, Green Street, Upton Park, London E13 9AZ
Telephone: Club (0181) 548 2748
Ticket Office (0181) 548 2700
Hammers ClubCall (0891) 121 165
Hammers Merchandising (0181) 548 2722
Official Website: http://www.westhamunited.co.uk/

The Upton Park area of east London is not exactly known for its haute cuisine. However, it could justifiably lay claim to honours for its 'basse cuisine' if such a phrase exists! In other words, leave room for the great British fry-up. There are at least five excellent cafés within a few hundred yards of the ground, including one selling (wait for it) hot eels. Unfortunately the same cannot be said for the local pubs, as most don't welcome visiting supporters. The area round the ground itself is multi-ethnic, made up of terraced housing and small downmarket shops. Parking can be difficult so it's much better, if possible, to leave the car somewhere along the District Line and take the tube.

HOW TO GET THERE

BY CAR (From North, East, West): Exit M25 at junction 27 and follow signs to 'M11 London (NE)' onto the M11 southbound. After 7.1 miles, where the motorway ends and road divides, keep left (s/p A12 London E, The City) onto the North Circular eastbound. Exit North Circular after 3.9 miles (s/p Barking, East Ham A124). At roundabout turn right (4th exit, s/p East Ham A124) onto Barking Road. After 1.5 miles turn right just after the 'Boleyn Tavern' (s/p Upton Park, Forest Gate) into Green Street. Ground is on RHS.
From South (M25): Approaching the Dartford Tunnel keep in left hand lane (s/p Dagenham A13). Go through tunnel and exit M25 after 0.8 miles at junction 31 (s/p Dagenham, Services, A13 West), and turn left at roundabout (s/p London, Rainham, Dagenham A13) onto the A13. Follow signs to London A13 over roundabout and two flyovers, for 10.1 miles. Stay in right hand lane, following signs to 'The City, Woolwich Ferry', passing under the North Circular. After 0.8 miles, at next junction, keep in right hand lane for 'The City, East Ham A117' and then turn right (s/p East Ham)

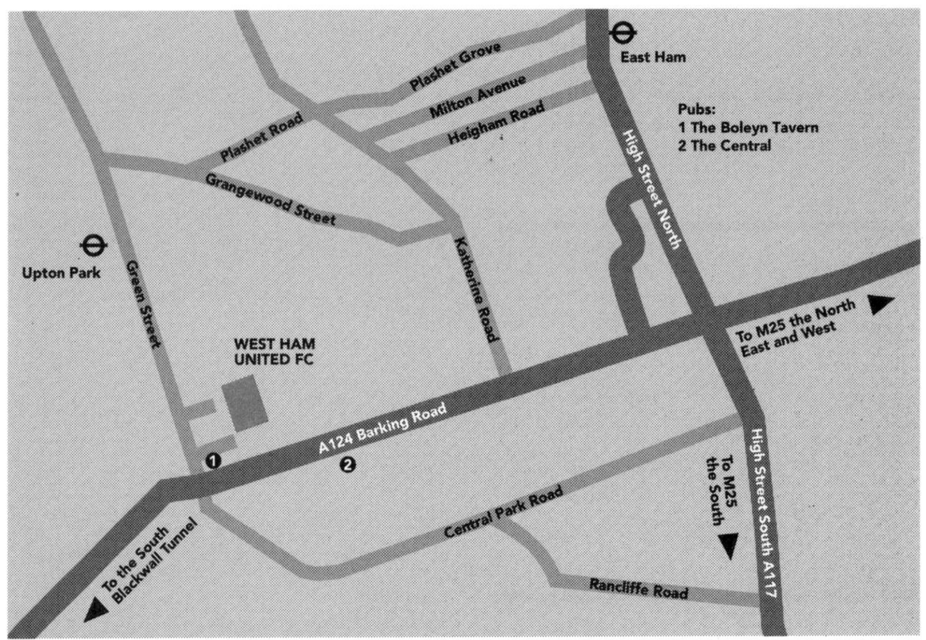

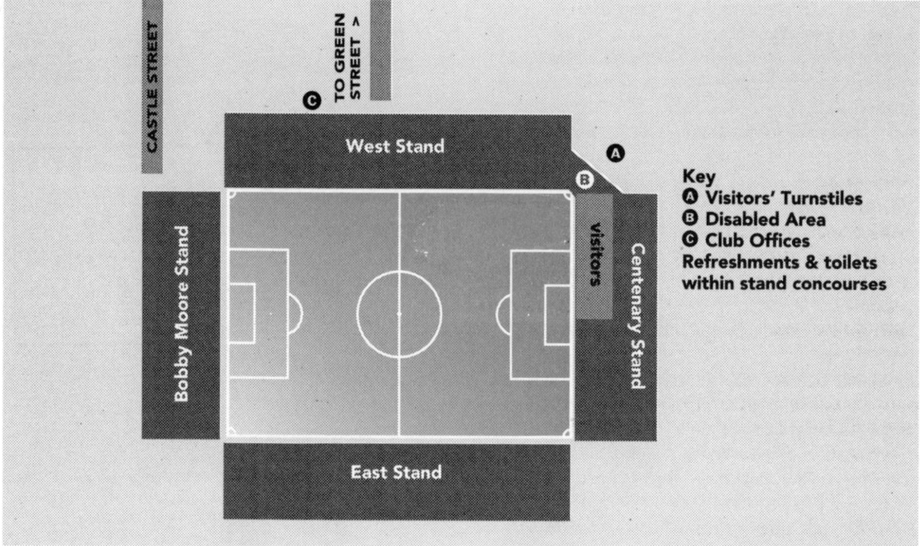

under the flyover into High Street South. At T-junction after 1.0 miles, opposite archway to shopping street, turn left (n/s) into Barking Road. After 0.7 miles, turn right at the 'Boleyn Tavern' (s/p Upton Park, Forest Gate) into Green Street. Ground is on RHS.

From South London (Blackwall Tunnel): See London Guide for directions to Blackwall Tunnel. Coming out of Tunnel, take 2nd exit, after 0.3 miles (s/p Tilbury A13, Canning Town). At lights, turn left (s/p Tilbury A13) onto the A13 Dock Road. Over flyover after 0.7 miles and 1.2 miles further on, at next major crossroads/lights, turn left (s/p Stratford A112, Plaistow) into Prince Regent Lane. After 0.6 miles, at first crossroads by 'The Castle', turn right (s/p Plaistow Hospital, East Ham) into Barking Road. After 0.5 miles, turn left in front of the 'Boleyn Tavern' (s/p Upton Park, Forest Gate) into Green Street. Ground is on RHS.

FROM UNDERGROUND STATION (Upton Park, District Line, Zone 3): 0.3 miles. *By foot:* Turn right out of station along Green Street, passing the covered market on RHS. Straight on for ground.

Last Midweek Trains: See London Guide at front of book.

BY BUS: Nos. 58, 104 and 330 run along Green Street. The no. 238 from Stratford to Barking runs along Plashet Road. Nos. 5, 58 and 147 run along Barking Road.

PARKING

It's street parking for all, and a real problem. For a start, the police warn about car crime. Secondly, new residents' parking schemes may soon be introduced to the east of the ground, and the council's buying thirteen new tow trucks!! You have been warned! The best areas to try are around Romford Road and the streets to the south of Barking Road. Finding a space is slightly easier at night, as many of the parking restrictions end at 6 pm. All roads near the ground are guaranteed to be gridlocked after the game.

THE GROUND

More than at any other ground, exciting moments in play at Upton Park are accompanied by the sound of hundreds of tip-up seats tipping-up back into place. In other words, even though the Centenary Stand is new, away fans on the bottom tier spring to their feet any time a striker advances over the half-way line. In the days of terracing, Upton Park was a ferocious ground, in more ways than one! The atmosphere was terrific, with 40,000 Hammers fans – especially those in the old Chicken Run – driving the team forward. Nowadays Upton Park is much more sedate, though that old atmosphere can still re-emerge, especially at night. The ground is made up of four separate stands: the West Stand, which dates back to the 1920s, the East Stand, opened in 1969, the impressive two-tier Bobby Moore Stand, opened in 1994, and the Centenary Stand opposite, opened in 1995. Amazingly, visiting fans are housed in this newest of stands, where the facilities are excellent.

Total Capacity: 26,024. For away fans: Seating (Centenary Stand Lower Tier) 2,274. Turnstiles 1-7 in Green Street.

Cost (98/99): Adults: Category 1 game £20, Category

2 game £24. Concessions (OAPs/juniors): £11.
Disabled Facilities: Space for up to six visiting supporters on a raised platform between the Centenary and West Stands. *Disabled Toilet:* In all areas. *Cost:* Free for disabled, £14 for helper. *Booking:* Yes. *Parking:* Small number of spaces available. *For the Blind:* Headphones linked into the ClubCall commentary.
Programme: £2.
Visitors' Toilets: *Male:* We approached with caution, crab-like from the side, yet still got soaked. Yep, the Upton Park water still comes out of the tap with the force of Niagara Falls. Apart from the tap-trap, the facilities were first class. *Female:* The facilities were clean, the tap-water icy and, as in the men's, spurting everywhere!
Food and Drink: 'The Hammer's Dog: a delicious jumbo frankfurter freshly cooked and served with a selection of relishes and pickles.' To you and me, mate, a hot-dog (£2) with ketchup or mustard, but no onions. The rather tasty beef-and-onion pies (£1.40) were steaming hot before the game, when fans were wolfing them down, but lukewarm at half-time. The lager, said Palace fans, tasted like a variety they'd had in Turkey ... 'cold and gassy'. In contrast the very British coffee (80p) was good (3.11.97).

PUB GUIDE

Several years ago the **Boleyn Tavern (1)** (Green Street/corner of Barking Road – Allied Domecq) was totally a West Ham preserve. It's still predominantly a home pub, but it does welcomes all supporters. It's obviously best to steer clear, however, on derby-days, or when tensions are high. A better bet is **The Central (2)** at 150 Barking Road. It's a large traditional Allied Domecq pub, serving sandwiches on matchdays. It welcomes families and has a pool table.

FOOD GUIDE

It's fry-up frenzy time! West Ham fans recommend the following:
a) 'Ken's Café, on Green Street, a football-mad family-run eatery with a huge classic menu (eg big breakfast £2.95, mugs of tea 30p).
b) The excellent value 'Green Street Café'.
c) 'Nathan's Pies and Eels', on Barking Road. For those who don't fancy hot or jellied eels, it also has pies (£1) and mash (50p).
d) 'Cassettaris' café on Barking Road, which does a set breakfast for £3.

For a post-match Indian meal try either the 'Raj Chatt House' (turn left out of Upton Park tube station and it's about 100 yards down the road) or the 'Ana Purna' on Plashet Road.

An alternative area for shopping and eating is the High Street at East Ham (see map), just one stop further out-of-town along the District Line.

LOCAL MEDIA

Local Radio: Capital Gold 1548 AM; Millennium Radio 106.8 FM; GLR 94.9 FM
Radio Phone-ins: Capital Gold, Saturdays 2-6.30, midweek 7-10 (or 7-8 if no match). Call (0845) 35 60 70 80; Millennium Radio, Sundays 7-8.30 pm, call (0181) 311 3111.
Saturday Sports Paper: None.

MISCELLANEOUS

Safety Factor: Few problems recently, but visiting fans should still approach with caution.
Rivals: The 'Ultimate Dream' lists Arsenal (more so because of the club's recent success) and Tottenham 'Flopspur', playing at 'Three Point Lane'.
Fanzines: 'Ultimate Dream', 33 Haskard Road, Dagenham, Essex, RM9 5XS; 'Over Land and Sea', PO Box 26, Dagenham, Essex RM10 8XY; 'On a Mission', PO Box 334, Taverham NR8 6QF; 'On the Terraces', PO Box 793, London, E6 1PJ; 'The Water in Majorca', 73a Belgrave Road, Ilford, Essex, IG1 3AL.
Unofficial Websites:
'Over Land and Sea': http://www.olas-hammers.co.uk
http://ourworld.compuserve.com/homepages/jeff_parkins/
http://easyweb.easynet.co.uk/~graeme.howlett/index2.htm
http://www.fortunecity.com/wembly/upton/6/
http://ds.dial.pipex.com/sean/westham/
http://www.dungeon.com/~express/whu.html
http://freespace.virgin.net/patrick.darragh/westham2.html
Tourist Information: None nearby.

Wigan Athletic

Springfield Park

Address: Springfield Park, Wigan, Lancashire WN6 7BA
Telephone: Club (01942) 244 433
ClubCall (0891) 121 655

A guided tour of 'Wigan Highlights' would include Wigan Pier, the rugby league ground Central Park, Haigh Hall, perhaps even the Heinz baked beans factory. A stopover at Springfield Park is unlikely, though anyone up for an 'Arctic Experience' could try out the open away terrace in January! The ground's about a mile from the town centre and railway stations, but thankfully there are some good, friendly pubs and a couple of decent takeaways nearby. However, all's about to change. In August 1999 Wigan Athletic is moving to a new 25,000-seater stadium, to be shared with Wigan Warriors Rugby League Club, about a mile away in Robin Park.

HOW TO GET THERE

BY CAR: From North: Exit M6 at junction 27 (s/p Wigan, Parbold) and follow the A5209 towards Standish and Wigan. After 0.4 miles, turn right at T-junction (s/p Shevington, Orrell A5206) into Shevington Lane. After 1.0 miles turn left (s/p Standish Lower Ground) into Old Lane, the B5375. The road winds downhill through country lanes for 1.9 miles. Go straight on at crossroads (s/p Town Centre B5375), and (*)after 0.7 miles, after passing between the 'Douglas Bank' and 'Belle Vue' pubs and past the 'Prince of Wales' on the left, turn sharp left at lights into Springfield Road. Take 2nd or 3rd turnings on LHS to ground.

From South and West: Exit M6 at junction 25 (s/p Wigan A49). At roundabout after 1.0 miles, take 1st exit (s/p Wigan A49) onto A49 Warrington Road. Follow signs for 'Wigan A49' and 'Town Centre A49' for 1.8 miles to a complex junction (by Homestyle). Aim for the left-hand lane (marked Preston A49) and follow left into Robin Park Road. Straight on for 1.5 miles, passing a large superstore complex and the Martland Mill industrial estate, and turn right at the next major junction (s/p Town Centre) into Woodhouse Drive. Then as From North(*).

From East: Exit M61 at junction 6 (s/p Chorley, Horwich A6027), and turn left at roundabout (s/p Westhoughton A6027) onto the A6027. At next roundabout, after 0.1 miles, turn left (s/p Westhoughton A6, Wigan B5238) into the A6 Chorley Road. After 0.3 miles, turn right (s/p Wigan B5238) into Dicconson Lane. Follow road for 1.8 miles, then turn left by Aspull war memorial (s/p Wigan B5238) into the B5238 Wigan Road. After 2.2

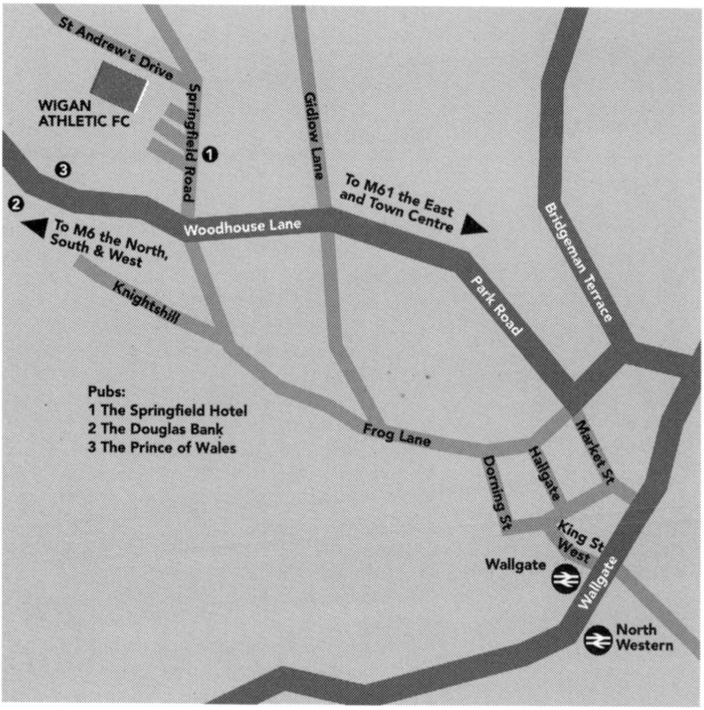

Pubs:
1 The Springfield Hotel
2 The Douglas Bank
3 The Prince of Wales

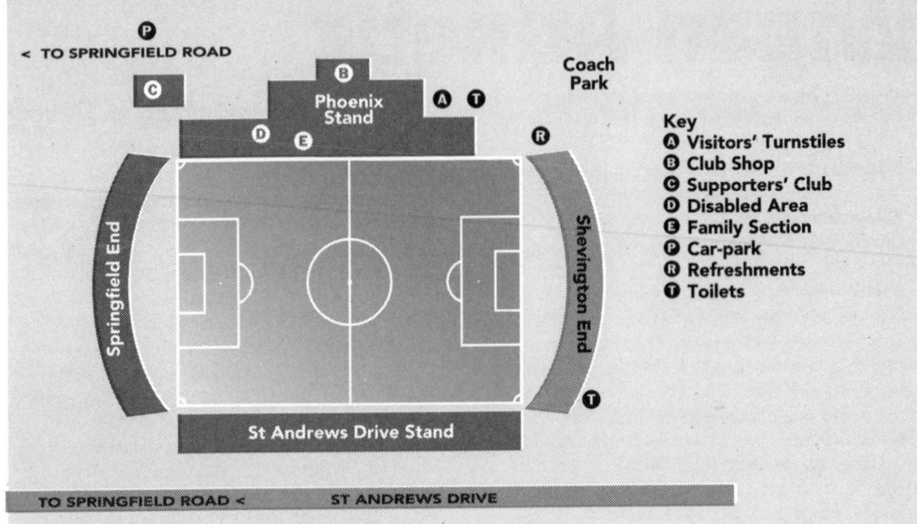

miles, just past the 'Earl of Balcarres' pub on RHS, turn right (s/p Infirmary, Wigan Pier) into Greenough Street. At traffic lights by the Wigan Rugby League ground after 0.2 miles, follow signs to 'Shevington, Standish'. Continue straight on through a further 5 sets of traffic lights, passing the 'Colliers Arms' and 'The Guardians' pubs on LHS. Just after passing the 'Brickmakers Arms', the Springfield Park floodlights become visible ahead. At traffic lights, turn right into Springfield Road.

FROM RAILWAY STATIONS (Wallgate or North Western): About 1.0 miles to ground. *By taxi:* Up to £2.50. *By bus:* Buses run from Hallgate. To get there: from stations turn left into King Street West, and then 2nd right into Crawford Street. This leads into Hallgate. Nos. 611, 612, 634 and 635 run along Woodhouse Lane, though only the 612 runs at night. *By foot:* The two stations face each other – Wallgate is for local rail services and North Western is the main line station. From North Western, cross the road towards Wallgate station and turn right. Take first left into King Street West. The road leads round to the left (becoming Dorning Street), and up to a T-junction by the 'Pear Tree' pub. Here, turn left into Frog Lane (s/p Shevington). Go straight on to the next major crossroads: Springfield Road is the middle of the three roads opposite.

Last Midweek Trains: The last train from Wigan to Manchester is at 23.08. Trains from Manchester run to York and Newcastle at 21.50, to York at 22.47, and to Nottingham and Derby at 22.28. It's not possible to get to London after a midweek game. Please double-check on (0345) 484 950.

BY BUS: As above.

PARKING

Parking is becoming increasingly difficult as more streets are coned off, or allow parking for limited periods only. Avoid parking in St Andrew's Drive or Woodhouse Lane. Instead, try one of the roads off Springfield Road, but late arrivals could be in for a long walk. Other than that, there are small car parks at 'The Springfield' pub (free) and the 'Douglas Bank' pub (£1, refundable).

THE GROUND

Those who like wide open spaces will be in their element at Springfield Park, which boasts just one isolated main stand and acres of covered and uncovered terracing. With Wigan Athletic progressing through the Football League, the ground is now looking tired and outdated. There's been talk of a ground move for years, but the financial backing only became available with the arrival of Chairman Dave Whelan, the multi-millionaire owner of 'JJB Sports', in 1995. The club's new 'JJB Stadium' at Robin Park, already under construction, is a joint venture between the sports company, Wigan Borough Council and the Wigan Warriers Rugby League Club. It's always sad to say goodbye to a traditional ground, but away fans, who for years have been soaked and frozen on the open Shevington End, will have few regrets. Oh, except for the long-gone grassy bank ... great for glory runs!

Total Capacity: 7,290. For away fans: Standing (Shevington End) 1,467. Turnstiles 10A, 10B, 11A and 11B. Seating (Phoenix Stand) 300. Turnstile 8B. Visiting fans are welcome in the Family Stand, which has 128

non-segregated seats. Tickets must be bought in advance at the ticket office. Turnstile 9B.

Cost (97/98): Seating: Adults £10, concessions (juniors and OAPs) £6. Terrace: £7/£4. Family stand: £10/£4.

Disabled Facilities: A portakabin with space for four wheelchairs, plus unlimited space outside on unused terracing. *Disabled Toilet:* In portakabin. *Cost:* Free for disabled and helper. *Booking:* Required. *Parking:* Available by prior arrangement. *For the Blind:* Commentary available, but supporters must bring their own headsets. Please book.

Programme: £1.50.

Visitors Toilets: *Male:* It was the traditional 'wall and gutter in cowshed' variety, plus a cubicle without a sink or paper. The sound-proofing wasn't good, so the gents listened in to an animated conversation going on in the ladies, which sounded like part of an Alan Bennett play. And historians should check out the other set of loos in the corner, which might turn out to be Churchill's wartime bunker. *Female:* 'Never mind the toilets, I was too worried about the spiders,' said one fan.

Food and Drink: No pies! In pie-eating land! Apparently they were available in the home end, but visitors were left disappointed. One Gillingham fan tried a burger (£2) and then ran around the terrace, waving his arms furiously gurgling: 'Don't touch the burgers!' The hot dogs (£2) were expensive but tasty. Tea and coffee were available in regular size (70p) and 'half pint cups' (£1) (21.10.97, 22.11.97, 20.12.97).

PUB GUIDE

The Springfield (1) 47 Springfield Road (01942) 242 072

Tetley/Walker. A traditional pub with a good matchday atmosphere, just a minute's walk from the ground. 'Feasting Fox Big Eat' menu, served 12-2 and 5-8. Pool table, darts, TV. Families welcome. Open: Saturdays all day from 12; from 5.30 for evening games.

The Douglas Bank (2) 213-215 Woodhouse Lane (01942) 829 005

Holts. No need for happy hours here, as the bitter is £1.05 and Premium lager £1.27 all the time! Pool table, darts, TV. Large car park – £1 refundable at the bar. Open: all day from 12.

The Prince of Wales (3) 202 Woodhouse Lane (01942) 241 795

Burtonwood. Friendly locals pub with pool table, darts and TV. Bar snacks served 12-5. Families welcome. Open: Friday-Sunday all day from 12; from 5 pm for midweek games.

FOOD GUIDE

One idea is to head along Woodhouse Lane, past the 'Douglas Bank' and the 'Prince of Wales', to the 'Stadium Chippy', which as well as the traditional fare offers Chinese dishes for around £4. For a similar price, try a

I NAME THIS CHILD....
TRACY WIGAN ATHLETIC,
1997 DIVISION 3 CHAMPIONS..
WIGAN ATHLETIC
cagle

pizza at the Pizzeria further along Woodhouse Lane. Those with cars can drive along Woodhouse Lane and follow signs to Robin Park, where there's a McDonalds. Those coming from the stations will pass a chippy on Frog Lane, while there's a fish and chip takeaway and a pie shop on Park Road.

LOCAL MEDIA

Local Radio: Wish FM 102.4 FM; GMR 95.1 FM; Red Rose Gold 999AM; Radio City 96.7 FM

Radio Phone-Ins: GMR, Saturdays 1-3 and 5-7, and after midweek games. Call (0161) 228 2255; Radio City, Saturdays 5-6 pm, call (0151) 4720 967.

Saturday Sports Paper: *The Manchester Evening News* produces a football pink.

MISCELLANEOUS

There was, wrote a Preston fan: 'A very strange mascot in a Wigan kit with a huge smiley head. I think he frightened some children.' The same object appeared before Cambridge fans the previous year, who decided it was a bath sponge. Gillingham fans guessed it was 'some sort of cartoon character.' The club, one of the friendliest in the league, wrote to say the mascot is called 'Mr Springy.' That's solved that puzzle then!

Safety Factor: Take precautions on derby days.

Rivals: The big games are with Burnley, Preston and Bolton.

Fanzines: The award-winning 'Latic Fanatic', 186 Hodges Street, Wigan, WN6 7JG.

Unofficial Websites:
http://www.btinternet.com/~jon.sanders/index.html
http://www.geocities.com/Colosseum/9766/
http://home.clara.net/ajhudson/

Tourist Information: (01942) 825 677.

W

Wimbledon

Selhurst Park

Address: Selhurst Park Stadium, London SE25 6PY
Telephone: Club (0181) 771 2233
Box Office (0181) 771 8841
Dons Call (0891) 121 175
Official Website: http://www.wimbledon-fc.co.uk

Milton Keynes, Sunbury, Gatwick Airport, Basingstoke, Cardiff, Dublin ... name a place, and it's likely that, over the last two years or so, someone has suggested that Wimbledon FC might move there! The proposed move to Dublin was undermined by a FIFA ruling, in June 1998, that clubs must play in the leagues of the country they're based in ... in other words, if Wimbledon transferred to Dublin, the team would have to play against Irish opposition. Most Wimbledon fans breathed a huge sigh of relief, as nearly all would prefer to return home, to Merton. This has proved extremely difficult, especially as most open spaces in the borough are public parkland. The redevelopment of the club's old ground, Plough Lane, is impossible, and the club's spent hundreds of thousands of pounds exploring other options. Longstanding plans for the conversion of Wimbledon Greyhound Stadium were shelved when both the club and Merton Council agreed that the site was inappropriate: for a start, the capacity would have been less than 20,000, with many supporters watching the game from behind glass! Meanwhile, the pressure for a move continues to mount, especially with clubs such as Bolton, Reading, Stoke and Sunderland – all presently outside the Premier League – opening brand-new super-stadiums. As the search continues, Wimbledon FC begins another season at Selhurst Park, its eighth year in exile.

'Oi'm not too keen on these English theme clubs that are cropping up, Patrick!'

HOW TO GET THERE

See details under the entry for 'Crystal Palace'.

PARKING

Parking is usually easier for a Wimbledon game, simply because the crowds are smaller.

THE GROUND

Wimbledon usually allocates the whole of the Arthur Wait Stand to the visiting support, and sometimes the Whitehorse Lane Stand as well, which gives away fans the chance to explore the facilities normally reserved for the home support. And is there a huge difference? Well, certainly not in the Arthur Wait Stand, though the view from the centre is better than in the corners.

Total Capacity: 26,309. For away fans: Up to 8,000. Entrances in Park Road.

Cost (97/98): £20, concessions (under 16s/OAPs) £10. Visiting fans are also welcome in the Family Stand (Blocks A and J of the Arthur Wait). Cost: £14/£8.

Programme: £2.

Visitors' Toilets (Whitehorse Lane Stand): *Male:* Some design fault surely? Those walking along the concourse tucking into their food are suddenly – when someone opens the loo door – faced with the vista of peeing males. The pee-ers don't care, but the eaters do! *Female:* Fans were happy that the loos looked recently redecorated, with new fittings and locks that worked. 'Better than usual' was the rather sad refrain.

Food and Drink: We approached a Barnsley supporter tucking into a pastie, and he said (honest!!): 'Eh-oop me ol' flower, me pastie's great, cos it's from Barnsley, I brought it wi' me.' Good start. Other fans had bought locally and thought the pasties (£1.40) were 'nice and warm, impressive', while the burgers (£2) were '******* horrible' (23.9.97).

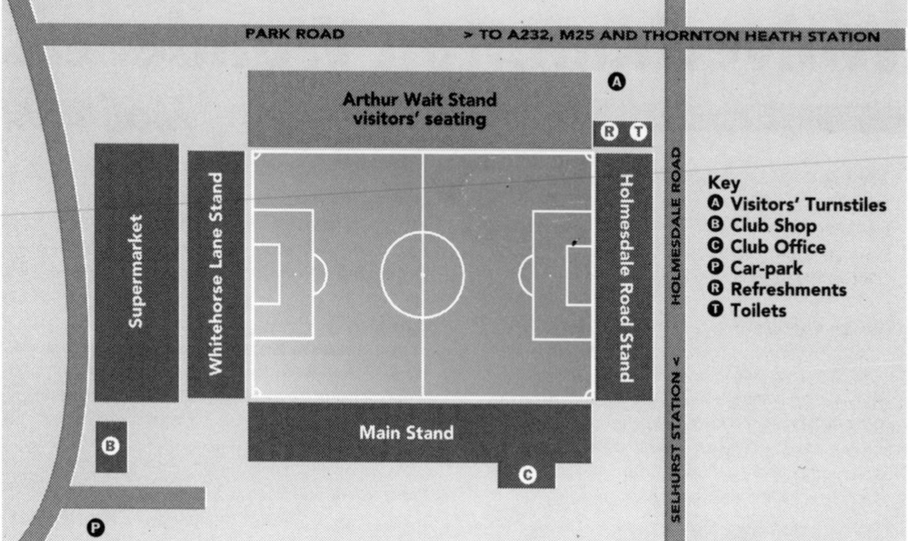

PUB/FOOD GUIDE

All the pubs listed under Crystal Palace are valid for Wimbledon. In addition, visiting supporters are welcome in the 'Crystals' club, above Sainsburys.

LOCAL MEDIA

Local Radio: Capital Gold 1548 AM; GLR 94.9 FM; XFM 104.9.
Radio Phone-ins: Capital Gold, Saturdays 5-6.30 pm; midweek every night 7-8 or after live match commentary. Call (0845) 35 60 70 80.
Saturday Sports Paper: None.

MISCELLANEOUS

Safety Factor: No problems here.
Rivals: The landlords, Crystal Palace, and Chelsea. 'Crazies' are also relishing the thought of a new South London derby, with Charlton.
Fanzines: 'Route One', 19 Arundel Avenue, Morden, Surrey, SM4 4DR; 'Sour Grapes', 90a Worcester Road, Sutton, Surrey, SM2 6QJ; 'Yidaho', 23 Ryecroft Avenue, Hither Green, London, SE13 6EZ; 'Hoof the Ball Up', 46 Oxford Street, London, W1N 9FJ; 'Big One Hans', address not known.
Unofficial Websites:
'WombleNet': http://www.geocities.com/SunsetStrip/Studio/6112/womblnet.html (which has excellent links)
'G's Spot': http://www.geocities.com/Colosseum/Loge/2092/
'Neil's Site': http://www.netkonect.co.uk/b/brenford/wimbledon/
'Steve's Homepage': http://www.russnet.force9.co.uk/steveweb/football/wimbledon/index.htm
'Reservoir Dons': http://members.aol.com/stevedons/Index/Html

W

Wolverhampton Wanderers

Molineux

Address: Molineux Stadium, Waterloo Road, Wolverhampton WV1 4QR
Telephone: Club (01902) 655 000
Ticket Office (01902) 653 653
Ticket News (0891) 121 823
ClubCall (0891) 121 103
Official Website: http://www.mbcis.co.uk/wolves/

It's difficult to miss Molineux, as it's right by the Ring Road, and it's painted gold! On paper, it looks to be in an ideal location, a short walk from the railway station and town centre, with several nearby car parks. However, on Saturdays, shoppers compete with football fans for every available parking space, and the local pubs are not keen on away fans. Basically, there are so many thirsty Wolves fans, they don't need the extra trade or the additional hassle! Thankfully, many of the pubs on the main roads into Wolverhampton are friendly, and with the town centre so close, no-one goes hungry.

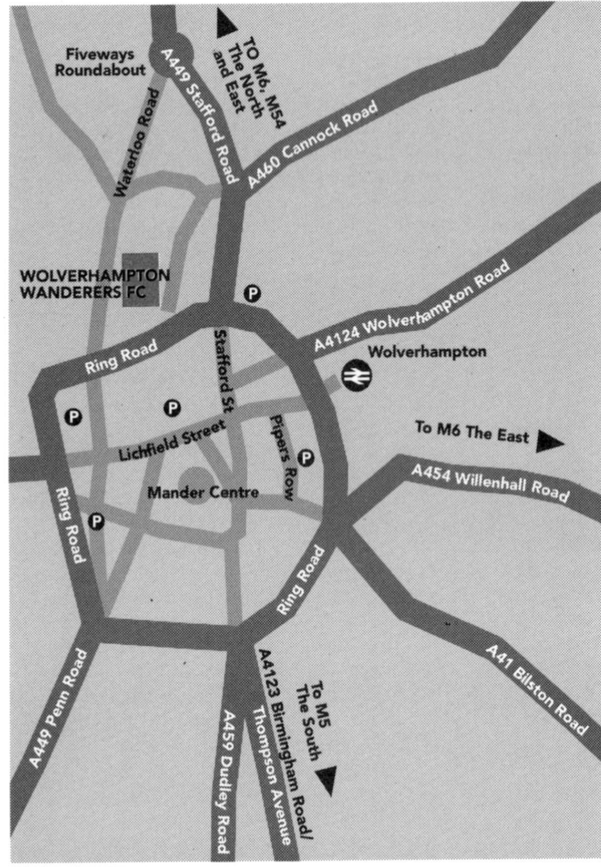

HOW TO GET THERE

BY CAR: Supporters travelling to evening games in Wolverhampton should remember that the M6 between junctions 6 and 10 is one of the busiest stretches of motorway in Europe. For evening games, approach Wolverhampton from junction 2 of the M5.

From North and East: Exit M6 at junction 13 (s/p Wolverhampton A449). From here the route is simple – keep following signs to 'Wolverhampton A449'. After 9.0 miles, go straight on under the M54. Go straight on for 2.7 miles, over three roundabouts, picking up signs to the Molineux Centre, to a 4th roundabout by the British Gas works. Go straight on (s/p Wolverhampton A449), under two railway bridges to 5th roundabout, dominated by a red-bricked building (the 'Five Ways' roundabout). Here take 3rd exit (s/p Molineux Centre, University North) into Waterloo Road. Ground is on LHS after 0.4 miles.

From East (Weekends Only): Exit M6 at junction 10. At motorway roundabout, follow signs to Wolverhampton A454, Dudley onto the A454 dual carriageway. Exit after 1.3 miles at the Keyway junction (s/p Wolverhampton A454, Willenhall). At next two roundabouts follow signs for Wolverhampton A454 onto the Willenhall Road (still the A454). After 2.2 miles all traffic swings to the left (s/p Ring Road, Town Centre A454) onto Middle Cross, to roundabout. Take 4th exit (s/p Ring Road, Stafford A449) onto Ring Road. Ground is on RHS after 0.6 miles.

From South: Exit M5 at junction 2 (s/p A4123 Dudley, Wolverhampton). At motorway roundabout take 1st exit, and then 3rd exit at next roundabout

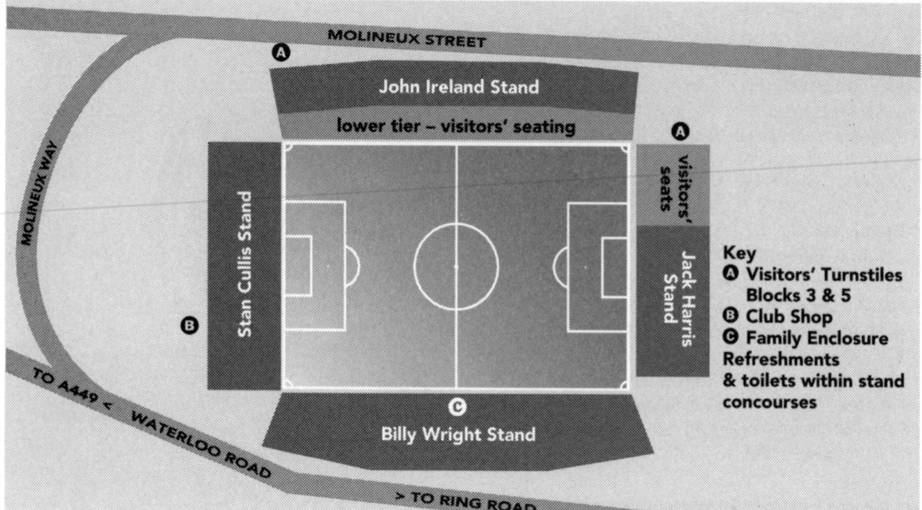

(s/p Dudley, Wolverhampton A4123) onto the A4123 dual carriageway. Follow signs to Wolverhampton A4123 for 7.6 miles, when all traffic swings left (s/p Wolverhampton Town Centre A4123), and then right (s/p Town Centre A4123) into Dudley Road. At Snow Hill Junction turn right (s/p Ring Road East, Motorway M6, Walsall A454) onto Ring Road. Ground is signposted right (Molineux Centre) off Ring Road after 1.0 miles.

FROM RAILWAY STATION (Wolverhampton): 0.5 miles. *By taxi:* £1.80-£2. *By foot:* Straight out of main entrance and over bridge. Keep left at clock tower and under covered walkway into Lichfield Street, passing the 'Grand Theatre' on the LHS. At lights turn right towards Prince's Square, passing between 'The Varsity' pub and the 'Midland and General'. Straight on, following signs to Stafford A449, to Ring Road. Ground is visible across road. Cross Ring Road at lights and turn left, where steps lead down to ground.

Last Midweek Trains: Trains leave for London Euston at 21.32 and 22.49, and there's a frequent service to Birmingham New Street. For onward connections, see under 'Birmingham City'. Please double-check on (0345) 484 950.

BY METRO: A new line is under construction from Snow Hill station in Birmingham to a new station in Bilston Street, Wolverhampton.

BY BUS: Buses run from Stand R of the bus station, by the railway station. Nos. 503, 504 and 506 run past the ground.

PARKING

The police advise visiting fans to leave their cars in the Faulkland Street car park (140 spaces, £1.70 all day). For those coming from the North via junction 13 of the M6, take the 2nd exit at the 'Five Ways' roundabout (s/p Wolverhampton Town Centre A449) onto Lower Stafford Street, and turn left onto the Ring Road (s/p Ring Road, Walsall A454). The car park is signposted left. For those travelling from the South, the car park is signposted off the Ring Road as a U-turn. If this car park is full, try the town centre car parks. The short stay car parks are signposted in brown (only two hours parking allowed before 6 pm, no restrictions thereafter), and the long stay car parks are signposted orange. A number of small unofficial car parks open up immediately around Molineux, but these are best avoided. The police strongly advise away fans against parking in the car park behind 'The Wanderer' pub by the ground, where many vehicles have been vandalised.

THE GROUND

Molineux is a Premiership ground awaiting Premiership football. Wolves fans have become philosophical: 'We're destined for a life in the First Division,' said one, still planning, however, to attend every home and away game! The ground is large, impressive, posh and ... well, gold! And the atmosphere, even without the traditional Wolves favourite, 'The Liquidator' theme, is excellent, not to mention a little intimidating. The oldest stand, the John Ireland, was built in the late 1970s, but supporters had to wait until 1993 for the rest of the ground to be redeveloped to the same high standard. The three new stands, built to match, cost £16 million, and facilities in all of them are first-class.

Total Capacity: 28,500. For away fans: From 1,500 in the Jack Harris Stand (turnstile 5), to 3,200 in the lower tier of the John Ireland Stand (turnstile 3).

Cost (98/99): Jack Harris Stand: Adults £12, concessions (juniors/OAPs) £8.50. John Ireland Stand: £13/£8.50.
Disabled Facilities: Space for 12 visiting supporters in the Jack Harris Stand. *Disabled Toilet:* Nearby. *Cost:* Free for disabled, £8 for helper. *Booking:* Tickets are sent to the away club for distribution. *Parking:* None available, but fans can be dropped off outside the stand. *For the Blind:* The club will do its best to provide commentary.
Programme: £1.80
Visitors' Toilets: *Male:* First class! *Female:* 'Everything smelt really fresh', said one mesmerized supporter.
Food and Drink: The cheeseburger (£2.15) came in a neat foil-lined bag with the Wolves logo emblazoned on it. Although it was pre-packed, and therefore presumably cooked beforehand, it was still piping hot and tasty, as was the excellent steak-and-kidney pie (£1.50). The tea (90p) and coffee (£1) were expensive but acceptable (14.3.98 and 29.3.98).

PUB GUIDE

From the North (A449):
The Moreton Arms Stafford Road, Fordhouses
(01902) 787 178
Banks's. Large, smart pub with a good mixture of fans. Full menu served 12-2, 6-8.30. Darts, TV, outdoor childrens' play area. Open: all day from 12.
From the South (A4123):
The Black Horse Thompson Avenue (A4123)
(01902) 629 921
Bass Taverns/M&B. Huge pub welcoming all. 'Top Twenty' menu (all meals cost £2.99) served 12-2.30, 6-8 (not Sunday). Pool, darts, TV, terrace. Disabled facilities. Open: all day from 12.
The Spread Eagle Birmingham New Road (A4123)
(01902) 663 564
Bass (with Banks's). Modern family-orientated pub welcoming all sports fans. Home-cooked food, including a prize-winning steak-and-kidney pie, served 12-2.30, 5.30-9.30. Pool, darts, TV, beer garden. Open: Saturdays all day; from 5 pm for midweek games.
The North Wolverhampton Working Men's Club (Carlsberg-Tetley) in Oxley Road, welcomes football supporters and their families for a small entrance fee (around 20p). Hot food. Darts, pool, snooker. Open: Saturday matchdays all day from 12; from 2.30 pm for evening games.
FOR FAMILIES:
The Staffordshire Knot, Birmingham New Road, Lanesfield (on the A4123) is a large attractive M&B pub/restaurant with separate dining area, pool table, TV and beer garden.

FOOD GUIDE

Loads of burger vans and the like set up around the ground, including the amazing pig roast outside 'The Feathers' pub, opposite the away turnstiles. For a greater choice, head for Dudley Street and the Mander Centre, the main shopping areas. The Mander Centre has a Pizza Hut, Wimpy and a KFC.

LOCAL MEDIA

Local Radio: BBC Radio WM 95.6 FM; Capital Gold 1152 AM; Wolf FM 107.7 FM.
Radio Phone-ins: Radio WM, Friday evenings 7-9, Saturdays 5-6 pm, and to 10 pm after midweek games, call (0121) 432 2000; Capital Gold, 1152 AM. Saturday 5-6.30 pm, midweek every night 7-8, or after live match commentary. Call (0845) 35 60 70 80.
Saturday Sports Paper: The 'Sports Argus' pink.

MISCELLANEOUS

Safety Factor: Although Molineux can be intimidating, there was little trouble in season 97/98.
Rivals: West Bromwich is the obvious rival, but many Wolves fans see Stoke as a major adversary.
Fanzines: 'A Load of Bull', PO Box 3483, Birmingham, B17 9SF.
Best Unofficial Websites:
http://home5.swipnet.se/~w-57029/wolves/index.htm
http://homepages.force9.net/grcampbell/wolves/
http://www.lazy-dog.demon.co.uk/wolves/index.htm
http://www.wolf.ndirect.co.uk/
Tourist Information: (01902) 556 110.

Wrexham

The Racecourse Ground

Address: The Racecourse Ground, Mold Road, Wrexham, Clwyd LL11 2AH
Telephone: Club/Ticket Office (01978) 262 129
ClubCall (0891) 121 642

Don't be misled ... there's not a horse or a winning post in sight at the Racecourse Ground! However, there is a pub on the corner, and the privileged few sit back to watch the game from the balcony. They could include the proprietors, as the brewers Marstons own the ground! The Racecourse stands on the northwestern edge of town, among the DIY stores and supermarkets, which severely limits the choice for food and drink.

HOW TO GET THERE

BY CAR: From South and East (M6-M54-A5-A483): Continue on the A483, which becomes the Wrexham Bypass. Exit bypass at signpost 'Wrexham, Mold A541'. (*)At next two roundabouts follow signs to 'Wrexham A541' (also yellow Football Car Park signs). The ground is on the LHS after 0.2 miles.
From North (M56-M53-A55-A483): Continue on the A483, which becomes the Wrexham Bypass, for 8.4 miles, exiting at signpost 'Wrexham, Mold A541'. Then as From South and East(*).
From East (via A534 from Crewe): Follow A534 along Wrexham Road, passing the Wrexham Industrial Estate to roundabout. Here, take 2nd exit (s/p Oswestry, Chester A483) onto the A5156 Acton Llan-Y-Pwll Link Road. At roundabout after 1.4 miles, take 2nd exit (s/p Wrexham, Oswestry A483) onto the Wrexham Bypass. Take 1st exit from bypass after 1.4 miles (s/p Wrexham, Mold A541). Then as From South and East(*).
FROM RAILWAY STATION (Wrexham): Two minutes' walk: turn right out of the station and up the steps to Mold Road, and turn right again.
Last Midweek Trains: A train to Leicester and Peterborough leaves at 22.17; to Chester at 22.00; and to Shrewsbury at 22.45. For most southern destinations, the vital train from Wrexham General is at 21.36. It goes to Shotton, from where there are connections to Crewe, London, Manchester Oxford Road and Birmingham. Please double-check on (0345) 484 950.
BY BUS: From the King Street bus station in the town centre, buses from Stand 5 run past the ground. The nos. 20, 21, 22 or 23 to Summerhill and the nos. 26 and 40 to Mold are the best bet.

PARKING

The best safe parking is at the Wrexham University Sector College, next to the ground on Mold Road. It costs £1.50 on Saturdays, and is free for midweek matches. In all other areas, there is car crime, especially in the evenings.

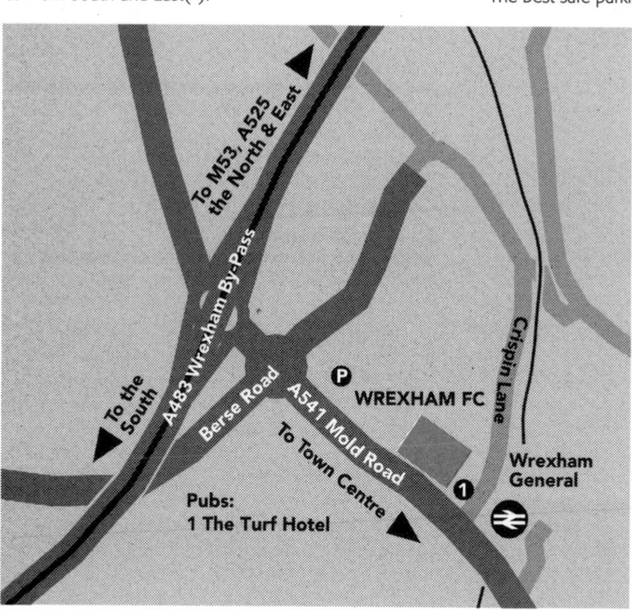

THE GROUND

Twickenham, Murrayfield, Parc des Princes, Wrexham. Oh yes, the Racecourse Ground has once again become an international venue, but this time for rugby union. The prospect of Wrexham hosting matches in the 1999 Rugby World Cup has given added impetus to plans to demolish the Mold Road Stand, closed for more than 13 years, and build a new 3,500-seater stand, complete with eight executive boxes. Work could begin as early as August 1998. The club also plans to add seats onto the Marstons and Yale Stand

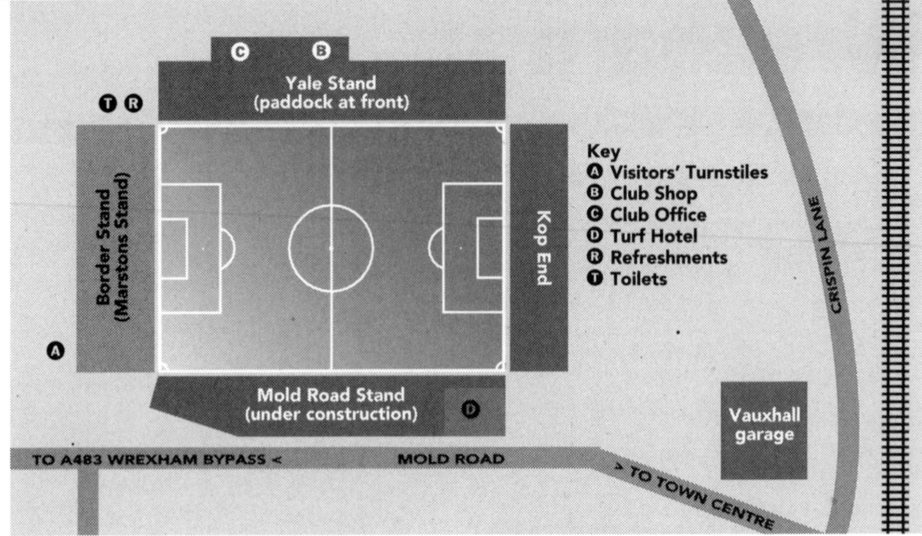

Paddocks, which will affect visiting fans. Until now, they have been allocated both the Marstons Stand (where the view and the facilities are good) and Marstons Paddock, the front of which is below pitch level.

Total Capacity: 11,400. For away fans: Marstons Stand 2,200. Turnstiles 40-42. Marstons Paddock 400. Turnstiles 36-39.

Cost (98/99): Seating: Adults £11, concessions £8. Terrace: Adults £8, no concessions.

Disabled Facilities: Space for 4 visiting supporters in an uncovered area in front of the Mold Road Stand. *Disabled Toilet:* Portaloo available. *Cost:* Free for disabled, terrace price for helper. *Booking:* Please phone Tony Millington on (01978) 351 332. *Parking:* Available. *For the Blind:* No special facilities.

Programme: £1.80.

Visitors' Toilets: Those in the stand have a much better deal – a new breeze block construction, with sinks, hot water and hot air dryers. Those on the terrace tried the toilet block between the Marstons and Yale Stands ... *Male:* Bunker-style toilets, dank, dark, smelly and cultivating their own ecosytems. Life on earth began in North Wales! *Female:* No-one wanted to venture in, even when offered a free pie.

Food and Drink: Just tasty, red-hot pies (£1.20). The coffee (60p) looked like coffee, but that was where the similarity ended. The club has brought in new caterers for season 98/99 (20.12.97, 8.11.97, 10.1.98, 25.4.98).

PUB GUIDE

Near the ground, there's only the welcoming **Turf Hotel (1),** a Marstons pub serving food from 11-2. However, it soon gets packed, and fans have to be turned away. It's only a short walk into town. A particularly football-friendly pub there is the small traditional **Horse and Jockey** on Hope Street.

FOOD GUIDE

Decision time: either eat from the burger van at the ground, or head into town. Regent Street has a McDonalds and Burger King, while nearby King Street has a 'Kebabs and Pizza', offering chicken and chips for £2.60; a 'Dino's Pizza', a 'King Chef' fish and chip shop, and an 'Ecclestons' bakers.

LOCAL MEDIA

Local Radio: Marcher Sound 1260 AM; BBC Radio Wales 882 MW.

Radio Phone-ins: BBC Radio Wales, Saturdays 6-7, call (01222) 578 928.

Saturday Sports Paper: None.

MISCELLANEOUS

Wrexham FC retains its 'Rockin' Robin' mascot, who was blamed for the team's total inability to score at home at the start of season 97/98. When the drought finally ended, the robin shot onto the pitch and did a 'Klinsmann Dive' into the net – and was reported to the FA!

Safety Factor: A safe ground to visit.

Rivals: Chester City, Shrewsbury and Cardiff.

Fanzine: 'The Sheeping Giant', 21 Dolafon, Penybontfawr, Near Oswestry, Shropshire, SY10 0PA.

Unofficial Websites:
http://www.csm.uwe.ac.uk/~klhender/wxm/index/html
http://www.apfscil.u-net.com/wrexham.htm

Tourist Information: (01978) 292 015.

Wycombe Wanderers

Adams Park

Address: Adams Park, Hillbottom Road, Sands, High Wycombe, Bucks HP12 4HJ
Telephone: Club (01494) 472 100
Shop 'Wanderers in Town' (01494) 450 957
Ticket Creditcard Hotline (01494) 441 118
Info Line 'Ringing the Blues' (0891) 446 855
Official Website:
http://www.wycombewanderers.co.uk

One visit to Wycombe and it's easy to see why the football team is called the 'Wanderers': visiting supporters looking for food and drink need to pack a good pair of hiking boots, a compass and a couple of sturdy mules! The ground's at the end of a cul-de-sac on an industrial estate, with only one way in and out, and with no away-friendly pubs for miles. Parking's a nightmare too, and one visiting fan concluded that the best way to avoid the post-match traffic gridlock was to leave at half-time! The good news, however, is that Adams Park itself is a rapidly developing ground with excellent facilities, and is easy to find by car from the M40. And the club's done its best to help ease the parking and travel problems by laying on special buses from the town centre and railway station.

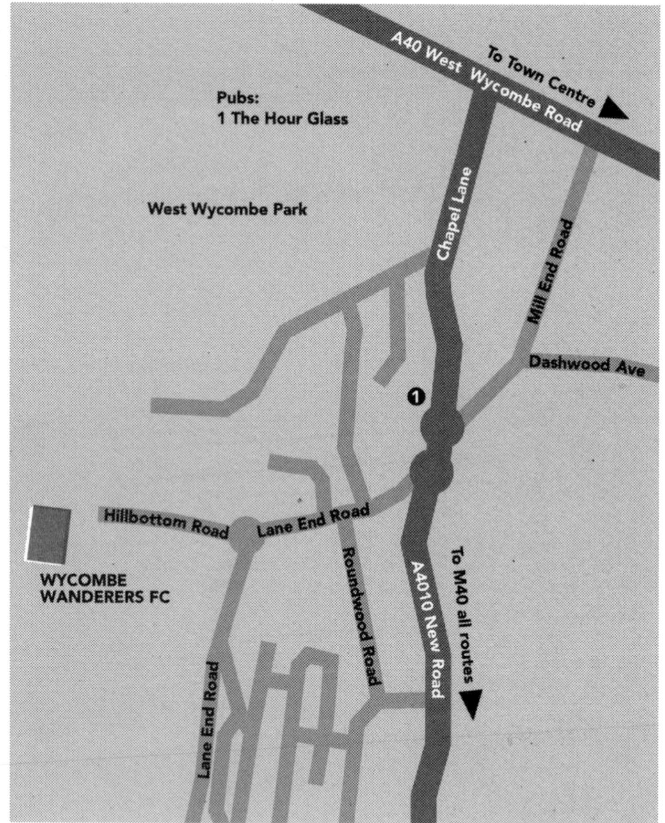

HOW TO GET THERE

BY CAR: From all directions: Exit M40 at Junction 4 (s/p A404 H. Wycombe, Marlow). At motorway roundabout, follow signs to 'Aylesbury A4010' onto the A4010. Straight on for 2.3 miles, over three roundabouts and down a long hill (New Road). At the first of two mini-roundabouts, turn left into Lane End Road. At next roundabout, after 0.5 miles, turn right (s/p Industrial Estate) into Hillbottom Road. For an easier get-away after the game follow the yellow AA signs to the M40, avoiding the town centre and some of the worst jams.

FROM RAILWAY STATION: (High Wycombe): 2.0 miles as the crow flies, further as the human walks. *By taxi:* £4.50-£5. *By bus:* The club runs special buses from the railway station, at 13.55 and 14.25 on Saturdays, and 18.35 and 19.05 for midweek games. They call in at the bus station in the Octagon Centre five minutes later. The journey takes about 15 minutes and costs £1 single, £1.50 return. In addition, the no. 338 bus runs past the end of Hillbottom Road.

Last Midweek Trains: Trains to London Marylebone leave at 21.58, 22.30 and 00.01. Please double-check on (0345) 484 950. For connecting trains from London, see London Guide at front of book.

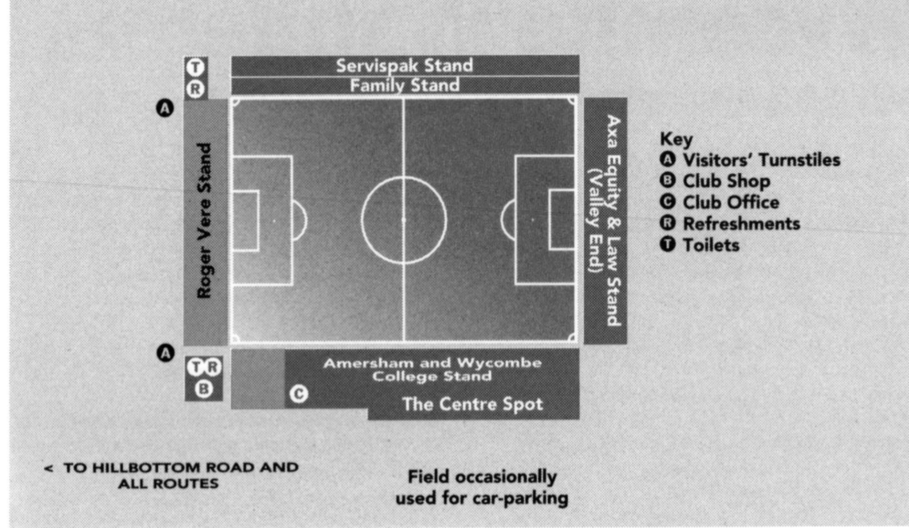

BY BUS: See above.

PARKING

Parking at the ground is limited to about 150-200 spaces on a nearby field (£1.50). In addition, some of the industrial units along Hillbottom Road allow matchday parking, charging between 50p-£1.50. Hillbottom Road is now one-way after the match, which has helped to ease the traffic congestion. To avoid the post-match gridlocks completely, park well away from the ground: try the area around Roundwood Road. Alternatively, leave the car in the large car park at the railway station, or in the town centre multi-storeys and catch the special football buses. The buses are given priority over other traffic after the match.

THE GROUND

Wycombe Wanderers FC, one of the most ambitious and well-organised clubs in the Football League, has simply outgrown the original Adams Park, built in 1990. The 'New Woodlands Stand' was demolished in 1996 and replaced with the two-tier, 5,000-seater 'Servispak Stand'. Home fans say it's simply 'brilliant', with excellent views. The new stand positively dwarfs the old Main Stand opposite, which has just seven rows of seats. The only remaining section of terracing is at the Valley End, and is reserved for the home support. For away fans, the Roger Vere Stand was successfully converted to seating in season 96/97, without a stanchion in sight. It's best to avoid the front rows, however, as fans walk past constantly to and from the toilets and refreshment kiosk. The facilities can get very crowded at half-time ... a Gillingham fan said some supporters in the tea queue had been 'fossilized in the Cretaceous period, judging from the waiting times!'

Total Capacity: 10,000. For away fans: 1,500. Entrance 2 for Roger Vere Stand, Entrance 1 for Amersham and Wycombe College Stand.

Cost (98/99): Adults £13, OAPs £12, juniors £11. Visiting family supporters are welcome in the family stand, the front section of the Servispak Stand. Cost: Adults £11, OAPs £9, Juniors £6. For all areas, tickets bought at least a day in advance are £1 cheaper.

Disabled Facilities: Space for 50 supporters in an area shared with the home support at the front of the Servispak Stand. *Disabled Toilet:* Two nearby. *Cost:* £6 for disabled, £11 for helper (£1 discount if bought a day in advance). *Parking:* Available, please book. *For the Blind:* Four seats in the Amersham and Wycombe College Stand.

Programme: £2.

Visitors' Toilets: *Male:* 'Spotlessly clean' and 'nice blue walls' were typical responses. *Female:* Quite simply football toilet heaven: clean, soft toilet paper, hooks to hang coats/bags, and with distorting mirrors (hooligan proof apparently) for added entertainment.

Food and Drink: Fans were impressed that the burgers were being freshly cooked. The end product (£1.70) was a bit thin and well done, though one fan said that was exactly how he liked it. Veggieburgers (£1.70) and American-style fries (£1) were also available. The tea (80p) was the powered-milk variety, which, even after a good stir, resembled weak cabbage soup. Stick with the coffee and the excellent hot chocolate (80p) (28.2.98).

PUB GUIDE

Away fans are welcome in the social club if they buy a £1 voucher from the commercial office before the game. Of the pubs listed below, only the 'Hour Glass' – which sometimes allows in away fans – is within reasonable walking distance.

The Hour Glass (1) 144 Chapel Lane (01494) 525 094

Allied Domecq. The nearest pub, and therefore immensely popular, with away fans admitted at the doorman's discretion. As it's a 'Mr Q's', there's three pool tables plus darts, big-screen TV and a lively atmosphere. Bar snacks. Open: all day.

Hungry Horse New Road, Booker (en route from M40) (01494) 529 419

Greene King. A very football-friendly pub with a great matchday atmosphere. Generous food portions, including an all-day breakfast or 10oz rump steak for £4.25, served all day. Children's menu/vegetarian selection. Big-screen TV, beer garden. Families welcome. Open: all day.

Also recommended: **The White Horse** 95 West Wycombe Road (A40). This is a Carlsberg/Tetley pub, very football friendly, but only for the adult crowd as 'exotic dancers' provide the lunchtime entertainment! There are a good number of excellent pubs in the town centre, especially along the High Street, though few wanted to be labeled as 'football pubs' and listed here. A good one to try, however, is the **The Hogshead** at 120-123 Oxford Road (A40), a large smart modern Whitbreads pub on two floors. Entry is at the landlord's discretion and colours are not advisable.

FOR FAMILIES:

The Bird in Hand 81 West Wycombe Road (A40) (01494) 523 502

Courage. Locals describe this traditional pub, with its conservatory area and open fires, as 'warm and friendly'. Home-made pies (£4.25) served 12-2.30, 6-9.30. Darts, TV, patio. Open: Saturday all day; from 5.30 for midweek games.

FOOD GUIDE

Home fans say the mobile burger vans are pretty good, which is excellent news as they're the only option near the ground. For choice, it's best to stop en route. The first turning to the left after the M40 roundabout leads to a small retail park, which has a 'Deep Pan Pizza', a 'TGI Fridays' and a 'Mongolian Barbeque'. A little further along the A4010, just past the first mini-roundabout and next to the 'Hungry Horse', is a fish and chip shop called 'Smarts Takeaway'. It's open all day on Saturday, and has a good menu. The nearest chippy to the ground, about a ten minute walk away, is 'The Corner Plaice' on the junction of Mill End Road and Dashwood Avenue.

'Wanderers? Yeah, we are – we've been wandering around looking for a pub for hours!'

LOCAL MEDIA

Local Radio: Radio High Wycombe 1170 AM; BBC Thames Valley 104.1, 104.4, 95.2 and 95.4 FM.

Radio Phone-ins: None.

Saturday Sports Paper: None.

MISCELLANEOUS

Adams Park has one celebrity fan – the commentator Alan Parry. In the matchday programme he writes of his ability to mention 'the Blues' as many times as possible on Sky. Quite how is a mystery! And why the nickname 'The Chairboys'? It was adopted about ten years ago, based on the town's traditional chair-making industry. There's even a Chair Museum, which Wycombe fans insist is an interesting place to visit.

Safety Factor: The police say Wycombe Wanderers is a 'family club' and trouble is unlikely.

Rivals: One Wycombe fan said: 'Enemies, what enemies? We're too friendly!' However the fanzine 'One-One' likes to have a go at Oxford, while Reading, now also in the Second Division, could come into the reckoning.

Fanzines: 'The Wanderer' (produced by the Independent Supporters Club), 22 Queen Street, High Wycombe, Bucks; 'One-One', c/o PO Box 589, High Wycombe, Bucks, HP15 7XL.

Unofficial Websites:
http://dialspace.dial.pipex.com/town/street/xnao6/
http://ourworld.compuserve.com/homepages/chairboys/
http://www.ndirect.co.uk/~chairboys/wwisc/

Tourist Information: (01494) 421 892.

York City

Bootham Crescent

Address: Bootham Crescent, York YO30 7AQ
Telephone: Club (01904) 624 447
City Hot Line (0891) 121 643

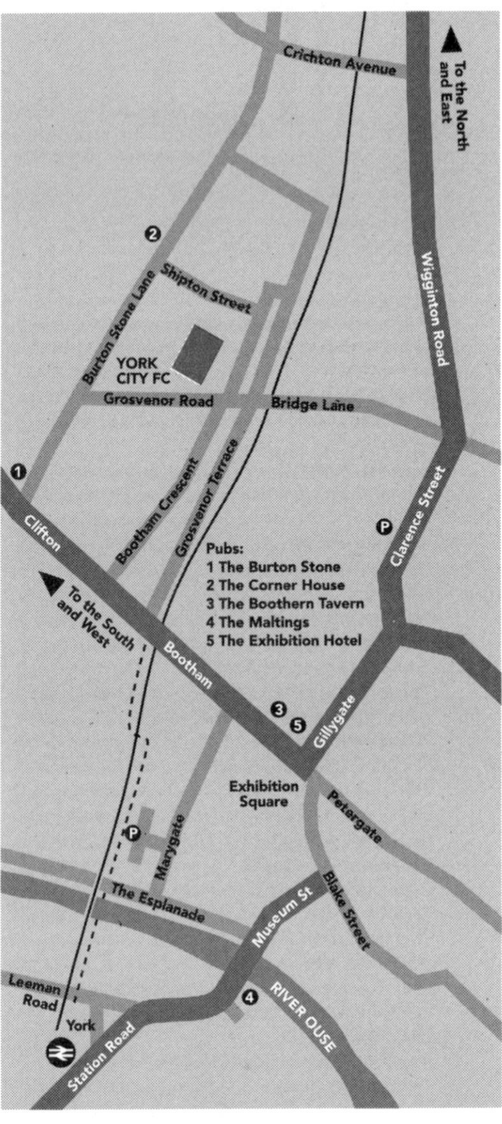

Relegation to the Second Division? It's not that bad if it involves a trip to York. Here's a possible itinerary: amble into town for a tour of the cathedral or a trip on the Viking time-train at the Jorvik Centre. Call in at the Petergate Fisheries for a top-class takeaway, then down a leisurely pint at a pub on Clifton village green before heading for the away terrace. Supporters travelling by car are well advised to avoid the congested city centre, and to allow a little extra time for finding a parking space. The railway station is a 15 minute walk away, but a possible route to the ground passes one of the best pubs in the north!

HOW TO GET THERE

BY CAR: From South (A1-A64): Exit A64 at signpost 'Leeds, York A64' and at the roundabout turn right onto the A64. Exit A64 after 9.3 miles (s/p York (North) A1237, Harrogate A59). At roundabout take 2nd exit (s/p York (North) A1237, Harrogate) onto the A1237. Go straight on, remaining on the A1237 for 5.2 miles, over three roundabouts and over River Ouse, to fourth roundabout. Here, turn right (s/p York A19) onto the A19 Shipton Road. (*)At lights after 1.6 miles by village green, go straight on (s/p City Centre). After 0.2 miles turn left by 'The Burton Stone' pub into Burton Stone Lane. Ground is on RHS.

From North (A19): Continue on the A19 to the roundabout junction with the A1237. Go straight on (s/p York A19) onto Shipton Road. Then as From South (*).

From East (Scarborough): Exit A64 at signpost York A1036, Thirsk, Harrogate A1237) onto the A1237. Continue on the A1237 for 3.5 miles to 6th roundabout. Here turn left (s/p B1363 York Centre, District Hospital) onto the B1363. Over level crossing after 1.2 miles, and a Nestle factory after a further 0.1 miles. After a further 0.4 miles turn right at lights (n/s) into Crichton Avenue and over bridge. Take 1st left into Burton Stone Lane. Grosvenor Road is the fifth turning on the left after 0.4 miles.

FROM RAILWAY STATION (York): A pleasant 15 minute walk. *By taxi:* £2.70-£3.50. *By bus:* 'Rider York' bus nos. 19 and 32 run from Rougier Street along Burton Stone Lane or Clifton. For evening games, the only option is the 'Pulman' bus no. Y20 from the Theatre Royal in St Leonard's Place, leaving at 18.48. *By foot:* Turn left out of station into Station

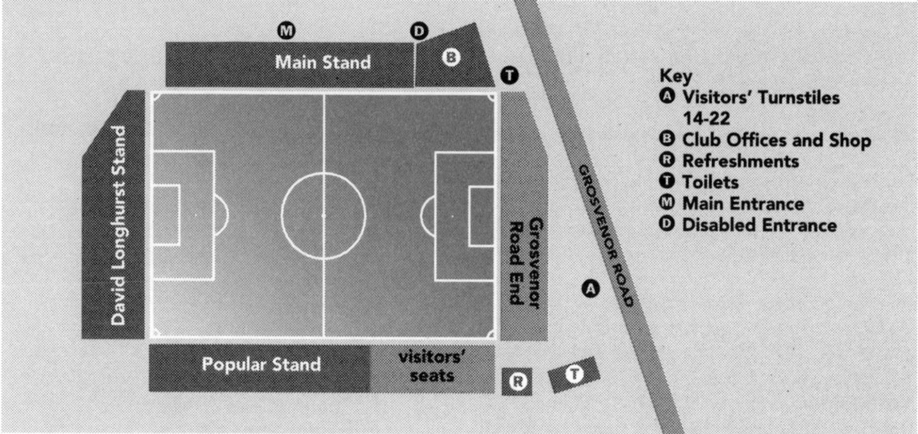

Road, past the Royal York Hotel. Take 1st left (s/p Leeman Road Industrial Estate, National Railway Museum). At end of road, in front of car park, follow the road round to the left, passing the Royal Mail depot. Just before railway bridge, turn right along pathway. Take footbridge over river, and then path between railway and Marygate car park. At end of car park turn left through underpass, and right into Bootham Terrace. At main road turn left, then take 2nd right into Bootham Crescent to ground.

Last Midweek Trains: The last train to London leaves at 21.37, and to Liverpool via Manchester at 21.21. Trains to Newcastle leave at 21.58 and 00.12. Please double-check on (0345) 484 950.

BY BUS: See above.

PARKING

Near the ground, the choice is between a small car park on Burton Stone Lane (£1.50 all day), and street parking. Roads near the ground have parking restrictions, but there are usually spaces a little further afield. Try around Cromer Street and Wilberforce Avenue, and to the west of the A19, on Westminster Road and The Avenue. Towards the city centre are two further options, the 'Marygate' car park and the 'Union Terrace' car park off Clarence Street (see map). Both charge £1.50 for three hours, £2.70 for four hours, £4 for five hours. There's a short cut from the far end of the Union Terrace car park, along Hospital Lane over a railway footbridge into Grosvenor Road.

THE GROUND

Bootham Crescent is a smart, traditional lower division ground, with a Main Stand, a seated Popular Stand, and terracing behind each goal. The home terrace is covered, the away one – the Grosvenor Road Terrace – is not. York City has plans to build a new 3,000-seater stand at the Grosvenor Road end, but only if the club gains promotion to the First Division. Until then, remember the sun-shades and/or the mac. However, it's usually possible to transfer from the terrace to the away seating in the Popular Stand on payment of £1. York City has made a brave attempt to improve its catering, but the loos are as bad as ever, and a large fence obscures the view from the lower terrace steps. The fence is, however, as one fan wrote, 'quite useful for hanging off when you've scored an 84th minute equaliser!'

Total Capacity: 8,975. For away fans: Standing 1,970; seating 990. Turnstiles 20-23. Visiting fans are welcome to use York City's Family Stand.

Cost (98/99): Seating: Adults £11 or £9, concessions (juniors/OAPs) £7 or £6. Terrace: Adults £8, concessions £5. Family Stand: Adults £8.50, children £5.

Disabled Facilities: Space for 20 supporters and their helpers in front of the Main Stand. *Disabled Toilet:* Nearby. *Cost:* Free for disabled, £8.50 for helper. *Booking:* Not necessary. *Parking:* Not available. *For the Blind:* Two seats available next to hospital broadcasting.

Programme: £1.50.

Visitors' Toilets: *Male:* A brick wall with a shallow mouldy gutter, plus a putrid, stinking shed. And probably some fairly unique strains of bacteria living on the walls. *Female:* York-on-Sea? One would think so from the amount of sand in the ladies loo. And when fans turned on the tap, it sounded like the entire portakabin was about to take off! No smell though.

Food and Drink: How's this for a footie menu? Pie, peas and chips £2.50, hamburger and chips £2.20 etc. Top marks for effort, but fans complained about the length of the queues – though thankfully there is a view of the game! Wycombe and Bristol City fans said the catering was one of the very best of the season, but Gillingham and Northampton fans were less impressed,

with comments such as: 'I've put loads of salt on the chips to soak up the grease', 'this hamburger meat looks like spam'. However, they did like the pies (£1.40) and the hot chocolate (30.8.97, 2.5.98).

PUB GUIDE

The Burton Stone (1) 34 Clifton (01904) 622 945
Bass. A large traditional football-friendly pub a couple of minutes walk from the ground. Sandwiches. Pool table, darts, big-screen TV, beer garden. Open: all day.
The Corner House (2) Burton Stone Lane (01904) 625 229
Mansfield. Locals pub with, says the landlord, very friendly staff! Big lounge bar, separate public bar with pool table and darts. Families welcome. Big-screen TV, beer garden. Open: all day.
The Maltings (4) Tanner's Moat (01904) 655 387
Free House. Classic traditional ale-house, recently voted 'Cask Ale Pub of Great Britain 1998'. Although it's a 20 minute walk from the ground, this pub is simply not to be missed! Well-behaved football fans and children welcome. Hot pub food and sandwiches served 12-2. Open: all day.
Also recommended: **The Bootham Tavern (3)**, a popular Tetleys pub at 29 Bootham, by the city walls.
FOR FAMILIES:
The Old Grey Mare Clifton Green (01904) 654 485
John Smiths. Top-rate traditional pub in a former coaching inn. English and Indian food served all day. Children's menu at £1.95. TV, pool table, beer garden. Disabled facilities. Open: all day. B&B at £25 pp.
The Exhibition Hotel (5) Bootham (01904) 624 248
Courage (with John Smiths). Popular pub/restaurant serving home-made food from 12-2.30 and from 5.30 pm. Vegetarian options plus children's menu at £2.50. Beer garden. B&B accommodation. Open: all day.
Also highly recommended: **The Riverside Farm,** Shipton Road, a massive new Tom Cobleigh pub with full menu served from midday. No colours please on teenagers or adults. To get there: At the roundabout junction of the A19 and the A1237, follow signs to 'Thirsk A19' onto the A19 northbound. Pub is on LHS.

FOOD GUIDE

The nearest fish and chip shop to the ground is 'Tony's Plaice' on Newborough Street and very good it is too. On Burton Stone Lane, the 'Star of Bengal' café serves English and Indian food, while the nearby 'Hong Kong House' takeaway has a good reputation, but doesn't open until 5.30 pm.

For something a little different, try a café called '76 Clifton', on the corner of Avenue Terrace. York fans strongly recommend the vegetarian sausage rolls, and it also offers 'Rarebit – a blend of Yorkshire ale, mature

'I don't care what you've found – fill it in!'

cheddar and mustard, served on toasted European bread with side salad' for £3.45. Bootham, the A19 towards town, has several cafés and takeaways, as does Gillygate near the city walls. Continue straight on at the end of Bootham through the city gates for the highly recommended 'Petergate Fisheries' in Low Petergate, which serves Pukka pies.

LOCAL MEDIA

Local Radio: Viking Radio 96.9 FM; BBC Radio York 103.7 FM; Minster FM 104.7.
Radio Phone-ins: BBC Radio York, 5-5.30 pm, call (01904) 641 641. Minster FM is also planning a 5-6 pm phone-in for season 98/99 – listen in for details.
Saturday Sports Paper: None.

MISCELLANEOUS

Safety Factor: The police advise fans to take care when walking back to the railway station. After dark, take the main road rather than the footbridge over the river.
Rivals: Scarborough, the only other team in North Yorkshire.
Fanzine: 'What a Shambles', address not known.
Unofficial Websites:
'Gary Morton's Unofficial Site:
http://www.alma.demon.co.uk/ycfc.html
'Joe Stoddart's Site':
http://www.shout.demon.co.uk/ycfc.htm
'MinsterNet': http://twie.lochnet.co.uk/ycfc/
Tourist Information: (01904) 621 756 and (01904) 643 700.

Credits and thanks

During our year's work on the *Football Fans Guide,* we have been greatly touched by the help and enthusiasm given to us by a huge number of people – from the fans, the clubs and the local police liaison officers. A lot of the information in this book has come from them, and we are immensely grateful:

The fans and the fanzines: Arsenal – Tony Madden of 'Highbury High'; Aston Villa – Dave Woodhall of 'Heroes and Villains'; Barnet – Steve Percy, Chairman of the Independent Supporters' Club, John Cosgrove of 'Two Together'; Barnsley – Supporters Gavin Talbot and John Wray; Birmingham – Author's local knowledge, Dave Small of 'The Zulu', supporter Dave McCoy; Blackburn – Paul Loftus of 'Loadsamoney', Ian F. Ferris of '4,000 Holes'; Blackpool – Mark Hillary, Chairman of the Blackpool Association of Supporters in London; Bolton – David Crook of the Bolton Wanderers Supporters' Club London, supporter Gill Ferris; Bournemouth – Mick Cunningham of the defunct fanzine 'Not the 8052'; Bradford – Richard Halfpenny of 'City Gent', supporter David Scally, additional research by David Goodman; Brentford – David Lane from 'Beesotted', supporter and cartoonist Cris Glascow, additional research by Mark Ainsbury; Brighton – Paul Whelch of 'Seagulls over London'; Bristol City – Rob Humphries of 'One Team in Bristol', Ben Jones of 'The Cider'Ed', Marcus Allin of 'Come In No. 7 Your Time Is Up'; Bristol Rovers – Hazel Potter, Chris Scargill and Ian Marriott of 'The 2nd of May'; Burnley – Ian Short of the defunct fanzine 'No Nay Never'; Bury – Warren Flood of 'Where Were You at the Shay?', supporter David Morris; Cambridge – Author's local knowledge, former fanzine editor Mark Johnson, Steve Jillings of 'The Abbey Rabbit'; Cardiff – Tony and Lorraine Jefferies, Brian and Shirley Morgan, Julie Morgan and Gareth Cartlidge, Rob Hughes of the London and South East England branch of Cardiff City Supporters Club; Carlisle – Bob Brookes and friends of the Carlisle United Supporters' Club, London Branch, Andy Baker of the defunct fanzine 'The Cumberland Sausage', Steve Warwick, Emily Jack; Charlton – Rick Everitt of 'Voice of the Valley'; Chelsea – Alan Collis of 'Red Card'; Chester – The Revd. Colin Mansley of 'Hello Albert'; Chesterfield – Dave Radford and Craig Thomas of the defunct fanzine 'The Crooked Spireite'; Colchester – Jason Skinner of 'The Blue Eagle'; Coventry – Terry Potts of Coventry City London Supporters' Club, supporter Adam Hewitt, former fanzine editor David Rose; Crewe – Jules Hornbrook of 'Super Dario Land'; Crystal Palace – Cris Lehmann of 'One More Point', supporters Mark Young, Chris Pattemore, Kate Sturtevant, Simon McHardy and 'Wags'; Darlington – Steve Harland and Dave Sowerby of 'Mission Impossible', supporter Richard Young; Derby – Nick Wheat of the defunct fanzine 'C–Stander', supporters Adrian, Andrew and Matthew Baseley, Paul Martin, Chris Wood and Jeff Davies, Mark Aldridge of 'Hey, Big Spender'; Everton – Supporters Daniel Magill and Andy Taylor, James Corbett of 'Gwladys Sings the Blues'; Exeter – Andrew Dye and Alan Crockford of the Exeter Exiles; Fulham – David Lloyd of 'There's only one F in Fulham'; Gillingham – Eddie Allcorn of 'Brian Moore's Head...', Chairman of the Supporters' Club Alan Liptrott; Grimsby – Bernard Morley, Terry Hall and Rachel Branson of the Grimsby Town Supporters' Club; Halifax – Supporters' Club Secretary Steve Kell, Club Historian Andrew Pinfield, Simon Denton of 'Shaymen Down South', supporters Nick Robinson and Roger Bottomley; Hartlepool – Paul Mullen of 'Monkey Business'; Huddersfield – Anne Richardson, Honorary Secretary of the Huddersfield Town Supporters' Club; Hull – Steve Maddison and Colin Smith of the Hull City Supporters' Club; Ipswich – Alasdair Ross and Annie Ross of 'Dribble', supporter Dave Kreamer; Leeds – Mark Monk of 'To Ell and Back', Steve Abbott of 'We are Leeds', Chris Stringer of 'The Hanging Sheep'; Leicester – Gary Silke of 'The Fox', supporter Merrick Prusinski, Ross Galbraith; Leyton Orient – Nick Madden of 'CheeryO's'; Lincoln – Gary Parle and Kevin Stow of 'The Deranged Ferret'; Liverpool – Author's local knowledge; Luton – Keith Heywood of 'Mad as a Hatter!'; Macclesfield – Supporters' Club Chairman Andy Ridgway, Committee Member Kenny Slater, Website Editors Clare Swift, Mike Griffiths and Nikki Welton; Manchester City – Sue and Dave Wallace of 'King of the Kippax', Noel Bayley of 'Bert Trautmann's Helmet', supporter Robin Dilks; Manchester United – Andy Mitten of 'United We Stand'; Mansfield – Steven Hartshorn of 'Follow the Yellow Brick Road', Jayne Danby of the Mansfield Town Supporters' Club, Steve Murray of 'Stags Outside Notts'; Middlesbrough – Robert Nichols of 'Fly Me to the Moon'; Millwall – George Craig of 'No-one Likes Us'; Newcastle – Mark Jensen of 'The Mag'; Northampton – Rob Marshall of 'What a Load of Cobblers'; Norwich – Darren Alcock of the defunct fanzine 'I Can Drive a Tractor', supporter Karen Buchanan; Nottingham Forest – Andy Lowe of 'The Tricky Tree', Richard Fisher of 'Forest Forever', Forest fans Helen Johnson and Dave Varley; Notts County – Ivan 'Bart' Bainbridge of 'No More Pie in the Sky'; Oldham – Pete Mason and Brian Green of 'Beyond the Boundary'; Oxford – Paul Beevers of 'Rage On'; Peterborough – Supporters Martin Thorpe and Kristen Gasson; Plymouth – Chris Reader of 'Way Out West', Supporters' Club Membership Secretary Keith Mitchell, Chris Errington of the Plymouth Evening Herald; Portsmouth – supporter Simon Bailey, Dave Benneworth of 'Frattonise', additional research by Jules Hornbrook; Port Vale – Gary Benson, match report by Craig Thomas; Preston – Supporter Mark Cassidy, Steve Brennan of 'Pie Muncher', Jonathan Richardson of the defunct fanzine 'Deepdale Rudge'; QPR – Howard Prosser of 'In the Loft'; Reading – Gary Purser of the defunct fanzine 'Taking the Biscuit'; Rochdale – Francis Collins and John Horrocks; Rotherham – Matt Norcliffe of 'Moulin Rouge', supporters Steve Brookes, Steve Exley and Hugh Vaughan; Scarborough – James Hunter of 'The Seadog Bites Back!'; Scunthorpe – Supporter Sean Coleman, Andy Skeels of the Scunthorpe United London and South–East Supporters' Club; Sheffield United – Matthew Bell of 'Flashing Blade', Martin Brammer, cartoonist Phil Maynard; Sheffield Wednesday – Graham Lightfoot of 'Spitting Feathers', supporters Daniel J. Hammond and Paul Haines, cartoonist Pete McKee; Shrewsbury – Kevin Bright of 'A Large Scotch', supporters Gary Bright, Adrian Plimmer, Mark Grice, Alan Follmer and Chris Smith; Southampton – Clive Foley of 'The Ugly Inside', supporters James Bonner and Jim Steele; Southend – supporter Tim Capp; Stockport – Dave Espley of 'The Tea Party', additional research by Steve Brennan; Stoke – Martin Smith of 'The Oatcake', supporters Dave Frith, Wayne Frith and Calvin Wagstaff; Sunderland – Ian Todd of the Sunderland AFC Supporters' Association (London and SE Branch), Martyn McFaddon of 'A Love Supreme'; Swansea – David Morgan of the Independent Travelling Swans, supporters Tony Pettican, Steve Griffiths, Ian Griffiths, Wesley Howard, Non Jones; Swindon – Supporters Alexander Deacon and Alex Cooke; Torquay – Hayden Jones of 'Bamber's Right Foot'; Tottenham – Supporters Stuart Young and Paul Peters; Tranmere – Supporter Tony Coombes, David Goat of 'Give Us an R'; Walsall – Pete Holland of 'Blazing Saddlers'; Watford – Matthew Bentote of 'Clap Your Hands...'; WBA – Simon Wright of 'Grorty Dick'; West Ham – Marc Williams of 'On the Terraces', Tony Fowles of 'The Ultimate Dream'; Wigan – Andrew Werrill of 'The Latic Fanatic', Simon Oldfield; Wimbledon – Chairman of the Supporters' Club Peter Tilbrook, supporter David Holdstock; Wolves – Charles Ross of 'A Load of Bull', supporter Phil Bradley, cartoonist Tony Eagle; Wrexham – Gavin Evans of 'The Sheeping Giant'; Wycombe – Dave Chapman of 'The Adams Family'; York – Supporters Annie Smith, Michael Howitt, Alison Cowdrey and Ian McManus.

Match and ground details: The following wonderful people either filled in our 'Travelling Fan's Forms', giving details of ground facilities and all the problems and delights of supporting their team away from home, or helped our researchers with the match reports: Gavin Hepworth, Ian Hepworth, Ian Bramall, Anthony 'Ronnie' Barker, Ben Schofield, Jill Martin, Lucy Burke, Steve Bannister, Rachel Roberts, Andrew Barnes, Dean Sadler, Graham Harris (all Doncaster); Trevor Bell (Arsenal); Steve Moore (Bournemouth); Alexander Betts (Bristol City); Sara Robb and Terry Potts (Coventry); Steve Addis (Crewe), Jason Henderson (Crystal Palace), Daniel Magill and Claire Gemma Hitchmough(Everton), Eddie Allcorn (Gillingham); Dave Kreamer (Ipswich); Rod Hadgraft (Luton); Robin Dilks and Barbara Ryding (Manchester City); Katie Phillips (Manchester United); Sandra Spurgin (Nottingham Forest); Mark Cassidy, Steve Brennan, Jonathan Richardson, Brian Baggley (Preston); Francis Collins (Rochdale); Steve Exley (Rotherham); Andrew Sloan (Stockport); Stuart Fuller and Stephen Gowers (West Ham); Alice Klein and Rod Gullit (Wimbledon); Alison Wheatley, Jo Dykes, Michael Hewitt (York City). In addition, we've used some of the ideas and the writings of Portsmouth supporter Simon Bailey. He's a writer of real wit and talent, and we hope very much to cooperate on future projects!

Clubs: All 92 Premiership and League clubs provided information for this book except for Newcastle United and Blackburn Rovers. Special thanks to Manchester United for kindly providing a complementary ticket when our writers had exhausted all other means.

Police: The police football liaison officers from all 92 Premiership and League clubs helped in the compilation of this book. Without their contribution, and their incredible local knowledge, the 'FFG' would simply not be possible.

Cartoons: All the cartoons in this book were drawn by: Cris Glascow (Tel: (01823) 698 033), Tony Eagle (Tel: (01782) 632 992), Phil Maynard (Tel: (0114) 249 2832), and Pete McKee (Tel: (0114) 237 4887), apart from: Bradford and Preston – Andy Roberts; Crystal Palace – Joe Gudgeon; WBA – Glyn Jones.

Janet Williams would like to thank the following: Chris Worrall for writing up several excellent match reports, checking pubs, compiling the Radio Phone-in guide, and for putting up with a year of disruption. I owe him about 100 dinners and six months of housework; Eddie Allcorn, as ever, has been a mine of football information, as he made his annual attempt to visit all 92 grounds; Tim Capp for the road directions and pub recommendations; Steve Day for help with the website listings; Mark Cassidy, Daniel Magill and Dave Kreamer for the particularly brilliant 'Travelling Fan's Forms'.

Victoria Bennett would like to give special thanks to: Adam Bonner for his continuous support and encouragement. I hope one day he'll forgive me for missing Birmingham's 7–0 win over Stoke! Thanks, too, to Dave and Len Thompson for coming up trumps with elusive tickets, and to June Bonner for turning her home into a hotel, complete with excellent fry-ups.

James Hilton would like to thank his parents, Josie and David Hilton, for the loan of the car, and Stuart Allen, Emily House, Steve Mullington and David Sturges for their research help. In addition, Janet and Derek Evans, Emily Jack and Simon Oldfield were kind enough to provide lodgings in the North West.